ATTENTION and PERFORMANCE IX

Proceedings of the Ninth International Symposium
on Attention and Performance
Jesus College, Cambridge, England, July 13-18, 1980

(ATTENTION and PERFORMANCE IX)

Edited by

John Long

Ergonomics Unit
University College London, England

Alan Baddeley

Medical Research Council
Applied Psychology Unit
Cambridge, England

Associate editors

Phil Barnard
John Duncan
Graham Hitch
Tony Marcel
Alan Wing

LAWRENCE ERLBAUM ASSOCIATES, PUBLISHERS
1981   Hillsdale, New Jersey

Lawrence Erlbaum Associates, Inc., Publishers
365 Broadway
Hillsdale, New Jersey 07642

Library of Congress Cataloging in Publication Data
International Symposium on Attention and Performance
   (9th : 1980 : University of Cambridge. Jesus College)
   Attention and performance IX.

   Includes bibliographical references and indexes.
   1. Attention—Congresses. 2. Performance—Congresses.
3. Visual perception—Congresses. 4. Perceptual-motor
processes—Congresses. I. Long, John B. II. Baddeley,
Alan D. III. Title.
BF321.I57 1980   153.7   81-9735
ISBN 0-89859-156-2   AACR2

Contents

PART III: AUTOMATICITY

PART IV: IMAGERY PROCESSES

PART VI: LONGER-TERM MEMORY

22. Encoding and Retrieval Effects in Human Memory: A Partial Review

23. Order Effects in Recall

24. Mentalmorphosis: Alterations in Memory Produced by the Mental Bonding of New Information to Old

Contributors and Participants

Invited Contributors

Stuart M. Anstis, Department of Psychology, York University, 4700 Keele St., Downsview, Ontario, Canada

Alain Berthoz, Laboratoire de Physiologie du Travail du CNRS., Département de Physiologie Neurosensorielle, 15 rue de l'Ecole de Médicine, 75270 Paris Cedex 06, France

John B. Black, Department of Psychology, Yale University, New Haven, Connecticut 06520, U.S.A.

Willem Bles, Academisch Ziekenhuis, 1007 MB Amsterdam, De Boelelaan 1117, Postbus 7057, The Netherlands

Claude Bonnet, Laboratoire de Psychologie Experimentale, Université Rene Descartes, 28 Rue Serpente, F-75006, Paris VIᵉ, France

William F. Brewer, Department of Psychology, University of Illinois, Psychology Building, Champaign, Illinois 81820, U.S.A.

Donald E. Broadbent, Department of Experimental Psychology, University of Oxford, South Parks Road, Oxford OX1 3UD, Great Britain

Claus Bundesen, Psychological Laboratory, Copenhagen University, Njalsgade 94, DK-2300 Copenhagen S., Denmark

Herbert H. Clark, Department of Psychology, Stanford University, Stanford, California 94305, U.S.A.

William E. Cooper, Department of Psychology, Harvard University, William James Hall, 33 Kirkland Street, Cambridge, Massachusetts 02138, U.S.A.

Fergus I. M. Craik, Department of Psychology, Erindale College, University of Toronto, Mississauga, Ontario L5L 1C6, Canada

Brian Craske, Department of Psychology, Memorial University of Newfoundland, St. John's, Newfoundland A1B 3X9, Canada

Carol A. Fowler, Department of Psychology, Gerry Hall, Dartmouth College, Hanover, New Hampshire 93755, U.S.A.

H. Frowein, Social Research Section (CASWO) of the PTT, Zeestrat 5, The Hague, The Netherlands

Simon Garrod, Department of Psychology, University of Glasgow, Adam Smith Building, Glasgow, G12 8RT, Great Britain

Richard L. Gregory, Brain and Perception Laboratory, Department of Anatomy, University of Bristol, The Medical School, University Walk, Bristol BS8 1TD, Great Britain

Margaret Hagen, Department of Psychology, Boston University, College of Liberal Arts, 64 Cummington St., Boston, Massachusetts 02215, U.S.A.

Geoffrey E. Hinton, MRC Applied Psychology Unit, 15 Chaucer Road, Cambridge CB2 2EF, Great Britain

Robert Hockey, Department of Psychology, Durham University, Science Laboratories, South Road, Durham DH1 3LJ, Great Britain

Marc Jeannerod, Laboratoire de Neuropsychologie Experimentale, Inserm U. 94, Avenue du Doyen Lepine, 69500 Bron, France

John Jonides, Department of Psychology, University of Michigan, Human Performance Center, 330 Packard Road, Ann Arbor, Michigan 48104, U.S.A.

J. A. Scott Kelso, Haskins Laboratories, 270 Crown St., New Haven, Connecticut 06510, U.S.A.

Stuart Klapp, Department of Psychology, California State University, Hayward, California 94542, U.S.A.

Stephen Kosslyn, Department of Psychology and Social Relations, Harvard University, William James Hall, 33 Kirkland St., Cambridge, Massachusetts 02138, U.S.A.

David LaBerge, Department of Psychology, University of Minnesota, Elliott Hall, Minneapolis, Minnesota 55455, U.S.A.

Elizabeth Loftus, Department of Psychology, University of Washington, Seattle, Washington 98915, U.S.A.

Gordon Logan, Department of Psychology, Erindale College, University of Toronto, Mississauga, Ontario L5L 1C6, Canada.

Peter MacNeilage, Department of Linguistics, University of Texas, Austin, Texas 78712, U.S.A.

G. Mulder, Department of Experimental Psychology, Rijksuniversiteit te Groningen, p a Biologisch Centrum Vleugel D., Karklaan 30, Haren, The Netherlands

Stephen Palmer, Department of Psychology, University of California, Berkeley, California 94720, U.S.A.

Jeroen G. W. Raaijmakers, Psychology Laboratory, University of Nijmegen, Erasmuslaan 4, Nijmegen, The Netherlands

Patrick Rabbitt, Department of Experimental Psychology, University of Oxford, South Parks Road, Oxford OX1 3UD, Great Britain

Eric Roy, Department of Kinesiology, University of Waterloo, Waterloo, Ontario N2L 3G1, Canada

Richard M. Shiffrin, Department of Psychology, Indiana University, Bloomington, Indiana 47405, U.S.A.

Robert Weber, Department of Psychology, Oklahoma State University, Stillwater, Oklahoma 74074, U.S.A.

Invited Participants

Alan D. Baddeley, MRC Applied Psychology Unit, 15 Chaucer Road, Cambridge CB2 2EF, Great Britain

Phil Barnard, MRC Applied Psychology Unit, 15 Chaucer Road, Cambridge CB2 2EF, Great Britain

Dominic G. Bouhuis, Department of Psychology, University of California, San Diego, La Jolla, California 92093, U.S.A.

Brian Butterworth, Department of Psychology, University College London, 26 Bedford Way, London WC1H OAP, Great Britain

D. Dubois, Chargée de recherches, CNRS, Laboratoire de Psychologie, Université de Paris 8, Route de la Tourelle, 75571 Paris Cedex 12, France

John Duncan, MRC Applied Psychology Unit, 15 Chaucer Road, Cambridge CB2 2EF, Great Britain

Daniel Gopher, Center for Work Safety and Human Engineering and Management, Technion-IIT, Haifa 32000, Israel

Nigel Harvey, Department of Psychology, University College London, 26 Bedford Way, London WC1H OAP, Great Britain

H. Heuer, Barladde 9, University of Bielefeld, Dr. 48, Bielefeld, W. Germany

Graham Hitch, Department of Psychology, University of Manchester, Manchester M13 9PL, Great Britain

Sylvan Kornblum, Mental Health Research Institute, The University of Michigan, Ann Arbor, Michigan 48109, U.S.A.

John B. Long, Ergonomics Unit, University College London, 26 Bedford Way, London WC1H OAP, Great Britain

Tony J. Marcel, MRC Applied Psychology Unit, 15 Chaucer Road, Cambridge CB2 2EF, Great Britain

Tom Moran, Xerox, Palo Alto Research Center, 333 Coyote Hill Road, Palo Alto, California 94304, U.S.A.

John Morton, MRC Applied Psychology Unit, 15 Chaucer Road, Cambridge CB2 2EF, Great Britain

Raymond S. Nickerson, Bolt, Beranek & Newman Inc., 50 Moulton St., Cambridge, Massachusetts 02138, U.S.A.

William Phillips, Department of Psychology, University of Stirling, Stirling FK9 4LA, Great Britain

Jean Requin, Centre National de la Recherche Scientifique, Institut de Neurophysiologie et Psychophysiologie, Departement de Psychobiologie Experimentale, 31 Chemin Joseph-Aiguier, 13274 Marseille Cedex 2, France

Andries F. Sanders, Institute for Perception, TNO, Soesterberg, Kampweg 5, Postbus 23, The Netherlands

Saul Sternberg, Human Information Processing Research Department, Bell Telephone Laboratories, Murray Hill, New Jersey 07974, U.S.A.

Anne Treisman, Department of Psychology, The University of British Columbia, 154-2053 Main Hall, Vancouver, B. C. Canada

Elizabeth Warrington, The National Hospital for Nervous Diseases, Queen Square, London WC1N 3BG, Great Britain

Alan T. Welford, 581 Kamoku St., Apt. 506, Honolulu, Hawaii 96826, U.S.A.

A. Wertheim, Institute for Perception, TNO, Soesterberg, Kampweg 5, Postbus 23, The Netherlands

Alan Wing, MRC Applied Psychology Unit, 15 Chaucer Road, Cambridge CB2 2EF, Great Britain

Co-Authors

C. Aquarius, Institute of Perception, TNO, Soesterberg, Kampweg 5, Postbus 23, The Netherlands

William Brown, Department of Psychology, Oklahoma State University, Stillwater, Oklahoma 74074, U.S.A.

Thomas Carlson, Department of Psychology, Stanford University, Stanford, California

Patrick Cavanagh, Department of Psychology, University of Montreal, Case Postale 6128, Montreal 101, Quebec, Canada

Paul Chase, Department of Psychology, University of California, Berkeley, California 94720, U.S.A.

Susan Dumais, Bell Telephone Laboratories, Murray Hill, New Jersey 07974, U.S.A.

Susan Ehrlich, Department of Psychology, Harvard University, William James Hall, 33 Kirkland St., Cambridge, Mass. 02138 U.S.A.

Joyce Farrell, Department of Psychology, Stanford University, Stanford, California 94305, U.S.A.

David Greim, Department of Psychology, California State University, Hayward, California 94542, U.S.A.

Peter Hamilton, Department of Psychology, University of Stirling, Stirling, Scotland

Larry Hochhaus, Department of Psychology, Oklahoma State University, Stillwater, Oklahoma 74074, U.S.A.

Judith Hutchinson, Department of Linguistics, University of Texas, Austin, Texas 78712, U.S.A.

Rebecca Jones, Department of Psychology, Elliott Hall, University of Minnesota, Minneapolis, Minnesota 55455, U.S.A.

Axel Larsen, Psychological Laboratory, Copenhagen University, Njalsgade 94, DK-2300 Copenhagen S., Denmark

Sarah Lasater, Department of Linguistics, University of Texas, Austin, Texas, 78712, U.S.A.

Edward H. Lichtenstein, Department of Psychology, University of Illinois, Psychology Building, Champaign, Illinois 81820, U.S.A.

Allan MacLean, MRC Applied Psychology Unit, 15 Chaucer Road, Cambridge CB2 2EF, Great Britain

Elizabeth Marshburn, Department of Psychology, California State University, Hayward, California 94542, U.S.A.

L. Mulder, Department of Experimental Psychology, Rijksuniversiteit te Groningen, p a Biologisch Centrum Vleugel D., Karklaan 30, Haren, The Netherlands

Lawrence Parsons, Center for Human Information Processing, University of California, San Diego, La Jolla, California 92093, U.S.A.

D. Reitsma, Institute of Perception, TNO, Soesterberg, Kampweg 5, Postbus 23, The Netherlands.

Eleanor Rosch, Department of Psychology, University of California, Berkeley, California 94720, U.S.A.

Tony Sanford, Department of Psychology, University of Glasgow, Adam Smith Building, Glasgow G12 8RT, Great Britain

Walter Schneider, Department of Psychology, University of Illinois, Psychological Building, Champaign, Illinois 81820, U.S.A.

Richard M. Shiffrin, Department of Psychology, Indiana University, Bloomington, Indiana 47405, U.S.A.

Steven Shwartz, Department of Psychology, Yale University, New Haven, Connecticut 06520, U.S.A.

Louis Tassinary, Department of Psychology, Gerry Hall, Dartmouth College, Hanover, New Hampshire 03755, U.S.A.

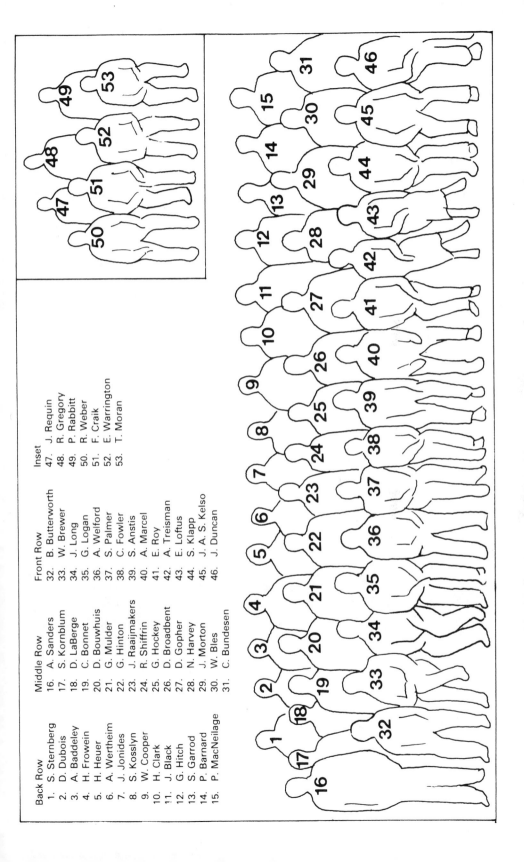

Back Row
1. S. Sternberg
2. D. Dubois
3. A. Baddeley
4. H. Frowein
5. H. Heuer
6. A. Wertheim
7. J. Jonides
8. S. Kosslyn
9. W. Cooper
10. H. Clark
11. J. Black
12. G. Hitch
13. S. Garrod
14. P. Barnard
15. P. MacNeilage

Middle Row
16. A. Sanders
17. S. Kornblum
18. D. LaBerge
19. C. Bonnet
20. D. Bouwhuis
21. G. Mulder
22. G. Hinton
23. J. Raaijmakers
24. R. Shiffrin
25. G. Hockey
26. D. Broadbent
27. D. Gopher
28. N. Harvey
29. J. Morton
30. W. Bles
31. C. Bundesen

Front Row
32. B. Butterworth
33. W. Brewer
34. J. Long
35. G. Logan
36. A. Welford
37. S. Palmer
38. C. Fowler
39. S. Anstis
40. A. Marcel
41. E. Roy
42. A. Treisman
43. E. Loftus
44. S. Klapp
45. J. A. S. Kelso
46. J. Duncan

Inset
47. J. Requin
48. R. Gregory
49. P. Rabbitt
50. R. Weber
51. F. Craik
52. E. Warrington
53. T. Moran

Preface

The first Attention and Performance Symposium was held in Soesterberg in 1966. The present volume is the ninth in the series and constitutes the proceedings of the meeting held in Cambridge, England from 13 to 18 July, 1980. The conference exemplified, we believe, many of the best features of previous meetings: papers of high quality, presented by new as well as established researchers; lively discussions and debates; and social and intellectual interaction among professional colleagues.

As with previous meetings, the program attempted to reflect the suggestions made by the members of the Council of the Association as to both topics and speakers. In the tradition of previous meetings, "Attention and Performance" was interpreted broadly to include most of human information processing; all papers were invited and the program consisted of sessions in which a longer tutorial review paper preceded a number of research papers. We felt obliged to cover a relatively broad range of topics, but within that range took advantage of the flexibility accorded to the organizers to emphasize certain areas and approaches. Firstly, we attempted to bias sessions somewhat more in the direction of ecological validity than is traditionally the case with Attention and Performance. We did so in some cases by selecting particular topic areas such as "Perception of Scenes and Objects" and "Language Comprehension and Knowledge," while in others we selected particular contributors likely to present work extending beyond the standard laboratory paradigm. The chapters by Loftus and by Rabbitt are examples of this. Secondly, we attempted to organize sessions linking areas of study that are often approached in isolation. The session on the "Perception and Effect of Visual Motion" is an example of this, while the sessions on "Motor Programming" and on "Speech Production" were intended to inter-relate. We felt more would be gained, both by contributors and by readers, especially general readers, from a concerted treatment of a particular issue by specialists than from a set of individually interesting but disparate papers addressing different issues.

Thirdly, with the encouragement of the committee of the Attention and Performance Association and our publisher, we attempted to produce a volume of an appropriate length within a reasonable time following the meeting (previous volumes had tended to be rather long and slow to appear). Rapid publication encourages contributors to publish their best and most recent research. A shorter volume attracts a lower price, making sales to individuals possible. To attain the goals concerning the length and timing of the volume, we adopted a two-tier system of editing. Following an initial evaluation by two reviewers, of which one was a conference attendee and one was not (a list appears below), associate editors integrated referees' comments with their own and where necessary recommended changes in the original manuscripts to the contributors (Phil Barnard was responsible for Parts 5 and 8; John Duncan for Parts 3 and 9; Graham Hitch for Parts 4 and 6; Tony Marcel for Parts 1 and 2, and Alan Wing for Part 7). Editing the revised manuscripts was carried out by the editors. They are fully responsible for the inclusion of papers and their final form. Sharing the editing in this way between several people meant that we were able to apply ourselves wholeheartedly to the manuscripts and most contributors (although not all) will agree that papers improved as a result. In short, our aim was to produce as soon as possible following the meeting an appropriately sized volume in which a current set of authentic issues, important in their own right and of concern to experimental psychologists, was addressed in a coherent manner at both the conceptual and the empirical level.

The extent to which our aims have been achieved, we leave to the reader. It is appropriate, however, for us to describe the difficulties associated with our approach. The attempt to reflect both our own interests and those of the Council meant that we spread our net wide, and while we believe strongly that Attention and Performance should not become too specialist; nevertheless the freedom to concentrate more narrowly might have made our task easier. For that reason, we note with approval the Executive Committee's suggestion that future organizers should feel free to organize a more specialized and concentrated program than has been the case in recent conferences. Second, by requiring contributors to speak within a limited topic area, we are aware that some contributors presented papers on issues that would not have been their own first choice. Lastly, meeting deadlines whether of length or of time, is never easy, and meeting both simultaneously can rarely be achieved without some wailing and gnashing of teeth on the part of contributors and considerable efforts on the part of our Associate Editors. We hope that the prompt publication of a reasonable-sized volume will convince all of us that the effort was worthwhile.

Symposia are social as well as professional affairs. It was the first Attention and Performance meeting to be held in England and we enjoyed inviting North American and European colleagues to Cambridge. We had a good time and have some happy memories to remind us. It was also a sad occasion in that Andries Sanders, initiator of the first meeting and mentor of the Association, resigned the Chairmanship of the Executive Committee. His commitment and contribution to the success of the Association and the symposia cannot be overestimated. He is replaced as Chairman by Saul Sternberg.

Finally, no conference of this kind comes into being without considerable dedication and effort. From the Attention and Performance Association, we would like to thank Council members for their helpful suggestions concerning possible contributors and members of the Executive Committee for their help and guidance and especially the Secretary, Sylvan Kornblum, for organizing the funding of American attendees. We thank the Medical Research Council for the use of the facilities at the Applied Psychology Unit, Cambridge, and particularly to staff involved in the organization of the conference: Lillian Astell, Alan Copeman, Marge Eldridge, Olive Fowles, Audrey Hull, Rob Milroy, Tina Purell and Derek Simmonds, and the office staff of the Applied Psychology Unit. Marge Eldridge also acted as editorial assistant and coordinator for the publication of the proceedings. She fulfilled both roles with enthusiasm and dedication and the timely appearance of the proceedings owes much to her efforts. Although both editors consider the conference and volume to have been very much a joint venture, it should be pointed out that the Executive Committee invited Alan Baddeley to be the organizer of the conference and responsible for the volume. He accepted on the understanding that John Long would be co-organizer. Since John Long undertook the lions share of the work, he appears as first editor.

Lastly, we would like to thank the contributors: for producing good papers and for taking our considerable demands seriously. Conventional wisdom suggested that contributors would not bring their manuscripts to the conference—but they did: we were warned that there was no reason to assume that deadlines would be met—but they were. Many thanks.

Alan Baddeley
John Long

List of Referees
(in alphabetical order)

Alan Benson	Tom Moran
Don Bouwhuis	Michael Morgan
Oliver Braddick	John Morton
Brian Butterworth	Bernard Moulden
Tom Carr	Ray Nickerson
Derek Corcoran	Ian Nimmo-Smith
Roddy Cowie	Alan Parkin
Anne Cutler	Bill Phillips
Johannes Dichgans	John Pickering
Mike Eysenck	Mike Posner
Gerald Gazdar	Jean Requin
Mark Georgeson	John Richardson
David Green	David Rosenbaum
Nigel Harvey	Andries Sanders
Harold Hawkins	Tony Sanford
Laurette Hay	Henry Shaffer
James Hoffman	Tim Shallice
Pete Howell	Philip Smith
Ian Hunter	Keith Stenning
Chris Idzikowski	Saul Sternberg
Greg Jones	Neil Thomson
John Kennedy	Anne Treisman
Ray Klein	Elizabeth Warrington
Sylvan Kornblum	Dave Wastell
David Lee	Alan Welford
Peter McLeod	Pat Wright
Ted Megaw	Richard Young
Stephen Monsell	

ATTENTION and PERFORMANCE IX

Proceedings of the Ninth International Symposium
on Attention and Performance
Jesus College, Cambridge, England, July 13-18, 1980

1 Association Lecture: From the Percept to the Cognitive Structure

Donald E. Broadbent
Department of Experimental Psychology
University of Oxford
Oxford, England

ABSTRACT

This chapter considers the problems of a system constructing a cognitive structure from a sequence of percepts each occurring separately in time. Thus a representation of each needs to be preserved temporarily, until the unified code for the combination can be established. But temporary memory seems to be limited in its performance. A way around this is to suppose that events are grouped hierarchically and the higher-order codes of the groups preserved in temporary memory; but recent evidence is difficult to reconcile with this. A fresh experiment is presented that shows that if a number of short lists are presented separately and then recalled together at the end of the session, such recall may be at least as good as similar recall of fewer but longer lists. This again is hard to handle with a model based on list codes that are unpacked and lost at recall. The preferred conclusion is that groups are not linked into higher-order codes but through common elements, each of which may occur in several fragments in storage.

INTRODUCTION

The purpose of this chapter is to take the border line between two traditional areas of cognitive psychology and to see what we can say about the way one fits into the other. One of the traditional areas is that of perception: the processes that take an event in the outside world and produce inside the person a representation that corresponds to it. In recent years, these processes have been studied with particular enthusiasm in the realm of identification of individual words. We now know a great deal about the effects of probability of a word in the language or of its imageability and meaningfulness or of the transition probabilities between its letters, on the chances of identifying it correctly. Some special paradigms have used slightly different tasks, such as the decision whether a letter string is a word or meaningless or whether a string contains a specified letter, to dissect the perceptual mechanism further. In some cases, experimenters have been greatly daring and gone into the effect of context. They have looked at the priming effects of showing another associated word shortly before the one that is to be perceived and demonstrated that this does improve performance. In general, however, research effort has concentrated on the factors affecting the reaction to the individual word.

My own last contribution to this series of meetings was in this tradition (Broadbent & Broadbent, 1980a), so naturally I think it eminently respectable. Even the most complex and complicated human skills do have to involve detection of one rather than another external event: If external events A, B, C, or D can influence performance, then some internal events α, β, γ, or δ have to take place representing, inside the person, the situation that has actually happened as opposed to all the others that might have happened. But linguists or people working in artificial intelligence can well criticize this tradition of looking at the isolated percept. They might rather say that the key feature of language lies in the structure connecting the individual percepts. Indeed even words themselves may be structures of more elementary units. Similar comments could be made about solving chess problems or going shopping. We bring these complex structures, as well as the function of perceiving the individual events, into our performance in any real situation.

There is therefore a second traditional area, the study of cognitive structure. When we are aware of some piece of knowledge such as that "in the park a hippie touched the debutante," or "yesterday at Luigi's Bar Carlo was bitten by Mary's dog," how should this knowledge of represented formally as existing inside the person? The usual line of attack on this problem has been to suggest a formalism and to elaborate it to discover any deficiencies or inconsistencies, perhaps with some experiments to check particular predictions. The various formulations have been reviewed a number of times, for example by Cohen (1977) and by Anderson (1976). They appear to differ quite widely, though in fact there may be translation rules between them. Some follow hierarchic structures, along a line from phrase structure grammar (Chomsky, 1957) through early formulations of semantic knowledge (Collins & Quillian, 1969) to propositional models (Anderson & Bower, 1973); others follow an approach through networks or matrices of relationships (Norman & Rumelhart, 1975). It is hard to devise any experiments that would really distinguish between approaches at such a high level of abstraction; Anderson (1976) is sufficiently sceptical of the possibility that he advocates thoughtful pursuit of one's own preferred formulation. At our last meeting, Kintsch (1980) also seemed dubious whether any agreed certainty had resulted from the fairly massive effort made in this area by psychologists over the past decade.

The point that I want to address is this. Whatever model one takes for cognitive structure, it is clear that some operations must take place to construct that structure from the successive percepts of individual events. This point is obscured by thinking of *simultaneous* visual presentation of information, as when one beholds the dramatic scene in Luigi's Bar. In that case we can be lured into thinking that, because the sensory information is all present at the same time, the percept is readily translatable into the cognitive structure. But, in hearing speech or in seeing words one at a time or of course frequently in watching a sequence of nonverbal events, the structure of meaning depends on taking the temporary representations of individual events and operating upon them. We see Carlo; later we see the dog approaching; subsequently we see Carlo's leg obscured by a massive pair of jaws; and only then do we see the dog withdraw and blood pouring from the wound. This then becomes recoded as "Carlo was bitten by the dog," and at a later time we may even be unable to retrieve the individual observations from which it was constructed (except of course by reconstruction from probable inference).

Earlier, we spoke of percepts α, β, and γ that represented various outside events A, B, and C. It would be easy to say that a further internal event 1 corresponds to ABC and a different internal event 2 corresponds to CBA. Code 1 might occur when "dog bites man" and 2 would occur when "man bites dog." Then all we need to get from the percept to the structure is that the percepts α, β, and γ should all persist in some temporary form until the last of them is in and that then translation should occur into the new code 1.

But the point that worries me is that experiments on temporary memory show some limits on its efficiency, which we discuss in the next section. These limits would make it harder to build up and use some kinds of cognitive structuring than others. So, much as students of perception can say that their area of interest is actually vital for cognitive structure and students of structure can say that perception alone is insufficient, one can argue that the area of transfer from one to the other can shed light on both.

THE POSSIBILITIES OF WORKING MEMORY

The Limits

The problem of holding simultaneously a number of independent percepts has of course been ably and amply discussed by Baddeley and Hitch (1974), under the term *working memory*. As they have shown, some temporary storage of this kind can take place in an internal articulatory loop, and in that case its scope is limited by the spoken duration of the words being used to describe the information. Fewer long words can be held than short one. This part of the mechanism seems usually to be used in serial learning to hold the earlier items in the sequence. There is also some other form of temporary or working memory, which is in general used for later items in the presentation sequence and is nonarticulatory. This second kind of code or representation can perhaps be regarded as the one described by Craik and Lockhart (1972) as maintaining material that is still undergoing processing. Of course, particular instructions or features of the task will doubtless alter the strategy of articulating early items and holding later ones elsewhere, but that seems to be a common or usual thing to do.

The nonarticulatory part of working memory is of particular importance in later sections of this chapter. The limit upon it seems to be one of number of items rather than duration of the corresponding spoken words; estimates derived from the recency portion of long lists put it at three or perhaps four items.

A rather similar limit is suggested by a number of other phenomena in short-term experiments; in particular, the grouping of a continuous series of items into subunits of three or four seems to be the most effective way of improving their recall. The benefits of grouping can be analyzed in the same way as we have looked at other forms of cognitive structures; each item is held temporarily after arrival and then reencoded into a new representation corresponding to the group (Broadbent, 1975). On such an analysis, the fact that the optimum group size is three or four suggests that the number of temporary representations of individual events cannot easily exceed three or four. At least this is so when the events are words rather than nonverbal occurrences. The traditional memory span with its considerably larger number of items is a special case, arising because all the items are inserted and then recalled without any requirement to hold some for later use. In a continuous process such as producing a response to each of a series of independent inputs, one cannot lag behind to the extent of six or seven items and still continue to follow efficiently (Poulton, 1954).

A limit of three or four independent items is however rather small. Is there any evidence that cognitive structure shows similar limits? In an earlier consideration of grouping, I pointed out that recall from long-term memory tended to occur in bursts. People asked to recall the countries of Europe, or Snow White's dwarfs, would give three or four and pause, then another burst, and so on (Broadbent, 1975). My techniques were crude; Graesser and Mandler (1978) have with much greater elegance taken recall from a variety of semantic categories and, for each subject, segmented the series of responses by counting as a burst all responses separated by less than a critical time interval. If a short critical time is used, the average length of burst is of course short; as longer and longer critical times are used, the average burst length also increases. There is, however, an inflection in the curve for each person, where the same average burst length is found for a substantial range of critical times. This is the point at which there is a distinct pause in the responding; and for each person it appeared between three and four items per burst.

Gruenewald and Lockhead (1980) used a different method but again found about 90% of clusters contained four or fewer words. The key point is that long-term memory does seem to be linked into bundles not too far different in size from the limits of the nonarticulatory working memory.

How Are the Temporary Representations Stored?

We have, however, gone ahead of ourselves; why should the temporary representations be in the nonarticulatory working memory rather than in the articulatory or indeed in some sensory or ikonic form? Indeed Broadbent (1975) presented some results that now seem to show fairly clearly that the temporary representations can be in sensory form, if the situation allows it. The experiment was one in which a series of items, grouped by threes, were presented in series, and recall was then required either in the order of presentation or starting with the last group. The theoretical point was that the last items could still be in the temporary code at the end of presentation. If that code was, for example, articulatory, it might well be simpler and more straightforward to output the last items immediately rather than to say earlier items first. In fact, Broadbent (1975) found that recall was better in the order of original presentation than it was if the last group was to be reported first; so I concluded that the temporary representations were not in a form available for immediate output.

This was an incautious argument, however, because the experiment was performed using acoustic stimulation. At that time, most of us thought that any difference between auditory and visual events could last only a short time, corresponding to the duration of a relatively brief precategoric acoustic store. It has since become clear that this is not so and that acoustic stimuli may show memory that is different from that for visual stimuli, even over quite long time intervals (Broadbent, Vines, & Broadbent, 1978; Frankish, 1976; Martin & Jones, 1979; Penney, 1979; Watkins & Watkins, 1977). As a result, the experiment has been repeated using visual stimulation. The results were then quite different (Broadbent, Cooper, Frankish, & Broadbent, 1980). With visual stimulation, it is better to respond with the last group first than it is to go through the groups in the order of arrival. Acoustic presentation creates one kind of temporary code, of a sensory type. With visual presentation this kind of code is unavailable, at least when items succeed each other in the same location (Broadbent & Broadbent, in press). The temporary code is then something other than sensory.

We have recently (Broadbent & Broadbent, 1980b) taken the obvious step of checking how far the grouping mechanism will work if the sensory store is eliminated by successive visual presentation and yet the person is hindered in using an articulatory loop by being asked to repeat aloud some repetitive phrase, as in the work of Levy (1971) or of Baddeley, Thomson, and Buchanan (1975). To do this we used a technique derived from that of Bower (1972), in which the material consists of letter trigrams, and in one condition the letters of each trigram make up a meaningful unit such as FBI or BBC. The advantage of meaningful units is just as great if articulatory suppression is being used. It seems fair to conclude that the temporary representations are not being held in an articulatory form.

Another piece of evidence from the same experiment is relevant. If we take less meaningful items such as digits and present them in groups, the recall of later digits in a group becomes heavily contingent upon the recall of the first digit of that group; you recall either the whole group or none of it. This effect also survives articulatory suppression.

To summarize this part of the argument, the temporary representation may be of a sensory type when the information arrives through the ear; when sensory and articulatory storage are made unlikely, grouping still occurs. Hence it seems to be mediated by a nonarticulatory working memory.

The Hierarchic Mechanism

In this section, we can put forward one account of the way the working memory builds up a cognitive structure. This account looked plausible a few years ago and still is one strategy by which the process may sometimes happen. But it ought to be said at this stage that it has severe limitations, so that in the end we shall come to a rather different point of view. The merit of stating the hierarchic approach is to introduce some of the topics important in the area, not to put forward a truly satisfactory theory.

To work through an example, let us consider sequences of letters and repre-sent the internal code for each triplet by a digit. Thus if a person receives the sequence BBC, the working memory holds each letter until the third arrives, when they are all cleared and replaced by some abstract symbol we shall call 1 (see Fig. 1.1). While this symbol is being held, the letters IBA arrive, and since these stand for *I*ndependent *B*roadcasting *A*uthority, they are replaced by the symbol 2. The working memory now holds 1 and 2, but both these have some connection with British television and can therefore be replaced by an even more abstract code that we shall call TV and suppose to hold only one place in working memory. The person therefore awaits the next letters holding only one code, TV, in working memory. (It is worth noting that these abstract symbols must be private codes of the person concerned and that we are only representing them for convenience by numbers or letters. They do not correspond to semantic features of the public language and therefore need not call up all the elementary units that the reader might understand by, say, TV.)

In a similar way, the person can then receive TUC and recode it as 3 and CBI and recode that as 4. The working memory then holds TV, 3, 4, but 3 and 4 are both large industrial organizations and can be represented by the abstract code IND. At this stage, the next input letters might be JFK, coded 5, but this reveals that the abstract codes TV, IND are all British and cry to be replaced by the

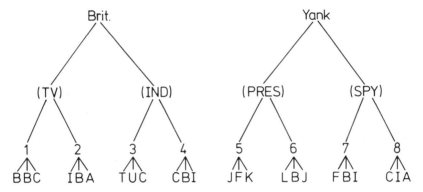

FIG. 1.1.   Hierarchic recoding of a sequence of meaningful letters, allowing temporary memory to hold only a few abstract codes.

single code Brit. (Notice that this code is at the third level of abstraction; TV and IND at the second; 1, 2, 3, and 4 at the first.) The working memory is still therefore only holding two items, Brit, 5. When the next letters are LBJ, coded 6, it becomes obvious that 5 and 6 should be coded as something like PRES, and the person is still only holding two codes while waiting for the next letters. These might be FBI, which become 7, and CIA, which become 8. The next step is clearly to recode 7 and 8 into something we might call SPY and to code PRES, SPY as Yank. The working memory is now holding only two items, Brit, Yank.

If the person is now asked to recall the sequence of letters, the code Brit can be expanded into TV, IND, while still holding Yank in working memory. TV can then expand into 1, 2, and 1 into BBC. The latter stage perhaps could be straight into overt output, and if so those who have been following closely will see that the whole operation of handling 24 letters has been performed with a working memory holding a maximum of only five separate items at a time. After presentation and until recall it can get by with only two codes, leaving some spare room for other activities. The trick is, in other words, to hold in working memory only the relatively abstract codes that will allow the more specific items to be retrieved, the addresses rather than the items themselves.

This notion will of course be familiar to you; it is only spelling out in detail the same general mechanism of chunking demonstrated so elegantly by Miller (1956) so many years ago. It builds a structure that is hierarchic, like a zoological classification, and tree structures of this kind are very familiar in our theoretical thinking. It was of course shown by Bower, Clark, Lesgold, and Winzenz (1969) that a very large number of words could be memorized by people if they were arranged in such a treelike structure rather than randomly; and studies of the grouping or categories into which naturally occurring words fall are an important growth industry in experimental psychology (Rosch, 1975). To take an example of the broader application of the principle, one can cite a fairly old-fashioned instance from Broadbent (1971). At that time, there was some evidence for the encoding of sentences into a single representation addressed predominantly through one higher-order code. The evidence came from studies of probed recall. The result suggesting this view was that, in simple active or passive sentences containing two nouns, the surface subject (the first noun to occur) was a better cue for recall of the sentence than the second noun was (Tannenbaum & Williams, 1968; Wright, 1969). This result could easily be described as grouping or nesting the remainder of the sentence under an address code identified as the surface subject of the sentence. It fitted well with the linguists' notions of "topic and comment" or "given and new" and with empirical data on the choice of active or passive sentences when describing pictures in which the agent of the depicted action was animate or inanimate (Harris, 1978). In a passage made up of many sentences it fitted with the relation between thematization and the choice of the noun to be the subject in a late-occurring sentence (Perfetti & Goldman, 1975). One could think therefore of the comprehension of a sentence as the building up of a complex code addressed through the subject.

These kinds of operation then can be seen as reconciling the limits of working memory with the ability to retain a widely extended cognitive structure. The structure tends to be hierarchic and to build up by class inclusion. Unfortunately, however, there are a number of difficulties in thinking of such a process as universal.

INADEQUACIES OF HIERARCHIC THEORY

Matrix Material Is Also Easy

The first difficulty that we have to recognize is that hierarchies have no special status in efficiency of memory. In the natural world, structure may be shown by organization on many independent dimensions rather by the appearing of nesting sets. Streets may be contained within cities, cities within nations, nations within continents; but regardless of their nation, cities may be large or small, windy or sheltered, on a river or not, high or low in altitude, and subject to many other classifications. These relationships form a table or matrix rather than a tree, as in Fig. 1.2. But if one presents material organized in such a way it is, like hierarchic material, much more easily recalled than random arrangements of words are, and there does not seem to be any difference on the average level of recall between hierarchy and matrix (Broadbent, Cooper, & Broadbent, 1978). This was true even though different experiments varied quantity of material and similar factors. Forms of representation can of course be translated, as we saw earlier in discussing the difficulty of testing between various approaches to cognitive structure. Hierarchies are only matrices with certain empty cells (Vickery, 1965). Conversely one can write out a matrix as if

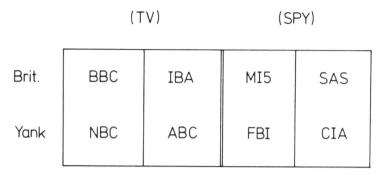

FIG. 1.2.   Matrix structuring of letter groups on two dimensions, requiring more codes in temporary memory.

it were hierarchic, by repeating the classificatory terms of each dimension over and over again under each of the terms used in other dimensions, as in Fig. 1.3. It is easy to see how a computer program using either type of data structure could transform an input of either type to fit its own preferred format.

Although such an operation is easy for computers, they do not necessarily have a limit of comparable size on their working memories. It is really quite difficult to see how a system of the kind described in the last section could store material that was matrix rather than hierarchic. To take up again our example of BBC, IBA, FBI, CIA, and so on: Suppose another two items had been NBC and ABC, which are of course TV but Yank rather than Brit. And suppose another two items had been MI5 and SAS, which are SPY but Brit rather than Yank. Now some of the tricks we used to group materials into chunks, and to avoid the limitations of working memory, will not do. In the earlier list, we dropped TV as well as IND, because both could be addressed by Brit; but now we need to hold both codes at once, because neither by itself can act as the address of a single chunk. The load on working memory needs therefore to be at least one code more.

One can imagine various dodges to get around this, but they create further difficulties. For instance, the categories could be doubled in size, so that working memory did not hold the codes for TV and SPY at all but simply remembered Brit and Yank as before. But we know experimentally that increasing the number of outputs dependent on a single cue code reduces the efficiency of recall; the phenomenon is known as cue overload (Moscovitch & Craik, 1976; Watkins & Watkins, 1975). If people were using this technique, therefore they ought to do worse with matrices. As a second try, we might suppose that people form codes that are private and do not correspond to our externally imposed ones. They might have a single code for Brit-TV and another for Yank-SPY, which could be chunked into a single more abstract code X. Similarly, the new items could be grouped into Yank-TV and Brit-SPY, and these represented by the more abstract

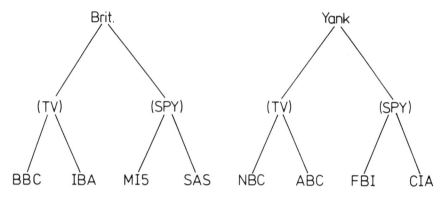

FIG. 1.3.   Hierarchic version of a matrix.

code Y. This would then allow performance to be as good as ever by a method that was in fact hierarchic although the material looks, from outside, like a matrix. The snag with this idea is that memory ought, in that case, to be the same for matrix and hierarchic material in every way and not just in the average level of recall but in the pattern of errors, the order of recall, and so on. Yet Broadbent, Cooper and Broadbent (1978) did not find that. In the hierarchy the recall of a group of words was conditional upon the recall of the superordinate cue, although for the matrix it was not; and in some of the experiments the pattern of clustering in recall was different for the matrix, as would be reasonable if words from different clusters were being retrieved by expansion of the same higher-order code, *not* different ones. Although equally efficiently recalled, and therefore presumably placing no more demand on working memory, matrix material does show the kind of differences that suggest that its structure is truly represented inside the person. How then do we encode matrix material without exceeding the limits of working memory?

Chunks Survive Recall

The second difficulty brings me to my one piece of new experimental material. The account of recall as due to hierarchical chunking of groups of items, with retention in working memory only of the abstract codes of chunks, makes the assumption that a single recall trial fills the working memory with the abstract codes, the addresses, of the material used in that trial. During recall each code in turn is unpacked and this means that each is replaced by the lower codes of its own and of later items; after recall the abstract codes for that list are no longer held in memory, If, therefore, they have been held *only* in working memory, they are lost. Peter FitzGerald has carried out the following experiment that makes this loss of abstract codes during recall very implausible. In essence, the experiment requires the same material to be presented either in two long lists or in six short ones. Each list is recalled immediately after presentation. The interest lies in comparison of the two conditions in a further final recall at the end of the session. If the abstract codes for each short list were lost in recall, and no higher-order codes were formed to connect material in one short list with that in another, the final recall of the short lists should be worse than that of the long ones. This is emphatically not so.

Materials.   Eighteen categories were selected from the Battig and Montague (1969) norms, and three were assigned to each of six lists. The best four exemplars from each category were chosen, and the resulting 12 words per list were placed in random order subject to the constraint that all four words from a category should not occur together and that no more than two words from any one category should occur in the last four serial positions. This then provided six short lists for the 6 × 12 condition; two long lists for the 2 × 36 condition were formed by joining together the first three and the last three lists of the 6 × 12, simply appending the first word of one list to the last of the other.

Subjects and Design.   Thirty-two women from the Oxford Panel were tested, all aged between 20 and 40. Half were tested individually and half in groups; no significant main effect or interaction of this difference was found, and it will be ignored from here on. Half the subjects were assigned to the 2 × 36 condition and half to the 6 × 12. Each subject went through the lists assigned to her condition, recalling each after presentation, then gave a final free recall for all the material in the session, and then gave cued recall to the names of the categories employed.

Procedure.   Each subject was given a response booklet, which had on the first page six numbered columns of 12 spaces (for the 6 × 12 group) or two columns of 36 spaces (for the 2 × 36 group). She was told that after each list had finished, she was to write down the words she had seen, in the order she remembered them, which need not be the order of presentation. (Subjects who failed to keep this instruction were discarded and replaced.) They were told that the lists were categorized and the number of categories per list. A short example list was shown; it had four words from each of four categories not otherwise used in the experiment. After any questions, subjects were reminded of their task, told the length of the response intervals, and then shown the lists.

Before each list a tone was given as a warning 2 sec before the first word. Each word was then presented on a video monitor screen for 2 sec each, with zero interstimulus interval. An asterisk signaled the end of the list. The response interval for the subject to record each list was 2.5 sec for each word presented; that is 30 sec for each list in the 6 × 12 condition and 90 sec in the 2 × 36 condition. By this time, recall appeared asymptotic to its maximum level.

At the end of the last list, subjects were asked to turn to the next page of the booklet, which then for the first time asked them to recall all the 72 words they had seen, in any order, writing the words in the sequence of recall. Three minutes were allowed for this final free recall. Lastly, subjects were again asked to turn to

TABLE 1.1
Recall of 72 Words, Presented as Six Short or Two Long Lists

Presentation Condition	Recall Condition	Words Recalled	Categories with at least one Word Recalled	Items per Category	C	Z	Tau
2 × 36	Immediate recall after list	40.69	13.69	2.97	.83	14.30	.46
	Final free recall	36.81;	12.62	2.91	.86	13.32	.01
	Final cued recall	48.19	16.44	2.92	—	—	—
6 × 12	Immediate recall after list	55.06	17.25	3.19	.84	19.87	.85
	Final free recall	38.50	13.00	2.96	.90	14.60	-.25
	Final cued recall	54.44	17.56	3.09	—	—	—

C and Z are the usual clustering scores. (Dalrymple-Alford 1970; Frankel & Cole 1971).
Tau is the correlation of input and output order.

the next page of the response booklet, which listed the 18 category names, as given by Battig and Montague, each accompanied by four spaces for responses.

Results and Discussion.   Table 1.1 summarizes the results. It is unsurprising that the immediate recall differs between the two conditions, as this is a familiar effect of list length. The main interest centers on the two tests of final memory, free and cued recall. Analysis of variance of these two conditions only shows an effect of type of recall on number of words correct, $F(1, 28) = 210.1, p < .001$; that is, unsurprisingly, cued recall is better than free recall. Much more surprising is the fact that the short lists give, numerically, slightly better overall recall than the long ones; the difference is in fact insignificant, $F(1, 28) = 2.268, p > .05$, but there is no question of inferiority of the short lists. This is still true even if we examine the free recall alone, $F(1, 30) = 0.434$. Indeed, there is an interaction of recall type and list length, $F(1, 28) = 5.862, p < .025$, which suggests that final cued recall does relatively better with short lists. Furthermore, the absence of inferiority of short lists is not due to the superior immediate recall; Table 1.5 shows that cued recall of long lists is if anything inferior to that of short lists even for items that have been successfully recalled on the first presentation.

The results quoted are for tests against the variance between subjects, but the conclusions still hold for tests against the variance between words, $F(1, 71) = 98.0, 12.7, 1.32,$ and 9.8, respectively. Further, there is no difference in final free recall between the list length conditions for number of categories recalled, for either of two measures of clustering or for the number of items recalled per category. The only difference lies in the correlation between order of output and order of presentation: The people who had received short lists were more likely to recall later items first than the people who had received long lists, $F(1, 28) = 10.816, p < .01$.

The simpleminded theory, therefore, does not work; people do not lose all the addresses for a list when they recall it nor even have a tendency to do so. Could they perhaps be formulating a higher-order code for each list, which they can somehow hold even during immediate recall, and then link to the higher-order code of the next list? If this were so, there are several features of the data that one might expect, none of which appear. First, if the list is retrieved through a single code, any forgetting of that code should lower the probabilities of recall for every category in the list. Conversely, if one category is successfully retrieved through the list code this should imply that other categories could be retrieved the same way. Therefore the probability of recall of items in one category of a list should be correlated with that of items in other categories of the same list; lists should tend to be recalled or forgotten as a whole. Admittedly, there might be tendencies in our particular material for categories from one list to be associated with categories from other lists and thus reduce the measure. But this can be checked by comparison of the tendency for all-or-none recall of the short lists in the people who received them as such and in those who had the long lists. The

TABLE 1.2
Tendency for Subjects to Recall Zero or Three Categories from the Same Short List

Group	First Half of Experiment		Second Half of Experiment		
	Actual Number of Lists with Zero or Three Categories Represented	Average of Number Predicted for Each Subject if Categories Independent	Actual Number of Lists with Zero or Three Categories Represented	Average of Number Predicted for Each Subject if Categories Independent	Average Difference
2 × 36	.9375	1.18	1.4375	1.4425	−.124 ($\sigma = .332$)
6 × 12	.9375	1.12	1.625	1.76	−.162 ($\sigma = .429$)

former should have a common code for the items in the same immediate recall, while the latter should have less tendency for the short lists to act as separate units.

For each subject, therefore, we count how many of the categories are represented by at least one item in free recall, in each half of the experiment. If the proportion of categories present is p, then if categories are independently recalled, the proportion of short lists having either zero or all three categories represented should total $p^3 + (1 - p)^3$ for that person. The excess of the observed proportion of lists over this chance prediction measures the tendency of that person to show all-or-none recall of individual lists.

In fact Table 1.2 shows that the 6×12 subjects show a predominance of negative values for this measure, as if they were showing *less* than a chance tendency for the list to survive as a whole. This however is not significant and could be due as already noted to some aspect of the distribution of categories between lists in our particular material. The key point is that the 6×12 subjects show no tendency whatever for the measure of all-or-none recall to be greater than that for the 2×36 subjects, $F(1, 30) = 0.074$, and the difference is numerically in the wrong direction.

If we separate across materials rather than subjects (Table 1.3), we find again that if a category occurs in recall the mean probability of recall of other categories in the same list can be compared with that in other lists; if this difference were greater for the 6×12 subjects than it was for a similar analysis of the 2×36 subjects that might suggest nonindependence. The difference is in that direction for three of the six lists but in the opposite direction for the other three, so against materials as against subjects there is no evidence for all-or-none recall of the list.

TABLE 1.3
Absence of Tendency of Categories in Same List To Be Recalled Together
in Final Free Recall

		List Number					
		1	2	3	4	5	6
2 × 36	In same list	.77	.37	.76	.80	.89	.54
	In other lists	.74	.59	.74	.70	.79	.64
6 × 12	In same list	.62	.63	.77	.76	.88	.81
	In other lists	.68	.62	.74	.73	.79	.74

This table is compiled by taking all cases in which at least one word has been recalled for a category and by calculating the probability of recall of other categories in the same list and in other lists. Note that half the lists show less difference for *same* and *other* when the lists are presented separately than when they are presented together.

Turning now to order of recall rather than probability, if each list has an integrated abstract code, we ought to find a tendency to cluster recall by lists as well as by meaning categories; that is, after recalling the items of one category of meaning people ought to go on to another category from the same list rather than change to another list; if they intrude from one category of meaning into another, they ought to be items from the same list; and so on. Yet Table 1.4 gives values of C (Dalrymple-Alford, 1970) and Z (Frankel & Cole, 1971) for the two conditions, scoring the whole of each long list as a category, and the differences between them are completely insignificant, $t(1, 30) = 1.02$ for C and 0.462 for Z.

Thus there is no sign at all that a list possesses a single more abstract code. If it did, items within a list should covary in probability of recall or of being forgotten, and they should be recalled in clusters. They are not. It may be worthwhile at this point to bring out the surprising nature of these findings, by emphasizing that the surprise does not depend solely on the theoretical analysis. At the empirical level it has been known for some years that final free recall of a number of lists shows a negative recency. The last items presented in each list tend to be well recalled in immediate recall but to be especially poorly recalled in final free recall (Craik, 1970). This is intelligible if those items are still being processed at the end of presentation, as in Craik and Lockhart's (1972) view; or in general terms if they are held in a very ephemeral type of storage. Yet the more lists, the more items ought to be in this position. We ought therefore to clarify what is happening to the items in the recency portion of the immediate recall, the last few presented. Also, because cued recall is more advantageous for the short lists than the long ones, we should consider what is happening in cued recall.

Table 1.5 presents the probabilities of final recall, given immediate recall, for items presented early in the list, for items presented late and recalled early, and for items presented late but not recalled early. The second type of item is especially likely to have been in some form of working memory at the end of presentation and indeed has a lower level both of free and of cued recall than do the other kinds of items. This is the usual negative recency of Craik (1970). Also,

TABLE 1.4
Extent to Which Items Cluster into the
First and Last 36 Presented

Group		C	Z
2 × 36	Mean	.822	3.990
	(σ)	(.831)	(1.055)
6 × 12	Mean	.786	3.762
	(σ)	(.1229)	(1.247)

The differences between the groups are totally insignificant; that is, items from a long list are no more recalled together than they are if presented in three short lists.

TABLE 1.5
Conditional Probabilities of Recall of Various Types for
Recent and Nonrecent Items

	Probability of Immediate Recall		Probability of Final Free Recall if in Immediate		Probability of Cued Recall if in Immediate but NOT in Final Free	
	2 × 36	6 × 12	2 × 36	6 × 12	2 × 36	6 × 12
Items early in the list (not in last three)	.55	.74	.83	.68	.75	+.86
Items in last three and in first three of immediate recall (i.e., recency effect)	.20	.39	.42*	.58*	.55	+.60
Items in last three and recalled later than first three of immediate recall	.48	.44	.80	.68	.78	+.88

*Indicates the usual negative recency effect in final free recall. The effect appears also in cued recall (i.e., the items making up the recency effect are less well linked to category names). This however does not unduly damage the 6 × 12 condition because negative recency is less marked for that condition and because the link of item to category is always greater for the short lists (see +).

This table is presented for a recency of three items for clarity; the results look similar if one, two, or four items are assumed.

short lists have more such items; not only are there more list ends in that condition, but a considerably higher proportion of the final items are immediately recalled if the lists were short. But, our surprising result still appears despite these facts, for the following reasons.

First, even for the items in recency, the short lists still give better final recall than the long ones do. Second, the items in true recency are only a small minority of all the items that were in immediate recall. Even of the last three items presented, the majority of immediate recalls were of the third type, recalled late and therefore likely to have been retrieved by category coding rather than directly from working memory. Correspondingly, the final recall of such items is very similar to that of items presented early. Thus the negative recency in final recall has only a small impact on the overall results, insufficient to balance the general tendency of other items to be recalled at least as well in short lists as in long.

Cued recall reveals the nature of the process particularly clearly. As Table 1.1 shows, when we give a category name as a cue for recall, the main benefit is to increase the number of categories from which at least one item is recalled. It is rather rare for a person, who has recalled three items from a category without prompting, suddenly to think of the fourth when the category name is given. Correspondingly, Table 1.5 shows that the probability of cued recall is high even for words that have been omitted from free recall; as seen by comparison with Table 1.1, cued recall is if anything higher for such words than it is for words in general. By looking at cued recall in such cases, we are obtaining a relatively pure measure of the link between the item and the rest of its category; and, as

Table 1.5 also shows, this link is at least as high for short lists as for long ones. Taking the early presented items to avoid the recency problem, $F(1, 30) = 1.34$, so the difference is insignificantly in favor of the short lists. The items are bound as closely to their categories in short lists as in long ones.

To summarize, negative recency effects in final recall do indeed appear as usual, but they do not make short lists worse than long because in the short lists the link of item to category is as strong as in long ones. The final free recall of the short lists is thus the same as that of long lists because the same number of categories are retrieved. We are left with the problem, how is it possible for a person to recall about a dozen categories at the end of a session of this type, if she is not chunking the categories in higher-order abstract supercategories?

Sentence Probing and the Fragment

We have seen two points against the theory of hierarchic chunking: materials that are hard to organize that way are nevertheless well retained, and a series of lists does not seem to be retained by abstract codes corresponding to whole lists. The third difficulty will lead toward a way out of these problems; it starts from the suggestion that a sentence is formed by the reader or listener into a unitary representation that can be reached through the surface subject of the sentence. The difficulty here is one that some readers will have realized as soon as the point was mentioned: Data more recent than those considered by Broadbent (1971) show that memory for sentences is sometimes equally good whether they are probed by their subjects or by their objects. The effect depends on the precise conditions of the experiment. To take two recent examples, Adams (1978) found that the effect could be exaggerated or reversed by various methods of training the people studied. If they were practiced at filling in a blank left in a sentence where the object word has been removed, then the subject was indeed a better probe than the object. If, however, they had been trained to fill in the subject word in a gap left in a sentence, then the object became a better probe. Wilhite (1980) noticed that in his results the effect depended on the precise method of scoring: If one scores the number of sentences recalled completely correctly, then his data did not show the effect. To find the traditional results it was necessary to score only the cases in which part of the sentence was forgotten. When Wilhite did that, he found that the verb was more likely to be recalled with a subject probe than an object probe, provided that in each case the other noun was forgotten; that is, people seem to have a higher probability of preserving the subject–verb part of the sentence than the object–verb part. But the whole sentence could as easily be retrieved by one noun as by the other.

These results again do not look like the recoding of the sentence into a single higher-order unit; rather, it looks like a collection of parts clinging together in a ramshackle and fragmentary way. It is time to see whether anything more satisfactory can be substituted for the notion of hierarchic chunking.

FRAGMENT THEORY AND THE DEVELOPMENT OF STRUCTURE

In a series of papers that are now deservedly conspicuous, G. V. Jones (1976, 1978, 1979) has put forward the notion that experience of a complex event gives rise to a representation of that event in fragments, each of which may contain several components of the event. If one such component is later used as a probe, it will obtain access to the fragment in which it is represented and allow recall of the other components in that fragment. The probability of this happening, that is of the right fragment existing after a given retention interval, is thus a major determinant of the probability of recall. The probability is also symmetrical, so if components A and B are present in the original event, the probability of recalling A given a probe B is the same as the probability of recalling B given a probe A. Jones has been able to fit a surprising amount of data with this set of assumptions, including data on the probed recall of sentences. The results of Wilhite (1980), mentioned previously, fit very well into Jones' approach: The apparent asymmetry in the success of subject and object as cues for the recall of a sentence lies in the greater probability that fragments containing the subject will exist. The probability of recalling the object given the subject is quite often no greater than the probability of recalling the subject given the object, but that is because sufficient fragments have been preserved for both to be available. The approach of Jones, then, can get us out of the problems raised by the data of Wilhite and Adams for the hierarchic addressing envisaged by Broadbent (1971). Can it get us out of the other problems?

Let us make the following plausible assumptions, which are similar to those of Jones but add a memory mechanism to produce the fragments. If a set of external events, $E_1, E_2, \ldots, E_n$, has occurred, then the later existence of a fragment relating any two of them, E_j, E_k, depends on the simultaneous existence at some time of representations of them, R_j, R_k, in working memory. The limits of working memory require that no single fragment will relate the full set of events unless n is less than the number of possible simultaneous representations R_{max}. Once a fragment has been formed, its continued existence does not depend on holding an abstract code of it within working memory, nor need any partial representation such as R_j persist until recall. But access to the fragment does depend on the later occurrence of one of the representations R_j contained within it. This occurrence of R_j can result either from a probe stimulus or from the holding of R_j in working memory throughout the retention interval or from the securing of access to some other fragment relating R_i to R_j where R_i is available at retrieval.

This suggested system sounds very like the notion of hierarchical chunking, and it can of course work in the same way. If several items are chunked together, any of them could act as the means of access to the whole chunk and act like the higher-level codes in the hierarchy. But the system can also work in some very different ways; the key notion of hierarchic chunking is that the means of access to the chunk is more abstract than the items themselves and has to be held in working memory or retrieved from a still higher level. In our alternative formulation there is indeed a special importance for those representations R_j that occur in more than one fragment. Through these, one fragment can call up another; yet, they need not be abstract and they need not be held in working memory throughout retention. Thus the load on working memory occurs primarily during learning, not later. To return to Fig. 1.1, this means that one might indeed generate Brit as an abstract code relating TV and IND but that the representation in working memory might then be not Brit but, say, BBC. This could gain access to a fragment containing TV, that in turn to Brit and so down to IND and TUC. The importance of Brit is that it occurs in many fragments and so, once retrieved, will allow access to many other items.

Does this distinction matter? Yes indeed, because our modified system can as well work with a matrix as with a hierarchy. If it were handling the data of Fig. 1.2, it could by holding CIA go to fragments containing Yank *or* to those containing SPY, from each of those back to lower-level items, and so on. The importance of structure in the material being remembered is not that there are abstract codes held in working memory but that there are in longer-term store a number of fragments that possess common elements. When one such fragment is retrieved and the elements that compose it entered into working memory, then any other fragment containing one of those elements can also be found. So elements with multiple relationships will help recall but do not themselves need to be held.

In the same way, thinking of the process in these terms makes our results on long and short lists very intelligible. To get back to early lists, after others have been learned, one needs only that an item from the earlier list should be accessible from one that is in working memory from the later list: perhaps from semantic memory, due to experiences outside the experiment, or perhaps merely to temporal association of the last response of one list and the first stimulus of another. Similar bridging links provide the basis for recall of the long lists themselves, and so the near equivalence of the two conditions. Lastly, this kind of approach can handle readily the results of sentence memory. There is indeed a particular importance for certain parts of a sentence; some words are more likely to be recalled and also are more effective as probes; that is, they are more likely to be encoded into fragments, but once two such words have been encoded the probability that each will cue the other will often be symmetrical. Furthermore, strategic factors may change the probability of encoding one part of the sentence rather than another.

A modified fragment system therefore avoids the weaknesses of hierarchic theory but also those of chained association between items.

It is interesting to note that a rather similar notion has been applied in computing science, to overcome the problems of possible mismatch between the data structure used in a mechanical system and the structure found natural by a human user. We knew that people find it easier to recall successfully with their own system of classificatory descriptors, rather than struggling with somebody else's and that the system they construct for themselves may vary widely in degree of hierarchization (Broadbent & Broadbent, 1978). Yet the designers of computer systems have to make some decision about the organization of the data in services intended for multiple users. Very often, some kind of hierarchic menu is used in which the user is offered a choice between alternatives, each choice is followed by another set of alternatives, and so on. Suppose however that the enquirer does not naturally think in hierarchies: What then? He might use a public data service and be offered a choice among Sport, Medicine, and What the Stars Foretell. But suppose his mind is such that he is really interested in the astrological omens for recovery from an ailment of his favorite football player: What should he do? Exactly the same problem applies to the rigid hierarchic mind encountering a structure laid out in matrix or tabular form.

One answer that has been suggested for this problem is a language called *Query-by-Example*. In this case, the user enters the structure, not by going down a tree but by providing particular items and relationships and calling for the other items that are linked to those provided in stated ways. For instance, the personnel records of a factory might conceivably be kept in hierarchic form corresponding to the management structure or in a linear list of names in alphabetic order or two-dimensionally on a map of the office or in many other ways. If an enquirer wishes to know the names of employees in a certain department, he would normally need to know the structure being used. If however he uses Query-by-Example, then he can specify any item that he happens to know in the structure and proceed to the desired goal through the items related to the starting point. For instance, if he knows that Smith works in the right department, he can ask for the names of all individuals supervised by a person defined as the supervisor of Smith. The mind of the enquirer can be as much hierarchic or matrixlike as it pleases (Zloof, 1976a, 1976b). The proposal we have been considering in human cognitive structure is itself built up and interrogated in a fashion rather like Query-by-Example and not according to the fixed tree or other structures beloved of most theorists.

CONCLUSIONS

To summarize, there is a problem of reconciling the possibility of creating cognitive structure, on the one hand, and the limited size of the working memory on the other. A way of reconciliation that has been much favored in the past is to suppose that successive items are built up into chunks accessed through a more abstract code and that the latter is held in working memory. But this encounters difficulties because it would imply differences in ease of recall between kinds of objective structure, and no such differences are found. It would also suggest that the same material would be better recalled from a few long lists than from many short ones, and it is not. Finally, it would suggest a kind of prior access in sentence memory that does not happen.

As against the notion of abstract codes, we have put forward the view that structure is represented inside people by relatively atomic fragments, connected by the fact that the same more primitive element may be represented in several such fragments. Because each fragment can be retrieved if one of its elements has been retrieved, this means that recall can proceed from fragment to fragment. The system is not, however, constrained to use any particular form of structure; some individuals may use one and some another. In either case, the relics of the process of formation of fragments will be seen in studies such as those of Graesser and Mandler (1978). As noted earlier, retention rather than learning will not load working memory very much.

One last point is worth making. The frequency with which an event has occurred can of course be counted in the nervous system without entering into a working memory of limited size. It is only the formation of fragments, the creation of structure, which needs the holding of temporary representations. This in turn means that structure is created only from selected aspects of the environment, those that have been encoded in working memory. Such a mechanism has an apparent evolutionary advantage, provided that good heuristic strategies are used by the system to select events for working memory. It should accelerate the speed of adjustment to novel environmental conditions, as compared with the speed possible for a mechanism that recorded unselectively the conditional probabilities between every possible pair of events in the environment.

Yet a working memory is necessary also, as many have pointed out (Anderson & Bower, 1973) for the comprehension and emission of speech, at a stage earlier than the motor process of articulation. There is therefore a logical link between the mechanism needed for the formation of structure and the mechanisms capable of producing a verbal report. Flint (1979) has produced a number of experiments supporting the view that empirically also these processes are connected. Events that cannot be consciously reported show, in his experiments, detectable aftereffects but do not show the formation of associative links. He therefore suggests that the working memory that underlies verbal introspection is also the system that has the main responsibility for the formation of associations between the items selected for entry to it and that this is the machinery that people usually describe under the somewhat ambiguous term *consciousness*. I would give to this intriguing idea the name of Flint's Conjecture. If that conjecture is sound, then it is not perceptual awareness (as is sometimes thought) that is conscious; it is the process of going from the percept to the cognitive structure, with which we have been concerned.

ACKNOWLEDGMENT

The author is employed and his research supported by the Medical Research Council.

REFERENCES

Adams, R. G. *Retrieval from remembered sentences.* Unpublished doctoral dissertation, N. E. London Polytechnic, 1978.

Anderson, J. R. *Language, memory, and thought.* Hillsdale, N.J.: Lawrence Erlbaum Associates, 1976.

Anderson, J. R., & Bower, G. H. *Human associative memory.* New York: Wiley, 1973.

Baddeley, A. D., & Hitch, G. Working memory. In G. H. Bower (Ed.), *The psychology of learning and motivation* (Vol. 8). New York: Academic, 1974.

Baddeley, A. D., Thomson, N., & Buchanan, M. Word length and the structure of short-term memory. *Journal of Verbal Learning and Verbal Behavior.* 1975, *14,* 575-599.

Battig, W. P., & Montague, W. E. Category norms for verbal items in 56 categories: A replication and extension of the Connecticut category norms. *Journal of Experimental Psychology Monograph,* 1969, *80,* No. 3.

Bower, G. H. Perceptual groups as coding units in immediate memory. *Psychonomic Science,* 1972, *27,* 217-219.

Bower, G. H., Clark, M. C., Lesgold, A. M., & Winzenz, D. Hierarchical retrieval schemes in recall of categorized word lists. *Journal of Verbal Learning and Verbal Behavior,* 1969, *8,* 323-343.

Broadbent, D. E. *Decision and stress.* London: Academic, 1971.

Broadbent, D. E. The magic number seven after fifteen years. In A. Kennedy & A. Wilkes (Eds.), *Studies in long term memory.* London: Wiley, 1975.

Broadbent, D. E., & Broadbent, M. H. P. The allocation of descriptor terms by individuals in a simulated retrieval system. *Ergonomics,* 1978, *21,* 343-354.

Broadbent, D. E., & Broadbent, M. H. P. Priming and the passive-active model of word recognition. In R. S. Nickerson (Ed.), *Attention and performance VIII.* Hillsdale, N.J.: Lawrence Erlbaum Associates, 1980. (a)

Broadbent, D. E., & Broadbent, M. H. P. *Articulatory suppression and the grouping of successive stimuli.* Manuscript in preparation, 1980. (b)

Broadbent, D. E., & Broadbent, M. H. P. Recency effects in visual memory. *Quarterly Journal of Experimental Psychology,* in press.

Broadbent, D. E., Cooper, P. J., and Broadbent, M. H. P. A comparison of hierarchical and matrix retrieval schemes in recall. *Journal of Experimental Psychology: Human Learning and Memory,* 1978, *4,* 486-497.

Broadbent, D. E., Cooper, P. J., Frankish, C. R., & Broadbent, M. H. P. Modality differences in relation to grouping in immediate recall. *British Journal of Psychology,* 1980, *71,* 475-485.

Broadbent, D. E., Vines, R., & Broadbent, M. H. P. Recency effects in memory, as a function of modality of intervening events. *Psychological Research,* 1978, *40,* 5-13.

Chomsky, N. *Syntactic structures.* The Hague: Mouton, 1957.

Cohen, G. *The psychology of cognition.* New York: Academic, 1977.

Collins, A. M., & Quillian, M. R. Retrieval time from semantic memory. *Journal of Verbal Learning and Verbal Behavior,* 1970, *9,* 143-148.

Craik, F. I. M., & Lockhart, R. S. Levels of processing: A framework for memory research. *Journal of Verbal Learning and Behavior,* 1972, *11,* 671-684.

Dalrymple-Alford, E. C. Measurement of clustering in free recall. *Psychological Bulletin,* 1970, *74,* 32-34.

Flint, C. R. *The role of consciousness in memory.* Unpublished doctoral dissertation, Oxford University, 1979.

Frankel, F., & Cole, M. Measures of category clustering in free recall. *Psychological Bulletin,* 1971, *76,* 39–44.

Frankish, C. *Organisational factors in short-term memory.* Unpublished doctoral dissertation, Cambridge University, 1976.

Graesser, M., & Mandler, G. Limited processing capacity constrains the storage of unrelated sets of words and retrieval from natural categories. *Journal of Experimental Psychology: Human Learning and Memory,* 1978, *4,* 86–100.

Gruenewald, P. J., & Lockhead, G. R. The free recall of category examples. *Journal of Experimental Psychology: Human Learning and Memory,* 1980, *6,* 225–240.

Harris, M. Noun animacy and the passive voice: A developmental approach. *Quarterly Journal of Experimental Psychology,* 1978, *30,* 495–504.

Jones, G. V. A fragmentation hypothesis of memory: Cued recall of pictures and of sequential position. *Journal of Experimental Psychology: General,* 1976, *105,* 277–293.

Jones, G. V. Tests of a structural theory of the memory trace. *British Journal of Psychology,* 1978, *69,* 351–367.

Jones, G. V. Multi-rate forgetting. *Journal of Experimental Psychology: Human Learning and Memory,* 1979, *5,* 98–114.

Kintsch, W. Semantic memory. In R. S. Nickerson (Ed.), *Attention and performance VIII.* Hillsdale, N.J.: Lawrence Erlbaum Associates, 1980.

Levy, B. A. The role of articulation in auditory and visual short-term memory. *Journal of Verbal Learning and Verbal Behavior,* 1971, *10,* 123–132.

Martin, M., & Jones, G. V. Modality dependency of loss of recency in free recall. *Psychological Research,* 1979, *40,* 273–289.

Miller, G. A. The magical number seven, plus or minus two: Some limits of our capacity for processing information. *Psychological Review,* 1956, *63,* 81–97.

Moscovitch, M., & Craik, F. I. M. Depth of processing, retrieval cues, and uniqueness of encoding as factors in recall. *Journal of Verbal Learning and Verbal Behavior,* 1976, *15,* 447–458.

Norman, D. A., & Rumelhart, D. E. *Explorations in cognition.* San Francisco: W. H. Freeman, 1975.

Penney, C. G. Interactions of suffix effects with suffix delay and recall modality in serial recall. *Journal of Experimental Psychology: Human Learning and Memory,* 1979, *5,* 507–521.

Perfetti, C. A., & Goldman, S. R. Discourse functions of thematization and topicalization. *Journal of Psycholinguistic Research,* 1975, *4,* 257–271.

Poulton, E. C. The eye-hand span in simple serial tasks. *Journal of Experimental Psychology: General,* 1975, *104,* 192–233.

Tannenbaum, P. H., & Williams, F. Prompted word replacement in active and passive sentences. *Language and Speech,* 1968, *11,* 220–229.

Vickery, B. C. *On retrieval system theory.* London: Butterworths, 1965.

Watkins, O. C., & Watkins, M. J. Buildup of proactive inhibition as a cue-overload effect. *Journal of Experimental Psychology: Human Learning and Memory,* 1975, *104,* 442–452.

Watkins, O. C., & Watkins, M. J. Serial recall and the modality effect: Effects of word frequency. *Journal of Experimental Psychology: Human Learning and Memory,* 1977, *3,* 712–718.

Wilhite, S. C. *Cued recall of sentences: A general structural account.* Unpublished doctoral dissertation, Oxford University, 1980.

Wright, P. Transformations and the understanding of sentences. *Language and Speech,* 1969, *12,* 156–166.

Zloof, M. M. Query-by-example: A data based language. *IBM Systems Journal,* 1976, *15–16,* 323–343. (a)

Zloof, M. M. Query-by-example: Operations on hierarchical data bases. *AFIPS Conference Proceedings,* 1976, *45,* 845–853. (b)

PERCEPTION AND EFFECT OF VISUAL MOTION

2 Intersensory Interaction in Motion Perception

Alain Berthoz
Départment de Physiologie Neurosensorielle
CNRS, Paris, France

ABSTRACT

This paper deals with the role of vision in (1) perceiving world versus self-motion; and in (2) regulating self-motion. The thesis advanced here is that the function of the visual system during motion perception cannot be studied in isolation but has to be considered in a framework of sensory and sensory-motor interaction.

INTRODUCTION

When an object or a visual scene is set into motion, two types of perception can be experienced by a subject: (1) perception of object motion or world motion with respect to the observer who perceives himself as stationary; or (2) perception of self-motion of the observer with respect to the visual world that is perceived as stationary. Object-motion perception is termed egocentric and self-motion perception is termed *exocentric* (Brandt, Dichgans, & Koenig, 1973).

Object-motion perception has been extensively studied, particularly in the case of small-sized objects moving in the center of the visual field (or when they are maintained there by active oculomotor pursuit). However, the question of which changes in the optic array may lead to either type of perception and, in the case of relative motion of parts of the visual field, which parts are taken as the *frame* relative to the body, are still open to theoretical and experimental controversy. In trying to answer such questions, the visual system has been divided in a number of ways. Psychologists such as Braddick (1980) and Anstis (this volume) suggest the existence of two processes for perceiving movement. They associate their fast (as opposed to slow) movement detection system with Trevarthen's (1968) *functional* concept of ambient (as opposed to focal) vision. A further distinction has been made both by psychologists and neurophysiologists concerning the central and peripheral visual field. The role of peripheral vision in static or motion perception has been largely underestimated in the past. However, it is now clear the the peripheral retina is the source of several noncortical pathways that allow patients with foveal scotoma or cortical hemianopia to recognize objects or point at them (Perenin & Jeannerod, 1978) or to process visual information for locomotion (Dichgans, unpublished observations).

Several reviews concerning the perception of world versus self-motion and the regulation of self-motion have been published recently (Berthoz, 1978; Berthoz, Lacour, Soechting, & Vidal, 1979; Dichgans & Brandt, 1978; Henn, Cohen, & Young, 1980; Johansson, von Hofsten, & Jansson, 1980). Specific points selected from the literature will be used to support the general thesis that the function of the visual system during motion perception cannot be studied in isolation. First, some of the factors influencing the perceived velocity of large segments of the visual field (egocentric motion perception) will be identified. Then, a brief review will be given of the basic properties of self- (or ego-) motion perception whether induced by a moving visual scene (which will be called *vection* after Tschermak, 1921) or induced by head movement and sensed by the vestibular system—the only other sensory system that specifically measures head motion *in space*. Next, the importance of visual–vestibular interaction in the case of circular or linear movements will be illustrated together with the influence of visual scene motion on the control of posture. This shows that the role of vision in motion perception is greatly modified when functionally relevant experimental situations are used rather than passive presentations to a seated subject. Finally, physiological evidence will be considered.

VISUAL MOTION PERCEPTION

Factors Influencing the Perceived Velocity of a Visual Pattern

The following section deals only with perceived velocity of a whole visual scene, even if it occupies only part of the visual field, and not with perceived velocity of an object moving relative to a fixed scene. When a stationary subject, with head fixed, views a moving visual scene covering a large part of the visual field, two types of oculomotor strategy can be adopted: The eye can be fixed in space or move with the visual scene. If the eyes looks at a fixed point in space, the angular velocity of the retinal image is equal to the angular velocity of the visual scene.

This would provide *afferent information*. If the eye follows the moving visual scene, optokinetic nystagmus (OKN) is induced. Visual scene velocity could then be estimated by the subject from eye velocity, if the gain of the OKN (eye velocity/visual scene velocity) is unity (i.e., when the image is clear). This would now provide *efferent information* (cf. Von Holst's, 1954, model) generated by the eye movement, about stimulus velocity.

These two oculomotor strategies induce two different perceived velocities of egocentric pattern motion. (Perceived velocity refers in this case to consciously judged velocity. It may however also reflect that tacit perception that permits grasping of a moving object or helps in driving a vehicle.) An overestimation of pattern velocity occurs with the eyes stationary and the ratio between afferent versus efferent perception is as high as 1.7. This effect is known as the Aubert–Fleischl phenomenon (Dichgans, Wist, Diener, & Brandt, 1975). In addition to these two eye-movement dependent factors, others related to the visual scene itself have been shown to influence perceived egocentric velocity. Of these one is spatial frequency. Diener, Wist, Dichgans, and Brandt (1976) have shown that perceived velocity increases with increasing spatial frequency of a periodic pattern (standard black and white stripe patterns in their case). The spatial frequency effect is independent of the angular extent of retinal stimulation. Spatial frequency, although it affects afferent object-referred motion perception, does not affect either pursuit movements of the eyes during slow phases of OKN or velocity perception during smooth pursuit eye movements. It has been proposed that perceived velocity (M) is related to angular pattern velocity ω and spatial frequency f_s by the relation

$$M = 0.61\omega f_s + b\omega \tag{1}$$

where b is the intercept of the relation of perceived velocity to real velocity. The factor b is independent of spatial frequency. The temporal frequency of the pattern, that is, the inverse of the time interval between successive stimulations of a given retinal receptor, is given by $f_t = \omega f_s$. The Aubert–Fleischl phenomenon depends on local temporal frequency stimulation caused by the repetitive passage of contrast borders over the retina, and consequently the multiplication factor also depends on pattern characteristics.

In summary, pattern velocity, oculomotor strategy, and pattern spatial frequency are some of the factors affecting perceived velocity of a moving visual scene. Two other factors have been shown to be of great importance: retinotopic stimulus localization (peripheral or central) and stimulus area or size. They will be discussed below in relation to self-motion perception.

Factors Influencing Self-Motion Perception Induced by a Visual Pattern

When designing laboratory simulators for car driving, authors such as Salvatore (1968) noticed that the best stimuli for producing movement sensation were large visual fields presented in the periphery. These observations confirmed the early observations of Mach (1875), Tschermak (1921), Fischer and Kormüller (1931), and Gibson (1954). Dichgans and Brandt (1978), working with the now classical combination of a large optokinetic drum and a rotating chair, were the first to make the observation that drum rotation induced a perception of self-motion ("circular vection") in the seated subject, even in the absence of real body rotation. Since then, the basic characteristics of circular, linear, and roll vection have been studied by several groups.

First some definitions in the interest of clarity: *Vection* is the perception of self-movement induced by and in the direction opposite to visual scene motion; *circular vection* (CV) is induced by a visual scene rotating around an head vertical axis; *roll vection* (RV) is induced by a scene rotating in the frontal plane around the optical axis of the eye; *linear vection* (LV) is induced by movement in the three orthogonal planes (X-anteroposterior, Y-lateral, or Z-vertical) of the head. In all cases, the remarkable fact is that it is stimulation of the *peripheral* visual field that is necessary to induce vection. It was shown for CV that when a conflict is created between the central visual field and the periphery, it is the peripheral stimulus that dictates the direction of vection, the central field inducing optokinetic nystagmus (Brandt et al., 1973). This experiment reveals nicely the independent processing of information and even motor activity arising from stimulation of different parts of the visual field, even when they lead, respectively, to egocentric and exocentric motion perception. It also reveals that the periphery is dominant in self-motion perception. Another result is that the minimal stimulus area necessary to induce a certain level of vection is smaller the more peripheral is the stimulus. It has even been argued by Johansson (1979) that a single spot of light in the periphery is sufficient to induce a small but clear sensation of vection.

The *periphery in depth* is also dominant for CV induction (Dichgans & Brandt, 1978). When two moving scenes are presented simultaneously at different distances, it is the distal one that dictates the direction of CV. *Latency* for the onset of vection varies according to the type of stimulus, with a range from 1 to about 10 sec depending on the size, velocity, and general setting of the subject's posture, his training, etc. *Thresholds* were defined as being the minimal visual scene velocity for the appearance of vection. They are extremely small and approach the thresholds for detecting the motion of an image or a signal light spot by the visual system (Berthoz, Pavard, & Young, 1975). *Saturation* has been reported for all types of vection. However, the saturation values are also dependent on experimental conditions. When image velocity increases above saturation values, pattern motion (in the opposite direction) is perceived in addition to vection. Another important result is the increase in linear vection with increasing spatial frequency or pattern density (Berthoz et al., 1975). This factor is extremely powerful.

The amount of adaptation to the environment shown by the mechanisms underlying visually elicited self-motion sensation is nicely illustrated by the fact that increasing spatial frequency increases LV. With linear motion in the antero-posterior direction, as experienced when driving on a straight road or in a tunnel, retinal image velocity is dependent on the distance between the pattern and the eye of the observer. The projection on the retina of the proximal portion of a "tunnel" has a higher angular velocity than the projection of a distal portion (see calculations in Berthoz et al., 1975). Spatial frequency, as imaged on the retina, is also distance-dependent but in a reciprocal way (a proximal portion of a pattern has a lower angular spatial frequency seen from the retina than a distal portion). So each of them tends to compensate in a reciprocal fashion for the other in depth. The invariant perceived self-motion is then a ratio of the two parameters. In circular vection (rotating drum), however, the angular speed of the retinal image of the pattern is independent of the distance between pattern and observer. In this case, then, a spatial frequency-dependent vection would disturb rather than subserve functional behavioral constancy of perceived self-motion.

It is interesting that large directional *asymmetries* in vection have been noted particularly in the case of LV: For instance, forward image motion induces a backward LV greater than the converse, and downward LV is weaker than upward LV. Also adaptation and habituation occur during vection. Adaptation to horizontal LV along the X-axis was noted by Salvatore (1968) in car driving and was also demonstrated by Berthoz et al. (1975). This short-term adaptation has a time constant of about 30 sec. Long-term adaptation probably exists but has not been measured.

The dynamics of vection have been studied by standard system analysis techniques using oscillatory visual scenes. The results of these dynamic tests (Reviews in Berthoz, 1978, and Henn et al., 1980) have shown that vection is intense particularly in the low-frequency range (below 0.1 Hz) of visual scene movements. However, it may depend heavily on experimental conditions and fast effects on postural control have in fact been found (Berthoz et al., 1979).

VISUAL-VESTIBULAR INTERACTION

Thresholds for Vestibular Detection of Angular or Linear Acceleration in Man

The early findings concerning CV and LV indicated clearly that visually induced vection interacted with vestibular self-motion detection. Convincing evidence comes also from the fact that pseudo-Coriolis effects (see Bles, this volume) and nausea can be obtained by combining visual rotation and head tilt. Other evidence originates from neurophysiological proof of convergence between visual and vestibular motion information at the level of the vestibular nuclei (Dichgans & Brandt, 1978).

It is still, however, believed by many that the vestibular system in man is an

archaic nonfunctional system, and the main argument given is that labyrinthec-
tomized patients apparently compensate well for the loss. In fact, when the
labyrinth is intact, it is a basic self-motion detection system of very high sensitivity. We know that the vestibular system (1) allows a highly accurate evaluation of
self-motion with very low acceleration thresholds; (2) complements visual motion perception for rapid self-motion; (3) allows a precise location of head position with respect to the direction of gravity; (4) modifies accommodation during
linear acceleration; and (5) is probably instrumental in the development of visual
control of posture in infants, etc. Some of these aspects will be underlined below.
The main properties of the vestibular system in man and its function in self-
motion perception have been well summarized by Guedry (1974).

We now briefly consider the detection of head movement by the vestibular
system in order to emphasize its extremely high sensitivity. Distributions of
thresholds for the perception of angular head accelerations around an earth vertical axis in darkness (horizontal semicircular canal stimulation) for 53 normal
men made by Clark and Stewart (1969) revealed a mean acceleration threshold of
about $.41°/sec^2$ with a standard deviation of $.35°/sec^2$ and a range from .05 to
$2.20°/sec^2$. Similar subjective threshold measurements have been made changing
the subject's body position for angular acceleration steps. The adaptation factors
that have to be taken into account in addition to the threshold values have been
quantified (Young & Oman, 1969).

The product of acceleration amplitude and the time necessary to detect an
acceleration is approximately constant, within a certain range. The evidence for
this is the hyperbolic relation between latency for acceleration detection and
acceleration amplitude. The suggestion has been made that a velocity threshold
mechanism is operating (Meiry, 1965; Melvill-Jones & Young, 1978). Elaboration of a model on these lines was made by Ormsby and Young (1976). A review
can be found in Levison and Zacharias (1978).

Detection of linear acceleration by the otolithic system is also extremely
sensitive. It has been argued by Malcolm and Melvill-Jones (1974) that the
subjective tracking of vertical motion with head erect is unreliable although the
threshold for vertical acceleration detection in the upright subject must be assumed to be much lower than the detection for horizontal (lateral or anteroposterior) linear acceleration. Recent evaluations by Gundry (1978) indicate that the
detection threshold for linear acceleration in the low-frequency range (below 1
Hz) can be as low as .001 g. A reevaluation concerning the detection of linear
acceleration by the otolith and the perception of static tilt was provided by
Ormsby and Young (1976). The important feature of the otolithic system that has
to be recalled here is that by their physical design the otolithic receptors detect
the component of the acceleration of gravity in the plane of their macula and
cannot therefore differentiate between *head tilt* and *linear acceleration* due to
linear head motion, if the acceleration vectors induced by these two types of
movement are of equal amplitude and direction. Such ambiguities require jet

pilots to be *taught* to ignore the g-factor and rely on instruments when flying in darkness or in the fog.

Influence of the Vestibular System on Visually Perceived Motion

In man a number of visual illusions are known to be due to stimulation of the vestibular organs even in the absence of eye movements. The *oculogyral illusion* (Clark & Stewart, 1969) is one example. It consists of the apparent movement of a spot of light (stable with respect to the head) presented in darkness to a subject submitted to an angular acceleration. Linear acceleration is also known to induce illusions such as the *oculogravic illusion* (Graybiel & Clark, 1975). The apparent tilt of a vertical line when body orientation is changed with respect to gravity was described long ago as the Aubert and Müller illusion (see Guedry, 1974).

In our laboratory, we have demonstrated a powerful influence of linear acceleration on perceived velocity in the course of a study on linear vection along the X-axis (Pavard & Berthoz, 1977). Using the apparatus reported in Berthoz et al. (1975), which allows independent manipulation of visual world motion and of body motion, we have shown that (1) transient acceleration modifies the perceived velocity of a moving visual scene; and (2) these changes are probably responsible for the transient loss of vection during linear acceleration also noted by Salvatore (1968) in car driving conditions. Salvatore observed that transient accelerations could seriously modify the subjective estimation of the average car velocity on the road.

Pavard and Berthoz (1977) applied small linear accelerations to subjects seated on a cart that could move horizontally in the X-axis. The subjects were suddenly transported forward or backward for about 1.5 sec. They were placed in a "visual tunnel" (as if in a train) and viewed a visual scene moving at constant velocity with respect to their head. Although the visual world was always moving at the same speed, they reported a transient immobilization of the visual scene during the acceleration of the cart. By calculating the time during which the subjects perceive the immobilization, Pavard and Berthoz (1977) were able to show that the time is linearly related to the peak acceleration of the cart during a triangular velocity waveform (step of acceleration). Because no eye movements were induced during the experiment by the linear acceleration, this suggests a direct effect of the otolithic system on visually perceived motion. The mechanisms underlying this effect have yet to be understood.

Apart from visual illusions, the vestibular system induces mainly, changes in perceived velocity by its action on eye movements through the vestibulo-ocular reflex whose basic circuitry is well known. It has been demonstrated that this reflex is instrumental for stabilizing the visual world on the retina and is therefore essential for reducing retinal slip during head movements in real life (Wilson & Melvill-Jones, 1979). The vestibulo-ocular reflex has been shown to contribute to retinal stabilization within a frequency range as high as 8 to 10 Hz or higher (Benson & Barnes, 1978). Recent results (Henn, personal communication) even suggest that in the monkey it can be as high as 20 Hz.

Modification of perceived visual scene motion can occur, whether it gives rise to vection or not, during both angular or linear acceleration, by an action of the vestibulo-ocular reflex on optokinetic nystagmus. This was demonstrated by Koenig, Allum, and Dichgans (1978) in the case of angular rotation around an earth vertical axis; they showed that vestibular nystagmus can modify optokinetic nystagmus slow phase velocity in such a way that the gain of OKN induced by rotation of an optokinetic drum can be even greater than one, therefore inducing a reversal of perceived motion of the visual pattern. In an experiment in which the vestibular stimulus was linear acceleration along the Y-axis, our group has demonstrated (Buizza, Léger, Droulez, Berthoz, & Schmid, 1980) that linear acceleration can modify the perceived velocity of a visual pattern moving linearly in the frontal plane and that this effect is produced at least in part by a change in the slow phase velocity of OKN. A 0.1-g sinusoidal acceleration at 0.2 Hz can induce a modulation of OKN slow phase velocity as large as 20°/sec and radically change the perceived velocity of the visual environmert.

Influence of Vision on Vestibular Self-Motion Detection

Just as a head movement that induces vestibular stimulation can modify perceived imaged velocity (probably that consciously judged and certainly that nonconsciously used for motor control), so reciprocally vision can radically modify vestibular processes.

The first important functional illustration of the effect of vision on the compensatory motor reactions induced by the labyrinth is visual suppression of the vestibulo-ocular reflex (Benson & Barnes, 1978). When the head rotates suddenly, for instance to the left, the vestibulo-ocular reflex produces a compensatory eye rotation in the opposite direction (right) with a gain which, in man and in the dark, varies according to several factors but is between .6 and 1, if one relates angular displacement of the eye to angular displacement of the head. During normal head rotation in the light, the gain can be 1 provided the frequency is not too high; visual world motion, being in the same direction as the compensatory eye rotation, adds to the efficacy of the image stabilization on the retina by the labyrinth. If the subject is rotated in a closed illuminated chamber that nulls the relative velocity between image motion and head motion, the vestibulo-ocular reflex is partly suppressed. Therefore, a visual scene or a target stabilized with regard to the head can induce suppression of the vestibulo-ocular reflex. However, a physical visual target is not always necessary; if the subject is asked to "look" at a virtual target in space, although he is in a dark room, this "intention to look" may induce the same effect. This is important when, for instance, a human operator wants to fixate a device or a target moving together with his body. Benson and Barnes (1978) have suggested that visual suppression has a dynamic range that is the same as pursuit eye movements (drop of gain above 1–2 Hz). The subjective velocity estimation during conflicting visual–vestibular stimulation by horizontal angular acceleration has been recently studied by Waespe, Waespe, and Henn (1980).

Another effect of vision on vestibular compensatory motor functions is the adaptation of the vestibulo-ocular reflex (VOR) by visual reversing prisms that has been demonstrated by Gonshor and Melvill-Jones (1976) in man. They showed that wearing reversing Dove prisms for a few weeks can modify and even reverse the direction of the horizontal vestibulo-ocular reflex tested by passive sinusoidal oscillations in the dark. Dove prisms reverse apparent visual world motion in both the horizontal (left–right) and the frontal (torsion) plane and thus leave visual world motion intact in the sagittal plane (up–down).

Berthoz, Melvill-Jones, and Bégué (in press) have recently shown that such adaptive modifications also include active transient head–eye movements for visual target acquisition, and they have shown that these modifications of the VOR occur only in the planes in which vision is reversed (horizontal and frontal) and not in the other (sagittal). As the vestibular receptors (vertical semicircular canals) responsible for the VOR in the frontal and sagittal plane are the same, this means that some identification process (possibly such as described by Longuet-Higgins & Prazdny, 1980) recognizing the geometrical features of visual scene motion with respect to the head is performed in the brain so that a direction and plane-specific adaptation occurs. These phenomena suggest the existence of central estimators that can recognize, store, and modify velocity and direction of apparent motion. Such central storage of the dynamic characteristics of head motion seems particularly indicated in the case of conflicting visual and vestibular cues.

ROLE OF VISION IN THE CONTROL OF POSTURE

In the preceding sections we have considered the role of vision and the vestibular system in modifications of perceived velocity. However, we have restricted ourselves to the case of a passive, seated subject submitted to rather selective sensory stimuli. In real life, in the course of phylogenetic or ontogenetic development, optic flow information (e.g., the changes in position of the array of points in the visual field that can be represented as a family of vectors providing a streaming perspective; Gibson, 1954) is used in sensory-motor coordination. It is therefore essential to ask whether perceived visual motion is integrated not only with head movement but also with the general organization of sensory-motor coordination.

Perhaps the most basic coordination is the maintenance of posture. Recently, Lee and Lishman (1974) designed an elegant experiment with a "swinging room" surrounding the subject. They showed that small oscillatory movements of the room induced two types of effect: (1) The subject perceived the swinging

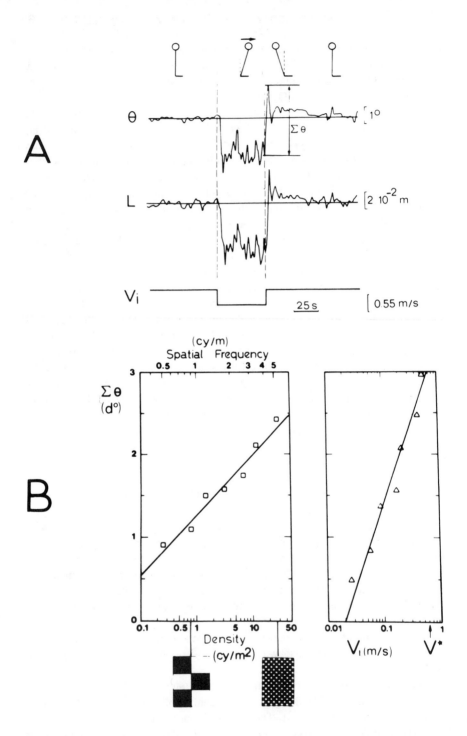

room as still and the floor as moving, therefore the swinging room induced linear vection; and (2) postural oscillations—the subjects perceived themselves as falling in the opposite direction and therefore adjusted their posture to the new perceived vertical, a reaction that eventually led them to fall over. By a subsequent systematic study of active or passive relative motions between the room and the subject, Lee and Aronson (1974) showed that these effects are strong in infants, and they hypothesized that vision could have a dominant role in postural control. A similar observation was made by Dichgans, Held, Young, and Brandt (1972) who showed that when an observer uses a wide angle display (disc) rotating around his line of sight, he both feels his body tilted and sees a vertical straightedge tilted with respect to the moving stimulus. Compensatory changes in posture occur during disc rotation and displacement of the perceived vertical increases with the angular speed of the disc until it reaches a maximum of about 15° at about 30°/sec (Dichgans et al., 1972; Mauritz, Dichgans, Allum, & Brandt, 1975). These motor effects were attributed to the modification of the apparent direction of gravity resulting from conflicting otolithic signals (indicating no acceleration) and visual cues (indicating angular rotation around the optic axis).

It should be stressed at this point that when an observer is stationary, the vestibular system does signal the fact that there is no head movement. Therefore it has been erroneous to assume that when a subject is stationary and a moving visual pattern is presented to him, only visual motion cues are available. In that case, there is visually perceived motion information, but also other information about the *absence* of body motion given by the vestibular and somatosensory system. However, an important alternative is that as long as vision is present, the vestibular information may be neutral (i.e., not taken into consideration).

FIG. 2.1.   Effects of linearly moving visual scenes on posture. A: A film projector allows the projection of visual scenes that move at constant velocity in the anteroposterior direction. This is obtained by a set of mirrors described by Lestienne et al. (1977). These schematic diagrams indicate the body pitch induced when the visual scene is moving in the direction of the arrow. θ is the angle of the body with respect to the vertical, $\Sigma\theta$ is the sum of the pitch during stimulation and the pitch during the powerful aftereffect at the cessation of stimulation (in degrees). L is the measure of the changes in the projection of the center of gravity. L parallels the measure of θ because for slow movements the body behaves as an inverted pendulum (in meters). V_i is image linear velocity (in meters per second). B: Effect of the image structure (density) and velocity (V_i) on the amplitude of postural readjustment. Left: variation of $\Sigma\theta$ (expressed in degrees) as a function of density between .26 and 28.1 squares per square meter (cycles per square meter). $V_i = 0.55$ m/sec in the forward direction. The inserts depict two of the patterns utilized. The "spatial frequency" as defined by the number of squares per meter is indicated for each point (in cycles per meter). Right: variation of $\Sigma\theta$ as a function of V_i (between .027 and .55 m/sec). The latter value, indicated by V_i (= 2 km/hr), equals one-half the mean speed of walking. Each data point is the mean value of three trials from one subject. (Redrawn from Lestienne et al., 1977).

Lestienne, Soechting, and Berthoz (1977), using a "visual tunnel," showed that body pitch is influenced by image velocity up to a point of saturation related to the saturation values of linear vection and not to biomechanical limitations. The most striking result was the influence of visual pattern spatial frequency that is illustrated in Fig. 2.1. The importance of the visual periphery was also clear although the exact tradeoff between temporal and spatial frequency could not be measured. Note that the basic nature of these effects was also demonstrated in field-insensitive subjects. The "distraction" of performing mental arithmetic served to remove some learned inhibition of these effects.

Various studies of the dynamic characteristics of visually induced postural reorganizations in the standing subject have led to the conclusion that vision improves postural stabilization in the low-frequency range (below .1 Hz; Berthoz et al., 1979; Dichgans & Brandt, 1978). We have complemented this conclusion by showing that vision also contributes to the initial rapid motor reactions that are triggered by a sudden perturbation of stance (Nashner & Berthoz, 1978; Soechting & Berthoz, 1979). This was investigated by placing standing human subjects on a platform that was suddenly moved. The motion of the visual surround could be manipulated by optical or mechanical means in order to suppress or increase visual information about head motion relative to platform motion. The results show that when, at the precise time of the postural perturbation, visual motion information is suppressed (but vision of an environment stable with respect to the head is maintained), early (within 100 msec) modification in the balancing reflexes is seen. This was further shown to be true for the reactions induced in the musculature of monkeys during free fall (Vidal, Lacour, & Berthoz, 1979).

The developmental course of visual control of posture is such that it seems to reach a maximum around 2-3 years of age, as observed by Lee and Aronson (1974), and then decrease slowly up to 16-18 years (Brandt, Wenzel, & Dichgans, 1977). This suggests that vision plays a very important role in the organization of sensorimotor coordination at an early stage of development but follows the maturation of the vestibular reactions that are present at birth. Butterworth and Cichetti (1978) have studied the disruption of posture in normal and motor-retarded (Down's syndrome) infants using the "swinging room" technique of Lee. Their results seem to fit with the view that "postural control depends on congruence between mechanical–vestibular and visual indices of postural stability."

However, in what has just been discussed, it would be an error to overstress visual–vestibular interaction and forget about the role of somatosensory cues. It has long been known that cutaneous cues contribute to righting reflexes. Clinical experience in neurology indicates also that vestibular compensation after labyrinthectomy in man also depends on cutaneous cues from the general somatosensory system (joints and pressure receptors).

In addition, although most of the presently available theories and data support the idea of a *continuous* role of vision in perceived motion and the control of posture, it may also be that in complex motor tasks such as locomotion the underlying operations are very different. In an elegant experiment Thomson (1977) showed that during locomotion to a predetermined point, visual cues were not necessary in order to attain the target as long as the visual information was available before starting and was not to be retained during more than about 8 sec. *Intermittent* control by visual information is therefore another mode of control that will use imagined internalized maps of the environmental space rather than the ongoing perceptual events.

NEUROPHYSIOLOGICAL BASIS OF
VISUAL–VESTIBULAR INTERACTION

Which are the pathways mediating visual motion perception? Where and how in the brain do visual and vestibular motion information combine? Comprehensive reviews of such questions are available (Baker & Berthoz, 1977; Fuchs & Becker, in press; Granit & Pompeiano, 1979; Henn et al., 1980; Wilson & Melvill-Jones, 1979). The main new findings have been that (1) there are not *two* but *several* afferent visual systems processing visual motion cues; and (2) visual and vestibular motion cues converge in a "meaningful" way at the levels of the so-called "vestibular" nuclei, cerebellum, thalamus, and even visual cortex. We shall summarize these findings only in order to introduce the reader to the literature rather than try to give an exhaustive review.

Afferent Visual Pathways

Two main afferent visual pathways were known in mammals: the cortical and the collicular. In recent years, another route relaying visual information to the cerebellum was discovered. Cerebellar Purkinje cells of the flocculus receive a visual climbing fiber input through the nucleus of the optic tract and the dorsal cap of the inferior olive and a visual mossy fiber input through the medial terminal nucleus (Fig. 2.2; see also Fuchs & Becker, 1981, in press). The essential finding is that the cells in the medial terminal nucleus are sensitive to large movements of the visual field at speeds around 1–2°/sec and have selectivity for speed that is similar to retinal ganglion cells. In addition, they have a direction selectivity that is functionally related to and derived from the three principal planes of the semicircular canals, allowing visual–vestibular interaction on the basis of one coordinate system. It seems that the accessory optic system may help to signal self-movement and complement the vestibular system in the low velocity range. It was initially thought that the visual input to the vestibular nucleus was mediated by a pathway through the cerebellum. However, lesions of the cerebellum do not suppress the visual modulation of vestibular neurons. Therefore, other possible pathways from the accessory optic system to the vestibular

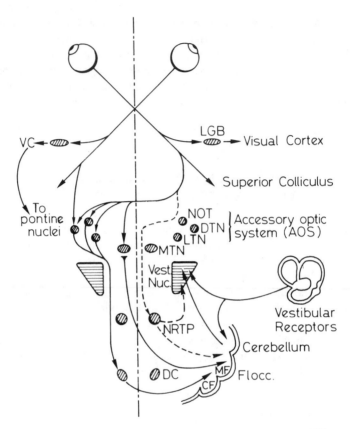

FIG. 2.2.   Visual pathways to the brainstem nuclei and cerebellum. In addition to the classical routes to the visual cortex and the superior colliculus, visual information is also distributed to the brainstem nuclei through at least two main routes: (1) The pontine nuclei from the visual cortex (linking between pontine nuclei and the vestibular system, however, has not been indicated). (2) The accessory optic system (AOS) that mediates a pathway to the flocculus of the cerebellum. Both climbing fiber (CF) and mossy fiber (MF) input are known to reach the flocculus by separate pathways. The CF pathway relays in the dorsal cap (DC) of the inferior olive. Other notations: LGB, lateral geniculate body; VC, visual cortex; NOT, nucleus of the optic tract; DTN, dorsal terminal nucleus; MTN, medical terminal nucleus; LTN, lateral terminal nucleus.

nuclei have been investigated and found in the reticular formation involving the nucleus reticularis tegmenti pontis.

In addition to these newly discovered pathways one should note that there exist corticopontine projections from visual areas 17, 18, and 19 corresponding to the peripheral retina. Neurons in the pontine nuclei have large receptive fields, are all movement and direction selective, and respond to a wide variety of visual patterns, although it is not known if these cells are linked with the vestibular system.

Visual–Vestibular Interaction at the Level of the Vestibular Nucleus

It has been traditionally thought that the vestibular nuclei were essentially a relay station conveying vestibular information to the spinal cord, reticular formation, cerebellum, and cerebral cortex. They were also recognized to be essential in the vestibulo-ocular reflex. A certain amount of sensory convergence was known to occur on these neurons from other sensory systems (from cutaneous and neck proprioceptors).

Using natural optic and vestibular stimulation in the goldfish, Dichgans, Schmidt, and Graf (1973) showed that the discharge rate of vestibular nucleus neurons could be modulated by angular rotation of a moving visual field surrounding the animal in the absence of any vestibular stimulus. This basic finding was confirmed in the rabbit, cat, and monkey (Waespe & Henn, 1977) and is probably also valid in man. Vestibular nuclei neurons therefore do not only respond to head motion in the dark but also respond to visual surround motion. During normal combined optic and vestibular stimulation, the discharge profile of type I neurons (second-order vestibular neurons increasing their discharge rate with ipsilateral head rotation in the horizontal plane) replicates nicely the head velocity profile *in space*. Therefore, it does seem that vision and the vestibular system cooperate, each with its particular dynamics, to produce an adequate speedometer function for head motion perception and that *each of these systems is insufficient by itself for all ranges of head velocities and accelerations*.

Visual–Vestibular Interaction at the Level of the Cerebellum

Another major line of research has been stimulated by the discovery of a visual influence on the discharge rate of cerebellar neurons. Purkinje cells in the vestibulo-cerebellum and particularly in the flocculus can respond either to vestibular or to visual stimuli and fire in relation with smooth eye movements during pursuit of a moving visual target. In the monkey, the functional consequence of the summation of these inputs is that vestibular nuclei neurons have a firing rate related to head velocity independently of head acceleration. In addition, it was shown first by Takemori and Cohen (1974) that lesions of the flocculus impair the visual suppression of vestibular nystagmus discussed in the first part of this review.

Ascending Vestibular Influence on the Visual System

In addition to the known projections of the vestibular system to the thalamus and cortex, three important recent findings have shown projections to the relay stations of the visual system. Magnin and Kennedy (1979) have identified in the cat a third distinct vestibular ascending pathway carrying eye movement, saccadic, and/or vestibular evoked activities to the intralaminar nuclei of the thalamus via the ventral lateral geniculate nucleus.

Another ascending vestibular influence was shown by Vanni-Mercier and Magnin (in press) who recorded saccadic and vestibular influences in visual cortical areas in the cat (area 18). The existence of an extraretinal input in the cerebral cortex was already suggested for these areas by Grüsser, Grüsser-Cornehls, and Saur (1959) and Kornhuber and Da Fonseca (1964) and in man by Jung (1977). Dichgans has suggested a model of interaction at the cortical level that could explain the occurrence of either object/self-motion perception (Dichgans & Brandt, 1978; Henn et al., 1980). Lastly, vestibular projections to the superior colliculus in the cat were suggested by Bisti, Maffei, and Piccolino (1974).

Thus, vestibular signals can be combined with visual signals at various levels of the brain. We now have to understand the role of these different interactions. A profitable hypothesis is to suppose that each of the pathways and centers for sensory interaction has an extremely specific function and therefore has to be explored with experimental paradigms using adequate natural stimulation and, in many cases, a combination of *sensory stimuli* with motor tasks involving self-generated movements.

For this purpose a close link between the human experimental approach, using behavioral and psychophysical methods, and the neuronal exploration of the underlying mechanisms will be very fruitful.

REFERENCES

Baker, R., & Berthoz, A. Control of gaze by brain stem neurons. *Developments in neuroscience* (Vol. 1). Amsterdam: Elsevier, 1977.

Benson, A. J., & Barnes, G. R. Vision during angular oscillation: The dynamic interaction of visual and vestibular mechanisms. *Aviation, Space and Environmental Medicine*, 1978, *49*, 340–345.

Berthoz, A. Rôle de la proprioception dans le contrôle de la posture et du geste. In H. Hécaen & M. Jeannerod (Eds.), *Du contrôle moteur à l'organisation du geste*. Paris: Masson, 1978.

Berthoz, A., Lacour, M., Soechting, J. F., & Vidal, P. P. The role of vision in the control of posture during linear motion. In R. Granit & O. Pompeiano (Eds.), *Progress in brain research: Reflex control of posture and movement* (Vol. 50). Amsterdam: Elsevier, 1979.

Berthoz, A., Melvill-Jones, G., & Bégué, A. Differential adaptation of vestibulo-ocular reflexes in horizontal, sagittal and frontal planes. *Experimental Brain Research 1981*, in press.

Berthoz, A., Pavard, B., & Young, L. R. Perception of linear horizontal self motion induced by peripheral vision (linear vection): Basic characteristics and visual vestibular interactions. *Experimental Brain Research*, 1975, *23*, 471–489.

Bisti, S., Maffei, L., & Piccolino, M. Visuo-vestibular interactions in the cat superior colliculus. *Journal of Neurophysiology*, 1974, *37*, 146–155.

Braddick, O. J. Low-level and high-level processes in apparent motion. *Philosophical Transactions of the Royal Society of London, B*, 1980, *290*, 137–151. Reprinted in *The psychology of vision*. London: The Royal Society, 1980.

Brandt, Th., Dichgans, J., & Koenig, E. Differential effects of central versus peripheral vision on egocentric and exocentric motion perception. *Experimental Brain Research*, 1973, *16*, 476–491.

Brandt, Th., Wenzel, D., & Dichgans, J. Die entwicklung der visuellen stabilisation des aufrechten standes beim kind. ein reifezeichen in der kinderneurologie. *Archiv für Psychologie und Nervenkrankheiten,* 1977, *223,* 1-13.

Buizza, A., Léger, A., Droulez, J., Berthoz, A., & Schmid, R. Influence of otolithic stimulation by horizontal linear acceleration on optokinetic nystagmus and visual motion perception. *Experimental Brain Research,* 1980, *39,* 165-176.

Butterworth, G., & Cicchetti, D. Visual calibration of posture in normal and motor retarded Down's syndrom infants. *Perception,* 1978, *7,* 513-525.

Clark, B., & Stewart, J. D. Effects of angular acceleration on man: Thresholds for the perception of rotation and the oculogyral illusion. *Aerospace Medicine,* 1969, *40,* 952-956.

Dichgans, J., & Brandt, Th. Visual-vestibular interactions: Effect on self-motion perception and postural control. In R. Held, H. Leibowitz, & H. L. Teuber (Eds.), *Handbook of sensory physiology: Perception* (Vol. VIII). New York: Springer, 1978.

Dichgans, J., Held, R., Young, L., & Brand, Th. Moving visual scenes influence the apparent direction of gravity. *Science,* 1972, *178,* 1217-1219.

Dichgans, J., Schmidt, C. L., & Graf, W. Visual input improves speedometer function of vestibular neclei in goldfish. *Experimental Brain Research,* 1973, *18,* 319-322.

Dichgans, J., Wist, E. R., Diener, H. C., & Brandt, Th. The Aubert-Fleischl paradox: A temporal effect on perceived velocity in afferent motion perception. *Experimental Brain Research,* 1975, *23,* 529-533.

Diener, H. C., Wist, E. R., Dichgans, J., & Brandt, Th. The spatial frequency effect on perceived velocity. *Vision Research,* 1976, *16,* 169-176.

Fischer, M. H., & Kormüller, A. E. Egocentrische localisation: 2. Mitteilung (Optische richtungslocalisation beim vestibularen nustagmus). *Journal fur Psychologie und Neurologie,* 1931, *41,* 383-420.

Fuchs, A., & Becker, W. (Eds.). *Progress in oculomotor research.* Amsterdam: Elsevier, in press.

Gibson, J. J. The visual perception of objective motion and subjective movement. *Psychological Review,* 1954, *61,* 304-314.

Gonshor, A., & Melvill-Jones, G. Extreme vestibulo-ocular adaptation induced by prolonged optical reversal of vision. *Journal of Physiology,* 1976, *256,* 381-414.

Granit, R., & Pompeiano, O. (Eds.). *Progress in brain research: Reflex control of posture and movement* (Vol. 50). Amsterdam: Elsevier, 1979.

Graybiel, A., & Clark, B. Validity of the oculogravic illusion as a specific indicator of otolith function. *Aerospace Medicine,* 1965, *36,* 1173-1181.

Grüsser, O. J., Grüsser-Cornehls, U., & Saur, G. Reaktionen einzelner neurone in optischen cortex der katze nach elektrischer polarisation des labyrinths. *Pflügers Archiv für Gesamte Physiologie des Menchen und der Thiere.* 1959, *269,* 593-612.

Guedry, F. E. Psychophysics of vestibular sensation. In H. H. Kornhüber (Ed.), *Vestibular system. Part 2: Psychophysics, applied aspects and general interpretations.* Berlin: Springer-Verlag, 1974.

Gundry, A. J. Thresholds of perception for periodic linear motion. *Aviation, Space and Environmental Medicine,* 1978, *49,* 679-686.

Henn, V., Cohen, B., & Young, L. R. *Visual-vestibular interaction in motion perception and the generation of nystagmus.* Cambridge, Mass.: MIT Press, 1980.

Johansson, G. Memory functions in visual event perception. In L. G. Nilsson (Ed.), *Perspectives on memory research.* Hillsdale, N.J.: Lawrence Erlbaum Associates, 1979.

Johansson, G., von Hofsten, C., & Jansson, G. Event perception. *Annual Review of Psychology,* 1980, *31,* 27-63.

Jung, R. An appreciation of early work on gaze control in man and of visuo-vestibular research before 1940. In R. Baker & A. Berthoz (Eds.), *Developments in neurosciences* (Vol. 1). Amsterdam: Elsevier, 1977.

Koënig, E., Allum, J. H. J., & Dichgans, J. Visual-vestibular interaction upon nystagmus slow phase velocity in man. *Acta Oto-laryngologica,* 1978, *85,* 397-410.

Kornhüber, H. H., & Da Fonseca, J. S. Optovestibular integration in the cat's cortex: A study of sensory convergence on cortical neurons. In M. B. Bender (Ed.), *The oculomotor system*. New York: Harper & Row, 1964.

Lee, D. N., & Aronson, E. Visual proprioceptive control of standing in human infants. *Perception & Psychophysics*, 1974, *15*, 529-532.

Lee, D. N., & Lishman, J. R. Visual proprioceptive control of stance. *Journal of Human Movement Studies*, 1974, *1*, 87-95.

Lestienne, F., Soechting, J., & Berthoz, A. Postural readjustments induced by linear motion of visual scenes. *Experimental Brain Research*, 1977, *28*, 363-384.

Levison, W. H., & Zacharias, G. L. Motion cue models for pilot vehicule analysis. *Aerospace Medical Research Laboratory Report*, 1978, *Tr 78-2*.

Longuet-Higgins, H. C., & Prazdny, K. The interpretation of a moving retinal image. *Proceedings of the Royal Society of London, B*, 1980, *208*, 385-397.

Mach, E. *Grundlinien der lehre von den bewegungsempfindungen*. Leipzig: Wilhelm Engelman, 1875.

Magnin, M., & Kennedy, H. Anatomical evidence of a third ascending vestibular pathway involving the ventral lateral geniculate nucleus and the intralaminar nuclei of the cat. *Brain Research*, 1979, *171*, 523-529.

Malcolm, R., & Melvill-Jones, G. Erroneous perception of vertical motion by humans seated in the upright position. *Acta Oto-laryngologica*, 1974, *77*, 274-283.

Mauritz, K. H., Dichgans, J., Allum, J., & Brandt, Th. Frequency characteristics of postural sway in response to self-induced and conflicting visual stimulation. *Pflügers Archiv für Gesamte Physiologie des Menschen und der Thiere*, 1975, *355*, supp. R 95.

Meiry, J. L. *The vestibular system and human dynamic space orientation*. Unpublished doctoral dissertation, Massachusetts Institute of Technology, Cambridge, Mass., 1965.

Melvill-Jones, G., & Young, L. R. Subjective detection of vertical accleration: A velocity dependent response? *Acta Oto-laryngologica*, 1978, *85*, 45-53.

Nashner, L., & Berthoz, A. Visual contribution to rapid motor responses during postural control. *Brain Research*, 1978, *150*, 403-407.

Ormsby, C. G., & Young, L. R. Perception of static orientation in a constant gravito-inertial environment. *Aviation, Space and Environmental Medicine*, 1976, *47*, 159-164.

Pavard, B., & Berthoz, A. Linear acceleration modifies the perceived velocity of a moving visual scene. *Perception*, 1977, *6*, 529-540.

Perenin, M. T., & Jeannerod, M. Visual function within the hemianopic field following early cerebral hemidecortication in man: I. Spatial localisation. *Neuropsychologia*, 1978, *16*, 1-13.

Salvatore, S. Velocity sensing. *Highway Research Record*, 1968, *282*, 79-90.

Soechting, J., & Berthoz, A. Dynamic role of vision in the control of posture in man. *Experimental Brain Research*, 1979, *36*, 551-561.

Takemori, S., & Cohen, B. Loss of visual suppression of vestibular nystagmus after flocculus lesions. *Brain Research*, 1974, *72*, 213-224.

Thomson, J. A. *Maps, programs and the visual control of locomotion*. Unpublished doctoral dissertation, Edinburgh University, 1977.

Trevarthen, C. B. Two mechanisms of vision in primates. *Psychologische Forschung*, 1968, *31*, 229-337.

Tschermak, A. Der exakte subjectivismus in der neuren sinnesphysiologie. *Pflügers Archiv für Gesamte Physiologie des Menschen und der Thiere*, 1921, *188*, 1-20.

Vanni-Mercier, G., & Magnin, M. Organisation of saccadic and vestibular influences in area 17 and 18 of the cat. In A. Fuchs & W. Becker (Eds.), *Progress in oculomotor research*, in press.

Vidal, P. P., Lacour, M., & Berthoz, A. Contribution of vision to muscle responses in monkeys during free-fall: Visual stabilisation decreases vestibular dependent responses. *Experimental Brain Research*, 1979, *37*, 241-252.

Von Holst, E. Relations between the central nervous system and the peripheral organs. *British Journal of Animal Behaviour*, 1954, *2*, 163-171.

Waespe, W., & Henn, V. Neuronal activity in the vestibular nuclei of the alert monkey during vestibular and optokinetic stimulation. *Experimental Brain Research*, 1977, *27*, 523-538.

Waespe, B., Waespe, W., & Henn, V. Subjective velocity estimation during conflicting visual-vestibular stimulation. *Archiv für Psychologie und Nervenkrankheiten*, 1980, *228*, 109-116.

Wilson, V., & Melvill-Jones, G. *Mammalian vestibular physiology*. New York: Plenum Press, 1979.

Young, L. R., & Oman, C. R. Model of vestibular adaptation to horizontal rotation. *Aerospace Medicine*, 1969, *40*, 1076-1080.

3 Stepping Around: Circular Vection and Coriolis Effects

Willem Bles
E.N.T. Department
Free University Hospital
Amsterdam
The Netherlands

ABSTRACT

A visual scene moving uniformly around a stationary observer induces illusory circular vection (CV) (i.e., the sensation of circular self-motion in the opposite direction). In the first experiment, reafferent somatosensory information from muscle and joint receptors was also found to be sufficient to induce an illusion of CV, with concomitant nystagmus in an objectively stationary subject, apparently stepping around (ASA) on a rotating platform in the dark. In addition to visual–vestibular convergence, a somatosensory–vestibular convergence underlying this phenomenon must be postulated. Active head tilts during ASA elicited Coriolis-like effects. In the second experiment, vestibular Coriolis effects were shown by magnitude estimation to be strongest when there was incongruity of afferent motion signals. In this respect, the phenomenon is similar to visual–vestibular interaction.

INTRODUCTION

To control postural balance during free standing or locomotion, adequate spatial orientation is necessary in both animal and man. Especially in man, whose upright stance encourages unstable equilibrium, the central nervous system needs a continuous provision of information about the actual as well as the expected position of the body, with respect to the field of gravity and the supporting surface of the earth. The most important sensory systems providing this information are the vestibular, the somatosensory, and the visual system.

47

The vestibular system comprises the semicircular canals for detection of angular accelerations and the otoliths for detection of linear accelerations (thus sensing the position of the head relative to the gravitational vector). The somatosensory system provides a gravitational frame of reference for the central nervous system and includes sensors in the skin and underlying tissue (which record the contact and pressure of the body on the supporting surface), as well as the sensory inputs from joints and tendons (signaling relative positions and movements of parts of the body). The visual system provides an additional reference frame because directionally structured stimuli in the visual field are preferentially perceived as vertical or horizontal. Moreover, the retinal periphery is important in deciding between self- and object motion.

Both the vestibular apparatus and the eyes are situated in the head, and the fact that the head can be moved relative to the trunk illustrates the necessity for an adequate integration of the sensory information to maintain constancy of space. The present study investigated the question of whether somatosensory–vestibular interactions are analogous to visuo–vestibular interactions when dealing with rotation about a vertical axis.

The horizontal semicircular canals within the vestibular labyrinths are detectors and transducers of angular accelerations applied to the head about the z-axis (i.e., in the medial plane). The mathematical description of the cupula-endolymph system, as a heavily damped torsion–pendulum system (van Egmond, Groen, & Jongkees, 1949; Steinhausen, 1933) is widely accepted. Of importance for the present study is that stimulation of the lateral semicircular canals, with a trapezoidal velocity profile, results in a decay of the nystagmus and circular self-motion sensation (circular vection, CV), during the constant velocity phase, with time constants of about 16 and 10 sec, respectively (Young, 1969). This illustrates the inadequacy of the semicircular canal system for detecting constant velocity rotation.

However, the vestibular system is not the only system that detects self-motion; vision is also important. Mach (1875) noted that looking at moving visible surroundings induces the sensation of self-motion. Dichgans and Brandt (1978) have extensively investigated optokinetically induced CV. Their most important finding is that, in a stationary subject, rotation of the entire visible surround invariably leads to an apparent self-rotation opposite in direction to pattern motion (optokinetic CV). Microelectrode studies in animals have demonstrated that second-order neurons in the vestibular nuclei exhibit a direction-specific modulation of resting discharge in response to body acceleration or optokinetic stimulation (Dichgans, Schmidt, & Graf, 1973; Klinke & Schmidt, 1970; Waespe & Henn, 1977). Waespe and Henn reported that more than 95% of the units recorded in the vestibular nuclei, which could be influenced by stimulation of the horizontal semicircular canals, also showed consistent frequency changes when the animals were exposed to moving visual fields. They infer the transmission of rather abstract information about the velocity of the visual surround. After onset of stimulation (e.g., a velocity step function), the visually induced modulation of the discharge rate has a latency of several seconds and it is usually some seconds before most units are maximally activated or inhibited by the visual stimulus. When human perception of such sensory stimulation is considered in the light of these neurophysiological findings, there are obvious similarities: Exposed to a moving pattern, the initial experience is only that of object or surround motion, relative to the ego (egocentric motion perception); after one to a few seconds the subject experiences self-motion as well (combined egocentric and exocentric motion perception), which is followed by a sensation of pure self-motion (exocentric motion perception), the surround appearing stationary, although it is actually moving (Dichgans & Brandt, 1972).

The finding that it is possible to induce Coriolis-like effects through head tilts during visually induced CV (the so-called Pseudo-Coriolis effects; Brandt, Wist, & Dichgans, 1971) provides further evidence for a functional visual–vestibular convergence. Because Coriolis effects are involved in the present study, some elucidation is required here. Tilt of the head toward a shoulder during constant velocity rotation results in a typical cross-coupled vestibular stimulation. In the literature, this kind of vestibular stimulation together with its perceptual consequences is referred to as the Coriolis effect. The perceptual aspects of the Coriolis effect are complex. The inexperienced subject reports at first a confused, unpleasant experience of motion. This is, however, often the case with sensation of rotation about axes other than the vertical. The reports are mostly of a combination of tilt and rotation, which can be understood by reference to a mathematical analysis of the stimulus. A comprehensive analysis has been provided by Guedry (1974). The point is that on completion of the head movement there is a discrepancy between the head tilt indicated by the otoliths and neck receptors and the direction of the angular velocity vector as sensed by the canals. When the head is tilted during optokinetically induced CV (Pseudo-Coriolis effect; Brandt et al., 1971), the perceptual experience includes tilt and dizziness too and is indistinguishable from real Coriolis effects. Because the Coriolis and Pseudo-Coriolis effect are qualitatively the same, it is postulated that both vestibular and visual information access the same central integrative mechanism.

In discussing these findings, Dichgans et al. (1973) state that the functional significance of the effect seems to be to provide the animal with an accurate velocity signal. Waespe and Henn (1977) predict from their experiments that congruent visual and vestibular stimulation would transfer velocity information over the whole frequency range up to about 1 Hz. They assume velocity to be the important parameter for the animal and that the combination of the visual and vestibular cues would reduce the weakness of each individual transfer function (i.e., the poor vestibular response at low frequencies and the poor visual response at high frequencies). They assume that convergence of vestibular and visual input, as low as the level of the vestibular nuclei, would ensure that motor reactions, like nystagmus and postural changes, should be the same and not depend on the peripheral channel by which the information about velocity or acceleration was obtained.

This assumption, however, is inconsistent with the fact that in subjects who experience a CV certain discrepancies in the direction of the CV, of nystagmus, and of postural sway occur, especially in those experimental conditions where the subjects are standing or stepping around (Bles, 1979; Bles & Kapteyn, 1977; Correia, Nelson, & Guedry, 1977; Guedry, Mortensen, Nelson & Correia, 1978; Kapteyn & Bles, 1977). So the question is whether the somatosensory information concerning rotatory motion in stepping around might also be interpreted (analogous to vision) as either object motion or self-motion. Stepping around in small circles provides a complex pattern of somatosensory stimulation in skin, muscle, and joint receptors, whose afferent signals, in combination, may represent the actual movement. However, under natural conditions, there is likely to be simultaneous, concomitant visual as well as vestibular information. Therefore, in order to study the contribution to somatosensory afferents, a dissociation of the various sensory loops is necessary. This can be achieved by the experimental situation of apparently stepping around (ASA) on a rotating platform in the dark, a stimulus situation in which somatosensory stimulation is unaltered while the canals and vision are not activated. Under these conditions, it is possible to induce CV and nystagmus (Bles & Kapteyn, 1977) and Coriolis-like effects (Bles & de Wit, 1978). The aim of the present study was to quantify by magnitude estimation the perceived CV and Coriolis effects, as induced by separate stimulation of specific sensory systems and by their congruent and incongruent combination.

APPARATUS AND METHOD

The apparatus used in the experiments was a rotating bar situated in a rotating drum (Tönnies, Freiburg im Breisgau). This is shown in Fig. 3.1. The drum was of cylindrical shape and had a diameter of 1.5 m. Its inner walls were painted with vertical black and white stripes, each subtending 7.5° of visual angle. The illumination in the drum could be switched on and off by the experimenter. The bar and the drum could be rotated separately or simultaneously at any desired speed up to 180°/sec in either direction. The bar and drum could also be coupled to each other by means of a clutch to obtain identical direction and speed. The angular velocity of the bar and of the drum were recorded continuously. The rotating bar also carried a small platform upon which the subject could stand upright. Subjects could indicate each subjective complete 360° body rotation by pushing a button on the bar. In some of the experiments, horizontal and vertical eye movements were recorded by means of electronystagmography (AC amplification, time constant 5 sec).

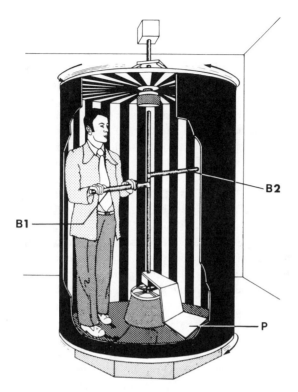

FIG. 3.1.   Diagram of equipment to show the rotating bar and drum. It should be noted that the drum consists not only of the walls but also of the floor and the ceiling. The bar and drum can be rotated separately. The subject can step behind the bar (B1) on the floor of the drum or stand on the platform (P), which rotates with the bar, with his hands on the bar (B2).

All signals were simultaneously recorded on a stripchart recorder (Siemens EM 81-80). Under all experimental conditions, a noise source was placed inside the drum in order to mask the faint motor noise. Reflections off the walls ensured the sound field was diffuse, so acoustic spatial orientation was impossible.

With the rotating bar/platform-drum combination, it is possible to pit the sensory systems against each other. However, because the floor of the drum is necessarily fixed to the walls of the drum, stimulation of both vision and the somatoreceptors is always congruent.

The experiments were performed with the following arrangement: The subject walked on the floor of the drum behind the bar with both hands on the bar (B1) or stood on the platform with his hands resting on the bar (B2) (Fig. 3.1).

Stimulation of the vestibular system alone was achieved by the subject standing on the counterclockwise (CCW) rotating platform in the dark. When the light in the stationary drum was switched on in this condition, vestibular and visual stimulation were congruent. If instead of rotating the bar the drum is rotated in the opposite direction, stimulation of the visual system alone was achieved. When the subject was walking on the floor of the drum, he was asked to stay behind the bar, which involved either real stepping around (RSA), in the case of CCW bar rotation, or apparent stepping around (ASA), in the case of clockwise (CW) drum rotation with the bar stationary. Both in RSA and ASA, he was stepping in circles, but only in the case of RSA was the vestibular system involved. Switching the lights on and off provided additional visual information.

EXPERIMENT 1: CONGRUENT SENSORY INFORMATION AND CIRCULAR VECTION

The aim of the first experiment was to compare the magnitude of the CV as induced by stimulation of the sensory systems, separately or in congruent combination. By using the platform as described in the previous section, it was possible to generate the stimulus conditions shown in Table 3.1.

Procedure

The stimulus consisted of an angular acceleration of $5°/sec^2$ for 12 sec, up to an angular velocity of $60°/sec$. The speed was maintained for 2 min followed by deceleration at $10°/sec^2$. The bar, the platform, or the drum rotated in such a way that the subjects would experience a CV to the left (rotation to the left is counterclockwise when viewed from above). In order to obtain reproducible stepping behavior, the step frequency was fixed. The subjects were instructed to adjust their stepping rhythm to the clicks of a metronome, set to a repetition rate of 1 Hz. The clicks were also presented when the subjects were standing still on the platform. Two conditions (stepping alone and stepping with vestibular stimulation) were repeated with a 2-Hz stepping frequency as well (conditions 3, 5, 8, and 9). The conditions were presented in random order. The subjects began stepping by command, 10 sec before motion stimulation took place, in order to

TABLE 3.1
Stimulus Conditions of CV Magnitude Estimation

1. Vest — —	: subject standing on CCW rotating platform with light off
2. — vis —	: subject standing on stationary platform with CW drum rotation and light on
3. — — somatos	: subject stepping behind stationary bar on CW rotating floor of drum with light off
4. Vest vis —	: subject standing on CCW rotating platform with light on in stationary drum
5. Vest — somatos	: subject stepping behind CCW rotating bar on stationary floor of drum with light off
6. — vis somatos	: subject stepping behind stationary bar on CW rotating floor of drum with light on
7. Vest vis somatos	: subject stepping behind CCW rotating bar on stationary floor of drum with light on

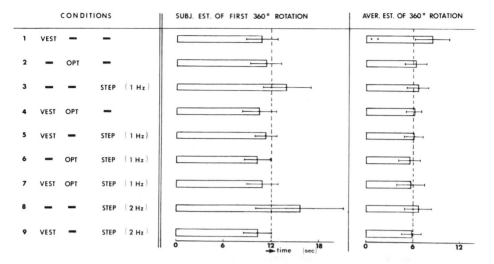

FIG. 3.2. Magnitude estimates of perceived circular vection reported by 10 subjects during congruent stimulation of the sensory systems. For detailed information about the test conditions, see text. The mean estimates ($\pm 1\sigma$) of the first 360° rotation (acceleration period) are shown as well as the mean estimates during the 2-min period following the initial acceleration. In condition 1 (vestibular stimulus only) responses were obtained only during the first two completed rotations at constant velocity.

suppress extra motion cues (Bles, 1979). By pushing a button on the bar, the subjects signaled each time that they felt they had rotated through 360°. In analyzing the data, the time between successive marks was used to calculate the mean subjective velocity.

Ten subjects, with no previous experience of such experiments, participated. They kept their eyes open at all times. Horizontal eye movements were recorded.

Results

Figure 3.2 shows the results. In all conditions CV to the left was reported. One subject did not experience CV in condition 8 (ASA, 2 Hz). The duration of the first subjective 360° rotation (which was actually 12 sec) was underestimated except for the ASA conditions, in which they were overestimated. The latter finding suggests a possible delay in the onset of the subjective rotation in ASA conditions. Indeed, discussing the experiment with the subjects afterward, three of them mentioned definite delays in these conditions. Because of the deficiency of the vestibular system in detecting rotation at a constant velocity, as mentioned in the introduction, CV in condition 1 was not maintained during the period of constant velocity rotation. Therefore, in an analysis of variance, the data of condition 1 have been omitted. The results of the analysis of variance performed on the CV magnitude data show no significant differences between the conditions, $F(7, 63) = 1.37$, $p > .05$.

The results indicate that stimulation of one sensory system alone is sufficient to obtain appropriate CV. The results obtained in conditions 3 and 8 indicate that stepping frequency does not significantly influence the magnitude of the CV. The subjects showed significant individual differences, $F(9, 1017) = 51.8$, $p < .001$, accounting for much of the variance (25.3%). Furthermore, the first-order interaction between subjects and conditions was highly significant, $F(63, 1017) = 11.7$, $p < .001$, and also contributed considerably to the variance (37.3%). The nystagmus tracings did not permit a quantitative evaluation because of artifacts during stepping. As an example, the original recordings for one subject obtained in conditions 1, 5, and 3, respectively, are shown in Fig. 3.3. They indicate prolonged vestibular nystagmus when the subject is stepping on the stationary floor of the drum behind the CCW rotating bar (condition 5), compared to when he is standing on the CCW rotating platform (condition 1). Both conditions were of course presented in total darkness. This finding is in accord with that of Guedry et al. (1978). Figure 3.3 also shows the nystagmic activity when the subject is stepping behind the stationary bar on the CW rotating floor of the drum (condition 3), and although the nystagmus is imperfect, the saccades are clearly directed to the left in accordance with earlier reports on ASA nystagmus (Bles & Kapteyn, 1977).

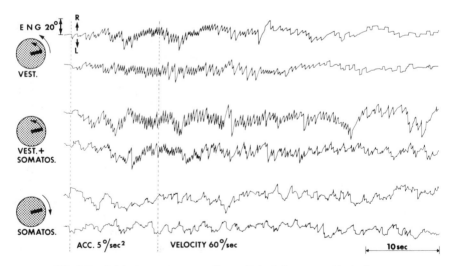

FIG. 3.3. Original nystagmus recordings, obtained from one subject who was tested twice during condition 1 (stimulation of the vestibular system), condition 5 (stimulation of the vestibular and the somatosensory system), and condition 3 (stimulation of the somatosensory system).

EXPERIMENT 2: CONGRUENT AND INCONGRUENT SENSORY INFORMATION AND (PSEUDO-) CORIOLIS EFFECTS

The aim of this experiment was to investigate the ASA-induced Pseudo-Coriolis effect and the modification of the vestibular Coriolis effect by supplementary visual and somatosensory motion information.

Procedure

The platform was removed, which means that the subject was standing or stepping on the floor of the drum behind the bar. The experimental conditions (detailed in Table 3.2) were chosen in such a way that vestibular stimulation was,

TABLE 3.2

Stimulus Conditions				Subject:	1	2	3	4	5	6	7	8	9	mean	σ
				Magnitude Estimates of Coriolis-like Effects											
A	bar drum	60°/sec → L 0°/sec	} light off		1	2	1	2	2	2	2	2	0	1.6	0.7
B	bar drum	60°/sec → L 60°/sec → L	} light off		4	3	4	3	2	3	5	5	5	3.9	1.1
C	bar drum	60°/sec → L 120°/sec → L	} light off		5	7	7	5	3	5	7	6	7	5.8	1.4
D	bar drum	0°/sec 60°/sec → R	} light off		1	0	0	1	1	3	2	1	0	1.0	1.0
E	bar drum	0°/sec 0°/sec	} light off		0	0	0	0	0	0	0	0	0	0.0	0.0
F	bar drum	0°/sec 60°/sec → L	} light off		0	1	0	2	1	3	0	2	0	1.0	1.1
G	bar drum	60°/sec → L 0°/sec	} light on		1	3	0	1	0	1	2	0	0	0.9	1.1
H	bar drum	60°/sec → L 60°/sec → L	} light on		4	6	5	3	2	1	5	5	5	4.0	1.7
I	bar drum	60°/sec → L 120°/sec → L	} light on		4	8	8	5	4	6	9	6	6	6.4	1.9
J	bar drum	0°/sec 60°/sec → R	} light on		2	6	4	4	2	3	3	2	5	3.4	1.4
K	bar drum	0°/sec 0°/sec	} light on		0	0	0	0	0	0	0	0	0	0.0	0.0
L	bar drum	0°/sec 60°/sec → L	} light on		0	6	2	0	3	5	2	5	6	3.2	2.4

if present, held constant and modified by congruent or incongruent information from the other sensory channels. For instance, in conditions A, B, and C the vestibular stimulus was held constant (CCW rotation of the bar) with modification of the somatosensory information; in condition A, the subject stepped forward on the stationary floor of the drum behind the CCW rotating bar; in condition B, the subject simply stood behind the CCW rotating bar on the floor of the drum, which also rotated CCW with the same velocity; in condition C, the subject stepped backward behind the CCW rotating bar, because the floor of the drum was also rotated CCW, but with twice the velocity of the bar. The last condition involves incongruent somatosensory and vestibular motion information. Conditions G, H, and I were exactly the same as A, B, and C, but with additional visual information. In condition E, no motion was involved at all. Condition D is a pure ASA condition: The subject apparently stepped around on the CW rotating floor of the drum behind the stationary bar. The difference between condition D and F is that the subject in condition F apparently stepped around backward. Conditions J, K, and L are exactly the same as D, E, and F, but with additional visual information. The accelerations chosen were $3°/sec^2$ for a terminal angular velocity of $60°/sec$ and $6°/sec^2$ for a terminal velocity of $120°/sec$. Consequently, the stepping acceleration forward or backward was always $3°/sec^2$. The subject was instructed to stay behind the bar, which meant that he was required to step forward or backward when there was motion of the bar relative to the floor of the drum; the stepping rhythm was not controlled.

Under each experimental condition, the subject started with his head tilted toward the left shoulder. On command, after rotating for 1 min at constant velocity, he returned his head toward the normal upright position within about 1 sec. Subsequently, he was asked to scale his subjective sensation in relation to the purely vestibular Coriolis effect, which served as a standard with an arbitrary value of 5. The absence of any sensation was given the value 0. This method, in which the head was returned from a tilted position rather than moved from the vertical to a tilted position, was chosen because it permitted the initial head tilt to be checked by the experimenter and so ensured a more reproducible condition of stimulation.

Nine subjects participated. First, they were trained to perform the correct head movements, after which they were exposed to the standard, exclusively vestibular stimulation (condition B, Table 3.2). Subsequently, the various conditions were presented in random order with sufficient time between each for all sensations of rotation to be dissipated.

Results

The results are shown in Table 3.2. Modification of the vestibular Coriolis-effect (condition B) by the presence of congruent (condition A) or incongruent (condition C) somatosensory motion information can be seen: The magnitude of the Coriolis effect in condition A is significantly lower than in condition B (p < .01; Wilcoxon Signed-Ranks test) and in condition B the effect is significantly less than in condition C (p < .01). Worthy of note is the subjects' reports that they had, prior to the head tilting, a motion sensation in accordance with the somatosensory information: In condition A they reported the sensation of stepping around forward, which was actually the case, whereas they reported stepping around backward in condition C, although they actually moved forward. When vision supplements the somatosensory information (conditions G, H, and I), the effects are similar. The estimates in condition G are again significantly lower than in condition H (p < .01), whereas in condition H the estimates are lower than in condition I (p < .01). Visual information enhances the modification of the vestibular Coriolis effect, because the differences of the estimates in conditions C and A are lower than in conditions I and G (p < .05). By comparing the results of conditions B, A, and G, it can be seen that congruent information from several sensory systems reduces the vestibular Coriolis effect.

It can be seen also from Table 3.2 that in the ASA conditions D and F compared to condition E a Pseudo-Coriolis effect is induced (p < .01). Although the ASA Pseudo-Coriolis effect is qualitatively similar to the vestibular Coriolis effect, its magnitude is significantly lower (p < .01). Additional visual information can be regarded as enhancing the ASA Pseudo-Coriolis effect, because the estimates obtained in conditions D and F are significantly lower than those obtained in conditions J and L (p < .01).

DISCUSSION

From the results just described, it may be concluded that the complex somatosensory information associated with stepping around is sufficient to induce a compelling illusion of self-motion. Several findings strongly suggest similarities of the perceptual and motor effects of ASA with those of optokinetic stimulation: namely that ASA is perceived as real stepping around, that during ASA nystagmus (Bles & Kapteyn, 1977) and Coriolis-like effects can be induced, and that latencies and positive aftereffects occur (Bles, 1979).

An important feature of the ASA-induced circular vection (CV) is the torsion of lower limbs, the ankles, and the feet. This seems to be essential for inducing CV because stepping on a treadmill induces linear vection (LV) and not CV. Stimulation of the vestibular system is similar during ASA and on a treadmill: The semicircular canals are not stimulated and the stimulation of the otolithic system is the same (vertical head movements due to the stepping). On the other hand, it is not torsion of the feet alone, because step size is important too. This can be deduced from the fact that the step size and joint torsion are integrated during the 1- and 2-Hz stepping rate in such a way that the magnitude of the perceived velocity remains unaltered (cf. Experiment 1: conditions 3–8, 5–9).

Such an integration has a functional value for maintaining appropriate spatial orientation: For example, stepping in circles with different radii should not lead to a mismatch of the actual angle of rotation. The integration of the step size and torsion of the feet might also be useful in more complex movement patterns (cf. idiothetic course control in millipedes and spiders; Mittelstaedt, 1977).

Also functional is the implication of the result of Experiment 1 that there is no difference in magnitude of the CV as induced by the sensory systems individually or by their congruent combination. In principle, this offers the possibility of maintaining correct spatial orientation, even in those situations in which not every sensory system provides information or when a system is impaired and incapable of transferring information. Whether apparent stepping around has some therapeutic value, like the optokinetic training employed in the treatment of patients with acute vestibular disorders (Pfaltz, 1977), remains to be evaluated.

Nystagmus has been reported to occur with stimulation of parts of the somatosensory system other than those directly involved in ASA. For example, torsion of the cervical column (cervical nystagmus; Bos & Philipszoon, 1963; Güttich, 1940) or passive rotation of the extended arm about a vertical axis in the shoulder joint (arthrokinetic nystagmus; Brandt, Büchele, & Arnold, 1977) each induce nystagmus. In both instances, there is no direct stimulation of the peripheral vestibular system. Arthrokinetic nystagmus is accompanied by a sensation of self-motion, and both the nystagmus and the CV exhibit latencies and positive aftereffects. Likewise, torsion of the cervical vertebral column induces a sensation of head movements as well as nystagmus (Bles, 1979; de Jong & Bles, 1981). Obviously, the role of the somatosensory system in providing information about rotation of the body is complex, because stimulation of different parts of the somatosensory system result in CV and nystagmus. Tilt of the head toward a shoulder during constant velocity rotation in the dark results in a typical cross-coupled vestibular stimulation (Lansberg, 1960), which, together with its perceptual consequences, is referred to as the Coriolis effect (Schubert, 1932). Typically, the sensation is unpleasant and features a reported combination of tilt and rotation, which can be understood in terms of a mathematical description of the stimulus (Groen, 1961; Guedry & Montague, 1961). The somatosensory-vestibular interactions in the Coriolis-effects as found in Experiment 2, conditions A, B, and C (Table 3.2) show exactly the same behavior as was found by Brandt et al. (1971) with visual modulation of the vestibular Coriolis effect. It is interesting to note the considerable differences in magnitude between conditions A and C despite the fact that the magnitude of the ASA-induced Pseudo-Coriolis effect (conditions D or F) is relatively small. In a previous study, the ASA-induced Pseudo-Coriolis effect was shown to be of the same magnitude as the optokinetic Pseudo-Coriolis effect (Bles & de Wit, 1978). When vision accords with the somatosensory cues of stepping around, the incongruity with the vestibular stimulus (condition I) results in a very strong reaction and some subjects even have serious difficulties in maintaining equilibrium. However, the Coriolis effect is reduced remarkably when the three systems produce congruent information (condition C), which is the normal daily-life situation (Bles & de Wit, 1978).

In discussing Coriolis and Pseudo-Coriolis effects, the Purkinje effect should also be mentioned. Purkinje (1820) induced sensations similar to those associated with the Coriolis effect by tilting the head, immediately on stopping a sustained constant rate turn. In this situation, there is, of course, a different conflict as now the Coriolis accelerations are absent. In fact, it is only the velocity vector associated with the skull that changes its position according to the head movement; a tilt of such a vector induces tumbling sensations and this is in conflict with the information of the graviceptors (Guedry, 1974). Guedry likens the optokinetic Pseudo-Coriolis effects to the Purkinje effect, because in the optokinetic Pseudo-Coriolis effect the Coriolis accelerations are absent too. It should be noted, however, that Purkinje performed his experiment with real active stepping around and with the eyes open, a situation in which optokinetic and somatosensory aftereffects are likely to play an important role (Bles & Kapteyn, 1977; Correia et al., 1977; Dichgans & Brandt, 1973; Guedry et al., 1978), which means that the real Purkinje effect is highly complex. In terms of definition, it is therefore reasonable to speak of (1) Coriolis effects, when we are dealing with head movements performed by subjects sitting in complete darkness, on a rotating chair that rotates at constant velocity; (2) optokinetically induced Pseudo-Coriolis effects, when we are dealing with head movements by stationary seated subjects viewing a rotating surround (Dichgans & Brandt, 1973); and (3) ASA-induced Pseudo-Coriolis effects, when we are dealing with head movements, performed by subjects stepping around in darkness on a rotating platform, such that they remain objectively stationary.

Joint receptors, which transfer information about position of the joint as well as the direction and speed of movement, are involved in kinaesthesis (Skoglund, 1973). Joint afferents project to the cortical somatic area, and especially to area 2, very near to the vestibular projection field (Frederickson, 1974; Frederickson, Figge, Scheid, & Kornhuber, 1966). Convergence of vestibular and somatosensory signals at cortical level has been established by several studies (Frederickson, 1974) and is of functional importance because both systems give information about position and movements of the body (Büttner & Buettner, 1978). There is also unambiguous evidence for the convergence of visual (Dichgans et al., 1973; Waespe & Henn, 1977) and somatosensory information (Deecke, Schwarz, & Frederickson, 1977; Frederickson, et al., 1966; Rubin, Liedgren, Odkwist, Milne, & Frederickson, 1978) at the level of the vestibular nuclei. Because the perceptual and oculomotor responses during ASA are similar to those evoked by optokinetic stimulation, it seems likely that a somatosensory–vestibular convergence at the level of the vestibular nuclei and thalamus is the basic integrative mechanism responsible for the phenomena observed during active stepping around.

ACKNOWLEDGMENTS

The author wishes to thank Drs. Th. Brandt, T. S. Kapteyn, E. R. Wist, and G. de Wit for their criticism and helpful comments and Mrs. Ineke Schmidt for preparing the manuscript.

REFERENCES

Bles, W. *Sensory interactions and human posture*. Thesis, Vrije Universiteit, Amsterdam, 1979.

Bles, W., & Kapteyn, T. S. Circular vection and human posture: I. Does the proprioceptive system play a role? *Agressologie, 1977, 18,* 325–328.

Bles, W., & de Wit, G. La sensation de rotation et la marche circulaire. *Agressologie, 1978, 19,* 29–30.

Bos, J. H., & Philipszoon, A. J. Some forms of nystagmus provoked by stimuli other than accelerations. *Practica Oto-Rhino-Laryngologica, 1963, 25,* 108–118.

Brandt, T., Büchele, W., & Arnold, F. Arthrokinetic nystagmus and ego-motion sensation. *Experimental Brain Research, 1977, 30,* 331–338.

Brandt, T., Wist, E., & Dichgans, J. Optisch induzierte Pseudocoriolis-effekten und Circularvektion. *Archiv für Psychiatrie und Nervenkrankheiten, 1971, 214,* 365–389.

Büttner, U., & Buettner, U. W. Parietal cortex (2v) neural activity in the alert monkey during natural vestibular and optokinetic stimulation. *Brain Research, 1978, 153,* 393–397.

Correia, M. J., Nelson, J. B., & Guedry, F. E. Antisomatogyral illusion. *Aviation Space and Environmental Medicine, 1977, 48,* 859–862.

Deecke, L., Schwarz, D. W. F., & Frederickson, J. M. Vestibular responses in the rhesus monkey ventro-posterior thalamus: II. Vestibulo-proprioceptive convergence at thalamus neurons. *Experimental Brain Research, 1977, 30,* 219–232.

Dichgans, J., & Brandt, T. Visual-vestibular interaction and motion perception. *Bibliotheca Ophthalmologica, 1972, 82,* 327–338.

Dichgans, J., & Brandt, T. Optokinetic motion and pseudo-coriolis effects induced by moving visual stimuli. *Acta Oto-Laryngologica, 1973, 76,* 339–348.

Dichgans, J., & Brandt, T. Visual-vestibular interaction: Effects on self-motion perception and postural control. In R. Held, H. W. Leibowitz, & H. L. Teuber (Eds.), *Handbook of sensory physiology* (Vol. VIII). Berlin-Heidelberg-New York: Springer, 1978.

Dichgans, J., Schmidt, C. L., & Graf, W. Visual input improves the speedometer function of the vestibular nuclei in the goldfish. *Experimental Brain Research, 1973, 18,* 319–322.

van Egmond, A. A. J., Groen, J. J., & Jongkees, L. B. W. The mechanics of the semicircular canals. *Journal of Physiology, 1949, 110,* 1–17.

Frederickson, J. M. Cortical projections of the vestibular nerve. In H. H. Kornhuber (Ed.), *Handbook of sensory physiology* (Vol. VII). Berlin-Heidelberg-New York: Springer, 1974.

Frederickson, J. M., Figge, U., Scheid, P., & Kornhuber, H. H. Vestibular nerve projection to the cerebral cortex of the rhesus monkey. *Experimental Brain Research, 1966, 2,* 318–327.

Groen, J. J. The problems of the spinning top applied to the semicircular canals. *Confinia Neurologia, 1961, 21,* 454–455.

Guedry, F. E. Psychophysics of vestibular sensation. In H. H. Kornhuber (Ed.), *Handbook of sensory physiology* (Vol. VI/2). Berlin-Heidelberg-New York: Springer, 1974.

Guedry, F. E., & Montague, E. K. Quantitative evaluation of the vestibular Coriolis reaction. *Aerospace Medicine, 1961, 32,* 487–500.

Guedry, F. E., Mortensen, C. E., Nelson, J. B., & Correia, M. J. A comparison of nystagmus and turning sensations generated by active and passive turning. In J. D. Hood (Ed.), *Vestibular mechanisms in health and disease*. New York: Academic Press, 1978.

Güttich, A. Ueber den Antagonismus der Hals- und Bogengangsreflexe bei der Bewegung des menschlichen Auges. *Archiv für Ohren-,Nasen- und Kehlkopfheilkunde*, 1940, *147*, 1-4.

de Jong, J. M. B. V., & Bles, W. *Nystagmus and self-motion perception during head and neck rotation*. Annals of the New York Academy of Sciences, 1981, in press.

Kapteyn, T. S., & Bles, W. Circular vection and human posture: III. Relation between the reactions to various stimuli. *Agressologie*, 1977, *18*, 335-339.

Klinke, R., & Schmidt, C. L. Efferent influence on the vestibular organ during active movement of the body. *Pflügers Archiv für Gesammte Physiologie des Menschen und der Tiere*, 1970, *318*, 325-332.

Lansberg, M. P. *A primer of space medicine*. Amsterdam/New York: Elsevier, 1960.

Mach, E. *Grundlinien der Lehre von den Bewegungsempfindungen*. Leipzig: Engelmann, 1875.

Mittelstaedt, H. Kybernetische Analyse von Orientierungsleistungen. In *Kybernetik* (1977). München-Wien: Oldenbourg, 1977.

Pfaltz, C. R. Vestibular habituation and central compensation. *Advances in Oto-Rhino-Laryngology*, 1977, *22*, 136-142.

Purkinje, J. E. Beiträge zur näheren Kenntnis des Schwindels aus heautognostischen Daten. Med. Jb. Oesterreich, 1820, *6*, 79-125.

Rubin, A. M., Liedgren, S. C. R., Odkwist, L. M., Milne, A. C., & Frederickson, J. M. Labyrinthine and somatosensory convergence upon vestibulo-spinal neurons. *Acta Oto-Laryngologica*, 1978, *86*, 251-259.

Schubert, G Die physiologischen Auswirkungen der Coriolisbeschleunigungen bei Flugzeugsteuerung. *Archiv für Ohren-,Nasen- und Kehlkopf-heilkunde*, 1932, *30*, 595-604.

Skoglund, S. Joint receptors and kineasthesis. In A. Iggo (Ed.), *Handbook of sensory physiology* (Vol. II). Berlin-Heidelberg-New York: Springer, 1973.

Steinhausen, W. Uber die Beobachtung der Cupula in den Bogengangsampullen des Labyrinthes des lebenden Hechts. *Pflügers Archiv für Gesammte Physiologie des Menschen und der Tiere*, 1933, *232*, 500-512.

Waespe, W., & Henn, V. Neuronal activity in the vestibular nuclei of the alert monkey during vestibular and optokinetic stimulation. *Experimental Brain Research*, 1977, *27*, 523-538.

Young, L. R. The current status of vestibular system models. *Automatica*, 1969, *5*, 369-383.

4

What Goes Up Need Not Come Down: Moving Flicker Edges Give Positive Motion Aftereffects

Stuart M. Anstis
York University,
Downsview
Ontario, Canada

and

Patrick Cavanagh
University of Montreal,
Montreal
Quebec, Canada

ABSTRACT

Motion aftereffects (MAEs) are usually negative (i.e., opposite to the direction of the stimulating motion). However, we report a positive MAE, in the same direction as the stimulating motion. A special horizontal flickering edge made small jumps downward, changing in polarity between black/white and white/black on each jump. Apparent motion (AM) downward was perceived, but it was followed by an MAE downward (not upward). So an invisible feature of the stimulus produced a visible aftereffect. This is interpreted as evidence for two separate systems for seeing visual motion (Braddick, 1974): A long-range system correctly perceived the change of location downward, but a short-range system sensed an illusory reversed apparent motion upward, caused by the changes in edge polarity from positive to negative (Anstis, 1970, 1978). The short-range signal was not consciously seen, but it is thought to adapt motion detectors to give a motion aftereffect.

INTRODUCTION

Many a physiologist has exposed the animal of his choice to a moving visual stimulus and recorded the responses of "motion-sensitive" neurons in the animal's visual system. (For a review, see Grüsser & Grüsser-Cornehls, 1973). At the same time, the physiologist himself would perceive movement when he turned his eyes toward the visual stimulus. It is often assumed that the perception of movement can somehow be explained by the physiology of motion-sensitive neurons. But we shall present an illusion of motion perception that cannot be explained in terms of motion detectors. We devised a stimulus that to an observer appeared subjectively to be moving upward but, as assessed by an adaptation technique, was probably registered by motion detecting neurons as movement downward.

This experiment was based upon combining three known phenomena: (1) the negative aftereffect of motion (MAE); (2) apparent motion (AM); and (3) reversed apparent motion (Anstis, 1970, 1980). We combined these in an apparent-motion display that (we believe) stimulated different parts of the visual system in opposite directions at the same time. Adaptation to this special display produced a new motion aftereffect that was positive (i.e., appeared to move in the same direction as the original stimulus). This new illusion was taken as evidence for Braddick's (1974) theory that there are two systems for seeing motion, namely a short-range system, mediated by neural motion detectors, which is thought to respond to small spatial jumps, and a more central long-range system, which responds to larger jumps.

We describe these three known phenomena in turn and then see how they were put together in the experiment.

1. Motion Aftereffect (MAE).   After an observer has looked at a moving display for awhile, a stationary test display will briefly appear to be moving in the opposite direction. The aftereffect is caused by retinal stimulation and is independent of eye movements (Anstis & Gregory, 1965). Sutherland (1961) and Sekuler and Pantle (1967) suggested that the effect was caused by selective fatigue of neural motion detectors. Such fatigue in motion-sensitive neurons was observed by Barlow and Hill (1963) in the rabbit retina and by Vautin and Berkley (1977) in the cat cortex.

(The neural adaptation theory commands wide agreement, but the evidence is not unanimous. Anstis and Reinhardt-Rutland (1976) found that induced motion of an actually stationary adapting field could produce motion aftereffects. However, this probably involved simultaneous and successive inhibition among neural motion detectors. Bonnet and Pouthas (1972) proposed two temporal phases in the MAE: a kinetic phase, which was localized to the adapted region of the retina and probably involved motion detectors, followed by a figural phase, which could spread to adjacent retinal areas, resulting from figural properties of the test field. Cavanagh and Favreau (1980) and Beverley and Regan (1979) found evidence for nonlocal, global components of motion aftereffects in special cases. Nevertheless we do not feel that these exceptions cast any serious doubts on the neural-adaptation theory of motion aftereffects.)

2. Apparent Movement (AM).   Motion is perceived during real movement (RM), when a contour moves smoothly and continuously, and also during stroboscopic or apparent movement (AM), when a contour makes discontinuous jumps but can still give a sensation of movement (Kolers, 1972).

Kolers (1972) and Anstis (1980) discuss the unresolved question of whether real and apparent movement are mediated by the same or different neural mechansims. Motion aftereffects provide some important evidence here. Adaptation to real movement produces MAEs, presumably because neural motion detectors adapt. Adaptation to apparent movement can also produce MAEs—but only if the jumps of the AM stimulus are kept small enough, below about 15' arc. Large jumps still give apparent movement but no motion aftereffects (Banks & Kane, 1972). This is puzzling. MAEs following AM suggest that the AM is sensed by neural motion detectors, which then adapt. But why should MAEs arise for small AM jumps and not for large ones? One might argue that small jumps resemble RM closely enough to fool the motion detectors. Larger jumps might give a poorer imitation of RM and fail to stimulate the motion detectors. But, in that case, what mechanism is involved in seeing motion from the large jumps? The trouble here is that large jumps can and do give a satisfactory percept of apparent movement, even though they do not generate aftereffects.

As a way out of this difficulty, it has been suggested (Anstis, 1978; Braddick, 1974, 1980; Braddick & Adlard, 1978; Gregory, 1966; Ramachandran, 1977) that there may be two separate perceptual systems for seeing apparent movement. Gregory (1966) proposed a positional system, which detects movement by comparing the position of an object with another object or with the background. This system might be responsible for some phenomena of phi movement and of relative movement. He also proposed a velocity system, which would give direct signals of movement, probably by interpreting local displacements of contours across the retina. Gregory pointed out that motion aftereffects seem to be a disturbance of the velocity system, not the positional system, because the aftereffect has illusory velocity but not illusory displacement. Braddick (1974) amplified these ideas. He proposed two motion-perceiving systems, which he called the "short-range" and the "long-range" systems. The short-range system responds to luminance edges that jump through 15' arc or less: This system is thought to be mediated by neural motion detectors, which can become adapted to give motion aftereffects. The long-range system is thought to respond to luminance edges that jump through larger distances. This system probably involves higher-order neurons of some kind, not neural motion detectors, and it does not adapt to give motion aftereffects. The long-range system might also be able to respond to "cyclopean" edges that are defined not by luminance but by higher-order properties such as spatial phase, stereo depth, textural properties, or flicker (Anstis, 1980).

The experiment to be reported here was designed to test Braddick's hypothesis of the two motion systems. We used flickering moving edges, and we believe that these stimulated both motion systems simultaneously in opposite directions: The temporal phase of the flicker defined an edge moving in one direction for the long-range system, while at the same time a step luminance edge defined an edge moving in the opposite direction for the short-range system.

3. Normal Apparent Movement (AM) and Reversed Apparent Movement (RAM). For normal apparent movement, two projectors can be arranged to project the same picture onto a single screen. Let the two pictures be overlapping but displaced out of perfect register by a few minutes arc. Now, if one picture replaces the other via a slow fade or dissolve, apparent motion will be seen. Moreover, adaptation to such fading apparent motion can give a motion aftereffect.

A new illusion of visual motion was reported by Anstis (1970) and further described by Anstis and Rogers (1975) and by Rogers and Anstis (1975). Suppose that one of the two projected pictures is now the photographic negative of the other. A fade or dissolve will now produce an apparent motion in a direction opposite to the direction of stimulus displacement. For instance, if a white disc is gradually replaced by an overlapping black disc that is shifted a few minutes arc downward, a strong upward apparent motion is seen. Moreover, exposure to this reversed apparent movement leads to motion aftereffects that are appropriate to (opposite to) the direction of the perceived illusory motion, not of the physical displacement (Anstis, 1978, 1980; Anstis & Rogers, 1975; Rogers & Anstis, 1975). In our example, a downward displacement of the disc would give an apparent motion upward, followed by a motion aftereffect downward. This would suggest that reversed apparent motion stimulated motion-sensitive neurons, and Blakemore and Anstis have confirmed this with some unpublished results. A pair of white spots was exposed in sequence on a screen, with the second spot lower than the first, to give a percept of downward apparent motion to human observers. They also produced firing of a motion-sensitive neuron, tuned to downward motion, in the cortex of an anesthetized cat that was looking at the same screen. When a negative (black) spot was substituted for one of the white spots, the apparent direction of motion reversed, and now an upward (not downward) physical displacement was necessary, both to give a sensation of downward motion to the two human observers and to produce firing of the downward-sensitive neuron in the cat's cortex.

These properties of reversed apparent movement, which we have just described, suggest that it occurs only in the short-range and not in the long-range system. To summarize the evidence: Reversed AM occurs only for small spatial shifts, say of 15' or less; it can give motion aftereffects in a direction appropriate to (opposite to) the illusory reversed direction and not to the direction of physical displacement; and it can directly stimulate neural motion detectors. It is probably caused by spatial brightness summation, either in or before the neural motion detectors. This summation effectively shifts the apparent positions of the positive/negative composites, in a direction opposite to the physical displacement.

Consider a white dot or picture element (pixel) as it gradually fades away and is replaced by a negative, black dot that is slightly displaced to the right (see Fig. 4.1). In our theory, each pixel is neurally blurred by a point-spread function,

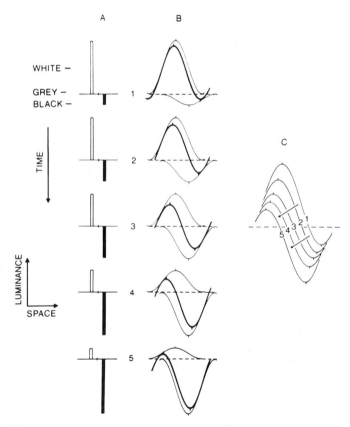

FIG. 4.1. Reversed apparent movement is explained by spatial summation. (a) Luminance profiles of white pixel as it fades over time and is gradually replaced by a black pixel that is displaced a few minutes arc to the right. (b) Spatial summation turns each pixel into a Gaussian point-spread function, which sum together to give an S-shaped curve (difference between displaced Gaussians). This combined point-spread function shifts gradually to the left. (c) Combined point-spread functions shown in (b) are superimposed. Shift to the left over time gives percept of reversed apparent movement to the left.

whose exact shape is not critical but may conveniently be taken as Gaussian. The point-spread function of an isolated white pixel will be exactly centered on the pixel. But when a black pixel is added, shifted slightly to the right, and the two pixel image profiles are convolved with the point-spread function, the combined luminance profile of the two pixels together will have its peak shifted slightly to the left (Fig. 4.1b). As the black pixel is gradually made more intense and the white pixel less so, the peak is shifted progressively farther and farther to the left. The point-spread function becomes S-shaped, like a sine wave that is being phase-shifted progressively to the left. What is true for a single pixel is also true for an edge or indeed for any complex picture. As a positive picture gradually dissolves to a negative picture that is displaced slightly to the right, reversed apparent movement will be seen apparently to the left.

There is no reason why this hypothetical spatial summation should be confined to dynamic moving stimuli. Rogers (1976) measured the spatial summation when an overlapping positive–negative pair was presented as a static vernier acuity target or else was embodied in a stereogram. He measured reversed apparent shifts in three conditions, using vernier, stereo, and AM targets. Consider the two stimuli shown in Fig. 4.1a (1) and (2), which would be blurred by spatial summation into Fig. 4.1b (1) and (2). In Roger's vernier condition, these two stimuli were presented one above the other and the subject was asked to set them into vernier alignment. Result: Figure 4.1a (2), which contains a negative image shifted to the right, appeared shifted slightly to the left, compared to Fig. 4.1a (1). In his stereo condition, the two stimuli were presented one to each eye. Result: The perceived depth was reversed (i.e., opposite to the direction of the physical disparity). Finally, in his apparent movement condition, the set of stimuli in Fig. 4.1 were presented dynamically, as a positive picture faded away and was replaced by a shifted negative. Result: reversed apparent movement.

Rogers found that the magnitude of reversed apparent vernier offset, depth, and AM, respectively, was an inverse function of the spatial displacement between positive and negative. Thus, as the spatial displacement was progressively inceased, the extent of reversed vernier offset, depth, or AM was progressively reduced and finally disappeared. However, the space constants found for the three tasks were different. The maximum physical displacements at which illusory reversed vernier, stereo, and AM could still just be seen were, respectively, 3', 6', and 10' arc.

Rogers attributed these findings to spatial summation and inhibition. Computer simulations of various hypothetical point-spread functions predicted the following:

1. Reversed apparent motion shifts only when the width of the hypothetical summatory region exceeded the displacement between positive and negative. This gave estimated foveal summatory zones of 3' arc for static vernier targets, 6' arc in the stereo disparity domain, and 10' arc for the short-range motion system.

2. Summatory point-spread functions without inhibition would give reversed shifts of contours that were relatively independent of the size of the displacement between positive and negative. This prediction was not supported by the data. The inverse relationship actually observed between physical displacement and amount of illusory shift could be predicted from a summatory zone surrounded by an inhibitory zone.

Rogers concluded that the visual pathways that respond, respectively, to static vernier targets, stereo, and apparent movement have point-spread functions consisting of summatory zones, respectively, 3', 6', and 10' arc wide, flanked in each case by inhibitory zones.

On this theory, reversed apparent movement will be seen only if the point-spread function is wider than the shift between positive and negative. In practice, the shift must be less than about 10-15' arc. (Larger shifts give indeterminate percepts of movement.) This gives a rough estimate of the size of foveal receptive fields. We have confirmed informally that larger shifts between pictures can still give RAM in two conditions: (1) peripheral vision, where the size of receptive fields is known to increase progressively with retinal eccentricity; and (2) when the stimulus pictures are optically blurred by defocusing the projectors. In this case, the optical blurring outside the head simply adds to the neural blurring inside the head.

These two phenomena—reversed apparent movement and the motion aftereffect—were combined in a special moving pattern whose movement, by design, could not be perceived exclusively by neural motion detectors. A moving, flickering edge was devised that was correctly perceived as moving downward. However, this moving edge contained a hidden, unseen component of reversed (upward) apparent motion, which adapted upward-specific neural motion detectors and subsequently gave a downward aftereffect of motion. We argue that the visible stimulus motion and the invisible motion that led to a subsequent aftereffect must have stimulated two different and independent motion-sensing systems. If the two opposite directions had been coded in separate motion detectors, say in the short-range system, such that the perceived output was some kind of vector sum of the two activities, then whichever direction was perceived during adaptation would have determined the direction of any subsequent—negative—aftereffect. However, we predicted that the moving step luminance change would stimulate the short-range system and give an aftereffect, whereas the temporal phase of the flicker would stimulate the long-range system, which would register the successive positional changes of the flicker edge but not lead to a subsequent aftereffect. A gradual fade or dissolve between a pair of pictures gives the best reversed AM, as in Fig. 4.1. A rapid cut or switch between two pictures comprises only the first and last stages of such a dissolve, and this gives less effective reversed AM. We once demonstrated this with a TV set in which alternate TV frames were successively positive–negative–positive–negative–.... We presented on the screen a moving real-life scene from a TV camera (Anstis, 1970). The result was a perceptual conflict between forward and reversed movement, in which the moving objects were seen moving in their true direction, with an overlaid effect of reversed AM that looked rather like sand streaming in the opposite direction.

In the present experiment, a horizontal edge was made to flicker or alternate in polarity between black/white and white/black at 15 Hz, which is well below flicker fusion frequency. When stationary, its position could be seen perfectly clearly; and when it made a series of small step movements downward, it gave a good, clear percept of movement, perhaps not as salient as a moving black/white edge that was not flickering but subjectively clear nonetheless. Adaptation to the apparent downward movement was followed by an upward (negative) motion aftereffect. This is just what one would expect if neural motion detectors responded to, and were adapted by, the apparent motion. But we devised a second, totally new flickering edge stimulus that was also correctly seen as moving downward but that introduced a hidden, unseen reversed apparent motion upward. Adaptation to this modified flickering edge gave a positive (upward) motion aftereffect. In the second case, the perception of motion cannot be mediated by motion detecting neurons.

Method

The horizontal edge, flickering at 15 Hz, was presented on a TV screen. On each flicker cycle the edge alternated in polarity between black/white and white/black and made a small jump downward.

The basis of the experiment is shown in Fig. 4.2. We manipulated the temporal phase relationships between the flicker and the movements. In the control condition, the edge alternately flickered and then moved; first it changed polarity (without moving), then moved (without changing polarity), and so on. This gave a series of movements, all downward. It was also true, but (we believe) irrelevant, that the moving edges were alternately black/white and white/black and were interspersed with static flickers or polarity changes.

In the experimental condition, a small but crucial change was made: the flicker and movement were now synchronized instead of being alternated, so that the edge jumped downward and simultaneously switched polarity, from black/white to white/black or vice versa. The purpose of this was to produce reversed AM, because the stimulus was now a positive edge being replaced by a displaced negative, which as we found in earlier papers (Anstis, *op. cit.*) would give a percept of apparent motion upward, followed by an MAE downward. However, the stimulus was different from the reversed AM stimulus in our earlier papers. We now had a flickering edge making a series of small discontinuous jumps, instead of a single pair of pictures making a slow fade. It was found that the experimental flickering edge was correctly perceived as jumping downward: There was no visible reversed AM effect of apparent motion upward.

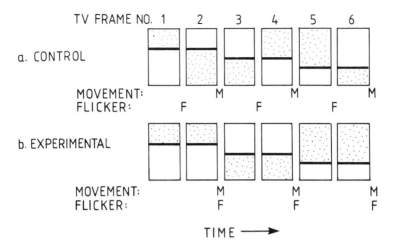

FIG. 4.2. Moving, flickering edges used as adapting stimuli in (a) control condition; (b) experimental condition. Edges were congruent in position in the two conditions. (a) Flicker and motion were out of phase. Edge alternately flickered or changed polarity without moving (frames 1-2, 3-4) and moved down without changing polarity (frames 2-3, 4-5). The flickers had no particular effect. The movements led to a negative motion aftereffect upward. (b) Flicker and motion were in phase. Nothing happened on frames 1-2, 3-4. The edge simultaneously changed polarity and jumped down on frames 2-3, 4-5. These jumps were correctly seen as being downward, but because the edge also changed from positive to negative on each jump, a hidden reversed apparent movement upward stimulated the neural motion detectors, leading to a downward motion aftereffect. The upward reversed apparent motion was not consciously seen. Conclusion: What the observer sees is not decided entirely by his neural motion detectors.

In the control condition, both the short-range and long-range motion signals were downward. In the experimental condition, the long-range motion signal was still downward, because the overall position of the flickering edge was being steadily displaced downward; however, the short-range signal was not upward, because the contrast reversal on each jump was giving a reversed apparent movement stimulus.

Why was the long-range downward motion seen and the short-range upward reversed AM not seen? The answer is that the stimulus time constants were carefully chosen to make the reversed AM suboptimal: strong enough to build up an aftereffect, but not strong enough to mask out the conflicting long-range movement signal. The moving flicker edges also gave a perceptual conflict, in which the downward displacement of the flicker edges completely masked out the reversed AM during the adaptation period. The reversed AM was able to reveal its presence only indirectly in the guise of an aftereffect.

Notice that the velocities, and the positions of the edges over time, were congruent in the two conditions: The only differences lay in the brightness

STIMULI

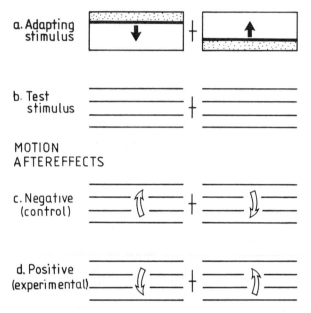

a. Adapting
   stimulus

b. Test
   stimulus

MOTION
AFTEREFFECTS

c. Negative
   (control)

d. Positive
   (experimental)

FIG. 4.3.   (a) Adapting stimulus: left-hand flickering edge moved downward; right-hand edge moved upward. (b) Test stimulus. (c) Apparent direction of a negative motion aftereffect (opposite to the adapting direction). This MAE was observed in the control condition. (d) Apparent direction of a positive motion aftereffect (same as the adapting direction). This MAE was observed in the experimental condition.

polarities of the edges. So the opposite aftereffects found in the two conditions were not determined by the actual positions of the adapting edges of the retina, because these were always the same. One confounding factor must be conceded: The flicker frequency in the zone adjacent to the experimental edge was half that at the control edge (Fig. 4.2), because the effective flicker rate was necessarily confounded with the phase of the movement/flicker combination. However, we do not feel that this confounding factor is important. Although the reduced flicker rate might alter the magnitude of the subsequent motion aftereffect, there is no clear theory, other than ours, that could predict the observed reversal in the direction of the aftereffect.

The moving flickering edge was generated by a program in an APPLE II microcomputer (Cavanagh & Anstis, 1980) and displayed on the screen of a good quality black and white TV monitor. The display, which was viewed from a distance of 2.1 m, is shown in Fig. 4.3. Two rectangles 1.3° wide and 0.5° high were placed on either side of a fixation cross, with their inner edges 0.17° apart. During the adapting phase, a moving, flickering edge scanned repetitively down the left-hand rectangle and a similar edge scanned up the right-hand rectangle, moving in a series of jumps of 3.8′ arc. Each scan took 1.1 sec, so the effective velocity of the edges was 0.46°/sec. The double display presenting step motions in opposite directions was intended to enhance any motion aftereffects.

During the test phase the moving edges were replaced by a field of four stationary horizontal lines, spaced 10′ arc apart, within each rectangle. A trial run consisted of 10 adapting periods each lasting 9 sec (eight scans of the rectangle), interspersed with 10 brief test periods. As soon as the test lines appeared, subjects reported any apparent motion aftereffects by pressing appropriate keys on the APPLE keyboard, whereupon the adapting scans resumed. Subjects were instructed to press a key on the left of the keyboard (A) if they saw a positive MAE and to press a key on the right of the keyboard (;) if they saw a negative

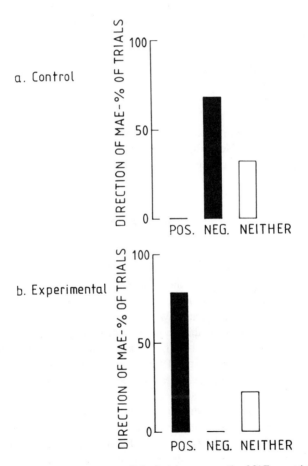

FIG. 4.4.   (a) Control condition: 68% of trials gave negative MAEs, no trials at all gave positive MAEs, and 32% gave no MAEs (or ambiguous ones). (b) Experimental condition: no trials negative MAEs, 78% gave positive MAEs, and 22% gave no MAEs (or ambiguous ones). See text.

MAE. They were told to press the spacebar if they saw any other direction of MAE or no MAE. After 10 test periods the computer printed out the total reports of positive and negative MAEs or otherwise, and these were recorded. Eight subjects were tested, including the two authors. Five subjects were naive about the purposes of the experiment.

Results

Results are shown in Fig. 4.4. They fulfil our predictions. In the experimental condition the motion aftereffects were positive (i.e., in the same direction as the adapting moving edges) in 78% of the trials; 22% of trials gave no MAE, but there were no (0%) reports of negative MAEs. In the control condition, on the other hand, the aftereffects were negative (i.e., in the opposite direction to the moving edges) in 68% of the trials; 32% of trials gave no MAE, and there were no (0%) reports of positive MAEs.

It should be noted that several subjects commented on how weak the MAEs in this experiment were. The experimental design constrained us to use small, flickering edges, so the MAEs were always brief and transitory, never lasting more than a second or two; a far cry from the robust, long-lasting motion aftereffects that are commonplace with an optimally chosen large, slowly moving, textured surface. Nevertheless, the MAEs, although small, were in the directions predicted by our theory.

DISCUSSION

We have argued that the flickering edges stimulated the long-range system in one direction and at the same time stimulated the short-range system in the opposite direction. These results support the idea that motion can be perceived in two ways: The short-range system does have a substrate of neural motion detectors that can be adapted, the alternative way is more central and is mediated by still unknown neural mechanisms that show little or no adaptation (Braddick, 1974, 1980; Braddick & Adlard, 1978). These ideas have been elaborated by Ramachandran (1977) and Anstis (1978, 1980). See also Ullman (1980).

When we pitted the long-range against the short-range system, the long-range system determined the perceived direction of the adapting motion, but the short-range system determined the direction of the motion aftereffect. This suggests that MAEs are much stronger in the short-range than in the long-range system. We cannot entirely rule out long-range MAEs; in fact, there have been reports of very brief long-range MAEs, lasting for 1 sec or less, following adaptation to long-range motion stimuli such as drifting cyclopean stereo gratings (Papert, 1964) and dichoptic AM of isolated spots that jumped through a few degrees (Anstis & Moulden, 1970). So the long-range system may show a very limited amount of adaptation. But it is undoubtedly much "stiffer" and less prone to adaptation than the short-range system.

Why should there be two separate systems for seeing movement, instead of just one? It may be economical to change visual strategy according to the size of the visual jump. An object in real movement makes infinitely small jumps. Larger jumps are very rare in the real world, perhaps occurring only for occluded motion when an object disappears behind an obstruction and reappears on the other side. Detecting these rare, large jumps would slow the system down considerably; in the worst case of a random-dot textured field, the number of comparisons needed to keep track of jumps through n dot diameters would increase according to n^2. In a serial processor, such as a modern computer, increasing the spatial range would impose an increased search time; in a parallel processor, which the visual system seems to be, it would increase the number of neural channels needed. So it may be efficient to restrict the spatial range of hard-wired motion detectors, say to $1/4°$, for the following reasons: (1) Receptive fields (or their subunits) cannot be made infinitely small; (2) time constants in the nervous system cannot be made infinitely small either, so to detect a useful range of velocities would require samples to be taken at certain spatial intervals; (3) even if the spatial distances could be made very small, a prohibitively large number of motion-detecting regions would then be needed to cover the visual field, each served by a different cell or subunit; and (4) it is useful to detect the motion of targets of finite size that move as wholes, and this would require some spatial integration for this region (Nakayama & Tyler, in press).

The psychophysics of the short-range system can be compared with the psyiology of the motion detectors that are thought to underlie it. Barlow and Levick (1965) found evidence that a neural motion detector compares inputs from two nearby retinal regions, A and B. Michael (1968) showed that a single small jump by a spot across any small subregion of a motion detector's receptive field could make the cell respond. The receptive field seems to be built up of many subunits, each containing an A region and a B region, and the jumping spot need stimulate only one subunit to make the cell fire.

We can speculatively equate short-range perceptual phenomena with the properties of neural motion detectors. The spatial integration range over which luminance is summated for an AM stimulus is about $10'$ arc (Rogers, 1976). (This will set an upper bound on dynamic visual acuity for moving targets.) It may correspond to the diameter of each A or B region within a subunit. The spatial range, or largest jump over which random-dot AM can be seen, is about $15'$ arc (Braddick, 1974). This may correspond to the mean separation between each A region and its corresponding B region. The largest region over which a field of uniformly moving random dots can be summated has been estimated to be about $2°$ arc (Nakayama & Tyler, in press). We conclude that the foveal units underlying the short-range system may have receptive fields as large as $2°$ in diameter. Each receptive field may be composed of many pairs of subregions, about $10'$ arc in diameter and separated by about $15'$ arc.

The short-range system will respond adequately to nearly all moving objects. Larger jumps can be detected by a backup system with a longer spatial range. It is not known whether this second, more global system has a fixed neural structure of higher-order cortical motion detectors or whether it is a set of perceptual strategies or procedures—a form of neural "software."

ACKNOWLEDGMENTS

This research was supported by Grant A 0260 to SMA and by Grant A 8606 to JPC, both from the Natural Science and Engineering Research Council of Canada (NSERC).

REFERENCES

Anstis, S. M. Phi movement as a subtraction process. *Vision Research*, 1970, *10*, 1411-1430.
Anstis, S. M. Apparent movement. In R. Held, H. Leibowitz, & H. L. Teuber (Eds.), *Handbook of sensory physiology: Perception* (Vol. VIII). New York: Springer-Verlag, 1978.
Anstis, S. M. The perception of apparent movement. *Philosophical Transactions of the Royal Society of London, B*, 1980, *290*, 153-168. Reprinted in *The psychology of vision*. London: The Royal Society, 1980.
Anstis, S. M., & Gregory, R. L. The after-effect of seen motion: The role of retinal stimulation and eye movements. *Quarterly Journal of Experimental Psychology*, 1965, *17*, 173-174.
Anstis, S. M., & Moulden, B. P. Aftereffect of seen movement: Evidence for central and peripheral components. *Quarterly Journal of Experimental Psychology*, 1970, *22*, 222-229.
Anstis, S. M., & Reinhardt-Rutland, A. H. Interactions between motion aftereffects and induced movement. *Vision Research*, 1976, *16*, 1391-1394.
Anstis, S. M., & Rogers, B. J. Illusory reversals of movement and depth during changes in contrast. *Vision Research*, 1975, *15*, 957-961.
Banks, W. P., & Kane, D. A. Discontinuity of seen motion reduces the visual motion aftereffect. *Perception & Psychophysics*, 1972, *12*, 69-72.
Barlow, H. B., & Hill, R. M. Evidence for a physiological explanation of the waterfall phenomenon and figural aftereffects. *Nature*, 1963, *200*, 1345-1347.
Barlow, H. B., & Levick, W. R. The mechanism of directionally selective units in rabbit's retina. *Journal of Physiology*, 1965, *178*, 477-504.
Beverley, K. I., & Regan, D. M. Separable aftereffects of changing-size and motion-in-depth: Different neural mechanisms? *Vision Research*, 1979, *19*, 727-732.
Blakemore, C., & Anstis, S. M. Unpublished results.
Bonnet, C., & Pouthas, V. Interactions between spatial and kinetic dimensions in movement afteref-fect. *Perception & Psychophysics*, 1972, *12*, 193-200.
Braddick, O. J. A short-range process in apparent motion. *Vision Research*, 1974, *14*, 519-527.
Braddick, O. J. Low-level and high-level processes in apparent motion. *Philosophical Transactions of the Royal Society of London, B*, 1980, *290*, 137-151. Reprinted in *The psychology of vision*. London: The Royal Society, 1980.
Braddick, O. J., & Adlard, A. Apparent motion and the motion detector. In J. C. Armington, J. Krauskopf, & B. R. Wooten (Eds.), *Visual psychophysics and physiology: A volume dedicated to Lorrin Riggs*. New York: Academic Press, 1978.
Cavanagh, P., & Anstis, S. M. Visual psychophysics and the APPLE II computer: Getting started. *Behavior Research Methods and Instrumentation*, 1980, *12*, 614-626.

Cavanagh, P., & Favreau, O. E. Motion aftereffect: A global mechanism for the perception of rotation. *Perception,* 1980, *9,* 175–182.

Gregory, R. L. *Eye and brain.* New York: McGraw-Hill, 1966.

Grüsser, O. J., & Grüsser-Cornehls, U. Neuronal mechanisms of visual movement perception and some psychophysical and behavioral correlations. In R. Jung (Ed.), *Handbook of sensory physiology* (Vol. VII/3). New York: Springer-Verlag, 1973.

Kolers, P. A. *Aspects of motion perception.* New York: Academic Press, 1972.

Michael, C. R. Receptive fields of single optic nerve fibers in a mammal with an all cone retina. II: Directionally selective units. *Journal of Neurophysiology,* 1968, *31,* 257–267.

Nakayama, K., & Tyler, C. W. Psychophysical isolation of movement sensitivity by removal of familiar position cues. *Vision Research,* in press.

Papert, S. *MIT Quarterly Technical Report,* 1964.

Ramachandran, V. W. *Studies on binocular vision.* Unpublished doctoral dissertation, University of Cambridge, England, 1977.

Rogers, B. J. *Perceptual consequences of spatial and temporal summation in the visual system.* Unpublished doctoral dissertation, University of Bristol, England, 1976.

Rogers, B. J., & Anstis, S. M. Reversed depth from positive and negative stereograms. *Perception,* 1975, *4,* 193–201.

Sekuler, R. W., & Pantle, A. A model for aftereffects of seen motion. *Vision Research,* 1967, *7,* 427–439.

Sutherland, N. S. Figural aftereffects and apparent size. *Quarterly Journal of Experimental Psychology,* 1961, *13,* 222–228.

Ullman, S. *The interpretation of visual motion.* Cambridge, Mass.: MIT Press, 1980.

Vautin, R. G., & Berkley, M. A. Responses of single cells in cat visual cortex to prolonged stimulus movement: Neural correlates of visual aftereffects. *Journal of Neurophysiology,* 1977, *40,* 1051–1065.

5 Processing Configurations of Visual Motion

Claude Bonnet
Laboratoire de Psychologie Experimentale
Universite Rene Descartes,
Paris, France

ABSTRACT

The aim of the present experiments was to examine the validity of linearity assumptions implied in the velocity vector model for the perception of motion configuration (Johansson, 1950) in the perspective of a neurosensory approach. Two orthogonally drifting gratings raise the phenomenal experience of an oblique motion of a gingham pattern. The first experiment explored the validity of the assumption according to which the perceived direction of the motion configuration is predicted by the resultant vector of the two orthogonal velocity components. Departures from the linear model are demonstrated. In a second experiment, it is confirmed that at threshold the detection of one directional component is independent of an orthogonal directional component, provided the contrasts of the latter are near threshold. In a third experiment, inhibitory interactions between the orthogonal directional components are shown both for the detection of one of these components and for the detection of the configuration. The latter requires more contrast than the former. These data suggest revision of the model, because linearity assumptions are not valid.

INTRODUCTION

Motion perception is currently studied mainly within either one or another of two *separate* approaches: a neurosensory approach exemplified in reviews such as those by Sekuler (1975) or Sekuler, Pantle, and Levinson (1978) or a

79

phenomenologically oriented approach exemplified recently by Johansson, von Hofsten, and Jansson (1980). In spite of their differences, it was felt that the theoretical gap existing between them could be reduced. The present chapter is such an attempt. A simple experimental situation appropriate for both approaches was chosen for the purpose.

When two completely superimposed patterns are independently moving in different directions, two opposite phenomenal effects can be experienced. On some occasions, a single motion configuration is perceived, in which the resulting unique motion can be predicted from a vector analysis of the stimulus (Johansson, 1950; Johansson et al., 1980). However, on other occasions, the two motions are seen as segregated, as shown in a recent experiment by Marshak and Sekuler (1979).

In a series of experiments, Johansson (1950) claimed to show that phenomenal experiences generated by simultaneous presentation of several visual movements can be accounted for by a velocity vector analysis of these movements. In his Experiment 19, two spots of light oscillated in phase at 90° trajectories to one another. The stimulus was described by the observers as a movement of the two spots toward and away from each other, along a common diagonal path. According to Johansson et al., 1980, this is just what would be expected if the visual system carried out a vector analysis of the stimulus in such a way as to "treat the relative movements in the pattern as a perceptual unit and the common component as a frame of reference for the motion of the unit [p. 33]." Following the gestalt tradition in stressing the phenomenal prominence of motion configurations, Johansson's model (1950) is an attempt to *describe* the proximal motion stimulus in a way that makes it similar to the percept. However, as we shall see, such a model implies very strong linearity assumptions that have not been validated.

Neurophysiological studies, using single-cell recording techniques, have demonstrated that some cells specifically code the direction of motion and that different cells have different directional selectivity (Grüsser & Grüsser-Cornhels, 1973). Psychophysically, through the use of a subthreshold summation paradigm, Levinson and Sekuler (1975) demonstrated that, at least at threshold, opposite directions of motion are coded independently. Such an assumption has been challenged by Moulden and Mather (1978), who argued in favor of nonindependent coding in the form of a ratio model (Barlow & Hill, 1963; Sutherland, 1961). Because directional selectivity as measured psychophysically is about ±30° (Sekuler et al., 1978), the use of orthogonal directions of motion in the present experiments makes neither set of claims directly applicable and the latter questionable.

The following experiments were undertaken before Marshak and Sekuler's recent (1979) paper was published. At that time, the perceptual synthesis of different directional motion components was assumed to be the case for visual processing. The velocity vector model was assumed to describe correctly the relationship between stimulus and percept. The question was then to show how such a model can be reconciled with a neurophysiological approach stressing characteristics of processing in the visual system. Consider a basic model that assumes a two-stage process for motion configurations. As a first stage, different directions of motion are coded in separate neural subunits. The second stage was initially assumed to be an integrator-like process, which received inputs from separate units and performed a velocity vector analysis. If such a vector model were valid, the linearity of the model would result from linearities in the underlying process. The first experiment evaluated the predictive value of the velocity vector model, whereas the following two experiments evaluated the linearity of the processes.

EXPERIMENT 1

The aim was to examine the velocity vector model for motion configurations resulting from two drifting, spatially superimposed, sinusoidal gratings, orthogonally oriented. Such patterns (termed *gingham*) allow one to examine how the perceived direction of the configuration is integrated as a result of only the *velocity* vectors, independently of the spatial and temporal frequencies of the pattern. It should, however, be stressed that the retinal projection of the two orthogonally drifting gratings contains an oblique motion component, the direction of which is obviously confounded with the resultant velocity vector. Certain aspects of moving ginghams deserve comment. First, the oblique motion component is given by angular contours and not by straightedges. Tentatively, one may suggest that the former are less effective in triggering directionally selective cells. Second, the two dimensional Fourier components of a stationary gingham pattern are only vertical and horizontal (De Valois, De Valois, & Yund, 1979). Apparently, motion does not change the spatial characteristics. Third, the alignments of the maxima (or minima) of the luminance regions of the gingham pattern are of an angle that differs considerably from the angle of the oblique motion component.

Nevertheless, a first experiment was undertaken in order to estimate the extent to which the perceived direction of a motion configuration is precisely predicted by the resulting vector of the two orthogonally oriented velocity vectors of the drifting gratings.

Materials, Apparatus, and Procedure

The moving patterns were sinusoidal gratings drifting on the face of an oscilloscope with a P-31 phosphor. Gratings were visible through an aperture 3° in diameter in the center of a lighted background of the same mean luminance (6 cd m^{-2}) and of the same green color. The background was seen through a large aperture, 13° in diameter, in binocular vision. A dark fixation point occupied the center of the moving field. The same two subjects participated throughout the experiment.

In a *preliminary experiment,* Michelson contrast thresholds for the detection of the direction of motion of a single drifting grating were measured for the two subjects. Contrast is defined as

$$C = \frac{L_{max} - L_{min}}{L_{max} + L_{min}}$$

where L_{max} is the maximum luminance of the grating and L_{min}, the minimum luminance. The gratings drifted at a rate of TF = 2 Hz, and the spatial frequency of the gratings varied from trial to trial between 0.4 cycle per degree (cpd) to 6 cpd. An adjustment method was used to establish the contrast. The optimum sensitivity was found to be at about 1 cpd.

In the *main experiment,* two orthogonally oriented gratings were simultaneously presented as optically superimposed. The horizontal grating drifted upward and will be referred to as the vertical motion component ($\dot{V}$); the vertical grating drifted rightward and will be referred to as the horizontal motion component ($\dot{H}$). The resultant vector indicating the configuration's predicted direction of drift ($\dot{D}$) is given by the arctangent value of the ratio of the velocity of the vertical motion component over the velocity of the horizontal motion component. Three directions of the configuration ($\dot{D} = 31.7°$, 45°, or 58.3°) were obtained for different spatial and temporal frequencies of the two gratings. A sample of eight stimulus conditions was obtained (see Table 5.1). Two subsets are distinguished: For stimulus conditions 1, 2, 3, and 4, the spatial (and temporal) frequency is in the low range; whereas, for conditions 5, 6, 7, and 8, it is in the high range. The limit between these ranges was the optimal spatial frequency of 1 cpd found in the preliminary experiment. For both subsets, similar velocities of medium value were obtained (1.85°, 3°, and 4.85°/sec). The Michelson contrast of the grating was 40%.

While keeping his gaze continuously on the fixation point, the subject was asked to match the perceived direction of drift of the gingham by appropriately adjusting by touch the orientation of a nonvisible rod. The rod was connected to a potentiometer that allowed digital measurement of the reported angle. Conventionally 0° referred to a horizontal direction and 90° to a vertical one. Matching started alternatively from a horizontal position of the rod or from a vertical position. Each subject experienced each of the eight stimulus conditions six times, presented in random order. Three sessions were necessary to test each subject.

In a *control experiment,* a single dark stationary bar was presented through the 3° aperture on a homogeneous green background at different orientations. The subjects were then asked to match each orientation with the response rod

TABLE 5.1
Stimulus Conditions of the Experiments

Conditions		*1*	*2*	*3*	*4*	*5*	*6*	*7*	*8*	
Vertical Grating	SF	0.21	0.56	0.56	0.21	1.47	3.85	3.85	3.85	cpd
	TF	0.63	1.68	1.68	1.02	4.41	11.55	11.55	7.13	Hz
	$\dot{H}$	3	3	3	4.85	3	3	3	1.85	°/sec
Horizontal Grating	SF	0.56	0.21	0.21	0.21	3.85	1.47	1.47	3.85	cpd
	TF	1.94	0.63	1.02	1.02	7.13	4.41	7.13	7.13	Hz
	$\dot{V}$	1.85	3	4.85	4.85	1.85	3	4.85	1.85	°/sec
	$\dot{D}$	31.7	45	58.3	45	31.7	45	58.3	45	deg.

SF, spatial frequency; TF, temporal frequency; $\dot{H}$, velocity of the horizontal motion component; $\dot{V}$, velocity of the vertical motion component; $\dot{D}$, resulting vector or predicted direction of the motion of the gingham.

used in the main experiment. The experiment was to validate the response technique, so as to check if the errors observed in the main experiment were due to response factors.

In the main experiment, as in the control experiment, every trial lasted until the subject was satisfied with the match. Practically all matches were accomplished within 5 sec.

Results and Discussion

The results of the *control experiment,* reported in Fig. 5.1, show a clear linear relationship between the orientation of the static bar and the response matched by touch. For each of the two subjects a correlation of .99 was observed. However, the slopes of the function are below unity, indicating an overestimation of the orientations close to the horizontal and an underestimation of the orientations close to the vertical. Nevertheless, the control experiment can be considered to have validated the response technique.

In the *main experiment,* a strong hysteresis effect was found. Direction estimates starting from a vertical position of the response rod are closer to a vertical direction (90°) than direction estimates starting from a horizontal position of the response rod. Such an effect was not found in the control experiment. Hence, the hysteresis effect is to be attributed to the motion stimulation itself. However, it does not affect the slopes of the relationship between estimated directions of the motion of the configuration nor the direction of the resultant velocity vector. Consequently the effect will be neglected in the following analyses, which were conducted on the pooled data of each subject.

The mean estimated directions of the motion configuration are reported in Fig. 5.1, separately for each subset of the spatial (and temporal) frequency range. In

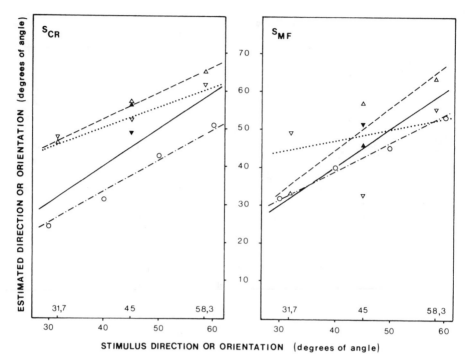

FIG. 5.1. Estimated direction of the motion configuration as a function of the direction of the resultant velocity vector. The continuous line represents a perfect estimate. ($\nabla \ldots \nabla$) are the mean results of stimulus conditions 1, 2, 3, and 4 in the low SF range; (Δ---Δ) are the mean results of conditions 4, 6, 7, and 8 in the high SF range; (0-.-.-.0) are the mean results of the estimated orientation of the static bar.

each condition, the variability was estimated by computing a variability coefficient that is, in percent, the ratio of the standard error of the mean over the mean. In spite of the hysteresis effect, such a coefficient is of 4.66% for S_{CR} and 6.75% for S_{MF}.

As for the estimation of the orientation of the static bar, the estimated direction of the motion configuration increases as a significant function of the stimulus direction, $F_{CR}(1, 40) = 29.7$, $p < .001$, $r = .50$; $F_{MF}(1, 40) = 41.9$, $p < .001$, $r = .68$. Generally, slopes are below unity. The slopes of the estimated direction of the motion configuration for stimulus conditions 5, 6, 7, and 8 (high spatial and temporal frequency range) are closer to the slopes of the estimated orientation of the static bar than the slopes of stimulus conditions 1, 2, 3, and 4 (low spatial and temporal frequency range). In the latter subset of data, although each individual slope is statistically significant, there is only a small effect of the change in the direction of the motion configuration. For stimulus conditions 1, 2, 3, and 4, the linear regressions are significant, $F_{CR}(1, 20) = 6.97$, $p < .02$, r

$= .20$; $F_{MF}(1, 20) = 20.47$, $p < .001$, $r = .66$. For stimulus conditions 5, 6, 7, and 8, the linear regressions are also significant, $F_{CR}(1, 20) = 65.9$, $p < .001$, $r = .82$; $F_{MF}(1, 20) = 22.06$, $p < .001$, $r = .72$.

None of the other possible within-subject comparisons is systematic enough to be considered further. The question remains of how to explain the large departure in the intercept values between the main experiment and the control experiment. The estimated directions of the motion configurations are systematically biased toward the vertical direction. Although the fixation of the gaze of the subject was not recorded, a correct fixation was necessary in order to perceive the oblique component. For that reason, eye movements are not believed to be the basic reason for the systematic bias in perceived direction.

The perceived direction of motion of the configuration differs from the direction of the resultant velocity vector in a way that cannot be attributed to the response system. The possibility that the subjects were in fact estimating the orientational alignment of the maxima (or minima) of luminance of the gingham was considered. Low and negative correlations between the alignments and the corresponding responses permit such an interpretation to be excluded.

Further experiments are necessary in order to clarify several aspects of the data. Nevertheless, the systematic differences in the slopes of the functions between the low and high spatial (and/or temporal) frequencies is a sufficient indication that the validity of the velocity vector model does not hold under the present conditions. A *linear* integration of the two orthogonal motion components should exclude any systematic effect of the spatial (and/or temporal) frequency content of the pattern.

EXPERIMENT 2

The aim of the second experiment was to evaluate the linearity assumptions that characterize the coding process of different directions of motion. For this purpose, the independence in the detection of two orthogonal directions of motion was tested by a summation technique.

Levinson and Sekuler (1975) have demonstrated that two motions of opposite direction can be assumed to be detected independently at threshold by using a subthreshold summation paradigm. Campbell and Kulikowski (1966) and Carlson, Cohen, and Gorog (1977) have demonstrated that two orthogonal stationary gratings are also detected independently.

Materials and Procedure

The same display was used as in Experiment 1. Now Michelson contrast thresholds for the detection of the direction of one motion were measured. In what follows, the modulation referred to is always the modulation of a single grating. In effect, when the two orthogonal gratings are superimposed, the modulation of the configuration is the mean of the contrasts of each of its two components.

In the first stage of the experiment, contrast thresholds were measured with each of the two gratings for each of the combinations of spatial and temporal frequencies used. The eight combinations of direction, spatial and temporal frequencies corresponding to the four stimulus conditions (1, 3, 5, 7) of Table 5.1, were used. Four replications of the adjustment of the contrast for detecting the direction of motion were made.

In the second stage, the contrast thresholds for the detection of the vertical motion component were measured when the horizontal component was presented at a contrast level below or above its own threshold. The thresholds are called $C_{\lim}$ $(\vec{V}/\vec{H})$. Five relative values of this "background" contrast were used: .33, .66, 1.00, 1.33, and 1.66 times the contrast threshold value for the horizontal motion component. For each of the four stimulus conditions, the relative contrasts of the horizontal motion component were presented in a random order using the constant method with four replications within a session. The order of presentation was different between the subjects and between the sessions. Each subject was tested in two sessions. The same two subjects took part as in Experiment 1.

Results and Discussion

Each measured threshold, $C_{\lim}$ $(\vec{V}/\vec{H})$, has been transformed into a relative value by dividing it by the threshold for the detection of the vertical motion component alone, $C_{\lim}$ $(\vec{V})$, obtained in the first stage of the experiment. The transformed results are presented in Fig. 5.2. If the independence hypothesis is true, each result should fall on a horizontal line with an intercept of unity.

Within each stimulus condition, the relative thresholds, $C_{\lim}(\vec{V}/\vec{H})/C_{\lim}$ $(\vec{V})$, were first compared to the unity level with a Student t test. On only one occasion for each subject (open symbols in Fig. 5.2) was a significant departure from unity demonstrated at the 5% level. Observe, however, that the mean tendency of the results of subject CR is toward facilitation, whereas for subject MF it is toward inhibition.

When the linearity of the regressions is tested, condition by condition, it is never significant.

In conclusion, within the range of the relative contrasts of the horizontal motion used in the present experiment, the assumption of the independence in the detection of orthogonal direction motion components is essentially valid. It is, however, obvious in Fig. 5.2 that the four conditions did not act consistently. In the two subjects, conditions 3 and 7 are statistically indistinguishable: The expected direction of their motion configuration is 58.3°, but their spatial and temporal frequencies are different. Conditions 1 and 5, for which the expected

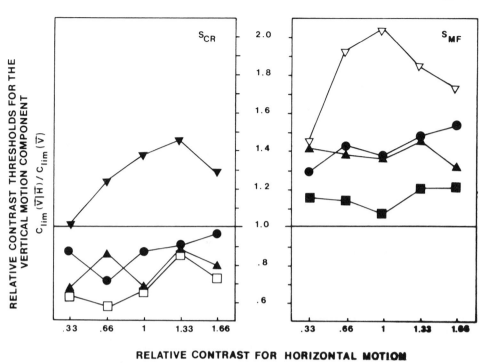

FIG. 5.2.   Relative contrast thresholds for the vertical motion component as a function of the relative contrast of the horizontal motion component. (Δ — Δ) represent results of stimulus condition 1; (0 — 0), condition 3; (∇ — ∇), condition 5; ($\square$ — $\square$), condition 7. See text.

direction of the motion configuration is 31.7°, give rise to extreme results. Sampling limitations of the present experiment do not warrant further analysis of the results.

EXPERIMENT 3

A third experiment was run in order to (1) show whether if the relative contrast of the horizontal component (background) is high enough, the detection of the vertical component will be degraded (inhibition); and (2) explore, in comparable conditions, the detection of the motion configuration. If the detection of the motion configuration resulted either from the presence of a real oblique motion component or from a linear summation process of the two orthogonal motion components, its contrast threshold should be the average of the contrast thresholds for the horizontal [$C_{\lim} (\dot{H})$] and for the vertical [$C_{\lim} (\dot{V})$] motion components. In fact, preliminary trials showed that more contrast is necessary to detect the oblique motion of the configuration than to detect its vertical component.

Materials and Procedure

The materials and procedure are essentially the same as those used in Experiment 2. However, two sets of instructions were used on separate occasions. In a first set, as in Experiment 2, the subject was asked to set the contrast of the vertical motion component when the horizontal motion component was present and visible: $C(\vec{V}/\vec{H})$. In a second set of instructions, the subject was requested to increase the contrast of the vertical component, while the horizontal motion component was present and visible, until an *oblique* motion of the gingham pattern was seen: $C(\vec{V} + \vec{H})$.

The same two subjects of Experiment 2 took part in this experiment, which was only run under stimulus condition 1. The relative contrasts of the horizontal motion component were 1.66, 3, 5, and 10 times its own threshold $[C_{\lim}(\vec{H})]$. Four replications were tested in every condition.

A third subject was then run in the four stimulus conditions (2, 4, 6, 8) with the two sets of instructions. The same relative contrasts of the horizontal motion component were used with the addition of a relative contrast level of 1. Four replications of each of the 20 conditions of each set of instructions were run on this subject.

Results and Discussion

The results of Experiment 3 are presented in Fig. 5.3 in terms of the liminal contrast of the vertical motion component relative to its own threshold, $C_{\lim}$ $(\vec{V}/\vec{H})/C_{\lim}(\vec{V})$, for each of the two phenomenal criteria and for each subject. Results of subject NC were averaged over the four conditions.

These results confirm the main feature of Experiment 2. The detection of the vertical motion component is statistically independent of the contrast of the horizontal motion component below some suprathreshold contrast of the latter. For a relative contrast of the horizontal motion component 10 times its own threshold, a clear inhibition in the detection of the orthogonal (vertical) motion component is present in each subject and under every stimulus condition. Within the sampling limits of the present experiment, only a linear trend can be shown to be statistically significant between the relative contrasts of the vertical motion component and of the horizontal motion component $F_{NC}(1, 60) = 159.74$, $p < .001$, $r = .69$. The trend remains significant within each subject and within each condition for subject $NC.F_{NC,2}(1, 15) = 68.23$, $p < .001$, $r = .87$; $F_{NC,4}(1, 15) = 166.12$, $p < .001$, $r = .95$; $F_{NC,6}(1, 15) = 14.62$, $p < .005$, $r = .69$; $F_{NC,8}(1, 15) = 62.23$, $p < .001$, $r = .89$.

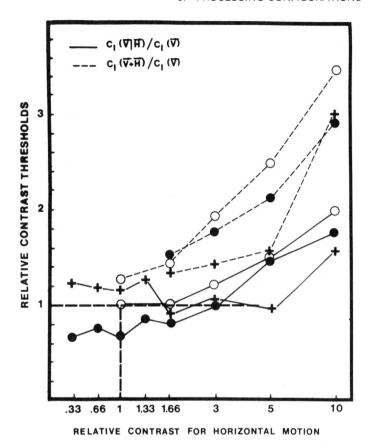

FIG. 5.3.   Relative contrast thresholds of the vertical component for detection of the vertical component (—) and for detection of the motion configuration (---) as a function of the relative contrasts of the horizontal component. (●) S_{CR}, (+) S_{MF}, (0) S_{NC}.

Now, the detection of the oblique motion configuration, $C_{\text{lim}}(\vec{V} + \vec{H})$, necessitates more contrast than the detection of the vertical motion component, $C_{\text{lim}}(\vec{V}/\vec{H})$. The relative liminal contrast of the vertical motion component for the detection of the oblique component, $C_{\text{lim}}(V + H)/C_{\text{lim}}(V)$, also increases linearly with the relative contrast of the horizontal motion component. The linear trends are statistically significant both within subject and within stimulus condition $F_{NC,2}(1, 15) = 283.72$, $p < .001$, $r = .92$, $F_{NC,4}(1, 15) = 111.75$, $p < .001$, $r = .93$; $F_{NC,6}(1, 15) = 29.80$, $p < .001$, $r = .81$; $F_{NC,8}(1, 15) = 50.17$, $p < .001$, $r = .87$. Their slopes are steeper than the slopes of the functions of the relative contrast thresholds for detecting the vertical motion component.

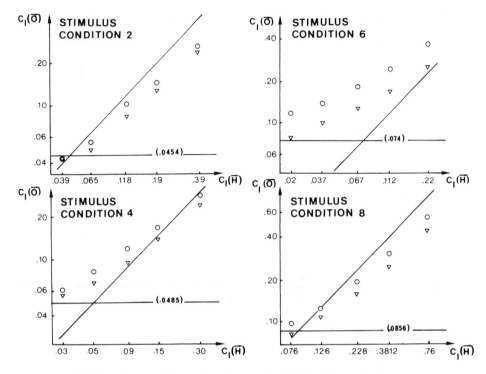

FIG. 5.4.   Contrast of the configuration for the detection of the vertical component (∇) and for the detection of the oblique component of the configuration (0)
as a function of the contrasts of the horizontal component.

Until now the data of Experiments 2 and 3 have been expressed in terms of the
subject's setting of the contrast of the vertically drifting grating, in the presence
of the horizontally drifting grating. The actual contrast of the configuration,
$C(\vec{O})$, is in fact the average of the contrasts of the vertical and of the horizontal
gratings. Further analysis of the results has been carried out on the actual contrasts of the configuration, $C(\vec{O})$. Results of the subject NC replotted in this way
are presented in Fig. 5.4 as a function of the contrasts of the horizontal motion
component.

In Fig. 5.4, the horizontal line refers to the contrast of the configuration, if the
two gratings were at their own threshold. The oblique line indicates the results
that would be obtained if the contrast of the vertical motion component for the
detection of the configuration increased proportionally with the contrast of the
horizontal motion component. Clearly, the data points fall on a line, the slope of
which is below unity. The present results show a statistically significant linear
trend within subject and within stimulus condition for subject NC. Within the
sampling limitations of the experiment, no systematic difference in slope could
be demonstrated either between conditions or between subjects. There is a ten-

dency for the slopes to be greater for the thresholds of the motion configuration than for the thresholds of the vertical motion component. However, the difference is not statistically significant. Finally, the ratio of the two thresholds is significantly greater than unity. Averaged over the 20 conditions of subject *NC*, the ratio has a value of 1.23 with a standard error of .032.

To summarize the results: For suprathreshold contrasts of the horizontal motion component (background) the thresholds either for the detection of the vertical motion component or for the detection of the motion configuration increase linearly with the contrast of the background drifting grating. Such a result demonstrates strong inhibitory interactions between the orthogonal components within a motion configuration. The fact that the contrast threshold for the detection of the motion configuration is 1.23 times greater than the contrast threshold for detecting a single directional component supports such a conclusion.

However, the latter result might be accounted for by meridional amblyopia (Blakemore, 1978). Apart from the fact that meridional amblyopia should be less important with drifting gratings of low spatial frequency (Levi & Harwerth, 1977), preliminary controls in which the two basic directional components of the configuration were oblique, while the direction of the motion configuration was horizontal, did not show very different results.

The basic question arises as to whether the inhibitory interactions are due to the directional components or to the orientational components of the gratings. Both components can be psychophysically separated (Sekuler, 1975). There is experimental evidence that the interaction occurs between directional components and not between orientational components, at least in the present experimental conditions. In a similar situation, Gorea (1979) has shown that a stationary flickering grating of one orientation strongly interacts with the motion detection of an orthogonally-oriented drifting grating. However, in a subsequent unpublished experiment, the same author showed that a stationary grating, *unmodulated in time*, does not affect motion sensitivity for an orthogonally oriented drifting grating. This holds true for modulation contrasts up to 50%. Therefore, it is extremely unlikely that the present results are due to the orientation of the gratings per se or to the effect of orientation of one on detection of direction of the other. It appears valid to infer that the inhibitory effects are indeed *due to* and *acting on* motion direction.

CONCLUSION

Even in the particularly favorable conditions of the present experiments, in which the oblique component does exist in the retinal image, it is obvious that the initial model of the processing of motion configurations is at best oversimplified. First, the perceived direction of the configuration is not strictly predicted by the resultant velocity vector and depends on the spatial (and/or temporal) frequency range of the directional motion components. High spatial (and temporal) frequency gratings produced more conspicuous motion configurations. Second, the independence in the detection of orthogonal motion components is only partially valid for subthreshold contrasts of the background. Third, strong inhibitory interactions prevail at suprathreshold contrasts of the gratings, a fact that rules out the assumption of linearity.

Subsequently, we examined informally the question as to whether such a motion configuration could be obtained when no oblique component was present in the retinal image. Dichoptic presentation of the two orthogonally drifting gratings was obtained by using crossed polarizing filters. With contrasts comparable to those of Experiment 1, a strong binocular rivalry always prevailed. When the contrast was reduced to very near threshold values, consistent phenomenal reports of an oblique motion of a gingham pattern were obtained. In other words, motion configuration seemed to occur only in situations in which no inhibitory interactions between the directional components were present.

As noted in the Introduction, while the present experiments were being run, Marshak and Sekuler (1979) published a paper treating the same problem. They used two random-dot patterns drifting with different angular separations. In their paper, there is no mention of reports concerning the perception of single-motion configurations. On the contrary, the two directions of the motion components are perceived as more different in direction than they really are. The maximum of this "repulsion" effect was obtained with an angular separation of 22°. The effect of repulsion was still conspicuous for an angular separation of 90°. Dichoptic presentation of the motion components reduced the amplitude of the repulsion effect, but as we were able to confirm, it did not allow the perception of a single-motion configuration at least for high-contrast patterns. Marshak and Sekuler (1979) have attributed the repulsion effect to an inhibition process occuring between separate directionally selective channels. Levinson, Coyne, and Gross (1980) reported that motion synthesis (i.e., the perception of a single-motion configuration) could be obtained in such circumstances with *low-contrast* random-dot patterns.

In conclusion, these arguments taken together suggest that the perception of motion synthesis is not the general outcome of presenting several directional components of moving patterns. Contrary to the expectation based on gestalt tradition, processing of such stimuli is characterized by *inhibition* between directional components. The inhibition may actually result in an improvement of discrimination between different directions of motion, as suggested by the results of Marshak and Sekuler (1979). In experimental conditions, motion synthesis is likely to occur near threshold (see also Levinson et al., 1980) (i.e., in conditions in which the linearity assumptions are valid).

With regard to the more general context of these experiments, a model dealing with the motion of several directional components should be able to explain what determines either the perception of a unique configuration or the perception of segregated motions; that is what determines whether one perceives a single part of the visual world moving unitarily or two parts of the visual world moving in different directions. Although segregation may be the rule for processing in the organism, flow models may nevertheless be relevant for more complex situations in which the different inhibitory relationships between directional components might compensate for each other.

REFERENCES

Barlow, H. B., & Hill, R. M. Evidence for a physiological explanation of the waterfall phenomenon and figural after-effects. *Nature, 1963, 200,* 1345-1347.

Blakemore, C. Maturation and modification in the developing visual system. In R. Held, H. W. Leibowitz, & H. L. Teuber (Eds.), *Handbook of sensory physiology: Perception* (Vol. VIII). Berlin: Springer-Verlag, 1978.

Campbell, F. W., & Kulikowski, J. J. Orientation selectivity of the human visual system. *Journal of Physiology, 1966, 187,* 437-444.

Carlson, C. R., Cohen, R. W., & Gorog, I. Visual processing of simple two dimensional sine-wave luminance gratings. *Vision Research, 1977, 17,* 351-358.

De Valois, K. K., De Valois, R. L., & Yund, E. W. Responses of the striate cortex cells to gratings and to checkerboard patterns. *Journal of Physiology, 1979, 291,* 483-505.

Gorea, A. Directional and non-directional coding of a spatio-temporal modulated stimulus. *Vision Research, 1979, 19,* 545-549.

Grüsser, O. J., & Grüsser-Cornhels, U. Neuronal mechanisms of visual movement perception and some psychophysical and behavioral correlations. In R. Jung (Ed.), *Handbook of sensory physiology* (Vol. VII/31). Berlin: Springer-Verlag, 1973.

Johansson, G. *Configurations in event perception.* Uppsala: Almqvist & Wiksell, 1950.

Johansson, G., von Hofsten, C., & Jansson, G. Event perception. *Annual Review of Psychology, 1980, 31,* 27-63.

Levi, D. M., & Harwerth, R. S. Spatiotemporal interactions in anisometropic and strabismic amblyopia. *Investigative Ophthalmology and Visual Science, 1977, 16,* 90-95.

Levinson, E., Coyne, A., & Gross, J. Synthesis of visually perceived movement. *Investigative Ophtalmology and Visual Science Supplement, 1980,* 105.

Levinson, E., & Sekuler, R. The independence of channels in human vision selective for direction of movement. *Journal of Physiology, 1975, 250,* 347-366.

Marshak, W., & Sekuler, R. Mutual repulsion between moving visual targets. *Science, 1979, 205,* 1399-1401.

Moulden, B., & Mather, G. In defence of a ratio model for movement detection at threshold. *Quarterly Journal of Experimental Psychology, 1978, 30,* 505-520.

Sekuler, R. Visual motion perception. In E. Carterette & M. Friedman (Eds.), *Handbook of perception: Seeing* (Vol. V). New York: Academic Press, 1975.

Sekuler, R., Pantle, A., & Levinson, E. Physiological basis of motion perception. In R. Held, H. W. Leibowitz, & H. L. Teuber (Eds.), *Handbook of sensory physiology: Perception* (Vol. VIII). Berlin: Springer-Verlag, 1978.

Sutherland, N. S. Figural after-effects and apparent size. *Quarterly Journal of Experimental Psychology, 1961, 13,* 222-228.

PERCEPTION OF SCENES
AND OBJECTS

6 Questions of Pattern and Object Perception by Man and Computer

Richard L. Gregory
Brain and Perception Laboratory
Department of Anatomy
Medical School
University of Bristol
Bristol, England

ABSTRACT

At least until recently, physiologists concerned with the senses have almost entirely limited their experiments to how sensory stimulus patterns are converted into neural signals and represented in the central nervous system. Much has been found out of the greatest interest; but this is a far cry from the psychologist's concern with how it is that perception is generally appropriate to characteristics of objects—many of which are not currently, or indeed ever, sensed. This at once suggests that perception and behavior are based on knowledge of objects: hence the importance of cognitive concepts. Distinctions between *pattern* and *object* are discussed, as a kind of prologomena to cognitive psychology, and this turns out to be tricky and confusing. Distinctions that may be made are related informally to selected classical and recent perceptual experiments, though not explicitly to clinical abnormalities of pattern or object perception.

INTRODUCTION

When discussing especially visual perception, we speak of *pattern perception* and *object perception,* though it is exceedingly hard to know what distinctions are or should be drawn between *pattern* and *object.* No doubt psychologists, philosophers, and physicists each prefer rather different distinctions between patterns and objects, and artists' views may be different again.

The aims of pattern and object recognition by computer no doubt change according to the uses to which they are put. One may say that over the last 20 or 30 years the emphasis has moved from pattern to object recognition in artificial intelligence (AI); and it might be suggested that mere pattern recognition does not justify the claim of intelligence. For AI as a tool for psychologists, the results may be deemed successful insofar as they illuminate or reflect the psychologist's general notion of how objects are perceived, which is bound up with how objects differ from patterns. This takes us to philosophy and physics.

The physicist is confronted with the amazing and ever-growing differences between how the world appears and what he believes it conceptually to be like. This applies especially to the very large and the very small—to things outside the scale of acceptance by human sense organs and control and manipulation by unaided limbs and fingers. Because the range of sensory acceptance and motor interaction is an arbitrary limitation, I propose to extend this discussion somewhat beyond the usual limits of recent psychological considerations—following the precedent of Aristotle who accepted no such limitations—to include physics in our discussion.

The physicist most concerned in recent times with the status of objects is Sir Arthur Eddington, who in his Tarner Lectures of 1939 wrote: "Does the scientist mean by 'physical objects' what the plain man would take it to mean? For example, when we give a scientific description of a chair according to the most modern physical theories, are we describing the object which in everyday life is called a chair? . . . Some of the pure philosophers deny that the scientific description applies to the objects which in ordinary speech are called physical objects [p. 159]." Eddington (1939) then quotes the logician–philosopher Susan Stebbing who says that the physicist: "Is not concerned with *chairs,* and it lies beyond his competence to inform us that the chairs we sit upon are abstract [p. 278]." To which Eddington replies, if the logician is correct, "why is it that a Transport Company, wishing to improve its arrangements for seating, consults a physicist who is not concerned with the chairs we sit upon, instead of a philosopher who is?". He concludes: "Do we have to take this sitting down?"

The issues here are nontrivial. Stebbing objects to Eddington saying, in a famous passage in *Nature of the Physical World* (1939):

> I am standing on a threshold about to enter a room. It is a complicated business
> . . . I must make sure of landing on a plank travelling at 20 miles a second round the
> sun . . . the plank has no solidity of substance. To step on it is like stepping on a
> swarm of flies. Shall I slip through? No, if I make the venture one of the flies hits
> me and gives me a boost up again; I fall again and an knocked upward by another
> fly; and so on. I may hope that the net result will be that I remain about steady . .
> . [p. 342].

Stebbing objects that this is: (1) a serious misuse of language; and (2) that stepping on a plank is not in the least like stepping on a swarm of flies. She objects, essentially, to Eddington's notion that because there are two descriptions—common sense and physicist's abstract—there are two sets and kinds of objects, as furniture of the earth. Here she is surely right; but it may be the case that what we accept as objects (rather than as patterns or whatever) depends on the prevailing usefulness of descriptions, in which so-and-so appear as objects, whereas such-and-such may be relegated, say, to patterns. When Stebbing says that stepping on a plank is not like stepping on a swarm of flies, she is objecting to the analogy *as it applies to us*. But, of course, for an atom it may indeed be as Eddington describes it, for the atom is of the scale where objects will appear as a swarm of flies. And because we are made of atoms, this scale does apply to us, though it is seldom in our perceptual appreciation. The "two worlds" here are, however, perceptual and conceptual.

The beautiful experiment by Hecht, Shlaer, and Pirenne (1942) showing that visual sensitivity is limited by quantum capture and is subject to the variance of a few quanta links vision (and similar considerations apply to the other senses) to the conceptual world of physics, and to the sub-atomic scale.

Should we expect congruence between perceptual and conceptual objects? No, surely, if "object" is always a highly theory-laden term. It is perhaps for this reason that Eddington rejects Herbert Dingle's description of an object as "a commonsense grouping of experiences." Eddington also rejects Bertrand Russell's (and so also Ernst Mach's) attempt to reduce objects to bundles of sense data. These accounts are inadequate if object perception is largely given by knowledge or assumptions.

To make matters even more confusing: When we consider earlier discussions, the words *objective* and *object* have, as pointed out by Michael Morgan in *Molyneux's Question* (1977, p. 79), drastically changed in meaning over the last 200 or 300 years. *Object* meant, for example, to Condillac and Locke, something more like *obstacle* does to us—rather than *sources* or *constructs* of perception, which we, according to our view of perception, might prefer.

If patterns are defined by internal relations—what of pictures? They bear relations to what they represent, generally to objects. A retinal image is a picture pattern bearing systematic relations to external objects and also a relation to the perceiver. It is related to objects by the laws of geometrical optics; but it is remarkable how recent in the history of ideas is this notion of retinal images as projections of the world. Euclid (1966), being faced with the problem of how the immensity of the universe could enter the tiny hole of the pupil, considered the eye as a mathematical point (entirely ignoring its structure) with rays shooting out somewhat like porcupine quills probing the world as by touch. As he saw the stars, immediately he opened his eyes; he deduced that the rays must shoot out of the eyes with infinite velocity. Loss of visual acuity with increasing distance was explained by the increasing separation of the quill-like rays so that distant objects could be lost between them. This is a theory of vision that did not involve reading objects from pictures. Most remarkable, this kind of account is still alive today; presumably because it has the attraction, though surely against all the evidence, that vision would be as "direct" and reliable as touch appears to be.

Touch discovers the shapes of nearby hard objects, either by "haptic" exploration, in time, or by simultaneous "passive" contact patterns of the interface with the skin. This does not introduce the intermediary pattern picture with its projective geometry of retinal images. The reading of optical images must have imposed extreme problems of interpretation at the early evolutionary stage of eyes, when presumably touch neural systems were taken over and developed for reading objects from projected patterns. This has been described (Gregory, 1967) as a hen-and-egg problem: For how did the computing necessary for vision develop before there was an eye to feed it, with (laterally and vertically reversed) picture patterns; and how did optically sophisticated eyes develop unless there was already nearly adequate neural computing? Possibly this hen-and-egg problem was resolved by vision taking over existing touch–pattern analyzers, when touch was sufficiently sophisticated for identifying objects by contact and exploration. It is interesting that cortical touch and visual maps are always in spatial accordance (both upside down, with respect to the world) so that, presumably, touch–vision correlations can be readily maintained in spite of the optical inversions of the retinal images. Providing this must have required radical rearrangement of the nervous system, when vision first fed into touch analyzers (Duke-Elder, 1958).

Given the confusing initial complexities, we can hardly hope to arrive at a consistent set of descriptions for defining object and pattern. In the hope that it may nevertheless be useful to explore the issues further, we start by discussing, magically, seven issues concerning patterns and objects and distinctions among them.

FIRST CONSIDERATION: THAT PATTERNS ARE DEFINED BY INTERNAL RELATIONS, OBJECTS BY EXTERNAL RELATIONS

Patterns, surely, consist of internal relations, whereas objects are defined by external relations. Objects can *form* patterns (such as the patterns of the stars) in which case the objects, which may be structureless dots, are entirely secondary. We are concerned only with relations and proportions of lengths and angles between the objects as markers defining positions, which could equally well be given as coordinates without visible or any object references. The pattern description is in terms of ratios, repetitions, and so on, which are internal relations without concern with external causal or any other considerations. Objects, on the other hand, are generally causal entities interacting with other objects according to causal laws, whereas patterns per se do not.

This distinction is, however, tricky, if only because patterns are generally carried by objects. Thus, a Willow Pattern dinner plate is an object bearing a pattern. We distinguish the plate as an object from the pattern that it bears, as the plate has causal properties and requirements—such that we eat off it and wash it—but none of these apply to the pattern. When we break the plate, though, we break the pattern. This particular instance of the pattern depends on the integrity of the plate as an object. This instance of the pattern does not exist without the plate; but the pattern can exist on any plate or on the surface of any unchanging object or even entirely independent of objects.

SECOND CONSIDERATION: THAT PATTERNS CAN BE IDENTICALLY MULTIPLIED; OBJECTS REPRODUCED ARE NEVER IDENTICAL, BECAUSE THEY ARE MADE OF MATTER

The question whether, ultimately, patterns require matter, or substance, is a question as old as philosophy. Traditionally, substance is invoked to give or to explain continuity through time though observations are intermittent. This notion of an underlying unobservable substance was challenged by Berkeley (1790), and it is now largely rejected in fundamental particle physics and wave mechanics, where one may speak of patterns without embodiment in substance.

Whatever we think about substance, criteria for permanence and maintenance through change are generally different for patterns and objects. Consider a chess game. The men and the board have an overall permanence through supposed causal continuity—even though bits break off or they become discolored or so worn as to be hardly recognizable. The men on the board set up patterns that change with each move; and these patterns have levels—some only significant to chess players. It is interesting that expert chess players can remember chess-sensible patterns far better than nonplayers can; but for chess-nonsense patterns, Grand Masters are no better than the rest of us.

One may say that there is a kind of continuity of pattern through a game and especially so with a satisfactory game. This is very much what one sees when watching a game—temporal patterns of several orders or levels of abstraction with switches to new patterns, not only at the start of a new game but sometimes after a switch of strategy or when possibilities change.

The abstract pattern invariances of chess are set by the rules and the strategies of the game. These invariances, only seen or appreciated by chess players, have nothing to do with substance or object properties; and they have nothing to do with laws of physics but only with the rules of the game.

THIRD CONSIDERATION: THAT PATTERNS MAY BE PERCEIVED AS OBJECTS; OBJECTS MAY FORM PATTERNS

Here we meet very different accounts, according to the kind of theory of perception adopted. That the only way of knowing patterns is from arrangements or structures of objects may be generally accepted; but that objects can only be perceived by reading from retinal images or other patterns is highly theory-laden and often denied. It is rejected in general by direct realists and in particular by Gibson (1950, 1966, 1979) who holds that objects are known by "direct pick-up of information from the optic array"—with an ethological optics that is not geometrical optics. This notion of pick-up of information is essentially different from what is usually meant by the reading of patterns, which is the essential notion in representational accounts of perception. This essential difference is that deriving information by reading from patterns depends not only on what is available but on the stored repertoire of *what might be*. This is the fundamental feature of the mathematical theory of information (Shannon & Weaver, 1949). Because alternative possibilities of what might be are stored knowledge and are not in the object world, this is essentially different from Gibsonian pick-up of information from the patterns of the ambient array of the world. So the word *information* has very different meanings for realist and representational accounts. This can be highly confusing.

In order to apply information theory quantitatively to perception, it is necessary to know the number of stored possibilities (the size of the ensemble) for selection and, at least roughly, their probabilities. But unfortunately it is extremely difficult to discover and measure these features of cognition. One may say that cognitive pyschology has so far failed to find adequate methods for investigating the probabilities, and numbers, of alternatives from which selections are made for object perception from sense patterns; though information theory may well be conceptually appropriate, at least for the present, it has failed to be useful practically for quantifying perceptual processes.

Possibly because information theory can hardly be applied to perception in practice, even though it gives important theoretical insights (such as the power of efficient selection procedures), representational accounts have recently stressed mapping and formal description rather than selecting from and testing among possibilities. An interesting account of perception as description is given by Sutherland (1968, 1973). He (1973) distinguishes between various levels of description, such as the "picture domain" and the "object domain," suggesting that: "Depending upon angle of regard, lighting conditions and so on, the descriptions a face gives rise to at the level of the picture domain will be very different, but if we are to recognize a face as the same when seen at different times, these different pictures must all be mapped onto the same descriptive structure in the object domain [p. 159]." Sutherland then points out that, on this account, there must "exist a set of rules that makes it possible to map from one domain onto another." He goes on to consider speech recognition as deriving words from characteristics of the wave, from phonemes, and so on, which may be different for each speaker and yet we hear the same words. Words are thus "objects," and for precise understanding of vision and hearing we need to know the generative rules (and also surely the context assumptions and local restraints) accepted under various conditions to know just how object perception derives or is generated from received patterns.

For Gibson, with his form of direct realism, the invariances are in the picture pattern of the "ambient array." He denies that the invariances are in retinal images, as he generally denied retinal images, until finally forced to admit (Gibson, 1974), in the face of objections put by Boynton (1974), that geometrical image-forming optics does apply to vision. Geometrical optics is an essential feature of retinal images—which are always an embarrassment for direct realists because they are patterns lying between the objects of physics and perception of objects, which therefore cannot be "direct." This presumably is why Gibson did not admit to retinal images much earlier.

On a representational account, the invariances with object rotation and so on, as discussed by Sutherland, are given from key features accepted as cues from which objects are inferred, partly by "bottom-up" procedures (the power of which is especially stressed by Marr, 1976, 1980) and by stored knowledge of objects providing "top-down" guides for search and decision among stored possibilities, which are somehow cognitively mapped and indexed for access. It is reasonable to suppose that many more key features remain essentially the same with changes of viewpoint than do complete complex patterns; as different key features come into view, they allow equivalent descriptions to maintain the object-domain map. So descriptions from named key features allow invariance with rotation. It is also reasonable to suppose that object knowledge can serve to select what features are likely to be useful for identifying objects from various viewpoints, or with parts hidden. So neither are acceptable to Gibson.

Gibson could, however, hardly allow this use of bottom-up key features for giving invariances, for he rejects inference for perception. He would not allow this use of top-down knowledge of objects, as he regarded perception as selections from patterns of the ambient array in the world and not as selections from stored accounts of the object world.

It is not at all clear how Gibson related received patterns to objects as they are known physically. Whether he regarded his account as a necessary stage toward object perception from patterns or as a full account of object perception is not clear. He has, however, established many of the features of patterns that are useful for bottom-up processing, and his findings are useful both for understanding perception by organisms and for the development of AI object recognition programs. His account has, however, grave difficulties with many phenomena of perception, such as ambiguities, distortions, and paradoxes—for these are surely characteristic of *description* rather than of the world of objects. It is for this reason that such trivial-looking phenomena are of great importance for unlocking the secrets of object perception on a representational account, whereas in direct realism they are embarrassments, to be brushed aside.

FOURTH CONSIDERATION: THAT PATTERNS ARE DEFINED BY FORMAL RESTRAINTS BUT MAY BE FREE OF LAWS OF PHYSICS; OBJECTS ARE DEFINED BY CONTINGENT RESTRAINTS AND ARE SUBJECT TO THE LAWS OF PHYSICS

We may point to differences between patterns and objects in terms of correspondingly different kinds of *restraints*. Here I ignore, for the moment at least, that some patterns may be quite arbitrary, or random.

Patterns having regularity, redundancy, or repetition are predictive from *internal* considerations. Objects are also predictive from *external* considerations—largely from their causal roles in relation to other objects. Patterns may be said to have conventional, arbitrary, or formal restraints allowing prediction into space and time; whereas objects have in addition interactive causal properties, obeying laws of physics, which may not apply to patterns. Thus, an artist is free to draw "impossible pictures" (Penrose & Penrose, 1958) and the retinal image of some three-dimensional objects can give rise to paradoxical object perception (Gregory, 1970), though here there is no correspondingly paradoxical object: for objects cannot be paradoxical, or logically impossible. Further, pictures can be ambiguous, whereas objects cannot be ambiguous. We often have problems *classifying* objects, or in naming objects, but objects per se cannot be ambiguous, though, of course, perceptions can be ambiguous. (This is a reason for not *equating* perceptions with objects, as known conceptually.)

It is interesting that picture patterns can be logically paradoxical, ambiguous, and they can represent nonsense or errors just as sentences can. This is a reason for thinking of percepts as descriptions.

Descriptions, like predictions, rely on restraints. Thus random patterns cannot be described in general terms, except statistically, and so far as this is possible, there are statistical restraints to the pattern. It must have higher-order invariances, or redundancies, to make description and prediction possible. Julesz (1962, 1980) finds that textures with second-order statistical invariance are readily discriminable, and third-order with difficulty. Some particular unit shapes, such as *corner* and *closure* stand out however, as giving discriminable textures though the power spectra are equated. Julesz (1980) suggests that these are fundamental building blocks of form—the essential nonlinearities of preattentive perception.

There are different kinds of perceptual ambiguity for patterns and for objects, as they have different kinds of restraints. This, we may suppose, is because perception selects between likely alternatives as set by formal and contingent restraints. Rubin's Double-Cross ambiguous figure is probably a *pattern* ambiguity, whereas his face-and-vases (and Boring's Mistress and Mother-in-Law and Jastrow's Duck-Rabbit) are *object* ambiguities, set up by probable object restraints. As we see later, the presence of contingent restraints is a key feature of AI programs for object recognition.

FIFTH CONSIDERATION: THAT PATTERNS CAN BE SYMBOLS MEDIATING INFORMATION AND BEHAVIOR; OBJECTS CAN BE TOOLS MEDIATING FORCES

Patterns as symbols select between hypothetical alternatives. The alternatives are not in the object world but are in the observer. Thus while objects interact according to physical laws, symbols affect organisms according to their repertoire of alternative states. MacKay (1969) suggests that meaning is given by the "states of readiness" in organisms, as these determine the effects of stimulus patterns. As the states of readiness are hypothetical, behavior (and so psychology) is essentially different from interactions of objects (including tools) according to physical laws.

SIXTH CONSIDERATION: THAT PATTERNS ARE PRIVATE; OBJECTS ARE PUBLIC

By "public" I mean shared, in the sense that we can share an apple but not the taste of the apple. We often speak, however, of patterns of stimulation as the proximal stimulus for perception. But this is confusing, for how can an object be a "distal stimulus"? This, on representational accounts, is nonsense; on a direct realism account (apart from solipsism), the shared object is the *only* stimulus. On any account of perception, the proximal–distal stimulus distinction is to be avoided.

It may be said that only patterns give evidence of objects, and so patterns may be read into object configurations, and these perceived patterns can change from moment to moment and be different for different observers. This is so for ambiguous figures of many kinds. It is also the case, in puzzle pictures, that alternate objects may be perceived, and different observers may perceive different objects in the same presented pattern.

On a representational account, which I support, it may be best to restrict *object* to the public domain; and for preference objects will generally be described as causal entities having interactive properties beyond what we know from immediate perception. Patterns will be, rather, relations between objects or object features and may be entirely abstract. It is, however, very difficult to maintain complete consistency here. We are left with the question: Granted that *objects* exist apart from observers—do *patterns* exist apart from appreciating relations? If one were convinced that they would not, a private-public distinction might be held consistently for distinguishing patterns from objects.

SEVENTH CONSIDERATION: THAT PATTERNS ARE ABSTRACT; OBJECTS ARE CONCRETE

This is perhaps the first pattern-object distinction to come to mind, and it is also the first to be discussed extensively in philosophy. To common sense, and generally for empiricism, objects are (apart from illusions) what we perceive by the senses, and relations are appreciated more or less intellectually. On rationalist philosophies following Plato, unsensed patterns represented mathematically, are the primary objects of the Universe, and sense objects such as chairs and houses merely provide premises for the body but not for the mind. The issue is whether these "deep structures" of the world are known directly to and inferred by the mind or whether they are discovered by experience. On a thoroughgoing rationalist account, objects of sense are regarded as obstructions to appreciating the underlying patterns of the world. (This is Plato's view.)

In any case, there are good reasons for questioning whether objects should be limited to what is sensed. In the first place, what is accepted for sensing is arbitrarily set by the transducer characteristics of the sense organs. In the second place, on any except an extreme passive-acceptance account of perception, the contribution of what is actually sensed may be quite small, even in normal object perception. This is an immediate consequence of perception being inference from sensory data. The issue becomes indeed: How much perceptual inference (by perceiving organism or computer) can there be before it becomes ridiculous to say that "objects are what are sensed"? On a Helmholtzian cue-based theory, this could be surprisingly little—and we know from many experiments with restricted displays as well as from the astonishing evocative power of cartoons that a great deal of object perception can be given by remarkably little sensed pattern. This may seem so familiar and obvious that it is hardly worth saying; but it does run counter to direct realist accounts (including Gibson's) and it is an embarrassment for describing perception and behavior by transfer functions, though they are adequate for typical engineering input-output systems. An important side effect of AI is to provide more adequate descriptions of input-output systems, where there is enrichment by stored knowledge.

On Helmholtzian representational accounts, it may be said that the direction of inference from sensed patterns is generally toward what are predictively useful. On this account, an object is a useful construct from sensed patterns. This readily generalizes to the notion that perceptions are hypotheses—essentially like predictive hypotheses of science (Gregory, 1980). Curiously, the empiricist approach ends up with the same conclusion as rationalism—that to be consistent we have to accept *public abstract objects.* (This is Aristotle's view.) In both accounts what is sensed is a quite minor part of perception.

Numbers, for example, are "public," in that we all agree that the number 13 is prime, is one less than 14, and is 3 greater than 10. This public consideration applies also to many unsensed features, and to features that cannot be sensed, of commonly perceived objects, such as centers of gravity. Centers of gravity may lie *between* objects, such as planets and stars, and indeed Newton took centers of gravity of bodies as the objects of his stellar dynamics, as the bodies were accepted, for convenience, as points of equivalent mass. Considerations such as these led the logician Frege (Dummett, 1974) to speak of "abstract objects." These he distinguished from "concrete objects."

If we accept numbers, centers of gravity, and other abstract entities as objects, it may be important to distinguish between concrete and abstract objects. The problem is to establish how distinct these are. If object perception involves knowledge of the world, it is largely conceptual—lying in a spectrum from sensed patterns to abstract conceptual understanding. We are left with difficult questions. Should mathematical scaffolding such as logarithms and $\sqrt{-1}$ be allowed object status? These are surely invented as tools. Or is $\sqrt{-1}$ an element in mathematical patterns rather than an (abstract) object? Should we preclude abstract objects or conceptual objects from the object pantheon on the ground that though they are public, they are not causal? But is it true that symbols are not causal? After all, we do speak of being affected by what we read; and clearly for computers it is symbol structures that matter, though the concrete objects of their components are necessary for the computer to function.

SOME IMPLICATIONS

Computing Objects from Patterns

Attempts at computer object recognition are based implicitly, and at least for Marr (1976) explicitly, on the extraordinary fact that we can recognize objects very well in simple line drawings. This at once suggests that texture gradients, and many other features of the sensed world, are far less important than edges forming lines, stripes, corners, and outline curves. If these are *named,* objects and scenes can be described by the presence (and sometimes absence) of these key features and their spatial arrangements. The problem of recognizing the line features is generally solved with mask filters, of simple shapes, which are tuned to these features—which are accepted according to how well the mask fits and its orientation to the features. It turns out that precise tuning is not necessary; so it is surprisingly easy to derive an initial rough account of pictures and scenes from mask-filtering data of patterns, to give in Marr's terms, a "primal sketch." This appears as a cumbersome set of intensity values of signals from the various masks, applied at various orientations. The masks need not of course be optical but can be electronic filtering of video scan signals. Because, as the evocative power of drawings shows, precise gray levels are not important, this can be crude and effective. It does, however, require a lot of (nonattentional) computing, and mistakes at the early stages of analysis are difficult to correct later. It is suggested that the cortical area 17 undertakes this computing for human vision. It remains an open question how far this nonattentional computing, without reference to knowledge of objects or object restraints, can be adequate. The fact that a human perceptual mistake when once recognized may not be repeated shows that specific high-level knowledge can be applied.

The changes of brightness of the shadow shape in Fig. 6.1 with changes of apparent depth is clear evidence in human perception of knowledge-based top-down effects of the probability of this being a shadow—as the probability changes according to whether the corner sticks in or out. Waltz (1975) has found it possible to take account of shadows and even use them as aids for computer object recognition. Perhaps the clearest example of object-probability biasing is the extreme difficulty of seeing the hollow mould of a face as indeed hollow—it appears as a normal nose-sticking-out face against evidence from texture, motion parallax, and even considerable stereopsis (Gregory, 1970). Here it is important to note that the hollow face does not reverse in depth—it never looks correctly hollow—whether the lighting is from above or below, though most objects will reverse according to shadow texture, from the general perceptual assumption that lighting is from above. Here the specific knowledge of faces overrides the usually appropriate generalization that lighting comes from above and that shadows occur below protruding features.

It is possible that face recognition is so important that it is handled by a specially dedicated neural computer. Evidence of single-cell recording of "hand-detectors" (Gross, Rochar-Miranda, & Bender, 1972) suggests this. There are analogies here to the well-established "fly-detector" found by Barlow (1953) in the frog retina. Such special analyzers, or object recognizers, are a trap for intercepting the plan of the system as a whole; but they might well be biologically useful for processing with maximum speed and accuracy crucial classes of objects, such as faces and hands; and for frogs, flies.

The feature detectors found in the frog's retina by Lettvin, Maturana, McCollough, and Pitts (1959) and also later discovery of cells responding to particular orientations, movements, and so on in the mammalian cortex by Hubel and Wiesel (Hubel, 1963; Hubel & Wiesel, 1968) seem to reveal features of general nonattentional pattern analyzing mechanisms, which perhaps carry out something of the procedures outlined by Marr for the "primal sketch." Just how

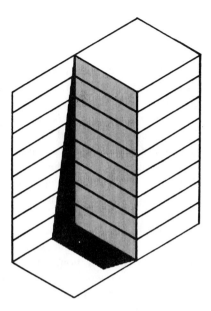

FIG. 6.1.   The dark rectangle is likely to be a shadow only when the corner is seen as inward, given typical lighting from above. For most observers it changes from dark to light each time the corner switches from outward to inward, when it is likely to be a shadow and not a mark on the wall. This change is evidence of modification by "top-down" processes of object perception, or pattern-signaled contours, and luminances.

knowledge of objects and restraints are then brought to bear is not known; but we can discover something of how they operate by looking at what happens when they are inappropriate. This is the point of studying visual illusions—on the paradigm that these distortions do not occur early on in the processing but are due to transfer of knowledge of objects and common restraints, to a given situation from past experience. The transfer is "negative" in situations where it is misleading (Gregory, 1970). The classical example is perspective convergence of line features, which is normally associated with increasing distance, by perspective. When presented on a picture plane, drawings and pictures including photographs of such objects as receding railway lines or corners, appear systematically distorted. The rule is that perceptual expansion occurs with increasing represented distance. This may be attributed to the size scaling normally compensating the shrinking of retinal images with increasing distance, normally to give size constancy. To read perspective shapes as distance cues depends on assumptions that edges often are parallel: and similarly for the arrowheads of the Müller-Lyer figure for corners. Given that this account of distortion illusions as "negative transfer" of knowledge of typical object shapes, it is interesting that even simple line figures are adequate for calling up object knowledge and affecting basic processing.

It is surprisingly difficult to design experiments for establishing whether these perceptual phenomena have their origins, as suggested here, in high-level object processing or at an early (perhaps primal sketch) stage. Until recently it was often thought that these distortions are retinal in origin, but clearly this is not the case; for as Julesz (1971) has shown, they occur just the same when presented as random-dot displays shared stereoscopically by the eyes—when neither alone has these patterns or indeed anything but random dots. Is it possible to show convincingly that their origin is high-level processing, where object knowledge operates?

There is some evidence that people brought up in different visual environments have correspondingly different distortion illusions. Dense forests and villages of round huts produce people with little or no perspective illusions, as found most recently and reliably by Segall, Campbell, and Herskovitz (1966) and by Deregowski (1974). Although this is not knockout evidence that object restraints are responsible for perceptual distortion, it is suggestive. The difficulty for finding convincing evidence, either way, is that objects cannot be seen except via sensory patterns. If pattern perception is necessarily involved in object perception, how can it be established that it is knowledge of typical object restraints that provides misleading evidence—to produce errors by ''negative transfer''? And, if we cannot show this, how can we show the converse—which is generally accepted—that object restraints are normally useful for seeing objects correctly in space by ''positive transfer'' of knowledge?

My colleague, John Harris, and I (Gregory & Harris, 1975) found that corners when seen correctly (i.e., in three dimensions using stereoscopic vision) do not appear distorted, though the retinal image patterns are the same as for the flat Müller–Lyer illusion figure. This result holds also for converging line illusions though these have greater experimental difficulties. The finding that the distortions reduce strictly to zero in this experimental situation indicates strongly that negative transfer of knowledge from object restraints is the *sole* significant source of these distortions. As this takes the phenomena away from physiology and into procedures of perceptual processing, naturally this move is resisted in some quarters!

Object Perception from Surprising Absence of Pattern

It is remarkable how little attention was paid to the striking phenomenon of *illusory contours*, before the beautiful examples provided by Kanizsa (1974, 1979) even though examples have been known and occasionally described (Woodworth, 1938, p. 637) for at least 70 years. Marr (1976), surely rightly, regards them as important for understanding perceptual processing. He considers three theories: (1) A local process tending to join neighboring ends of lines; (2) that the illusory contour is produced by the placing of an edge-shaped mask that

FIG. 6.2.   Kanizsa illusory triangle figure. On a "physiological" account, in terms of pattern perception, this might be attributed to receptive field effects. A "cognitive" account, in terms of object perception, might be that unlikely gaps forming a likely kind of object set up the hypothesis of an eclipsing object.

picks up spurious signals from these patterns; and (3) that the lines of these figures cause a " 'Gestalt' (of an object) . . . to be used for describing the situation. This very high-level concept then imposes the contour of the figure." (p. 498). It has also been suggested (Gregory, 1972) that the visual system postulates nearer eclipsing objects to account for unlikely gaps, when the form of the gaps is a likely object. This takes the explanation away from specific stimulus patterns, to procedures allowing objects to be recognized though partly hidden, which is often extremely important. Illusory contours (see Fig. 6.2) occur with a great variety of stimulus patterns (Kanizsa, 1979), and this Bayesian strategy seems by inspection to fit the examples. It is interesting that these completions and inventions of missing features seem to grade from clearly perceptual to purely conceptual. Support for this postulation of eclipsing objects from surprising absence of pattern comes from an experiment by Gregory and Harris (1974) that showed that when the putative eclipsing features are forced behind the rest of the figure, using stereopsis, the illusory contours and associated areas of different brightness disappear—as should happen, since to mask they must be in front.

Object Perception with Displacements (Mirrors)

An object with remarkably interesting though curiously ignored perceptual properties is the common plane mirror. It seems, from recent experiments by Gallup (1977), who studied chimpanzees, babies, and other animals peering into mirrors, that no animals lower in the evolutionary scale than chimpanzees ever learn that it is *themselves* they see; and this does not take place in human infants before about 10 months. Part of the evidence is whether they point correctly to a mark placed (in the animals while anesthetized) on the side of their face and not to its mirror reversal (Desmond, 1979).

More generally, if we consider a highly reflecting clean mirror (and where it is not reflecting, it is not strictly a mirror) so that we do not sense its surface but only reflections, we generally see or realize that we are looking at a mirror—though what we are seeing are dislocated and right-left reversed features of the visual scene. The point is that we can see mirrors *only* from dislocation of scenes, or from objects being in the wrong place or in the wrong orientation. A mirror in a random world would be invisible. It would be interesting to make a dislocated room: We would surely see a mirror that is not there; and indeed painters show the presence of mirrors by dislocation of patterns or objects. It would, indeed, be interesting to know whether dislocations of *patterns* per se would suggest a mirror or whether *objects* are required. If pattern alone is not sufficient, this could be a test for what is perceptually pattern and what is perceptually accorded object status.

The already classical studies of Lettvin et al. (1959) on what the frog's eye tells the frog's brain, and Barlow's (1953) discovery of the frog retina's "bug detector," and Hubel and Wiesel's "feature detectors" of the striate cortex of cat (Hubel, 1963), monkey (Hubel & Wiesel, 1968), and presumably man, are extremely important in showing that there are, in the visual pathway, specifically tuned filters that signal preselected features of retinal image patterns including orientations of borders, movement, and probably also corners and textures. The positions of edges as imaged on the retina during a fixation by no means however set the spatial positions of objects in perceived space. The problem is how the selected signaled features are normally put together to form stable object perceptions; and here neurology has no answers. Suggestions are likely to come from Anne Treisman and her colleagues' experiments on discrepancies between color and form in short exposure (Treisman, Sykes, & Gelade, 1977). Illuminating also are experiments showing criteria of object permanence and change in illusory movement (Anstis, 1970; Kolers, 1972).

It is not known how feature detector outputs are combined for simple shapes, such as the letter A. Whether the striate feature detectors are entirely prewired or are produced or modified by early experience remains controversial, though the consensus opinion (Barlow, 1975) favors prewiring with "fine tuning," to adjust for standing errors and changes with growth, especially of increasing interocular distance affecting stereopsis through childhood. As a general principle, it is likely that the usually more reliable senses serve for "calibrating" the weaker brethren (Howard & Templeton, 1966) presumably with overall criteria for consistency. Many adaptation phenomena may be seen in this light, but it is difficult to know how far adaptations reveal physical inadequacies of neural components and how far they are necessary for setting up criteria of invariance for object recognition, by reflecting object restraints.

Signals from the different senses generally arrive at different times (as sight and sound from a ball hitting a bat), and this is true also for different intensities, or colors, from the retina. So why do contours or edges not break up—with gaps or overlaps—as the image moves across the retina? This problem, for parallel channel systems, seems to be largely unrecognized. The problem here is: What holds the visual world together? Different signal arrival times, drift of components, and different processing times surely make this a problem, both for the nervous system and for robotic seeing machines. And yet we seldom experience mismatches or misregistrations between color regions and edges in object perception. Gaps and overlaps and general instabilities do, however, occur when adjacent regions of different color have the same luminance. We have suggested that there are processes of *border locking,* which literally pull together discrepancies to maintain the integrity of the visual world in spite of signaling errors (Gregory & Heard, 1979). The suggestion is that there is a hierarchy of locking signals, such that, for example, color is slave to luminance. When the usually present common luminance boundary between contiguous color regions is removed—by setting the colors to isoluminance—the locking luminance signals are no longer present, and then the world appears unstable. Actually a great deal of perception is lost: It is difficult to read large red letters on an equal luminance green background, and even common objects such as faces appear but meaningless shapes, though they are fully resolved optically. It is also interesting that the random-dot stereo depth of Julesz figures is lost when the dots are isoluminant to the background, as shown by Lu and Fender (1974), and confirmed by us (Gregory, 1977). The general conclusion here is that perception largely depends on brightness differences: Color signals do not feed into cross-correlating and various other mechanisms. As color vision came late in the mammalian evolutionary sequence, it is not surprising to find that it is tacked on, rather like "painting by numbers"; but just how it is tacked on is an important question.

The Observer in Current Physics

Paradigms of physics are seldom discussed explicitly by psychologists, in spite of Wittgenstein's discussions in *Philosophical Investigations* (1953), the highly pertinent discussions by Hanson in *Patterns of Discovery* (1958) and *Observation and Explanation* (1971), and the current emphasis on assumptive "paradigms" for hypotheses following Kuhn's *The Structure of Scientific Revolutions* (1962). Because physicists tend toward operationalism, in which the observer has little and preferably no part to play, as in Einstein's earlier papers, physicists themselves have contributed little to understanding perception; but there is now a growing interest among writers on the philosophy of quantum mechanics, as here it is impossible to separate "what is" from the limits of observation.

It was pointed out by Heisenberg (1958) that extracting information from the world is not a one-way process but is interactive, somewhat like the difficulty of touching a soap bubble without destroying it, at the quantum level. And ultimately all perception is at the quantum level: Photons providing patterns for seeing affect what is sensed. This is of great practical importance in electron microscopy, and Heisenberg's uncertainty principle applies in practice with light microscopes and conceptually for all observation and measurement. All observation is ultimately interactive, for the sensor and sensed object both change as information is extracted.

This issue of the *interaction* between sensing and what is being sensed is a fundamental issue that is receiving considerable theoretical attention in wave mechanics. The problem is that in wave mechanics there are not particles or discrete values but only probability distributions—"wave packets"—and yet observations have specific values. Somehow the probability spread of the wave packets, which are the objects of wave mechanics, are collapsed to give specific values for perception. Heisenberg made the somewhat bizarre suggestion that consciousness is involved in the collapsing of wave packets for perception. This, however, involves the notion, which generates paradoxes, that the object reality of physics is deeply affected by the act of perception, when consciousness is involved. This step goes radically beyond the earlier considerations of uncertainty and detector interaction. The American physicist Shimony (1963) has pointed out the difficulties, though he recognizes as does d'Espagnat (1976) that there are very real problems for physics and perception at this level of analysis. Paradoxes are generated when we consider two or more observers. Are we to suppose that the act of perceiving of the first observer collapses wave packets to set specific values for all later observers? But if this were not so, why should later observers of the same "object" agree with the first, or with each other? This bizarre suggestion that specificity of object reality is created for all time by individual acts of perception is to say that conscious beings create the world according to how they see it. Even for one observer this has difficulties, for the behavior of objects is not obviously affected by their being perceived. So we might have to say that causal processes are in terms of the probability distribution of the wave packets for unobserved objects and that physical causes are not affected by the collapse of wave packets into specific values by perception. But then, what we perceive should bear little relation to what happens causally in the physical object world. Or, is it just possible that what we observe is so insignificant that the wave packets we collapse have negligible effects? If this were so, it would follow that by increasing the power or range of perception we could change the Universe—even to its destruction. Somehow, though, this seems hardly likely. We may however conclude that destroying the Universe by object perception would be the ultimate demonstration of human *attention and performance*.

REFERENCES

Anstis, S. M. Phi movement as a subtraction process. *Vision Research,* 1970, *10,* 1411-1430.

Barlow, H. B. Summation and inhibition in the frog's retina. *Journal of Physiology,* 1953, *119,* No. 69.

Barlow, H. B. Visual experience and cortical development. *Nature,* 1975, *258,* 199-204.

Berkeley, G. *A new theory of vision.* London: Everyman's Library, Dent, 1790.

Boynton, R. M. The visual system: Environmental information. In E. C. Carterette & M. P. Friedman (Eds.), *Handbook of perception* (Vol. 1). New York: Academic Press, 1974.

Deregowski, J. Illusion and culture. In R. L. Gregory & E. Gombrich (Eds.), *Illusion in nature and art.* London: Duckworth, 1974.

Desmond, A. *The ape's reflection.* New York: Quartet Books, 1979.

D'Espagnat, B. *Comceptual foundations and quantum mechanics* (2nd ed.). Boston: Benjamin, 1976.

Duke-Elder, S. (Ed.). *System of ophthalmology: The eye in evolution* (Vol. 1). London: Henry Kimpton, 1958.

Dummett, M. *Frege: The philosophy of language.* London: Duckworth, 1974.

Eddington, A. *Nature of the physical world.* Cambridge, England: Cambridge University Press, 1939.

Euclid. Optics. In M. R. Cohan & I. E. Drabkin (Eds.), *A source book of Greek science.* Boston: Harvard University Press, 1966.

Gallup, G. G. Self recognition in primates: A comparative approach to bidirectional properties of consciousness. *American Psychologist,* 1977, *32,* 329-338.

Gibson, J. J. *The perception of the visual world.* Boston: Houghton-Mifflin, 1950.

Gibson, J. J. *The senses considered as perceptual systems.* Boston: Houghton-Mifflin, 1966.

Gibson, J. J. A note on ecological optics. In E. C. Carterette & M. P. Friedman (Eds.), *Handbook of perception* (Vol. 1). New York: Academic Press, 1974.

Gibson, J. J. *The ecological approach to visual perception.* Boston: Houghton-Mifflin, 1979.

Gregory, R. L. The evolution of eyes and brains—a hen-and-egg problem. In S. J. Freeman (Ed.), *The neuro-psychology of spatially oriented behavior.* Illinois: , 1967. (Reprinted in R. L. Gregory, *Concepts and mechanisms of behavior.* London: Duckworth, 1974.)

Gregory, R. L. *The intelligent eye.* London: Weidenfeld and Nicolson, 1970.

Gregory, R. L. Cognitive contours. *Nature,* 1972, *238,* 51-52.

Gregory, R. L. Vision with isoluminant colour contrast: A projection technique and observations. *Perception,* 1977, *6,* 113-119.

Gregory, R. L. Perceptions as hypotheses. *Philosophical Transactions of the Royal Society of London, B,* 1980, *290,* 181-197.

Gregory, R. L., & Harris, J. P. Illusory contours and stereo depth. *Perception & Psychophysics,* 1974, *15,* 411-416.

Gregory, R. L., & Harris, J. P. Illusion-destruction by appropriate scaling. *Perception,* 1975, *4,* 203-220.

Gregory, R. L., & Heard, P. Border locking and the cafe wall illusion. *Perception,* 1979, *8,* 365-380.

Gross, C. H., Rochar-Miranda, C. E., & Bender, C. E. Visual properties of neurons in infratemporal cortex of the macaque. *Journal of Neurophysiology,* 1972, *35,* 96-111.

Hanson, R. H. *Patterns of discovery.* Cambridge, England: Cambridge University Press, 1958.

Hanson, R. H. *Observation and explanation.* Cambridge, England: Cambridge University Press, 1971.

Hecht, S., Shlaer, S., & Pirenne, M. H. Energy, quanta, and vision. *Journal of General Physiology,* 1942, *25,* 819-840.

Heisenberg, W. *Physics and philosophy.* New York: Harper, 1958.

Howard, I. P., and Templeton, W. B. *Human Spatial Organization,* New York. Wiley, 1966.

Hubel, D. H. The visual cortex of the brain. *Scientific American,* 1963, *209,* 54-62.

Hubel, D. H., & Wiesel, T. N. Receptive fields and functional architecture of monkey striate cortex. *Journal of Physiology,* 1968, *195,* 215-243.

Julesz, B. Visual pattern discrimination. *I.R.E. Transactions on Information Theory,* 1962, *IT-8,* 84-92.

Julesz, B. *Foundations of cyclopean vision.* Chicago: Chicago University Press, 1971.

Julesz, B. Spatial nonlinearities in the instantaneous perception of textures with identical power spectra. *Philosophical Transactions of the Royal Society of London, b,* 1980, *290,* 83-94. (Reprinted in H. C. Longuet-Higgins & N. S. Sutherland (Eds.), *The psychology of vision.* London: The Royal Society, 1980.)

Kanizsa, G. Contours without gradients. *Italian Journal of Psychology,* 1974, *1,* 93-112.

Kanizsa, G. *Organization in vision: Essays on gestalt perception.* New York: Praeger, 1979.

Kolers, P. *Aspects of motion perception.* Oxford, England: Pergamon Press, 1972.

Kuhn, T. S. *The structure of scientific revolutions.* Chicago: Chicago University Press, 1962.

Lettvin, J. Y., Maturana, H. R., McCollough, W. S., & Pitts, W. H. What the frog's eye tells the frog's brain. *Proceedings of the Institute of Radio Engineers,* 1959, *47,* 1940-1951.

Lu, C., & Fender, D. H. The interaction of color and luminance in stereoscopic vision. *Investigative Ophthalmology,* 1974, *11,* 482-489.

MacKay, D. M. *Information, mechanism and meaning.* Boston: MIT Press, 1969.

Marr, D. Early processing of vision information. *Philosophical Transactions of the Royal Society of London, B,* 1976, *275,* 483-524.

Marr, D. Visual information processing: The structure and creation of visual representations. *Philosophical Transactions of the Royal Society of London, B,* 1980, *290,* 199-218. (Reprinted in H. C. Longuet-Higgins & N. S. Sutherland (Eds.), *The psychology of vision.* London: The Royal Society, 1980.)

Morgan, M. *Molyneux's question: Vision, touch and the philosophy of perception.* Cambridge, England: Cambridge University Press, 1977.

Penrose, L. S., & Penrose, R. Impossible objects: A special type of illusion. *British Journal of Psychology,* 1958, *49,* 31-3.

Segall, M. H., Campbell, T. D., & Herskovitz, M. J. *The influence of culture on visual perception.* Indianapolis: Bobbs-Merrill, 1966.

Shannon, C. E., & Weaver, W. *The mathematical theory of communication.* Champaign, Ill.: University of Illinois Press, 1949.

Shimony, A. Role of the observer in quantum theory. *American Journal of Physics,* 1963, *31,* 755-773.

Sutherland, N. S. Outlines of a theory of pattern recognition in animals and man. *Proceedings of the Royal Society of London, B,* 1968, *171,* 297-317.

Sutherland, N. S. Object recognition. In E. C. Carterette & M. P. Friedman (Eds.), *Handbook of perception* (Vol. 3). New York: Academic Press, 1973.

Treisman, A. M., Sykes, M., & Gelade, G. Selective attention and stimulus integration. In S. Dornic (Ed.), *Attention and performance VI.* Hillsdale, N.J.: Lawrence Erlbaum Associates, 1977.

Waltz, D. L. Understanding line drawings of scenes with shadows. In P. H. Winston (Ed.), *The psychology of computer vision.* New York: McGraw-Hill, 1975.

Wittgenstein, L. *Philosophical investigations* (Trans. by G. E. M. Anscombe). Oxford, England: Blackwell, 1953.

Woodworth, R. S. *Experimental psychology.* New York: Henry Holt, 1938.

7 Plane Surface Information as a Determinant of Pictorial Perception

Margaret A. Hagen
Boston University
Boston, Massachusetts, U.S.A.

Rebecca K. Jones
University of Minnesota
Minneapolis, Minnesota
U.S.A.

ABSTRACT

Adults were asked to scale the distances of five isosceles triangles at five different distances under 17 viewing conditions. The smallest distance was 15.2 cm and the largest was 127 cm from a small marker placed 45.8 cm from the observer. The conditions were designed to approximate pictorial viewing with real scenes through the interposition of a flat surface between viewer and scene and through limitation of the size of the available field of view; two conditions simulated the interposition of a flat surface; four conditions were designed to test the effects of removing flat surface information from pictures to approximate real scene perception. The obtained distance functions were all linear. Relative to a real scene monocular control function, the slopes of all surface addition and field limitation functions were lower and the intercepts higher. The two conditions of simulation of surface addition showed the same functions. These functions did not differ from those obtained with distance scaling in slides and prints of the scenes tested here. Surface addition and field limitation alone or together approximate pictorial perception in the scaling of distance. The attempt to remove flat surface information from pictures failed to approximate the function obtained with the real scene monocular control. The results are interpreted in terms of probable interactions among multiple pictorial variables.

INTRODUCTION

Traditionally, investigators within the field of picture perception have concentrated on analyzing the types of information that the pictorial field retains and presents relative to that from ordinary scenes. It has been argued extensively by Gibson (1971), Kennedy (1974), Pirenne (1970), and Hagen (1974), among others, that perspective pictures carry the same kind of information for spatial layout as the scenes they represent. Thus the perception of distance and size in pictures should be equivalent roughly to their perception in the real world. However, it has been noted repeatedly, particularly in the cross-cultural and developmental literatures, that both children and adults experience difficulty in perceiving depth in pictorial materials (Deregowski, 1968, 1972; Hudson, 1960; Jahoda & McGurk, 1974; Miller, 1973; Wilcox & Teghtsoonian, 1971; Yonas & Hagen, 1973). It is generally assumed and sometimes reported that the perception of relative distance and size are inferior in pictures relative to their perception in the ordinary environment, although good controls are usually lacking in this literature (Hagen & Glick, 1977). Those investigators who have analyzed the nature of pictorial stimuli frequently have attributed the observed difficulties to the coexistence of conflicting flatness and depth information in pictures (Gibson, 1969; Gregory, 1970; Hagen, 1974); that is, pictures carry information that specifies both a scene in depth and merely a flat surface. Schlosberg (1941), Attneave and Frost (1969), Gregory (1970), Hagen (1974), and others have argued that if flatness cues were weakened, the picture would take on a stronger appearance of depth.

Working on the converse side of this hypothesis, Hochberg (1962) attempted to add surface information with cellophane and a frame to real scenes in order to produce pictorial perception. He found that in the presence of such flatness cues a picture could not be distinguished from its real scene counterpart. Along similar lines, Hagen, Glick, and Morse (1978) found that looking through a clear pane of glass significantly increased observer's error rates on a comparative size judgment task with real objects. Also, looking through a single-lens reflex camera with a 50-mm lens significantly increased the error rate. The authors argued that the camera condition increased the error rate primarily through truncation of the available field of view and the glass condition through the addition of conflicting flat surface information.

In a further complication of the proposed role in picture perception of surface information, Pirenne (1970) argued that perception of a picture's projection surface, be it canvas, paper, wall, or ceiling, is critical for successful perception of the depicted spatial relations because such perception triggers compensation for the distortions attendant on oblique views of pictures. Because observation from the geometrically correct center of projection is a rarity in normal viewing, compensation is usually necessary. Pirenne's hypothesis received some support from Hagen (1976), who found that for adults the perception of the sizes of objects, placed at various distances and then photographed, was facilitated by oblique view of the picture surface of prints and disrupted by oblique view of slides. It seems to follow, then, that picture perception is not necessarily improved by diminishing the flat surface information available. However, the task in the Hagen (1976) study was judgment of relative size and involved an indirect measure at best of distance perception. All the other work just cited assumes that flat surface information in pictures (canvas, paper, frame, etc.) somehow directly affects perception of the amount of depth depicted within the picture, either the overall distance depicted or the relative distances between objects. It may be the case, as Rosinski and Farber (1980) have argued, that an oblique view of pictures creates distorted *shape* information without affecting depicted distance information. Hence, Hagen's (1976) relative size measure, which involved simple judgments of whether two forms were of the same or different size, might be seen as resting on the perception of depicted shapes distorted by oblique picture viewing rather than on the perception of relative distance depicted. If this interpretation is correct, there is no real conflict expressed in the views of Pirenne and the other workers cited.

Recently, Hagen, Jones, and Reed (1978) argued that both theoretical and empirical analyses of picture perception have failed to consider the perceptual effects of the pictorial truncation of the visual field. This truncation, particularly of the foreground, is necessarily entailed by the limited size of ordinary pictures. In their study, Hagen, Jones, and Reed demonstrated the importance of this variable both for methods of testing pictorial information and for theory building. They asked adults to scale the distances of five isosceles triangles placed on an 8-ft long checkered tabletop at five different distances, under four different viewing conditions. These conditions were unobstructed static monocular view, peephole view, view through a rectangular frame that truncated the visual field the way a picture does, and slide views of all the stimuli viewed through the truncation frame. The authors hypothesized that restricting the available field of view, with a peephole, frame, or limited pictorial field, would *decrease* the amount of distance perceived, hence *lowering* the slopes of the psychophysical distance functions, relative to the amount perceived in an unrestricted but stationary monocular view of the scene.

The results are shown in Fig. 7.1. The prediction received support in all conditions. For the distance judgments, the slopes of the scaling functions for the peephole, truncation, and slide conditions were all significantly lower than the slope of the untruncated monocular condition and the y-intercepts for peephole and slide were greater. The mean intercept for the function obtained in the truncation condition lay between the untruncated monocular condition and the peephole and slide conditions without differing significantly from any of them.

Hagen, Jones, and Reed (1978) interpreted these results as supporting the hypothesis that the truncation that occurs both in pictures and peephole views of scenes results in a lack of specific information for foreground distance. This lack

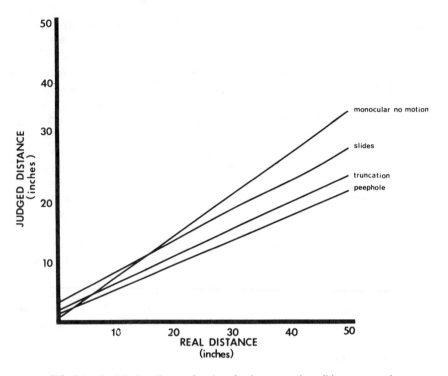

FIG. 7.1.   Straight-line distance functions for the truncated conditions compared
to the slides 90° and to the control. From Hagen, Jones, and Reed, 1978.

of specification of the foreground introduces a highly variable nonzero distance
intercept and causes a frontal shift in the location of the visual field. They noted
that, in the ordinary environment, the visual field begins at the face. If the same
assumption is made in pictorial or truncated perception, then the relatively slow
rate of change of visual angle with distance specifies short distances. Thus the
mean slopes for the functions obtained in truncated conditions were significantly
lower than that for the untruncated condition. The depressed slopes and elevated
intercepts of the obtained distance functions provided excellent support for Hagen, Jones, and Reed's interpretation of truncation of the visual field as a
signnificant but neglected variable in pictorial perception.

   Because Hagen, Jones, and Reed (1978) demonstrated the importance of
truncation of the visual field as a variable in picture perception, the purpose of
the present set of studies was to examine further the role of flat surface information in the perception of pictures. The 17 conditions studied are outlined briefly
in the following and presented fully in Methods on p. 123. We used the tasks of
distance scaling of isosceles triangles resting on a textured surface (4 × 8 ft
checkered tabletop) in order to facilitate specification of the exact nature of the

problems with picture perception and to allow comparison with previous work (see Fig. 7.2). (1) We first ran a real scene control condition in which view of the table was monocular, untruncated, and with no head motion. We combined these data with those obtained in an identical condition in an earlier study (Hagen, & Teghtsoonian, 1977) in order to obtain a reliable comparison function. The mean function for distance to be used for comparison in the work that follows was $y = 0.67x + .86$. In addition to the (2) full color slide condition previously reported in Hagen, Jones, and Reed (1978) and cited previously, we also created (3) photographic color prints of all our stimuli, photographed from the point of observation of the real scene control. In line with the thinking of Gregory and E. J. Gibson discussed earlier, we hypothesized that distance perception in back-projected transparencies, *where the surface information is minimal,* would be more accurate than with prints; that is, that the distance slope of the scaling function for slides would be higher than for prints and the intercept lower.

Following Hochberg's (1962) work on the addition of flat surface information to real scenes, we (4) interposed a sheet of light yellow cellophane mounted on glass between the observers and real scenes in order to approximate "pictorial perception" with those real scenes. (5) We also tested the effects of the glass alone. We hypothesized that, like truncation of the visual field, the pane of glass

FIG. 7.2.   View of the display from the monocular viewpoint: a 3-in. (7.62-cm) triangle at 6-in. (15.24-cm) distance. The triangle and disc were red; the checkered surface was black and white.

and the sheet of cellophane would depress the slopes and elevate the intercepts of the obtained distance functions relative to the values of the real scene monocular condition. In addition, we replicated the previously reported (6) truncation and (7) peephole conditions (Hagen, Jones, & Reed, 1978) with the addition of a pane of glass to each (8) and (9) to determine if the effects of truncating the field of view and adding a flat surface were additive. A colleague in art history, John Ward, argued that the effect of truncating the field of view might not be that of cutting off available information for the foreground but of simply facilitating the projection of forms seen behind the frame onto a projection surface. Accordingly, Ward designed and ran two additional conditions: in the first (10) the subject looked through a frame of the same dimensions as the truncation frame, but that was formed by the intersections of four strings and that allowed the viewer to see the space on all sides; in the second (11) the subject looked through a frame identical to the truncation frame at the top and sides but without a bottom and therefore occluding nothing of the foreground. The truncation frame was similar to looking through a window, whereas Ward's "frame" was similar to looking through an open doorway. Ward hypothesized that both strings and archway would produce effects identical to those obtained either by truncation or by surface addition.

In the next condition, we undertook to pursue a suggestion of Gregory (1970, p. 92) that the depth indicated in perspective figures in pictures is countermanded by the texture of the background surface. Gregory suggested that pictorial stimuli might be made with luminous paint and be presented in the dark to remove surface characteristics. We followed this suggestion. We duplicated all our pictures with Day-Glo on matte black backgrounds and had subjects view them under ultraviolet light in several viewing conditions. (12) View was at the correct center of projection in a vertical view condition that oriented the axes of pictorial space with those of the surround and (13) in a horizontal view condition that rotated those axes 90°. The pictures were also viewed (14) with the addition of head motion and (15) the presence of white light to provide information for the surface of the plane of projection, through motion parallax and texture, respectively. We hypothesized that under static view with black light in either the vertical or the horizontal condition the obtained distance functions would approximate those obtained in the real scene monocular control. We also hypothesized that with the addition of either head motion or white light, the functions would revert to those obtained in ordinary picture viewing.

Lastly, following Pirenne's argument that the normal case of picture viewing involves observation from an arbitrary viewpoint and not from the geometrically correct center of projection, we had subjects view the slides and prints from a point from which the line of sight was at a 45° angle to the picture plane, of (16) reinforced paper for the prints, and (17) glass screen for the slides. We hypothesized that oblique view of both prints and slides would increase awareness of the surface of the plane of projection and trigger the compensation mechanism hypothesized by Pirenne, thus elevating the slopes and decreasing the intercepts of the obtained distance functions relative to those obtained with view from the correct station point. The data for the (6) truncation, (7) peephole, and (2) slide conditions (*without* the addition of glass) were taken from Hagen, Jones, and Reed (1978). (See Fig. 7.1.)

Method

Subjects

Volunteers from introductory psychology classes participated in the experiment. There were 15 subjects in each of the conditions, except for the monocular control with 45 subjects. About half of the subjects in each condition were female and about half were male.

Apparatus and Procedure

Stimuli to be judged for distance were presented vertically on a 4 × 8 ft (1.22 m × 2.44 m) flat textured tabletop. They were isosceles triangles whose heights and bases were 2, 3, 4, 5, and 6 in. (5.08, 7.62, 10.16, 12.7, and 15.24 cm). They were cut from Day-Glo red–orange posterboard and mounted upright with L-shaped hardware (see Fig. 7.2). The tabletop was covered with black, white, and gray checked gingham stretched tight over 3/4-in. (1.91-cm) plywood. The entire table was surrounded by 4-ft (1.22-m) high off-white curtains suspended from the ceiling; these occluded the view of everything in the room but the stimulus field. Subjects judged the distance between a small (2 cm in diameter) circular marker placed flat on the table 18 in. (45.75 cm) from the edge and the bases of the triangles presented vertically 6, 10.2, 17.3, 29.5, and 50 in. (15.24, 25.9, 44, 75, and 127 cm) beyond the marker. At each of the five distances, subjects made five distance judgments to the bases of the five different-sized triangles. Thus every subject was given 25 stimulus presentations in which he/she judged the distance of the presented triangles. This order was randomized as was the order of the 25 presentations for each subject. This design produced five judgments from each subject for every distance.

Viewing Conditions

All viewing conditions were monocular, with each subject indicating his/her perferred eye. The nonpreferred eye was covered with an eye patch. In the untruncated monocular condition, the eye was positioned 6 in. (15.24 cm) above the table and 18 in. (45.75 cm) from the circular marker. Head motion was constrained by use of a chin rest with temple guides, Biometrika Model #115-4. Subjects viewed the stimulus field through a 35 × 15 cm slot that allowed proper orientation without truncating the field of view. In the glass condition, a pane of framed glass was placed behind the nontruncated slot on the table, 2 in. (5 cm) beyond the slot. In the cellophane condition, a sheet of light yellow cellophane, .76 × 1.2 m, was mounted flat on the framed glass in the same position. The glass was somewhat pitted so that in addition to the surface color of the cellophane some minimal texture information for the glass was available. However, the absence of any lens properties or distortion in the glass was determined by photographic comparison. In the rectangular truncation condition, view was constrained by a small slot (6.5 × 4.5 cm). In the strings condition, strings were placed to duplicate the framing of this slot. In the archway condition, the bottom of the truncating slot was simply removed and the sides extended vertically to the table. The size and shape of the available field of view was identical to that in the fourth and fifth conditions, slides and prints. The photographs were taken in color with a 50-mm SLR camera placed at the station point described previously and developed as both slides and prints. The prints were duplicated as closely as possible using Day-Glo lines and triangles against a matte-black construction paper background. The dimensions of the truncated field, the slides, the prints, and the Day-Glo pictures were determined by projecting the slides until the images were identical to those obtained when viewing the real scenes. In the slide, rectangular truncation and print conditions view was constrained not only by the cardboard frame but by the head rest as well. In The Day-Glo conditions, view was constrained by a peephole except in the head-motion condition, where a 4 in. × 6 in. (10.16 cm × 15.24 cm) viewing slot was used. Day-Glo stimuli were mounted inside a large box, approximately 30 in. high, 30 in. wide, and 15 in. deep (76.20 cm × 76.20 cm × 38.10 cm), lined with black velvet and illuminated with ultraviolet light in the black light conditions. The illumination in the surrounding room was low, from an ordinary incandescent bulb.

Subjects were permitted to view each presentation once and were instructed to match the distance from the circular marker to the base of the triangle by extending a tape measure held in the right hand and pulled out by the left in front of the subject. The numbers on the tape were not visible to the subjects. They were instructed to retract the tape after each trial.

Results

Distance Functions

The least-squares technique was used to fit a straight-line function to the mean distances judged for every subject. This regression technique yielded three scores for every subject: slope, y-intercept, and coefficient of determination as a measure of goodness of fit of the linear functions. The mean slopes, intercepts, and coefficients of determination for each condition are tabulated in Table 7.1. As seen from the table, the very high r^2's are indicative of the appropriateness of the linear functions. Indeed, there was so little variability that the coefficients of determination were not subjected to analysis.

The slopes and intercepts of the obtained functions were tested by planned comparisons against the real scene monocular control function in accordance with the individual hypotheses. For all four picture conditions, we had

TABLE 7.1
Linear Functions for Distance with Attendant Coefficients of Determination

Condition	Function	r^2	$m < .67$	$c > .86$	$c > 0.0$	
Monocular control	$y = .67x + .86$	.99				
Pictures 90°						
Slides	$y = .49x + 2.91$	.98	*	**	**	
Prints	$y = .35x + 2.97$	.98	**	**	**	
Pictures 45°						
Slides	$y = .32x + 3.19$	.98	**	**	**	$.32 < .49, p < .05$
Prints	$y = .29x + 2.52$	.98	**	**	**	$.29 = .35$
Truncations						
Frame	$y = .44x + 2.01$	.99	**	*	**	
Peephole	$y = .42x + 1.22$	.99	**		**	
Surface addition						
Glass	$y = .54x + 2.07$	.98	*	*	**	
Cellophane + glass	$y = .48x + 2.21$	.98	**	**	**	
Truncations + surface						
Frame + glass	$y = .48x + 2.01$	.98	**	**	**	
Peep + glass	$y = .48x + 1.82$	.99	**	*	**	
Specification of surface						
Strings	$y = .53x + 1.64$	.99	*		**	$.05 < p < .10 \ (1.64)$
Archway	$y = .50x + 1.21$	.99	*		**	
Subtraction of surface						
PHBL	$y = .41x + 7.10$	.90	**	**	**	
PHWL	$y = .36x + 8.32$	.86	**	**	**	
MHBL	$y = .44x + 5.29$	.93	**	**	**	
PVBL	$y = .36x + 4.85$	.93	**	**	**	

$* = p < .05$
$** = p < .01$
P = peephole
M = head motion
H = horizontal
V = vertical
B = black light
W = white light
m = slope
c = intercept

hypothesized that the slopes of the distance functions would be lower than that of the control function, $m = .67$, and the intercepts higher than $y = .86$ (see Fig. 7.3). The results were as predicted: slides 90°, $t(14) = 2.45$, $p < .025$ for the slope and $t(14) = 2.92$, $p < .01$ for the intercept; prints 90°, $t(14) = 6.13$, $p < .01$ for the slope and $t(14) = 4.77$, $p < .01$ for the intercept; slides 45°, $t(14) = 5.36$, $p < .01$ for the slope and $t(14) = 5.66$, $p < .01$ for the intercept; prints 45°, $t(14) = 10.1$, $p < .01$ for the slope and $t(14) = 2.58$, $p < .025$ for the intercept. Further, we had hypothesized that under 90° observation, the slide function would more closely approximate the real scene control than would the print function, but we obtained no reliable differences between slides and prints.

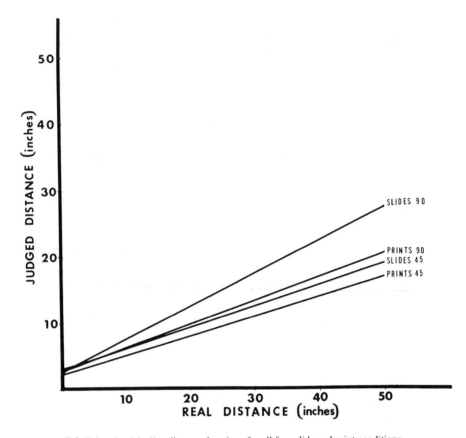

FIG. 7.3.   Straight-line distance functions for all four slide and print conditions.

We had also hypothesized that under oblique view (pictures 45°) the slopes of the picture functions would be higher and the intercepts lower than under the condition of observation from the correct station point (pictures 90°). We were quite mistaken. The intercepts do not differ, and the slopes of the oblique view conditions are lower than those of the correct station point conditions, the slide slope reliably so, $t(28) = 1.72$, $p < .05$.

For the surface addition conditions, we had hypothesized that, like the truncation of the visual field with frame or peephole, the pane of glass and the sheet of cellophane would depress the slope and elevate the intercept of the obtained distance functions relative to the values of the real scene control. All four surface addition conditions affected the distance functions as predicted, the glass alone least so, (see Fig. 7.4). The t-values for the obtained slopes relative to the control slope of .67 were as follows: glass, $t(14) = 2.22$, $p < .025$; cellophane, $t(14) = 4.18$, $p < .01$; frame + glass, $t(14) = 4.56$, $p < .01$; peephole + glass, $t(14) = 3.09$, $p < .01$. The t-values for the obtained intercepts relative to the control intercept of .86 were glass, $t(14) = 1.94$, $p < .05$; cellophane, $t(14) = 3.25$, p

< .01; frame + glass, $t(14) = 2.84$, $p < .01$; peephole + glass, $t(14) = 1.98$, p
< .05. We also expected the combination of truncation and surface addition to
have additive effects at least in terms of a lower range and less variability of
slopes in the combined conditions relative to the several ones. It can be seen from
Table 7.1 that surface addition to real scenes in combination with truncation of
the field or alone is indistinguishable in mean effect from truncation by framing.
It is also similar to the peephole effect except that the peephole intercept of 1.22
was not significantly greater than the control intercept of 0.86, whereas all the
other truncation and addition intercepts were significantly greater. Moreover,
inspection of the data did not indicate for the truncation plus surface conditions
either a more limited range of scores or a decrease in variability masked by the
similar group means.

John Ward's hypothesis that pictorial perception might be induced by simple
specification of a surface without truncation received partial support. The slopes
of both the strings and the archway conditions were depressed significantly

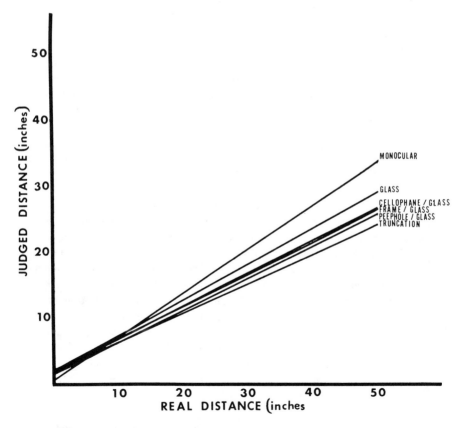

FIG. 7.4.   Straight-line distance functions comparing surface information with
truncation of the visual field.

relative to the control slope; for the strings, $t(14) = 2.95$, $p < .025$; for the archway, $t(14) = 2.42$, $p < .025$. However, the intercepts for these two conditions did not differ significantly from the control intercept of .86.

For the conditions involving the subtraction of surface information from pictures through black light observation of Day-Glo stimuli, we had hypothesized that both black light peephole conditions would produce functions similar to the real scene control and would differ reliably from the white light and head motion conditions. It is clear from Table 7.1 that these predictions were not borne out. All four slopes are depressed significantly below the control slope of .67 and do not differ from the ordinary picture slopes: PHBL, $t(14) = 3.68$, $p < .01$; PHWL, $t(14) = 5.22$, $p < .01$; MHBL, $t(14) = 3.26$, $p < .01$; PVBL, $t(14) = 5.06$, $p < .01$. All four intercepts are not only significantly greater than the control intercept of .86 but are greater than all four standard picture intercepts. The closest comparisons involve PVBL, and the relevant t-values are PVBL versus S190°, $t(28) = 1.85$, $p < .05$; PVBL versus Pr90°, $t(28) = 2.09$, $p < .025$; PVBL versus S145°, $t(28) = 1.89$, $p < .05$; PVBL versus Pr45°, $t(28) = 2.33$, $p < .025$. Because all the peephole conditions necessarily are truncated and the head motion condition truncated by the limited extent of the picture itself, as well as the slot, this result is not perhaps surprising. The Day-Glo composition of the pictures seems only to have made them less comprehensible as representations of anything familiar. They did not seem to have greater or more effective information for depth. The high intercept values were accompanied by disproportionately greater variability and the linear functions were less good fits in these conditions than in any others.

DISCUSSION

Several variables distinguish the viewing of pictures from the ordinary viewing of real scenes. The information provided by pictures is essentially static and monocular although pictures are usually viewed binocularly by an observer who is moving. In addition, pictures offer to the viewer a much smaller field of view than that available to a one-eyed observer scanning a scene from a stationary point of observation. Looking at pictures is like standing still in a darkened room looking through a window at a lighted scene outside—with one additional factor. Pictures are usually created on perceptually discriminable flat surfaces—canvas, paper, walls, and such. These surfaces have visible texture and they look flat. They are flat. Thus the perception of pictures involves the pickup of artificially truncated, static, monocular information for the scene in depth depicted in conjunction with the information for the flat surface media of canvas, paint, paper, frame, stucco, etc. The effect of all these factors on the perception of pictured scenes is not terribly clear, but many investigators have noted that "depth perception" in pictures, however measured, is not as "good" as depth perception with real scenes. It is generally agreed that the "goodness" of depth perception is reasonably measured by the degree of match of perceptual judgments to tape-rule measurements of depth. Thus, if depth perception in pictures is defective, the amount of depth judged to be present between two points in the pictured scene should be less than that metrically present. In the limiting case of defective picture perception, the distance between two points pictured at different depths should be zero. Much of the cross-cultural literature testing picture perception with non-Western samples finds just such a result. However, the pictorial depth perception work with Western samples finds not the complete absence of depth perception but diminished depth perception. The study providing the clearest comparison between static, monocular view of a real scene and view of a picture of that scene was Hagen, Jones, and Reed (1978) cited previously. They found that relative to the real scene control the distance function obtained in slide viewing showed a lower slope and a higher intercept. In both cases, absolute amount of distance perceived in slides was less than in the real scene controls. This result is slightly modified by the fact that the intercept for the slide function differed reliably from zero, whereas the control intercept did not. Hagen, Jones, and Reed showed too that similar results could be obtained by artificially truncating the field of view with a slot or a peephole. Thus they argued that the critical variable in determining the diminished distance perception with pictures was that of truncation of the field necessarily attendant upon the creation of an ordinary picture.

However, the study by Hagen, Jones, and Reed (1978) was only an initial pass at the several variables influencing picture perception listed previously. Their study made no attempt to examine the role of the flat surface information provided by pictures in the perception of the depicted scene in depth. It was to that end that the additional conditions reported herein were addressed. In the present study, the amount of surface information provided by pictures themselves was extended by examining the perception of photographic prints as well as the slides previously studied and by attempting to heighten surface awareness through oblique viewing of both slides and prints. Generally, our manipulations were inconsequential. Slides did not differ reliably from prints in either slope or intercept. Oblique viewing certainly did not enhance distance perception in the pictures; it further disrupted it. In the slide condition the slope of the distance function was reliably lower under oblique view than at the geometrically correct point of observation. We have no explanation for this finding because we are in accord with Rosinski and Farber's (1980) mathematical determination that the distance gradient information is not altered by oblique view of pictures. It is tempting to dismiss the finding as a fluke, but it would be rash to do so especially as the data from the photographic-print condition show the same tendency. We must fall back on the inevitable observation that further work is required to clarify the situation.

We are in a considerably more desirable position with respect to our attempt to add surface information to real scenes in order to approximate pictorial distance perception. These conditions involved the interposing of sheets of glass and cellophane between the viewer's point of observation and the table on which the triangles were placed, as well as the addition of a pane of glass to the conditions in which view was limited by a truncation frame or a peephole. We had predicted that the addition of the flat surface information provided by the cellophane or glass would depress the slope of the distance function and elevate the intercept relative to the control function; we had hoped as well to find that surface information and truncation of field of view would have additive effects. In the first case, our predictions were borne out. Both glass and cellophane plus glass diminish the amount of distance perceived while leaving the functions linear. The intercepts differ reliably from zero. We feel confident then in arguing that picture perception can be approximated in real scenes by the simple addition of a flat surface similar to the canvas, paper, or projection screen provided by real pictures.

We would like to argue as well that we have demonstrated that the diminished distance perception that occurs in picture viewing is therefore a simple product of the truncation of the field of view and its attendant depth information in conjunction with the additional flat surface information occasioned by pictures; but the data do not permit us to do so. Either variable alone generates distance functions that do not differ significantly from the combined picture conditions under normal observation; that is, the mean distance function for slides and prints each viewed 90° to the picture plane is $y = .42x + 2.94$. Not only does this function not differ from the two truncation functions (frame and peephole) or from the two surface addition functions (glass and cellophane plus glass), it is nearly identical to them. All we accomplished through combining truncation and surface information was two more replications of approximated pictorial perception. We were aware of these statistical limitations beforehand, but we had hoped that additive effects might be revealed either through a decrease in the range of the scores or through a decrease in ordinary variability. Our hopes were in vain. There is no evidence to suggest a decrease in either type of variability. Because we feel confident that the psychophysical scaling measure used in this study was finely graded enough to reveal such effects if present, we are forced to consider whether the stimuli themselves may be at fault (not to mention the hypothesis). We examined only five distances all within a range from 6 in. to 50 in. (15 cm to 127 cm). Perhaps a greatly extended range of several meters would separate the effects of the two variables. This is a reasonable hypothesis because truncation of the visual field (i.e., removal of specific information for the extent of the foreground) should have its greatest effect at the near distances. As seen from Fig. 7.5, the curve of change in visual angle with distance falls off abruptly with ever-increasing distance from the self. It follows then that the effect of chopping off the nearest section of the curve on the gradient information for distance should diminish as the depicted section of the curve is moved farther and farther away. (The mathematical exposition of this argument is present admirably in Lumsden, 1980.) However, the addition of surface information should have a constant effect regardless of the distance pictured. This explanation again puts us

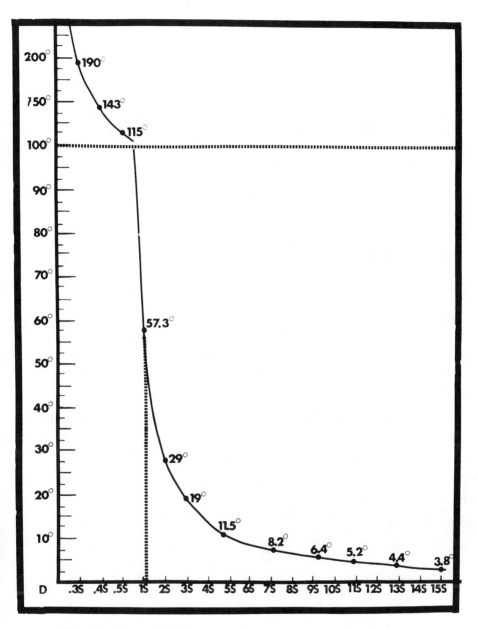

FIG. 7.5. Change in visual angle with distance where distance is plotted as a multiple of size.

in the position of saying that further work is indicated, but in this case the promissory note is rather more substantial than previously.

The last set of conditions addressed the role of surface information in picture perception from the opposite angle. Instead of trying to add surface information to ordinary scenes, we attempted in these conditions to substract it from pictures. Following a suggestion from Richard Gregory's (1970) work, we constructed stimuli out of luminous Day-Glo lines and figures and had subjects view them under black light. The luminous stimuli were the same size as the ordinary pictures and the triangles pictured subtended the same visual angles. We had predicted that the slope of the distance function in the black light conditions would approximate that of the real scene control. We found instead that the slope was the same as for the ordinary slides and prints. The intercepts, however, were considerably larger than in any other condition. It should be noted that even with the larger intercepts the perceived distance is not as great with Day-Glo pictures as it is in the perception of real scenes. We would like to account for the much heightened intercepts, as well as the much greater variability, by noting that black light view of luminous figures provides no information whatsoever for the location of the figure in space relative to the observer. Yet, this is not completely true. Our subjects know that they are in an ordinary room and that they are looking in a not-very-big box. This environmental surround no doubt serves as an anchor for a spatial reference frame. The heightened variability and increased intercept values are more likely to be due to the lack of specific information from the pictures regarding their subject matter. As seen from observation of Fig. 7.2, the checkered fabric covering the table pictured in the slides and prints *looks like* a checkered fabric. When the fabric checks are replaced in the Day-Glo pictures with a simple perspective grid of very thin Day-Glo lines, the size of the units in the grid is unspecified. Each unit could be a meter square or a centimeter square. The observer has no information to set the scale (other than his/her beliefs about the experiment). We now believe that the only reason that distance judgments did not vary, subject to subject, from centimeters to kilometers, is that subjects were constrained in the range of their judgments by the response measure. After all, one can only pull out a tape rule so far between the right and the left hand. If we used a scaling technique that had allowed individual subjects to set their own values, however great, it is likely that the range of values would have been enormous. If this is the case, then the absolute distances judged in such a condition would be in the direction predicted from Gregory's work. Gregory's response measure did not limit the range of subject responses as ours did. However, the inadequacy of the response measure in limiting the range of judgments does not address the issue of the slopes of the black light functions. They are significantly lower than the slope of the control, and there is no reason to believe that altering the response measure will elevate the slopes. It may be the case that pictorial truncation of the field of view will always depress the slopes of distance functions in pictorial perception.

The study reported here was intended to be quite comprehensive and definitive in its examination of the role of plane surface information in pictorial perception, alone and in conjunction with other variables. Yet in its execution we have discovered new variables to be considered and promising directions rather than definitive answers. A direction not much examined here is that suggested by the findings in the two conditions suggested by the art historian, John Ward. Ward's simple specification of a surface of projection through the use of strings and archway also came close to approximating pictorial perception. The slopes are not quite so low, nor the intercepts so high as in the other picture approximation conditions, but the differences between the Ward conditions and the real scene control are reliable. This aspect of surface information in pictorial perception has never been considered before, and it is barely touched on here. So at the end of this somewhat involved investigation of the interlocked roles of surface specification, surface texture, and truncation of the available field of view on the perception of distance in pictures, we are left mainly with the assurance that each is no doubt important, and we have much more work to do.

ACKNOWLEDGMENTS

This research was supported by a grant from the National Institute of Mental Health to the first author, Grant No. 1-R01-MH27947-01. The authors gratefully acknowledge the conceptual assistance of Martha Teghtsoonian and John Ward. Requests for reprints should be sent to the first author at 64 Cummington Street, Department of Psychology, Boston University, Boston, Massachusetts 02215, U.S.A.

REFERENCES

Attneave, F., & Frost, R. The determination of perceived tridimensional orientation by minimum criteria. *Perception & Psychophysics,* 1969, *6,* 391–396.

Deregowski, J. B. Difficulties in pictorial depth perception in Africa. *British Journal of Psychology,* 1968, *59,* 195–204.

Deregowski, J. B. Pictorial perception and culture. *Scientific American,* 1972, *227,* 82–88.

Gibson, E. J. *Principles of perceptual learning and development.* New York: Appleton-Century-Crofts, 1969.

Gibson, J. J. The information available in pictures. *Leonardo,* 1971, *4,* 27–35.

Gregory, R. L. *The intelligent eye.* New York: McGraw-Hill, 1970.

Hagen, M. A. Picture perception: Toward a theoretical model. *Psychological Bulletin,* 1974, *81,* 471–497.

Hagen. M. A. Influence of picture surface and station point on the ability to compensate for oblique view in pictorial perception. Developmental Psychology, 1976, *12,* 57–63.

Hagen, M. A., & Glick, R. Pictorial perspective, perception of size, lines and texture perspective in children and adults. *Perception,* 1977, *6,* 675–684.

Hagen, M. A., Glick, R., & Morse, B. The role of the two-dimensional surface characteristics in pictorial depth perception. *Perceptual and Motor Skills,* 1978, *46,* 875–881.

Hagen, M. A., Jones, R. K., & Reed, E. S. On a neglected variable in theories of pictorial perception: Truncation of the visual field. *Perception & Psychophysics,* 1978, *23,* 326–330.

Hagen, M. A., & Teghtsoonian, M. *Size and distance scaling: Binocular and monocular view with and without head motion.* Paper presented at the meeting of the Eastern Psychological Association, New York, 1977.

Hochberg, J. E. Psychophysics of pictorial perception. *Audio-Visual Communication Review,* 1962, *10,* 22–54.

Hudson, W. Pictorial depth perception in sub-cultural groups in Africa. *Journal of Social Psychology,* 1960, *52,* 183–208.

Jahoda, G., & McGurk, H. Pictorial depth perception: A developmental study. *British Journal of Psychology,* 1974, *65,* 141–149.

Kennedy, J. M. *A psychology of picture perception: Information and images.* San Francisco: Josey-Boss, 1974.

Lumsden, E. A. Problems of magnification and minification: An explanation of the distortions of distance, slant, shape and velocity. In M. A. Hagen (Ed.), *The perception of pictures I.* New York: Academic Press, 1980.

Miller, R. J. Cross-cultural research in the perception of pictorial materials. *Psychological Bulletin,* 1973, *80,* 135–150.

Pirenne, M. *Optics, painting & photography.* Cambridge, England: Cambridge University Press, 1970.

Rosinski, R. R., & Farber, J. Compensation for viewing point in the perception of pictorial space. In M. A. Hagen (Ed.), *The perception of pictures I.* New York: Academic Press, 1980.

Schlosberg, H. Stereoscopic depth from single pictures. *American Journal of Psyhology,* 1941, *54,* 601–605.

Wilcox, R. L., & Teghtsoonian, M. The control of relative size by pictorial depth cues in children and adults. *Journal of Experimental Child Psychology,* 1971, *11,* 413–429.

Yonas, A., & Hagen, M. A. Effects of static and kinetic depth information on the perception of size in children and adults. *Journal of Experimental Child Psychology,* 1973, *15,* 254–265.

8 Canonical Perspective and the Perception of Objects

Stephen Palmer, Eleanor Rosch, and Paul Chase
University of California, Berkeley, California, U.S.A.

ABSTRACT

It is argued that there is a privileged or canonical perspective for perceiving objects. Three operational definitions are shown to converge on an underlying psychological variable consistent with this notion: (1) subjective ratings of the goodness of different perspective views; (2) the perspective from which people first imagine a common object; and (3) the perspective from which they choose to take the "best" photograph. A speeded performance experiment demonstrates that canonicalness affects perceptual processes during identification. Highly canonical perspectives are identified more quickly than others, with response latencies being a monotonically decreasing function of canonicalness. Finally, it is shown that canonicalness of a perspective view can be well predicted from (1) the visibility of information about the object in a given perspective view; and (2) the subjective importance of that information for the identity of the object. These results support the claim that canonical perspectives maximize the amount of salient information about an object that is available for perceiving it.

INTRODUCTION

The basic job of visual perception is to recover information about the properties of environmental objects from information in light. There are many aspects of this problem that make it a difficult one. Not the least of these is that the same object gives rise to an infinite number of different two-dimensional images when viewed from different positions. In fact, only a portion of the entire three-

135

dimensional object is visible from any given perspective, and that portion differs from one perspective to another.

This chapter concerns some implications of these facts for object perception. Specifically, we consider the possibility that the internal knowledge structure for an object is maximally accessible from a privileged or "canonical" perspective. Four diverse traditions in the study of cognition and perception suggest that this might be so.

First, within the information-processing tradition, object recognition is thought to occur when a stimulus "accesses" or "makes contact with" the appropriate internal object representation. It is generally believed that this internal knowledge structure contains information about the whole object and that stimulus information is mapped into this knowledge structure as a subset (Minsky, 1975; Palmer, 1975). From these assumptions plus the fact that different views reveal different information about the object, it follows that some views should provide better access to the internal representation of the corresponding object than others. That view containing the most information of the highest salience should be maximally recognizable.

Second, research on categorization suggests that categories contain "prototypical" exemplars having privileged status. Such members have more attributes in common with other exemplars and contain more information about the category as a whole (Mervis & Rosch, 1981; Rosch, 1975, 1978). If one considers the concept of an individual perceptible object to be, in itself, a very low-level category and its perspective views to be exemplars of that category, then there should be some "best" or "most typical" perspective view of the object: the canonical perspective. Within such a framework, certain predictions become obvious by analogy. People should have a good intuitive idea of which perspectives are most canonical and be able to make consistent ratings of "canonicalness." Canonical perspectives should be the first to come to mind when people are asked to imagine the object. These perspectives should be most similar to other views of the same object and most different from views of other objects. They should contain the most information of greatest salience about the object. Of particular concern for the present chapter, canonical perspectives should be most easily categorized ("recognized") as perceptual instances of the object depicted.

A third tradition that unexpectedly converges on the idea of canonical perspective is that of phenomenology. Merleau-Ponty (1962) argues that a stable object with objective properties emerges in perception only after the spatial field has been organized such that the observer has a "maximum grip" (*prise maximale*) on the object; that is, the object appears at the distance and perspective in which there is maximum sharpness of detail for visual exploration and maximum potential coordination between body and object for ordinary use of the object. In Merleau-Ponty's analysis, therefore, not only is there a privileged perspective from which an object is most perceivable, but this perspective is prior to and a necessary precondition for definition of the object and its attributes.

A fourth body of theory, the Gibsonian concept of affordances (Gibson, 1979), is actually quite similar to the phenomenological view. Organisms directly perceive the affordances for interaction that objects in the environment provide. However, the affordance structure of an object can only be perceived from certain perspectives (e.g., that a cup can hold liquid is not perceivable from underneath but only from perspectives where the rim, sides, and bottom of the cup are all in view). It is reasonable that the organism will respond maximally to the perspective of an object from which its affordance structure is most perceivable. And if the perception of affordances is an integral part of object recognition, objects will be most easily recognized from just such a perspective.

In this chapter, we present empirical evidence that common objects have standard or canonical perspectives. First, three converging operations show high agreement among different measures of canonicalness of object perspectives. Second, speed of object recognition is shown to be highly correlated with canonicalness. Finally, canonical perspectives are shown to be those that present the most information of greatest salience about the object.

CONVERGING OPERATIONAL DEFINITIONS

The first experiments investigate three operational definitions of canonical perspective: (1) subjective ratings of the goodness of different perspective views of an object; (2) the first perspective from which people imagine an object; and (3) the perspective from which people choose to take the best photograph of the object. These will be referred to as the *goodness rating, imagery,* and *photography* tasks, respectively.

In the goodness rating task, subjects were shown a series of different perspective views of an object and asked to make direct ratings of how good an example the picture was of the object depicted. For this experiment an extended series of pictures of 15 real objects was taken by the experimenters. Each object was photographed from 11 different perspectives: front (F), back (B), side (S), top (T), front-side (FS), front-top (FT), side-top (ST), back-top (BT), back-side (BS), front-side-top (FST), and back-side-top (BST). An additional picture was taken that reflected the experimenters' intuitions about the best or most canonical picture for each object. These photographs will be referred to as the *standard set* of pictures. Subjects made goodness ratings of each picture.

The rationale for the imagery task is that people should spontaneously generate the canonical perspective when asked to imagine an object. Although subjects may then manipulate the image—for example, by mentally rotating it (Shepard & Metzler, 1971) or by mentally "walking around" it—to generate other perspectives, the perspective of the first image that comes to mind is one operational definition of canonical perspective. Rather than making direct judgments of perspective, however, subjects were simply asked to rate the amounts of the front, back, side, and top surfaces of the object they could "see" in their images.

The photography experiment was undertaken to obtain more objective measurements of the most canonical perspective. Because peoples' images are not open to inspection by others, subjects in this task were asked to take a photograph from the perspective that best captured their image of an object. In order to compare the results of this task with those of the imagery task, independent judges rated the amounts of front, back, side, and top surfaces visible in each photograph. In order to compare both of these tasks with the goodness rating task, the same judges also rated the amounts of front, back, side, and top surfaces visible in each of four standard pictures of each object: those receiving the highest, lowest, and two equally spaced intermediate goodness ratings. Thus, the results of all three tasks can be compared in terms of ratings of surface visibilities.

All the present experiments used 12 common objects familiar to everyone or realistic, small-scale models of such objects: chair, car, grand piano, horse, house, camera, steam iron, telephone, teapot, shoe, (manual) pencil sharpener, and alarm clock (see Fig. 8.1). The first six were detailed small-scale models of real objects, and the last six were full-scale, real objects. The particular objects were carefully chosen to be as representative as possible of the categories to which they belonged. Other selection criteria included bilateral symmetry to reduce the number of different perspectives (although the grand piano, shoe, and house were only approximately symmetrical), familiarity, and the availability of

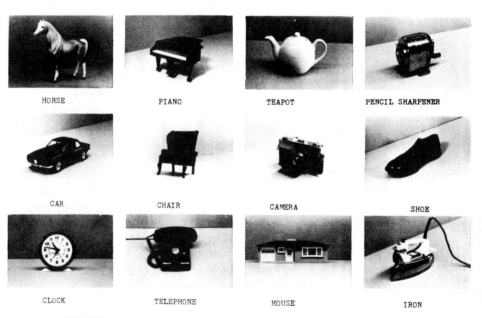

HORSE   PIANO   TEAPOT   PENCIL SHARPENER

CAR   CHAIR   CAMERA   SHOE

CLOCK   TELEPHONE   HOUSE   IRON

FIG. 8.1.   Examples from the standard picture set showing each of the 12 experimental objects from the perspective rated most canonical.

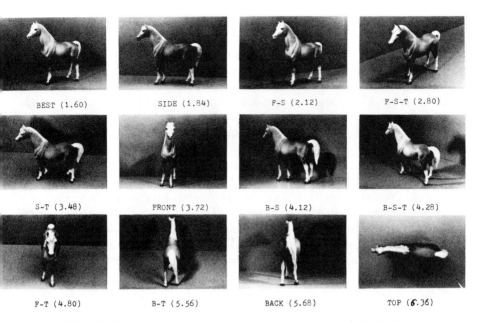

BEST (1.60) SIDE (1.84) F-S (2.12) F-S-T (2.80)

S-T (3.48) FRONT (3.72) B-S (4.12) B-S-T (4.28)

F-T (4.80) B-T (5.56) BACK (5.68) TOP (6.36)

FIG. 8.2. Examples from the standard picture set showing all 12 perspective views of the (model) horse together with their perspective descriptions and mean goodness ratings.

realistic models for large objects. Three other objects were also photographed in the same way for use as practice and demonstration objects in the experimental tasks: a real cup, a model dog, and a model train.

Method

Goodness Rating. Twelve perspective views of each of the 12 experimental objects were taken according to the general scheme just discussed. For each type of picture, the experimenters took the picture they believed represented the best view of that particular type (e.g., the front-side perspective was taken from what appeared to be the most representative viewpoint that included both the front and the side of the car but not its top or the back). These 12 pictures (F, S, B, T, FS, FT, BS, ST, BT, FST, BST, and Best perspectives) were made into slides for group presentation. Figure 8.2 shows all views of the horse from the standard set.

These 12 views of each object were presented twice to 24 psychology undergraduates, in groups of 5 to 10 people. The first presentation familiarized the subjects with the 12 views of a single object. Immediately afterward, the same 12 pictures were shown again for about 20 sec each. During this time the subjects recorded their goodness ratings. They were instructed to use a scale from 1 (very good) to 7 (very bad). The actual instructions were a slightly modified version of the instructions used by Rosch (1975). Subjects were told to rate how good or typical the presented picture was of the object shown. After all the pictures of one object had been rated, the procedure was repeated for the rest of the experimental objects.

Imagery Task.   Forty psychology undergraduates participated in groups of 5 to 10 people. First, they became familiar with the complete set of 12 objects by inspecting them closely. The experimenter then showed the subjects 11 different slides of the model train, each from a different perspective. He pointed out the amounts of front, back, side, and top surfaces visible in each picture. The subjects were then informed that their task would be to form a clear mental image of a specific object and to judge the amounts of front, back, side, and top surfaces "visible" within that image. They were instructed to report their responses in terms of numbers from 0 (not visible at all) to 100 (completely visible) for each surface and that the numbers need not sum to any particular number. They were further advised that their judgments should be based upon the first clear image that came to mind and that they should try to hold that image until they had performed the four judgments. These additional instructions were included because a pilot study revealed that some subjects performed various transformations on their images while making the judgments. These four judgments were performed for all 12 experimental objects. The task required a single session lasting about 30 min.

Photography Task.   Twenty-eight undergraduate subjects were run individually in a single session. Each subject first familiarized himself/herself with the 12 objects. The experimenter then pointed out that each object could be viewed from many different perspectives using a model of a dog as an example. The subject was then told that he/she was to imagine clearly a particular object and then to use the camera to take a photograph of the object that best depicted the image they generated. The subject was further instructed to base the photograph on the first image that came to mind. The experimenter then gave the subject an instant camera and instructed him/her in its use. After imagining each object named, the subject placed the object on a tabletop, photographed it according to the instructions, and then removed the object.

Judging Perspectives from Photographs.   Eight paid subjects were each given a packet of 40 photographs for each of the 12 experimental objects. Each packet consisted of 28 photos taken by subjects in the photography experiment and the 12 photos used as stimuli in the goodness rating experiment. These pictures were randomly ordered within packets and the order of packets was randomized across subjects. The judges were asked to determine the visibility of the front, back, side, and top surfaces in each picture using the real object as a reference. Each surface was rated on a scale from 0 (not visible) to 100 (completely visible). They were told to use the same criterion for each picture of the same object. As soon as the subject had finished rating all 40 pictures of an object, he/she continued with another packet until all 12 objects had been rated. The judges worked independently.

Results and Discussion

To provide an intuitive feel for the qualitative results of the goodness rating task, consider Fig. 8.1 and 8.2. The pictures shown in Fig. 8.1 are, in fact, those that received the highest mean goodness ratings for each of the 12 experimental objects. Figure 8.2 shows mean goodness ratings beneath each view of the horse from the standard set. Not unexpectedly, there was very high agreement among subjects on the best and worst views, with more variability at intermediate levels of the scale.

The primary quantitative data consist of the visibilities of front, back, side, and top surfaces for each of six perspective views of each of the 12 objects. The six views correspond to (1) the internal image generated by subjects in the imagery task; (2) the picture taken in the photography task; (3) the standard picture given the highest mean rating (H); (4) the standard picture given the lowest mean rating (L); and (5 and 6) the two standard pictures whose goodness ratings were closest to equal spacings between the best and worst pictures (MH and ML). These data were analyzed for agreement across different tasks in several ways.

Correlations between Surface Visibilities. Correlation coefficients were computed on the mean visibility ratings of front, back, side, and top surfaces for pairs of perspective views. That is, for a given pair of views—say, the best standard picture of the car and the subject's image of the car—the correlation was computed between the mean visibility ratings of the front, back, side, and top surfaces of the best standard picture and the mean visibility ratings of the front, back, side, and top surfaces in the image. To the extent that the best standard picture and the image are from the same perspective, these two sets of visibility ratings should be highly correlated for corresponding surfaces. Such correlations were computed for individual objects (on just 4 data points for each object) as well as for the whole object set (on 48 data points). These correlations among the imagery task, photography task, and best picture from the goodness rating task are all quite high, as shown in Table 8.1. The only exception is the piano for which the correlation fell substantially below the .80 to .99 range typical for the rest of the objects. The difference is mainly that the imagery and photography subjects included a substantial amount of the top surface of the piano, whereas the goodness ratings did not reflect as much salience for the top.

As another indication of the consistent relationship among the results from the three tasks, correlation coefficients were also computed between surface visibility ratings from the imagery and photography tasks versus the medium good, medium bad, and worst pictures as well as the best picture from the standard set. These correlations (averaged over objects) are plotted in Fig. 8.3. Note that correlations for both tasks fall off sharply with mean rated goodness of the standard pictures. Thus, the pattern of correlation is just what would be expected if the imagery, photography, and goodness rating tasks were measuring the same underlying variables: High ratings were given to standard pictures whose perspective is most similar to that in subjects' images and photographs, and low ratings were given to those whose perspective is most different.

Canonical Correlations.   Caution must be exercised in interpreting these correlations, however, because they are not simple correlations in the usual statistical sense of a measure of the relationship between one simple variable and another. The visibilities of the front, back, side, and top surfaces of an object in a particular view are actually four different and highly dependent variables that collectively are presumed to define the perspective view. Thus, in order to compare one view (in terms of the visibilities of their component surfaces in both cases), a correlational analysis is required that treats these visibilities as a set of measures that collectively define a single variable: the perspective view of the object. This technique, known as *canonical correlational analysis,* may be conceptualized as the simple correlation between two composite variables (or canonical variates). One canonical variate is a linear composite of the visibilities of the front, back, side, and top surfaces in one perspective view, and the other is a linear composite of the visibilities for the same surfaces in another perspective view. (Both linear composites are determined by estimating weights for each variable in both composites in order to maximize the resulting canonical correlation.) To the extent that (1) the correlation between these canonical variates is statistically significant; and (2) the linear composition of the canonical variates is the same for the two data sets, one is justified in concluding that the two data sets are related to each other by the same underlying psychological variable.

Canonical correlations were performed for a number of different pairs of perspective views. First, the visibilities of fronts, backs, sides, and tops of

TABLE 8.1
Correlations among Surface Visibility Ratings for Different Examples of
Canonical Perspective

Object	Best/Photo	Best/Image	Photo/Image	Mean
Pencil sharpener	.99	.99	.99	.99
Clock	.99	.99	.99	.99
Horse	.99	.98	.98	.98
Car	.99	.96	.99	.98
Teapot	.99	.96	.97	.98
Steam iron	.99	.96	.96	.97
Telephone	.95	.88	.97	.94
Shoe	.99	.88	.90	.93
House	.77	.98	.82	.86
Chair	.73	.85	.97	.85
Camera	.89	.68	.94	.83
Grand piano	.42	.43	.98	.61
All objects	.85	.84	.94	.88

Note: Best = best standard picture, Photo = photograph taken by subjects, Image = image generated by subjects.

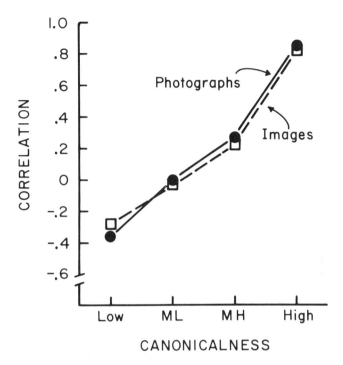

FIG. 8.3.   Correlation coefficients comparing four standard pictures (H, MH, ML, and L goodness levels) with subjects images and photographs in terms of visibilities of front, back, side, and top surfaces.

objects in subjects' images were compared to those in the H, MH, ML, and L standard pictures. The only photographs to correlate significantly with the image data were the highly canonical (H) pictures, $R = .9912$, $X^2(16) = 36.48$. In addition, the compositions of the canonical variates over the visibility ratings are quite similar for the two data sets. Therefore, we conclude that the two canonical variates have the same underlying structure and both correspond to the same perspective view.

A second set of canonical correlations were performed in the same way for surface visibilities in the subjects' own photographs and the H, MH, ML, and L standard pictures. Once again, only the highly canonical pictures from the standard set correlated significantly with the subjects' photographs, $R = 0.9996$, $X^2(16) = 64.80$. The compositions of the canonical variates for this analysis again indicate that they correspond to the same perspective view.

Finally, canonical correlations were performed comparing surface visibilities of objects in images with those in subjects' own photographs. These two sets of data are also highly correlated, $R = .9915$, $X^2(16) = 58.44$. Once more, the analysis indicates that the canonical variates have the same underlying structure and correspond to the same perspective view. Therefore we conclude that there is a reliable relationship between the results of each pair of tasks and that the three tasks converge on an underlying variable related to canonicalness.

OBJECT RECOGNITION

Given that there is a canonical perspective for an object, our central hypothesis is that it should be the most recognizable view. If it contains more of the salient information about the object than any other view, and if this information can be processed simultaneously, then it should be more quickly and easily mapped into the appropriate internal object category than any other view.

Subjects were shown a picture of an object and were asked to name it from a known set of alternatives as quickly as possible. Response latency and accuracy were taken to reflect facility of object recognition. Four pictures from the standard set were used to define high (H), medium high (MH), medium low (ML), and low (L) levels of canonicalness for each of the 12 experimental objects. We expected recognition latencies to decrease monotonically as a function of increasing canonicalness.

A second aspect of perspective in object recognition was also investigated in this experiment. We were interested in the extent to which prior information about perspective would affect performance in the object-naming task. Prior perspective information was given in the form of a description of the surfaces that were visible—front, back, side, top, or some combination of these. If canonicalness affects object recognition simply because of showing unexpected surfaces (e.g., the top and back sides), then prior knowledge about the presence of such surfaces should eliminate the difference between views high and low in canonicalness. However, if the effect of canonicalness depends only on the information available in different views rather than on the type of view per se, then prior perspective information should not decrease it.

Method

Stimuli.   Each of the 12 experimental objects was shown at four different levels of canonicalness: high (H), medium high (MH), medium low (ML), and low (L). The pictures were chosen from the set described previously and were classified into the four levels of canonicalness based on the subjective ratings from the previous study.

The pictures were selected such that no subject saw the same picture twice. Two different sets of pictures were constructed, one for the primed trials and another for the umprimed trials, for different groups of subjects. These two sets were balanced across subjects so that half saw one set in the primed trials and half saw that same set in the unprimed trials. The two sets were equated as much as possible for goodness ratings within canonicalness conditions and for types of perspectives.

Procedure.   Subjects first familiarized themselves with each of the 15 objects (12 experimental plus 3 practice objects) and were given the names for each that would be used in the experiment. They were encouraged to pick each one up and to view it from all perspectives. They were told that their task would be to name each test picture as quickly as possible and that the pictures would show the objects from different points of view.

On half the trials, subjects received no prior information about perspective (unprimed trials) and on half the trials they saw a perspective description (primed trials). Unprimed trials began with the appearance of an asterisk. Subjects were told that on such trials they were to respond as soon as they were ready to see the next picture. The response was to press a "clicker" with their thumb; this noise triggered the voice-operated relay that, in turn, stopped the clock. After a 500-msec delay, the test object was presented, and subjects were required to name the object as quickly as they could. The naming latency was measured using the voice-operated relay that was activated by onset of the naming response. The experimenter recorded the verbal response.

Primed trials began with the description of a perspective. Subjects were asked to use this description by imagining a pedestal on which the to-be-presented object would be placed in the described perspective and to make the preparatory "clicker" response after having done so. Following a 500-msec delay, the test picture was presented, and the subject named the object as quickly as possible.

The experiment began with 24 practice trials identical to the following experimental trials except for the objects used (a dog, cup, and train). The 96 experimental trials were presented in four blocks of 24. One primed and one unprimed trial for each of the 12 objects were included in each block. Each level of canonicalness appeared three times per block in random order. Four orderings of the blocks were constructed according to a Latin-square design, each of which was presented to 14 subjects. A total of 56 undergraduates participated. They were tested individually in a single session of about 45 min.

Results and Discussion

Latencies for both initial preparation responses and later recognition responses were recorded to the nearest millisecond. Error trials were discarded so that only latencies for correct trials entered the anlaysis.

Average latencies to name objects in test pictures are plotted in Fig. 8.4 as a function of canonicalness for primed and unprimed conditions. The overall analysis of these data indicated significant effects due to canonicalness, $F(3, 120) = 107.74$, $p < .01$, perspective priming, $F(1, 40) = 9.22$, $p < .01$, and the interaction of these two factors, $F(3, 120) = 5.86$, $p < .01$. Several higher-order interactions were also significant, particularly those involving the two different stimulus sets used in balancing, but they are of no particular theoretical interest.

For both the primed and unprimed conditions, naming latencies decreased monotonically as a function of increasing canonicalness. The fact that naming

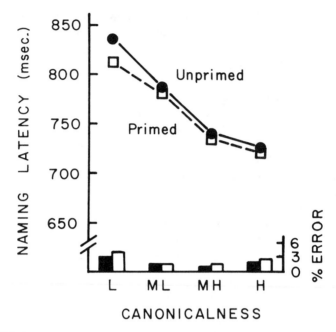

FIG. 8.4.   Mean recognition latencies and error rates for the naming task plotted
as a function of canonicalness in primed and unprimed perspective conditions.

was faster on trials primed with perspective information indicates that subjects *are* able to make use of prior perspective information. It reduces the slope of the function by reducing latencies at the lowest level of canonicalness. This suggests that knowing the general perspective can aid in perceiving very bad views of objects. Even for these extreme cases, however, the facilitating effect of prior knowledge is only about 30 msec.

Error rates for naming were very low (see bottom of Fig. 8.4). The only significant effect was due to canonicalness, $F(3, 120) = 4.41$, $p < .05$. Errors were slightly more frequent for the worst views than for others. The decrease in latency for primed trials was not accompanied by any significant increase in errors, $F(1, 40) = 1.42$, $p > .10$, implying that a speed/accuracy tradeoff was not responsible for the latency effect.

In general, then, highly canonical views of objects are more quickly and accurately identified than highly uncanonical views. The latency results show that the majority of the effect takes place for the poorest views, as though object recognition is impaired primarily in those cases in which very few characteristics of the object are represented in the picture. Prior information about perspective decreases the effect of canonicalness slightly, but only for the poorest views. It does not seem that people are able to prepare themselves perceptually for an unknown object in a specific perspective. In this respect, the current results are consistent with previous studies showing that people cannot prepare for an unknown letter in a particular orientation (Cooper & Shepard, 1973). However, it may be possible to eliminate the effects of canonicalness on object processing by giving prior information about both the object and its perspective in a verification task.

DETERMINANTS OF CANONICALNESS

Thus far we have shown that several operational definitions converge on the construct of canonical perspective and that canonicalness influences perceptual processing in object recognition. The final experiment concerns predicting canonicalness from stimulus attributes of pictures, knowledge of objects, and the relation between the two.

We said at the outset than an object's canonical perspective is the view that reveals the most information of greatest salience about it. There are two main components to this definition: the revealing of "object information" and the "salience" of that information. The first has to do with the fact that any two-dimensional projection of a three-dimensional object reveals some aspects of the object and not others. The second concerns the perceiver's familiarity with the revealed aspects and their importance within his/her knowledge about objects. Together, the objective, geometrical information and its perceptual salience determine the "subjective information content" of a given view. This, we claim, is what is maximized in canonical perspective.

In the following experiment this idea was pursued. We use surface visibility ratings for all 12 views of each object to try to predict the goodness ratings obtained for them. The rationale is that these visibility ratings reflect the amount of information available about the object in the picture. If information content is an important variable, then the goodness ratings should be predictable from visibility ratings. Other subjects rated the importance of each of these four sides for each object to determine whether the surfaces whose visibilities best predict the goodness ratings are felt to be the most important ones according to their intuitions.

Method

Surface Visibility Rating.   Eight paid graduate student judges rated each of the 12 standard perspective views of each of the 12 experimental objects for the visibilities of the front, back, side, and top surfaces. The procedure for obtaining these ratings was the same as reported earlier except that the ratings were made on a scale from 1 (highly visible) to 7 (not visible at all).

Surface Importance Rating.   Eight other graduate students, tested in a single group session, were shown each object in turn and asked to rate the importance of each surface (front, back, side, and top) for the object's identity. The ratings were made on a scale from 1 (very important) to 7 (very unimportant).

Results and Discussion

Surface Visibility Ratings. Regression analyses were performed on the goodness rating data for the standard pictures of real objects using the visibility ratings of the front, back, side, and top surfaces as predictors. Separate analyses yielded significant multiple correlations for each individual object. These ranged from .99 for the car and clock to .83 for the pencil sharpener, with the average correlation being .95 across all objects. These results are presented in more detail in Table 8.2. The regression weights for each surface are presented in this table to give some indication of the predictive power of different surfaces for different objects. By and large, the front and side surfaces accounted for most of the variance, although the particular surfaces with highest weightings differed greatly from one object to another. For example, the front of the clock, the side of the horse, and the top of the shoe are all highly weighted, whereas the side of the clock, the top of the horse, and the front of the shoe are not. Still, a single analysis for all 12 objects together showed that the visibility of the front and side surfaces alone accounted for over 50% of the variance. This is rather remarkable, considering that the identity of the object is not taken into account.

The weighting parameters for front, back, side, and top estimated by the regression model have a natural interpretation as surface salience. If the canonicalness of perspective is assumed to be an additive, linear function of the amount

TABLE 8.2
Regression Weights (beta), Importance Ratings (Imp.) and
Multiple Correlations (*R*) for Surfaces of Experimental Objects

	Front		*Back*		*Side*		*Top*		
	beta	*Imp.*	*beta*	*Imp.*	*beta*	*Imp.*	*beta*	*Imp.*	*R*
House	.55	1.25	.47	3.50	.09	4.50	−.33	5.75	.97*
Chair	.51	1.50	.00	5.00	.13	2.25	−.23	5.25	.95*
Car	.26	2.00	.27	2.90	.34	1.13	−.16	3.75	.99*
Horse	.17	1.88	−.15	3.75	.46	1.50	−.27	4.75	.94*
Camera	.46	1.13	−.08	4.25	.08	4.37	.15	3.37	.98*
Iron	.27	3.25	.07	4.75	.49	1.37	.11	3.50	.96*
Telephone	.49	1.12	.03	3.25	.08	2.12	.05	1.87	.96*
Teapot	.14	4.12	.04	5.62	.69	1.12	.32	3.37	.98*
Piano	.65	1.62	.07	4.25	.31	2.88	.12	2.38	.97*
Shoe	.16	3.50	.00	4.62	.37	1.25	.35	1.65	.93*
Pencil sharpener	.11	2.75	.03	3.62	.33	1.75	−.16	4.00	.83*
Clock	.77	1.00	.32	4.37	.08	4.87	−.05	5.75	.99*

*p < .01

and salience of the information it contains, and if the amount of information is measured (albeit crudely) by the visibility ratings, then the weights estimated for the visibilities should correspond to the saliences of the information on that surface. To determine whether these weights are psychologically meaningful, they are compared to the importance ratings for the same surface of the same object (see Table 8.2). The correlation between these ratings and the regression weights was .77, $t(46) = 8.29$, $p < .01$. This is a highly respectable amount of agreement, considering that the visibility and importance ratings were made by different subjects (who may have different ideas about what constitutes these surfaces for some objects) and for many different objects (which may not have been rated on exactly the same scale). Perhaps even more impressive is the fact that there are only four violations out of 72 ordinal predictions that can be made for the importance ratings of the surfaces of an object on the basis of the corresponding beta weights.

Together these results demonstrate a clear relationship between the canonicalness of a perspective view and the subjective information it contains about an object. Both the visibility of surfaces and their importance for the identity of the object are critical aspects of canonicalness. The fact that fronts are the most important surfaces for predicting the goodness ratings and are also the most frequently interacted with surfaces of most objects suggests that familiarity and function play a substantial role in determining the importance of various aspects of objects.

Of course, in the case of many objects, the front also contains the most information, and so familiarity and information content are confounded. Further research using novel three-dimensional objects (similar to those used by Shepard & Metzler, 1971) shows that similar effects of canonicalness are present even for objects that subjects have never seen before. The importance of informational variables in this case is unquestionable: Factors such as the number of visible edges and surfaces account for about 80% of the variance in goodness ratings of pictures taken from 35 different viewpoints.

GENERAL DISCUSSION

We began by pointing out that several diverse traditions lead one to expect there to be privileged or canonical perspectives for perceiving objects. We then showed that three operational definitions converge on an underlying psychological variable consistent with this idea. A speeded naming task demonstrated that this variable substantially influenced the ease of object recognition. Perspectives judged highly canonical were identified more quickly and accurately. These results also showed that perspective priming alters the effects of canonicalness, but only slightly. Finally, we showed that canonicalness is strongly associated with informational variables—the visibility of aspects of objects—for the real-world objects used in the preceding experiments.

In discussing the notion of canonical perspective we have focused exclusively on the *direction* of view. If canonical perspective is conceived as a particular real-world point of view, then there should also be a *distance* component. The same object from the same direction but at different distances should produce different goodness ratings, different identification performance, different preferences among images, and so forth. Along these lines, Hagen and Elliott (1976) have shown that when picture size is held constant, people prefer pictures taken from relatively long distances in which perspective convergence is not extreme. There is some question, of course, about the extent to which preference for pictorial representations coincides with superior perceptual performance.

In its most general form, then, the concept of canonical perspective for viewing an object is a particular station point from which it is optimally perceivable. Put this way, it becomes obvious that canonicalness is not really concerned with two-dimensional pictures but with any sort of stationary view of three-dimensional objects. It would be equally sensible to talk about canonicalness as a variable operating *after* depth information were processed from a real, three-dimensional scene. The reduced information available from two-dimensional projections probably increases the potential effect of canonicalness, but it is fundamentally a phenomenon associated with *viewpoint* rather than with reduced stimulus dimensionality.

There are many possible interpretations of the present phenomena in terms of process models. In many ways the most obvious is that given in the introduction: There may exist an essentially perspectiveless representation of the object in memory onto which the current representation is mapped as a subset. To the extent that some perspectives include more information about the object (i.e., constitute a larger informational subset) than others, they will have better access to the appropriate object representation. Such a view attributes the effects of canonicalness to the nature of the mapping process. It is also possible, however, that canonicalness reflects the nature of the underlying representation in memory. There is a tendency to assume that "deep" object representations are perspectiveless in the sense of representing all surfaces in equal degree simultaneously. There are a number of ways in which this might be untrue. The memory representation might be (1) some composite, object-centered description in which perspective is implicitly represented by differential weighting of various parts; (2) some organized collection of representations of particular views; or even (3) the representation of a particular view together with heuristic rules and/or transformations for mapping other views onto it. Although the last two ideas seem rather implausible, they are still possibilities and cannot be dismissed out of hand. In fact, they are, if anything, more easily reconciled with the close relationship between object recognition and imagery than the more abstract alternatives.

Canonical perspectives were described as being *privileged* with respect to people's internal conceptions about objects. We used this language deliberately in order to point to the empirical nature of our results and to avoid commitment to one or another of the previous alternatives. Although the mechanisms underlying the effects of canonical perspective are not clear, the phenomenon itself is undeniable. That certain perspectives are judged ''better'' than others, that the same perspectives are spontaneously experienced in imagery, and that these perspectives are also the most easily recognized views, all demonstrate that people's concepts of objects contain at least implicit aspects of perspective.

ACKNOWLEDGMENTS

This research was supported in part by Grant 1-R01-MH33103-01 from the National Institute of Mental Health to the first author and by Grant 1-R01-MH24316-02 from the National Institute of Mental Health to the second author. We wish to thank Ruth Kimchi and Dan Morrow for their help in collecting and analyzing some of the data reported here.

REFERENCES

Cooper, L. A., & Shepard, R. N. Chronometric studies in the rotation of mental images. In W. G. Chase (Ed.), *Visual information processing*. New York: Academic Press, 1973.

Gibson, J. J. *The ecological approach to visual perception*. Boston: Houghton-Mifflin, 1979.

Hagen, M. A., & Elliott, H. B. An investigation of the relationship between viewing condition and preference for true and modified linear perspective with adults. *Journal of Experimental Psychology: Human Perception and Performance*, 1976, *2*, 479–490.

Merleau-Ponty, M. *Phenomenology of perception*. London: Routledge & Kegan Paul, 1962.

Mervis, C. B., & Rosch, E. Categorization of natural objects. In M. R. Rosenzweig & L. W. Porter (Eds.), *Annual review of psychology*, 1981.

Minsky, M. A framework for representing knowledge. In P. H. Winston (Ed.), *The psychology of computer vision*. New York: McGraw-Hill, 1975.

Palmer, S. E. Visual perception and world knowledge: Notes on a model of sensory-cognitive interaction. In D. A. Norman & D. E. Rumelhart (Eds.), *Explorations in cognition*. San Francisco: Freeman, 1975.

Rosch, E. Cognitive representations of semantic categories. *Journal of Experimental Psychology: General*, 1975, *104*, 193–233.

Rosch, E. Principles of categorization. In E. Rosch & B. Lloyd (Eds.), *Cognition and categorization*. Hillsdale, N.J.: Lawrence Erlbaum Associates, 1978.

Shepard, R. N., & Metzler, J. Mental rotation of three-dimensional objects. *Science*, 1971, *171*, 701–703.

9 Intersegmental Coordination During Reaching at Natural Visual Objects

Marc Jeannerod
Laboratoire de Neuropsychologie Experimentale
I.N.S.E.R.M. - Unite 94
Bron, France

ABSTRACT

The perception of scenes and objects can be studied by examining motor interactions with them. The question addressed here is the relation between the use of visual information related to extrinsic properties of an object (its location and orientation relative to the perceiver) and that related to its intrinsic properties (its shape and size). Reaching and grasping movements directed at natural objects were studied by film records. It is assumed that such movements involve a transportation component carrying the hand to the object's location and a manipulation component shaping the hand in anticipation of the grasp. Time-course and dynamic aspects of these components were measured in a normal situation (i.e., allowing visual cues from the moving hand) and in a situation where the hand was not visible during the movement (open-loop situation). Movement duration, peak velocity of each component, and hand shaping were unaffected by the open-loop situation. Only terminal precision of the transportation component was affected, resulting in undershooting with respect to object location. The two components appeared to have a significant covariation on the time axis. A single point on the two curves of instantaneous velocity was found to remain time-invariant across different conditions of movement execution (e.g., normal or open-loop, different distances, different size for the target object). Within this time constraint, an unexpected alteration of the object size when the movement started only influenced the manipulation component. The transportation component was not affected by this perturbation. These results are interpreted in terms of an open-loop control of independent visuomotor channels by visual input. A temporal frame common to all the participating channels seems to limit the expression of this control. The treatment of object location is not affected by object shape. However, the perceptual-motor consequences of object shape are constrained by those of object location. In the person–scene interactions studied here, information about extrinsic and about intrinsic properties have a hierarchic relationship in the organization of perception and action.

INTRODUCTION

Objects located within visual space are phenomenal entities. They give rise to the subjective experience of perceptual unity and constancy, whereby a given object will still appear as the same, despite different orientations, different angles of exposure, or different distances of viewing. This can be taken as an indication that objects are internally represented as holistic events rather than as the mere addition of their physical properties. Sensory systems, however, are known to detect features, not objects. Perceptual unity is thus the net result of complex processes involving a parallel activation of different sensory channels. Objects have to be split into "elemental" visual features (or properties) like size, shape, texture, or color, each of them being assumed to activate a specific visual mechanism. Such properties belong intrinsically to objects (we shall refer to them as their intrinsic properties) and are constituents of their identity.

When object perception is considered in the behavioral context, another set of properties emerges. The fact that objects are handleable or graspable implies that they are distinct from the perceiver (i.e., that they are located at some distance from the body surface). One school of thought would even argue that object-oriented action is a condition for perceptual "reality" of objects. According to Von Fieandt (1974), for example, objects are discriminated from one another only to the extent that they are independent objects of manipulation or activity. This would radically differentiate objects from patterns that are purely perceptual events and do not represent goals for action. In the case of patterns, viewer-centered spatial location would represent an irrelevant property. Concerning objects, however, egocentric spatial or extrinsic (as opposed to intrinsic) properties like orientation, distance with respect to the body, location in the frontal plane, or direction and velocity of motion are essential attributes for directing action. In addition, determination of spatial coordinates of an object results from neural mechanisms involving activation of structures or "channels" that are probably different from those accounting for detection of intrinsic properties (Trevarthen, 1968).

The question now arises whether intrinsic and extrinsic properties represent independent sets of descriptions of the same object or whether they are mutually dependent as postulated by the previously mentioned action–perception continuum theory. A study of object-directed movements such as reaching and grasping might represent a good approach to this problem. Accordingly, the question now becomes: Are these movements organized on the basis of separate motor components corresponding to dissociable sensory channels and perceptual descriptions, or can they be considered as unitary? And a subsidiary question could be: How can unity of the object-directed movement be achieved out of the probable channel organization at the input level?

The first hypothesis postulates the existence of visuomotor channels activated in parallel by a specific visual input and controlling a specific part of the arm musculature. Accordingly, processing of the spatial properties of the object would result in activation of proximal muscles (e.g., at the shoulder joint) although processing of its intrinsic properties would feed into muscles of more distal segments (e.g., fingers). As a consequence, reaching and grasping can be tentatively divided into components, one component dealing with transportation of the hand at the vicinity of the target and another one dealing with forming a finger grip properly sized and oriented.

As already stated, this hypothesis implies that properties like location in space and shape are independent paramaters of an object. It implies that the hand has to be brought near the object in order to grasp and manipulate but that the spatial locus where grasping occurs will in no way affect it (provided the target remains within reach). This is better conceived when the reaching movement is directed at a moving object. In that case, the hand can be observed to keep a fixed anticipatory posture while it is transported by the proximal segments that act as a pure tracking system.

Neurophysiology provides other justifications for dividing reaching into transportation and manipulation components. Neural pathways controlling the proximal and distal muscle groups have a different organization (Brinkman & Kuypers, 1973) and their maturation follows a different time course (Kuypers, 1962). Specific lesions can alter visually controlled grasping without significantly affecting the transportation component (Haaxma & Kuypers, 1975). (See Jeannerod & Biguer, 1981, for review.)

Another hypothesis about the organization of reaching is that of a single act based on a unified percept of the object. Although this notion would be more difficult to formalize in neurophysiological terms, it appears to be closer to current thinking about "motor programming." According to this hypothesis, one assumes that a reaching movement is controlled by a unique program containing motor commands for accommodating the main graspable properties of the object (i.e., both intrinsic and extrinsic properties). The program would thus bear strong relationships to the internal "holistic" representation of the object. One consequence of this attitude is that a movement directed at a given object should no longer be described as the result of separate components aiming at individual goals. It would be more accurately described as the displacement of a single point in space. A good analogy would be the trajectory in the dark of a small luminous source placed somewhere at the center of gravity of the fingertips. The resulting description of the movement would consider only the matching of the luminous source with, say, the center of gravity of the object and would ignore elemental aspects of the movement, such as the number of joints involved. Along the same lines, Kugler, Kelso, and Turvey (1980) postulate the existence of "coordinative structures," understood as a group of muscles temporarily constrained to act as a single functional unit. The timing of the impulses to individual muscles would arise from the design specifications of the muscle collective. Hence, the program would contain only minimal instructions and would rely for its execution on peripheral constraints. Such a model certainly represents an extreme case of holistic programming where the motor act would be only grossly specified by the building up of the appropriate coordinative structure.

However, at least in the case of reaching movements, the notion of uniqueness of the program is not incompatible with that of parallel visuomotor channels. Bernstein (1967), for instance, expresses the view that "elementary engrams" controlling the execution of individual elements of a movement have to exist independently from the other, more general, engram (the "ecphorator") that controls the law of succession of these elements. He also states that the pattern of impulses over time (as released by the "ecphorator") may have very little in common with the picture of the movement, becasue the program in fact adjusts to the external force field generated by the moving segments. A similar duality has been expressed by Arbib (1980) in formalizing our own early results on object-directed reaching movements (Jeannerod & Biguer, 1981). Arbib's model involves a distributed motor program accounting for the various components of the movement. "Motor schemas" for each component represented in the program shape their parameter values on the basis of identification algorithms received from closely related "perceptual schemas." Besides these data paths, a control path is supposed to activate the motor program as a whole.

In our experiment we had recorded the onset of EMG activation of the different muscle groups controlling, respectively, the transportation component (biceps brachii) and the manipulation component (extensor digitorum). The typical pattern of results was that both muscle groups begin to contract at about the same time, that is, within less than 25 msec (with a constant advantage, though not statistically significant, for the finger extensor). Similar patterns of synchronous activation can be observed in movements involving orientation of gaze toward a target and pointing the hand at the same target (Jeannerod & Biguer, 1981); in movements involving orientation of head and eyes (Warabi, 1977); and in movements involving both arms (Kelso, Southard, & Goodman, 1979). Quasisimultaneity of commands for the several components of the same motor act seems an obvious argument for the existence of a unique program structure controlling its execution. Peripheral constraints (Bernstein's external force field) would then account for the phenomenal appearance of the motor act, a notion that is also implicit in Kugler et al.'s (1980) model.

The experiments to be reported here are aimed at describing natural reaching and grasping movements. For the sake of description, we assume that reaching (transportation) and grasping (manipulation) are separable components of a global act directed at an object. We shall try to determine how these two components are matched in time and/or space with respect to their common goal and then discuss the implications of our findings for theories of perceptual-motor programming.

GENERAL METHOD

Apparatus

During the experimental session, subjects were seated in front of a cubicle (68 cm high × 100 cm wide × 70 cm deep) placed on a tabletop on which target objects were displayed. The cubicle was separated horizontally into two equal compartments by a semireflecting mirror. Subjects looked through a 15 cm × 18 cm window in the upper compartment and placed their hand in the lower compartment. In the first situation, the target object was placed on the table in the lower compartment, so that the subject could see it directly through the semireflecting mirror. During movements directed at the target the subject could also see his hand. This situation will be referred to as the "normal" situation. In the second situation, a mask was inserted below the mirror, so that the lower compartment was no longer visible. In this case, target objects were displayed from the top of the upper compartment. Because the mirror was placed halfway between the object display and the table, subjects could see in the mirror a virtual image of the object projecting at the level of the table. Another object identical to that displayed in the mirror was placed directly on the table in coincidence with the virtual image seen in the mirror. This setup resulted in a situation where the subject reached for the virtual image below the mirror without seeing his hand and met the second, real, object at the expected location. This situation is referred to as the "visual open-loop" situation (Held & Gottlieb, 1958).

Procedure

Subjects were required to perform rapid and accurate movements and to grasp the objects as precisely as possible and lift them. At the beginning of each trial, they had to place their hand on a stand near their body axis and keep it in a relaxed posture (i.e., in the prone position with the fingers semiflexed). While a new object was displayed, subjects kept their eyes closed, until they heard an acoustic signal. Finally, the subjects had to wait between 2 and 10 sec, until a small light in front of them was turned off, before performing the reaching movement.

Data Processing

Reaching movements were recorded on 16 mm cine-films, by using a camera running at 50 frames per second. Film data were processed by projecting single frames on a screen with a one-to-one magnification. The position in space of the subject's wrist was plotted across successive frames. In addition, for each frame, the distance between the tip of the thumb and the tip of the index was measured. Finally typical hand postures were drawn for each movement directly from the screen (see Fig. 9.1).

EXPERIMENT 1

The main goal of the first experiment was to assess the principal characteristics of the transportation and manipulation components of reaching movements, in both the normal and the visual open-loop situation.

The targets were simple three-dimensional objects, namely a small rod (10-cm length × 2-mm diameter) displayed vertically, a heavy cylinder (10-cm length × 5.5-cm diameter) displayed horizontally, and a sphere (4-cm diameter). These are shown in Fig. 9.2. Shape and orientation of objects were chosen in order to minimize wrist rotation during the movement. Objects were displayed in the frontal medial plane, at 40 cm from the body. In one session, however, distance from the body was varied randomly over trials (25, 32, and 40 cm). Presentation of the three objects was randomized across trials. A maximum of 30 trials per subject were recorded on film. Five subjects were studied.

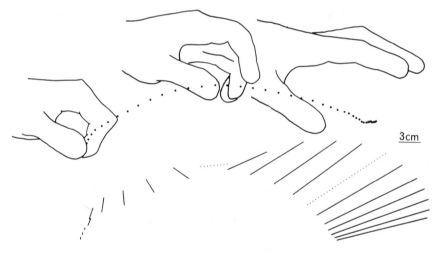

3cm

FIG. 9.1.   Methods used for data processing. Upper row: Processing of the transportation component. Dots represent successive positions of the hand every 20 msec. Outlines of the hand are redrawn directly from the screen. Lower row: Processing of the manipulation component. Each line represents the size of the finger grip on successive frames (in this case, every 40 msec). The two dotted lines correspond to the two finger grips drawn in the upper row. The single movement represented here is a reaching movement directed at the cylinder, in the open-loop situation.

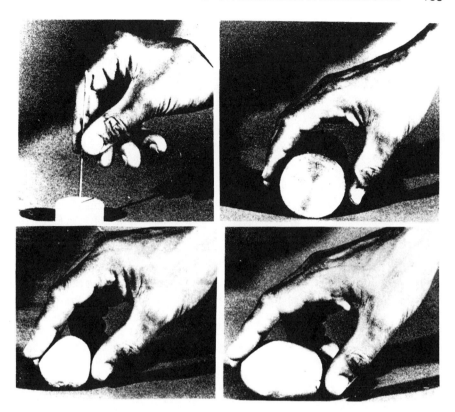

FIG. 9.2.   Objects used as targets. The two upper objects (rod and cylinder) and the sphere at the lower left were used in Experiment 1. The two lower objects were used in Experiment 2.

Results

Movement duration varied widely across subjects, but variation was less marked within individual subjects. For movements of an amplitude of 40 cm, mean duration ranged between 718.6 msec (s.d. = 102.1) in the fastest subject and 1176.6 msec (s.d. = 124.7) in the slowest. Standard deviation ranged between 10% and 17% of the mean, except for one subject where it reached 25%. As often observed for this type of movement since Woodworth (1899), the position-against-time profile of the transportation component consistently fitted an S-shaped curve. The first derivative of the position curve (movement velocity) showed a fast rise time with a sharp peak (see Fig. 9.3, upper figures). Maximum velocity also varied from one subject to another, between about 80 cm/sec and about 135 cm/sec (for 40-cm movements). Although maximum velocity was found to be uncorrelated with movement duration on the overall sample (r =

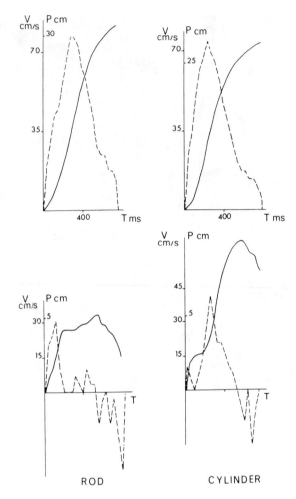

FIG. 9.3. Velocity and position profiles of two reaching movements. The two diagrams on the left correspond to a movement directed at a small object (rod); the two diagrams on the right, to a large object (cylinder). Upper row: Transportation component. Note similar position (*P*, solid line) and velocity (*V*, dashed line) profiles for the two movements. Lower row: Manipulation component. Note different position and velocity profiles according to the object size.

0.13, n.s.), subjects making movements of shorter duration tended to have higher velocities.

In one session, where the distance of the target was varied systematically, maximum velocity was found to increase almost linearly ($r = 0.96$) with movement amplitude.

The part of the velocity-against-time curve corresponding to movement deceleration was consistently marked by a rather brisk change in slope. Beyond this "breakpoint," and until completion of the movement, deceleration tended to be slower. In some subjects a constant velocity plateau was maintained during this terminal part of the movement until it came to an abrupt stop on contact with the object. Duration of this low-velocity phase was between 150 msec and 250 msec, although it never exceeded one-third of the total movement duration.

The previously mentioned dynamic characteristics of reaching movements were not affected by whether the visual feedback loop was open or closed. Duration and maximum velocity were similar in both situations. The low-velocity phase at the end of the movement was present both when the hand was visible during the movement and when it was not. The only significant difference between movements in the two situations was the frequent occurrence of a small undershoot of the hand with respect to the target, when the visual loop was open (see Fig. 9.4).

The manipulation component appeared to have more complex position profiles than the transportation component. This may be partly due to the planar two-dimensional projection of the fingers' trajectory made during measurement on the screen. The first obvious feature of this component was that the fingers opened up to a maximum grip aperture, which was a function of the anticipated object's size, although it was always greater than that which the actual size of the object would require. Hence, after the maximum grip aperture had been reached, the fingers began to close in anticipation of contact with the object. Position in

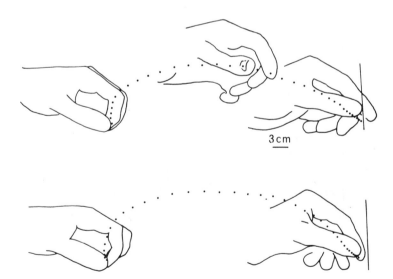

FIG. 9.4. Pattern of reaching movements in the open-loop situation. In this situation only the object, not the moving limb, is seen by the subject. Notice perfect shaping of the hand according to the size and to the shape of the object (a small rod). In the lower movement, notice a final error, due to hypometria. As in Fig. 9.3, the slowing down of the transportation component at the end of the trajectory is clearly present, even in the open-loop situation.

time of the point of maximal aperture was independent of the size of the aperture itself; rather, this point appeared to be located at a constant time whatever the amplitude of the grip (i.e., whatever the size of the object). This feature is exemplified in Fig. 9.5 where position profiles of finger aperture for two objects of different size are shown for two different subjects.

As the lower part of Fig. 9.3 shows, the velocity pattern of the manipulation component also depended on the object's size and shape.

Closing or opening the visual feedback loop did not influence the timing of the grip, nor the grip pattern itself. As seen from Fig. 9.4, anticipated finger posturing with respect to object size and shape appears to be remarkably preserved in the open-loop situation.

An attempt was made to correlate the temporal invariance of the point of maximum grip aperture (from the manipulation component) with aspects of the transportation component. This is illustrated in Fig. 9.6. Transportation components from 25 reaching movements (selected at random from different subjects) have been plotted from the upper to the lower part of the diagram. Each movement has been normalized in amplitude ($P = 1$), in order to eliminate individual differences due to reaching errors. Dots on the diagram are samples of the hand position taken from single frames every 40 msec. Greater concentration of dots

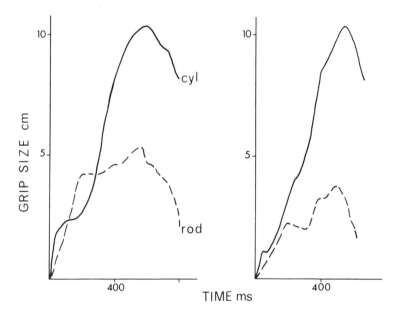

FIG. 9.5.   Position profile of the manipulation component in two different subjects reaching either for a small object (rod, dashed line) or for a large object (cylinder, solid line). For each given subject, maximum grip aperture (grip size, in centimeters) occurs at a relatively constant time in the movement whatever the size of the object.

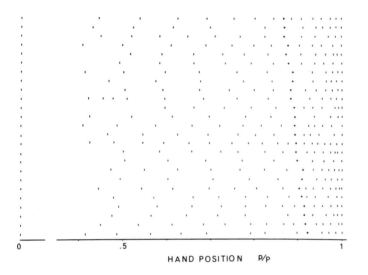
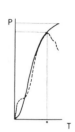

HAND POSITION   P/p

FIG. 9.6. Co-occurrence of maximum finger grip aperture and of slowing down of the transportation component. Diagram on the left: The values *p* of the transportation components (sampled every 40 msec) of 25 reaching movements (from the upper to the lower part of the figure) have been plotted after being normalized in percent of the total value of the trajectory amplitude (*P*). The time value of the maximum finger grip aperture (+) has been reported at the corresponding location for each movement. Diagram on the right: Superimposition of the position profile of the transportation component (solid line) and of the manipulation component (dashed line). *P* is the amplitude of the transportation component; + is the time of occurrence of the maximum finger grip aperture. The ordinate value of the same point corresponds to the + mark reported on the diagram on the left.

on the right side of the diagram corresponds to the previously mentioned slowing down of the arm near the end of the movement. The position in time of the maximal grip aperture has been plotted on the same diagram by putting a mark at the corresponding dot. A close coincidence in time appears between the occurrence of the change in velocity of the hand transportation and the beginning of finger closure. This is true for movements directed at both large and small objects and also for movements of different amplitude.

This co-occurrence has been further tested in 65 fully analyzed movements from the five subjects and for the three different test objects used in this experiment. The curves of velocity against time of the transportation component and of the manipulation component have been superimposed for each individual movement. In 49 cases (68.9%) the time at which the velocity of the finger movement became negative (crossing of the time axis in Fig. 9.3, lower figures) corresponded exactly to the time of the breakpoint on the velocity curve of the transportation component. In the 16 other cases, the two curves were out of phase by no more than 80 msec.

EXPERIMENT 2

This experiment must be considered as a preliminary attempt at testing the degree of independence of the two components of reaching movements described in Experiment 1.

The apparatus and procedure described in General Method, p. 157, were used. Subjects always performed their reaching movements in the visual open-loop situation (i.e., no visual feedback from the moving hand was available throughout the experiment). For this experiment subjects were asked to grasp the object and put it in a small box at the side. Three subjects were studied.

The particular feature of this experiment was that the object to be reached could be suddenly modified in size and shape during the reaching movement, without change in its absolute spatial location. This was realized by placing an ellipsoid object (7 cm × 4 cm) above the mirror and rotating it by 90° in a plane perpendicular to the mirror plane. According to the orientation of the object, the subject saw (in the mirror) either a sphere (4-cm diameter) or an elongated ellipsoid (7-cm length) at the table level (see Fig. 9.2). Rotation was produced by a small motor triggered by raising the hand from the starting stand. Rotation was completed within a few milliseconds, which produced the subjective appearance of a sudden expansion of the object shape.

Each trial was started with the presentation of a sphere. Transformation into an elongated shape occurred randomly across trials. In each case, a real object of the corresponding target shape was placed at the expected location on the table, so that the shape of the object grasped by the subject at the end of the movement actually fitted the virtual image present in the mirror at the same time. The number of trials was limited to about 20 per subject.

Results

Whether the shape of the target object was changed or not at the onset of the movement did not affect the transportation component. Duration, maximum velocity, and location of the breakpoint on the curve of velocity against time remained within the same range as that described for Experiment 1. No significant intrasubject difference could be detected between normal and "perturbed" trials.

In the three subjects, however, the grip pattern differed according to whether the object shape remained constant throughout a given trial or whether it was unexpectedly changed at the onset of the movement. The difference in anticipatory hand shaping, as studied from drawings taken from frames near the end of the movement, is quite clear in one subject (Fig. 9.7A), and this difference was completely reliable. In the two other subjects, the difference in hand shaping was more subtle and appeared in measurements of respective finger positions near the end of the movement. The difference between values obtained in the normal and

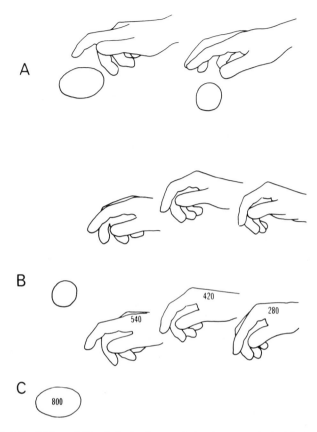

FIG. 9.7.   Differential hand shaping in perturbed and nonperturbed trials, in one subject. (A) Pattern of anticipatory hand shaping in movements directed at a sphere (nonperturbed trials) or at an ellipsoid shape (perturbed trials). (B) Nonperturbed. (C) Perturbed trials. Hand posture has been drawn at corresponding times of the movements (i.e., 280, 420, and 540 msec after the occurrence of the perturbation). Both movements have the same total duration (800 msec). Notice the beginning of a detectable differential shaping on the frame at 540 msec.

in the perturbed trials was significant at the 0.01 level in one subject and at a level between 0.1 and 0.05 in the other (Cochran test).

The time at which a difference in hand shaping could be first detected can be only grossly evaluated from Fig. 9.7B and C, representing our best subject. Although 420 msec after the perturbation has occurred the grip pattern is still similar for the two objects, a clear difference is visible some 120 msec later. From this it can be suggested that at least 500 msec are needed for processing of the visual change and for elaborating new motor commands. It must also be taken into account that changes in the grip pattern must be effected before the beginning of finger closure, which occurs roughly some 200 msec before the end of the movement. This rather tight time constraint may explain differences in amplitude of the effect across subjects. Indeed, the subject with the least significant effect made movements of a relatively short duration (720 msec to 840 msec), which allows little time for elaborating the new commands required by the perturbed trials.

In summary, it does appear that the two components of reaching are dissociable in that the velocity pattern of transportation remains unaltered in a situation where the grip pattern has to be altered. On the other hand, the temporal organization of grip adjustments is highly dependent on that of transportation and remains so when distance is varied from one trial to another.

DISCUSSION

Because we are dealing with object perception in terms of motor interactions, we discuss the implications of the results for motor control in some detail before finally placing them in the context of a perceptual framework.

In many respects, the reaching movements described here are in accordance with current conceptions of motor programming. A motor program is classically conceived of as "a set of muscle commands that are structured before a movement sequence begins, and that allow the entire sequence to be carried out uninfluenced by peripheral feedback" (Keele, 1968; see also Glencross, 1977). This definition would account for the relative paucity of the effect produced by opening the visual loop during reaching movements. A previous study by Prablanc, Echallier, Komilis, and Jeannerod (1979) dealing with pointing at small targets (i.e., a type of movement close to our transportation component) has also shown that such parameters as latency and duration of the movements were unaffected by suppression of peripheral feedback. The only aspect of pointing movements that Prablanc and colleagues found to be strongly dependent on vision of the moving hand was terminal precision. This finding is consistent with the terminal errors due to undershooting that we have observed here in the open-loop situation.

However, it remains to be discussed where (or when) closed-loop visual control, as reduced as it appears to be, takes place during reaching movements. A common idea is that this could be during the low-velocity, terminal part of the trajectory, often considered as a guided phase, by contrast with the earlier, high-velocity, ballistic phase (Navas & Stark, 1968). Indeed, the fact that the low-velocity phase is still present in the open-loop situation does not imply that closed-loop visual control would not occur at this point when visual feedback from the movement is present. As a matter of fact, it is known that visual control can be effective anywhere during the trajectory after the minimum time for a visual-motor loop to be completed (Keele & Posner, 1968; Megaw, 1974). Visual cues concerning the static position of the hand relative to the body prior to the movement could be used as well to improve terminal precision (Prablanc, Echallier, Jeannerod, & Komilis, 1979).

Persistence of the low-velocity phase in the open-loop situation only means that this phase is also part of the motor sequence predetermined by the program prior to the movement. Our conception of the low-velocity phase would be that of a target-acquisition phase (homing in on a target; Welford, Norris, & Shock, 1969), that is, a necessary constraint for movements requiring a high degree of precision, like reaching at small or fragile objects. This view is consistent with our observation that the slowing down of the transportation component closely corresponds in time with the closure of the fingers. Thus it could be tentatively suggested that a certain state has to be reached simultaneously by the different segments involved in the movement, a state that would be defined as the goal for the high-velocity ballistic parts of all the movement components. It is a logical speculation to assume that, for the sake of precision of reaching, the point in time where the velocity curves of the different components are phased must be different from the final state of the movement (i.e., the stop at contact with the object).

We have no arguments as to whether this point (goal state) on the time axis is defined in the program itself or whether it results from some peripheral equilibrium of forces acting on the limb (as proposed by Schmidt, 1980). At any rate, this view tends to make the problem of the internal representation of the movement to be performed less critical. A "holistic" program could be conceived more simply as a temporal frame defining a limited number of critical points on the time axis; among those points would be the time of simultaneous release of the ballistic commands and the point of convergence of the velocity curves. However, this does not obviate the fact that, within a given temporal frame, generation of the velocity curves for each component of a movement are the result of processes independent from each other, according to our channel hypothesis (see Introduction). Experiment 2 clearly shows that motor commands specified by a certain visuomotor system can be selectively modified during execution of the movement. A sudden change in object shape (an equivalent of a sudden increase in visual "load") affects only the relevant channel, in this case the mechanism responsible for anticipatory hand shaping in relation to object shape. We have no evidence as yet for similar behavior of the system in the reverse situation (i.e., a perturbation imposed upon the "distance channel" without changing object size or shape).

This result might suggest that some degree of visual-load compensation remains continuously possible during the execution of a reaching movement and that the movement is subjected to continuous open-loop central monitoring. However, the fact that a change in object shape affects only the "shape channel" and not the others implies that the load compensation in the perturbed channel will have to be constrained within the time limits required for the execution of the other, nonperturbed, channels. The temporal frame imposed on all the channels participating in the movement as a consequence of holistic programming thus limits the expression of the open-loop control of the movement by ongoing visual input.

Given the foregoing discussion of motor control, we can now speculate on its implications for how different kinds of visual information relate to subjects' interactions with objects. It appears that object distance is treated for motor purposes independently of object shape. However, the ulitization of shape and size is affected by time taken to cover the distance. Thus in person–scene inter-actions one hypothesis is that the use of viewer-centered (extrinsic) information and that of object-centered (intrinsic) information are hierarchically ordered: Location has priority in determining the overall frame of an action (in time) and constrains the degrees of freedom open to the use of shape orientation. Two reservations need to be made. First, we have not investigated the counterpart of Experiment 2, where distance but not shape would be altered after initiation of the movement. Our present position predicts an alteration of the dynamics of grip to fit with those of transportation. Second, object orientation has here been con-sidered an intrinsic property and has not influenced transportation. However, for certain object orientations where the perceiver has one or other purposes, the specific grip plausibly influences the type and direction of the transportation component. Although such experiments may alter the details of a perceptual-motor theory, nonetheless conceptually they only reinforce the validity of the approach adopted here: that the organization of object perception is profitably studied in terms of our purposes in interacting with objects.

ACKNOWLEDGMENTS

Helpful comments by Tony Marcel and two reviewers on an early version of this chapter are gratefully acknowledged.

REFERENCES

Arbib, M. A. Interacting schemas for motor control. In G. Stelmach & J. Requin (Eds.), *Tutorials in motor behavior*. Amsterdam: North Holland, 1980.

Bernstein, N. *The coordination and regulation of movements*. Oxford: Pergamon Press, 1967.

Brinkman, J., & Kuypers, H. G. J. M. Cerebral control of contralateral and ipsilateral arm, hand and finger movements in the split-brain rhesus monkey. *Brain*, 1973, *96*, 663–674.

Glencross, D. J. Control of skilled movements. *Psychological Bulletin*, 1977, *84*, 14–29.

Haaxma, M., & Kuypers, H. G. J. M. Intrahemispheric cortical connections and visual guidance of hand and finger movements in the rhesus monkey. *Brain*, 1975, *98*, 239–260.

Held, R., & Gottlieb, N. Technique for studying adaptation to disarranged hand-eye coordination. *Perceptual and Motor Skills*, 1958, *8*, 83–86.

Jeannerod, M., & Biguer, B. Visuomotor mechanisms in reaching within extrapersonal space. In D. Ingle, M. Goodale, & R. Mansfield (Eds.), *Advances in the analysis of visual behavior*. Boston: MIT Press, 1981.

Keele, S. W. Movement control in skilled motor performance. *Psychological Bulletin, 1968, 70,* 387-404.

Keele, S. W., & Posner, M. I. Processing of visual feedback in rapid movements. *Journal of Experimental Psychology,* 1968, *77,* 155-158.

Kelso, J. A. S., Southard, D. L., & Goodman, D. On the coordination of two-handed movements. *Journal of Experimental Psychology: Human Perception and Performance,* 1979, *5,* 229-238.

Kugler, P. N., Kelso, J. A. S., & Turvey, M. T. On the concept of coordinative structures as dissipative structures: I. Theoretical lines of convergence. In G. Stelmach & J. Requin (Eds.), *Tutorials in motor behavior.* Amsterdam: North-Holland, 1980.

Kuypers, H. G. J. M. Cortico-spinal connections: Postnatal development in the rhesus monkey. *Science,* 1962, *138,* 678-680.

Megaw, E. D. Possible modification to a rapid on-going programmed manual response. *Brain Research,* 1974, *71,* 425-441.

Navas, F., & Stark, L. Sampling or intermittency in hand control system dynamics. *Biophysical Journal,* 1968, *8,* 252-302.

Prablanc, C., Echallier, J. F., Komilis, E., & Jeannerod, M. Optimal response of eye and hand motor systems in pointing at a visual target: I. Spatiotemporal characteristics of eye and hand movements and their relationships when varying the amount of visual information. *Biological Cybernetics,* 1979, *35,* 113-124.

Prablanc, C., Echallier, J. F., Jeannerod, M., & Komilis, E. Optimal response of eye and hand motor systems in pointing at a visual target: II. Static and dynamic visual cues in the control of hand movement. *Biological Cybernetics,* 1979, *35,* 183-187.

Schmidt, R. A. On the theoretical status of time in motor program representations. In G. Stelmach & J. Requin (Eds.), *Tutorials in motor behavior.* Amsterdam: North-Holland, 1980.

Trevarthen, C. B. Two mechanisms of vision in primates. *Psychologische Forschung,* 1968, *31,* 299-337.

Von Fieandt, K. Some psychological constituents and aspects of object perception. In R. B. MacLeod & M. L. Pick (Eds.), *Perception: Essays in honor of James J. Gibson.* Ithaca, N.Y.: Cornell University Press, 1974.

Warabi, T. The reaction time of eye-head coordination in man. *Neuroscience Letters,* 1977, *6,* 47-51.

Welford, A. T., Norris, A. H., & Shock, N. W. Speed and accuracy of movement and their changes with age. In W. G. Koster (Ed.), *Attention and performance II. Acta Psychologica,* 1969, *30,* 3-15.

Woodworth, R. S. The accuracy of voluntary movements. *Psychological Review Monograph Supplement.* 1899, *3,* 114.

AUTOMATICITY

10 Automatic Information Processing: A Review

David LaBerge
University of Minnesota
Minneapolis, Minnesota
U.S.A.

ABSTRACT

This review attempts to clarify some current theoretical issues concerning automatic processing in the light of recent research. Two selected properties of automatic processes, absence of capacity limitations and unavoidability, are examined in relation to a dual-stage hypothesis of perception. Other topics discussed include some recently proposed limits to automatic processing in both early and late stages of processing and mechanisms underlying the acquisition of automaticity.

INTRODUCTION

Automaticity, like attention, has been described in several different ways. Among the more frequent properties proposed are processing that is unavoidable, without capacity limitations, without awareness, without intention, with high efficiency, and with resistance to modification. Whether or not one could devise a useful and widely acceptable definition of automaticity based on all or a proper subset of these properties, or including other properties as well, is not yet clear, because different experimental tasks continue to reveal different combinations of these descriptive properties of automaticity. In the event, the properties of unavoidability and absence of capacity limitation dominate the descriptions of automaticity in the research studies reviewed here. Therefore, the presence of either of these two properties will be considered a sufficient condition for use of the term *automaticity* in this chapter.

The plan of the review is to describe how recent research studies illuminate currently active theoretical issues in automatic processing. The remainder of the chapter divides into four general topics. The first topic concerns the hypothesis that perception of patterns occurs in two stages, of which the first is automatic and the second attention-demanding; the second topic examines more specifically the possible limits to automatic processing in early stages; the third topic examines the role of automatic processing in the concurrent performance of two complex tasks; the fourth topic discusses the theoretical mechanisms by which automaticity in different tasks may be acquired.

THE TWO-STAGE HYPOTHESIS OF PERCEPTION

Absence of Capacity Limitations

The layman's view of automaticity is often tied to the idea of doing two things at the same time. One thinks of examples such as carrying on a conversation while driving a car or listening to a newscast while writing a letter. In these examples, there are two task operations and two separable types of input to the tasks. Which of the aspects is mainly responsible for the difficulty commonly reported in attempting dual tasks? Can both tasks be done at the same time? The investigator usually aims to demonstrate that the processing of one or both tasks is free of capacity limitations when two conditions are met: (1) The performance level of each task separately shows no decline when they are performed simultaneously. (2) There is clear assurance that attention cannot be alternated or time-shared between the tasks. The first condition is apparently easier to satisfy than the second. Performance levels can be measured objectively, but the presence or absence of attention switching must be inferred.

Many studies that attempt to meet these requirements have used some variation of the dichotic listening task. In these tasks, subjects are required to shadow a message in one ear while monitoring a message in the other ear, for example, listening for the occurrence of the word *tap* to which the subject responds by striking a stick against the table (Treisman & Geffen, 1967). Though performance on one of the tasks usually suffers when they are performed simultaneously, this may no longer be so when extended practice is given (Ostry, Moray, & Marks, 1976; Underwood, 1974). If one is assured that the performance and time-sharing criteria are indeed satisfied in these studies, then one concludes that after practice one or both of the tasks is being performed automatically. Much of the discussion of dichotic listening experiments seems to be concerned with whether or not these criteria are met.

A careful application of the criteria for presence or absence of capacity limitations during early and late stages of perception was embodied in a visual task recently by Duncan (1980). He used simplified versions of search tasks in an elegant design that allowed him to compare performance under single-task and double-task conditions. The subjects were asked to search for digits among distracting letters. The display consisted of four characters arranged in the shape of a cross, but the display could be reduced to only two characters making up either the horizontal or the vertical limb of the cross. For the one-response task, there was a single response key to be pressed if a digit appeared anywhere in the display. For the two-response task, the subjects pressed one key if a digit appeared on the horizontal limb and another key if a digit appeared on the vertical limb. Both keys were to be pressed if digits appeared on both limbs. In the one-response task, the comparison of the condition in which the display contained four items with the condition in which it contained only two showed only a very small difference in performance (accuracy of digit detection), whereas with the two-response task large differences in performance were obtained, favoring the smaller display. The results suggest that, in these experiments, it is the existence of two detection responses, not two inputs, that is the main cause of interference in performance. Evidently, the two-response task could not be performed in parallel, that is, automatically, but required attention. Duncan interpreted the results of his study as supporting a theory of late selection, in which much stimulus analysis is performed automatically up to the point of full stimulus identification. At this point, automatic processing gives way to limited capacity attentional processing. The picture that emerges is that stimulus identification generally occurs without capacity limitations during the first stage of perceptual processing, but thereafter outputs must pass through a limited-capacity system before a response is activated.

Unavoidability of Processing

The other main property of automatic processing that has been attributed to early perceptual operations is unavoidability. When a subject is instructed to respond to a particular target item in a multielement display, nontarget items or attributes of items, which presumably pass the first stage of identification, may influence the selection of a response in the second stage. This phenomenon, which is a manifestation of automatic first-stage processing, has been investigated in numerous designs, from dichotic listening tasks to the Stroop task and its variations. Consider experiments in which a subject is required to shadow a message in one ear, while words are presented simultaneously to the other ear. When a word in the unattended ear is a synonym of the simultaneously presented word in the shadowed ear, the shadowing slows down (Lewis, 1970; Treisman, Squire, & Green, 1974). This supports the view that unattended words may access their meanings automatically. Similarly, MacKay (1973) found that ambiguous sentences in the attended ear can be resolved by a word in the unattended ear, and Underwood (1977) found that context presented in the unattended ear facilitated shadowing of target words. One way to interpret findings such as these is to conclude that complete early selection is not possible when stimuli are sufficiently meaningful. Another way is to suggest that meaningful information may get through without attention but that perceptual identification of the source or location of that information requires the follow-up of attentional processing.

The particular method of presenting one task with two (or more) inputs (one to be attended and the other ignored) in a continuous shadowing experiment can also be used in a discrete trial experiment by using one of the many forms of the well-known Stroop (1935) task. In the original Stroop task, the subjects name the color of the ink in which a word is printed. When the word is a color name that is different from the ink color, the response is slowed. Even neutral words apparently produce interference (Klein, 1964; Regan, 1978). These results are often used to support the claim that word meanings are automatically processed.

Other tasks that are variations on the Stroop task include naming visually presented digits while hearing other auditorally presented digits (Greenwald, 1972); naming line drawings of common objects that have an unrelated word printed inside them (Rayner & Posnansky, 1978; Underwood, 1976); and pressing one of two buttons to the category of a target word that has words of another category printed above and below the target word (Shaffer & LaBerge, 1979). Another button-pressing version of the flanker display used letters positioned to the right and left of the target (Eriksen & Eriksen, 1974; Taylor, 1977). Most interpretations of the substantial Stroop interference observed in all of these tasks maintain that the locus of interference is at the point of response selectivity (Dyer, 1973; Eriksen & Eriksen, 1974; Posner & Snyder, 1975b). However, the word-flanker study of Shaffer and LaBerge (1979) and a letter-digit identification task of LaBerge (in press) indicate that interference can ocur at the earlier stage of semantic categorization, because flanking items assigned to the same response as the target, but of a different category, produced substantial interference. Nevertheless, the results from these numerous variations of the Stroop task appear to support the hypothesis of an initial stage of perceptual processing in which item information is processed unavoidably. As we see in the next section, this hypothesis has recently come under attack on both theoretical and empirical fronts.

AUTOMATIC PROCESSING IN EARLY STAGES

Early parallel extraction of stimulus information of familiar items is a very basic assumption in current theories of automatic processing (LaBerge, 1975; Posner, 1978; Shiffrin & Schneider, 1977). According to straightforward interpretations of these theories, all familiar items in the sensitive portion of the visual field are processed to their representative perceptual code and, in some cases, to the phonological name codes and meaning networks as well. This implies, for example, that all clearly presented digits and letters in the sensitive visual field should be processed without attention up to the level of perceptual identification regardless of their color or position.

Perhaps the strongest current theoretical and empirical challenge to early automatic processing of patterns is offered by Treisman and her associates (Treisman & Gelade, 1980; Treisman, Sykes, & Gelade, 1977). According to their feature-integration theory, separable features such as colors, orientations, spatial frequencies, brightness levels, and directions of movement are initially registered automatically, and in parallel, but percepts or objects, which are conjunctions of features, are identified only by focusing attention at the point in the visual field where the features are located. Thus, attention serves as the "glue" that conjoins features into a unitary percept or object. Perception of location is apparently necessary to enable attention to focus on an item and unitize its features. Converging support for these hypotheses was provided from experiments using visual search, texture segregation, identification, and localization. For instance, 1664 trials with a particular colored letter (e.g., a green T) as a target in a search task did not appreciably reduce evidence of serial processing, as measured by the slope of the function relating search time to display size. The conclusion would seem to be that focal attention is required during early perceptual processing of items that are conjunctions of separable features. This implies that unattended items in a Stroop-type task should not access their meanings or response assignments, if the items could be identified only by conjunctions of separable features. Treisman and Gelade (1980) point out that some visual patterns (e.g., some letters) may not be based on conjunctions of feature sets and therefore may be processed in parallel. It is possible, then, that restricted sets of items used in some Stroop-type designs could be discriminated on the basis of single features, so that attention would not be necessary for these items to access their meanings.

In view of these considerations, it would seem that the feature-integration theory may be sharply at odds with theories of early automatic processing in accounting for the processing of conjunctions made up of particular separable features (e.g., searching for a green T in a field of green X's and brown T's). Another area of potential contrast between the theories arises in an account of the results of two recent empirical studies that seriously question early automatic processing.

Kahneman and Henik (1979) showed that in a Stroop color-naming task interference is substantially greater when the distracting information is in the same location as the target item as opposed to being in a different location (but still within the central fixation area). In their task, subjects were shown a circle and square, side by side, and asked to search first for a circle within which a colored word was printed. The response was to name the color. When the target word spelled another color, there was much more interference than when that color word appeared in the adjacent square. Early-automatic-processing theories should predict no difference in the amount of interference between the two conditions.

A somewhat similar result was shown by Francolini and Egeth (1980) with a task in which subjects counted the number of red items among black items, all of which were arranged in a circular display. Counting two red 3's among black letters produced Stroop interference, but counting two red A's among black 3's produced no interference. Again, an early-automatic-processing theory would expect interference in both conditions.

It would seem that the feature-integration theory of Treisman and Gelade (1980) could account for the pattern of results of these two experiments on the assumption that attention serially scans locations in space and conjoins features existing only at particular locations. Both experiments presumably employ attention during the search that precedes the processing of the Stroop-sensitive item. In the case of the Kahneman and Henik (1979) experiment, a circle was cued; in the Francolini and Egeth (1979) experiment, the color red was cued. Cuing a form or a color speeds its processing over noncued items (LaBerge, Van Gelder, & Yellott, 1970; Posner & Snyder, 1975a) and thereby draws attention to the cued item first, inducing an orienting response to that item's location where the spotlight of attention subsequently begins to process the conjunction of features related to the Stroop part of the trial. Features in other locations (inside the square of Kahneman and Henik or the black digits of Francolini and Egeth) are likely to receive little or no attentional "glue" to form conjunctions and subsequently access their meanings, because the uncued square or color does not attract the spotlight. Therefore, items in uncued locations show little or no Stroop interference.

For these tasks, then, we conjecture that two kinds of attention are operating: (1) attention to the features of form or color during initial search for these cued features; and (2) attention to integrating the set of features at the location found by the search. The first type of attention functions much like Broadbent's (1958) filter conception. The second type of attention allows the integration of features within a location (Treisman & Gelade, 1980).

Kahneman and Henik (1979) give a theoretical account that is close to the one derived here from the feature-integration model. They assume that attention is allocated to objects that are identified preattentively. Thus, greater interference is produced when the target color and distracting word are within some object than when they are within separate objects.

AUTOMATIC PROCESSING IN LATER STAGES

Thus far our discussion has centered on tasks that investigated automatic processing in the detection of items such as digits, letters, or words. Now we turn to some recent studies of automatic processing in tasks that emphasize the processing that follows the detection of an item.

Logan (1979) explored automatic aspects of the preparatory period just prior to the onset of a stimulus in a choice task. The choice task assigned eight different letters to eight different button responses that used the four fingers of each hand. Letters were presented singly, and subjects performed the task under conditions of varying difficulty in which two-, four-, or eight-choice alternatives were required. Prior to the onset of each choice trail, the subjects in one condition were given a memory load consisting of a string of eight digits that they were required to recall after the letter-to-button choice had been made. In the other condition, the subjects were given no memory load prior to the choice task on a trial.

The data of main interest here were the choice reaction-time curves plotted as a function of number of response alternatives for the two memory load conditions. On the first day, the RT curves for the high memory load and zero memory load were approximately linearly related to number of choice alternatives, with the range (difference between two- and eight-choice RTs) of the high memory load condition being about 1200 msec and the range of the zero memory load condition about 900 msec. The interaction of memory load with number of choice alternatives decreased and apparently vanished by the sixth day of testing. Also the slope of the zero load curve decreased to a range of about 300 msec by the sixth day.

These results showed, first of all, that lengthy practice in the choice task lowered the slope of the reaction time curves, indicating progress toward the high efficiency level found in the zero-slope curves of well-practiced and highly compatible S–R choice tasks (Fitts, 1964; Mowbray & Rhoades, 1959). Of particular interest in Logan's study are the data showing a reduction in the amount of interaction between memory load and choice alternatives. The interaction found on the first day disappears and the effects of the two factors become additive by the sixth day, implying that some component of the choice task has been developing automaticity. Logan suggests that the interaction of memory load with choice alternatives is related to preparation for the choice task; that is, the rapid, strategically controlled "tuning" of components of the choice task during the moments just prior to the onset of the choice stimulus. Presumably, divided attention between the encoding of items of the memory task and the preparation for the choice task is located just prior to the onset of the choice stimulus. We may suggest that when the attention demands of encoding and preparation coincide in time, extensive practice is needed on the combination. But when preparation or "tuning" can be accomplished sufficiently quickly, then attention switching is effective for encoding the memory task and then preparing for the choice task.

Traditionally, considerations of automaticity in multiple-choice tasks have been restricted largely to the high efficiency observed in the accessing of the appropriate response by the stimuli. Logan's concurrent memory load design apparently taps another major aspect of performing a choice task that shows development of automaticity, namely, the preparation stage.

The preparation or "tuning" prior to the onset of a stimulus in a choice task seems somewhat similar to the priming or cuing of a letter prior to a matching operation. Posner and Boies (1971) presented two letters successively; at the time the second letter appeared, subjects were asked to judge whether the two letters were the same or different. In order to measure the attention demands of preparation for the second letter, the investigators presented an auditory white noise probe at various times between the first and second letter. (They also presented probes at other points during the trial to measure attention demands of other events.) The reaction times to the noise probes increased markedly just prior to the display of the second letter. This finding was replicated by Posner and Klein (1973) and more recently by Ogden, Martin, and Paap (1980). Apparently the task of preparing to perceive a particular letter and perform a matching operation draws upon attentional capacity. Whether or not intensive practice would appreciably reduce the attentional demands of preparation in this matching task, as it apparently did in Logan's choice task, is, to my knowledge, not yet determined.

We now consider an example of a particularly complex stage of late processing: comprehension. Comprehension of a sentence has traditionally been regarded as a heavy consumer of attention resources, especially in reading new text (LaBerge & Samuels, 1974). In view of this assumption, one would predict that an individual could not perform two comprehension tasks simultaneously without a decrement in the performance of one or both tasks. In an attempt to test this prediction, Hirst, Spelke, Reaves, Cahavack, & Neisser (1980) trained two subjects to copy dictated sentences while reading. After what must be considered heroic amounts of practice, the two subjects came close to matching performance criteria on copying errors, reading speed, and comprehension when the tasks were done singly and together. In addition, these subjects showed evidence of comprehension of the dictated words. One interpretation of the results is that some of the semantic components of these tasks became automatic. The authors, on the other hand, adopt the strong a priori assumption that comprehension, which includes the understanding of new sentences and the integration of ideas, cannot in principle be automatic, even in the highly practiced dual task that their subjects performed. Furthermore, the authors assume that the ability to divide attention is not dependent on resource considerations but rather on the level of skill achieved by an individual (Neisser, 1976). This conception of attention, which is tied to the level of a skill, departs sharply from traditional notions of attention that grew out of the limited capacity characteristics of performance observed in some of the other, less highly practiced, tasks reviewed in this chapter. In effect, the assumptions of Hirst et al. (1980) concerning the role of attention would seem to eliminate the need for the notion altogether in accounting for how highly practiced activities are performed. But, in a sense, this elimination of attention is consistent with what is usually meant by the term *automaticity,* which applies when there is freedom from capacity limitations.

ACQUISITION OF AUTOMATICITY

The traditional view of achievement of automaticity has placed much faith in the role of practice, implying that repetition of processing is the major factor in the development of the underlying mechanisms. In this section, we discuss two current theories, one (LaBerge, 1975) that maintains that there are factors other than repetition in the acquisition of automatic processing of certain types and one (Treisman & Gelade, 1980) that maintains that some perceptual processes cannot be automatized regardless of practice.

An earlier theoretical report (LaBerge, 1975) proposed that the mechanisms involved in the acquisition of automaticity may not be the same for all processes or tasks. In particular, the mechanism of unitizing a perceptual pattern, such as a letter or a word, is assumed to require a convergence of feature detector outputs into a higher-order representation or code. In contrast, the association of a visual letter code to its name or semantic category seems to be a matter of a consistent mapping of a visual code to a phonological or semantic code. If the theoretical distinction is valid, then the implication for methods of training automatic processing of naming a letter or a word is simply to provide repetitive practice in viewing the pattern and making the correct response. On the other hand, learning to perceive automatically a visual letter or word as a unit may require something more than the association of a stimulus and response representation through repetition alone.

The additional factor is regarded as a combination operation on the several feature inputs that converge on a perceptual representation or code. When a complex pattern, such as a letter, a word, or a face, is presented, the pattern presumably activates several feature detectors. At this point, it may be assumed that the subject directs attention narrowly to the location of each component feature or directs attention widely to the location of the entire array of features given by the pattern or to subsets of the array of intermediate width.

If the subject's attention is directed to features as single units, then one would expect processing time of a pattern to increase with the number of component features, because attention must shift from component to component. On the other hand, if the subject's attention is directed widely to encompass the entire pattern, then one might expect processing time of the pattern to be constant as the number of component features increases (within reasonable limits), because only one fixation of attention is required.

One line of indirect support for this view of variable attention allocation to patterns comes from studies of reaction time to words of varying length. When subjects attend to components, reaction time is expected to increase with word length, on present assumptions. However, when subjects attend to the word as a whole, then reaction time is expected to be constant within reasonable limits of word length.

Some word tasks in the literature appear to emphasize component processing, whereas other tasks seem to emphasize holistic processing. Matching two words requires that corresponding letters be the same, and a lexical decision task requires that a word be spelled properly. Thus, both tasks draw attention to letter-level components of a word. On the other hand, judging whether a word is a member of a category (e.g., press the button if the word is an animal) would seem to place less emphasis on examination of component letters and may draw attention to the entire word.

The effect of word length on reaction time shows significant, and usually substantial, slopes in matching studies (Bruder, 1978; Eichelman, 1970) and significant slopes in a lexical decision task (Butler & Hains, 1979). In contrast, the word length effect shows zero slope in a categorization task (Terry, Samuels, & LaBerge, 1976). All of these studies used adult subjects.

When subjects from second, fourth, sixth, and college grades are compared in a word categorization task, the results show substantial word length slopes for second graders but a decrease in slope to zero at the college level (Samuels, LaBerge, & Bremer, 1978). Apparently, both the type of task and the level of development influence the word length effect in ways that seem to be consistent with the assumption that attention can be allocated narrowly to locations of components of a word or widely to the whole word.

The foregoing theoretical view of pattern perception differs from that of Treisman and Gelade (1980) mainly on the issue of the effect of practice on the automatization of perception. Their claim is that perceptual processing of patterns based on conjunctions of features always requires attention (except when the patterns can be predicted top-down from context and past experience), whereas the present position maintains that appropriate practice procedures eventually eliminate the need for attention. However, the position of Treisman and Gelade (1980) is apparently based on evidence taken from conjunctions of color and shape. They suggest the possibility that combinations of other features (e.g., parts of shapes) may initially require attention to be conjoined, but after appropriate practice they may be utilized without attention, perhaps by the development of new unitary features during practice. We would stress that appropriate practice involves procedures that induce attention to be focused widely across a pattern as opposed to focusing narrowly on components. For example, displays containing background items that draw attention to component features of patterns may narrow the spotlight of attention so that the target item is also processed in component fashion and thereby is likely to require attention.

Evidence for the withdrawal of attention in the unitization of features of letterlike forms has been described in an earlier study (LaBerge, 1973). In the study, the target items were chosen so that discrimination among them required two features. The items were presented in displays that did not require search through distractor items. The only context that might have influenced the mode of attention (narrow to features versus wide to the whole pattern) was the type of item that occurred on the majority of trials (LaBerge, Petersen, & Norden, 1977; Petersen & LaBerge, 1977). In the LaBerge (1973) study, the majority of items were familiar letters, which presumably induced a single, wide mode of attentional focus to all items. The result of interest here was the 48-msec longer reaction time to unfamiliar items as compared to familiar letters on the first day of testing. The difference was taken as an indication of the amount of attention required to unitize the features of the novel items. By the fifth day, the difference between novel items and familiar letters disappeared, suggesting that the features of the novel items became unitized automatically.

These data are consistent with the view that automatic processing of the category of a letter or the meaning of a word has two main parts. In the first part, features are automatically unitized or integrated into a perceptual representation or code. In the second part, the code is associated with a category code or a meaning network. The first type of acquisition is located within the perceptual system. It requires the convergence of several feature detector outputs into one perceptual code. The second type of acquisition, which occurs between the perceptual and semantic systems, may be characterized by the association of a code in one system to a code in another system and is said to be produced by repeated stimulus–response mapping as in the acquisition of automatic categorizing reported by Shiffrin & Schneider (1977). Thus, acquisition of automaticity between systems seems mainly to imply the strengthening of associative links, whereas acquisition of automaticity within a system such as perception may also involve combining or recombining links from feature detectors to the perceptual code that is being automatized.

This distinction between processes that occur within systems as opposed to those that occur between systems suggests that the automatization of representations within other systems, such as networks in the semantic system and programs in the motor system, might also be acquired not by repeated pairings of the same situations and responses but with regard to the role of attentional modes that organize networks during training. In the case of motor programs, for example, one would not expect the pianist to achieve an automatic execution of a fast arpeggio by diligently giving attention to each separate finger movement. Rather, the effective way to practice is by focusing on groups of finger movements (Lashley, 1951) to determine suitable ways to organize them within the hand (Bernstein, 1967).

The point being made here is that the mechanisms tacitly assumed to underlie operations within systems may be quite different from the mechanisms tacitly assumed to underlie operations between systems. In particular, this section of the chapter has attempted to suggest that the within–between systems distinction may be helpful in clarifying differences in the mechanisms of automatic processing and in suggesting differences in the ways that automatic processing may be acquired.

ACKNOWLEDGMENTS

Part of this research was supported by a grant from the National Science Foundation (BNS-7904677) to the author and by a grant from the National Institute for Child Health and Human Development (HD-01136) to the Center for Research in Human Learning, University of Minnesota. The author thanks John Duncan, Ray Klein, Anne Treisman, and an anonymous reviewer for helpful comments.

REFERENCES

Bernstein, N. *The coordination and regulation of movements.* Oxford, England: Pergamon Press, 1967.

Broadbent, D. E. *Perception and communication.* New York: Pergamon Press, 1958.

Bruder, G. A. Role of visual familiarity in the word superiority effects obtained with the simultaneous matching task. *Journal of Experimental Psychology: Human Perception and Performance,* 1978, *4,* 88-100.

Butler, B. & Hains, S. Individual differences in word recognition latency. *Memory & Cognition,* 1979, *7,* 68-76.

Duncan, J. The locus of interference in the perception of simultaneous stimuli. *Psychological Review,* 1980, *87,* 272-300.

Dyer, F. N. The Stroop phenomenon and its use in the study of perceptual, cognitive, and response processes. *Memory & Cognition,* 1973, *1,* 106-120.

Eichelman, W. H. Familiarity effects in the simultaneous matching task. *Journal of Experimental Psychology,* 1970, *86,* 275-282.

Eriksen, B. A., & Eriksen, C. W. Effects of noise letters upon the identification of a target letter in a nonsearch task. *Perception & Psychophysics,* 1974, *16,* 143-149.

Fitts, P. M. Perceptual-motor skill learning. In A. W. Melton (Ed.), *Categories of human learning.* New York: Academic Press, 1964.

Francolini, C. M., & Egeth, H. A. On the nonautomaticity of "automatic" activation: Evidence of selective seeing. *Perception & Psychophysics,* 1980, *27,* 331-342.

Greenwald, A. G. Evidence of both perceptual filtering and response suppression for rejected messages in selective attention. *Journal of Experimental Psychology,* 1972, *94,* 58-67.

Hirst, W., Spelke, E. S., Reaves, C. C., Cahavack, G., & Neisser, U. Dividing attention without alternation or automaticity. *Journal of Experimental Psychology: General,* 1980, *109,* 98-117.

Kahneman, D., & Henik, A. Perceptual organization and attention. In M. Kubovy & J. R. Pomerantz (Eds.), *Perceptual organization.* Hillsdale, N.J.: Lawrence Erlbaum Associates, 1979.

Klein, G. S. Semantic power measured through the interference of words with color naming. *American Journal of Psychology,* 1964, *527,* 576-588.

LaBerge, D. Attention and the measurement of perceptual learning. *Memory & Cognition,* 1973, *1,* 268-276.

LaBerge, D. Acquisition of automatic processing of perceptual and associative learning. In P. M. A. Rabbitt & S. Dornic (Eds.), *Attention & performance V.* New York: Academic Press, 1975.

LaBerge, D. Unitization and automaticity in perception. In J. H. Flowers (Ed.), *1980 Nebraska Symposium on Motivation.* Lincoln: University of Nebraska, in press.

LaBerge, D., Petersen, R. J., & Norden, M. H. Exploring the limits of cueing. In S. Dornic (Ed.), *Attention and performance VI.* Hillsdale, N.J.: Lawrence Erlbaum Associates, 1977.

LaBerge, D., & Samuels, S. J. Toward a theory of automatic information processing in reading. *Cognitive Psychology,* 1974, *6,* 293-323.

LaBerge, D., Van Gelder, P., & Yellott, J. A cueing technique in choice reaction time. *Perception & Psychophysics*, 1970, *7*, 57-62.

Lashley, K. S. The problem of serial order in behavior. In L. A. Jeffress (Ed.), *Cerebral mechanisms in behavior*. New York: Wiley, 1951.

Lewis, J. L. Semantic processing of unattended messages using dichotic listening. *Journal of Experimental Psychology*, 1970, *85*, 225-228.

Logan, G. D. On the use of a concurrent memory load to measure attention and automaticity. *Journal of Experimental Psychology: Human Perception and Performance*, 1979, *5*, 189-207.

MacKay, D. Aspects of the theory of comprehension, memory and attention. *Quarterly Journal of Experimental Psychology*, 1973, *25*, 22-40.

Mowbray, G. H., & Rhoades, M. V. On the reduction of choice reaction times with practice. *Quarterly Journal of Experimental Psychology*, 1959, *11*, 16-23.

Neisser, U. *Cognition and reality*. San Francisco: Freeman, 1976.

Ogden, W. C., Martin, D. W., & Paap, K. R. Processing demands of encoding: What does secondary task performance reflect? *Journal of Experimental Psychology: Human Perception and Performance*, 1980, *6*, 355-367.

Ostry, D., Moray, N., & Marks, G. Attention, practice, and semantic targets. *Journal of Experimental Psychology: Human Perception and Performance*, 1976, *2*, 326-336.

Petersen, R. J., & LaBerge, D. Contextual control of letter perception. *Memory & Cognition*, 1977, *5*, 205, 213.

Posner, M. I. *Chronometric explorations of mind*. Hillsdale, N.J.: Lawrence Erlbaum Associates, 1978.

Posner, M. I., & Boies, S. J. Components of attention. *Psychological Review*, 1971, *78*, 391-408.

Posner, M. I., & Klein, R. M. On the functions of consciousness. In S. Kornblum (Ed.), *Attention and performance IV*. New York: Academic Press, 1973.

Posner, M. I., & Snyder, C. R. R. Facilitation and inhibition in the processing of signals. In P. M. A. Rabbitt & S. Dornic (Eds.), *Attention and performance V*. New York: Academic Press, 1975. (a)

Posner, M. I., & Snyder, C. R. R. Attention and cognitive control. In R. L. Solso (Ed.), *Information processing and cognition: The Loyola symposium*. Hillsdale, N.J.: Lawrence Erlbaum Associates, 1975. (b)

Rayner, K., & Posnansky, C. Stages of processing word identification. *Journal of Experimental Psychology: General*, 1978, *107*, 64-80.

Regan, J. Involuntary automatic processing in color-naming tasks. *Perception & Psychophysics*, 1978, *24*, 130-136.

Samuels, S. J., LaBerge, D., & Bremer, C. D. Units of word recognition: Evidence for developmental changes. *Journal of Verbal Learning and Verbal Behavior*, 1978, *17*, 715-720.

Shaffer, W. O., & LaBerge, D. Automatic semantic processing of unattended words. *Journal of Verbal Learning and Verbal Behavior*, 1979, *18*, 413-426.

Shiffrin, R. M., & Schneider, W. Controlled and automatic human information processing: II. Perceptual learning, automatic attending, and a general theory. *Psychological Review*, 1977, *84*, 127-190.

Stroop, J. R. Studies of interference in serial verbal reactions. *Journal of Experimental Psychology*, 1935, *18*, 643-662.

Taylor, D. A. Time course of context effects. *Journal of Experimental Psychology: General*, 1977, *106*, 404-426.

Terry, P., Samuels, S. J., & LaBerge, D. The effects of letter degradation and letter spacing on word recognition. *Journal of Verbal Learning and Verbal Behavior*, 1976, *15*, 577-585.

Treisman, A. M., & Geffen, G. Selective attention: Perception or response? *Quarterly Journal of Experimental Psychology*, 1967, *19*, 1-17.

Treisman, A. M., & Gelade, G. A feature-integration theory of attention. *Cognitive Psychology*, 1980, *12*, 97-136.

Treisman, A. M., Squire, R., & Green, J. Semantic processing in dichotic listening? A replication. *Memory & Cognition,* 1974, *2,* 641-646.

Triesman, A. M., Sykes, M., & Gelade, G. Selective attention and stimulus integration. In S. Dornic (Ed.), *Attention and performance VI.* Hillsdale, N.J.: Lawrence Erlbaum Associates, 1977.

Underwood, G. Moray vs. the rest: The effect of extended shadowing practice. *Quarterly Journal of Experimental Psychology,* 1974, *26,* 368-372.

Underwood, G. Semantic interference from unattended printed words. *British Journal of Psychology,* 1976, *76,* 327-338.

Underwood, G. Contextual facilitation from attended and unattended messages. *Journal of Verbal Learning and Verbal Behavior,* 1977, *16,* 99-106.

11 Voluntary versus Automatic Control over the Mind's Eye's Movement

John Jonides
University of Michigan
Ann Arbor, Michigan
U.S.A.

ABSTRACT

Three experiments are reported that test the hypothesis that shifts of attention can be mediated by automatic as well as voluntary control. In these experiments, subjects were induced to shift their attention, but not their fixation, through the use of two types of visual cue. The experiments examined differences between the cues on three criteria for comparing automatic versus nonautomatic processes: capacity demands, resistance to suppression, and sensitivity to changes in expectancy. According to all criteria, one of the cues was shown to induce shifts of attention more automatically than the other. This indicates two separable modes of control over the allocation of attention.

INTRODUCTION

Attention can be shifted from one locus in the visual field to another without shifting eye position. Two experimental results invite this conclusion: First, subjects are faster and more accurate at detecting or recognizing a target in a visual array if the position of the target is known before the array is presented than if it is not (Jonides, 1976; Smith & Blaha, 1969; Eriksen & Hoffman, 1974; Posner, Nissen, & Ogden, 1978). Second, misinforming subjects about a target's location harms performance relative to giving no location information (Jonides, 1976; Posner et al., 1978). Moreover, these "benefits and costs" in performance are not caused by movements of fixation. They persist even with stimulus presentations too brief to permit a saccade, and they are found when eye position is measured and remains fixed.

What controls movements of attention? An examination of the experimental procedure that is frequently used to elicit attention shifts suggests one answer. Frequently, subjects are presented with a visual marker in advance of each stimulus array, with the marker located near the impending location of the target item (Eriksen & Hoffman, 1972, 1973, 1974; Eriksen & Rohrbaugh, 1970; Holmgren, 1974; Van Der Heyden & Eerland, 1973). Such a marker would be a high contrast, salient discontinuity in a nonfoveal area of the visual field. Intuition and some experimentation suggest that such a cue may automatically capture attention much as it might automatically elicit an eye movement to the cued location, if a functional eye movement were permitted in these experiments (Todd & Van Gelder, 1979).

But peripherally located visual cues are not necessary to cause shifts of attention. Helmholtz (1925) realized this long ago when he remarked that "it is possible, simply by a conscious and voluntary effort, to focus the attention on some definite spot in a field" Various casual observations lead one to the same conclusion. For example, in order to detect the dim illumination of distant stars, many astronomers have developed the ability to focus attention *voluntarily* on a part of the peripheral visual field while maintaining fixation at the center. But one does not even need to be extensively skilled or practiced to engage in a voluntary shift of attention: We have all, at one time or other, watched an event "out of the corner of our eyes" without actually foveating the event of interest.

Experimental data also support the claim that the location of attention is subject to voluntary control. Posner et al. (1978), for instance, gave subjects *centrally* located visual cues (arrows) to indicate the *peripheral* positions of impending targets in a detection task. Introspection suggests that such cues, unlike the peripheral visual markers just described, do not automatically draw attention to the cued location; rather, they seem to stimulate a voluntary shift of attention.

These and other experiments (Jonides & Somers, 1977; Shaw, 1978; Shaw & Shaw, 1977) support the hypothesis that attention shifts can be guided by two mechanisms: On the one hand, certain salient stimuli have reflexive control over attention allocation such that when one of these stimuli occurs, a shift of attention to the stimulus is automatically elicited. On the other hand, subjects have internal control over the spatial allocation of attention so that, when motivated, they can voluntarily shift attention from one part of the field to another.

We tested this hypothesis by having subjects engage in a visual search task under the guidance of one of two cues. One was chosen because of its likelihood of automatically drawing attention (an arrowhead in the periphery), whereas the other (an arrowhead at the point of fixation) was chosen because it was presumed to cause a voluntary shift of attention (see Todd & Van Gelder, 1979, for a discussion of stimuli that control shifts of the eyes, and presumably attention, in a voluntary or reflexive manner).

The hypothesis, then, was that the two types of cues would mediate shifts of attention in qualitatively different ways—one via automatic control and one via voluntary control. Evaluation of the hypothesis required some empirical criteria of automaticity. To avoid ambiguous results, a strict position was adopted by choosing three criteria for automatic processes and testing whether a difference in automaticity between the types of cues could be demonstrated according to *all three* criteria. The experiments that follow report the results of tests against these criteria.

EXPERIMENT 1: CAPACITY

Perhaps the most frequently cited feature of an automatic process is its minimal use of mental capacity. According to many accounts, as a process becomes more automatic, the operations involved are executed with ever lessening demands on attentive resources. Presumably, this is due in part to the stereotypy of operation that characterizes most (if not all) automated processes.

In the present experiment, a standard laboratory paradigm was used to assess capacity demand. Subjects engaged in a memory span task while performing visual search under the direction of either peripheral or central cues. If peripheral cues are processed more automatically than central cues, subjects should be disrupted less by the memory task when using peripheral cues during search.

Method

Design.   There were two conditions in the experiment, in both of which the primary task was the identification of an L or R that appeared among seven other letters. In the peripheral cue condition, each search display was preceded by an arrowhead that was placed near one of the letter positions. In the central cue condition, an arrowhead was also used as a locational cue, but it was placed in the center of the display where subjects were told to fixate. The delay between cue and search array was 90 msec.

The cost–benefit technique of Posner et al. (1978) was used to assess shifts of attention. On 70% of the trials (valid trials) with either cue the arrowhead correctly indicated the position of the impending target. On the remaining 30% of the trials (invalid trials), the arrowhead pointed to a nontarget location. We diagnosed shifts of attention by examining differences in performance between valid and invalid trials. This corresponds to adding together costs and benefits in the sense defined by Posner et al. (1978).

Subjects.   Eight undergraduates served as paid volunteers in two experimental sessions of 1 hr each.

Apparatus.   A computer controlled the presentation of stimuli, which were displayed on a graphic display device. Subjects were seated such that the viewing distance from the screen was approximately 60 cm. The testing room was kept dimly illuminated throughout the experiment.

Stimuli.   The stimulus arrays consisted of letters evenly spaced around the circumference of an imaginary circle of 7.5° diameter. Each letter was 1.2° in height and .8° in width. Each stimulus array was constructed by first locating an uppercase L or an uppercase R at one of the eight array positions and then randomly selecting uppercase letters from the remainder of the alphabet without replacement to fill the seven remaining display positions. On peripheral cue trials, the stimulus arrays were preceded by an outline arrowhead (.8° in length) that pointed to one of the eight array locations. The arrowhead was positioned in the display such that its tip was .7° from the closest position of the letter to which it pointed. On the central cue trials, an arrowhead also preceded the letter displays, but it was always positioned in the center of the imaginary circle on which the letters were placed.

In the first experimental session, a subject received three blocks of 80 trials from one of the two conditions, preceded by 30 practice trials appropriate to that condition (peripheral for half the subjects, central for the other half). The second session contained trials from the remaining cue condition. In both conditions, there were 56 valid and 24 invalid trials with targets appearing equally often at each display position for each type of trial. The practice trials were constructed using the same principles as those used for the test trials. Data from the practice trials are not included in the analyses presented below.

Procedure.   Subjects were told about the design of the experiment and about the two conditions in which they would participate. This included instructions about cue validities. Then they were told the order of events on each trial: First, they would be read a list of three, five, or seven randomly chosen digits. Following this, they could initiate a trial that began with a dot appearing in the center of the screen and remaining in view for 2 sec. The dot would be replaced by the cue which was displayed for 25 msec. Next, the screen would be blank for the duration of the delay (90 msec), and then an eight-letter display would be presented for 25 msec. Subjects were told to press a left response key if the display contained an L or a right key if it contained an R. They were instructed to respond as quickly yet as accurately as possible. Finally, subjects were instructed to recall aloud the digit string in serial order. Subjects were told to regard the digit task as secondary and not to let it detract from performance on the search task. Nevertheless, they were told to be accurate in their recall.

We exercised two precautions to ensure that subjects maintained fixation throughout the trials. First, we vigorously instructed and reminded subjects about the importance of maintaining fixation throughout the experiment. Second, we used a delay, 90 msec. for which the total duration of cue plus delay plus display was 140 msec. This value is about one-half of the average saccade latency reported in experiments similar to the present one (Colegate, Hoffman, & Eriksen, 1973). Thus, even the fastest saccades to the target should have been rendered nonfunctional.[1]

Results and Discussion

Reaction Times and Errors.   Figure 11.1 presents the mean response times and error rates for central and peripheral cues as a function of memory load. Separate analyses of variance for each dependent measure were used to analyze these results. The analyses included the factors of cue type (central versus peripheral) and memory load (three versus five versus seven items) in addition to a subjects factor.

The analysis of response times revealed a reliable main effect of memory load, $F(2, 14) = 95.24$, $p < .001$, and a reliable interaction of this factor with cue type, $F(2, 14) = 10.07$, $p < .01$. The main effect of cue type was not significant ($F < 1$). Examination of Fig. 11.1 shows the cause of the reliable interaction: Response times to central cues are affected by memory load more than responses to peripheral cues.

The analysis of error rates revealed no reliable interaction of cue with memory load, $F(2, 14) = 1.76$, $p > .05$, although each of the main effects was significant, $F(1, 7) = 10.13$, $p < .02$ for cue type, $F(2, 14) = 10.44$, $p < .01$ for memory load.

Memory Scores.   On the basis of assumptions underlying the use of dual-task methodology, the reaction-time results indicate that processing the central cue is a more capacity-demanding task than processing the peripheral cue. To ensure that this conclusion is warranted, we examined the accuracy of subjects' memory scores. The result of this examination was the following: For list lengths of 3, 5, and 7, respectively, subjects correctly recalled 2.93, 4.53, and 5.56 items in the peripheral cue condition and 2.93, 4.38, and 4.75 items in the central cue condition. The data reflect the use of a strict scoring criterion in which a digit was counted as correct only if it was recalled in the correct serial position. Notice that on the average (and especially with list length = 7) performance is worse on trials with a central cue than on those with a peripheral cue. Analysis of the memory scores confirmed that there was a reliable main effect of cue, $F(1, 7) = 19.95$, $p < .001$, and memory load, $F(2, 14) = 87.35$, $p < .001$, and a reliable interaction of these two variables, $F(2, 14) = 9.02$, $p < .01$. So both the

---

[1]Pilot experimentation confirmed the success of these precautions. In this pilot work, subjects' fixations were monitored while the same two precautions as in Experiment 1 were exercised. We found that subjects refixated the display on 7% or less of all trials. The results of the pilot study were unchanged by deleting the trials on which refixations occurred.

response times and the memory scores indicate the greater difficulty of process-ing the central cue.

   Costs and Benefits.   A final analysis confirms the position presented here. We subtracted response times and error rates for valid trials from the comparable scores for invalid trials. The difference scores are measures of costs plus benefits in performance. Our hypothesis was that the greater automaticity of the peripheral cue should render it more invulnerable to interference by the memory task. This would be indicated by a greater invariance of costs plus benefits as a function of memory load for the peripheral than for the central cue. Our analyses confirm this prediction.

   Figure 11.2 plots costs plus benefits in response times as a function of memory load. There is an overall effect of cue type, $F(1, 7) = 22.59$, $p < .01$, and of memory load, $F(2, 14) = 4.52$, $p < .05$. Of greater interest, however, is the reliable interaction of these two effects, $F(2, 14) = 4.73$, $p < .05$. The interac-tion was also found for the error rates reported in Fig. 11.2, $F(2, 14) = 8.87$, $p < .01$, although neither main effect was reliable, $F(1, 7) = 1.98$, $p > .05$ for cue, $F(2, 14) = 1.35$, $p > .05$ for memory load.

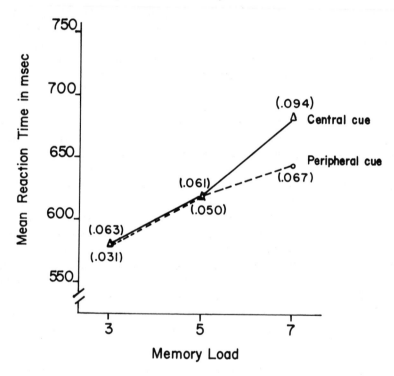

FIG. 11.1.   Experiment 1: Mean reaction times as a function of memory load for central and peripheral cues. Numbers in parentheses represent proportions of er-rors.

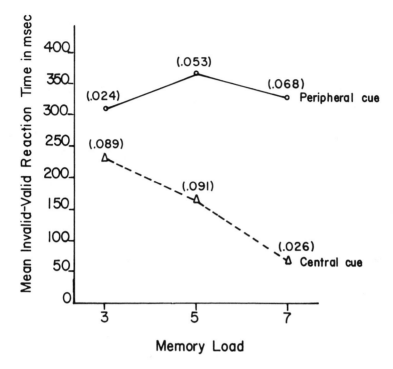

FIG. 11.2.   Experiment 1: Mean invalid-valid reaction times as a function of
memory load. Numbers in parentheses represent proportions of errors.

Thus, the attention-capturing power of the peripheral cue is relatively unaffected by increased alternative demands on processing capacity. This is exactly
what one would predict if the peripheral cue were operating in a more automatic
fashion than the central cue.

We consider now two further criteria used to assess the automaticity of processing in this task.

EXPERIMENT 2: RESISTANCE TO SUPPRESSION

One of the most striking aspects of an automatic process is its resistance to
suppression. By this, we mean that, given the proper initiating conditions (i.e.,
the proper stimulus), an automatic process will begin and end in an autonomous
fashion. An attempt to suppress or interrupt processing will either completely fail
or be less successful than a similar attempt to interrupt a nonautomatic process.

The classic example of resistance to suppression is the Stroop effect. The
problem for subjects here is that the names of the words intrude on the naming of
the hues in which the words are printed. But, subjects are aware of this. Their

problem is that, try as they may, they cannot seem to suppress processing of the word names sufficiently to eliminate the interference.

This and other similar phenomena (Shiffrin & Schneider, 1977, Experiment 4d) suggest that measuring the degree to which one can suppress a particular process will provide an indication of the level of automaticity for that process. Consequently, in Experiment 2 we introduced a condition in which subjects were instructed to ignore the arrows that preceded the letter displays. We reasoned that if a peripheral arrow cue provides a more automatic basis for an attention shift than a central cue, then subjects should have more difficulty ignoring it.

Method

Subjects.   Eighteen undergraduates were paid for participation in one experimental session.

Apparatus and Stimuli.   The apparatus and stimulus displays were identical to those of Experiment 1 with three exceptions. First, a delay of 50 msec between cue and display was used. Second, the validity of the cue in the peripheral and central cue conditions was reduced to 12.5%. Because there were eight possible target locations, the one indicated by the cue was therefore only randomly related to the actual location of the target. The reason for the decrease in valid trials is made clear later. Third, the memory load task was eliminated.

Procedure.   The trial-by-trial procedure was similar to that of Experiment 1, except for the elimination of the memory load task. Subjects received two consecutive blocks of 80 trials for each cue condition, resulting in a total of 320 test trials. The blocks of each cue condition were preceded by a block of 30 practice trials appropriate for that condition. The order of cue conditions was counterbalanced across subjects.

Subjects in the "attend" group were given instructions that were similar to the visual search instructions of Experiment 1. In addition, these subjects were told that there was a "fairly low" cue validity, although they were not told that the validity was at a chance level. Throughout the session, these subjects were frequently instructed to attend to the cue because on the average, they were told, it would improve their performance.

The second group of subjects was instructed to ignore the arrow cues. They were told about the actual cue validity and the random relationship between cue and target. Furthermore, these subjects were shown data similar to those of Experiment 1 to convince them that the experimenter could assess whether they had actually ignored the cue. In this way, the need to ignore the directionality of the cues in both peripheral and central conditions was emphasized.

Results and Discussion

Reaction times and error rates are presented in Table 11.1. Two analyses of variance, one for each group, assessed the effects of cue (peripheral versus central) and validity (valid versus invalid) for each of the dependent measures.

The analyses of reaction times revealed the following effects. For the group that was instructed to attend to the cue, there was a reliable main effect of validity, $F(1, 8) = 20.83$, $p < .001$; no reliable effect of cue types ($F < 1$); and an insignificant interaction of the two variables, $F(1, 8) = 1.43$, $p > .05$. The interaction is consistent with the finding of Experiment 1 that there is a smaller difference between valid and invalid trials for the central than the peripheral cue. That this interaction is not reliable may be attributed to the increased variability of the valid trials in this experiment due to their small number.

Analysis of the reaction times for the group instructed to ignore the cues revealed a somewhat different pattern of results. Again, there was no main effect of cue type ($F < 1$). Also, there was no reliable effect of validity overall, $F(1, 8) = 2.98$, $p > .05$. However, there was a reliable interaction of these two variables, $F(1, 8) = 6.25$, $p < .05$. As Table 11.1 suggests, this interaction is due to the fact that there is a reliable difference between valid and invalid peripheral cues ($p < .05$ by Scheffé post hoc test) but no reliable difference between valid and invalid central cues ($p > .05$).

The analysis of the low error rates for each group revealed no reliable effects ($p > .05$).

These results indicate that, when given instructions to ignore an attention-directing cue, subjects can comply when the cue appears in the center of the display, but they cannot do so when it appears in the periphery. In other words, subjects have more difficulty in suppressing an attention response to the peripheral cue, a result that is consistent with our hypothesis that this cue acts in a more automatic fashion than does its central cue counterpart.

There is one aspect of these results that may appear strange initially. The mean difference between response times for valid and invalid trials in the "attend" condition is 95 msec for peripheral cues and 61 msec for central cues. The comparable values for Experiment 1 are 337 msec and 153 msec, respectively. Why is there such a large discrepancy between the experiments?

One obvious possibility is that Experiment 1 also included a memory load variable that may have exaggerated the invalid–valid difference. But as we shall

TABLE 11.1
Mean Reaction Times and Mean Error Proportions for the
Two Conditions of Experiments.[a]

Condition			Attend		Ignore	
Validity			Valid	Invalid	Valid	Invalid
	Peripheral	RT	666 (155)	761 (120)	714 (150)	812 (131)
		Errors	.039 (.042)	.067 (.029)	.061 (.042)	.086 (.026)
Cue						
	Central	RT	679 (149)	740 (113)	763 (197)	761 (122)
		Errors	.045 (.046)	.070 (.026)	.050 (.035)	.045 (.020)

[a] The values in parentheses each represent one standard deviation from the respective means.

see, a similar size effect also obtains in Experiment 3 in which no memory load variable is involved. A more plausible possibility involves the cue validity. In Experiment 1, validity was 70%, whereas in the present experiment it was 12.5%. In another series of experiments, Jonides (1980) has shown that there are systematic and roughly symmetrical reductions in the magnitudes of costs and benefits with reductions in cue validity. The discrepancy between the first two experiments can be resolved on the basis of these findings.

The fact that cue validity can have an effect on the magnitude of costs and benefits for a peripheral cue as well as a central cue suggests that subjects do have some measure of control over whether they attend to the peripheral cue. Of course, as the data of the "ignore" condition in the present experiment show, subjects do not have total control: They cannot completely ignore the peripheral cue even if motivated to do so. Thus, a reasonable conclusion might be that the operation of the peripheral cue is not completely automated. Perhaps there are two components to its processing, an automatic and a nonautomatic one. The automatic component is revealed by the identical differences between invalid and valid trials for the attend versus the ignore conditions. The nonautomatic component is revealed by the change in invalid minus valid response times with cue validity. This may be an interesting hypothesis for future research; but for the present our main purpose is to demonstrate a difference in the processing of central and peripheral cues. The present experiment is support for such a hypothesized difference.

EXPERIMENT 3: EXPECTANCY

In Experiment 2, we discovered that it is difficult to ignore a peripheral cue when it precedes a stimulus display, apparently because the presence of such a cue initiates a shift of attention on many trials regardless of instructions to ignore the cue. The result suggests the following generalization: The proper stimulus conditions alone may often be sufficient to trigger an automatic process in the present task. From this it follows that a peripheral cue should remain an effective stimulus to capture attention regardless of whether subjects expect it to be presented or not. This stands in contrast to the effectiveness of a central cue. Here we hypothesize that the controlled processing that is required to render this cue effective would leave it subject to changes in expectation. The present experiment tests this notion: that is, whether the potency of the two types of cues is influenced by subjects' expectations about their occurrence. We predict that the automaticity of the peripheral cue should render it less subject to such influence. We test this prediction by mixing trials with the two types of cues and varying the probability that each cue will be presented. Presumably, if one cue is made much more probable than the other, then subjects will come to expect its occurrence more frequently.

Method

General Design.   There were two groups of subjects in the experiment. Each group was presented a series of visual search trials as in Experiment 1 (though without the memory load task) with either peripheral or central cues preceding each trial in a mixed random order. For one group (80 C–20 P), central cues occurred on 80% of all trials and peripheral cues occurred on the remaining 20%. For the other group (80 P–20 C), peripheral cues appeared on 80% of the trials, whereas central cues appeared on 20%.

Subjects.   Twenty-four undergraduates were paid for participation in two 1-hr sessions. Twelve were assigned to the 80 C–20 P group, 12 to the 80 P–20 C group.

Apparatus and Stimuli.   The apparatus was identical to that described for Experiment 1. The test stimuli likewise were constructed according to the same principles used for Experiment 1. In the present experiment, two delay values were used, however: 25 msec and 100 msec. Subjects were presented with 400 test trials in each session at one of these two delays. The order in which subjects were presented with the two delay conditions was determined randomly.

Procedure.   In addition to general instructions about stimulus events, 70% cue validity, and cautions about speed and accuracy, subjects were told about the uneven probability of central and peripheral cues. They were further instructed that although the two cues were randomly intermixed, a trial-by-trial expectation for the more frequent cue would be correct much more often than not.

Results and Discussion

Reaction Times.   Figure 11.3a and b display the reaction-time results for the 80 P–20 C and 80 C–20 P groups, respectively. An analysis of variance was used to examine trends in the data. It included the factors of expectancy condition (80 P–20 C versus 80 C–20 P), delay (25 msec versus 100 msec), cue type (peripheral versus central), validity (valid versus invalid), and subjects. The analysis revealed several reliable effects. As the figures clearly show, valid cues produce responses that are faster than those produced by invalid cues, $F(1, 22) = 77.70$, $p < .001$. Furthermore, as in Experiment 1, the difference between valid and invalid cues is greater for peripheral than central cues, $F(1, 22) = 89.82$, $p < .001$. The most relevant interaction for the hypothesis underlying the experiment, however, is the reliable four-way interaction among expectancy, cue, validity, and delay, $F(1, 22) = 20.51$, $p < .005$. Its interpretation is revealed by examining Fig. 11.3. Note first that the difference between valid and invalid central cues is much smaller (and, in fact, not statistically reliable by post hoc test) in the 80 P–20 C than in the 80 C–20 P condition at a delay of 25 msec. At the same delay, however, the difference between valid and invalid peripheral cue trials is about the same magnitude in the two expectancy conditions. This pattern of results is different at a delay of 100 msec. Here, the difference between valid and invalid central cues as well as the difference between valid and invalid peripheral cues remains the same in the two expectancy conditions. So it appears that, at a short delay, varying the probability of the central cue has marked consequences for resulting costs and benefits; varying the probability of the peripheral cue has no such effect. Subjects can, however, compensate for the unexpectedness of the low probability central cue if given sufficient delay between its presentation and the presentation of the display. For the peripheral cue, no compensation is necessary. It retains its potency in capturing attention regardless of its probability of occurrence within the range explored. This confirms the hypothesis that the peripheral cue operates in a more automatic manner than does

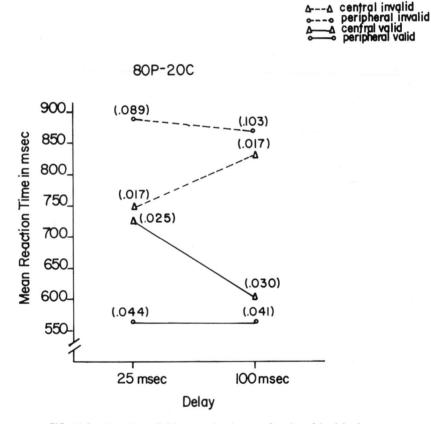

FIG. 11.3.   Experiment 3: Mean reaction time as a function of the delay between cue and display for the valid and invalid trials with central and peripheral cues. Numbers in parentheses represent proportions of errors. Panel a displays data for the 80 P–20 C expectancy condition; panel b displays similar data for the 80 C–20 P condition.

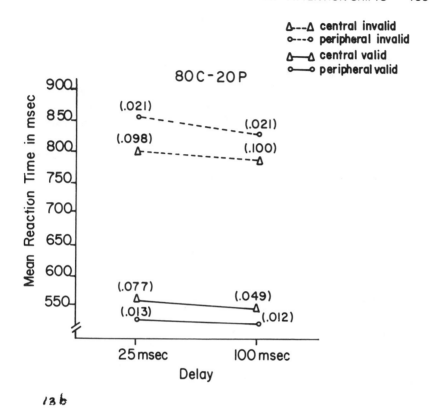

13 b

the central cue, insofar as automatic processing is characterized by insensitivity to variations in expectancy.

The remaining reliable effects in the analysis of variance can all be interpreted in light of the reliable four-way interaction. The interaction of delay with validity, $F(1, 22) = 5.78$, $p < .05$, is a result of the overall smaller effect of cue validity at a delay of 25 msec. That this is due to the 80 P-20 C expectancy condition is indicated by the reliable interaction of these two variables with condition, $F(1, 22) = 9.75$, $p < .01$. Finally, the reliable three-way interaction of expectancy condition, validity, and cue type, $F(1, 22) = 19.31$, $p < .001$, also follows from the previous analysis: Although there is a larger effect of validity on peripheral than central cues, this is more true of the 80 P-20 C condition than of the 80 C-20 P condition.

Errors. As Fig. 11.3 shows, the error rates were generally quite low. An analysis of variance identical to the one for reaction times was used to analyze the data. The only reliable main effect was that for cue validity, $F(1, 22) = 40.22$, $p < .001$. Two interactions were also highly significant: The first was an interaction of expectancy condition by cue type, $F(1, 22) = 191.03$, $p < .001$; the second was a three-way interaction between these two variables and validity,

$F(1, 22) = 59.17$, $p < .001$. These two interactions are apparently due to higher error rates for the trials on which expected cues appear than for trials on which unexpected cues appear. It is not immediately clear why this should have been so. In any case, because the error rates are different from the contrasts of interest for the reaction times, we are confident that subjects are not trading speed for accuracy to affect the interaction of interest in the reaction times.

Overall, the results of the experiment support the hypothesis that motivated it: If a peripheral cue attracts attention more automatically than a central cue, it should be less subject to changes in subjects' expectations about its occurrence. It is.

GENERAL DISCUSSION

The experiments just described have established four properties of peripheral cues:

1. The processing of the cues does not draw heavily on cognitive resources, at least in comparison with the processing of central cues.

2. It is more difficult to suppress a shift of attention induced by a peripheral cue than one induced by a central cue. This conclusion is supported by the persisting costs and benefits that accrue to a peripheral cue when subjects are instructed to ignore it. Such effects do not persist when subjects ignore central cues.

3. Peripheral cues maintain their attention-capturing property even when subjects do not particularly expect their occurrence. This is not true of central cues: Their effectiveness in causing attention shifts is directly related to subjects' expectations about their occurrence.

4. Peripheral cues are more effective in drawing attention in the sense that they produce greater costs plus benefits in processing times and accuracy than central cues.

Taken together, these results support the hypothesis that the two cues differ in the extent to which they engage attention automatically. One could attribute this difference in automaticity to any or all of several differences between the cues: One possibility is that the peripheral cue, by dint of its position in the display, is more precise in its localization of the cued letter. A second alternative is that the central cue is rendered relatively less effective than the peripheral cue because "deeper" encoding of it (analysis of the direction in which it points, as opposed to simple determination of its position) is required before its indicated location is revealed to the subject. Finally, a third plausible account of the effectiveness of the peripheral cue hinges on its similarity to visual stimuli that elicit reflexive saccades. According to this possibility, the peripheral cue effectively captures attention because it exploits a predisposition of the visual system to be especially sensitive to salient discontinuities off the fovea (Todd & Van Gelder, 1979).

Whatever the difference between the cues, however, they both seem to have one common effect: They concentrate a disproportionate share of subjects' processing resources on the cued location. As Jonides (1980) has shown, a class of models that accounts nicely for this effect is one in which processing resources are initially spread evenly over all potential target positions. When a cue appears, it causes more of these resources to be assigned to the cued location than to the others, producing costs and benefits in performance. According to this class of models, the peripheral cue of the present experiment is simply more effective in causing a reallocation of resources, because it has automatic control over these resources. This greater control is not shown as a faster shift of attention compared with a central cue (overall reaction times to the cues do not differ). Rather, the peripheral cue seems to differ from the central by virtue of its ability to attract attention on a greater proportion of trials. It is in this sense that it is more effective.

We should make clear, of course, that we are not here claiming that the visual characteristics discussed above are *necessary* to engage selectively an automatic processing mechanism, only that they are sufficient. One may well imagine that some experimental manipulation could cause a central cue to act automatically as well. For example, the work of Shiffrin and Schneider (1977) suggests that training regimens that use consistent versus varied mapping with a *single* type of cue may cause the cue to act automatically or not. This might be tested in the present paradigm in two ways: One might provide subjects with extensive consistent mapping training with a central cue to produce its effect automatically; or one might provide varied mapping training with a peripheral cue to try to eliminate its automatic effect (actually, the question of how a process once automated can be made nonautomatic is itself an interesting one). In any case, the *present* experiments suggest only that certain stimulus characteristics may be sufficient to engage automatic shifts of attention.

Significance

What is the significance of having established two modes of control over attention shifts? First of all, in doing so, these experiments add to the growing body of literature concerned with voluntary versus automatic control over perceptual and cognitive processes. This literature has begun to establish a range of phenomena in which automatically guided mechanisms can develop. At some point, this collection of phenomena will contribute to a general theory of automaticity that will help us better understand the executive mechanisms that control cognitive activity.

But there is also a more specific implication of the present experiments that merits further exploration. Although the psychological literature has long contained evidence of our ability to shift attention, there has only been sparse concern with the role that these shifts may play in general perceptual processing. Recently, Nissen, Posner, and Snyder (1978) have commented on the possible "functional relationship" between attention shifts and saccades. Both phenomena are characterized by benefits in processing information at the attended location and costs in processing nonattended stimuli. Both are characterized in terms of a spotlight metaphor according to which attention can be devoted to only one location at a time. Furthermore, both seem typically to occur together (although they can be separated, as our experiments, for example, show). Perhaps the demonstration of automatic and nonautomatic control over attention shifts adds further evidence to the emerging similarity between saccades and attention shifts, especially in view of the fact that a similar feature seems capable of eliciting automatic shifts in both systems. This strengthens the case for a "functional relationship" as proposed by Nissen et al. (1978). Further research, however, will be required to establish the nature of that function.

ACKNOWLEDGMENTS

This research was supported by National Science Foundation Grants BNS 77-16887 and 79-07373. I thank David Bauer, Laren Birenbaum, Bruce Iden, Deborah Reyher, and Barbara Zeeff for their help in collecting data and David Bauer and David Irwin for their help with data analyses. Requests for reprints should be addressed to Department of Psychology, University of Michigan, 330 Packard Road, Ann Arbor, Mich. 48104.

REFERENCES

Colegate, R. L., Hoffman, J. E., & Eriksen, C. W. Selective encoding from multielement visual displays. *Perception & Psychophysics*, 1973, *14*, 217-224.
Eriksen, C. W., & Hoffman, J. E. Some characteristics of selective attention in visual perception determined by vocal reaction time. *Perception & Psychophysics*, 1972, *11*, 169-171.
Eriksen, C. W., & Hoffman, J. E. The extent of processing of noise elements during selective encoding from visual displays. *Perception & Psychophysics*, 1973, *14*, 155-160.
Eriksen, C. W., & Hoffman, J. E. Selective attention: Noise suppression of signal enhancement? *Bulletin of the Psychonomic Society*, 1974, *4*, 587-589.
Eriksen, C. W., & Rohrbaugh, J. W. Some factors determining efficiency of selective attention. *The American Journal of Psychology*, 1970, *83*, 330-342.
Helmholtz, H. von. *Handbuch der physiologischen detik.* English translation. Southall, J. P. C., 3, 1925.
Holmgren, J. E. The effect of a visual indicator on rate of visual search: Evidence for processing control. *Perception & Psychophysics*, 1974, *15*, 544-550.
Jonides, J. *Voluntary versus reflexive control of the mind's eye's movement.* Paper presented at the meeting of the Psychonomic Society, November, 1976.
Jonides, J. Toward a model of the mind's eye's movement. *Canadian Journal of Psychology*, 1980, *34*, 103-112.

Jonides, J., & Somers, P. *Voluntary control of the allocation of attention in the visual field.* Paper presented at the meeting of the Midwest Psychological Association, May, 1977.

Nissen, M. J., Posner, M. I., & Snyder, C. R. R. *Relationships between attention shifts and saccadic eye movements.* Paper presented at the meeting of the Psychonomic Society, November, 1978.

Posner, M. I., Nissen, M. J., & Ogden, W. C. Attended and unattended processing modes: The role of set for spatial location. In H. Pick & E. Saltzman (Eds.), *Modes of perceiving and processing information.* Hillsdale, N.J.: Lawrence Erlbaum Associates, 1978.

Shaw, M. L. A capacity allocation model for reaction time. *Journal of Experimental Psychology: Human Perception and Performance,* 1978, *4,* 586-598.

Shaw, M. L., & Shaw, P. Optimal allocation of cognitive resources to spatial locations. *Journal of Experimental Psychology: Human Perception and Performance,* 1977, *3,* 201-211.

Shiffrin, R. M., & Schneider, W. Controlled and automatic human information processing: II. Perceptual learning, automatic attending, and a general theory. *Psychological Review,* 1977, *84,* 127-190.

Smith, S. W., & Blaha, J. *Preliminary report summarizing the results of location uncertainty experiment I-VIII.* The Ohio State University, 1969.

Todd, J. T., & Van Gelder, P. Implications of a transient-sustained dichotomy for the measurement of human performance. *Journal of Experimental Psychology: Human Perception and Performance,* 1979, *5,* 625-638.

Van der Heyden, A. H. C., & Eerland, E. The effect of cueing in a visual signal detection task. *Quarterly Journal of Experimental Psychology,* 1973, *25,* 496-503.

12

Attention, Automaticity, and the Ability to Stop a Speeded Choice Response

Gordon D. Logan
Erindale College, University of Toronto
Mississauga, Ontario
Canada

ABSTRACT

This chapter reports an investigation of people's ability to inhibit their responses in choice reaction-time tasks, when given a signal not to respond at various delays after the onset of the choice stimulus. Responses that could not be stopped were considered ballistic; responses that could be stopped were considered subject to attentional control. Two experiments were conducted. The first varied event and temporal predictability of the stop signal to examine strategies that subjects use to control the probability of inhibition, and the second varied discriminability and stimulus–response compatibility to localize the point in processing at which responses become ballistic. The findings suggest that people have some strategic control over whether or not they respond in choice reaction-time tasks, which they can exercise up to the point at which the physical response is initiated.

INTRODUCTION

The distinction between automatic and attentionally controlled modes of processing is generally considered to be important in understanding the mechanics of complex cognitive activity. Very generally, the distinction reflects a difference between processing that is controlled by the "stimuli" in the task environment and processing that is controlled centrally, by attentional mechanisms. This general view has several empirical interpretations, each focusing on a different implication of the same idea. For example, the dual-task method for distinguishing the two modes of processing exploits the idea that the capacity for attentional control is limited (Logan, 1979; Posner & Snyder, 1975). The unattended-channel method exploits the idea that automatic processes are stimulus driven. Stimuli or stimulus dimensions are presented outside the focus of attention and their effects on the attended task are measured (Posner & Snyder, 1975).

The present experiments explore a third empirical interpretation that reflects the distinction between stimulus control and attentional control more directly. They investigate subjects' ability to stop a speeded response after the eliciting stimulus has appeared. Subjects are engaged in a choice reaction-time task and, occasionally, a tone sounds which indicates that they should not respond on that trial. Whether or not subjects are able to inhibit their responses is the main variable of interest: Responses that can be stopped in response to the signal are clearly subject to attentional control, whereas responses that cannot be stopped are clearly beyond attentional control, hence automatic.

A similar distinction has proved useful in the study of rapid movements of the eyes and hands: Responses that can be modified to accommodate changes in the eliciting stimulus are considered *controlled,* whereas responses that cannot be modified to accommodate changes in the stimulus are considered *ballistic* (Lisberger, Fuchs, King, & Evinger, 1975; Megaw, 1974). These studies show that simple movements are neither purely ballistic nor purely controlled.

The present experiments investigated a similar distinction in choice reaction time using three types of parameters: The first, and most important, was the delay between the onset of the choice stimulus and the onset of the stop signal. Surely, all subjects would be able to inhibit their responses if the stop signal occurred well before the choice stimulus appears, and no subject could inhibit a response if the stop signal occurred after it. The points between these extremes describe an *inhibition function,* relating the probability of inhibiting a response to the delay between the onsets of the choice stimulus and the stop signal. Inhibition functions were obtained in each of the two experiments in the present investigation.

The second type of parameter affected subjects' ability to predict the occurrence of the stop signal and was used in the first experiment to investigate strategies that subjects may develop to exploit the predictability. Predictability was varied in two ways: The probability that a stop signal would occur on a given trial was varied (*event predictability, $p = 0.1$ or 0.2*), and the delay of the stop signal varied randomly within blocks or was fixed for a block of trials (*temporal predictability*). Stop signals with low probability or with delays that vary randomly would be unpredictable relative to stop signals with higher probability or with delay fixed for a block of trials. Increasing predictability generally improves performance with the predicted stimuli; thus, subjects should be better able to inhibit responses when the stop signal is more predictable.

Studies using the stop-signal methodology with simple reaction-time tasks suggest that subjects improve their ability to inhibit by sacrificing speed in the reaction time task: They appear to impose a delay between detecting the reaction-time stimulus and responding to it that is proportional to stop-signal delay, in order to increase the chances of detecting the stop signal (if it occurs) before responding (Lappin & Eriksen, 1966; Ollman, 1973). In choice reaction-time tasks, this sort of strategic adjustment should be apparent as a speed-accuracy tradeoff: In choice tasks, evidence for one response or the other is generally believed to accumulate over time, so if a delay were imposed before responding in order to improve the chances of inhibiting, any responses that resulted would be based on more evidence and hence would be more accurate. Moreover, if *latency operating characteristics* were calculated to reveal the fundamental relation between speed and accuracy, conditions that yield different mean reaction times, error rates, and probabilities of inhibition should yield equivalent latency operating characteristics. These possibilities were explored in Experiment 1.

The third type of parameter, varied in Experiment 2, affected the elementary processes recruited to perform the task (i.e., encoding and response-selection operations). They were included to provide information about structural limitations on the ability to inhibit. By observing the effects of these parameters on inhibition functions as well as on reaction time, it may be possible to estimate the point in processing at which responses become ballistic.

EXPERIMENT 1

Method

Subjects.   Sixty-four undergraduate students from Erindale College participated in one 1-hr session to fulfill a course requirement.

Apparatus and Stimuli.   The stimuli for the choice task were the letters A and B (uppercase), presented singly in the center of a cathode-ray tube (Tektronix Model 604 equipped with P31 phosphor) under the control of a PDP-11/03 laboratory computer. The letters were formed by illuminating approximately 20 points in a 5×7 dot matrix. One point was illuminated every 78 μsec. Viewed at a distance of 60 cm, each letter subtended $0.43 \times 0.57°$ of visual angle (constant viewing distance was maintained by using a headrest). The letters were exposed for 500 msec following a 500-msec foreperiod during which a fixation point was illuminated in the center of the screen. The interval between trials (i.e., from the termination of a letter to the beginning of the next foreperiod) was held constant at 2.5 sec.

The stop signal was a 500-msec, 1000-Hz tone presented through a speaker behind the cathode-ray tube. It occurred on 10% or 20% of the trials (see following) either 100, 200, 300, or 400 msec after the onset of the letter.

Subjects responded by pressing one of two telegraph keys mounted on the table in front of them. The computer measured reaction time and recorded which key had been pressed.

Procedure. This experiment manipulated stop-signal delay (100, 200, 300, and 400 msec), the probability that a stop signal would occur (event predictability; $p = 0.1$ or 0.2) and the temporal predictability of the stop signal (blocked or randomized delays). Stop-signal delay was varied within subjects, whereas event and temporal predictability were varied between subjects, forming four groups of 16 subjects.

Each subject completed four blocks of 160 trials. The letter A appeared on half of the trials, and the letter B occurred on the other half. At each delay, half of the stop signals occurred when A was presented and half occurred when B was presented. Half of the subjects in each group pressed the right key for A and the left key for B, and the other half did the opposite.

The order of delays was balanced for the two groups for whom the stop-signal delay was blocked. They received one block of 160 trials at each of the four delays, in an order determined by a balanced Latin square. Within each group, four subjects received each order, and the order of delays was orthogonal to the assignment of stimuli to responses. For the two groups for whom the stop-signal delay was random, the four delays occurred equally often within each block of 160 trials. Note that in the random conditions there is a danger that the delays "age"; that is, the stop signal becomes more probable as time passes. However, the aging effect is slight: In the 20% random condition, the probability that a signal will occur at any one delay is .05. Thus, the probability that the signal will occur if it has not already is .050, .053, .056, and .059, for the 100- to 400-msec delays, respectively. In the 10% random condition, the aging effect is half as large.

Whether the delay was blocked or random, every subject received the choice stimuli and the stop signals in a different random order. Subjects were not told of the temporal or event predictability of the stop signal. The instructions emphasized the reaction-time task over the inhibiting task.

Results and Discussion

Probability of Inhibition. The mean probabilities of inhibiting responses when the stop signal occurred are displayed for each group as a function of stop-signal delay in Fig. 12.1A. The figure shows that subjects could inhibit their reaction-time responses if the stop signal occurred early enough, but their ability to do so declined roughly linearly as stop-signal delay increased. The probability of inhibition was affected by both event and time predictability: Increasing the probability that a stop signal would occur from .1 to .2 increased the "intercepts" of the inhibition functions by about .1 but had no effect on the "slopes." Increasing the temporal predictability of the stop signal also increased the probability of inhibition, having a stronger effect at the longer delays (i.e., temporal

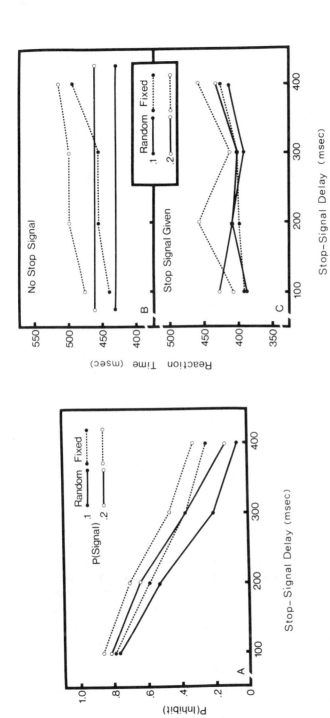

FIG. 12.1. (A) Probability of inhibiting a response as a function of stop-signal delay in Experiment 1. (B) Reaction time in the choice task as a function of stop-signal delay for responses from trials in which no stop signal was presented. (C) Reaction time in the choice task as a function of stop-signal delay for responses from trials in which the stop signal was presented but subjects responded anyway.

predictability affected the slopes but not the intercepts of the inhibition functions).

These conclusions received some support in an analysis of variance on the inhibition data: The main effect of delay and the interaction between delay and temporal predictability were significant, F's $(3,180) = 215.0$ and 3.51, respectively, p's $< .02$, MSe $= .022$. However, the main effects of event and temporal predictability only approached conventional levels of significance, F's $(1, 60) = 2.83$ and 3.23, respectively, $p < .10$, MSe $= .210$. No other effects were significant in the analysis.

Reaction Times.   Mean reaction times from trials on which no stop signal occurred are displayed for each group as a function of stop-signal delay in Fig. 12.1B. Note that for the random-delay groups reaction times cannot be associated with particular delays, so the points are "stretched" horizontally across the figure to facilitate comparison.

In general, the figure shows that subjects seemed able to adjust the probability of inhibition by trading speed in the reaction-time task for an improvement in the ability to inhibit; reaction times increased in conditions in which the probability of inhibition increased (relative to controls). In particular, reaction times were longer when the stop signal occurred on 20% of the trials than when it occurred on 10%; in the groups for whom delay was blocked, reaction time increased with stop-signal delay.

These conclusions received rather weak support in analyses of variance performed on the reaction-time data: In an analysis of the fixed-delay conditions by themselves, the main effect of stop-signal delay was significant, $F(3, 90) = 8.16$, $p < .01$, MSe $= 1513.44$. In an analysis comparing the random-delay conditions with the averages over delay from the fixed-delay conditions, the F-ratios for temporal and event predictability were greater than unity but not significantly so, F's $(1, 60) = 2.44$ and 2.34, respectively, MSe $= 7904.03$. These findings replicate those of Lappin and Eriksen (1966) and Ollman (1973) and extend them to choice reaction-time tasks.

Mean reaction times from those trials on which a stop signal was presented but subjects responded anyway (i.e., failed to inhibit) are displayed in Fig. 12.1C for each group as a function of stop-signal delay. Although in general there were too few responses for any stable pattern to emerge (especially at the longer delays), these reaction times were slightly faster than reaction times from no-stop-signal trials. However, the stop-signal-given reaction times were within the range of no-stop-signal reaction times.

Latency Operating Characteristics.   In order to evaluate the possibility that the covariation between reaction time and the probability of inhibition was primarily a strategic phenomenon, latency operating characteristics were calculated. For each subject, reaction times in each condition were rank ordered, and the mean reaction time and probability of error in each successive 10% of the distribution were calculated (Lappin & Disch, 1973). The mean functions across subjects in each condition are displayed in Fig. 12.2.

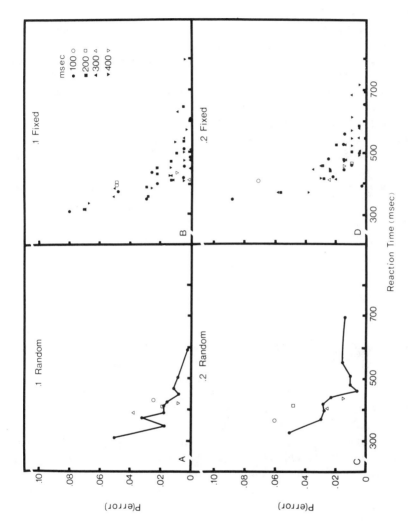

FIG. 12.2. Latency operating characteristics from each condition of Experiment 1.

If subjects delayed reaction time to improve their ability to inhibit (either by increasing the amount of time or evidence required to reach a decision), the error rates should decline proportionately, and conditions that yield different mean reaction times, error rates, and probabilities of inhibition should yield equivalent latency operating characteristics.

Both of these predictions were confirmed in the fixed-delay conditions: Mean error rate declined as delay and reaction time increased (the means were .021, .020, .020, and .016, respectively), and the operating characteristics from the different delays were indistinguishable (see Fig. 12.2B and D). However, the change in the probability that a signal would occur from .1 to .2 actually increased mean error rate (from .019 to .020), though the operating characteristics seemed similar (compare Fig. 12.2A and B with C and D).

Reaction times and error rates from trials on which the stop signal was presented but subjects responded anyway are displayed in Fig. 12.2 as the open symbols. The figure suggests that much of the difference in reaction time can be accounted for by differences in error rate; stop-signal reaction times appear to come from the fast, inaccurate end of the no-stop-signal reaction-time distributions.

EXPERIMENT 2

This experiment was conducted to determine the point in processing at which responses become ballistic. The idea was to manipulate parameters of the experimental situation that were associated with different stages of processing and to observe their effects on the inhibition functions. In general, parameters that affect stages prior to the point at which responses become ballistic should affect the inhibition functions, increasing the probability of inhibition as they increase the duration of the stage. Parameters that affect stages subsequent to the point at which responses become ballistic should have no effect on the inhibition functions, because at that point responses would be beyond attentional control.

The experiment required that subjects indicate the position of an X on the cathode-ray tube by pressing the appropriate telegraph key. The positions were easy or difficult to discriminate, and the responses were compatible (e.g., "press the key under the X") or incompatible (e.g., "press the key opposite the X") with the judged position. Previous research has shown that both these variables affect reaction time, but their joint effects are additive (Egeth, 1977). Following Sternberg's (1969) additive-factors logic, this means that they affect different stages, discriminability affecting an encoding or comparison stage and compatibility affecting a response selection stage.

If responses become ballistic after the first few milliseconds of stimulation (as Lappin & Eriksen, 1966, suggested was true of simple reaction-time responses), neither discriminability nor compatibility should affect the probability of inhibition. If responses become ballistic after the encoding or comparison stage, discriminability should affect the probability of inhibition but compatibility should not. If responses become ballistic after the response selection stage, both discriminability and compatibility should affect the probability of inhibition.

Method

Subjects.   Sixteen undergraduate students from Erindale College were paid to participate in four 1-hr sessions.

Apparatus and Stimuli.   The stimuli for the choice task were capital X's, displayed singly to the left or right of fixation. The separation between the X's on the left and right varied between blocks. In the wide-spacing conditions, the separation was about 3.01° of visual angle center to center; in the narrow spacing condition, the separation was about .60° of visual angle. Again, the viewing distance, maintained by a headrest, was 60 cm, and each X subtended .43 × .57° of visual angle.

Each X was exposed for 50 msec, preceded by a 500-msec foreperiod and followed by a 2950-msec intertrial interval. A central fixation point was illuminated for the first 250 msec of the foreperiod and extinguished for the last 250 msec.

In all other respects, the apparatus and stimuli were the same as in Experiment 1.

Procedure.   Each subject completed four sessions of 640 trials. Each session was divided into four blocks of 160 trials, representing the factorial combination of the two discriminability conditions and the two compatibility conditions (i.e., these variables were manipulated within subjects). In each block, the stop signal occurred on a random 20% of the trials. Stop-signal delay varied randomly within blocks (i.e., low temporal predictability). Four delays were used (i.e., 75, 150, 225, and 300 msec), and half of the stop signals at each delay occurred with X on the right and half with X on the left.

The order of conditions varied between subjects each session and within subjects over sessions according to a balanced Latin square. The instructions emphasized the reaction-time task over the inhibiting task.

Results and Discussion

Probability of Inhibition.   The mean probabilities of inhibiting responses when the stop signal occurred are displayed as a function of delay and experimental conditions in Fig. 12.3A. The data in the figure are collapsed over subjects and sessions.

Again, the probability of inhibition declined roughly linearly as stop-signal delay increased. It was clear that the probability of inhibition was affected by discriminability and compatibility; reducing discriminability and reducing compatibility both increased the ''intercepts'' of the inhibition functions, and neither

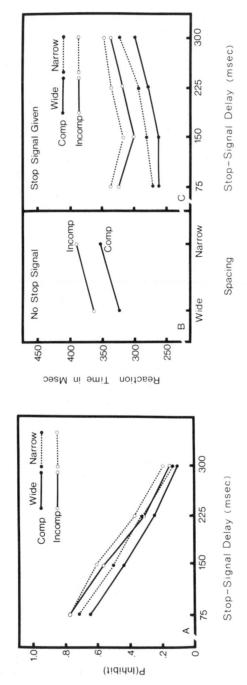

FIG. 12.3. (A) Probability of inhibiting a response as a function of stop-signal delay in Experiment 2. (B) Reaction time from no-stop-signal trials as a function of spacing and compatibility. (C) Reaction time from stop-signal trials as a function of stop-signal delay.

affected the "slopes." These conclusions were supported by an analysis of variance on the inhibition data in which the only significant effects were the main effects of the stop-signal delay, $F(3, 45) = 100.79$, $p < .01$, MSe $= .163$, discriminability, $F(1, 15) = 16.28$, $p < .01$, MSe $= .033$, and compatibility, $F(1, 15) = 26.41$, $p < .01$, MSe $= .052$.

These data suggest a locus for the point at which responses become ballistic: Parameters that affect stages prior to the point should influence the probability of inhibition, whereas parameters that affect the ballistic processes should not. Since both discriminability and S–R compatibility affected the probability of inhibition, it follows that responses become ballistic after the response selection stage.

Reaction Times.   Mean reaction times from trials on which no stop signal was given are displayed as a function of discriminability and compatibility in Fig. 12.3B. Note that delay is not a factor because delay varied randomly within each block.

The results replicate previous findings: Reaction time increased as discriminability was reduced and increased as compatibility was reduced; moreover, these effects were additive (Egeth, 1977). These conclusions were supported by an analysis of variance on the reaction-time data, in which the main effects of discriminability, $F(1, 15) = 67.36$, $p < .01$, MSe $= 756.16$, and compatibility, $F(1, 15) = 28.72$, $p < .01$, MSe $= 3065.20$, were significant, but the interaction between them was not, $F(1, 15) = 1.91$, MSe $= 300.42$. The main effect of sessions, $F(3, 45) = 3.06$, $p < .05$, MSe $= 3944.33$, and the interaction between sessions and compatibility, $F(3, 45) = 7.03$, p $< .01$, MSe $= 720.62$, were also significant, reflecting improvements in performance with practice.

The mean reaction times from those trials on which a stop signal was presented but subjects responded anyway (i.e., failed to inhibit) are displayed as a function of stop-signal delay and experimental conditions in Fig. 12.3C. Again, there were too few responses for statistical analysis to be reliable, but these reaction times resemble the no-stop-signal reaction times in Fig. 12.3B (i.e., both discriminability and compatibility effects are apparent and seem to be additive). Again, reaction times from responses that escaped inhibition were faster than reaction times from no-stop-signal trials but remained within the same range (see following).

Latency Operating Characteristics.   Latency operating characteristics were calculated for each of 14 subjects (2 subjects' data were lost due to disk damage) by pooling reaction times from the same conditions over days, rank ordering them, and calculating mean reaction time and probability of error in each successive 10% of the reaction-time distributions. The average functions across subjects appear in Fig. 12.4.

From the figure, it is clear that latency operating characteristics varied dramatically between conditions; the differences in reaction time and error rate were not simply due to an adjustment of a temporal or evidential criterion. Moreover, the

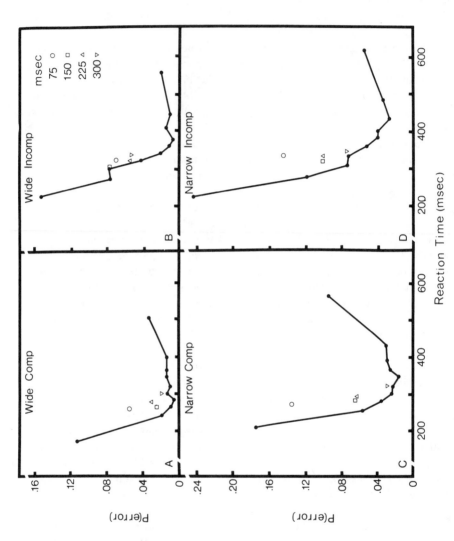

FIG. 12.4. Latency operating characteristics from each condition of Experiment 2.

different manipulations appeared to affect the functions in different ways: Changing the separation between alternative positions from wide to narrow tended to increase the proportion of slow erroneous responses (compare the rightmost points in Fig. 12.4A and B with C and D), while increasing mean error rate from .032 to .060. By contrast, reducing the compatibility of S–R mapping tended to increase the proportion of fast erroneous responses (compare the leftmost points of Fig. 12.4A and C with B and D), while increasing mean error rate from .036 to .056.

Reaction times and error rates from stop-signal trials are plotted in Fig. 12.4 as well (open symbols). Again, they were relatively close to the functions, but in some cases the error rates appeared too high for the reaction times (e.g., the 75-msec delay in the narrow-compatible condition).

Reaction-Time Distributions. The conclusion that responses become ballistic after the response selection stage entails two predictions about the relation between the probability of inhibition and the distribution of choice reaction times: The stop-signal task may be modeled as a "horse race" between the processes responding to the stop signal and the processes responding to the choice stimulus, in which the probability of inhibition represents the probability that the processes responding to the stop signal will finish before the processes responding to the choice stimulus. This probability will depend on both the distribution(s) of finishing times for the stop-signal processes (which will depend on stop-signal delay) and the distribution(s) of finishing times for the choice processes (which will depend on the subject's strategy and the difficulty of the choice task). This means that the probability of inhibition may be increased by presenting the stop signal at an earlier delay or by delaying the choice response, either strategically or by making the choice task more difficult. Thus, the time between the presentation of the stop signal and the response to the choice task should be a better predictor of inhibition than stop-signal delay by itself.

The logic behind this prediction can be seen by comparing the different situations depicted in Fig. 12.5. In Fig. 12.5A, the choice reaction-time distribution is delayed relative to Fig. 12.5B, but the probability of inhibition remains the same because the stop-signal delay has been increased by the same amount. In Fig. 12.5C, the choice distribution is delayed relative to Fig. 12.5B, but the probability of inhibition is different because there was no compensating change in stop-signal delay.

To test this prediction, the inhibition data from both experiments were plotted against the difference between mean reaction time and stop-signal delay in Fig. 12.6A and B. This is equivalent to shifting the points in Fig. 12.1A and 12.3A to the left by an amount corresponding to the differences in reaction time between conditions. Note that the interactions apparent in Experiment 1 disappear in this plot; differences in reaction time provide a nearly perfect account of differences in probability of inhibition. The correlation between the means is .991 in Fig. 12.6A and .992 in Fig. 12.6B.

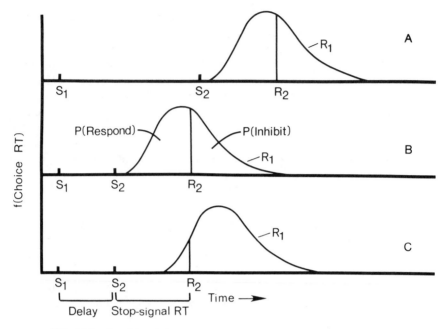

FIG. 12.5.   Possible relations among choice reaction-time distributions, stop-signal delay, and "reaction time" to the stop signal (S_1 = choice stimulus; R_1 = distribution of responses to choice stimulus; S_2 = stop signal; R_2 = internal response to stop signal).

The assumption that choice responses can be inhibited up to the point at which the physical response is initiated suggests that it should be possible to predict reaction time to the stop signal, given the probability of inhibition, stop-signal delay, and the distribution of choice reaction times. The logic can also be seen in the situations depicted in Fig. 12.5. To a first approximation, probability of inhibition reflects the proportion of the reaction-time distribution that is slower than the average response to the tone. In the distributions in Fig. 12.5, this represents the area to the right of R_2, the response to the tone. Thus, it should be possible to estimate the time at which a response occurs to the tone by integrating the reaction-time distribution (from zero to infinity) and by finding the point at which the integral equals (one minus) the probability of inhibition. In Fig. 12.5, this amounts to drawing a vertical line through the distribution such that the area to the right of the line equals the probability of inhibition and using the point at which the line intersects the time axis as an estimate of the time at which the stop signal was responded to.

These estimates were calculated for all subjects in Experiment 1 and for 14 of the subjects in Experiment 2. The means across subjects appear in Fig. 12.6C and D for Experiments 1 and 2, respectively. The sloping lines in the two figures

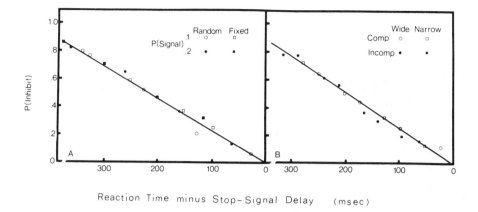

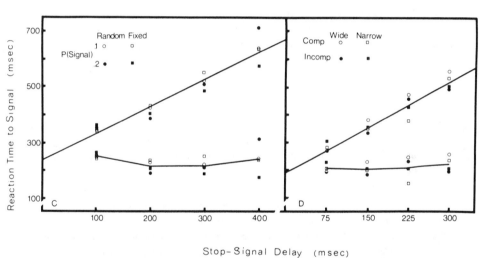

FIG. 12.6. (A) Probability of inhibition as a function of the time between the onset of the stop signal and the onset of the choice repsonse in Experiment 1. (B) Probability of inhibition as a function of the time between the onset of the stop signal and the onset of the choice response in Experiment 2. (C) Predicted reaction times to the stop signal, relative to the onset of the choice stimulus (upper sloping line) and relative to the onset of the stop signal (lower flatter line) in Experiment 1. (D) Predicted reaction times to the stop signal relative to the onset of the choice stimulus (upper sloping line) and relative to the onset of the stop signal (lower flatter line) in Experiment 2.

are drawn through estimates of the time at which the stop-signal response occurred relative to the onset of the choice stimulus and so include stop-signal delay. The zero intercepts of these best-fitting functions are estimates of reaction time to the stop signal, 239 msec for Experiment 1 and 195 msec for Experiment 2. The correlations between the means providing these estimates were .968 and .964, for Experiments 1 and 2, respectively.

The lower, flatter lines in Fig. 12.6C and D are drawn through estimates of reaction time to the stop signal, calculated by subtracting stop-signal delay from estimates of the time at which the response to the stop signal occurred relative to the onset of the choice stimulus. The average of these estimated reaction times was 231 msec for Experiment 1 and 212 msec for Experiment 2. Calculated either way, these estimates are close to what would be expected for simple reaction time to a tone, and the agreement between experiments is encouraging. It is interesting that the estimated reaction times were so fast and were not affected by tone delay. This suggests that the response to the stop signal and the response to the choice task developed in parallel with no interference. This finding stands in marked contrast with typical results when the tone requires a separate, manual response; in those situations, tone reaction time is elevated substantially and strongly affected by tone delay (e.g., Posner & Klein, 1973).

GENERAL DISCUSSION

The experiments have shown that people have some strategic control over whether or not they respond to a stimulus in a choice reaction-time task, and that they can exercise this control up to the point at which the motor system initiates a physical response. Of course, these conclusions may be limited somewhat by the details of the experiments. For example, the experiments involved relatively little practice, and it is possible that, with extended practice, reaction-time responses would become automatic enough to be difficult to inhibit at premotor stages. Further, the experiments provide little evidence on the extent to which having to respond to the tone affected the reaction-time task. Despite these limitations, the experiments have some interesting implications.

First and foremost, the stop-signal method is a measure of automaticity, and the conclusions drawn from the experiments may be compared with conclusions drawn from experiments using other measures of automaticity. Though the stop-signal method addresses the question of attentional control versus stimulus control more directly than do dual-task and unattended-channel methods, it is not a more appropriate measure that should be explored at the expense of the others. Rather, conclusions drawn from the different methods should converge to provide a more accurate picture of the nature of attentional control.

At first glance, the conclusions drawn from the different methods appear to be at variance: Dual-task and unattended-channel measures suggest that reaction-time tasks are largely automatic (e.g., Logan, 1978; Posner & Snyder, 1975), whereas stop-signal measures suggest that reaction-time tasks are largely controlled. However, it is important to recognize that the conclusion, drawn from Experiment 2 and the analysis of distributions from both experiments, that subjects can control reaction-time tasks up to the point at which the motor response is initiated does not mean that the processes prior to motor initiation are necessarily controlled. The experiments merely identify a point of control; it remains possible that processes prior to this point are automatic. For example, the stages underlying performance may each function automatically, and attention may have its controlling influence at the interface(s) between stages. Viewed this way, the present results are relatively easy to reconcile with results from other methods: By and large, dual-task and unattended-channel methods measure the automaticity of component processes, whereas the stop-signal method measures the automaticity of the whole task. Possibly, the components are automatic, but their organization as a set to perform a task requires attentional control (Logan, 1978; 1979).

Possibly, the most important aspect of the present investigation is the relatively direct focus on the function of attention (i.e., to control the execution of mental processes) rather than on derived properties like capacity and selectivity. There are surprisingly few experiments and theories on control processes in the literature, despite a general belief that attention is primarily a control process. Perhaps experiments using the stop-signal methodology, or derivatives of it, can remedy this situation.

ACKNOWLEDGMENTS

This research was supported by Grant No. A0682 from the Natural Sciences and Engineering Research Council of Canada. I am grateful to Kathy Constantinou for running the subjects and to Jane Zbrodoff for valuable discussion throughout the development of the project.

REFERENCES

Egeth, H. Attention and preattention. In G. H. Bower (Ed.), *The psychology of learning and motivation* (Vol. 11). New York: Academic Press, 1977.

Lappin, J. S., & Disch, K. The latency operating characteristic: III. Temporal uncertainty effects. *Journal of Experimental Psychology*, 1973, *98*, 279–285.

Lappin, J. S., & Eriksen, C. W. Use of a delayed signal to stop a visual reaction-time response. *Journal of Experimental Psychology*, 1966, *72*, 805–811.

Lisberger, S. G., Fuchs, A. F., King, W. M., & Evinger, L. C. Effect of mean reaction time on saccadic responses to two-step stimuli with horizontal and vertical components. *Vision Research*, 1975, *15*, 1021–1025.

Logan, G. D. Attention in character-classification tasks: Evidence for the automaticity of component stages. *Journal of Experimental Psychology: General*, 1978, *107*, 32-63.

Logan, G. D. On the use of a concurrent memory load to measure attention and automaticity. *Journal of Experimental Psychology: Human Perception and Performance*, 1979, *5*, 189-207.

Megaw, E. D. Possible modification to a rapid on-going programmed manual response. *Brain Research*, 1974, *71*, 425-441.

Ollman, R. T. Simple reactions with random countermanding of the "Go" signal. In S. Kornblum (Ed.), *Attention and performance IV*. New York: Academic Press, 1973.

Posner, M. I., & Klein, R. On the functions of consciousness. In S. Kornblum (Ed.), *Attention and performance IV*. New York: Academic Press, 1973.

Posner, M. I., & Snyder, C. R. R. Attention and cognitive control. In R. L. Solso (Ed.), *Information processing and cognition: The Loyola symposium*. Hillsdale, N.J.: Lawrence Erlbaum Associates, 1975.

Sternberg, S. Memory scanning: Mental processes revealed by reaction-time experiments. *American Scientist*, 1969, *57*, 421-457.

13 Characteristics of Automatism

Richard M. Shiffrin
Indiana University
Bloomington, Indiana

Susan T. Dumais
Bell Laboratories
Murray Hill, New Jersey

Walter Schneider
University of Illinois
Champaign, Illinois
U.S.A.

ABSTRACT

In this chapter we propose a definition of and some tests for *automatism* and describe certain characteristics of automatism. The development of automatism is explored by assessing the role of consistency of training and by considering the effects of searching for versus finding targets. What can and cannot be automatized is examined by search for conjunctions of features. What is learned during automatism is assessed by transfer and generalization tests.

INTRODUCTION

It is our aim in this chapter to offer a definition and some tests of automatism and to review certain characteristics of automatism, including the conditions under which it develops and the nature of the automatic state.

AUTOMATISM AND CONTROLLED PROCESSING

The acquisition of almost any cognitive or motor skill involves profound changes that have impressed researchers since the earliest days of psychology (James, 1890; Solomons & Stein, 1896). Consider, for example, the changes that occur while learning to type, to play a musical instrument, to read, or to play tennis. At first, effort and attention must be devoted to each smallest movement or minor decision, and performance is slow and error-prone. Eventually, long sequences of movements or cognitive processes are carried out with little attention, and performance may be quite rapid and accurate. The changes that occur are striking enough that a qualitative change seems to have occurred. Such a view has been espoused by many recent workers (Laberge, 1975; Posner & Snyder, 1975; Shiffrin & Schneider, 1977). Some theorists, however, prefer to consider the changes that occur with practice to be quantitative in nature, reflecting continuous improvements along a continuum (Hirst, Spelke, Reaves, Caharack, & Neisser, 1980).

Part of the difficulty in resolving this two-process versus continuum issue lies in the confusion of observable states with theoretical states. An analogous situation occurred when multistore memory models were first being developed. Short-term and long-term *tasks* were confused with short-term and long-term *stores;* it is of course the case that recall in almost all tasks (regardless of test delay) consists of information retrieved from both long-term and short-term stores. Similarly, it must be realized that automatism and controlled processing are theoretical states and that performance in almost all tasks will be carried out with a contribution from both types of processes. The proportions of the contribution will surely vary as skill development proceeds, but the measurement of the proportions is a delicate and difficult undertaking, especially because the components themselves may be unknown. The same problem makes it difficult to set forth necessary and sufficient distinguishing characteristics.

These considerations led Schneider and Shiffrin (1977) and Shiffrin and Schneider (1977) to choose a task utilizing two extreme conditions, each tending to lead subjects to use one of the two ideal processing modes, controlled and automatic. The task utilized memory and visual search, in both single-frame (reaction time) and multiple-frame (accuracy) settings. The type of processing was manipulated by varying the relationship between target and distractor stimuli across trials. Automatic detection occurred when there was a *consistent mapping* (termed CM) of targets and distractors. In the CM conditions, the target and distractor sets never changed over trials. When automatic detection is used by subjects, load (the product of memory set size and display size) has little effect on performance, detection is rapid and accurate, and the attention and effort required are minimal. Conversely, controlled search occurred in *varied mapping* (termed VM) conditions where the target and distractor stimuli were thoroughly mixed across trials. When controlled search is used, performance becomes slower and less accurate as load increases, and subjects report that high levels of attention and effort are required to accomplish the task. The limited capacity search process that was used in the VM conditions could be well modeled as a serial self-terminating comparison process requiring about 40 msec per comparison.

Because the search task seems to provide a well-controlled method to decompose processing into automatic and controlled components, it has been used in several subsequent experiments by Schneider and by Dumais to further our understanding of automatism. Results from these new studies are presented in this chapter to bolster our arguments. However, our main concern is not with automatic detection and controlled search in particular but with automatism and controlled processing in general.

TOWARD A DEFINITION OF AUTOMATISM

There are numerous characteristics that have been proposed, and that could be proposed, to distinguish automatic from controlled processing. At the present time we know of no completely satisfactory definition, certainly none that is necessary and sufficient to establish the presence and absence of these types of processing. In this chapter, we adopt a sufficient condition for the presence of automatism, a condition dependent on two characteristics: "resource utilization" (or limited capacity) and "control."

The basic idea holds that an automatic process should not require resources or reduce capacity. Our definition is based first and foremost upon the factor of resource utilization (or limited capacity). Shiffrin and Schneider (1977, Section III) showed that controlled search required processing resources, at least in the context of other search tasks. Two search tasks competed with each other for resources (and the competition appeared to involve a virtually perfect trading relationship, so that the total number of comparisons that could be carried out in both tasks in a given time equaled the total number that could be carried out in either task alone in that same time). On the other hand, our definition suggests that if two tasks were to be carried out simultaneously, and one could be carried out using automatic detection, then the other search task could be carried out unhindered, even though involving controlled search.

Schneider and Fisk (1980b) have recently examined joint automatic and controlled search. The basic paradigm involved search through a sequence of 12 visual displays called *frames*. Each frame consisted of four alphanumeric characters arranged in a square. One diagonal of the square was always the VM diagonal, on which subjects searched for a single digit among digit distractors. On the other diagonal, subjects performed a CM search task, looking for one of seven letters among digit distractors. (For half of the subjects, the letter and number sets were reversed.) Four subjects each had approximately 19,000 trials

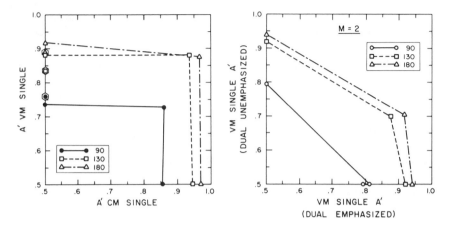

FIG. 13.1.   The left panel shows dual-task performance compared with single-task controls, when one search task is automatic (CM) and the other is controlled (VM), for three frame times (levels of difficulty). The rectangular form of the POC curve indicates that both CM and VM tasks can be carried out simultaneously without loss. The curves in the right panel are for dual controlled (VM) searches showing a simultaneous dual processing loss in VM search. A' is a measure of search accuracy independent of the subject's criterion for response emission (after Schneider and Fisk, 1980b).

in VM and CM search combined. Subjects participated in both single- and dual-task conditions. In the single-task conditions, subjects were presented a single letter or digit to search for. In the dual-task condition, subjects were presented a VM digit and a dot indicating that they were to search for any letter. At the end of the trial, subjects pushed a button indicating whether they detected a VM target, a CM target, or no target. Note that dual CM and VM targets could not both appear on a single trial. In the single-task conditions the probability of a target was .25 and no target .75. In the dual-task condition, the probability of a CM target was .25; a VM target, .25; and no target, .50.

The results of these studies are shown in Fig. 13.1. In the left panel, performance in the single-task conditions requiring only automatic detection (CM conditions) is shown on the horizontal axis. Performance in the single-task conditions requiring only controlled search (VM conditions) is shown on the vertical axis. In the interior of the square are graphed joint performance levels in which *both* tasks had to be performed simultaneously. The different curves correspond to different frame times; the frame time determines the level of difficulty. The rectangular form of the POC curves indicates that both tasks could be carried out together without noticeable loss (Norman & Bobrow, 1976). At least one of the tasks, presumably the CM one, required no resources. Note that the measures on the axes are A', a nonparametric analog of d' (Craig, 1979; Norman, 1964). The A' measure is used here because a considerable bias shift occurred for the CM task in the dual condition; that is, subjects in the dual-task condition were much less likely to emit a CM response than in the CM single condition. This conservatism reduced the "hits" when targets were present but also dropped "false alarms" when targets were absent, so that sensitivity for CM items remained unchanged. The independence results shown in the left panel of Fig. 13.1 were obtained when subjects were instructed to devote their processing resources to the VM diagonal and task. When subjects tried to divide their attention between the two diagonals, the VM performance decreased. This finding suggests that subjects do not realize that automatic detection requires no resources—given free choice, they devoted unneeded resources to the diagonal that could be handled by automatic detection. Finally, a control condition was used in which controlled processing was required on both diagonals. In this condition, A' was lowered by 10% to 15% on each diagonal compared with the single-task controls (Fig. 13.1, right panel).

Results like these suggest that resource utilization (or capacity reduction) could provide a basis for a definition distinguishing automatic from controlled processing. In practice, however, there are some problems that must be considered. One important problem has to do with the concept of capacity. Any automatic process involves a sequence of neural–muscular events, the components of which surely are unavailable for system use while the process is engaged. This is obvious in the motor domain. For example, playing a well-learned sequence on the piano may be automatized, but the fingers are unavailable during this time for other activities. The same sort of problem can arise in the domain of internal, neural processing. This situation can be saved by proposing:

RULE 1: Any process that does not use general, nonspecific processing resources and does not decrease the general, nonspecific processing capacity available for other processes is automatic.

It is understood in this definition that general, nonspecific processing refers to processing not directly involved in the automatic sequence. For example, the presentation of a visual character should not interfere with the ability to add two auditorily presented digits. We realize that the actual measurement of capacity usage is a most difficult problem, filled with unexpected pitfalls (Duncan, 1980). However, space does not allow us to discuss this problem in the present chapter.

Rule 1 is a sufficient, but not necessary, criterion for automatism. The reason is that some automatic process can interfere with ongoing processing even when specific interference is not a factor. As an example, detection of a CM target (presented on a to-be-ignored display diagonal) interferes with the detection of a VM target presented at the same instant in time on a to-be-attended display diagonal (Shiffrin & Schneider, 1977, Section III). It seems reasonable to conclude that the CM target attracted attention automatically, thereby causing a performance decrement for VM detection. (Note that the previously discussed independence results obtained by Schneider & Fisk, 1980b, occurred in conditions where VM and CM targets never appeared at the same moment in time.) The Shiffrin and Schneider results show that an automatic process can interfere with an ongoing controlled process. In effect, capacity has been reduced; so, some automatic processes can reduce capacity. In this study, however, attention demands occurred whenever CM targets were presented, despite subject attempts to ignore them. This *mandatory* distraction suggests Rule 2, which utilizes the characteristics of "control."

RULE 2: Any process that demands resources in response to external stimulus inputs, regardless of subjects' attempts to ignore the distraction, is automatic.

Rules 1 and 2 together still do not provide necessary conditions for automatism, because some automatic processes can be initiated by control processes. For example, stopping a car by depressing the clutch pedal and then the brake pedal may be an automatized sequence. It could be initiated by an external stimulus, such as a red light, or by an internal decision, such as that following a recollection that luggage has been left behind. We leave further generalizations of these rules for future research.

SOME CHARACTERISTICS OF AUTOMATISM

We propose the general position that controlled and automatic processing are two qualitatively different forms of processing rather than the two ends of a continuum. It is admitted that almost all tasks normally encountered are accomplished with a mixture of automatic and controlled processes. Furthermore, we allow for the possibility that each of these types of processing may develop in a *continuous* way. We do not feel that these facts detract from the usefulness and validity of the two-process distinction. In the rest of the chapter, the two-process dichotomy is assumed correct (though we will have occasion to comment on it briefly). Under this assumption, a number of important questions concerning automatism are discussed.

The Development of Automatism

In this section we consider a number of related questions: What training conditions are needed for the development of automization? What stimuli control the automatic response? What can and cannot be automatized?

Consistency.   In the earlier work on the development of automatism, only two training conditions were typically used. Training was either perfectly consistent (CM conditions) or inconsistent (VM conditions). These two extremes, of course, occur only in controlled laboratory settings. In real-life situations, training is unlikely to be perfectly consistent; yet, automatic responses appear to develop (Cherry, 1953).

In a recent series of experiments, Schneider and Fisk (1980a) examined whether automatic detection would develop under varying degrees of consistency. They manipulated consistency by holding constant the number of times various items appeared as targets and by varying the number of times these items appeared as distractors. The target and distractor sets were selected from a set of nine consonants. Five consistency conditions were used: (1) always target and never distractor (CM control); (2) target twice as often as distractor; (3) target and distractor equally often; (4) target half as often as distractor; and (5) target approximately one-seventh as often as distractor (VM control, because this is a typical ratio of target-to-distractor presentations of an item in VM conditions). During each block of 85 trials, each of four selected characters was presented as a target item 10 times. In addition, one appeared as a distractor 0 times (condition 1), one 5 times (condition 2), one 10 times (condition 3), and one 20 times (condition 4). The remaining trials in the block were VM-only trials involving other characters.

These experiments used nine subjects in a multiple-frame (12) search-detection task in which accuracy of spatial detection was the primary response measure. On each trial, a target was presented in a series of four-position frames, and the subject had to indicate in which of the four quadrants the target appeared. A single memory set item (the target) was presented prior to each trial. Subjects received six cycles of 12 training blocks (85 trials each) and then one test block of 100 trials (20 per conditon). During the test blocks none of the CM target letters (conditions 1–4) appeared as distractors.

By the end of training, performance was a monotonic function of the ratio of target frequency to distractor frequency of a given stimulus (Fig. 13.2, tests 5–6). Conditions 1, 2, and 3 were all statistically superior to the VM control. However, performance in condition 4 did not improve much during the course of training and was not statistically higher than the VM control. Remember that targets were presented as often in this condition as in the other CM conditions. It would take an infinite training series to be certain, but it appears that inconsistency both slows the rate of development of automatism and also inhibits automization completely in certain cases. In particular, when an item is presented as a target only half as often as it appears as a distractor, automatism may not develop at all.

Searching Versus Detecting.   In the studies just discussed, a target was presented on each trial. In many of the previous studies, targets were presented on only half of the trials. One might ask: Does searching for a target without finding it help or hurt automization? Schneider and Fisk (1980c) have examined this question.

A multiple-frame detection task was used, with memory set size of one, and frame size four. Subjects searched for a single letter target in letter distractors

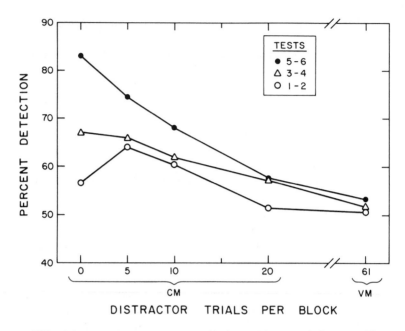

FIG. 13.2. Detection accuracy on test blocks (which occurred after every 12 training blocks) as a function of consistency, for three levels of training (after Schneider and Fisk, 1980a).

and made a forced-choice response on every trial as to the spatial position of the target even when there was no target. Eighteen subjects were used, and letters were counterbalanced across subjects. In all CM conditions, the consistency was held at 100% (no target was ever a distractor). During the training phase of the experiment, two factors were varied. First, the absolute number of times that subjects searched for CM target items was either 6 or 20 per block. Second, the number of times that an item that subjects searched for was actually present was varied (2 or 4 out of 6; and 4 or 16 out of 20). All conditions (including a VM control) were mixed within a block of 12 trials. Subjects were not informed about different target probabilities. Subjects received seven blocks of training. They were then tested in a condition in which a target was presented on every trial. The frame time was 150 msec during training and 110 msec during the test.

The results indicated that detection accuracy increased as the number of detections increased (with the number of searches held constant): from .64 to .71, as the number of target presentations increased from 2 to 4 per block, and from .57 to .72 as the number of target presentations increased from 4 to 16 per block. All of these detection rates were higher than the VM control .45. These results suggest that the rate of automization is a function of the number of times that an item is detected, when the total searches for the item is held constant. In addition, when total detections were held about equal, an increase in the number of nondetection searches slowed the rate of automization. To be precise, when the trials without targets rose from 2 to 16 (while detections remained about constant), performance dropped from .71 to .57. There are also some interesting tradeoffs. Doubling the number of detection opportunities and quadrupling the number of nondetection searches decreases performance from .64 to .57. Apparently two searches without a detection hinders automization as much as a single successful detection helps. These results were replicated in an experiment in which target probability during the test blocks was .50, indicating that the benefits of target detections and decrements due to nondetection searches were not due to differential training and test target detection probabilities.

These detection- and nondetection-search effects taken together seem to suggest that the ratio of detection to nondetection trials is the single largest determinant of automization. It hardly seems possible that this could be true in the extreme. Could one detection in two attempts be as valuable as 500 detections in 1000 attempts? Nevertheless, these results are intriguing and have important practical consequences (e.g., when learning tennis, on what proportion of swings should the learner be allowed to miss?).

Other Factors Affecting Automization.   Although we cannot describe the results in any detail, it is useful to list several other factors affecting the rate of automization: (1) Similarity or feature overlap between target and distractor sets. Learning is faster with greater dissimilarity. (2) The massing or distribution of training. This factor appears to have only minor effects. (3) History of training. Prior antagonistic CM training obviously hinders automization. In addition, prior VM training appears to slow automization compared with no prior training. (4) Type of task. Multiple-frame tasks involving accuracy measures appear to lead to faster automization than single-frame tasks involving reaction times. The stress on processing speed and effort may be the reason.

What Can and Cannot Be Automatized?

Automatic attention responses can be attached to the name of a stimulus (Laberge, 1973; Shiffrin & Schneider, 1977) and the name itself generated automatically. In addition, a category name may be generated automatically, even for new categories learned in an experiment (Shiffrin & Schneider, 1977) as long as the category *name* is consistently assigned (or assignable) to the stimuli.

There has been a small amount of research directed toward the question of whether automatic detection can be learned for spatiotemporal combinations that are more complex than simple alphanumeric characters. For example, can automatic attention be directed to conjunctions of stimuli; to combinations of stimuli and spatial positions; to the absence of features; etc.? Some recent experiments have begun to explore these and related questions in an attempt to establish the limits of automatic processing.

Schneider and Eberts (1980) and Treisman and Gelade (1980) have reported experiments in which subjects searched for items that were specified by conjunctions of features. In particular, Schneider and Eberts used a single-frame task on

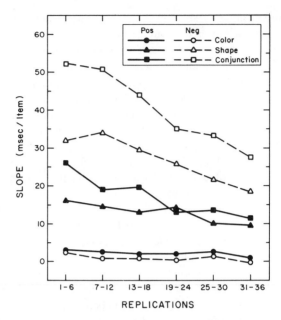

FIG. 13.3.   Slope of search function as a function of the amount of consistent training, for color, for shape, and for the conjunction of color and shape. Each replication consists of 106 trials (after Schneider and Eberts, 1980).

six subjects and compared single-feature search (for either color or shape; e.g., a red letter; a T) with conjunction-feature search (for both color and shape; e.g., a red T). Because the dimensions of color and shape have been classified as separable dimensions according to several criteria (Garner, 1970), an interesting question concerns whether consistent training will result in the "unitization" of these separable dimensions. Treisman and Gelade suggest the answer is "no." In the Schneider and Eberts study, large amounts of training were used (10,728 trials per subject). Some of the results are presented in Fig. 13.3, in terms of the slopes of search functions. Results show conjunction search remains inferior to shape search, though both improve with training. Color search is best of all and has no room to improve because the slope starts near zero. Although conjunction search is more difficult than shape-only search, both improve at similar rates with practice. The improvement may be ascribed to automatization, because VM control conditions show slopes that do not change much with training. (In a second study, the CM slopes dropped during training by a factor of about one-half, while the VM positive slope dropped from 14.9 to 12.8 and the negative slope dropped from 24.2 to 22.3.) In this experiment, there was still a 2:1 ratio of positive to negative slopes, which according to Treisman and Gelade (1980) suggests that both the shape and conjunction conditions are being performed by focal attention. We do not feel that a 2:1 slope ratio provides a sufficient condition for a search process to be a control process. Because dual automatic and control processing can occur jointly, a mixture of automatic and control processing could produce a 2:1 slope ratio if the subject waited for the control process to be completed on some proportion of the trials.

The Schneider and Eberts (1980) experiment suggests that conjunctions of features can be automatically processed after appropriate training, although the amount of learning may be small and the difficulty of training may be large.

What Is Learned During Automization?

Although the change in search tasks from a controlled to automatic mode of processing with consistent training has been well documented, less is known about the processes and mechanisms that underlie the resulting automatism (Kristofferson, 1977; Schneider & Shiffrin, 1977). What is learned in consistent mapping conditions that enables subjects to detect target items automatically? Do subjects learn to attend to relevant information (targets), ignore irrelevant information (distractors), or both? Does learning in a search task generalize to other situations?

Target Versus Distractor Learning. In order to examine the relative importance of targets and distractors in automatism, a transfer of training design was used by Dumais (1979, Experiments I and II). A single-display search task was employed, and reaction time was the dependent variable of interest. At the beginning of each trial, a single target item was presented; then a display of 4 or 16 items (arranged in a 4 × 4 square matrix) was presented and the subject indicated as quickly as possible whether the target item was or was not in the display. In this experiment, the target item was present on half of the trials.

The two CM training conditions used are denoted T1(D1) and T2(D2); where T1 and T2 represent two different memory sets, and D1 and D2 represent two different distractor sets. Each memory set and each distractor set consisted of 2 letters, 1 number, 1 Hebrew letter, and 1 Greek letter. Six subjects received 4000 trials of training in each of these two CM conditions [and 12,000 trials in a VM training condition, denoted VM(VM)]. After training, subjects were transferred to five different CM conditions for testing. Two of the conditions are examples of *positive transfer*. In the *target-transfer* condition [T1(VM)], the T1 target items remain the same, but the D1 distractor set is replaced with a set of VM items. In the *distractor-* (or *background*) *transfer* condition [VM(D1)], the D1 distractor items are still distractors, and a VM target set is used. There are also two examples of *reversal conditions*. In the *target-reversal* condition [VM(T2)], the T2 items (which had previously been targets) are now used as distractors and a VM target set is used. And, in the *background-reversal* condition [D2(VM)], the previously trained distractor set D2 becomes the target set and a VM set is the distractor set. The final condition is a *control* condition in which both target and distractor sets had been used for training only in VM conditions.

The data from the training and transfer phases of this experiment are presented

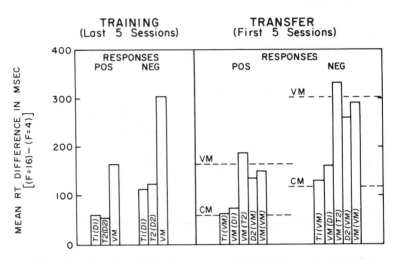

TI(VM): Target Transfer   VM(T2): Target Reversal
VM(DI): Background Transfer   D2(VM): Background Reversal
VM(VM): Control

FIG. 13.4. Data from the last five sessions of training (left panel) and the first five sessions of transfer (right panel). The bars give the reaction-time difference between display sizes of 4 and 16, a small difference implying automatic performance and good transfer. The dashed lines in the right panel give the pre-transfer performance levels, for both CM and VM (after Dumais, 1979).

in Fig. 13.4. The bar graphs represent the mean difference in RT between display size 16 and display size 4. Short bars reflect smaller differences between different loads (display sizes), implying automatic performance. Data from the last five training sessions (averaged over subjects) are shown in the left panel. As expected, the CM differences are considerably less than those observed in the VM conditions.

RT differences from the transfer phase of the experiment are shown in the right panel. First, consider the results of the two positive transfer conditions [T1(VM) and VM(D1)]. Performance in the target-transfer condition [T1 (VM)] is the same as that in the background-transfer condition [VM (D1)]. Furthermore, performance in these two positive transfer conditions is no different than that observed in the CM training conditions. Essentially perfect transfer has taken place when *either* the targets or distractors remain the same and are paired with VM trained items. (We mention in passing the very interesting result from a companion study in which the transfer conditions did not use VM items. Instead, they used totally new items in place of the VM items. The results were identical.)

We now consider the results of the two reversal conditions [VM(T2) and D2 (VM)]. Performance in the background-reversal condition [D2 (VM)] is the same as that in the target-reversal condition [VM (T2)], and both of these conditions are the same as the VM control. Subjects appear to revert without loss to a normal controlled search when either the targets or distractors are reversed. This result is at apparent odds with data reported by Shiffrin and Schneider (1977) in which a reversal of target and distractor sets resulted in performance that was much worse than that observed in VM conditions. Several procedural differences might account for this discrepancy: multiple-frame accuracy versus single-display reaction-time tasks; reversal of both targets and distractors versus reversal of either targets or distractors; number of distractors; and display sizes of 2 versus 16 (see Dumais, 1979, for additional details). In the present study, up to 16 previously trained CM targets could appear as distractors in a display after reversal. We propose that subjects find it difficult to attend to items attracting attention in many disparate spatial locations. Consequently, they revert to a controlled search through displays that consist primarily of previously trained CM targets. (Note that Shiffrin & Schneider, 1977, Section II, also found VM-like performance when subjects searched through a display composed entirely of previously trained CM targets.)

A simple model of automatic attending can account for these results. We assume that items newly introduced in a study have an average distribution of strength with which they tend to draw attention. During training, this distribution is altered considerably. Items that are consistently targets and never appear as distractors (i.e., the CM target items—T1 and T2 here) will accumulate the greatest attention strength. VM items that are sometimes targets and sometimes distractors will maintain an intermediate strength, perhaps not much different from the starting strength (because "new" items and VM items were equivalent). CM distractors (D1 and D2 here) that are never targets will loose a considerable part of their initial strength. Performance during training, positive transfer, and reversal is assumed to be based on the strength of the target items relative to the distractors. In addition, the results suggest that attention cannot be drawn simultaneously to multiple disparate spatial locations.

In sum, we observed excellent transfer for both the target and background sets suggesting that the learning that underlies automatic detection depends on both target accentuation (target attending) and distractor inhibition (distractor ignoring). The results follow from a model in which the consistency of training determines an item's tendency to draw attention.

Generalization of Automatic Learning.   The previously mentioned transfer of training experiment is certainly one measure of the generalizability of automatic learning. We now report a different, but also interesting, test of generalization (Dumais, 1980). Three subjects were trained (for about 20,000 trials) in a CM visual search task in which they searched for letter target items in a background of number distractors. They were then transferred, not to another search task but to a counting task. More specifically, subjects were asked to count the number of letters in a circular display (of at most eight items) composed of both numbers and letters. The results of this and other counting tasks are shown in Fig. 13.5. The main finding of interest for present purposes is that the time required to count the number of letters is not much affected by the number of irrelevant numbers in the display (Fig. 13.5, right panel, condition 4). This result suggests that the automization of detection that results from CM training in the search task produces a perceptual saliency of letters that can be used (perhaps as a basis for preliminary segregation) in the counting task. When three subjects who had not previously received CM training with letter targets and number distractors were asked to perform the same counting task, there were marked effects of the number of irrelevant digits (Fig. 13.5, left panel, condition 4). These subjects had, however, received a comparable amount of training in search and counting tasks not having consistent letter in number conditions (see also Francolini & Egeth, 1979).

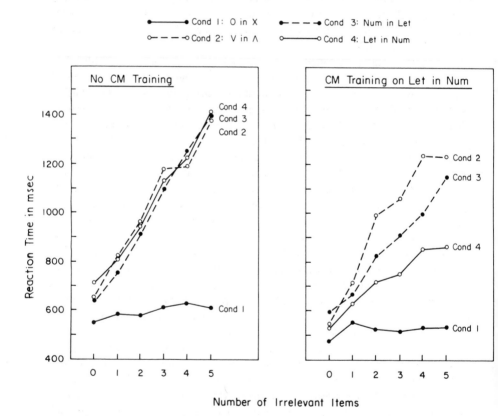

FIG. 13.5.   Time to count the number of letter targets among number distractors. Data in the right panel are from three subjects who had been trained in a letter–number CM situation. Data in the left panel are from three different subjects who had not received consistent letter–number training (after Dumais, 1980).

CONCLUDING REMARKS

The recent upsurge of research on automatism has raised more questions than it has answered. In this chapter we have taken some first steps toward generating a definition that can be used to distinguish automatism from controlled processing and have a few tests that might be carried out. The definition is based on the concepts of "capacity limitations" and "control," but we admit that other plausible definitions could be proposed. It is an interesting anomaly that research has proceeded apace on automatism in the absence of an accepted definition and a generally practical test.

In the second part of this chapter, we have described a number of interesting findings that help elucidate our understanding of automatism. The present chapter has presented preliminary results in a number of areas. These include the conditions needed for automatism, the processes that can be automatized, and what is learned during automization (including generalization). Most of this work has been carried out in the framework of search and detection tasks, but these tasks merely provide a convenient and powerful vehicle for explorations. As other research paradigms are utilized, we would hope to see the present results confirmed in these new settings.

ACKNOWLEDGMENTS

This research was supported by PHS Grant 12717 to the first author and ONR Grant 14-78-C-0012 to the third author. Part of the work was carried out while the second author was working at Bell Laboratories.

REFERENCES

Cherry, E. C. Some experiments on the recognition of speech with one and two ears. *Journal of the Acoustical Society of America*, 1953, *25*, 975-979.

Craig, A. Nonparametric measures of sensory efficiency for sustained monitoring tasks. *Human Factors*, 1979, *21*, 69-78.

Dumais, S. T. *Perceptual learning in automatic detection: Processes and mechanisms.* Unpublished doctoral dissertation, Indiana University, Dept. of Psychology, September, 1979.

Dumais, S. T., *Perceptual selectivity with consistently trained items.* Unpublished paper, 1980. (Available from Susan T. Dumais.)

Duncan, J. The demonstration of capacity limitation. *Cognitive Psychology*, 1980, *12*, 75-96.

Francolini, C. M., & Egeth, H. E. Perceptual selectivity is task dependent: The pop-out effect poops out. *Perception & Psychophysics*, 1979, *25*, 99-110.

Garner, W. R. The stimulus in information processing. *American Psychologist*, 1970, *25*, 350-358.

Hirst, W., Spelke, E. S., Reaves, C. C., Caharack, G., & Neisser, U. Dividing attention without alternation or automaticity. *Journal of Experimental Psychology: General*, 1980, *109*, 98-117.

James, W. *Principles of psychology.* New York: Holt, 1890.

Kristofferson, M. W. The effects of practice with one positive set in a memory scanning task can be completely transferred to a different positive set. *Memory & Cognition*, 1977, *5*, 177-186.

Laberge, D. Attention and the measurement of perceptual learning. *Memory & Cognition*, 1973, *1*, 268-276.

Laberge, D. Acquisition of automatic processing in perceptual and associative learning. In P. M. A. Rabbitt & S. Dornic (Eds.), *Attention and performance V*. London: Academic Press, 1975.

Norman, D. A. A comparison of data obtained with different false alarm rates. *Psychological Review*, 1964, *71*, 243-246.

Norman, D. A., & Bobrow, D. J. On the analysis of performance operating characteristics. *Psychological Review*, 1976, *83*, 508-519.

Posner, M. I., & Snyder, C. R. R. Attention and cognitive control. In R. L. Solso (Ed.), *Information processing and cognition: The Loyola symposium*. Hillsdale, N.J.: Lawrence Erlbaum Associates, 1975.

Schneider, W., & Eberts, R. *Automatic processing and the unitization of two features*. (Report No. 8008). Champaign, Ill.: University of Illinois, Dept. of Psychology, Human Attention Research Laboratory, 1980.

Schneider, W., & Fisk, A. D. *Degree of consistent training and the development of automatic processing*. (Report No. 8005). Champaign, Ill.: University of Illinois, Dept. of Psychology, Human Attention Research Laboratory, 1980a.

Schneider, W., & Fisk, A. D. *Dual task automatic and controlled processing in visual search, can it be done without cost?* (Report No. 8002). Champaign, Ill.: University of Illinois, Dept. of Psychology, Human Attention Research Laboratory, 1980b.

Schneider, W., & Fisk, A. D. *Visual search improves with detection searches, declines with nondetection search*. (Report No. 8004). Champaign, Ill.: University of Illinois, Dept. of Psychology, Human Attention Research Laboratory, 1980c.

Schneider, W., & Shiffrin, R. M. Controlled and automatic human information processing: I. Detection, search, and attention. *Psychological Review*, 1977, *84*, 1-66.

Shiffrin, R. M., & Schneider, W. Controlled and automatic human information processing: II. Perceptual learning, automatic attending, and a general theory. *Psychological Review*, 1977, *84*, 127-190.

Solomons, L., & Stein, G. Normal motor automatism. *Psychological Review*, 1896, *3*, 492-512.

Treisman, A. M., & Gelade, G. A feature-integration theory of attention. *Cognitive Psychology*, 1980, *12*, 97-136.

IV
IMAGERY PROCESSES

14 Empirical Constraints on Theories of Visual Mental Imagery

Stephen M. Kosslyn
Harvard University
Cambridge, Massachusetts
U.S.A.

Steven P. Shwartz
Yale University
New Haven, Connecticut
U.S.A.

ABSTRACT

Our knowledge about visual mental imagery has increased dramatically during the last decade. Any theory of mental imagery must now provide accounts for a sizable body of data. This chapter reviews the results that seem to place the most severe constraints on theories of mental image representation and processing. In addition, the chapter identifies a number of holes in the data base, issues that have yet to be addressed in the literature. Although the data are presented in the context of a discussion of basic issues about imagery, we have not attempted to resolve the issues nor to argue in depth for any particular theory.

INTRODUCTION

The recent advent of information-processing models in cognitive psychology has had a profound effect on the study of mental imagery. Whereas rigorous experimental studies of imagery had previously been focused primarily on the *function* of images in helping one perform some task (Paivio, 1971), researchers have now begun to ask about the *structure* of the imagery representation and processing system per se. That is, visual mental images are now considered as particular kinds of representations that are processed in particular ways, and the goal is to specify the nature of the mental structures and processes that allow images to serve as repositories of information in memory. The advent of this conceptual framework has resulted in the collection of numerous and interesting empirical findings about image representation and processing, and these results must be explained—in some way or another—by any viable theory of mental imagery: The time when one could take a free rein in armchair theorizing about imagery is definitely now a part of history. In this chapter we summarize the major empirical findings that seem to place the strongest constraints on theories of the visual imagery representation and processing system. Because much of this data was collected in the course of researchers considering issues about the structures and processes underlying imagery (see Anderson, 1978; Kosslyn, 1980, 1981; Kosslyn & Pomerantz, 1977; Pylyshyn, 1973, 1981), it seems both sensible and convenient to organize our review around the major issues in the field.

Following the emphasis in the literature itself, we begin by considering the properties of putative structures that may underlie imagery processing. In considering the properties of structures we have found it helpful to make use of a distinction originally introduced by Plato in the *Theaetetus,* between data structures and the medium in which they occur. In Plato's theory, memory representations (data structures) are like inscriptions etched on a wax tablet (the medium). Importantly, properties of the medium, such as the consistency of the wax, were posited to influence how easily information could be stored in data structures. Data structures, then, are the information-bearing representations in a processing system. Data structures can be specified with respect to three properties: their *format, content,* and *organization*. The format is determined by the nature of the ''marks'' used in the representation, such as ink, magnetic fluxes on a tape, or sound waves, and the way these marks are interpreted (the mark ''A'' could be interpreted as a token of a letter of the alphabet or as a picture of a particular pattern). The format specifies the nature of the primitive elements and the relations among them—or even whether a code makes use of primitives. The content, in contrast, is the actual information conveyed by a given data structure. It is important to realize that any given content can be represented using a number of formats. The information in the previous sentence, for example, could be stored on a magnetic tape, as dots and dashes etched on a gold bar, or in a sentence written in Hebrew. Finally, the organization is the way elementary representations can be combined. The format of a representation places constraints on the possible organizations but does not dictate them; for example, a list of features can be ordered in any number of ways.

In contrast to data structures, media do not carry any information in their own right. Rather, media are structures that support particular kinds of representations. Media can be specified with respect to their *formatting* and *accessibility*. Formatting places restrictions on the sort of data structures that can be supported by a medium. A short-term store, for example, might have five "slots" that take representations in a verbal format—but not visual images or abstract propositions. The accessibility characteristics of a medium constrain how data structures within it can be processed. A short-term store, for example, might have slots that can be accessed only in a given order.

It is important to realize that all the properties of both kinds of structures, data structures and media, are by necessity defined in the context of a particular processing system because the functional properties of structures depend on the way processes access them (see Kosslyn, 1980). This fact is especially important regarding media: A medium need not actually *be* a physical space in order to function as one. For example, the way processes in a computer can access the elements of an array allow the array to function as a coordinate space (with cells being different "distances" from each other and standing in various geometrical relations to each other) although the "words" in the computer's memory representing the various cells need not even be in the same room, let alone be actually physically organized into an array (Kosslyn, 1980, 1981).

In each of the following sections we first describe a general issue and then turn to data that bear on it. We do not try to defend a particular position on the issue but merely provide the data that have been taken to bear on some aspect of it; however interpreted, these data must be dealt with by any reasonable theory. In many instances there is little or no data relevant to an issue, in which case we offer an open invitation for future research.

ISSUES CONCERNING THE ACTIVE MEMORY DATA STRUCTURE

Perhaps the most argued issues in the field concern the status of the data structures in active memory that underlie the images most people report experiencing. In the remainder of this chapter we use the term *image* exclusively to refer to a data structure in active memory that underlies the experience of imaging.

Format

Is there a special kind of data structure underlying the experience of imaging, which is distinct from that underlying language and other forms of thought? It is possible, but not necessary, that the properties of images apparent to introspection, such as the depiction of spatial extent, index properties of the underlying representation. If images do in fact *depict* information, each part of the representation must correspond to a part of the object, and the relative interpoint distances among parts of the image must mirror the corresponding interpoint distances among parts of the object itself. Hence, information about size and orientation are necessarily specified when a shape is depicted.

Most of the research relevant to the issue of image format has attempted to demonstrate that images depict information. The logic of the experiments has been to demonstrate that distance, size, or orientation affects the ease of interpreting shape information represented in images—which would not be expected if images represent information in a descriptive, languagelike format (see Kosslyn, 1980, Chap. 3, for a detailed treatment of the properties of depictive formats as contrasted with the properties of "propositional" formats).

Scanning Visual Images.   If asked to begin by mentally focusing on the tail of an imaged German Shepherd dog, most people report scanning along the dog's body in order to "see" the ears when asked whether they are rounded or pointed. And in fact a number of experiments have been conducted that validate this sort of introspection, indicating that the experience of scanning corresponds to a continuous (or incremental, with small increments) internal transformation. The amount of time necessary to scan across an image is *linearly* related to the distance scanned. Importantly, scanning time increases with distance scanned per se and not simply with the amount of material scanned. Although Lea (1975) found that scan time did increase as one had to scan over more items, Kosslyn, Ball, & Reiser (1978) showed that distance and amount of material scanned had independent, additive effects on scan time. In addition, if subjects are asked to alter the apparent size of an image and then scan it, scan times reflect the size scale of the image—and not just the size at which a stimulus was originally presented (Kosslyn et al., 1978). This finding occurs only with very simple imaged stimuli, however; with more complex stimuli, subjects seem to slow down their scanning rate when an image is mentally reduced in size. In addition, time to scan to a part of an image that is not visible in the image initially, because it has "overflowed" (i.e., it falls beyond the bounds of the medium in which images seem to occur), is the same as time to scan an equal distance to a part that is initially visible (Kosslyn, 1978). Finally, scanning is equally easy left to right as right to left (Kosslyn, 1973, 1978; Kosslyn et al., 1978).

The results on scanning images, then, are exactly as expected if images depict objects or scenes and scan rate is constant (at least for images of a given size). In this case, scan time is a kind of "tape measure," indicating that distances are in fact embodied in the image.

Image Manipulation.   There has been an enormous amount of work on the processes of image transformation; however, as discussed shortly, most of this work pertains to the transformation process itself and not to the nature of the data structure being manipulated. There is one class of work on image transformation that may allow us to draw inferences about the format of the data structure, however, namely the effects of image size on the rate of mental rotation. If images are spatial representations that depict, one would expect larger images to require progressively more time to rotate than smaller ones (because more processing would be required to transform a greater area, and this additional effort would be compounded as more processing is required—at least according to the Kosslyn & Shwartz, 1977, 1978, theory; see Shwartz, 1979). If images do not depict, there is no reason to expect the value of a size parameter to affect the ease of altering the value of an orientation parameter (c.f., Anderson, 1978). Thus, Shwartz's (1979) finding that images of larger figures required increasingly more time to rotate further amounts (relative to images of smaller figures) would seem to place strong constraints on theories of image representation. This was true even though the complexity of the Attneave random polygons being rotated was equated at the two sizes.

Subjects in Shwartz's (1979) experiments were shown a stimulus and then were shown an orientation cue. Time to rotate mentally an image of the figure to the cued orientation was measured. This "preparation paradigm" is potentially flawed, however, in that one cannot be certain that the subject has in fact rotated the image all the way to the cued orientation prior to responding. The alternative paradigms, to be discussed shortly, also have drawbacks. For example, if a subject is shown a figure at a nonstandard orientation and simply asked to judge whether it is facing normally or is mirror-reversed (the standard Cooper & Shepard, 1973, paradigm), there is no guarantee that the subject rotates the entire figure rather than only selected parts (c.f., Anderson, 1978). Further, the subject may adjust his or her "attention field" (Larsen & Bundesen, 1978) such that the large and small figures are the same "phenomenal size" (i.e., are mapped into the same area in the spatial medium in which images are represented), or the subject may normalize the size of the image itself (Sekuler & Nash, 1972).

Image Size. Parts of smaller images are more difficult to detect (Kosslyn, 1975, 1976), which is easily explained if images are data structures that depict and that occur in a spatial medium that has a limited "grain." Because these findings may speak more directly to questions about properties of the image medium, they are discussed in more detail in Active Memory Medium on p. 247.

Content

The primary issue here is: Are images representations that depict objects as seen from a particular vantage point, or are they descriptions of the three-dimensional shape of objects as seen from no particular vantage point? The data most relevant here concern the question of "hidden line removal"; if images are representations of objects seen from a given vantage point, only information that would be visible from that vantage point should be represented in the image. Neisser & Kerr (1973) asked people to form images from three types of descriptions of objects interacting in scenes: In *pictorial* scenes two objects were visible and neither occluded the other (e.g., "A harp is sitting on top of the torch of the Statue of Liberty"); in *concealed* scenes one object completely occluded the other (e.g., "A harp is hidden inside the torch held up by the Statue of Liberty"); and in the *separated* scenes two objects were not interacting (e.g., "Looking from one window, you see the Statue of Liberty; from a window in another wall, you see a harp''). Subjects recalled concealed scenes and pictorial scenes equally well, so well that this null result could simply reflect a "ceiling effect" (see Kosslyn & Alper, 1977, for a discussion of problems with this experiment). Further, when Keenan and Moore (1979) ensured that subjects actually imaged objects as concealed in the concealed scenes, now memory for these scenes *was* worse than for pictorial scenes. This result is what is expected if the image only represents what is "visible," and if subjects utilize the stored imagistic representation of the scene as a retrieval aid (Kosslyn & Alper, 1977).

Organization

Do images have an internal organization? Reed (1974) and Reed & Johnsen (1975) report that people found it more difficult to "see" some segments of images than others, presumably because some of the segments (e.g., a triangle as part of a Star of David) corresponded to the "natural" units that actually were constituent parts of an image, whereas others (e.g., a hexagon at the center of a Star of David) did not. In these experiments subjects were asked to view geometric shapes, to image them, and then later to indicate whether various fragments were or were not parts of the figure. However, qualitatively similar results occur in "embedded figures" tests (see Gottschaldt, 1926, in Ellis, 1938) where the stimuli are physically in front of the subject. Thus, one cannot argue with confidence that Reed's findings show that the image itself is so structured but only that the interpretive mechanisms that "look at it" obey certain rules (e.g., they organize according to the Gestalt Laws of perception). These rules may reflect properties of the data structures, properties of the interpretive processes, or properties of both the structure and the process.

Hinton (1979) also presents findings that are relevant to the issue of whether images have an internal organization. For example, subjects were asked to image a wire-frame cube that had been rotated so that the diagonal from the bottom, front, left-hand corner to the top, back, right-hand corner was vertical. They then had to point out where the remaining corners were. This task was very difficult, whereas other ones that made use of the natural units and axes of a form were much easier. In addition, Palmer (1977) asked subjects to combine patterns mentally into a single form and found that the organization of the patterns greatly affected the ease with which they could be combined. Again, although the data suggest that images have an internal organization, the data could also be interpreted at least in part to reflect properties of the processes that access images. (See Chapter 6 of Kosslyn, 1980, for an account of how units are preserved in images.)

In closing this section, it is worth noting that although images may have an internal organization, they *can* serve as wholistic templates that are matched all of a piece against percepts. Smith and Nielson (1970) and Nielson and Smith (1973) found that time to match an imaged face against a picture of a face, and determine if the two were identical, was independent of the number of relevant features when three to five features were varied. Similarly, the results of the Cooper and Shepard (1973), Cooper (1975), and Cooper and Podgorny (1976) studies indicate that subjects can match a correctly oriented image to a percept, again using the image as a kind of template. In these studies the complexity of the image also did not affect the time to make the comparison, which would be expected if the image were in fact being matched wholistically.

ISSUES CONCERNING THE ACTIVE MEMORY MEDIUM

Much of the present debate about imagery has focused on the claim that images derive some of their properties from the medium in which they occur (see Kosslyn, 1981, versus Pylyshyn, 1981). In this chapter, we do not engage in this debate but simply present the data that some people take to reflect properties of the medium; any theory must explain these data, if not by appeal to properties of a medium in which images occur then by appeal to the data structures per se and how they are processed. One reason the following data have been interpreted to reflect constraints imposed by the medium is that these constraints are independent of the particular object being imaged. If the constraints were a consequence of properties of the data structures themselves, the reasoning goes, they would not necessarily generalize to all instances.

Formatting

Evidence that the Medium Has a Fixed Spatial Extent.   If asked to image an object far away and mentally walk toward the object, most people report that the object seems to subtend a progressively larger angle and eventually "overflows"; that is, the entire image is not "visible" to the "mind's eye" at the same time. Kosslyn (1978) hypothesized that the reason for this might be that images exist in a spatial representational medium of limited extent. If so, then the larger an imaged object, the farther away it should seem at the point it seems to overflow. And in fact, in a series of experiments, Kosslyn (1978) found this to be true. Further, in most cases a constant angle was subtended by different-sized objects at the point of apparent overflow. Importantly, the greatest single extent measured across an imaged object (usually along a diagonal) was the best predictor of the distance estimates (and not area or the like), as would be expected if overflow was dictated by the confines of a spatial medium. The finding that the medium has a specifiable extent was corroborated in a mental image scanning task and a simple gestural task (Kosslyn, 1978).

If there is a spatial medium with a fixed extent, one can sensibly ask about its shape. And in fact Finke and Kosslyn (1980) demonstrated that the medium has an eliptical shape, having greater extent along the horizontal axis.

Dimensionality of the Medium.   Another issue about the medium focuses on its dimensionality: is it two-dimensional or three-dimensional? It is important to realize that the dimensionality of the medium places an upper bound on the dimensionality of image data structures. Not all image data structures need utilize the full potential of the medium; it is possible to have two-dimensional data structures in a three-dimensional space. Thus, the fact that images can display two-dimensional properties does not imply that the medium itself is only two-dimensional. In fact, there is considerable evidence that images can represent information about three-dimensional shape. Shepard and Metzler (1971) and Metzler and Shepard (1974) found that subjects can rotate images in three dimensions. In addition, Pinker (1980), Pinker and Finke (1980), and Pinker and Kosslyn (1978) report evidence that images can represent three-dimensional space per se. In the Pinker and Kosslyn experiment, for example, subjects first memorized the positions of several children's toys hanging inside a box. Each subject was then instructed to image this three-dimensional scene and to scan between pairs of objects in the image. Scan times increased linearly with increases in the three-dimensional distances between the objects.

However, Pinker (1980) also found that two-dimensional distances are preserved in three-dimensional images. In another experiment, he asked subjects to image the same box, but this time they were to image it with a clear plate of glass over the front. On this glass were cross-hair cursors, and the subject's task was to image moving the cross hairs from one object to another. This time he found that scan times depended on the two-dimensional, not the three-dimensional, distances. Pinker and Finke (1980) report another series of experiments that demonstrate that subjects can image the emergent perspective effects of three-dimensional images from viewing angles they never actually saw.

The data taken together, then, are consistent with a three-dimensional medium in which two-dimensional data structures can sometimes appear or a two-dimensional medium that is processed to produce foreshortening and perspective effects. The two-dimensional theory must posit that three-dimensional information is represented in long-term memory, and that new information is generated into the medium as an image is rotated and previously obscured parts come into view. This notion leads us to the following prediction: If two-dimensional information is directly accessible, whereas three-dimensional information requires accessing long-term memory, then transformations in the picture plane ought to be easier. And in fact this is generally true: Pinker (1980) found a two-dimensional scanning rate of 11.4 msec/cm and a three-dimensional scanning rate of 33.8 msec/cm. Although Shepard and Metzler (1971) found that three-dimensional rotations of their blocklike stimuli were generally no more difficult than two-dimensional rotations, when the ease of locating corresponding parts of figures is equated the two-dimensional rotations tend to be slightly faster (by 10°/sec). When Shwartz (unpublished) ensured that two-dimensional rotations were in fact performed in the picture plane (subjects report a three-dimensional component, a "tumbling motion," even with the two-dimensional rotations of the Shepard & Metzler figures) and equated the ease of locating corresponding parts, now two-dimensional rotations were accomplished at a rate of 264°/sec and three-dimensional rotations at a rate of 117°/sec (*Note:* In the Shepard & Metzler experiment, figures were rotated at a rate of 60°/sec, at least partly because of the difficulties in locating corresponding parts and the tendency to add a three-dimensional component to two-dimensional rotations).

Processing Capacity Allocation.   If media are in fact fixed structures, their properties should not change depending on what data structures are being supported. Alternatively, if Pylyshyn (1981) is correct, there is no spatial medium as such in which depictive images occur. Rather, images are symbolic representations that merely mimic depictive ones. One property of internal media is that "processing resources" (Kahneman, 1973) need not be allocated for the storage of information in the medium. Rather, there is a fixed amount of resources allocated to the medium, and this constitutes one of the "formatting" properties of the medium. General-purpose processing resources should not be required for the storage of image data structures, then, if these data structures occur in a specialized spatial medium. In contrast, if there is no special-purpose spatial medium but rather data structures are used to simulate representations in a medium, then general-purpose processing resources will be required in order to store data structures. This implies that the more complex is a given data structure, the more capacity will be required to keep it activated. Shwartz (1979) investigated this aspect of the putative medium by measuring the time to detect a signal while subjects were simultaneously performing either a simple image maintenance task (i.e., maintaining a visual image in order to make a later "same" versus "different" judgment) or performing an image rotation task. Of principal interest was whether or not detection time would be slower when processing large mental images than when processing small mental images and whether or not detection time would be slower when processing complex images (10-point geometric figures) than when processing images of lower complexity (6-point geometric figures). If the storage of data structures in the medium does not draw on general-purpose processing resources, then although the size and complexity of an image should affect the density and the amount of information in the medium, these variables should not affect how general-purpose processing resources are allocated. Thus, there should be the same amount of such general-purpose processing resources available for performing the detection task regardless of the contents of the medium, leading one to expect no differences in time to detect a visual signal in the different conditions. And in fact this is exactly what was found. The result could not have been due to an insensitivity of the experimental design because detection time did in fact increase as a function of other manipulated variables (e.g., detection time was significantly slower during counterclockwise rotation than during clockwise rotation).

Storage Capacity.   Images clearly can represent only a limited amount of information at any one time. Kosslyn (1975) showed that more time was required to see parts of an animal when it was imaged in a relatively complex scene (with a 16-cell matrix being imaged next to it rather than a 4-cell matrix or 4 digits rather than 2). Weber and Harnish (1974) present evidence that images of letters of longer words are more decayed than those of shorter words. In addition, they found that people reported being able to maintain images of only about 5 or 6 letters at once. The problem with taking this estimate as a measure of capacity per se is, of course, that the subjects may not have been holding each letter as a separate unit but may have organized them into multiletter "chunks."

Accessibility Considerations

The other way of characterizing media that we have found useful is to consider the constraints a medium places on how information in data structures may be accessed. Again, the motivation for treating the following results as reflecting properties of the medium, and not the individual data structures, is that these constraints seem independent of the particular image being accessed.

Grain Effects.   If images occur in a medium with a fixed grain, then details of smaller images ought to be more difficult to discern.[1] And in fact Kosslyn (1975) found that parts of animals imaged at small sizes required more time to "see" than parts of animals imaged at larger sizes. This was true when size was manipulated directly (i.e., subjects were cued a given size to picture a beast) or indirectly. Size was manipulated indirectly by asking subjects to imagine a target animal (e.g., a duck) next to either a very large animal (an elephant) or next to a very small animal (a fly). As would be expected if the medium has only a limited spatial extent, subjects reported that the target animal was imaged smaller when next to the elephant than when next to the fly.

An alternative, nonimagery account of this result is, however, possible. It could be argued that the functional representation is not a spatial image but rather a list of the animal's properties and that for larger images more properties are activated. Thus, it is more likely that the queried property is already activated when the subject is queried after being asked to image a "large" object, and hence the subject is faster than when a smaller image was requested. Kosslyn (1976) argued that proponents of such a representation would predict that association strength, not image size, would determine the time to "see" a part of an

---

[1]The actual locus of these effects could be in the medium or in the processes that access it. This "structure/process tradeoff" is characteristic of "accessibility constraints" of media, which by their very nature necessarily involve a dynamic interplay between properties of the structure and properties of the process. Thus, accessibility constraints must be regarded as applying to a structure/process pair, and the precise locus of the constraint may be particularly difficult to isolate.

animal because more highly associated parts should be higher on the list (given that the list is ordered in terms of how distinctive parts are, and association strength reflects this property). Kosslyn (1976) varied image size and association strength orthogonally and found that when imagery was not used, times increased with increased association strength. But when imagery was used, image size overrode any effects of association strength and determined inspection time. For example, it took longer to "see" a cat's claws than a cat's head even though claws are more strongly associated with a cat than is head.

Kosslyn and Alper (1977) demonstrated the effects of grain using a different paradigm. They asked subjects to image the referents of two concrete nouns and to rate the vividness of the resultant image. For some pairs, both named objects were imaged at a normal size, whereas for others the second object was imaged at a subjectively tiny size. Later, a surprise memory test was given by presenting subjects with the first noun and asking for the noun it was paired with. Recall was poorer when the second noun was imaged subjectively small. This result is not surprising if subjects retrieved a long-term memory encoding of the image constructed earlier, and it was more difficult to identify the second object if it was initially imaged at a small size.

Resolution Distribution.   Given that the medium has a grain, one can then ask whether this grain is homogeneous throughout the medium; that is, there is no need that the resolution of the medium be the same at all locations (although it would be surprising if it were not fixed at some value for any given location). And in fact Finke and Kosslyn (1980) and Kosslyn (1978) present evidence that the resolution decreases toward the periphery. Furthermore, it appears that the most resolved region of the medium is roughly circular but that acuity drops off more sharply along the vertical axis than the horizontal one.

THE LONG-TERM MEMORY REPRESENTATION OF VISUAL IMAGES

In the foregoing sections we considered data relevant to the nature of the visual image representation in active memory. Logically, the active memory image must be dependent on more long-term storage of information. The present section focuses on the structure of the long-term memory information and on image generation—the process that takes as input the long-term memory information and produces as output an active-memory visual image.

The Data Structures

Format.   Virtually nothing is known about the format of the long-term memory representations that may underlie active memory representations in a depictive format. There is evidence, however, that discursive information can be stored and used to coordinate images of individual objects into a single scene (Kosslyn, 1980, Chap. 4 and 6). Beech and Allport (1978) and Kosslyn, Reiser, Farah, and Fliegel (1980) showed that descriptions of relations could be used to image named objects in a specified configuration, and Weber, Kelley, and Little (1972) showed that verbal information is sometimes used to prompt individual images used to form a composite image. The representations of the "mental pictures" themselves, however, could be in a number of formats, ranging from a Fourier transform to, at least in part, the sort of structural description suggested by Marr and Nishihara (1978).

Content. The underlying data structures must contain information sufficient to form the active memory images. As such, they must contain information about the appearance of *surfaces* of objects. Thus, some formats, such as the generalized cone format suggested by Marr and Nishihara (1978), would have to be supplemented in order to store the necessary content. Information about the three-dimensional structure of objects must often be stored, as must information about the name, time, place, or some other form of identification that will make it possible to retrieve a given image upon receiving a later cue.

Organization. Images can be formed from information stored in separate encodings. These encodings seem to be activated individually, as witnessed by the fact that image generation time generally increases linearly with the number of units in the image (Beech & Allport, 1978; Kosslyn, 1980; Weber & Harnish, 1974). In addition, remembered verbal information can be used to organize separate objects into a single scene. But what about cases in which subjects are to image a single stimulus just as it was presented to them? Are these stimuli also encoded into separate units that are later amalgamated into a single image, or are they encoded wholistically and later simply activated? Kosslyn (1975) found that larger images required longer to form, which would not be expected if images of single objects were simply stored wholistically and later retrieved. However, if multiple units are stored even for single objects, one may place fewer of them on a smaller image because the grain of the medium impairs "seeing" where parts belong. Kosslyn et al. (1980) found that it takes longer to form images of pictures of animals drawn with many details included than to image pictures with few details included. This too was taken as evidence for a constructive image generation process that accessed long-term memory encodings of units and the relations among them. Interestingly, a control group asked simply to indicate when they were prepared for a question about the drawing did not require more time to prepare for more detailed drawings.

The actual organization of the long-term memory data structure has not been studied in detail; many, such as Kosslyn and Shwartz (1977, 1978), have posited that it is hierarchical, with a "global" image being stored and encodings of local regions (with a high resolution also being stored). But the fact is that we know almost nothing about how image representations in long-term memory are organized.

The Medium

Virtually nothing is known about the medium in which long-term memory encodings of images occur. It would be interesting if different media were used in storing information in different formats (discursive, depictive), and if these media could be directly identified with neural structures in the brain (e.g., perhaps in different cerebral hemispheres). This could be studied by examining patients with very localized forms of brain damage. It would be especially interesting if it could be demonstrated that the medium used in storing discursive information had different accessibility constraints than the medium used in storing depictive information (e.g., one might be processed serially, the other in parallel; c.f., Paivio, 1971).

IMAGE TRANSFORMATIONS

In the preceding sections we discussed data that have been taken to bear on properties of structures. We assumed that the functional properties of structures arise only in conjunction with the appropriate kinds of processes (e.g., a procedure that "reads" spatial displays), but the specific nature of these processes has been left open. There is a considerable body of data about the process of image transformation, however, that must be considered in its own right. To date, the most substantial sets of results exist for transformations of apparent size and apparent orientation of images. The major findings can be summarized as follows.

Size Alterations

When subjects are asked to image a stimulus and then to match it to a second one, the time to make the match increases linearly with the disparity in the size of the two stimuli (Bundeson & Larsen, 1975; Larsen & Bundesen, 1978; Sekuler & Nash, 1972). These results are consistent with the view that subjects mentally alter the apparent size of an image of the initial stimulus until it is at the same size as the second stimulus and then match the image against the stimulus. This interpretation is buttressed by the finding that the same linear increases are found when subjects are asked to image a stimulus and then to adjust it to a given size, pushing a button when the adjustment is completed. In all cases, the rate of alteration is the same when images are expanded as when they are contracted (see Kosslyn, 1980, Chap. 8).

Mental Rotation

Since the now-classic paper by Shepard and Metzler (1971) there have been numerous reports of experiments on the mental rotation of imaged objects (letters, digits, blocklike forms, hands, or Attneave random polygons; Kosslyn, 1980; Shepard, 1975). The standard result is that the farther one must rotate an image, the more time is required. However, this increase in time is only linear in certain conditions. If a letter or digit is presented at some orientation about the circle, and the subject must decide whether it is a standard or a mirror-image version, the rate of rotation seems to increase for the smaller angular disparities from the standard upright. Hock and Tromley (1978) present evidence that this effect is due not to a change in rotation rate per se but to subjects only rotating the figure until its top is at the top of the picture plane; they argue that this is as far as one needs to rotate a figure in order to categorize the direction in which it faces. When subjects are asked to decide whether a given Attneave random polygon is the same as one in a set learned initially, and the distractors include similar forms as well as the mirror-reversal, now times do increase linearly with the angular disparity from the learned upright orientation (Cooper & Podgorny, 1976). Taken together, the data suggest that we do not have evaluation procedures that can be used to make subtle judgments about stimuli in arbitrary orientations and, hence, mentally rotate them prior to making an evaluation. With very familiar stimuli, such as letters and digits, we have seen them misoriented often enough to have developed evaluation procedures that are effective even when the stimuli are not fully upright. With unfamiliar figures, and/or when one must sometimes distinguish a figure from a similar distractor (not simply its mirror-reversal), our evaluation procedures are not as robust, and hence one must rotate an image of a misoriented stimulus to the full upright before performing an evaluation. It would not be surprising if one could develop evaluation procedures with practice that would eliminate the need for any mental rotation.

If subjects are informed about the identity (by being shown an upright version) and the orientation of a to-be-presented stimulus before it is actually presented, the time to prepare for the stimulus increases linearly with the amount to be rotated to the cued orientation. The time to evaluate the direction or shape of the test stimulus is now relatively independent of its orientation (Cooper, 1976; Cooper & Podgorny, 1976; Cooper & Shepard, 1973). However, if subjects in these experiments were informed about *only* the orientation or *only* the identity of an upcoming figure, the time to evaluate the figure increased with the angular disparity of the figure from the standard upright. The inference drawn from this finding has been that these subjects could not prepare by rotating an empty "orientation frame" or cannot use an orientation parameter to adjust the image in a single step after the test stimulus is presented. One interpretation of the findings presented by Hinton & Parsons (this volume) would contradict this inference, however, leading us to be cautious in drawing firm conclusions at the present time.

Cooper & Shepard (1973, Experiment 2) and Cooper (1976) present evidence that the image actually moves through intermediate positions along a trajectory as it is mentally rotated. Cooper's (1976) very impressive demonstration relied on her obtaining prior estimates of the rate at which her subjects rotated images. She then cued them to begin rotating a specific stimulus and then, after a variable interval, presented a stimulus that was the same or different. The test stimulus was presented either at the orientation at which the image should be or at a different orientation, and subjects were to judge whether the test stimulus was the same as the imaged one irrespective of orientation. Importantly, decision times were independent of the actual orientation of the test stimulus if it was presumed to be congruent with the image—exactly as one would expect if the image were moving through intermediate positions and the stimulus caught it just right. However, the time to compare the image and stimulus increased linearly with the disparity in the orientations of the two when the orientations did not match, suggesting that subjects had to rotate the image to the orientation of the test stimulus if the two did not initially match. Lastly, Cooper's results allowed her to infer that if images are rotated in discrete intervals, these intervals can be no larger than 30°.

To many people's surprise, it has been found repeatedly that the complexity of a stimulus does not affect the rate at which it is mentally rotated. Cooper (1975), Cooper and Podgorny (1976), and Shwartz (1979) found no effects of the complexity of Attneave random polygons on rotation rate, although Shwartz found that less complex forms required less time in general to process than did more complex forms (see also the Adelson and Kosslyn experiment described in Chapter 8 of Kosslyn, 1980). Although the Cooper and Podgorny (1976) experimental design has been criticized (Anderson, 1978; Shwartz, 1979), the Shwartz experiment corrected the flaws and essentially replicated the earlier results. These results are important because many theories of representation posit that images are stored as sets of discrete units, which are transformed individually; if so, and if only limited "processing capacity" is available, then more complex images ought to require more time to rotate (Anderson, 1978). Pylyshyn (1979) presents some data that can be taken to support this prediction, in part (he also presents some data that directly contradict it), but these experiments may have nothing to do with image transformations per se for reasons discussed in detail in Kosslyn (1981). Thus, we shall not review them again here.

Finally, it should be noted that subjects *can* transform images without going through the intermediate steps, but this requires more time generally than the corresponding incremental transformation. Further, when left to their own devices, subjects almost invariably spontaneously transform images gradually, seeming to pass through intermediate points along a trajectory (Kosslyn, 1980, Chap. 8).

IMAGERY AND PERCEPTION

Perhaps the one common thread running through all conceptions of imagery is the notion that imagery and like-modality perception share at least some of the same specialized mechanisms. Ideally, we would like to specify the similarities and differences among image and percept representations in terms of their format, content, and organization, and we would like to discuss in detail the nature of the media involved. Unfortunately, the data are simply not available. Most of the work reported in the literature is intended simply to demonstrate that images and percepts are in some sense functionally analogous. Finke (1980), Paivio (1971), Segal (1971), and Shepard and Podgorny (1978) review this literature, and we will not repeat their efforts here. However, to obtain a sense of this kind of work, and the problems in interpreting it, consider an experiment reported by Brooks (1968). Brooks used two different tasks. One involved imaging a block letter (e.g., F) and categorizing its corners, for example in terms of whether or not they are on the extreme top or bottom of the figure. The other involved categorizing each word in a sentence in terms of whether or not it was a noun. Brooks used three response modes, two of which are of most interest: In one, subjects indicated *yes* or *no* by working their way down a staggered column of Y's and N's, pointing to the correct letter; in the other, subjects simply said aloud *yes* or *no*. The interesting finding here is that the visual response mode impaired letter classification more than did the auditory response mode, but the response modes had the opposite effect in the noun-classification task.

Unfortunately, in the Brooks study, as in most of the studies in this genre, the interference could be due either to competition for modality-specific processing resources or to competition for modality-specific media in which to store the results of intermediate computations; that is, most of these tasks require modality-specific *processing* as well as modality-specific *data storage,* and it is not clear which of these is causing the modality-specific interference. In addition, it is unclear whether these effects are due to interference between the *content* of the representations, independently of their formats; that is, simply the similarity in the information about spatial extent in image and percept representations could cause the interference—even if the representations were in different formats. And even if it could be shown that interference is due to similarity in the formats of the representations, these results would tell us nothing about the format actually used in either kind of representation (Kosslyn & Pomerantz, 1977).

CONCLUSIONS

In this chapter we have briefly reviewed some major empirical findings that constrain theories of how visual mental images are represented and processed. This review is not exhaustive, either in scope or in depth (Denis, 1979; Kosslyn, 1980; Paivio, 1971), but it should serve to convey a sense of how difficult it will be to formulate an adequate theory of imagery. Further, many of the important issues are currently open questions, and additional results are needed to help delimit the class of viable theories. We have intentionally attempted to identify holes in the data base, loci where theories are virtually unconstrained, in hope of inspiring further research in the area that will speak directly to these issues. If enough constraints become available, it seems to us that a convergence on a true theory is virtually inevitable. Whether this is justifiable optimism or hopeless naivete is, of course, impossible to judge at this tender stage in the development of the field.

ACKNOWLEDGMENT

The preparation of this chapter was supported by NSF Grant BNS 79-12418, awarded to the first author.

REFERENCES

Anderson, J. R. Arguments concerning representations for mental images. *Psychological Review,* 1978, *85,* 249–277.
Beech, J. R., & Allport, D. A. Visualization of compound scenes. *Perception,* 1978, *7,* 129–138.
Brooks, L. Spatial and verbal components of the act of recall. *Canadian Journal of Psychology,* 1968, *22,* 349–368.
Bundesen, C., & Larsen, A. Visual transformation of size. *Journal of Experimental Psychology: Human Perception and Performance,* 1975, *1,* 214–220.
Cooper, L. A. Mental rotation of random two-dimensional shapes. *Cognitive Psychology,* 1975, *7,* 20–43.
Cooper, L. A. Demonstration of a mental analog of an external rotation. *Perception & Psychophysics,* 1976, *19,* 296–302.
Cooper, L. A., & Podgorny, P. Mental transformations and visual comparison processes: Effects of complexity and similarity. *Journal of Experimental Psychology: Human Perception and Performance,* 1976, *2,* 503–514.
Cooper, L. A., & Shepard, R. N. Chronometric studies of the rotation of mental images. In W. G. Chase (Ed.), *Visual information processing.* New York: Academic Press, 1973.
Denis, M. *Les images mentales.* Paris: Presses Universitaires de France, 1979.
Ellis, W. D. (Ed.). *A source book of gestalt psychology.* New York: Humanities Press, 1938.
Finke, R. A. Levels of equivalence in imagery and perception. *Psychological Review,* 1980, *87,* 113–132.
Finke, R. A., & Kosslyn, S. M. Mental imagery acuity in the peripheral visual field. *Journal of Experimental Psychology: Human Perception and Performance,* 1980, *6,* 126–139.
Hinton, G. Some demonstrations of the effects of structural descriptions in mental imagery. *Cognitive Science,* 1979, *3,* 231–250.
Hock, H. S., & Tromley, C. L. Mental rotation and perceptual uprightness. *Perception & Psychophysics,* 1978, *24,* 529–533.
Kahneman, D. *Attention and effort.* Englewood Cliffs, N.J.: Prentice-Hall, 1973.
Keenan, J. M., & Moore, R. E. Memory for images of concealed objects: A reexamination of Neisser and Kerr. *Journal of Experimental Psychology: Human Learning and Memory,* 1979, *5,* 374–385.
Kosslyn, S. M. Scanning visual images: Some structural implications. *Perception & Psychophysics,* 1973, *14,* 90–94.

Kosslyn, S. M. Information representation in visual images. *Cognitive Psychology*, 1975, *7*, 341-370.

Kosslyn, S. M. Can imagery be distinguished from other forms of internal representation? Evidence from studies of information retrieval time. *Memory & Cognition*, 1976, *4*, 291-297.

Kosslyn, S. M. Measuring the visual angle of the mind's eye. *Cognitive Psychology*, 1978, *10*, 356-389.

Kosslyn, S. M. *Image and mind*. Cambridge, Mass.: Harvard University Press, 1980.

Kosslyn, S. M. The medium and the message in mental imagery: A theory. *Psychological Review*, 1981, *88*, 46-66.

Kosslyn, S. M., & Alper, S. N. On the pictorial properties of visual images: Effects of image size on memory for words. *Canadian Journal of Psychology*, 1977, *31*, 32-40.

Kosslyn, S. M., Ball, T. M., & Reiser, B. J. Visual images preserve metric spatial information: Evidence from studies of image scanning. *Journal of Experimental Psychology: Human Perception and Performance*, 1978, *4*, 47-60.

Kosslyn, S. M., & Pomerantz, J. R. Imagery, propositions, and the form of internal representations. *Cognitive Psychology*, 1977, *9*, 52-76.

Kosslyn, S. M., Reiser, B. J., Farah, M. J., & Fliegel, S. L. *Generating visual images*. Harvard University manuscript, 1980.

Kosslyn, S. M., & Shwartz, S. P. A simulation of visual imagery. *Cognitive Science*, 1977, *1*, 265-295.

Kosslyn, S. M., & Shwartz, S. P. Visual images as spatial representations in active memory. In E. M. Riseman & A. R. Hanson (Eds.), *Computer vision systems*. New York: Academic Press, 1978.

Larsen, A., & Bundesen, C. Size scaling in visual pattern recognition. *Journal of Experimental Psychology: Human Perception and Performance*, 1978, *4*, 1-20.

Lea, G. Chronometric analysis of the method of loci. *Journal of Experimental Psychology: Human Perception and Performance*, 1975, *2*, 95-104.

Marr, D., & Nishihara, H. K. Representation and recognition of the spatial organization of three-dimensional shapes. *Proceedings of the Royal Society*, 1978, *200*, 269-294.

Metzler, J., & Shepard, R. N. Transformational studies of the internal representation of three-dimensional space. In R. Solso (Ed.), *Theories in cognitive psychology: The Loyola symposium*. Hillsdale, N.J.: Lawrence Erlbaum Associates, 1974.

Neisser, U., & Kerr, N. Spatial and mnemonic properties of visual images. *Cognitive Psychology*, 1973, *5*, 138-150.

Nielson, G. D., & Smith, E. E. Imaginal and verbal representations in short-term recognition of visual forms. *Journal of Experimental Psychology*, 1973, *101*, 375-377.

Paivio, A. *Imagery and verbal processes*. New York: Holt, Rinehart & Winston, 1971.

Palmer, S. E. Hierarchical structure in perceptual representation. *Cognitive Psychology*, 1977, *9*, 441-474.

Pinker, S. Mental imagery and the third dimension. *Journal of Experimental Psychology: General*, 1980, *109*, 354-371.

Pinker, S., & Finke, R. A. Emergent two-dimensional patterns in images rotated in depth. *Journal of Experimental Psychology: Human Perception and Performance*, 1980, *6*, 244-264.

Pinker, S., & Kosslyn, S. M. The representation and manipulation of three-dimensional space in mental images. *Journal of Mental Imagery*, 1978, *2*, 69-84.

Pylyshyn, Z. W. What the mind's eye tells the mind's brain: A critique of mental imagery. *Psychological Bulletin*, 1973, *80*, 1-24.

Pylyshyn, Z. W. The rate of "mental rotation" of images: A test of a holistic analogue hypothesis. *Memory & Cognition*, 1979, *7*, 19-28.

Pylyshyn, Z. W. The imagery debate: Analogue media versus tacit knowledge. *Psychological Review*, 1981, *88*, 16-45.

Reed, S. K. Structural descriptions and the limitations of visual images. *Memory & Cognition*, 1974, *2*, 329-336.

Reed, S. K., & Johnsen, J. A. Detection of parts in patterns and images. *Memory & Cognition*, 1975, *3*, 569-575.

Segal, S. J. Processing of the stimulus in imagery and perception. In S. J. Segal (Ed.), *Imagery: Current cognitive approaches*. New York: Academic Press, 1971.

Sekuler, R., & Nash, D. Speed of size scaling in human vision. *Psychonomic Science*, 1972, *27*, 93-94.

Shepard, R. N. Form, formation, and transformation of internal representations. In R. L. Solso (Ed.), *Information processing and cognition: The Loyola symposium*. Hillsdale, N.J.: Lawrence Erlbaum Associates, 1975.

Shepard, R. N., & Metzler, J. Mental rotation of three-dimensional objects. *Science*, 1971, *171*, 701-703.

Shepard, R. N., & Podgorny, P. Cognitive processes that resemble perceptual processes. In W. K. Estes (Ed.), *Handbook of learning and cognitive processes* (Vol. 5). Hillsdale, N.J.: Lawrence Erlbaum Associates, 1978.

Shwartz, S. P. *Studies of mental image rotation: Implications for a computer simulation of visual imagery*. Unpublished doctoral dissertation, Johns Hopkins University, 1979.

Smith, E. E., & Nielson, G. D. Representation and retrieval processes in short-term memory: Recognition and recall of faces. *Journal of Experimental Psychology*, 1970, *85*, 397-405.

Weber, R. J., & Harnish, R. Visual imagery for words: The Hebb test. *Journal of Experimental Psychology*, 1974, *102*, 409-414.

Weber, R. J., Kelley, J., & Little, S. Is visual imagery sequencing under verbal control? *Journal of Experimental Psychology*, 1972, *96*, 354-362.

15 Frames of Reference and Mental Imagery

Geoffrey E. Hinton
and
Lawrence M. Parsons
Center for Human Information Processing
University of California, San Diego, California
U.S.A.

ABSTRACT

Successively perceived parts of a scene or object must be related to one another
to create a representation of the whole (Hochberg, 1968), and the same object
when seen from a different viewpoint must be seen to have the same three-dimensional spatial structure. These perceptual requirements can be met by a system
that explicitly represents and manipulates relationships between a viewer-centered
frame of reference and frames of reference that are embedded in external objects.
The computational apparatus that is required for handling these relationships during
normal perception can also be used for simulating continuous spatial transformations and for performing imagery tasks. The use of a three-dimensional, viewer-
centered frame of reference as a common space in which to coordinate the various
frames embedded in objects may be what distinguishes visual imagery from other
methods of spatial reasoning.

A major objection to the view that people explicitly represent and manipulate
relationships between frames of reference is a finding by Cooper and Shepard (1973)
that suggests that people cannot mentally rotate an abstract frame of reference. We
present an experiment that shows that under suitable conditions, predicted by our
theory, people do mentally rotate an abstract frame.

A THEORY OF SPATIAL REPRESENTATIONS

Figure 15.1 depicts a three-dimensional spatial structure composed of six rods. To help depict the structure it is embedded in a solid object. When people are shown the configuration of six rods by itself, they can perceive it in several distinct ways. They can "parse" it into the groups *ab, cd, ef,* and see it as a "crown" consisting of three triangular flaps that slope upward and outward. Alternatively, they can group *a* and *d* together as the ends of a central tilted rectangle and see *b* and *c* as a triangular flap sloping downward and outward and *e* and *f* as a flap sloping upward. Figure 15.2 shows two structural descriptions that represent these alternative perceptions.

Each part of the structure appears to have its own intrinsic frame of reference. One of the triangular flaps in the crown interpretation, for example, has an intrinsic frame that has three orthogonal directions defined by the axis of symmetry of the triangle, the normal to the plane of the triangle, and the "sideways" direction parallel to the base of the triangle. Each flap defines a different intrinsic frame of reference, but relative to its own frame of reference each flap is identical. Rock (1973) provides considerable experimental evidence for intrinsic frames of reference, and Marr and Nishihara (1978) and Hinton (1979a) discuss their theoretical importance.

An intrinsic frame of reference serves two functions. The object can be given a shape description that is independent of the subject's viewpoint by describing the orientations and dispositions of the object's features relative to its own intrinsic frame. That is why the three flaps in the crown are seen as having the same shape even though their retinal images are very different. Second, the relationship of an object to its context can be specified by specifying the relation-

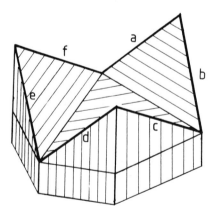

FIG. 15.1.   The spatial structure formed by the six rods (heavy lines) can be perceived either as a "crown" composed of three triangular flaps or as a "zigzag" composed of a central rectangle with one triangular flap sloping up from the bottom edge and another sloping down from the top edge.

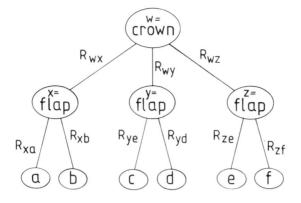

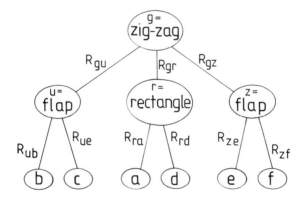

FIG. 15.2.   Two alternative structural descriptions corresponding to the alternative ways of seeing the six rods in Fig. 15.1. The nodes represent objects or their parts, and the labels on the arcs represent spatial relationships.

ship between the object's intrinsic frame of reference and an intrinsic frame of reference embedded within the context. The relationship of one flap to the whole crown, for example, is determined by the relationship of the intrinsic frame of the flap to the intrinsic frame of reference of the whole crown.

Relationships between Frames of Reference

Frames of reference themselves cannot be directly described. They can only be specified by their relationships to other frames of reference. If nonrigid transformations like shear and elongation are discounted, the relationship between two

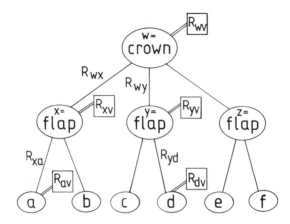

FIG. 15.3. A structural description with some attached viewpoint information in the form of relationships like R_{av} that specifies how the intrinsic frame of a is related to the common, viewer-centered frame.

three-dimensional frames of reference has 7 degrees of freedom: 3 for translation, 3 for rotation, and 1 for scale. So relationships between two intrinsic frames of reference could be represented by 7 real-valued variables. It is unlikely that the representation of a spatial relationship in the brain is anything like the natural representation in a digital computer, but whatever it is like, it must have the same number of degrees of freedom each of which must be capable of having a more or less continuous range of values.

It is possible to simulate continuous spatial transformations (Shepard & Feng, 1972; Shepard & Metzler, 1971) by simply modifying the representations of the spatial relationships in a structural description. For example, the transformation in which the three triangular flaps of the crown fold outward and downward can be simulated by changing R_{wx}, R_{wy}, and R_{wz} in Fig. 15.2. There is evidence that this is what is happening when people imagine a continuous transformation (Hinton, 1979a). Each structural description makes some relationships explicit and leaves others implicit, so the number of explicit relationships that have to be changed to simulate a given physical transformation may depend on which of several alternative structural descriptions is used. People find transformations easier to imagine if they use a structural description in which only a few of the explicit relationships need to be changed.

The structural descriptions shown in Fig. 15.2 are useful for recognizing objects and providing stable representations of the structure of the environment because they are independent of viewpoint. However, in addition to this kind of viewpoint-independent knowledge, people are also aware of how objects and their parts are related to the current viewer-centered frame of reference. Figure 15.3 shows how this knowledge can be represented by attaching to all or some of the object nodes in a structural description information about the relationship between the intrinsic frame of reference of that object and the current viewer-centered frame.

Inferring Relationships between Frames of Reference

Some of the relationships between frames can be computed from others, and a visual system that uses intrinsic frames needs to be able to do this. One type of computation yields the intrinsic relationship between two intrinsic frames, a, b, from information about the relationship of each frame to a common, viewer-centered frame, v. This kind of computation must occur when we "just see" an intrinsic relationship because what is perceptually available is the relationship of each object to the viewer-centered frame. The computation may be expressed as follows:

$$R_{av} \ \& \ R_{bv} \Rightarrow R_{ab}$$

Another type of computation must be performed when an object has been perceived and recognized as a whole, and the system uses its stored knowledge of the spatial structure of the object to help it pick out a particular part of the object. The system must figure out where the part is in viewer-centered terms so that it can make the appropriate eye movement or internal change of attention. So the relationship of the part to the viewer-centered frame must be computed from the intrinsic relationship between the whole, a, and the part, c, and the relationship of the whole to the viewer-centered frame, v:

$$R_{av} \ \& \ R_{ac} \Rightarrow R_{cv}$$

If these two types of computation are occuring all the time during normal perception, it is reasonable to suppose that people have special-purpose hardware for implementing them efficiently. We show that this same hardware could also be used in performing imagery tasks.

Mental Images and Pictures

When a person forms a mental image of a spatial structure, he/she can often "just see" new spatial relationships that were not explicitly used in forming the image. Imagine, for example, the following journey. Go a mile north, then a mile east, and then a mile north again. Now, what is the direction back to your starting point? Most people report that they form an image and read off the answer without any conscious inference. It seems to them that they create something like a picture in their mind that they can then perceive. A crucial question is: In what ways do the internal representations involved in imagery resemble pictures and in what ways to they differ?

There are two separable properties of pictorial or arraylike representations, and we shall argue that mental images have one of these properties but not the other.

To create a picture of an object or scene it is necessary to adopt a specific viewpoint. This is equivalent to choosing a relationship between a frame of reference embedded in the scene and the frame of reference of the picture. As well as this "commitment to viewpoint," pictures have a further property that we shall call "atomic depiction." For simplicity we shall assume that a picture is like an array in which each cell may be given a number of properties like color or intensity but cannot have internal spatial structure. Notice that it is the mapping from scene to picture and the structure of the pictorial medium, not the structure of the scene itself, that defines how the scene is carved into separate atomic parts each of which is depicted by averaging its visible properties.

A representation can have the property of commitment to viewpoint without necessarily having the further property of atomic depiction. The kind of representation in which each node in a structural description is given a relationship to a common, viewer-centered frame of reference is committed to a specific viewpoint, but it does not require decomposition into elements defined by the grain size of the pictorial medium. Instead, the viewpoint information is attached to the units that are meaningful within the scene, and it is possible to attach viewpoint information to some units without necessarily attaching it to all. For example, it is possible to represent where a large elephant is in viewer-centered space without being forced to represent the orientation of its trunk.

Much of the evidence that is normally taken to corroborate the idea that a mental image is like a picture actually only shows that mental images are committed to viewpoint. One line of evidence for the further property of atomic depiction is that people seem to zoom in mentally in order to see details in mental images. Kosslyn (1975) claims that zooming is necessary because mental images have a finite grain size. However, Hinton (1979b) shows how the need for zooming is also predicted by a model in which there is some noise in the representation of the parameters of a spatial relationship.

The following section shows why commitment to viewpoint is a computationally useful property in solving mental imagery tasks.

Computing Spatial Relationships in Mental Images

It is possible to define a spatial structure by giving some but not all of the spatial relationships between its parts. The remaining relationships can then be inferred from the ones that are explicitly given. The imagery task presented in the previous section required this kind of inference. The obvious way of inferring the relationship between two nodes in a structural description that are not directly connected is to find an indirect pathway of known intrinsic relationships. Each relationship is equivalent to a matrix, and the product of these matrices is the required relationship between the two nodes.

There is, however, an alternative method of computation that requires commitment to viewpoint and is therefore a more plausible model of what occurs during visual imagery. The computation involves three stages:

1. One of the nodes in the structural description is given a relationship to the viewer-centered frame of reference. This relationship can be chosen arbitrarily. In effect, it defines the imagined viewpoint.

2. Consistent relationships to the viewer-centered frame can then be propagated to other nodes by using the intrinsic relationships and computations of the form: R_{av} & $R_{ab} \Rightarrow R_{bv}$. The process of propagating consistent relationships is what is required to form a mental image.

3. Finally, *any* relationship between two nodes can be computed immediately by using a computation of the form: R_{av} & $R_{bv} \Rightarrow R_{ab}$. Notice that this is the same primitive computation as is used during perception to "just see" a relationship. This may explain why people introspectively describe the process of computing a new relationship in a mental image as "just seeing" it.

This method enables a system that uses a hierarchy of intrinsic frames to compute an unperceived relationship by making use of the mechanisms that must already be available for normal perception. It is like the process of drawing a picture in that it uses the intrinsic relationships to give every object a consistent relationship to a common, viewer-centered frame. Once everything has been related to one frame, it is possible to read off implicit relationships without performing long chains of inference. However, the computational advantages of a common frame of reference are achieved without requiring atomic depiction. Objects do not need to be decomposed into pieces of a size defined by the picture grain or the individual array cells in order to represent their relationships to the common frame of reference.

THE FUNCTION OF MENTAL ROTATION

A major problem for the theory just presented is why mental rotation is necessary at all for the kind of task in which a subject has to judge whether two objects at different orientations are the same or are mirror images of each other. Shepard (1979), Kosslyn, Pinker, Smith, and Shwartz (1979), and Pinker and Finke (1980) argue that the fact that people use mental rotation is evidence that they do not have a representation of the shape of an object that is independent of the object's orientation. If they did, the argument goes, they should be able to judge the identity or nonidentity of two shapes in different orientations without performing mental rotation.

This argument certainly appears to rule out any theory that claims that the internal representation of the shape of an object is generated by imposing an intrinsic frame of reference on the object and describing its features relative to

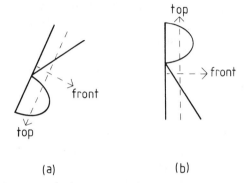

(a)   (b)

FIG. 15.4.   Two versions of an R, with the intrinsic frames of reference that
people impose on them. Relative to their intrinsic frames, they have identical
features. The differences lie in the orientation, position, and handedness of the
imposed frames.

that frame of reference. Given two objects in different orientations, it should be
possible to impose appropriately oriented intrinsic frames on each of them and
then to check whether the resulting shape descriptions were identical. It is hard to
see how this kind of process could account for the mental rotation data. The time
take to assign tilted intrinsic frames might depend on the tilt, but this would make
the wrong predictions. In experiments where two objects are presented simultaneously, it would predict that the reaction time should depend on the sum of the
two tilts, not on the difference. Furthermore, it would not explain subjects'
introspections that they mentally rotate one of the objects from its current orientation into alignment with the other object.

There is, however, a simple additional assumption that makes the theory
being proposed entirely consistent with the mental rotation data. Mental rotation,
it will be argued, is necessary to overcome a peculiar and normally irrelevant
deficit in our way of representing spatial structures: Although we can rapidly
perceive the shapes of objects in unusual orientations, we do not normally know
and are not normally interested in the handedness of these objects. (*Handedness*
is the property that distinguishes a right-hand glove from a left-hand one.)

Introspectively, we do not perform mental rotation in order to recognize a
tilted object like the *R* in Fig. 15.4a. We can see that it is an *R* and that it is
roughly upside down without any mental rotation. Indeed, we must be able to
identify the letter and to see which way up it is in order to decide what rotation to
perform to make it upright. Cavanagh (1977) has shown that the effects of
orientation on the time required to identify letters are much smaller than the times
required for mental rotation.

Mental rotation does seem to be required in order to decide whether the *R* is a
normal or mirror-image version (i.e., to decide on its handedness). It appears that
we can only compare the handedness of two objects if their orientations are

aligned, and we use mental rotation to achieve this alignment. Deciding whether the R is forward or backward is a special case in which one of the objects is remembered rather than perceived.

The need for alignment in judging relative handedness is a subtle consequence of the assignment of intrinsic directions to an object. The problem is that we can assign either a left-handed or a right-handed intrinsic frame, and we use the intrinsic frame that yields a familiar shape representation (see Fig. 15.4a). If there are two objects of opposite handedness, we use intrinsic frames of opposite handedness and obtain the same shape representation. This means that to compare the handedness of the objects it is necessary to compare the handedness of their intrinsic frames. This would be possible without any mental rotation if we knew the absolute handedness of each frame. It appears, however, that we do not have an explicit representation of the handedness of an intrinsic frame (this is our additional assumption). So, in order to compare handedness we mentally rotate one frame until all but one of its significant directions align with the corresponding directions in the other frame, and then we compare the remaining direction. In two dimensions this means rotating one frame until its top/bottom direction aligns with the other one and then comparing the front/back directions. (Generally, equivalent arguments about handedness apply in both two dimensions and three dimensions, but they are easier to present in two dimensions.)

Mental rotation, in our theory, does not affect the representation of the object's shape. It simply involves altering the explicit representations of two spatial relationships, one between the object and the viewer and the other between the object and its context. The alterations must preserve handedness (a property of continuous rotations), but this requirement does not, in itself, explain why mental rotation appears to be continuous. There are many possible reasons. If, for example, people only have the computational hardware for rotating through a small angle, then large rotations would require repeated use of this hardware, just as large shifts require repeated operations in a simple shift register. We must emphasize, however, that the aim of this chapter is not to explain why mental rotation times depend on angle of rotation. We merely aim to show that the phenomena of mental rotation are compatible with the assignment of intrinsic frames of reference for generating shape descriptions.

The idea that we can know both the top/bottom direction and the front/back direction of a two-dimensional intrinsic frame and yet not know its handedness may appear strange, because these two directions determine the handedness of the frame. However, neither direction by itself determines handedness, so a system that represents the two directions separately may lack an explicit representation of the handedness, even though this is implicit in the representations of the two directions.

It is not theoretically necessary to use a continuous rotation to bring two frames into alignment. A sequence of more discrete operations could also be used. For example, the top/bottom direction could be changed by 30° and the front/back direction could then be changed by the same amount so as to restore perpendicularity of the two directions. It is not possible, however, to use large steps like 90°, because it would then be possible to reverse the handedness of the frame when restoring perpendicularity. Reversal could not occur if the top/ bottom and front/back directions were changed either both clockwise or both counterclockwise. However, this strategy involves labeling angles as clockwise or counterclockwise, which is equivalent to knowing the handedness of systems in arbitrary orientations. It is just this kind of explicit representation of handedness that we are postulating is absent in people.

Normal adults must have knowledge that is equivalent to knowing the absolute handedness of a vertically aligned frame of reference because they can distinguish correct letters from backward ones. However, this knowledge may consist in knowing which way the front of a normal version points when the character is upright. This would mean that knowledge of shape and handedness were separate, even for characters whose handedness we know. Some such separation appears to be necessary to explain how certain dyslexics can know the shapes of characters but not know which way round they go. Explicit knowledge of handedness is normally ecologically irrelevant. There are very few objects in the world whose properties depend on their handedness, and for man-made artifacts like writing where handedness is crucial, people have unusual difficulty. Normally, we want to classify objects that differ only in handedness as having the same shape. A person's profile seen from the other side is a good example.

In order to reconcile the need for mental rotation with the idea that people achieve invariant representations of the shapes of objects by assigning intrinsic frames of reference, we have postulated that people do not know the handedness of the tilted frames that they assign.

THE EXPERIMENT

Introduction

The hypothesis about the function of mental rotation predicts that it should be possible to rotate mentally an upright frame of reference of known handedness to the appropriate orientation before a tilted letter is presented. The subject could then judge whether the letter was forward or backward without performing any further mental rotation. Cooper and Shepard (1973) claim that people cannot do this under their particular experimental conditions. They found that giving subjects advance information about the orientation of a letter did not remove the need to rotate the letter mentally to upright in order to judge its handedness. This is an important result because it suggests that people cannot use the advance orientation information to rotate an abstract frame of reference of known handedness to the appropriate orientation, and this inability corroborates the view that shape and orientation are not separately represented.

We decided to investigate whether Cooper and Shepard's (1973) results might depend on special characteristics of their experimental design. In particular, we were interested in whether the subjects had simply failed to discover the strategy of rotating a frame of reference and whether the difficulty of using this alternative strategy might depend on the particular character set being used and the particular form of the required response.

Cooper and Shepard (1973) presented subjects with a character from the set G, J, R, 2, 5, 7, displayed in one of a number of orientations, and required them to respond with a right-hand button press if the character was a normal version and a left-hand button press if it was a mirror image. We reasoned that the particular character set might make it hard to put advance information about orientation to good use because there is no common relationship to a frame of reference that is shared by just the normal versions. The characters in the set F, R, G, L, on the other hand, all seem to have a "front" that faces to the right, so the normal versions all "agree" with a frame of reference that has its front on its right. This allows subjects to use the following strategy: When they see the arrow indicating the top/bottom direction of the upcoming character, they mentally rotate an abstract frame of reference that initially has a vertically aligned intrinsic top/bottom direction and a front pointing to the right. They note which way the *front* of this frame points when its top/bottom direction aligns with the arrow. When the character appears, they have only to judge whether its front points in the same or the opposite direction.

In a pilot experiment, we discovered that when a normal character was upside down so that its front was on the left of the screen, there was a strong tendency to press the left-hand button, because the button location "agreed" with the direction in which the front of the character pointed. To avoid this type of intrusion of the spatial characteristics of the response, we required subjects to press a key if the character was normal and to make no response to mirror images.

One group of subjects was explicitly instructed in how to make use of the advance orientation information. They were given trials both with and without the advance information. Initially, they were given characters from the set F, R, G, L. Later, they were given characters from the set F, R, J, 7, and they were instructed to try to see the J and the 7 as pointing to the right.

A second group of subjects was used as a control to show that it was the particular character set and the explicit instruction in the strategy that caused us to obtain different results from Cooper and Shepard (1973). The group was presented with characters from the set F, R, J, 7, both with and without advance orientation information, but they were not explicitly instructed in the strategy.

Method

Subjects.   Twelve right-handed University of California students participated in this study for credit in a lower-division course in psychology.

Stimuli.   The test stimuli were asymmetrical alphanumeric characters—one Arabic numeral, 7, and five uppercase letters, F, R, G, L, J. Each of the six characters could be presented in any of 12 equally spaced orientations in the picture plane, in either its normal or mirror-image version. Advance information for the orientation of the upcoming character consisted of an arrow drawn through the center of the field and pointing to the position at which the top of the character was about to appear. All stimuli were displayed visually in the center of the bit-mapped display of a TERAK microcomputer. They subtended about 5° of visual angle.

Design.   The 12 participants were randomly divided into 6 experimental and 6 control subjects. Experimental subjects performed 24 blocks (of 96 trials each) as follows. The first 12 blocks consisted of trials with the character set F, R, G, L. In half of these blocks, a trial was always preceded by advance information for orientation. In the other 6 blocks, subjects received no advance information and the trial began with the onset of the test character. In the second half of the experiment (the second 12 blocks) the character set was F, R, J, 7 (two characters from the first set and two new characters). Again, all the trials in 6 of these blocks were preceded by advance orientation information, and all trials in the other 6 blocks were without the advance information.

The control subjects were told to do the best they could to use the arrow in preparing for the trial, but they were not instructed in the strategy. Apart from this, the control subjects exactly replicated the *second* 12 blocks (i.e., those with F, R, J, 7).

The order of conditions for the 12 blocks with each character set was identical for all subjects: Blocks 1, 2, 5, 6, 11, 12 were in the advance orientation information condition, and Blocks 3, 4, 7, 8, 9, 10 were in the no-advance information condition. The first four blocks with each character set provided subjects with practice in the two conditions. Practice trials were identical in all respects to test trials. This order of conditions was designed to equate effects due to practice for blocks with and without advance information for orientation and to minimize the number of times a subject had to change between the two conditions.

Each block contained a trial for every possible combination of one of the four characters, one of the 12 orientations, and normal or mirror-image version. The trials were randomly ordered for each subject.

Procedure.   Subjects were seated before a CRT screen with their right-hand index finger on a key of the microcomputer keyboard. They were told the task was to press the key as quickly as possible if the character was a normal version, regardless of the character's orientation. If it was a mirror-image version, they were told not to press the key. They did not make any large head movements.

On trials without advance information for orientation, a stimulus character would appear on the screen until a response was made or 1.5 sec had elapsed with no response. Trials with advance information for orientation began with the display of the arrow for 2 sec, followed by a stimulus character as before. For all blocks, there was a 2-sec intertrial interval.

Subjects were given immediate feedback information as to the accuracy and duration of their responses. At the occurrence of an incorrect response, the microcomputer made a readily audible buzzing sound. Subjects' reaction times (RTs) in milliseconds were displayed in a column along the left-hand margin of the CRT screen. The RT (± 1 msec) and accuracy of each response were recorded by the computer.

Results and Discussion

Figure 15.5 shows the mean RTs of correct positive responses, as a function of the orientation of the test stimulus, for experimental subjects with the F, R, G, L character set in the advance and no-advance information conditions. Clockwise and counterclockwise rotations of equal magnitude yielded comparable RTs; therefore they have been combined for all analyses.

For 5 of the 6 experimental subjects, and for the group as a whole, the advance orientation information condition yielded significantly lower values than the no-advance information condition for both the mean RTs averaged over

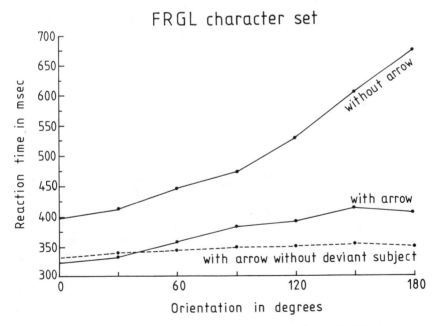

FIG. 15.5. Mean RT plotted as a function of orientation from vertical for the advance and no-advance information conditions. The second plot of the advance information condition is without the data of the one subject who failed to follow the strategy that subjects were instructed to use.

orientation [for the group, $t(19) = 3.34$, $p < .01$] and for the slope of the linear regression lines of RT on orientation [for the group, $t(925) = 3.15$, $p < .01$]. One subject appeared to be incapable of using the strategy. For the other 5 subjects, RT was only very slightly affected by orientation in the advance information conditions (see Fig. 15.5). The magnitude of this effect (19 msec in 180°) is much smaller than any reported times for mental rotation. In terms of our theory, this implies that it takes very slightly longer to impose a nonvertical frame of reference and to represent a stimulus relative to this frame.

The condition without advance information yields data typical of mental rotation. The linear regression equation accounts for 41% of the variance in the raw data, $t(1095) = 2.72$, $p < .01$. With advance orientation information, it accounts for 11%, $t(1098) = 2.81$, $p < .01$, but if the deviant subject is excluded, the variance accounted for drops to 1%. Even this is significant at the .01 level because of the large sample size. Subjects' mean error rates vary from 2% to 9%, with an overall mean of 6%. The error rates did not show any significant main effects or interactions of the factors of character, orientation, normal or mirror-image version, and advance or no-advance information.

As a result of the differences between our design and that used by Cooper and Shepard (1973), our subjects are able to use advance orientation information to prepare for the discrimination of a normal from a mirror-image character at various orientations. Moreover, subjects reported doing this by first rotating, as per instructions, a frame of reference that denotes top and front directions and then noting whether the front of the displayed character was facing in the direction specified by the frame of reference.

Our hypothesis was tested once more, this time using two members of the previous character set (F, R) and two new characters (J, 7). Figure 15.6 shows the correct positive RTs as a function of the angular difference from upright of the stimulus character. The figure shows the group data for both experimental and control subjects, with and without advance orientation information.

For control subjects, the linear regression equation accounts for a significant amount of the variance: In the advance information condition it accounts for 42% of the total variance, $t(1082) = 2.84$, $p < .01$, and in the no-advance information condition it accounts for 38% of the total variance, $t(1095) = 2.97$, $p < .01$. These subjects had significantly lower mean RTs for the advance than for the no-advance information condition (57 msec, $t(23) = 2.21$, $p < .05$). This difference may be due to a reduction in recognition time for the character when the top/bottom direction is known in advance or to the use of the advance orientation information to decide which way to rotate the character. For 4 of the 6 control subjects, and for the group as a whole, the advance orientation information did not significantly affect the slope of the regression line. For one of the two exceptional control subjects, both the regression slope and mean RTs were significantly lowered by advance orientation information, $t(185) = 2.21$, $p < .05$, and $t(358) = 2.02$, $p < .05$, respectively; conversely, for the other exceptional subject, advance orientation information significantly increased the slope of the

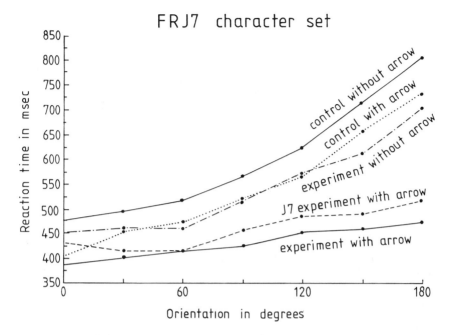

FIG. 15.6.   Mean RT plotted as a function of orientation with and without advance information for experimental and control subjects. Data from the deviant experimental subject is not included. The data for the experimental subjects on the J and 7 trials is plotted separately to show that the advantage of advance information is not restricted to the F and R trials.

linear regression line, $t(188) = 2.15$, $p < .05$. The control subjects' overall error rates varied from 3% to 9% for individual subjects, with a mean of 5%. There were no significant interactions with any experimental factors.

Thus, the control subjects were apparently unable to use advance orientation information to avoid mental rotation in discriminating normal from mirror-image characters. This result, which can be considered a replication of the Cooper and Shepard (1973) finding, contrasts clearly with the experimental subjects' performance with this same character set (see Fig. 15.6). For 5 of these 6 experimental subjects, and for the group as a whole, there were significant effects of advance orientation information on the mean RTs averaged over orientation [for the group, $t(23) = 3.52$, $p < .01$]. (The subject failing to show this difference with the F, R, J, 7 character set was the one who also failed on the simpler F, R, G, L set.) Further, the RTs and regression-line slopes for just the trials with the two new characters J and 7 (see Fig. 15.6) again revealed significant differences between advance and no-advance information conditions [for 5 subjects, $t(19) = 3.01$, $p < .01$, and $t(450) = 2.97$, $p < .01$]. The small slope for the J and 7 trials with advance information (even omitting the deviant subject) suggests that some subjects occasionally revert to mental rotation for these characters.

The experimental subjects' overall error rates with the F, R, J, 7 set varied from 3% to 9% (with a mean of 6%). Again, the error data did not yield any significant effects.

Thus, subjects with the appropriate instructions, training, and response conditions are able to use the advance orientation information to avoid mental rotation even with a character set in which there are no obvious features that discriminate normal characters from mirror images.

SUMMARY

We have presented a specific alternative to the view that mental images are like pictures or arrays. The alternative is a hierarchical structural description containing explicit representations of quantitative spatial relationships. One type of relationship represents the intrinsic, viewpoint-independent spatial structure of a scene or object. A second type represents the relationships of objects and their parts to the viewer. These relationships to a viewer-centered frame of reference facilitate spatial reasoning, and it is their presence that characterizes mental imagery.

Continuous spatial transforamtions like mental rotation can be mentally simulated by continuously changing the representations of the spatial relationships.

It is commonly claimed that models that include viewpoint-independent representations of shape cannot explain why mental rotation is necessary to compare two shapes at different orientations. We have shown how the normally useful ability to describe shapes relative to imposed frames of reference of either handedness may lead to a specific inability to compare the handedness of two nonaligned shapes or to judge whether a single nonupright shape has its normal handedness. Our argument requires us to postulate that people do not have an explicit representation of the handedness of the nonupright frames of reference that they impose on nonupright shapes.

Experimental evidence has been presented that shows that, with proper instruction and under conditions predicted by our theory, subjects can judge the handedness of a nonupright character without mentally rotating it. This result corroborates our explanation of why mental rotation is necessary and shows that its use is not incompatible with the existence of internal, viewpoint-independent representations of shape.

ACKNOWLEDGMENTS

This research was conducted while the first author was a Visiting Scholar with the Program in Cognitive Science, supported by the Sloan Foundation. The second author was supported by Grant No. BNS 7915336 from the National Science Foundation to George Mandler.

REFERENCES

Cavanagh, P. Locus of rotation effects in recognition. *Bulletin of the Psychonomic Society,* 1977, *10,* 152–154.

Cooper, L. A., & Shepard, R. N. Chronometric studies in the rotation of mental images. In W. G. Chase (Ed.), *Visual information processing.* New York: Academic Press, 1973.

Hinton, G. E. Some demonstrations of the effects of structural descriptions in mental imagery. *Cognitive Science,* 1979, *3,* 231–250. (a)

Hinton, G. E. Imagery without arrays. Commentary on: S. M. Kosslyn, S. Pinker, G. E. Smith, and S. P. Shwartz, "On the demystification of mental imagery." *The Behavioral and Brain Sciences,* 1979, *2,* 555–556. (b)

Hochberg, J. In the mind's eye. In R. N. Haber (Ed.), *Contemporary theory and research in visual perception.* New York: Holt, Rinehart and Winston, 1968.

Kosslyn, S. M. Information representation in visual figures. *Cognitive Psychology,* 1975, *7,* 341–370.

Kosslyn, S. M., Pinker, S., Smith, G. E., & Shwartz, S. P. On the demystification of mental imagery. *The Behavioral and Brain Sciences,* 1979, *2,* 535–581.

Marr, D., & Nishihara, H. K. Representation and recognition of the spatial organization of three-dimensional shapes. *Proceedings of the Royal Society, Series B,* 1978, *200,* 269–294.

Pinker, S., & Finke, R. A. Emergent two-dimensional patterns in images rotated in depth. *Journal of Experimental Psychology: Human Perception and Performance,* 1980, *6,* 244–264.

Rock, I. *Orientation and form.* New York: Academic Press, 1973.

Shepard, R. N. Psychophysical complementarity. In M. Kubovy & J. R. Pomerantz (Eds.), *Perceptual organization.* Hillsdale, N.J.: Lawrence Erlbaum Associates, 1979.

Shepard, R. N., & Feng, C. A chronometric study of mental paper folding. *Cognitive Psychology,* 1972, *3,* 228–243.

Shepard, R. N., & Metzler, J. Mental rotation of three-dimensional objects. *Science,* 1971, *171,* 701–703.

16 Mental Transformations of Size and Orientation

Claus Bundesen and Axel Larsen
Copenhagen University, Denmark

Joyce E. Farrell
Stanford University
Stanford, California
U.S.A.

ABSTRACT

Mental transformations of size and orientation were investigated in a successive matching reaction-time experiment. Mean reaction times increased approximately linearly with both the linear size ratio and the angular difference in orientation within stimulus pairs, and the effects of angular and size disparities were additive. The results suggest that mental transformations corresponding to compositions of external size transformations and rotations were composed from mental transformations corresponding to simple size transformations and simple rotations. Each of the component transformations, in turn, appeared to be sequential-additive in structure. The linear size functions were explained on the dual hypotheses that (1) disparities of size were visually resolved as differences in depth; and (2) mental transformation times were directly proportional to these differences in depth.

INTRODUCTION

Subjectively we seem capable of mentally transforming the visual size and orientation of objects in space, that is, transforming mental images of objects in given sizes and orientations into mental images of objects of the same shapes but in

279

other sizes and orientations. Experimental evidence on the nature and function of such mental transformations accumulated during the last decade (see Cooper & Shepard, 1978, for a general review). In a basic experiment, Shepard and Metzler (1971) found that the time taken to recognize that two perspective drawings depicted objects of the same three-dimensional random shape was a linearly increasing function of the angular difference in orientation between the two objects. Shepard and Metzler conjectured that the task was performed by mentally rotating one of the objects into the orientation of the other one and then testing for a match, and their account was supported by subjective reports. In similar experiments on mental size transformation (Bundesen & Larsen, 1975), the time required to recognize that two random figures were the same in shape was found to be a linearly increasing function of the ratio of their linear sizes. Moreover, Sekuler and Nash (1972) found that the time taken to recognize that two rectangles had the same shape increased with both their linear size ratio and their angular difference in orientation such that effects of these factors were approximately additive. Only two levels of angular difference (0° and 90°) were investigated, but assuming that both mental size transformation and mental rotation were invoked, the additivity suggests that mental transformations corresponding to combinations of external size transformations and rotations actually are composed from mental transformations corresponding to simple size transformations and simple rotations. To further investigate this hypothesis, we conducted a more extensive experiment on the joint effects of disparities of size and angular orientation in successive visual matching.

Studying the structure of combined transformations of size and orientation should elucidate the nature of the component transformations themselves. We particularly considered the question whether the internal processes corresponding to simple size transformations and simple rotations are individually sequential-additive in structure.

Method

Subjects.   Six subjects with normal or corrected vision participated, including one of the authors (A.L.) and five students or members of the staff at Copenhagen University. All subjects had served for at least 10 hr in similar experiments.

Stimuli.   The stimuli were normal or right–left mirror-inverted versions of six asymmetrical characters, *3, 4, 7, J, P,* and *R.* The characters appeared in any of three fixed-size formats with linear size ratios of 1:1.5:4 and in any of 12 orientations differing from the standard upright by 0°, 30°, 60°, . . . , or 330° of positive (i.e., counterclockwise) rotation in the frontoparallel plane. To ease perceptual determination of the orientation of the characters, each one was supplied with a bar extending from the center through the top and scaled to the format of the character.

For each of the six characters, 1728 stimulus pairs were constructed by combining different transforms of the same character. For each of the possible versions (normal versus inverted) and sizes of the two stimuli, each of the 12 orientations of the first stimulus was paired with four orientations of the second stimulus corresponding to rotations of 0°, 30°, 60°, and 90°, respectively. The directions of rotation were randomly determined with the constraint that positive and negative rotations be equally frequent.

Each of the six sets of 1728 stimulus pairs was used with three subjects such that each of the six subjects was presented with a random sequence of 5184 stimulus pairs.

Apparatus and Procedure. The subject was seated in front of a computer-driven cathode-ray tube (Digital Equipment Corporation GT44 graphics system equipped with a P-39 phosphor) at a viewing distance of 1 m. All stimulus characters were centered on the face of the tube where the largest format spanned approximately 13.2 cm × 8.8 cm (i.e., 7.56° × 5.04°) and the smallest format approximately 3.3 cm × 2.2 cm (i.e., 1.89° × 1.26°). The stimuli were displayed by periodic intensifications at a rate of 40 Hz, each with a luminous directional energy of approximately 0.6 cd-μsec/cm (Sperling, 1971); background luminance of the screen was about 3.1 cd/m². Viewing was binocular and fixation was free.

The stimuli were presented in 87 blocks of about 60 pairs. When the subject pressed a starting key, the first member of the first stimulus pair in a block appeared with a latency of 4000 msec. The stimulus was refreshed for 500 msec; during the next 1100 msec, the stimulus decayed, and the second member of the stimulus pair was then exposed. The subject was instructed to decide ''as quickly as possible'' whether the two stimuli were identical except for change in size and rotation in the frontoparallel plane. A positive decision was indicated by pressing a right-hand button; a negative decision, by pressing a left-hand button. Reaction time (RT) was measured in milliseconds from the onset of the second stimulus. The exposure of the second stimulus was terminated by the reaction, and after a fixed intertrial interval of 2000 msec the next pair of stimuli was presented. The subject was allowed a rest after each block of trials, and the blocks were distributed over three to five sessions depending on the subject.

Throughout the experiment, trials on which errors were made were later repeated until a complete set of errorless RTs had been obtained.

Results

All analyses were based on trials that were immediately preceded by correct reactions, and only correct reactions were analyzed with respect to latency. Individual mean error rates ranged between .02 and .105. The grand mean RTs for the six subjects were 508, 514, 514, 548, 643, and 665 msec, respectively. Group data were separately analyzed for the four faster and the two slower

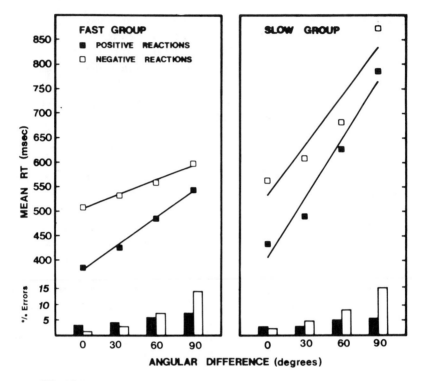

FIG. 16.1.   Mean correct positive and negative RTs as functions of angular difference in orientation within stimulus pairs. (Data are for pairs of same-sized stimuli. Left panel: group data for fast subjects; right panel: group data for slow subjects; bottom subpanels show rates of false alarms [solid bars] and misses [open bars]. Estimated standard errors of the mean RTs ranged between 5 msec and 11 msec with a mean of 8 msec for the fast group and between 9 msec and 36 msec with a mean of 21 msec for the slow group.)

subjects; for each of these groups, the individual patterns of RTs closely resembled the group data.

Overall, positive and negative mean RTs were approximately linearly increasing functions of the angular difference in orientation within stimulus pairs. The group data for pairs of same-sized stimuli are displayed in the left and right panels of Fig. 16.1 for fast and slow subjects, respectively. For the fast group, the product-moment correlation of mean RT with difference in orientation was .997 and .992 for positive and negative reactions, respectively, and the deviations from linearity were not significant; for positive reactions, $\chi^2(2) = 2.53$, $p = .29$; for negative reactions, $\chi^2(2) = .89$, $p = .64$; in sum, $\chi^2(4) = 3.42$, $p = .49$. The slope constants for positive and negative reactions were about 1.80 and .98 msec/°, respectively. For the slow group, the correlation between RT and difference in orientation was .98 and .95 for positive and negative reactions, respectively, though in this case the deviations from linearity were significant;

for positive reactions, $\chi^2(2) = 10.4$, $p = .005$; for negative reactions, $\chi^2(2) = 9.8$, $p = .008$; in sum, $\chi^2(4) = 20.2$, $p = .0005$. The fitted slope constants for positive and negative reactions were about 4.00 and 3.35 msec/°, respectively. For both groups, the interaction between difference in orientation and type of response in mean RT was accompanied by an interaction in the rate of errors: With increasing difference in orientation, both miss and false-alarm rates increased, but the miss function crossed the false-alarm function by increasing more steeply (see bottom subpanels in Fig. 16.1).

The values shown in Fig. 16.1 were produced by averaging data for stimulus pairs with size ratio 1 over format combinations 1:1, 1.5:1.5, and 4:4. The effects of absolute size format were small and inconsistent. Averaged across angular differences in orientation, mean RTs for all subjects for pairs of same-sized stimuli in formats 1, 1.5, and 4, respectively, were 505, 495, and 505 msec for positive reactions and 589, 588, and 604 msec for negative reactions. As a test of the hypothesis that, for the fast group, mean RT for same-sized stimuli was linearly increasing with angular difference in orientation but independent of the size format, $\chi^2(10) = 9.57$, $p = .48$, for positive reactions; $\chi^2(10) = 16.69$, $p = .08$, for negative reactions; $\chi^2(20) = 26.26$, $p = .16$, in sum. For the slow group, testing the hypothesis that mean RT for same-sized stimuli was independent of the size format for each level of angular difference, $\chi^2(8) = 8.12$, $p = .42$, for positive reactions; $\chi^2(8) = 9.86$, $p = .28$, for negative reactions; $\chi^2(16) = 17.98$, $p = .33$, in sum.

When averaged over absolute orientations, mean RTs were approximately linear functions of angular difference in orientation within stimulus pairs (Fig. 16.1), but a strong interaction was found between the angular difference in orientation and the absolute orientation of the probe (i.e., the second stimulus in a pair). Figure 16.2 shows mean RT for same-sized stimuli averaged across response types as a function of angular deviation of probe from upright (taking values between 0° and 180°). Angular difference in orientation within stimulus pairs is the parameter. The data displayed are for the group of fast subjects, but results were similar for the slow group. Mean RT increased with angular deviation of probe from upright and with angular difference in orientation within stimulus pairs, and the higher the level of one of these factors, the greater was the effect of the other one. The same pattern was evidenced for each of the four combinations of versions (normal versus inverted) of the first and second members of stimulus pairs.

The three solid curves in Fig. 16.2 are theoretical fits to the data for stimulus pairs with differences in orientation of 30°, 60°, and 90°. The fits were made on the hypothesis that, for a pair of stimulus orientations spanning a specific sector of a circle, of size $i30°$ (where $i = 1$, 2, or 3), the RT was a sum of a base RT b and i additive increments in latency, one for each of the i nonoverlapping subsectors of 30°. The base time b was estimated by simply averaging RTs for same-orientation combinations (0°, 0°), (30°, 30°), (330°, 330°), (60°, 60°), and (300°, 300°), corresponding to the three lowest data points in Fig. 16.2. Let $t(u, w)$ be

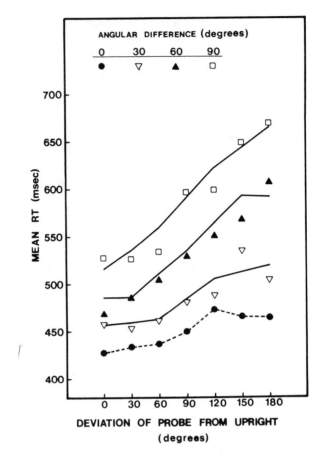

FIG. 16.2. Mean correct RT across response types (positive versus negative) as a function of angular deviation of probe from upright with angular difference in orientation within stimulus pairs as the parameter. (Data are for pairs of same-sized stimuli and for the group of fast subjects. A theoretical fit is indicated by solid curves. Estimated standard errors ranged between 8 msec and 37 msec with a mean of 15 msec.)

the additive increment in latency for orientation combination (u, w). Estimates of t for sectors of $30°$ of the circle were computed from b and the observed RTs to stimulus pairs with a difference in orientation of $30°$. With the constraint that $t(u, w) = t(w, u) = t(360° - u, 360° - w)$,[1] estimates of $t[(j - 1) 30°, j30°]$, for $j = 1, 2, \ldots, 6$, were 24, 29, 30, 74, 72, and 87 msec, respectively. From these six values and b, theoretical RTs to stimulus pairs with differences in orientation of

---

[1]For observed RTs, RT $(u, w) \cong$ RT $(w, u) \cong$ RT $(360° - u, 360° - w)$, even if some trend existed that RT (u, w) was greater than RT (w, u) when the angular deviation from upright was greater for the orientation of w than for the orientation of u. For $|u - w| = 30°$, $|w - 180°| < |u - 180°|$, and $0° \leqslant u, w \leqslant 360°$, the mean of RT (u, w) − RT (w, u) was 14 msec.

60° and 90° were determined by the hypothesis of additivity. The fit was remarkably good, $\chi^2(14) = 15.40$, $p = .35$.

Effects of the linear size ratio (s) of pairs of stimuli in the same orientation are shown in Fig. 16.3, summarized across the six subjects. Positive and negative mean RTs increased approximately linearly with s, measured such that $s \geq 1$. The rate of increase was higher when the second stimulus was smaller than the first one (demagnification pairs), but for both magnification and demagnification pairs the rate was nearly the same for negative as for positive reactions. By test of the hypothesis that, for each type of pair, positive and negative mean RTs were

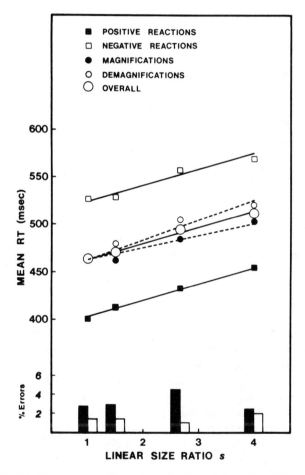

FIG. 16.3.   Mean correct positive and negative RTs, their mean, and the means for correct responses to magnification and demagnification stimulus pairs as functions of linear size ratio. (Data are for pairs of stimuli in the same orientation across all subjects. Bottom panel shows mean rates of false alarms [solid bars] and misses [open bars]. Estimated standard errors of the mean RTs ranged between 3 msec and 6 msec.)

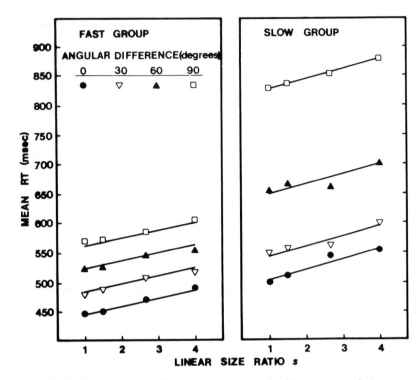

FIG. 16.4.   Mean correct RTs across response types (positive versus negative) as functions of linear size ratio with angular difference in orientation within stimulus pairs as the parameter. (Left panel: group data for fast subjects fitted by equidistant lines; right panel: group data for slow subjects fitted by parallel lines. Estimated standard errors ranged between 4 msec and 8 msec with a mean of 6 msec for the fast group and between 8 msec and 23 msec with a mean of 15 msec for the slow group.)

linear and parallel functions of size ratio, $\chi^2(10) = 17.43$, $p = .07$. In the best fit, the slope constants for magnification and demagnification pairs were about 12 msec and 20 msec, respectively.

The effects on RT of disparities of size and angular orientation within stimulus pairs were approximately additive. Figure 16.4 shows mean RTs for the groups of fast and slow subjects as functions of linear size ratio with angular difference in orientation as the parameter. Data are averaged over types of response (positive versus negative), directions of size transformation (magnification versus demagnification), absolute size formats, and absolute orientations. For the group of fast subjects, four equidistant minimum chi-square lines, one for each level of the parameter, account for 98.8% of the variance. For the group of slow subjects, four parallel minimum chi-square lines account for 99.7% of the variance. The results for the two slow subjects agreed with the hypothesis that, for each direction of size transformation, mean RT was a linearly increasing function of size ratio with the same rate of increase for each level of angular difference in orientation and each type of response, $\chi^2(46) = 52.14$, $p = .25$. For the four fast subjects, testing the same hypothesis with the further constraint that, for each type of response, mean RT was a linearly increasing function of angular difference in orientation, $\chi^2(50) = 63.43$, $p = .11$.

The error rates corresponding to the patterns of mean RTs in Fig. 16.4 were similar for the two groups. Table 16.1 shows the mean rate of errors for all six subjects as a function of linear size ratio and angular difference in orientation within stimulus pairs. For each size ratio, errors increased with angular difference in orientation, $\chi^2(12) = 477.9$, $p < 10^{-9}$. With difference in orientation kept constant, the effect of size ratio on error rate was not significant, $\chi^2(12) = 12.26$, $p = .42$.

Subjective Reports

All subjects reported that, during the interstimulus interval, the first stimulus of a pair was retained as a more or less schematic visual image. Subjects were less confident in reporting upon subsequent stages of processing. Three subjects gave clear reports that, in order to compare the two stimuli, they tried to imagine how the first one would appear if transformed to the size and orientation of the second one. These subjects agreed that the transformed image of the first stimulus appeared to result from a process in which its imagined orientation was changed by degrees. Two of the three subjects claimed that mental changes in visual size and orientation were concurrent such that, when mentally passing intermediate orientations, imagined visual sizes were also intermediate between those of the two stimuli. One of these subjects felt that a mental size transformation involved a mental change in depth, but the other subject did not. Otherwise, the subjective reports were not inconsistent, but they lacked in specificity. Variations between subjects in explicitness of report and regularity or pattern of measured RTs and error rates showed little relationship.

TABLE 16.1
Mean Rate of Errors as a Function of
Linear Size Ratio and Angular Difference
in Orientation (in degrees) within Stimulus Pairs

Angular Difference	Size Ratio			
	1.00	1.50	2.67	4.00
0°	.022	.022	.028	.023
30°	.034	.032	.033	.034
60°	.065	.064	.050	.056
90°	.104	.104	.086	.091

DISCUSSION

The pattern of RTs obtained in the experiment confirms and extends a series of previous findings on temporal effects of disparities of size and orientation in visual comparison of confusable objects with respect to shape. Mean decision times across absolute orientations increased approximately linearly with both the linear size ratio and the angular difference in orientation within stimulus pairs (Bundesen & Larsen, 1975; Shepard & Metzler, 1971), and the temporal effects of angular and size disparities were approximately additive (Sekuler & Nash, 1972).[2] The results are consistent with the hypothesis that subjects encoded the first stimulus in a pair as a mental image that was retained during the interstimulus interval. When the second stimulus appeared, the mental image was transformed to fit the visual size and orientation of that stimulus. Following the transformation, the image was used for position-wise comparison with the second stimulus. If they matched, a positive reaction was made, otherwise a negative reaction.

Additivity of the temporal effects of disparities of size and angular orientation within stimulus pairs suggests that mental transformations corresponding to combinations of external size transformations and rotations are composed from mental transformations corresponding to simple size transformations and simple rotations. Some subjects insisted that mental changes in visual size and orientation were gradual and concurrent in the sense that, in intermediate states of mental transformation, imagined visual size and orientation were both intermediate between the initial and final state; and no subjects explicitly reported otherwise. The reports speak against the hypothesis of a simple two-stage organization by which one of the component transformations (i.e., mental rotation or mental size transformation) is initiated when the other one is completed. But consider the assumption that both of the component processes themselves are sequential-additive in structure such that, for instance, a mental rotation over a large sector of the circle is a sequence of mental rotations over smaller subsectors, the durations of these steps being additive. Both temporal additivity and apparent concurrence can then be explained by the hypothesis that mental transformations of size and orientation are performed by sequentially alternating smaller steps of mental size transformation with smaller steps of mental rotation.

---

[2]From a reanalysis of the data obtained by Sekuler and Nash (1972), Besner (1978) reported a significant interaction between disparities of size and orientation in rates of errors. Besner (1978) felt that, by additive stages logic (Sternberg, 1969), this finding suggests that effects of the two factors be located at the same stage of processing. Formally this suggestion seems unwarranted. If the stages affected by disparities of size and orientation are sequentially organized, additive stages logic (Sternberg, 1969) implies that effects of the two factors be additive in mean RTs; but even if the stages are completely independent, there is no implication that effects of the factors be additive in rates of errors.

Mental Rotation

A strong interaction between angular difference in orientation within a stimulus pair and absolute orientation of the probe was observed. The greater the angular deviation of probe from upright, the stronger was the increase in mean RT with angular difference in orientation between the stimuli in the pair (see Fig. 16.2). Apparently, for the alphanumerical stimulus characters employed, the rate of mental rotation was a decreasing function of the angular deviation between the imagined orientation and the vertical. Analysis of the interaction confirmed that, using estimated times for mental rotations over sectors of 30° of the circle, RTs corresponding to rotations over sectors of 60° and 90° could be predicted on the hypothesis that mental rotations are sequential-additive in structure. By the same hypothesis, the mean duration of mental rotation should be directly proportional to the angular extent of the transformation, when averaged over a set of segments adding to a full circle. This explains why, across absolute orientations, the increase in mean RT with angular difference in orientation within stimulus pairs was approximately linear (see Fig. 16.1).[3]

Although the suggested account explains the main features of the data on mental rotation, some systematic deviations from the expected pattern of results should be noted. First, for the two slower subjects, deviations from linearity in mean RTs as functions of angular difference in orientation within stimulus pairs were highly significant, the functions being positively accelerated (see Fig. 16.1). Predictions of RTs associated with rotations over larger sectors of the circle from RTs associated with rotations over smaller ones would be too low for these subjects. Second, for all subjects, mean RTs showed some increase with angular deviation of probe from upright even when the angular orientations of the two stimuli in a pair were the same (cf. Fig. 16.2, the broken bottom curve). However, both deviations from expectation may be explained by assuming some variability in the imagined orientation of the first stimulus in a pair at the time the probe was presented, as follows.

Consider the effects of a displacement of w degrees, $-90 \leq w \leq 90$, in the imagined orientation of the first stimulus at the time the second one is presented. Let the angular deviations of the first and second stimuli from the standard upright be u and $(u + v)$ degrees, respectively ($0 \leq u \leq 360$ and $-90 \leq v \leq 90$). At the time the second stimulus is presented, the imagined orientation of the first is $(u + w)$ degrees from the standard upright. A mental rotation of $(v - w)$ degrees is therefore required to align the imagined orientation of the first

---

[3]The present results resemble those provided by Cooper and Shepard for a related task (compare Fig. 16.2 with Fig. 14 in Cooper & Shepard, 1973), but the present method of predicting RTs associated with rotations over larger sectors of the circle from RTs associated with rotations over smaller ones fails if directly applied to their data. The failure supports the contention that, in the previous task, subjects used a mixture of different strategies (Cooper & Shepard, 1973, pp. 154–155).

stimulus with the second. Assuming that positive and negative mental rotations are equally fast, only the numerical value $|v - w|$ is important. When $|v| \leqslant |w|$, and the sign of v is determined at random, it can easily be shown that the expectation of $|v - w|$ equals $|w|$, but when $|v| > |w|$, the expectation of $|v - w|$ equals $|v|$. In general, as the angular difference in stimulus orientations $|v|$ increases, the expected angular extent of the required mental rotation stays constant at $|w|$ degrees, the error in imaging the orientation of the first stimulus, as long as $|v| \leqslant |w|$; but for $|v| > |w|$, the expectation is $|v|$ degrees, regardless of w.

The result implies that, if $|w|$ is a continuous random variable ranging between 0 and max $(|w|)$ with expectation $E(|w|)$, then the expected angular extent of the required mental rotation as a function of $|v|$ equals $E(|w|)$ degrees for $|v| = 0$, increases with positive acceleration for $0 < v < $ max $(|w|)$, and equals $|v|$ degrees for $|v| \geqslant$ max $(|w|)$. Post hoc, then, we suggest the deviant results for the two slower subjects be explained by the conjecture that these subjects sometimes attempted to anticipate the (unpredictable) orientation of the probe by making some mental rotation of the first stimulus before the arrival of the second one. Their anticipatory mental rotations should sometimes exceed an angle of 30° (cf. Fig. 16.1). For the four faster subjects, however, the variability in the imagined orientation of the first stimulus should be small and supposedly result from an inability to keep the image strictly constant during the interstimulus interval, and not from attempts to anticipate the orientation of the probe. With max $(|w|)$ less than 30°, only RTs for pairs of stimuli in the same orientation should be affected. The analysis of additivity in the results (cf. Fig. 16.2) suggests that effects of this source of variation in the imagined orientation of the first stimulus were negligible at angular departures from upright of 0°, 30°, and 60° but were observable as an increase in RTs to same-oriented stimuli at the more extreme orientations, where the rate of mental rotation was slower and, presumably, the orientational uncertainty was greater.

Finally, although the patterns of positive and negative RTs were generally similar, the temporal effects of differences in angular orientation within stimulus pairs were stronger in positive than in negative reactions (see Fig. 16.1). A corresponding interaction was observed in rates of errors. With increasing difference in angular orientation, error rates increased, but the miss function crossed the false-alarm function by increasing more steeply. Both interactions may be explained by hypothesizing that, the greater the discrepancy in angular orientation for a stimulus pair, the more the subject was biased toward a negative reaction and against a positive one.

Mental Size Transformation

For pairs of same-oriented stimuli, positive and negative mean RTs were linearly increasing and nearly parallel functions of the linear size ratio of the stimuli, for both magnification and demagnification, though the rate of increase was higher for demagnification. This pattern of results is the same as that found by Larsen and Bundesen (1978) for successive matching of random shapes, but some limitations on the generality of the pattern should be noted. First, the effect of magnification versus demagnification apparently depends on minor variations in procedure. For successive matching of random shapes, Howard and Kerst (1978) also found that positive and negative mean RTs were linear and parallel functions of the linear size ratio of stimuli, but in their study the effect of size ratio was greater for magnification than for demagnification. Second, the finding that temporal effects of size ratio and response type were additive seems critically dependent on the fact that, within negative pairs, stimuli were visually highly confusable. A number of experiments have shown that, when members of negative pairs are grossly different in shape, the slope of the negative RT function degenerates (Besner & Coltheart, 1976).

Earlier, we raised the question of whether mental changes in depth were involved in mental size transformations. The subjective evidence was ambiguous. However, on the assumption that mental size transformation is a sequential-additive process, the linear increase in mean RT as a function of the linear size ratio of stimuli does suggest that mental changes in depth were implicated, as the following argument shows.

Suppose that a mental size transformation of a stimulus character corresponds to a geometric multiplication about the center of the character. Let x, y, and z be stimulus characters in the same position, shape, and orientation, but in size formats 1, 1.5, and 4, respectively. By sequential additivity, a mental transformation of stimulus x from size format 1 to size format 4 should consist in a mental transformation of x to size format 1.5 followed by a transformation to size format 4, the durations of these steps being additive. If each of the transformations corresponded to a geometric multiplication about the center of the character, then the transformed mental image of x should be the same as an untransformed image of stimulus y after the first step in the sequence and the same as an untransformed image of stimulus z after the second step. The duration of the mental size transformation of x required for comparison of x against z should therefore equal the sum of the durations of the mental size transformations required for comparisons of x against y and y against z, respectively; in symbols,

$$t(x, z) = t(x, y) + t(y, z). \qquad\qquad 1$$

But from the observed linear increase in mean RT as a function of the linear size ratio s of stimuli α and β, $t(\alpha, \beta)$ is a linear function of s such that $t(\alpha, \beta) = 0$ if $s = 1$; that is,

$$t(\alpha, \beta) = c(s - 1), \qquad\qquad 2$$

where c is a positive constant. Hence, $t(x, z) = 3c$, $t(x, y) = c/2$, and $t(y, z) = 5c/3$, which violates Equation 1. Thus if the mental size transformation is sequential-additive in structure, and its duration is a linear function of size ratio, it cannot correspond to a geometric multiplication about the center of the stimulus, effecting no change in spatial position.

The linear relation between RT and size ratio and the assumption that the underlying transformation is sequential-additive suggests that the transformation operates on a representation of the size ratio itself or of something linearly related to it. There is a way of making the depth of one of the stimuli be linearly related to the size ratio, and this would allow the transformation in relative size to be performed by a sequential-additive transformation of the mental depth of one stimulus.

Suppose the mental size transformation investigated in matching tasks is based on two simple operations, one corresponding to a geometric multiplication with respect to the subject's point of view and the other corresponding to a translation in three-dimensional space. The first operation affects apparent size and distance in three-dimensional space while keeping apparent size in the two dimensions of the visual field constant. This operation should be useful in reconstructing three-dimensional scenes from two-dimensional representations.[4] The second operation transforms the representation of distance and proximal size but not of distal size; it seems adaptive for a creature moving in a world of rigid or semirigid objects. By combining the two operations in sequence, counterparts of geometric multiplications about any points can be constructed. Specifically, by combining the first operation with a mental translation in depth, the equivalent of a change in size with no change in spatial position can be effected.

Consider the implications for visual matching of two stimulus patterns, x and y, presented in a frontoparallel plane at a distance D from the subject (see Fig. 16.5). Let L_x and L_y, where $L_x \leq L_y$, be the linear sizes (i.e., the greatest linear extents) of x and y, and let $s = L_y/L_x$. The first operation envisaged should correspond to central projection of the patterns onto frontoparallel planes at distances d_x and d_y, respectively, such that apparent distal sizes l_x and l_y are equalized. The second operation should be a mental translation over the distance $d = |d_x - d_y|$. By simple geometry, $l_x/d_x = L_x/D$ and $l_y/d_y = L_y/D$. Given that $l_x = l_y$, it follows that $L_x d_x = L_y d_y$ and therefore $d_x = s d_y$. Accordingly

$$d = d_y(s - 1). \qquad\qquad 3$$

Hence, on the assumptions that (1) the represented distance of the larger pattern, d_y, is a constant, regardless of L_x and L_y; and (2) internal transformation time is directly proportional to the extent d of the mental change in depth, a linear increase in matching RT with the linear size ratio s should be expected.

To summarize: From additivity of effects of disparities of size and angular orientation in RTs and subjective reports that performance was based on mental changes in size and orientation that were gradual and concurrent, we argued that

---

[4]A few monocular projections of a rigidly moving object is normally sufficient for computing the three-dimensional structure and motion of the object up to a geometric multiplication with respect to the point of view (Ullman, 1979). The correct scaling factor, however, is not computable by geometric analysis.

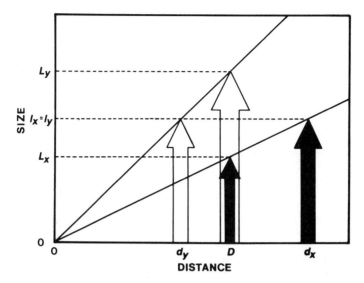

FIG. 16.5. Resolving a disparity of size as a difference in depth. (Objects x [smaller solid arrow] and y [larger open arrow] with linear sizes L_x and L_y are shown at a distance D from a subject. By geometric multiplications with respect to the subject's point of view [the origin of the coordinate system], the disparity of size between x and y is resolved as a difference in depth between the images of x [larger solid arrow] and y [smaller open arrow]. The sizes and distances of the images are designated by ls and ds.)

mental transformations corresponding to simple size transformations and simple rotations are both sequential-additive in structure; the combination of temporal additivity and apparent concurrence could then be explained by the hypothesis that mental transformations of size and orientation were performed by sequentially alternating smaller steps of mental size transformation with smaller steps of mental rotation. From the assumption that mental size transformation is sequential-additive in structure and the finding that mean RT was a linearly increasing function of the linear size ratio of stimuli, we further argued that the mental transformation in question did not correspond to a geometric multiplication about the center of the stimulus, effecting no change in spatial position. On the contrary, the linear size functions support the dual hypotheses (1) that disparities of size were visually resolved as differences in depth; and (2) that mental transformation times were directly proportional to these differences in depth.

ACKNOWLEDGMENTS

This research was part of a project planned at Stanford University in collaboration with Roger N. Shepard. The work was supported by a traveling grant from the Danish Research Council for the Humanities to Claus Bundesen, a traveling grant from Copenhagen University to Axel Larsen, a National Institute of Mental Health training grant to Joyce E. Farrell, and National Science Foundation research grant BNS-75-02806 to Roger N. Shepard. The authors are indebted to Roger Shepard for helpful discussions and generous support during all phases of the project. Important technical assistance was provided by Jørgen Rathje, Copenhagen University.

REFERENCES

Besner, D. Pattern recognition: Are size and orientation additive factors? *Perception & Psychophysics*, 1978, *23*, 93.

Besner, D., & Coltheart, M. Mental size scaling examined. *Memory & Cognition*, 1976, *4*, 525–531.

Bundesen, C., & Larsen, A. Visual transformation of size. *Journal of Experimental Psychology: Human Perception and Performance*, 1975, *1*, 214–220.

Cooper, L. A., & Shepard, R. N. Chronometric studies of the rotation of mental images. In W. G. Chase (Ed.), *Visual information processing*. New York: Academic Press, 1973.

Cooper, L. A., & Shepard, R. N. Transformations on representations of objects in space. In E. C. Carterette & M. P. Friedman (Eds.), *Handbook of perception* (Vol. 8). New York: Academic Press, 1978.

Howard, J. H., Jr., & Kerst, S. M. Directional effects of size change on the comparison of visual shapes. *American Journal of Psychology*, 1978, *91*, 491–499.

Larsen, A., & Bundesen, C. Size scaling in visual pattern recognition. *Journal of Experimental Psychology: Human Perception and Performance*, 1978, *4*, 1–20.

Sekuler, R., & Nash, D. Speed of size scaling in human vision. *Psychonomic Science*, 1972, *27*, 93–94.

Shepard, R. N., & Metzler, J. Mental rotation of three-dimensional objects. *Science*, 1971, *171*, 701–703.

Sperling, G. The description and luminous calibration of cathode ray oscilloscope visual displays. *Behavioral Research Methods and Instrumentation*, 1971, *3*, 148–151.

Sternberg, S. The discovery of processing stages: Extensions of Donders' method. *Acta Psychologica*, 1969, *30*, 276–315.

Ullman, S. *The interpretation of visual motion*. Cambridge, Mass.: MIT Press, 1979.

17 Equivalence of Perceptual and Imaginal Representation: Developmental Changes

Robert J. Weber,
Larry Hochhaus,
and
William D. Brown
Oklahoma State University
Stillwater, Oklahoma, U.S.A.

ABSTRACT

The degree of equivalence between perceptual and imaginal modes of representation was examined across three age levels, 9-, 20-, and 68-years of age. The
perceptual and imaginal systems were most equivalent, in terms of time scores,
at age 20. Several hypotheses concerning the development and decline with age
of imaginal and perceptual modes of representation were considered. The results
were most consistent with a percept-first development hypothesis in which the
perceptual system matures before the imagery system in the age transition from 9
years old to 20 years old. In contrast, an image-first decline hypothesis was most
consistent with the age transition from 20 years old to 68 years old. There were
also systematic differences in the correlational structure of the data. The results
suggest that 9-year-olds begin with an overlapping perceptual and imaginal processing capacity. This capacity has become more differentiated or specialized by
age 20. Then by age 68 the capacity has once again become general purpose in
nature.

INTRODUCTION

This study is concerned with the degree of equivalence of perception and imagery
and how that equivalence may vary with age. Finke (1980) discusses equivalence
between perceptual and imaginal systems. We borrow some of his concepts, add

others, and use a somewhat different terminology. In addition to phenomenal similarity there are at least two possible forms of equivalence that may exist between the visual perceptual and imaginal systems.

1. Performance Equivalence. Two systems have performance equivalence to the extent that they produce, say, comparable time scores for a given task. Insofar as measures like time are used, it is possible to talk about degrees of equivalence. Note that time scores may be equivalent without underlying processes being identical.

2. Process Equivalence. Two systems have process equivalence to the extent that the same underlying processes are involved. Actually, there are two subspecies of process equivalence. One type would have the perceptual and imaginal systems sharing some of the very same processes; in this case a high correlation between them would be expected. The other type would have the perceptual and imaginal systems drawing on separate capacities that were nonetheless highly similar to one another. The similarities might occur through a kind of parallel development due to the capacities having to deal with related information, such as spatial relations; in this case there is no reason to expect a high correlation.

The issue of performance equivalence has been addressed by several investigators: Finke (1980), Hebb (1966, 1968, 1972), Podgorny and Shepard (1978), Shepard and Podgorny (1978), and Weber and Harnish (1974). The work of Hebb and Weber and Harnish is most germane to the present discussion. Hebb argued that the image system was in essence epiphenomenal; that is, one did not really use its properties to process information (Kosslyn & Shwartz, 1977). Hebb based his claim on a backward spelling test. He argued that if the image system was actually used for information extraction, it ought to be possible to spell an imagined word backward about as rapidly as forward—presumably this can be done if the word is visually present. Because spelling an imagined word backward is much slower than spelling it forward, Hebb concluded that the image system did not really function like a mental picture; the picturelike appearance of images was misleading. Mental images whatever their nature were not like visual perceptions.

Weber and Harnish (1974) point out a number of difficulties with Hebb's spelling test that serve to obscure the possible performance equivalence between the two systems. For example, the spelling test may involve an asymmetrical use of verbal and visual image representation, with backward spelling drawing on the imagery system and forward spelling on the verbal system. Because previous findings (Weber & Castleman, 1970) have shown that the verbal system is faster than the image system for the sequential processing of letters, it would not be surprising to find more rapid processing for forward than for backward spelling. If the visual image system is of more limited capacity than the visual perception system for the simultaneous representation of letters, then Hebb's use of long words like *university* may have further biased the results in favor of the perceptual system over the imagery system.

Weber and Harnish (1974) took several steps to address these and other problems. It seemed to them that there was both phenomenal and potential performance equivalence between the perceptual and imaginal systems, and if the problems associated with the spelling test could be overcome, that equivalence might be revealed. To ensure image processing, subjects were required to categorize the height of imagined lowercase letters as tall (b, d, f, . . .) or not (a, c, e, . . .). Also to allow for maximum simultaneous representation of multiple letters in a visual image and to avoid building in sequential processing habits, a partial-report procedure was used. A digit probe was presented immediately after an auditory presentation of a word (image condition) or a visual presentation of a word (perception condition). These procedures resulted in processing times that did not differ significantly for perceptual and imaginal conditions. Under the appropriate experimental conditions, there was indeed a performance equivalence between perceptual and imaginal representation.

Developmental Changes in Representation

Does the degree of equivalence as measured by comparability of processing times and correlations between representation modes change with age? The present study is concerned with this question as age ranges from childhood to college age to over 65. The approach is to study performance on the ''same'' task (equivalent information requirements and common response requirements) but with varying modes of representation (Weber & McManman, 1977), as a function of age. Several hypotheses may be considered. The percept-first hypothesis of development is illustrated in the left half of Fig. 17.1. It asserts that any given response time (or more generally any given response time deviation from an optimal minimal time on a function) will occur at an earlier age for the percept

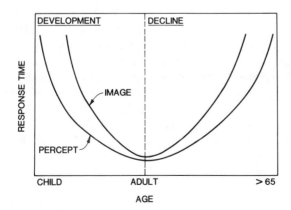

FIG. 17.1.   Hypothetical results for the percept-first development hypothesis and the image-first decline hypothesis.

system than for the image system. The right half of Fig. 17.1 illustrates an image-first decline hypothesis. The image system, relative to the percept system, declines at an earlier age in that processing time increases earlier. The same-time development hypothesis is not depicted, but it would assert that the perceptual and imaginal systems display the same development and decline patterns, with the percept and image functions superimposed. A generalization on the same hypothesis would not require superimposition but only that there be no representation mode by age interaction. Another possible pair of hypotheses arises from reversing the labels on Fig. 17.1, so that the image system develops before the perceptual system; this seems unlikely. But on the right side of the resulting function it is certainly possible that the percept system would begin to decline before the image system. It is of course possible to have function types very different from those of Fig. 17.1, but these functions seem to be quite plausible psychologically. (It is not necessary that the functions be symmetrical about any given age.)

It should be noted that all of these hypotheses are concerned with *perceptual* rather than *sensory* functioning, so that a person could have bifocals, a hearing aid, etc., without any necessary decline in perceptual functioning: the ability to process stimulus patterns and relations.

It seems to us that everyone of the hypotheses noted is somewhat plausible. Rather than make an extensive case for each, we simply note that each is testable based on a particular pattern of percept–image mode by age interaction.

Consider next the hypotheses dealing with the correlation of time scores from the different modes of representation. Three hypotheses may be considered. The divergence hypothesis asserts that the perceptual and visual imagery systems are closely yoked or less differentiated in children than in adults, in the sense of drawing on a common, shared processing capacity that differentiates or specializes with increasing age. Under this hypothesis, percept–image correlations would be expected to be higher for children than for adults, because of the common capacity for children and the specialized capacity for adults. The idea of capacity becoming more differentiated with age is a common view in the mental testing literature (Anastasi, 1970; Friedman, 1974). In contrast, the convergence hypothesis would state that the perceptual and imaginal systems are relatively independent in children but with increasing age the two systems become more closely articulated. Or said in another way, their underlying processes would become more equivalent. This would imply relatively low correlations in children and higher correlations with adults. A third possibility, the steady state hypothesis, would claim that there is no consistent age-related change in the overlap of representation modes. This would imply no systematic correlational change across ages.

A final introductory comment is in order. The work presented here does not make use of the sophisticated age change designs that are often recommended in the aging literature (Schaie, 1977). Thus we ignore cohort effects (i.e., those effects that are attributable to one's birth date). This is done for practical and conceptual reasons. The cohort designs that embody both longitudinal and cross-sectional components are simply not practical for exploratory, preliminary efforts such as the present one. Moreover, the focus in the present work is not on main effects at all, but rather interactions and correlations between conditions and how these may change with age. Of primary interest are questions like how differences between perceptual and imaginal processing change with age and how patterns of correlations change with age. It seems to us that a cohort or birth date effect is not as likely to influence such measures as it is to change main effects. Of course, there is nothing to preclude a third-order interaction in which cohort effects influence the nature of an age by mode of representation interaction. But one must stop somewhere.

In brief, the goals of the present study are to examine the degree of equivalence between perceptual and imaginal representation as shown by time scores and by correlations of time scores, to determine how those forms of equivalence change with age and to test several of the proposed hypotheses about age changes in perceptual and imaginal representation.

Method

Subjects

The subjects were 20 children (age range 95 to 132 months, mean age 9 years and 1 month); 20 college students (age range 19 to 23 years, with a mean age of 20 years and 2 months); and 20 older people (age range 66 to 72 years, with a mean age of 68 years and 10 months). there were 10 males and 10 females in each group. The 9-year-old group was composed of volunteers from a community summer recreation program; the 20-year-old group consisted of college students who served for extra credit; and the 68-year-old group was formed of volunteers from a local senior citizen's center. The center was paid $3.00 for each person participating. Particular care was taken in selecting the 68-year-old group. Any visual or auditory acuity was acceptable, provided that with corrective lenses the individual could read the materials presented at twice the distance actually used in the experiment or with hearing-aid could hear and repeat back the spoken materials at twice the distance actually used. The members of the 68-year-old group seemed to be far above average for their age in outgoing attentive behavior. They were regular participants in the senior citizens center and its activities. In many cases they were retired professionals. The members of the 9-year-old group came from an area of the city with a heavy concentration of university and professional families. The entire experimental session took about 60 min for the 9-year-old and 68-year-old age groups; it took about 40 min for the college age group. Sometimes during the session individuals in the 9-year-old or 68-year-old groups would stop briefly to rest.

Task 1: Sentences

Each subject was given preliminary training in classifying lowercase alphabetic letters as to whether they were tall (b, d, g, . . ., y) or not (e, c, e, . . ., z). The subject was required to respond *yes* orally to a letter that was tall and *no* to other letters. There were two kinds of target letters, those in the first (leftmost) letter position of a word and those in the last (rightmost) letter position of a word. Sixteen words were taken from a second-grade reader and arranged into four meaningful sentences. The actual sentences were: "sail this able boat"; "race with fast time"; "bake that same meat"; and "jump over tall alps." some of these sentences were a bit unusual, but they allowed for a careful statistical balancing. Each sentence had four words, each word had four letters, and across sentences each target letter position (first, last) had an equal number of yes and no letters. Each of the four sentences was used once in each of six conditions for a total of 24 trials.

The six conditions consisted of three modes of representation (image, percept, mixed) by two target letter positions (first, last). For the image condition the experimenter spoke the sentence, and to ensure accurate perception the subject was instructed to repeat the sentence aloud. After the subject had repeated the sentence, the experimenter said either *first* or *last* (and simultaneously started a clock) indicating the letter location in the word that the subject should respond to. Thus for the sentence "sail this able boat", the correct oral response sequence for the first target letter location in each word would be *no, yes, no, yes,* corresponding to the letters s, t, a, b. For the last target letter location in each word the correct response sequence would be *yes, no, no, yes,* corresponding to the letters l, s, e, t. The subjects were instructed to imagine the words of a sentence as if they were projected on an imaginary movie screen. Also, subjects in this and all other conditions were to respond quickly and as accurately as possible. The principal dependent variable was response time defined from onset of the first/last target position cue to completion of the string of four yes/no responses for a given sentence.

For the percept condition the subject read aloud the sentence from a 13 × 20.5 cm card placed in front of him/her. The letters were 3 cm high for the tall lowercase characters and 1.5 cm high for the characters that were not tall. The sentence remained visually present during the trial. The subject read the sentence on the card to ensure accurate encoding. Then the experimenter said *first/last,* and the trial proceeded as before. For the mixed condition, elements of both the percept and image conditions were combined. All the letters were presented in *uppercase.* The procedure was identical to that in the percept condition, except that the subject was instructed to "translate" in imagination from uppercase to the corresponding lowercase representation on which his/her responses were to be based. Thus the mixed condition did not require a memorial representation of the sentence (it was perceptually available), but it did require a translation from uppercase to a spatial representation of the lowercase letters. Finally, extensive practice was given, particularly to the 9-year old and the 68-year-old groups, to ensure that the task was understood.

Task 2: Forms

Each subject was given preliminary training in classifying the corners of block uppercase letters as to whether they were located at the extreme top or bottom of the letter or not (Brooks, 1968). If a corner was at the extreme top or bottom, the subject was to respond *yes*, and all other corners were to receive *no* responses. The letters used were block capital equivalents of I, E, H, and M, each of which had 12 corners (it was sometimes necessary to 'flatten' points, as with the M, to get the 12 corners). The subjects were instructed to begin at the upper left-hand corner of a letter and classify all corners in either a clockwise or counterclockwise direction. Thus for the letter I the correct oral response sequence for clockwise would be *yes, yes, no, no, no, no, yes, yes, no, no, no, no.* For the counterclockwise sequence the correct oral response would be *yes, no, no, no no, yes, yes, no, no, no, no, yes.*

The stimulus forms were employed in the following six conditions: three modes of representation (image, percept, mixed) by two scan directions (clockwise, counterclockwise). These six conditions combined with the four letters used gave a total of 24 trials. For the image condition the experimenter spoke the letter name, the subject repeated it back to ensure correct coding, and the experimenter said either *clockwise* or *counterclockwise* (and the clock was simultaneously started). Again, the principal dependent variable was response time defined from onset of the clockwise/counterclockwise cue to the completion of the string of 12 yes/no responses for a given letter. For the percept condition, the subject was presented with a block uppercase letter on a 13 × 20.5 cm card that remained visually available during the trial. (The block letters were 3 cm high.) After the subject pronounced the letter name, the experimenter said *clockwise/counterclockwise,* and the trial proceeded as before. For the mixed condition, elements of both perceptual and imaginal conditions were combined. All the letters were presented in *lowercase.* The procedure was identical to that in the percept condition except that the subject was instructed to "translate" in imagination to the corresponding block letter imaginal representation on which his/her responses were to be based.

Results

Time Data

Figure 17.2 presents the principal results for sentences, with processing time in seconds as a function of conditions and age, and with the sex variable pooled. Because the various development and decline hypotheses depended on interac-

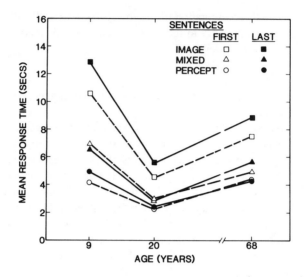

FIG. 17.2.   Mean response time per sentence as a function of age, mode of representation, and target position.

tions between adjacent age groups, two separate analyses were performed, 9-year-olds versus 20-year-olds and 20-year-olds versus 68-year-olds. Consider first the 9-year-old versus 20-year-old groups. The results of interest include the following. There is a significant age effect, $F(1, 36) = 83.23$, $p < .001$, with 20-year-olds taking less time than 9-year-olds. There is a significant representation mode effect, $F(2, 72) = 32.27$, $p < .001$, with perceptual representation taking the least time and followed by the mixed and imaginal forms of representation. There is a significant target position effect, $F(1, 36) = 50.11$, $p < .001$; and a significant representation mode by target position interaction, $F(2, 36) = 22.74$, $p < .001$. There is no significant sex effect ($p > .05$), and the sex variable is not involved in any higher-order interactions. The finding of greatest interest is the significant age by representation mode interaction, $F(2, 72) = 32.27$, $p < .001$. This interaction is most consistent with the percept-first development hypothesis of Fig. 17.1. As seen from Fig. 17.2, the percept conditions are faster (take less time) than the image conditions for the 9-year-old group, but the difference between the two representation modes becomes smaller for the 20-year-old group.

For the second analysis of sentences, the 20-year-old group was compared with the 68-year-old group. The right half of Fig. 17.2 shows the summary results. There are significant effects for age, $F(1, 36) = 42.56$, $p < .001$, with 68-year-olds taking more time than 20-year-olds; for representation mode, $F(2, 72) = 153.27$, $p < .001$, with perceptual representation taking the least time and image representation the most time, $F(1, 36) = 8.50$. $p < .006$. There is also a representation mode by position interaction, $F(2, 72) = 10.17$, $p < .001$. Again, there is no significant effect for sex nor is the sex variable involved in any higher-order interactions. Of particular interest is the age by representation mode interaction, $F(2, 72) = 4.00$, $p < .02$. This interaction indicates that there is a larger difference in image–percept processing for the 68-year-old group than for the 20-year-old group. Such a result is consistent with the image-first decline hypothesis depicted in the right-hand panel of Fig. 17.1. Overall, the results for sentences indicate a much closer performance equivalence between imagery and perception for 20-year-olds than for either 9-year-olds or 68-year-olds.

Figure 17.3 reveals the main results for forms, with processing time in seconds as a function of conditions and age and pooled with respect to sex and direction of scan. Once more, adjacent pairs of age groups were analyzed. For the 9-year-old and 20-year-old groups the following results are of interest. There is a significant age effect, $F(1, 36) = 71.07$, $p < .001$, with the 20-year-olds taking less time than the 9-year-olds; a significant representation mode effect, $F(2, 72) = 89.08$, $p < .001$, with percept, mixed, and image conditions in order of increasing time; and a significant scan direction effect, $F(1, 36) = 8.82$, $p < .005$. Even though the scan direction effect is significant, the absolute size of the effect is small (0.54 sec, pooled across all conditions, with clockwise scanning slightly faster than counterclockwise scanning). Because the effect is small, scan direction is pooled in Fig. 17.3 to avoid clutter. There is no significant sex effect. The result of greatest interest is the age by representation mode interaction, with $F(2, 72) = 13.83$, $p < .001$. Although this interaction is not large, it is consistent. As seen from Fig. 17.3, the image–percept difference is smaller for

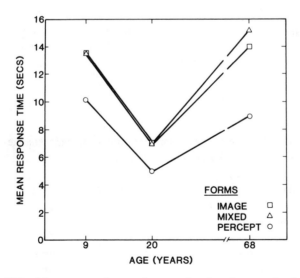

FIG. 17.3. Mean response time per form as a function of age, mode of representation, and target position.

20-year-olds than for 9-year-olds. This result supports the percept-first development hypothesis that is illustrated in Fig. 17.1.

The next analysis for forms is for the 20-year-old and the 68-year-old groups. The right half of Fig. 17.3 indicates the graphic results. There is a significant age effect, $F(1, 36) = 51.84$, $p < .001$; a significant representation mode effect, $F(2, 72) = 69.22$, $p < .001$; and a significant scan direction effect, $F(1, 36) = 9.48$, $p < .01$. Once more, the absolute size of the scan direction effect (pooled across the six conditions) is sufficiently small (0.34 sec) to warrant pooling in Fig. 17.3. Again there is no significant sex effect. The most important result is the age by representation mode interaction, with $F(2, 72) = 23.73$, $p < .001$. This interaction is very large and it is consistent with the image-first decline hypothesis of Fig. 17.1.

The overall results for forms also indicate a greater degree of performance equivalence between imagery and perception for 20-year-olds than for either 9-year-olds or 68-year-olds.

Error Data

Error data generally paralleled the response-time data. There was usually an increase in errors in the progression from perceptual to mixed to imaginal conditions, but not always. The minimum error rate for sentences was 0% (percept-first), and the maximum error rate was 9% (image-last). For forms the error results were more variable. The minimum error rate was less than 1% (percept-clockwise), and the maximum error rate was 5.7% (mixed-clockwise). There were also age effects with the 20-year-old group usually producing fewer errors than the other age groups. Analyses of variance for the error data generally yielded similar if somewhat fewer significant effects than for comparable analyses with the time data. Thus conditions with high error rates also tended to have large time scores, a result incompatible with a speed–accuracy tradeoff. Because the error data was less sensitive than the time data, it is not considered further.

Correlational Data

The question of interest is whether there are systematic changes in process equivalence across ages. To answer this question, time scores at a given age level were intercorrelated. Three types of correlation matrix were constructed: (1) one for the six sentence conditions based on three representation modes (percept, mixed, image) by two target positions (first, last), with a total of 15 intercorrelations; (2) another for the six forms conditions based on the three modes by two directions of scan (clockwise, counterclockwise), also with a total of 15 correlations; and (3) a third with the six sentence conditions paired with the six forms conditions, for a total of 36 correlations. Figure 17.4 depicts the summary results by stimulus materials and age. The top left panel for the sentence conditions indicates that the median correlation decreases from the 9-

year-olds to the 20-year-olds (this happened for 14 of the 15 correlations) and then increases again for the 68-year-olds (13 of 15 correlations). Also, the median correlation is slightly less for 9-year-olds than for 68-year-olds (9 of 15 correlations). This result is consistent with the divergence hypothesis for the transition from childhood to young adulthood. Shared processing capacity becomes more specialized in the sense of having proportionally less overlap of common processes or capacity. It is also consistent with the convergence hypothesis for the transition from young adulthood to an aging state. Previously specialized processes give way to shared processing capacity. Hence the age at which there is the least process equivalence between perception and imagery is for the 20-year-olds, a result apparently at odds with the time data.

The second panel of Fig. 17.4, for forms, displays the same ordinal results but the differences among ages are much smaller and more inconsistent. For the transition from 9 years to 20 years of age, 9 of 15 correlations are in the same direction as the medians. For the transition from 20 years to 68 years, 9 of 15 correlations are in the same direction as the medians. And last, for the transitions from 9 to 68, only 5 of the 15 correlations are lower for the 9-year-olds. The forms condition does have the distinction of having produced the highest correlations among perceptual, mixed, and imaginal modes of representation across all age groups, suggesting a great deal of processing overlap. Finally, the right panel for both sentences and forms shows that the median correlation between tasks decreases substantially from 9-year-olds to 20-year-olds (34 of 36 correlations) and then increases dramatically again for 68-year-olds (36 of 36 correlations). For the comparison of 9-year-olds versus 20-year-olds, the correlations also increase with age (36 of 36 correlations).

With the possible exception of the forms conditions, there is substantial evidence that correlations among conditions decrease from age 9 to age 20 and then

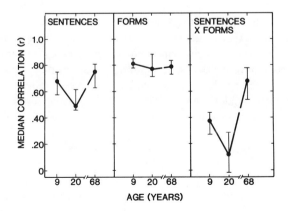

FIG. 17.4.   Summary characteristics of correlation matrices. First quartile, median, and third quartile as a function of age and stimulus materials.

increase again from age 20 to age 68. These results as a whole are clearly consistent with the divergence hypothesis for the transition from 9 to 20 years old and the convergence hypothesis for the transition from 20 to 68 years old.

DISCUSSION

The response-time results clearly support the percept-first development hypothesis and the image-first decline hypothesis. Thus the perceptual system matures earlier than the image system, and the image system begins to decline before the perceptual system. (It is understood that by the *perceptual system* is meant the ability to discern patterns and relations rather than any particular measure of acuity.) Because the various development and decline hypotheses were based on interaction patterns, the comparisons across age groups are relatively immune to age changes that might occur in either the response system or the perceptual system.

In particular, the response-time results illustrate that the degree of performance equivalence between the perceptual and imaginal systems changes as a function of age. Percepts and images more closely approximate performance equivalence in the 20-year-old group than either the 9-year-old or 68-year-old group. There is some generality for this result because it holds for both the sentence and forms tasks. To be sure, the performance equivalence is not complete at any age. Thus for sentences in particular but also for forms there are large time differences between image and percept processing, even at age 20. Also for sentences there is a substantial difference in response time between first and last target positions for the image condition but not for the percept condition. Both of these results are consistent with the findings of Weber and Harnish (1974, Experiment 2) where it was found to take longer to generate images than percepts and longer to process the properties of letters at the end of a word than at the beginning, even though retrieval from existing percepts and images produced equivalent times (Experiment 1). For sentences, the mixed conditions fell squarely between the percept and image conditions. Having the sentence visually present seemed to save the time of generating it from memory. For forms, there was very little difference between mixed and image conditions.

An interpretive problem remains. Because the present results are based on interactions, is it not possible that they are merely an artifact of the scale of measurement used? In other words, if the time scores were transformed to some other scale, a very different pattern of results might have occurred. Such a point can be raised about virtually any set of results, but we wish to make two specific rejoinders. First, the use in psychology of units of fundamental measurement such as time is still rare enough that one ought not to transform a time score unless there is some compelling reason for doing so. There was none here.

Second, the most important answer is that much of the present experiment was motivated by theoretical and/or conceptual issues. These issues are most simply and succinctly stated against a backdrop of time. Until there is a clearer statement of these issues that requires a measure other than time, it seems only fitting to stay with the time scale.

The correlation results support the divergence hypothesis for the transition from 9 to 20 years old, and the convergence hypothesis for the transition from 20 to 68 years old. Thus children appear to have a general-purpose processing capacity that the different modes of representation share. Because the processing capacity is general purpose or shared, a variety of tasks will show relatively high correlations with one another. With increasing age that processing capacity becomes more specialized so different tasks will become less correlated with one another, at least to young adulthood. For the transition from young adulthood to over 65, processing capacity begins to lose its specialized character and correlations begin to increase again.

It is important to note that the correlation results cannot be explained as a simple restriction of range phenomenon. In mental testing, a restriction of range means that a distribution has been truncated in some way, as by using a cutoff or criterion score, so that predictor variance decreases while error variance is roughly constant. That was not the case here.

A troubling question remains. Why is the degree of performance equivalence as measured by response time the greatest at age 20 and the degree of process equivalence as indexed by correlations the least at age 20? This perplexing situation may be resolved by the following ad hoc account. We assume that response time is inversely related to the amount of capacity that is available for a representation system. It is further assumed that the degree of overlap in processes or capacity between the perceptual and imaginal systems is indexed by the size of the correlation. Based on these assumptions, at age 9 most of the available capacity is taken up by the perceptual system; therefore the response times are faster for perceptual than imaginal processing. The image capacity that is available overlaps substantially with some of the perceptual processing capacity. Hence there will be moderately high correlations between the two modes of representation. By age 20 the processing capacity for both the perceptual and imaginal systems has increased, with the image system increasing more. This would explain the overall more rapid responding at age 20 and also the greater degree of performance equivalence. Although capacity of the two modes has increased, the proportion of shared capacity has actually decreased. Because the perceptual and imaginal systems are both concerned with common problems (spatial information), they continue to develop in a similar way, a parallel evolution attributable to confronting similar spatial processing tasks. By age 68, processing capacity has begun to diminish, with imagery capacity declining first. Hence response times go up, and the degree of performance equivalence diminishes. At the same time any task that requires imaginal processing will force the imaginal system to draw in part on shared perceptual capacity. The correlations between the two modes will once again increase.

The foregoing account is quite consistent with other findings in the literature that support the existence of a somewhat abstract imaginal system that is not modality specific. Thus Brooks (1968) found a tactual spatial task interfered with image scanning, presumably because both required the processing of spatial relations. Baddeley and Lieberman (1980) obtained a similar result. Pointing to an auditory signal occurring at different spatial locations while concurrently engaged in imagery also interfered with imagery processing, whereas a visual task involving a brightness discrimination did not interfere. The critical factor was spatial information, whatever its modality of origin. Such findings suggest strongly a processing separation between the perceptual and imaginal systems. The present results confirm just such a separation with the low correlations at age 20. The results also provide a developmental perspective consistent with the view that the perceptual and imaginal systems have a common origin, specialize or differentiate in parallel ways at least to young adulthood, and then in old age begin to converge again to an earlier organization with more shared processes or capacity. It is believed that the present use of both response time and correlations has been helpful in constraining the number of possible relations between the perceptual and imaginal modes.

ACKNOWLEDGMENTS

This research was funded in part by a Biomedical Sciences grant to the first author and in part by the Education Research Foundation, Oklahoma State University.

The authors wish to thank Cindy Daugherty and Matt Ferrara for testing subjects and James Price and James Phillips for statistical advice.

Requests for reprints should be sent to Robert J. Weber, Department of Psychology, Oklahoma State University, Stillwater, Okla. 74078, U.S.A.

REFERENCES

Anastasi, A. On the formation of psychological traits. *American Psychologist,* 1970, *25,* 899–910.
Baddeley, A. D., & Lieberman, K. Spatial working memory. In R. S. Nickerson (Ed.), *Attention and Performance VIII.* Hillsdale, N.J.: Lawrence Erlbaum Associates, 1980.
Brooks, L. R. Spatial and verbal components of the act of recall. *Canadian Journal of Psychology,* 1968, *22,* 349–368.
Finke, R. A. Levels of equivalence in imagery and perception. *Psychological Review,* 1980, *87,* 113–132.
Friedman, H. Interrelation of two types of immediate memory in the aged. *Journal of Psychology,* 1974, *87,* 177–181.
Hebb, D. O. *A textbook of psychology* (2nd ed.). Philadelphia: Saunders, 1966.

Hebb, D. O. Concerning imagery. *Psychological Review,* 1968, *75,* 466–477.

Hebb, D. O. *A textbook of psychology* (3rd ed.). Philadelphia: Saunders, 1972.

Kosslyn, S. M., & Shwartz, S. P. A simulation of visual imagery. *Cognitive Science,* 1977, *1,* 265–295.

Podgorny, P., & Shepard, R. N. Representations common to visual perception and imagination. *Journal of Experimental Psychology: Human Perception and Performance,* 1978, *4,* 21–35.

Schaie, K. W. Quasi-experimental designs in the psychology of aging. In J. E. Birren, & K. W. Schaie (Eds.), *Handbook of the psychology of aging.* New York: Van Nostrand-Reinhold, 1977.

Shepard, R. N., & Podgorny, P. Cognitive processes that resemble perceptual processes. In W. K. Estes (Ed.), *Handbook of learning and cognitive processes* (Vol. 5). New York: Lawrence Erlbaum Associates, 1978.

Weber, R. J., & Castleman, J. The time it takes to imagine. *Perception & Psychophysics,* 1970, *8,* 165–168.

Weber, R. J., & Harnish, R. Visual imagery for words: The Hebb test. *Journal of Experimental Psychology,* 1974, *102,* 409–414.

Weber, R. J., & McManman, K. Visual representations of words in perceptual and image modes as a function of age. *Bulletin of the Psychonomic Society,* 1977, *9,* 33–36.

V LANGUAGE COMPREHENSION AND KNOWLEDGE

18

Context for Comprehension

Herbert H. Clark and Thomas B. Carlson
Stanford University, Stanford, California, U.S.A.

ABSTRACT

Although the notion of context plays a central role in most current explanations of language understanding, what can count as context is generally left undefined. If it includes any information a listener can make available to himself, then it loses much of its power to explain. After reviewing experimental attempts to elucidate context, we take up a more analytic approach. We first define the *intrinsic context* as that information available to a process that is potentially necessary for it to succeed. Our proposal is that the intrinsic context for understanding what a speaker means on some occasion is the common ground that the listener believes holds at that moment between the speaker and the listeners he or she is speaking to. By common ground, we mean the knowledge, beliefs, and suppositions that the two people share in a technical way. Finally, we review some of the evidence for this proposal.

INTRODUCTION

In the past 20 years, the word *context* has become a favorite in the vocabulary of cognitive psychologists. It has appeared in the titles of an astonishing number of articles. It has been used to describe phenomena under labels ranging from "environmental" and "pharmacological context" to "thematic" and "knowledge context." "Context effects" are everywhere. "Contextualism" has been coined as the name of a theory of memory (Jenkins, 1974).

What then *is* context? According to the dictionary, it is the "parts of a discourse that surround a word of passage and can throw light upon its meaning." We call this the *standard definition*. In psychology, its use has been extended far beyond the standard definition. And the further its uses have been extended, the murkier its denotation has become. Smith, Glenberg, and Bjork (1978) have complained that context has become "a kind of conceptual garbage can."

For most purposes in psychology, this may not matter. Context, one could argue, is a term that is useful precisely because it is vague and general and can accommodate many different ideas. In some areas, however, context has been used not merely to *describe* phenomena, where vagueness and generality could be virtues, but to *explain* them, where vagueness and generality are vices. One of these areas is language comprehension, in which the theories appeal directly to context to explain how people decide what a speaker means. Theories of how people decide between two meanings of a word like *bank,* for example, appeal to people's knowledge of the "context," which includes not only the "parts of the discourse that surround" the word but also a good deal more. In theories like these, the characterization of context must be precise before their predictions can be precise.

Our goal is to outline a theory of the context that is intrinsic to language comprehension. First, we review some of the uses of the term "context" in the experimental literature, concentrating on the literature in language comprehension, and draw out their essential features; that is, we try to summarize the *experimental approach* to the role of context in psychological processes. Second, we make our own proposal, which is based largely on an *analytic approach* to context. What we argue, briefly, is that for a listener to understand a speaker's meaning, he can confine himself to a certain limited domain of information, namely, the speaker's and his listener's common ground, that part of the speaker's and his listener's knowledge, beliefs, and assumptions that are shared. We then review some of the evidence for this proposal.

VARIETIES OF CONTEXT

Context has long been used in psychology to describe certain parts of the experimental subject's surroundings. In visual perception, it has been used for the content of the visual stimuli surrounding or preceding the object to be perceived or identified (Brigell, Uhlarik, & Goldhorn, 1977) and for the "contextual relations" among objects depicted in a scene (Biederman, 1972; Palmer, 1975). In learning and retention, it has been used in a broad sense both for "stimulation from the external environment, such as the furniture in the room, the experimenter, and the apparatus" (McGeoch, 1939, p. 347) and for the "inner states of the experiencing person which affect the way he views or remembers the same stimulus material" (Reiff & Scheerer, 1959, p. 19). The inner states have been given such names as "pharmacological context" (Eich, 1980) and "mood contexts" (Bower, Monteiro, & Gilligan, 1978). Context has also been used in a narrower sense for the items presented along with the target item on each study trial in learning (Tulving & Thomson, 1973), as well as for larger units of organization, under such names as "list context" (Anderson & Bower, 1974).

In word perception, most uses of context have been close to the standard definition. It has appeared in such notions as "context-conditioned" acoustic cues (Liberman, Cooper, Shankweiler, & Studdert-Kennedy, 1967), "syllable contexts" (Dorman, 1974), and "acoustic contexts" (Warren & Obusek, 1971). In the identification of words in printed texts, context has also been used in a sense close to the standard definition (Tulving & Gold, 1963). In other studies, the notion has been drastically extended under such labels as "sentence context," "word association context," "category contexts" (the name of a semantic category), and "letter contexts" (the first few letters of the word being identified) (Rubenstein & Pollack, 1963), and "semantic context" (associated words or incomplete sentences) (Meyer, Schvaneveldt, & Ruddy, 1975; Schuberth & Eimas, 1977). These uses refer, as Miller, Heise, and Lichten (1951) put it, to the subject's "knowledge of the conditions of stimulation." This tradition has been continued in Morton's (1964, 1969) "logogen model," in which there are word unit detectors, or "logogens," that are sensitive to information provided by the unspecified workings of a "context system" ("cognitive system" in later formulations). In this model, all information is treated equally, with no restriction on what is to count as context (Morton, 1970).

Contexts for Language Use

In studies of language use, context could have been limited to the standard definition, but even here it has been extended from the very beginning. In 1951, in his classic text *Language and Communication,* Miller said, "The verbal context of any particular verbal unit is made up of the communicative acts that surround it." But then he added, "What a man says cannot be predicted entirely from the verbal context. . . . A discussion of the complete context of a communicative act must include the talker's needs, perceptions, audience, and cultural background (pp. 81–82)."

In studies of the ongoing processing of sentences, most uses of context refer to selective parts of the context as specified in the standard definition, as in "semantic and syntactic context" (Marslen-Wilson & Welsh, 1978) and "prior semantic context" (Foss & Jenkins, 1973; Swinney & Hakes, 1976). What "syntactic and semantic context" refer to here are the constraints placed on a word by the syntax and meaning of the sentence up to that point. Similarly, Carroll, Tanenhaus, and Bever (1978) have spoken of the "discourse context" provided by a preceding sentence. On the other hand, what Dooling (1972) meant by "context" was not just syntactic and semantic constraints but some sort of mental representation of the *content* of the previous discourse.

Two related uses of context can be found in the study of memory for utterances. In Brewer and Harris's (1974) study, they spoke of "deictic context"—the relation of an utterance to "the particular time, place, person, or discourse context." And in a study by Keenan, MacWhinney, and Mayhew (1977), memory for utterances was examined in "the context of natural, purposeful communication" or "interactional context," which includes "degree of previous involvement with the speaker, the formal identity of speech acts represented by particular statements, the organizational structure of the interaction . . . , and the amount of active participation on the part of the listener (p. 559)." For these to be considered part of the standard definition, discourse must be taken as including a good deal more than just the linguistic expressions that have gone before.

Context has also been used to refer to things that are clearly nonlinguistic. In studies of the verification of sentences against pictures, the pictures have sometimes been called the "context" (Tanenhaus, Carroll, & Bever, 1976). And in work by Huttenlocher and Weiner (1971), the physical situation in which children were to carry out instructions was called the "extralinguistic context" of the instructions. The idea of calling these context may be traced to Wason's (1965) classic study of the "contexts of plausible denial," in which he referred to the pictures that his assertions and denials were meant to describe as the "objective context." This he contrasted with the "subjective context," the speaker's beliefs about the listener's beliefs about a situation.

It is Bransford and his colleagues (Bransford & Johnson, 1972, 1973; Bransford & McCarrell, 1974) who have been most closely associated with the study of context in comprehension; yet they have been even less clear about what they meant by it. Bransford and Johnson (1972), for example, speak of the "context picture," "appropriate semantic structures," "appropriate context" as "part of the pre-experimental knowledge," and "the context underlying a stimulus," all in relation to their general claim that "relevant contextual knowledge is a prerequisite for comprehending prose passages." Doll and Lapinski (1974) attribute to Bransford and Johnson two additional terms, "thematic context" and "referential context." Later, Bransford and Johnson (1973) speak of "activated semantic context" or "activated knowledge structures," arguing that in general "the ability to understand linguistic symbols is based not only on the comprehender's knowledge of his language, but also on his general knowledge of the world (p. 383)." Still later, Bransford (1979) equates "context" with "appropriately activated knowledge." What knowledge is "relevant" or "appropriately activated" Bransford never says.

ESSENTIALS OF CONTEXT

There are six features of context that appear to be common to most of the uses we have reviewed.

1. Information.   Context is information in the sense used in "information-processing" psychology. It is information about objects, events, states, or processes. It may be generic, characterizing what, for example, trees are like in general, or particular, characterizing what a particular tree—say, the tree after which Palo Alto was named—is like. It may come from direct experience, from being told, or from inferences based on these sources. It may include, but is not limited to, a person's knowledge, beliefs, or suppositions.

2. Person Relativity.   If context is information, it must be in someone's possession. In most of the uses we have reviewed, the context is usually relativized, not to people in general but to each particular person.

3. Process Relativity.   Not all information a person possesses is considered to be context. Investigators always speak of the context *of* something—of a word, of a list, or of the subject in an experiment. What they mean, we suggest, is that context is relative to a *process* a person is carrying out. In a sentence, the context of a word is really information a person has relative to his interpretation of that word.

4. Occasion Relativity.   For most investigators, context is information a person possesses in the carrying out of a particular process *on a particular occasion.* To be able to speak of the context changing from one pass through a list to the next or from one hearing of a sentence to the next, we must treat context as occasion relative.

With features 2 through 4, context can be thought of as a function with three arguments—the agent A, the process p, and the occasion or time t. Context is context(A, p, t), not just context(A, p), context (p, t), or context(A, t). This is another way of saying that when investigators talk about context, they talk about the context for a particular person doing a particular task at a particular time (see Bower, 1972).

5. Availability.   In most usages, context is only that information that is *available* to the person carrying out the particular process on that particular occasion. When Joe Bonnano was reading the word *today* in his newspaper at 9:13 A.M. on July 4, 1980, his memory was full of all sorts of information. He knew the map of Eastern Europe, knew how to change tires, knew the Catholic catechism, believed that at age 13 one day he saw a flying saucer, and so on. But only the part of this information that was available to Joe for the task at hand would be considered part of the context.

6. Interactibility.   For information to be called context in most usages, it must also be able to interact with the process at hand. Even if the catechism were available to Joe Bonnano as he was reading *today* in the newspaper, it wouldn't be considered part of the context unless it could somehow interact with the reading and understanding of that word.

To sum up, context is information that is available to a particular person for interaction with a particular process on a particular occasion. From now on, we take this to be *the* definition of context.

Intrinsic and Incidental Context

Psychologists study context—in our now technical sense—because of its role in the processes they are interested in. Their accounts of those processes would not be complete without describing its role. Take the psychologists who study how people identify objects in visual scenes. The surroundings of an object in a scene are often crucial to people's identification of that object. One and the same visual configuration—say, a blacked-in circle—will be identified in one surrounding as a ball, in another as a tire, and in a third as a hole in a door. Most visual configurations are ambiguous in this way—look at Magritte. Psychologists recognize, therefore, that their theories of object identification must specify the role that the surroundings play.

Yet most psychologists try to distinguish between two parts of the context (still in our technical sense). For example, take Margaret in an experimental room viewing a slide and trying to identify an object in the middle of it. The process she goes through, and hence her identification, errors, and reaction time, can be influenced by many things. One category includes her identification of the surroundings of the object, her knowledge of the plausibility of the object in those surroundings, and her knowledge of the categories of objects the experimenter said she would be identifying. Another category includes her thoughts about the exam she has been studying for, her irritation with the experimenter, her perseveration on the mistake she made on the last slide, her awareness of her sore throat, her hunger, and her discomfort in the chair. Technically, both categories are part of Margaret's context in identifying the object. Both have been studied, and both continue to be worth studying.

These two categories, however, bear different relations to the task Margaret is carrying out. The things in the first category would generally be considered parts of the context that are *intrinsic* to the process of object identification. They belong to the process and, most psychologists would feel, need to be accounted for in any adequate theory of the process. The things in the second category would generally be considered *incidental* to the process as carried out on that occasion. They affect the process only indirectly, by limiting Margaret's attention to the task, interrupting the process, or making her less efficient. They do not belong to the process of object identification per se and do not need to be accounted for directly in a theory of that process. Let us call these two parts of the context the *intrinsic context* and the *incidental context*.

The intrinsic context, we stipulate, is that part of the context that, a priori, has the potential of being necessary on some occasion for carrying out the process in question. Although Margaret may sometimes be able to identify the typewriter in the middle of the slide without checking its visual surroundings, in general she could not. For the process of object identification to succeed *in general,* it must make use of the visual surroundings. The incidental context is what remains, the parts of the context that never need to be consulted.

An adequate theory for any psychological process must make reference to the intrinsic context, without which the process won't generally succeed. An important goal in studying such a process, then, is to distinguish the intrinsic from the incidental context. Indeed, in the study of comprehension, psychologists have tried to identify those parts of the discourse, broadly conceived, that a listener appears to have to consult in order to succeed in understanding what the speaker meant. Most of this effort has been experimental. Psychologists have tried out this and that part of the context to see which parts are potentially needed in comprehension. We now turn to a more analytic approach to intrinsic context. We argue that there are certain a priori grounds for characterizing the intrinsic context for comprehension in one particular way.

INTRINSIC CONTEXT IN COMPREHENSION

Most of the characterizations of context we have reviewed allow almost anything a person knows to belong to the context in comprehension. This is implied by such terms as "interactional context," "appropriate semantic context," "relevant contextual knowedge," "thematic context," "referential context," "activated knowledge structures," "appropriate knowledge structures," and "cognitive system." The modifiers that might limit this range—"relevant," "activated," and "appropriate"—have been left undefined. As characterizations of intrinsic and incidental context together, these descriptions may be accurate, but they aren't very helpful as characterizations of intrinsic context alone, which is what we are seeking. The problem is a practical one. When a listener tries to understand what a speaker means on some occasion, it would be advantageous if the process he uses could limit what it retrieves from memory to some portion of the total information that could be made available. In particular, it should limit itself to the intrinsic context, that portion of the information that may be needed for the process to succeed.

Our proposal is straightforward: *The intrinsic context for a listener trying to understand what a speaker means on a particular occasion is the common ground that the listener believes holds at that moment between the speaker and the listeners he or she is speaking to.* There are two technical notions here that need explaining. The first is *what the speaker meant,* or *speaker's meaning* (Grice, 1957, 1968; Schiffer, 1972). Our proposal is about how a listener tries to determine what the speaker intended him to determine, in part by means of his recognition of the speaker's intentions. Our proposal is *not* about the further inferences that a listener carries out on the basis of what the speaker meant; that is, it is about the "authorized" and not the "unauthorized" inferences made by the listener, two sorts of inferences that listeners ordinarily keep quite distinct (Clark, 1977).[1] The second technical notion is *common ground*.

Common Ground

As a first approximation, the common ground between two people can be thought of as the information the two of them share. When Ann and Bob, for example, are standing together in a gallery looking at a Picasso painting, they share a good deal of information—about the objects depicted in the painting, about its colors, about its position on the wall, about Picasso, about modern painting, about each other, and so on. When Ann and Bob are later discussing their opinions of the painting with each other, they also share information about what each other has just said, meant, and implied. The common ground between them consists, roughly, of the knowledge, beliefs, and even suppositions shared in this way.

The obvious first problem is that what Ann takes to be the common ground between them won't exactly match what Bob takes to be the common ground between them. Discrepancies of this sort are a major source of misunderstanding between people. Furthermore, we can speak of a third party's beliefs in the common ground between Ann and Bob—say, the beliefs of Connie. In general, Connie's beliefs about Ann's and Bob's common ground will be less veridical and less complete—often very much so—than will either Ann's or Bob's. Non-veridicality and incompleteness are two major sources of misunderstandings by third persons.

As we will see, however, this first approximation to common ground will not do. It isn't enough for both Ann and Bob to know or believe certain things. They must each know or believe that they both know or believe these things—and they must know or believe that the other knows or believes that they both know or believe these things, and so on. What is required is the technical notion of "common" or "mutual" knowledge, beliefs, and suppositions (Lewis, 1969; Schiffer, 1972). Mutual knowledge of a proposition p is defined by Schiffer as follows:

A and B mutually know that p = $_{def}$.

---

[1]So in the understanding of what the speaker meant, one could also define two further notions of context. One is the *intended context*, the information that the speaker intended the listener to consult in understanding his utterance on a particular occasion. The second is the *actual context*, the information that the listener actually did consult. Ideally, the actual context should be identical to the intended context, and both should be part of the intrinsic context. In everyday performance, these relations doubtless fall short of the ideal.

1. *A* knows that *p*.
1'. *B* knows that *p*.
2. *A* knows that *B* knows that *p*.
2'. *B* knows that *A* knows that *p*.
3. *A* knows that *B* knows that *A* knows that *p*.
3'. *B* knows that *A* knows that *B* knows that *p*.
etc., ad infinitum

Mutual beliefs and mutual suppositions are like mutual knowledge but with the verb *know* replaced everywhere by the verb *believe* or the verb *suppose*. In short, the common ground between two people consists of their mutual knowledge, mutual beliefs, and mutual suppositions.[2]

Sources of Common Ground.   An immediate problem with the definition of common ground is that it is infinite in length. For *A* and *B* to mutually know something, it appears that they must represent in memory an infinite number of knowledge statements—namely, 1, 1', 2, 2', etc., ad infinitum. This is clearly impossible. Clark and Marshall (1981), however, have argued that the problem is only apparent.

The central idea is that mutual knowledge is an elementary mental representation that is inductively inferred from certain special kinds of evidence. Imagine that Ann and Bob are standing together looking at the Picasso painting and that each is aware of the other doing this; that is, Ann sees Bob looking at the painting, and she sees him noticing her doing this at roughly the same time. If she assumes that Bob is rational and that he is attending to both her and the painting, it is easy to show that she can immediately jump to the conclusion that they mutually know about the painting. The evidence Ann requires is an event in which she, Bob, and the painting are "co-present," that is, openly present together in a certain way. She can jump to this conclusion by using this evidence along with certain auxiliary assumptions in a "mutual knowledge induction schema." She can then add to her beliefs about the common ground between her and Bob certain beliefs about the Picasso painting. For the induction schema to apply, the evidence has to be of just the right kind. Clark and Marshall identified three major types of evidence: physical co-presence, linguistic co-presence, and community membership.

Among the strongest evidence that something is common ground is *physical co-presence*. An example of this is Ann and Bob viewing the Picasso painting at the art gallery. The two of them are experiencing it together, simultaneously, in the near-certain awareness that the other is experiencing it too. What better

---

[2]As Gerald Gazdar has pointed out to us, this definition is probably insufficient, because there are almost certainly mixtures of knowledge, belief, and suppositions in which 3, for example, might read *A supposes that B believes that A supposes that p*, or *A knows that B knows that A believes that p*, etc. This is not the place to take up these complications.

evidence could Ann want that she knew about the painting, knew that he knew about the painting, knew that he knew that she knew about the painting, and so on? The auxiliary assumptions she needs are minimal—mainly that Bob is rational and is paying attention, just as she is. This experience constitutes an *event* of physical co-presence, and it is that event, along with the assumptions, that allows her to infer mutual knowledge of the picture. The experience, of course, can be visual, auditory, tactile, and so on, or any combination of the senses.

In contrast with physical co-presence is *linguistic co-presence*. Imagine that Ann had seen the painting and Bob hadn't, and Ann says to Bob *I saw an extraordinary painting by Picasso today*. In mentioning the painting in this way, she is bringing it into linguistic co-presence with Bob; that is, whereas in physical co-presence Ann, Bob, and the picture are openly present together in a single event, in linguistic co-presence Ann, Bob, and Ann's *mention* of the picture are what are openly present together. If Ann assumes that Bob understands her correctly and is otherwise rational and paying attention, she can infer that they now mutually suppose the existence of the Picasso painting. Whereas physical co-presence relies on "natural" evidence of the joint presence of Ann, Bob, and the painting, linguistic co-presence relies on "symbolic" evidence of their joint presence. In this way, the two types of evidence are distinct.

The last major type of evidence for common ground is *community membership*. Once Ann and Bob mutually establish that they both belong to a particular community, they can infer that what is universally known within that community is mutually known to the two of them. Imagine, for example, that Ann and Bob mutually discover that they are both on the Stanford University faculty. Ann can then infer that they mutually know where the Stanford Post Office is, who the president of the university is, and so on. Ann and Bob, of course, each belong to many communities and subcommunities, some in common and others distinct. To assume mutual knowledge for anything known by some community, they must first establish that they mutually know that they are both members of that community. If Ann knew that Bob was on the Stanford University faculty but knew that he didn't know that she was, she couldn't assume mutual knowledge of the post office, the president, and so on.

As evidence for common ground, physical and linguistic co-presence constitute single time-bounded events, whereas community membership constitutes an enduring state of affairs. Once Ann and Bob have mutually established that they are both members of some community, they can return again and again to that membership as a basis for inferring what is in their common ground. With physical and linguistic co-presence, in contrast, the single events are generally of limited use. Ann can later refer to the painting she and Bob had just seen or talked about, but only so long as the events are still fresh in memory. Evidence of physical and linguistic co-presence is generally pretty transitory.

Most inferences of common ground are based on a combination of these three types of evidence. After Ann tells Bob *I saw an extraordinary painting by*

Picasso today, she can infer that they mutually believe not only that she saw the painting but also that it was modern. She can draw the second inference because they both belong to the community of educated people who almost universally know that Picasso was a modern painter. Similarly, after Ann and Bob view the painting together, she can infer mutual knowledge not only of its existence but also of the manner in which it was probably created—from oils applied to canvas with a brush. This inference is also justified and drawn quite naturally on the basis of their joint membership in the community of educated people. If Bob had been a child or a stone-age food gatherer, Ann would not have been willing to draw this inference.

A Classification of Contexts

If the intrinsic context for comprehension is the speaker's and addressee's common ground, then the contexts mentioned in the literature as relevant to comprehension should be classifiable into one or more of the three main sources of common ground. And they are.

A major source for common ground in comprehension is, naturally enough, linguistic co-presence. The listener takes as common ground between him and the speaker all of their conversation up to and including the utterance currently being interpreted. Likewise, the reader takes as common ground between him and the narrator of the written discourse all the text up to and including the utterance he is currently considering. So linguistic co-presence quite naturally subsumes such types of context as "prior linguistic context," "semantic context," "discourse context," "syntactic context," and even "interactional context."

A second source for common ground is physical co-presence. The listener takes as common ground what he and the speaker are currently experiencing and have already experienced. This subsumes such notions as "extralinguistic context," "perceptual context," and Wason's "objective context." As they stand, these earlier notions are untenably broad, because they include perceptual information that is available to the listener but is known, believed, or supposed by the listener *not* to be part of his and the speaker's common ground. By reference to common ground, we can cut these gargantuan contexts down to size.

The least understood source of evidence is community membership. If something is universally known in a community, then two people in that community can assume that they mutually know it. This will cover, while narrowing down, a good deal of Bransford's allusions to "preexperimental knowledge," "appropriate knowledge framework," and "relevant contextual knowledge." It will also subsume other notions often included under the rubric of context, such as frames (Minsky, 1975), scripts (Schank & Abelson, 1977), schemata (Rumelhart & Ortony, 1977), and story grammars (Mandler & Johnson, 1977). These notions are each too inclusive as they now stand. An American wouldn't assume that an Egyptian has the script for what happens in American fast-food restaurants. The mutuality of such knowledge is essential for understanding the speaker's intent.

WHY COMMON GROUND?

What evidence is there that common ground is the right notion of intrinsic context? Most of it is formal. There are, for example, formal demonstrations that common ground is the necessary ingredient in conventions (Lewis, 1969), in speech acts (Schiffer, 1972), and in definite reference (Clark & Marshall, 1981). Other investigators have appealed to these demonstrations in their own arguments in favor of common ground. Yet most of the argument depends on a common sense analysis of language use. In our review, we try to convey as much of this common sense analysis as we can.

Conventions

The first formulation of mutual knowledge was proposed by Lewis (1969) to account for conventions. Consider the convention of using *chien* to denote dogs. For Ann to use *chien* with Bob to denote dogs, she must know that he knows it means "dog." But what if he knows it means "dog," but believes *she* thinks it means "cat"? Then Ann must suppose that he knows that *she* knows it means "dog." But what if he knows that she knows that it means "dog" but believes that *he* thinks it means "cat"? Ann must therefore suppose that he knows that she knows that *he* knows it means "dog." And so on, as Lewis demonstrated, ad infinitum. More generally, Lewis showed that for any convention to be usable by two people, it has to be mutually known (in the technical sense) by those two people.

If mutual knowledge—one aspect of common ground—is an essential part of conventions, then it must also be an essential part of language use because so much of language is conventional. The relations between most words and their meanings are conventional and so are phonological, morphological, and syntactic rules, the rules of semantic composition, and even, some would argue, much of pragmatics. What is represented in a person's mental lexicon and mental grammar are conventions that are common ground for that person and any other person who speaks the same language or dialect.

The source of common ground for conventions, then, is community membership. Trivially, to use English phonology, syntax, and semantics, the speaker must establish that he and his listener mutually know that they are both members of the community of English speakers. For many aspects of language, even the subcommunities to which the speaker and listener belong are critical. Words like *Jacobian, Bessel function,* and *quark,* for example, have conventional meanings only for the subcommunity of physicists, and ordinary words like *bug, tea,* and *attention* have additional conventional meanings in the subcommunities of computer workers, drug users, and psychologists. Whenever a speaker from one of these subcommunities talks to someone outside it, he can take as common ground only the vocabulary of the larger communities to which they both belong (Nunberg, 1978).

Speech Acts

In uttering sentences like *It's raining out* and *Who is coming tonight?,* a speaker is performing certain speech acts. He has certain attitudes he wants to express for certain listeners—for example, his belief that it is raining out or his desire to know from his addressees who is coming that night—and in uttering these sentences he intends those listeners to recognize these attitudes by means of their recognition of his intentions (Grice, 1957; 1968; Searle, 1969; Bach & Harnish, 1979). Our working assumption is that understanding what the speaker meant consists largely in trying to recognize the attitudes the speaker intended his listeners to recognize—the speech acts he performed.

How do listeners recognize the attitudes the speaker is expressing? According to a formal demonstration by Schiffer (1972), they do so by means of certain evidence—the words the speaker used and certain other "contextual" information. The critical point in Schiffer's demonstration is that this evidence has to be mutually known or believed by the speaker and his addressees. If it isn't, the speech act can fail, and it will be only accidental if the listeners manage to recognize the speaker's attitudes. What Schiffer's demonstration shows, then, is that the intrinsic context for understanding speech acts is mutual knowledge or beliefs—that is, common ground.

One source of evidence listeners use here is community membership, which leads them to the conventions governing the phonology, syntax, and semantics of the sentence uttered. The interrogative mood of *Who is coming tonight?,* for instance, can conventionally be used for asking questions (although it can also be used for other speech acts). The two other main sources of evidence for common ground—physical and linguistic co-presence—are also important. With *Who is coming tonight?,* they are needed for identifying when "tonight" is and where the people are "coming" to. Identifying the speech act being performed generally requires some combination of the three main sources of evidence for common ground.

Every conversation can be viewed as a series of speech acts that each increment the common ground of the parties in the conversation (Gazdar, 1979; Stalnaker, 1978). The idea, roughly, is this: Before Joe says in the middle of a conversation *Bill left for New York yesterday,* he will have assessed the common ground of his conversational partners and found it to be common ground who Bill is but not that he left for New York yesterday. Joe, of course, believes that Bill left for New York the day before (if he is being sincere) and perhaps that a few others might believe it but that not all the parties believe that all the parties believe it. Joe makes his assertion, therefore, in an attempt to increment the common ground among the parties—otherwise, there would be no point to it. They now *all* believe—indeed, mutually believe—that he believes that Bill left for New York yesterday. Once this is common ground, the next speaker, Sally, can say, for example, *Did he go by plane?*, in which she presupposes that it is common ground that Bill left for New York the day before.

Common ground is essential to speech acts that are indirect too. Imagine that Joe says to Sally *Do you know what time it is?* In the right situation, he could mean, literally, that she is to say whether or not she knows what time it is. He could also mean, indirectly, that she is to go to an appointment she has forgotten. What is the intrinsic context for Sally's recognition of this reminder? All the evidence suggests (Clark, 1979; Cohen & Perrault, 1979) that it is once again common ground. To be able to make this reminder, Joe must know about the appointment, know that she knows about it, know that she knows that he knows about it, and so on. Joe cannot expect her to refer to information that is not part of their common ground.

Definite Reference

Imagine Judy saying to David at a party *The woman in the blue dress is the mayor of San Francisco*. In uttering *the woman in the blue dress*, Judy is making a definite reference. She is trying to enable David to identify the person to whom she is referring—a particular woman—and with the rest of her utterance she is asserting something about that woman.

What information is necessary for David's identification of that woman? According to a formal demonstration by Clark and Marshall (1981), it is once again mutual knowledge or beliefs. If Judy's definite reference is sincere, she has good reason to believe that on this occasion David can readily and uniquely infer mutual knowledge of the identity of her referent. Most often, that means that the referent itself is *already* mutually known, and it is a matter of picking out the right referent from a mutually known array of possible referents. Describing the referent as the woman in a blue suit will do the trick. On other occasions, the referent *isn't* yet mutually known, but its identity can be inferred on the basis of mutual knowledge, beliefs, or suppositions. In short, the part of the context that David is intended to use as intrinsic to understanding Judy's reference is his and her common ground.

The three traditional types of definite reference—deixis, anaphora, and proper names—generally reflect the three main sources of mutual knowledge by which they are interpreted (Clark & Marshall, 1981). With deixis, as in *this woman, that box over there*, or *you*, the speaker prototypically depends in part on the physical co-presence of the speaker, addressee, and referent, which he often secures by gestures and eye contact. With anaphora, as in *the woman, the box I just mentioned,* and *itself,* the speaker depends primarily on the *linguistic* co-presence of the speaker, addressee, and referent. And for proper names, as with *George Washington, Napoleon,* and *World War II,* the speaker relies mainly on community membership—that he and his addressee belong to a community in which it is universally known who George Washington and Napolean were, and what World War II was. What listeners take as intrinsic context for interpreting definite reference is just the evidence that allows them to infer common ground.

Contextual Expressions

Contextual expressions are constructions whose senses vary indefinitely depending on the occasion on which they are used (Clark & Clark, 1979). Imagine that Ed and Joe have a mutual friend named Max, who has the odd habit of carrying a teapot and occasionally sneaking up and rubbing the back of people's legs with it. One day Ed says to Joe, "Well, Max did it this time. He tried to teapot a policeman." On this occasion, the verb *teapot,* based on the noun *teapot,* has the meaning "rub the back of the leg of with a teapot." However, with a change in the story about Max, it could have meant something else entirely. Because there are indefinitely many distinct stories one could tell about Max and teapots, there are indefinitely many distinct senses one could ascribe to the constructed verb *teapot.*

The main defining feature of contextual expressions is that, like the verb *teapot,* they have indefinitely many potential senses. They are different from ordinary ambiguous constructions like *virtualness,* which have a small finite number of distinct senses that either are conventional and are listed separately in the mental lexicon or are identifiable from conventional rules of composition applied to the conventional meanings of their parts (here, *virtual* and *-ness*). It is only in context that listeners can create the intended senses of expressions like *teapot,* hence the name *contextual expression.* Contextual expressions are not on the periphery of language, linguistic oddities to account for in a special way. They are ubiquitous and are thought to be a natural part of language (Clark, 1981).

The point is that for contextual expressions the intrinsic context is the speaker's and the target audience's common ground. Ed could not have said *Max tried to teapot a policeman* to just anyone and expected him to recognize the meaning "rub the back of the leg of with a teapot." Ed had to be sure that his addressee knew about Max's odd habits, knew that Ed knew about them, knew that Ed knew that he knew about them, and so on. It is easy to demonstrate that, like definite reference, contextual expressions have interpretations that require, in general, reference to the speaker's and audience's mutual knowledge, beliefs, and suppositions. The intrinsic context is their common ground.

CONCLUSIONS

What we have proposed is that when a listener tries to understand what a speaker means, the process he goes through can limit memory access to information that is common ground between the speaker and his addressees. At the very least, it must distinguish between information that is and is not part of the common ground, because otherwise in certain situations it will systematically misinterpret conventions, direct and indirect speech acts, definite reference, and contextual expressions. So the comprehension process must keep track of common ground, and its performance will be optimal if it limits its access to that common ground. Whether its design is actually optimal in this respect is a question that can only be answered empirically.

The intrinsic context for comprehension is different in one fundamental way from most other notions of intrinsic context. In areas like visual perception, the notion of common ground isn't even definable, because there are generally no agents involved other than the perceiver himself. Defining the intrinsic context in terms of common ground appears to be limited to certain processes of communication. Context, therefore, cannot be given a uniform treatment across all psychological domains. In language comprehension, indeed, the intrinsic context is something very special.

ACKNOWLEDGMENTS

The writing of this chapter was supported in part by Grant MH-20021 from the National Institute of Mental Health. We are indebted to a number of colleagues and reviewers for constructive comments on earlier drafts of this chapter. These include Philip Barnard, Larry Barsalou, Irving Biederman, Eve V. Clark, Simon Garrod, Gerald Gazdar, Gregory Murphy, and Keith Stenning.

REFERENCES

Anderson, J. R., & Bower, G. H. Interference in memory for multiple contexts. *Memory & Cognition,* 1974, *2,* 509–514.

Bach, K., & Harnish, R.M. *Linguistic communication and speech acts.* Cambridge, Mass.: MIT Press, 1979.

Biederman, I. Perceiving real world scenes. *Science,* 1972, *177,* 77–80.

Bower, G. H. Stimulus-sampling theory of encoding variability. In A. W. Melton & E. Martin (Eds.), *Coding processes in human memory.* Washington, D.C.: V. H. Winston, 1972.

Bower, G. H., Monteiro, K. P., & Gilligan, S. G. Emotional mood as a context for learning and recall. *Journal of Verbal Learning and Verbal Behavior,* 1978, *17,* 573–585.

Bransford, J. D. *Human cognition: Learning, understanding, and remembering.* Belmont, Calif.: Wadsworth, 1979.

Bransford, J. D., & Johnson, M. K. Contextual prerequisites for understanding: Some investigations of comprehension and recall. *Journal of Verbal Learning and Verbal Behavior*, 1972, *11*, 717–726.

Bransford, J. D., & Johnson, M. K. Consideration of some problems of comprehension. In W. G. Chase (Ed.), *Visual information processing*. New York: Academic Press, 1973.

Bransford, J. D., & McCarrell, N. S. A sketch of a cognitive approach to comprehension: Some thoughts about what it means to comprehend. In W. B. Weimer & D. S. Palermo (Eds.), *Cognition and the symbolic processes*. Hillsdale, N.J.: Lawrence Erlbaum Associates, 1974.

Brewer, W. F., & Harris, R. J. Memory for deictic elements in sentences. *Journal of Verbal Learning and Verbal Behavior*, 1974, *13*, 321–327.

Brigell, M., Uhlarik, J., & Goldhorn, P. Contextual influences on judgements of linear extent. *Journal of Experimental Psychology: Human Perception and Performance*, 1977, *3*, 105–118.

Carroll, J. M., Tanenhaus, M. K., & Bever, T. G. The perception of relations: The interaction of structural, functional, and contextual factors in the segmentation of sentences. In W. J. M. Levelt & G. B. Flores d'Arcais (Eds.), *Studies in the perception of language*. New York: Wiley, 1978.

Clark, E. V., & Clark, H. H. When nouns surface as verbs. *Language*, 1979, *55*, 767–811.

Clark, H. H. Inferences in comprehension. In D. Laberge and S. J. Samuels (Eds.), *Basic processes in reading: Perception and comprehension*. Hillsdale, N.J.: Lawrence Erlbaum Associates, 1977.

Clark, H. H. Responding to indirect speech acts. *Cognitive Psychology*, 1979, *11*, 430–477.

Clark, H. H. Making sense of nonce sense. In G. B. Flores d'Arcais & R. Jarvella (Eds.), *The process of language understanding*. New York: Wiley, 1981.

Clark, H. H., & Marshall, C. R. Definite reference and mutual knowledge. In A. K. Joshi, I. Sag, & B. Webber (Eds.), *Linguistic structure and discourse setting*. Cambridge: Cambridge University Press, 1981.

Cohen, P. R., & Perrault, C. R. Elements of a plan-based theory of speech acts. *Cogitive Science*, 1979, *3*, 197–212.

Doll, T. J., & Lapinski, R. H. Context effects in speeded comprehension and recall of sentences. *Bulletin of the Psychonomic Society*, 1974, *3*, 342–344.

Dooling, D. J. Some context effects in the speeded comprehension of sentences. *Journal of Experimental Psychology*, 1972, *93*, 56–62.

Dorman, M. F. Discrimination of intensity differences on formant transitions in and out of syllable context. *Perception & Psychophysics*, 1974, *16*, 84–86.

Eich, J. E. The cue-dependent nature of state-dependent retrieval. *Memory & Cognition*, 1980, *8*, 157–173.

Foss, D. J., & Jenkins, C. M. Some effects of context on the comprehension of ambiguous sentences. *Journal of Verbal Learning and Verbal Behavior*, 1973, *12*, 577–589.

Gazdar, G. *Pragmatics: Implicature, presupposition, and logical form*. New York: Academic Press, 1979.

Grice, H. P. Meaning. *Philosophical Review*, 1957, *66*, 377–388.

Grice, H. P. Utterer's meaning, sentence-meaning, and word-meaning. *Foundations of Language*, 1968, *4*, 225–242.

Huttenlocher, J., & Weiner, S. L. Comprehension of instructions in varying contexts. *Cognitive Psychology*, 1971, *2*, 369–385.

Jenkins, J. J. Remember that old theory of memory? Well, forget it! *American Psychologist*, 1974, *29*, 785–795.

Keenan, J. M., MacWhinney, B., & Mayhew, D. Pragmatics in memory: A study of natural conversation. *Journal of Verbal Learning and Verbal Behavior*, 1977, *16*, 549–560.

Lewis, D. K. *Convention*. Cambridge, Mass.: Harvard University Press, 1969.

Liberman, A. M., Cooper, F. S., Shankweiler, D. P., & Studdert-Kennedy, M. Perception of the speech code. *Psychological Review*, 1967, *74*, 431–461.

Mandler, J. M., & Johnson, N. S. Remembrance of things parsed: Story structure and recall. *Cognitive Psychology*, 1977, *9*, 111–151.

Marslen-Wilson, W. D., & Welsh, A. Processing interactions and lexical access during word recognition in continuous speech. *Cognitive Psychology*, 1978, *10*, 29-63.

McGeoch, J. A. Learning. In E. G. Boring, H. S. Langfeld, & H. P. Weld (Eds.), *Introduction to psychology*, New York: Wiley, 1939.

Meyer, D. E., Schvaneveldt, R. W., & Ruddy, M. G. Loci of contextual effects on visual word-recognition. In P. Rabbitt & S. Dornic (Eds.), *Attention and performance V*. New York: Academic Press, 1975.

Miller, G. A. *Language and communication*. New York: McGraw-Hill, 1951.

Miller, G. A., Heise, G., & Lichten, W. The intelligibility of speech as a function of the context of the test materials. *Journal of Experimental Psychology*, 1951, *41*, 329-335.

Minsky, M. A framework for representing knowledge. In P. H. Winston (Ed.), *The psychology of computer vision*. New York: McGraw-Hill, 1975.

Morton, J. The effects of context on the visual duration threshold for words. *British Journal of Psychology*, 1964, *55*, 165-180.

Morton, J. Interaction of information in word recognition. *Psychological Review*, 1969, *76*, 165-178.

Morton, J. A functional model for memory. In D. A. Norman (Ed.), *Models of human memory*. New York: Academic Press, 1970.

Nunberg, G. Slang, usage-conditions, and l'arbitraire du signe. In *Papers from the parasession on the lexicon*. Chicago: Chicago Linguistic Society, 1978.

Palmer, S. E. The effects of contextual scenes on the identification of objects. *Memory & Cognition*, 1975, *3*, 519-526.

Reiff, R. R., & Scheerer, M. *Memory and hypnotic age regression*. New York: International Universities Press, 1959.

Rubenstein, H., & Pollack, I. Word predictability and intelligibility. *Journal of Verbal Learning and Verbal Behavior*, 1963, *2*, 147-158.

Rumelhart, D. E., & Ortony, A. The representation of knowledge in memory. In R. C. Anderson, R. J. Spiro, & W. E. Montague (Eds.), *Schooling and the acquisition of knowledge*. Hillsdale, N.J.: Lawrence Erlbaum Associates, 1977.

Schank, R. C., & Abelson, R. P. *Scripts, plans, goals, and understanding: An inquiry into human knowledge*. Hillsdale, N.J.: Lawrence Erlbaum Associates, 1977.

Schiffer, S. R. *Meaning*. Oxford: Clarendon Press, 1972.

Schuberth, R. E., & Eimas, P. D. Effects of context on the classification of words and nonwords. *Journal of Experimental Psychology: Human Perception and Performance*, 1977, *3*, 27-36.

Searle, J. R. *Speech acts*. Cambridge: Cambridge University Press, 1969.

Smith, S. M., Glenberg, A., & Bjork, R. A. Environmental context and human memory. *Memory & Cognition*, 1978, *6*, 342-353.

Stalnaker, R. C. Assertion. In P. Cole (Ed.), *Syntax & semantics 9: Pragmatics*. New York: Academic Press, 1978.

Swinney, D. A., & Hakes, D. T. Effects of prior context upon lexical access during sentence comprehension. *Journal of Verbal Learning and Verbal Behavior*, 1976, *15*, 681-689.

Tanenhaus, M. K., Carroll, J. M., & Bever, T. G. Sentence-picture verification models as theories of sentence comprehension: A critique of Carpenter and Just. *Psychological Review*, 1976, *83*, 310-317.

Tulving, E., & Gold, C. Stimulus information and contextual information as determinants of tachistoscopic recognition of words. *Journal of Experimental Psychology*, 1963, *66*, 319-327.

Tulving, E., & Thomson, D. M. Encoding specificity and retrieval processes in episodic memory. *Psychological Review*, 1973, *80*, 352-373.

Warren, R. M., & Obusek, C. J. Speech perception and phonemic restorations. *Perception & Psychophysics*, 1971, *9*, 345-349.

Wason, P. C. The contexts of plausible denial. *Journal of Verbal Learning and Verbal Behavior*, 1965, *4*, 7-11.

19 Bridging Inferences and the Extended Domain of Reference

Simon Garrod and Tony Sanford
University of Glasgow
Glasgow
Scotland

ABSTRACT

A major issue that continues to concern the literature on sentence interpretation is the extent to which a reader incorporates his prior knowledge into the semantic representation of a sentence. A related question is whether sentences containing complex verbs are encoded in terms of a decomposed and extended semantic representation or encoded in a simpler propositional format. Two experiments are presented consistent with the hypothesis of decomposition at encoding. The rationale of the studies assumes that an extended representation for an antecedent sentence makes resolution of a subsequent related reference easier, when the bridging information is included in the representation. The results show this to be the case under certain conditions for antecedent sentences containing complex verbs.

INTRODUCTION

Text comprehension may be defined at least in part as the production of a coherent representation of the text in the mind of the reader. Central to the production of such a representation is the need to decide to what the phrases of a text refer, and whether, or how, they relate to one another. A case for study is that of anaphoric reference, in which a noun phrase refers to something denoted by an antecedent noun phrase, for example:

1. The tin soldier had a leg missing.
1'. *The toy* was not very well made.

331

In this case, the phrase *The toy* is taken to refer to an entity denoted by the antecedent phrase *The tin soldier,* and the reader has to make use of the knowledge that a ''tin soldier'' is a specific instance of the class ''toys.'' Other nominal references are not so straightforward, however:

2. Mary sewed her new dress.
2'. *The needle* was a little too large for the delicate work.

In this case, there is no direct antecedent noun phrase leading to a representation to which the mention of *The needle* might also lead. Rather, the link between sentence 2 and 2' seems to be through the verb *sewed,* which implies using a needle and thread.

In both sets 1 and 1' and 2 and 2', background knowledge has to be used for a reader to interpret correctly the referential expression. This chapter addresses two related aspects of the problem: First, how much background knowledge is made available when a reader interprets an antecedent sentence; second, to what extent is this reflected in the ease with which a subsequent related reference may be resolved. We begin by considering what is already known about the use of inferences in resolving reference and then go on to consider the nature of the meaning representation one might expect to be set up for an antecedent sentence. It is easy to see how these two components of the reference problem are related. Suppose, for example, that on reading sentence 2 the mental representation that resulted carried the information that Mary was using a needle. On encountering 2' the phrase *the needle* will lead to the appropriate part of the extant representation. In short, the inferential bridge between *sewing* and *needle* may have been made before 2' is even encountered. By contrast, if the representation set up by 2 does not contain this information but can only be used as a starting point to get at it, then the necessary bridge will be made only when 2' is encountered. The questions are: How much computation is left until needed? How much is carried out in the expectation that it might subsequently be useful?

BRIDGING AND DECOMPOSITION

Haviland and Clark (1974) demonstrated that it takes a measurable amount of comprehension time to draw such bridging inferences. As a baseline, they measured the time taken to read the second of a pair of sentences in which no inference had to be drawn. This was achieved by using pairs of sentences in which the referring expressions of interest were cast in the form of the same noun phrase; for example:

3. Mary got some beer out of the trunk.
3'. *The beer* was warm.

The critical target sentences, exemplified by 3', were read more rapidly with such a *direct* antecedent than when preceded by one requiring bridging computation; for example:

4. Mary unpacked the picnic supplies from the trunk.
4'. *The beer* was warm.

Although it was the same sentence, 4' was read considerably more slowly than 3', presumably because, in the absence of a direct antecedent, one has to be searched for and resolved on the basis of the description *"The beer"* in 4'. Because "beer" can be a member of the set denoted by "The picnic supplies," this affords a bridging link between the two sentences. Since then, Garrod and Sanford (1977, 1978), Sanford and Garrod (1980), and Kennedy (1979) have demonstrated that the time to map one noun phrase onto another may depend on the nature of the class-membership relation between antecedent and anaphor.

Evidence such as this strongly suggests that Haviland and Clark (1974) were dealing with materials in which inferences had to be drawn on encountering the target sentence [Clark's (1975) "backward-inferences"] and carries with it the implication that the mental representation of 4, for example, does not contain information directly concerning "beer." But the question remains as to whether a greater degree of complexity can be ascribed to the meaning representation of a sentence in *any* circumstances. Pertinent to this question is the issue of lexical decomposition, which we consider in the context of the semantic description of complex verbs.

The semantics of verbs can be described in terms of related sets of atomic concepts that together make up their complete meaning. There are a variety of analyses of verb meaning based upon the notion of decomposition, and from these analyses three kinds of element emerge:

1. Primitives describing actions or states (e.g., TRANSFER, MOVE) (Schank, 1973). Thus "give" can be described in terms of an *agent* TRANS-FERRING something to a *recipient*.

2. Logical primitives (e.g., NEGATION). So, "prohibit" may be seen as equivalent to "allow," but with an additional NEGATIVE component (Just & Clark, 1973).

3. Entities necessarily entailed in the descriptions of actions or states. For instance, moving a FOOT is entailed by "kick," BEAK by "peck."

This type of analysis has proved particularly useful in formulating computer programs that produce coherent representations of text (Norman, Rumelhart & LNR, 1975; Schank, 1973). From the point of view of human language processing, an important question therefore is whether a sentence is automatically represented in a "decomposed" form in terms of the elements of meaning sketched previously or whether such decomposition only occurs when needed. Three basic methods have been used to evaluate the decomposition hypothesis in adults: ease of remembering, reading time, and statement verification.

In the context of memory, a number of early studies seemed to suggest that decomposition did not occur at the time of encoding. Thus Kintsch (1974) argued that with a sentence that would give rise to a complex decomposition, memory should be poorer than for a sentence giving rise to a simpler decomposition, because memory for the explicit sentence would be confused with the additional information introduced into the representation. Because Kintsch found no such effects, he concluded that decomposition had not occurred. The problem with this argument is that it is assumed that complexity interferes with retrieval. More recently Gentner (in press) has argued that such an assumption is unwarranted. She suggested that what is important at retrieval is how well connected the elements of the sentence are, connection being defined in terms of decomposition. Some verb decompositions will be complex and yet relate other entities in the sentence closely through the primitive elements of the decomposition. Using a cued recall procedure, Gentner demonstrated that retrieval of sentences based on complex structures giving rise to high degrees of relatedness was in fact superior to retrieval of those containing simpler verbs. She concluded that decomposition did occur and that Kintsch's materials could not discriminate these possibilities.

In a similar vein, Kintsch (1974) and Carpenter and Just (1977) found that sentences using verbs that should give more complex decompositions took no longer to read than ones that should give simpler decompositions. Again, decomposition should take up comprehension time, and because no increase in reading time was observed, the results were taken as going against the decomposition hypothesis. However, it might be countered that verb meanings in the form of decompositions are represented as modules in memory, and there is no need to suppose that differences in complexity of the modules would lead to differences in retrieval time. In terms of reading-time measurements, then, it could be argued that the issue is undecided. Indeed, some recent evidence is compatible with the idea that more complex but more specific words may facilitate the ease of encoding a sentence (Tabossi & Johnson-Laird [1980] for verbs; Sanford & Garrod, [1980] for noun phrases).

On the other hand, when we turn to studies utilizing a verification procedure, there is evidence suggesting some relationship between the nature of a decomposed representation and verification time. Thus, Carpenter and Just (1977) have demonstrated that subjects treat verbs like "forget" as equivalent to "NOT remember," and in these circumstances the inherently negative (and so more complex) verb does take longer to process in verification. Furthermore, the pattern of results from these studies gives strong support to the decomposition hypothesis for the logical operator NOT. Similar results obtain for adjective comparisons using examples such as "bad," taken as equivalent to "NOT good" (Clark, 1969). Although these studies may be taken as giving broad support to the hypothesis of decomposition at encoding in the case of logical operators, they should not be confused with the general complexity hypothesis. The time to process sentences in a verification task cannot be directly equated with reading time in general.

If the working representations of sentences are in a decomposed form, as some of the studies previously cited suggest, then this has an important consequence for the processing of subsequent sentences. In our original argument, it was proposed that a newly encountered noun phrase may be resolved in two ways— either by being mapped directly into an extant structure set up by the antecedent sentences or by implementing a search for a bridge, using general knowledge. A decomposed representation might enable mappings to be made not *only* onto explicitly mentioned entities but also onto elements of the decomposition. An important class of these elements are those deriving from implied entities, as introduced previously. It is to this specific issue that the remainder of the chapter is devoted.

The issue of implied entities requires the determination of what might be considered plausible components of a decomposed representation. When this is done, some components seem more central than others. For instance, the verb "to dress" necessarily implies "to transfer clothes"—it is a logically necessary part of the dominant sense of the verb, and it is not merely the "transfer" part that is necessary but also "clothes." On the other hand, the verb "to scratch (something)" requires an instrument but does not severely restrict what that instrument might be. For any experimental study, it is essential to use verbs that very strongly imply (and preferably require) the existence of certain entities, if we are to test the idea that these implicit entities may form part of the representation of a sentence.

The design of the first study is based on the established technique of measuring reading times for critical (target) sentences, in a self-paced reading situation. If a noun phrase can be resolved referentially through an extant decomposed representation, then the time to comprehend the sentence should be no longer than that taken if it is presented in the context of a sentence, which has used that noun phrase directly. Consider 6 and 6′.

6. Mary dressed the baby.
6′. *The clothes* were made of pink wool.

If a representation incorporating *clothes* is set up by 6, then 6′ should be resolved as rapidly as it would if preceded by the direct antecedent 7;

7. Mary put the clothes on the baby.
6′. *The clothes* were made of pink wool.

EXPERIMENT 1. DIRECT AND INDIRECT ANTECEDENTS

Materials

As indicated, a very strict criterion is desirable in order to determine what is likely to be present in a semantic representation. In selecting the materials, therefore, two criteria were employed. In the first case, an informal method was used in which the noun phrase of interest was incorporated into a sentence already implying its existence. For instance:

8. Mary dressed the baby with *clothes*.

The strictest criterion of implication is revealed in this way if the result is a tautology or, more strictly, a pleonasm. This test provides an important means of grading predictability, as we shall see in the general discussion.

The second procedure used in gathering materials was to have 15 subjects produce brief descriptions of verbs. They were asked to base their responses on examples like:

9. CARVE: Use a knife to slice meat.

The requirement was a high percentage of responses to each verb that included mention of the noun phrase that was to provide the test item in the main experiment. Questionnaires were given to 15 subjects in order to elicit definitions for the verbs. The results from this pretest are shown in Fig. 19.1, presented in terms of the number of verbs for which a given criterion percentage of subjects included the implied entity. It will be noticed that in all but three of the verbs used, more than 70% of the subjects included mention of the implied entity in their definitions. In the case of the remaining three verbs, it was clear that a few subjects had not interpreted the verbs in the sense used in our materials. For example, when given the verb "to fly" this can be interpreted in terms of a nonhuman animal moving itself through the air by means of wings or in the sense of a human being using an aircraft to travel through the air. When inappropriate sense definitions are removed from consideration, then all verbs reach at least the 70% criterion.

For the experimental comparison, 16 sentences were produced leaving the noun phrases only implied (*unstated*) and 16 paraphrases were generated in which the noun phrase was explicitly mentioned. So, for the verb "unlocked" and the noun phrase "key," there was an *unstated* version, "she unlocked the door," and a *stated* version, "she opened the door with a key."

For each pair of sentences, a subsequent target sentence was generated in which the entity was identified with an anaphoric reference; so for the pair just shown, the target sentence was "The key belonged to her father." In order to make the passages coherent, an initial neutral sentence was always added, giving the subject three sentences to read on each trial. In addition, a yes/no question

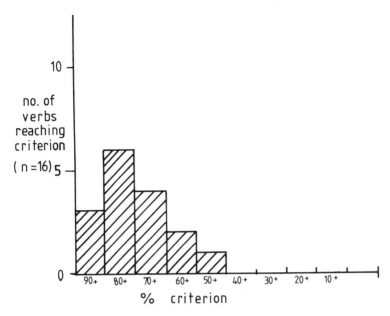

FIG. 19.1. Frequency of verb definitions reaching percentage choice criterion indicated. The verbs and implied entities were BAKE—OVEN, BUY—MONEY, CUT (HAIR)— SCISSORS, DRESS—CLOTHES, DRIVE—CAR, FLY—PLANE, FREEZEOVER—ICE, GROW—HEIGHT, KISS—LIPS, PHOTO-GRAPH—CAMERA, POST—LETTERBOX, RIDE—HORSE, SAIL—BOAT, SELL—MONEY, SMOKE—CIGARETTE, UNLOCK—KEY.

was presented at the end of each trial to ensure that the passages were being read for meaning. An example of the materials, from matching trials in the implied and stated conditions, is shown in Table 19.1.

Subjects

Twenty male and femal undergraduates from Glasgow University were employed as subjects. (These were different from the 15 used in the verb selection pretest.) They were paid at the rate of 50p. per hr and were naive as to the aim of the experiment.

Design and Procedure

Each subject was presented with 16 trials, half of these in the implied antecedent condition and half in the stated antecedent condition, the two conditions being randomized across a sequence of trials. Furthermore, the materials were counterbalanced across the subjects in such a way that if subject n saw a given triplet in the stated condition, subject $n + 1$ would see the matching triplet in the implied condition or vice versa.

TABLE 19.1

Stated Antecedent	
Keith was giving a lecture in London:	
He was taking his car there overnight.	
The car had recently been overhauled.	
QUESTION:	
Did Keith go to London by car?	*Yes*
or	
Did Keith go to London by train?	*No*
Unstated Antecedent	
Keith was giving a lecture in London.	
He was driving there overnight.	
The car had recently been overhauled.	
QUESTION:	
Did Keith go to London by car?	*Yes*
or	
Did Keith go to London by train?	*No*

The procedure used was essentially the same as that reported in Garrod and Sanford (1977). The subject was seated in front on an Imlac visual display unit on which the sentences and questions were exposed one at a time. At the beginning of each trial, the subject pressed a space key to bring on the first sentence. After reading it, he pressed the same key for the next sentence, and so on until the question appeared. The subject then pressed one key to indicate a *yes* response and another key for a *no*. To initiate a new trial, the subject pressed the space key again. All the time intervals between key presses were recorded automatically for subsequent printout.

The sequence of events for any subject was the following. First there were two forms of practice; the initial practice consisted of reading about 200 lines of connected text, in order to introduce the general task requirements, character font, etc. The second phase consisted of the presentation of 20 sentence triplets with associated questions, of the kind used in the main study, thus familiarizing the subject with shorter passages. The subject was then presented with 16 experimental trials, as described previously, having been instructed to read the materials carefully at a normal rate. Mixed in with these were trials of a comparable length from another experiment that was being run simultaneously, thus reducing the possibility of subjects developing specific, artificial strategies for processing the experimental materials.

Results and Discussion

Two sets of reading times are of interest here: times for the critical target sentences under the two conditions and the response times for the questions. The first times were estimated from the interval between the subject pressing the space bar to call up the target sentence and pressing the bar for the question. The second times were measured from this point to pressing one of the response keys.

The mean reading times for the targets were, for *stated* 1287 msec and *implied* 1302 msec, yielding a small difference of 15 msec in favor of the stated condition (S.E. = 20 msec). In order to check the reliability of this difference, analyses of variance were carried out on the means both by subjects and materials. By subjects the difference was unreliable, $F_1(1, 19) = 0.1383$; also by materials, $F_2(1, 15) = 0.202$. Furthermore, when the subjects' means were considered individually, half of the subjects showed faster target reading times under the implied condition. As far as bridging goes, we would suggest that there is no appreciable advantage to stating an antecedent rather than implying it as part of the meaning of the verb.

There are two other possibilities, however, that might throw doubt on this conclusion. The first is that the subjects may not have integrated the information until they had finished reading the material. It is possible though to make an independent check for this with the response times for the questions.

The questions were specifically designed to check whether the appropriate bridge had been made. Thus in order to answer *yes* questions correctly, the subjects would have had to form the bridge between antecedent and anaphor for both implied and stated conditions. For instance, in the material illustrated, to determine whether "Keith went by car" requires knowing that *the car* was the one used to drive to London in the context material. Now if the subjects had not already determined this relationship before encountering the question, they would have to do so when answering it. In other words, we would expect to find an effect in the *yes* question times corresponding to the extra time needed to make the bridging inference. No such difference emerged: For the *stated* condition, the question times were 1871 msec and for the *implied* condition they were 1858 msec (S.E. = 32 msec), with associated error rates of 0.06% for implied and 2.3% for stated. Thus, questions were answered in marginally *less* time (13 msec) under the implied condition, suggesting that integration was occurring at the time of reading.

The second possibility is that the reading-time technique as applied to this situation is not sensitive to the comprehension consequences of making bridging inferences. Although there is no way of directly addressing this question with the data from the first experiment, it may be possible to demonstrate reading-time increase under conditions where inferential bridging would be predicted for the implied condition but not the stated. Such a prediction emerges from a closer look at the nature of the complex underlying representations.

Until now it might appear to have been assumed that the underlying representation for a sentence containing a verb implying an entity is the same as that for a sentence in which the entity is explicitly stated, but of course this need not be so. As pointed out by Woods (1975), it is important to make a distinction between general and structural information and specific and asserted information in a semantic representation. That "dressing" will entail the transfer of clothes is part of the structure of the concept "to dress." However, a statement such as "Mary put the clothes on the baby" asserts something about a specific set of clothes.

By whatever means "clothes" is explicitly introduced ("the clothes," "some clothes," "clothes"), it is possible to make an attributional statement about the set of clothes so introduced. Indeed, in almost all cases, it is impossible to introduce an entity explicitly without asserting something about it. A direct outcome of explicit mention is the possibility of subsequent pronominal reference. Thus it is in order to say:

10. Mary put the clothes on the baby.
10'. They were made of pink wool.

but not with the implicit antecedent:

11. Mary dressed the baby.
11'. They were made of pink wool.

A common way of dealing with such implicit entities as structural information in work on conceptual representation is to treat them as variables, say ⟨clothes⟩ or ⟨vehicle⟩, which can accept as a value any specific reference that passes the critical tests for clothes or vehicles (Rumelhart, 1977). This makes it possible both to map appropriate subsequent references directly onto the representation and to keep the asserted and structural information marked as distinct.

The distinction between treating something as a specific asserted piece of information or as a variable has implications for inferential bridging. These become apparent when we consider what happens if an indirect attributional statement is made about an entity that was previously implied but not specifically introduced. Consider for instance the two sample passages given here:

12. Keith drove to London overnight.
12'. The engine had recently been overhauled.

13. Keith took his car to London overnight.
13'. The engine had recently been overhauled.

In both passages, it is necessary to draw the inference that the engine is conceptually dependent on the vehicle in question. However, in 13 and 13' this can be done directly through the stated antecedent "car," whereas in 12 and 12' it is necessary to set up an antecedent with the inference:

14. Driving implies traveling by vehicle; a vehicle possesses an engine; this engine is antecedent to *the engine*.

The fact that the representation for the verb "drive" contains a variable ⟨vehicle⟩ is of no help here because "the engine" does not pass the critical test for vehicle. Instead, it is necessary to generate some antecedent that both maps into the variable ⟨vehicle⟩ and qualifies as a governor for the entity "*the engine.*" We would therefore expect additional reading time to be associated with this extra step in the bridging process.

The second experiment was designed to test this prediction.

EXPERIMENT 2

Method

Subjects

Twenty undergraduates from Glasgow University were recruited as subjects. They were paid at the rate of 50p. per hr.

Materials, Design, and Procedure

The context materials were generated in exactly the same fashion as in Experiment 1 except that 6 of the 16 verb-paraphrase pairs had to be changed in order to generate plausible target sentences. The target sentences were all designed in such a way that they contained a definite reference to an entity that was dependent on what had been implied by the verb in the context material. A set of materials under both the implied and stated condition is shown in Table 19.2.

The procedure was exactly the same as that used in the first experiment.

Results and Discussion

In this experiment the reading times of interest were for the critical target sentences under the two conditions. The mean times under the *stated* condition were 1339 msec and under the *implied,* 1404 msec yielding an advantage of 65 msec for the stated over implied condition. To test the reliability of this difference, analyses of variance were carried out on both the subject means and the means by materials. By subjects the implied/stated factor was reliable; $F_1(1, 19) = 4.4123$,

TABLE 19.2

Stated Antecedent

Keith was giving a lecture in London.
He was taking his car there overnight.
The engine had recently been overhauled.

Unstated Antecedent

Keith was giving a lecture in London.
He was driving there overnight.
The engine had recently been overhauled.

$p < .05$), and also by materials, $F_2(1, 15) = 6.2162, p < .025$. From these two F values, a min F' was estimated that was marginally significant, min $F'(1, 34) = 2.581, p < .1$). The fact that an effect is demonstrated here reinforces the conclusion that the failure to demonstrate such an effect in Experiment 1 cannot be attributed to any lack of sensitivity with the reading-time procedure.

GENERAL DISCUSSION

We began this chapter with the question of how newly introduced noun phrases are resolved referentially. On the basis of Experiment 1, we would claim that certain entities implied by verbs are represented as a subset of the sentence representation set up when sentences containing these verbs are understood. Consequently, any subsequent mention of noun phrases referring to these entities may be mapped directly onto the entity representation. At once this raises two issues. First, what are the limits on any extended representation set up by sentences? Second, through which processing operations is an extended representation turned to advantage in reading?

In Experiment 1, strict criteria were used in determining which entities were strongly suggested by the verbs. The entities themselves were necessary parts of the meaning of the verb. Singer (1979) carried out a test similar to ours, using *instruments* implied by action descriptions, and obtained rather different results. We begin by considering a typical example of the sentence pairs used in Singer's study. In the implied antecedent condition, a typical example was:

15.   The boy cleared the snow from the stairs.
15'. *The shovel* was heavy.

The idea is that *cleared the snow* suggests *shovel* and, in norms for implied instruments, this certainly appeared to be the case (Singer, 1977). In the direct antecedent condition, the matching sentence was:

16.   The boy cleared the snow with the shovel.
16'. The shovel was heavy.

Singer found that the reading time for the target sentence 16' was considerably shorter under direct than indirect antecedent conditions, a finding that is superficially at variance with ours. However, there are clear differences between the antecedent sentences used in our experiment and his, and examination of the differences throws some light on possible limitations of the extended semantic representation. In the first place the implied instrument in Singer's example does not appear to derive from the verb "to clear." If subjects were asked to give a definition of the verb (as in the pretest for Experiment 1), it seems most unlikely that they would include "shovel" as part of it—consider for instance "The boy cleared the luggage from the stairs." It is perhaps for this reason that sentence 17 is not pleonastic in the way that 18 is:

17. They cleared the snow with *shovels*.
18. Mary dressed the baby *with clothes*.

This would suggest two things. First, that in Singer's case the implied instrument could not be attributed to the decomposed representation of the verb; second, that however popular a candidate *the shovel* might be as an instument, it is still optional, and from Singer's results this seems to mean that it will not be specified in the representation unless it is mentioned directly. Furthermore, the design used by Singer could well be unsuitable for testing our own hypothesis: If the same verb can be used for both direct and indirect antecedents, then either the added noun phrase will produce a strained example in the direct condition, as a result of its pleonastic quality, or the entity will not be necessarily implied in the indirect condition. For instance, if one did use an antecedent like "Mary sailed to Ireland in a boat," then the effect of this might be to emphasize "boat" in some way (for instance, an unusual contrast may follow in a later sentence). In such a case, a subsequent reference to "boat" may be resolved more rapidly than it would with an indirect antecedent, simply because of the additional foregrounding afforded to it (Chafe, 1972, see also Sanford & Garrod, 1981).

Although it is still unclear precisely how much information is present in the mental representation of a sentence, the results at hand suggest that at least some of the extended meaning is represented and does not have to be computed "when needed." However, the nature of the extended representation itself creates some problems. Clearly, there is a difference between an explicitly mentioned entity and one that is merely implied. As suggested earlier, the implied entity may be considered as a variable, such as ⟨CLOTHES⟩, which may be realized as a series of tests to be applied to the concept underlying any definite noun phrase. A phrase that matches will be taken as referring to the ⟨CLOTHES⟩ slot. With such a process, some terms will provide a better and quicker fit than others. In our own experiments, only words chosen in the description norms or high conjoint frequency exemplars of these categories were used as target noun phrases, as it was assumed that others may take longer to process. However, one would antici-pate that a term like "the socks" would be processed fairly quickly in the example containing the verb "dress." Indeed, Garrod and Sanford (1977) found that with explicitly mentioned antecedents, the conjoint frequency (Wilkins, 1971) of the anaphoric noun phrase with the antecedent was an important deter-minant of resolution time. Presumably, if a stated antecedent perfectly matched the specifications of the variable, one would expect a minimal conjoint frequency effect here.

The limited extended representation that is set up by a sentence seems to provide a processing advantage to noun phrases that refer to it, because a ref-erential "bridge" has already been formed, in effect. However, in order to produce such an advantage, certain limitations have to guide referential search processes. Sanford and Garrod (1981) have suggested ways in which the search process may be controlled by a noun phrase. For instance, we suggest that a definite noun phrase serves as a processing directive to seek a referent in a partition of memory, which we term *focus* (following Grosz, 1977). Focus is assumed to be a currently privileged part of memory, comprising two components—*explicit* and *implicit* focus. Implicit focus in part consists of the current extended representation, whereas explicit focus consists of tokens of individuals explicity mentioned in the text. With such a scheme, a definite noun phrase may be resolved unambiguously within a restricted search set. For instance, "the clothes" could refer, in theory, to any clothes of which the reader has prior knowledge. However, if a search is made for the referent, it will begin with a search of focus and, with the examples just described, either a token for "clothes" (explicit focus) will be found or a variable slot admitting "clothes" will be found (implicit focus).

According to Sanford and Garrod's (1981) account, such resolution exemplifies *primary processing* (see also Garrod & Sanford, 1980). The result of the mapping is that "the clothes" are identified as the same "clothes" in the focused representation. Of course, this sometimes fails, and then *secondary processing* takes over. Secondary processing basically entails a broader search of memory for what Haviland and Clark (1974) term a bridge. There are many ways in which this could occur, but the basic principle underlying them is that it would be necessary to attempt resolution on the basis of a longer sample of text. So, for instance, a longer parse may result in the discovery of a restrictive relative clause—for example, "the clothes worn to the party." This longer description may enable a search of other (long-term) partitions of memory. At the other extreme, we suggest that *pronouns* serve almost always as primary processing directives and, furthermore, direct the search to tokens within explicit focus only. As shown earlier, pronouns cannot be used to refer to implied entities (pairs 10 and 11).

Reading-time data do indeed support the view that a pronoun reference, having a more restricted search domain, is resolved more rapidly than a noun-phrase reference (Sanford & Garrod, 1981).

In this way we argue that a focus system with an implicit component serves as a means for the rapid resolution of nonanaphoric definite reference. The advantage of the system is that short descriptions may be rapidly mapped into a small (and hence unambiguous) prior representation that nevertheless extends beyond that which has been explicitly mentioned. However, some writers who have presented evidence favoring bridge-building rather than decomposition (Singer, 1979) have stressed that language usage is so flexible that the extent of implicit focus would have to be extremely large if all sentences following an antecedent were to be handled through what we have called primary processing. However, we would counter this by saying that a discourse is usually constructed in such a way that, at any point, the writer is able to produce a judicious mixture of primary and secondary processing in a reader. Whereas primary processing produces basic *coherence,* secondary processing allows a unique and novel text representation to unfold. Some of our recent research is aimed at investigating the upper limits of implicit focus and at identifying those cues in language that control the availability of and changes in its content (Garrod & Sanford, 1980; Sanford & Garrod, 1981; Sanford, Henderson & Garrod, 1980). In the present chapter, we have attempted to demonstrate its importance in resolving simple nominal references.

REFERENCES

Carpenter, P. A., & Just, M. A. Reading comprehension as eyes see it. In M. A. Just & P. A. Carpenter (Eds.), *Cognitive processes in comprehension.* Hillsdale, N.J.: Lawrence Erlbaum Associates, 1977.

Chafe, W. Discourse structure and human knowledge. In J. B. Carroll & R. O. Freedle (Eds.), *Language comprehension and the acquisition of knowledge.* Washington, D.C.: V. H. Winston, 1972.

Clark, H. H. Linguistic processes in deductive reasoning. *Psychological Review,* 1969, *76,* 387–404.

Clark, H. H. Bridging. In R. Schank & B. Nash-Webber (Eds.), Theoretical issues in natural language processing. Proceedings of a conference at the Massachusetts Institute of Technology. Cambridge, Mass., 1975.

Garrod, S., & Sanford, A. J. Interpreting anaphoric relations: The integration of semanic information while reading. *Journal of Verbal Learning and Verbal Behavior,* 1977, *16,* 77–90.

Garrod, S., & Sanford, A. J. Anaphora: A problem in text comprehension. In R. N. Campbell & P. T. Smith (Eds.), *Recent advances in the psychology of language.* New York: Plenum Press, 1978.

Garrod, S., & Sanford, A. J. *Topic dependent effects in language processing.* Paper presented at the XXII International Congress of Psychology, Leipzig, July 1980.

Gentner, D. Verb semantic structures in memory for sentences: Evidence for componential representation. *Cognitive Psychology,* in press.

Grosz, B. J. *The representation and use of focus in dialogue understanding.* Technical Note 151, Artificial Intelligence Centre SRI International, Menlo Park, Calif., 1977.

Haviland, S. E., & Clark, H. H. What's new? Acquiring new information as a process in comprehension. *Journal of Verbal Learning and Verbal Behavior,* 1974, *13,* 512–521.

Just, M. A., & Clark, H. H. Drawing inferences from the presuppositions and implications of affirmative and negative sentences. *Journal of Verbal Learning and Verbal Behavior,* 1973, *12,* 21–31.

Kennedy, R. A. Eye movements and reading. In M. M. Gruneberg, P. E. Morris, & R. N. Sykes (Eds.), *Practical aspects of memory.* Proceedings of the International Conference, London: Plenum Press, 1979.

Kintsch, W. *The representation of meaning in memory.* Potomac, Md.: Lawrence Erlbaum Associates, 1974.

Norman, D. A., Rumelhart, D. E., & LNR. *Explorations in cognition.* San Francisco: W. H. Freeman, 1975.

Rumelhart, D. E. *Introduction to human information processing.* New York: Wiley, 1977.

Sanford, A. J., & Garrod, S. Memory and attention in text comprehension: The problem of reference. In R. S. Nickerson (Ed.), *Attention and performance VIII*. Hillsdale, N.J.: Lawrence Erlbaum Associates, 1980.

Sanford, A. J., & Garrod, S. *Understanding written language: Explorations in comprehension beyond the sentence.* Chichester: Wiley, 1981.

Sanford, A. J., Garrod, S., & Henderson, R. *Topic shift as a variable in text cohesion: Experimental evidence from studies in reading time.* Paper presented at the Experimental Psychology Society, Cambridge, July 1980.

Schank, R. C. Identification of conceptualizations underlying natural language. In R. C. Schank & K. M. Colby (Eds.), *Computer models of thought and language.* San Francisco: W. H. Freeman, 1973.

Singer, M. *Inferences about instruments: Response norms.* University of Manitoba, 1977.

Singer, M. Processes of inference during sentence encoding. *Memory and Cognition,* 1979, 7(3), 192-200.

Tabossi, P., & Johnson-Laird, P. N. Linguistic context and priming of semantic information. *Quarterly Journal of Experimental Psychology,* 1980, *32,* 595-603.

Wilkins, A. J. Conjoint frequency, category size and categorization time. *Journal of Verbal Learning and Verbal Behavior,* 1971, *10,* 383-385.

Woods, W. A. What's in a link: Foundations for semantic networks. In D. G. Bobrow & A. Collins (Eds.), *Representation and understanding in cognitive science.* New York: Academic Press, 1975.

20 The Effects of Reading Purpose on Memory for Text

John B. Black
Yale University
New Haven, Connecticut, U.S.A.

ABSTRACT

Reading a text for different purposes influenced the drawing of inferences during reading as measured by the false recognition of inference lures on a later memory test. When subjects read a text only to rate its comprehensibility, they recognized falsely fewer inferences than subjects who read the text for either a memory test or an essay test. In particular, the rating subjects recognized fewer inferences requiring real-world knowledge and integration of information from different parts of the text than did the memory and essay subjects.

INTRODUCTION

Texts typically omit many statements that are easy to infer from common knowledge. To understand texts fully, readers need to make these inferences. However, too many inferences are possible for any given text, so a reader must be selective. This chapter examines how different purposes affect which inferences are made during reading and stored as part of the memory for the text. The approach combines three separate areas of research: (1) inferencing during reading; (2) how activities during reading affect learning; and (3) the effects of processing levels on memory.

INFERENCING DURING READING

Most studies of the inferences made during language comprehension have used memory tests to measure inferencing. They have provided two kinds of evidence: false memory for inferences, implied but not stated in the text, and better memory for texts connected by cohesive inferences. In the case of false memory, if subjects falsely recall or recognize an inference during a memory test, it is assumed that the inference was made during comprehension and stored in memory in a form indistinguishable later from information that was stated explicitly.

As primary initiators of the false-memory approach, Bransford, Barclay, and Franks (1972) found that subjects made appropriate spatial inferences and later erroneously remembered them. Also, Johnson, Bransford, and Solomon (1973) showed that subjects inferred the appropriate instruments needed for actions in the text. False-memory evidence has also been found for referential (Anderson & Bower, 1973) and causal inferences (Bower, Black, & Turner, 1979). The latters' subjects recognized and recalled standard actions in descriptions of common situations even if they were not explicitly stated. The actions falsely remembered were part of the standard causal chains connecting the stated actions.

The second kind of memory evidence indicates better recall for text statements connected by inferential relations. The subjects are assumed to infer the additional connections while reading. Similar evidence has been found for referential and causal inferences. De Villiers (1974) found that subjects recalled texts better if they read the same texts will all *a*'s replaced by *the*'s. Similarly, Black and Bern (in press) found that pairs of sentences in texts that enable causal linking inferences are remembered better than those that block such inferences.

One problem is that the memory measurements are made long after the supposed inferencing has taken place. More direct evidence is provided by reading time. Haviland and Clark (1974) showed that reading time increased when subjects had to infer referential connections between sentences. Haberlandt and Bingham (1978) found that subjects read causally related sentence triples faster than ones that were not causally related. If readers always try to infer causal connections between statements in narratives, they spend more time processing statements when they cannot find such a connection. Consistent evidence is provided by Bower et al.'s (1979) finding that reading time was longer when readers made more than one inferential step to establish a causal connection between two narrative statements.

All the studies summarized here have shown that inferences vary with the nature of the text. Text structure, however, is not the only factor that might plausibly affect inferencing: Reading purpose is also a likely candidate. The next section summarizes research on the effects of reading purpose.

EFFECTS OF READING PURPOSE ON LEARNING

Educational psychologists studying reading have generally focused on the reader's purpose for reading. Purpose has been manipulated by either asking questions about the text (e.g., How many moons does each planet have?) or providing explicit goals for reading the text (e.g., Learn the number of moons each planet has.). Much of this research has been stimulated by Rothkopf's concept of "mathemagenic activity" (Rothkopf, 1970). The basic idea is that what readers learn from a text depends on the way in which they processed the text during reading.

Anderson and Biddle (1975) in their survey found that asking questions before a text was read improved later memory for the answers to the identical questions but was detrimental to other information in the text, even when it was the same kind as that being queried. However, asking the question after the text was read improved memory for both the exact information questioned and for other similar information. Subjects thus adapted their reading of the text to accent the kinds of information contained in the questions.

Stating explicit study goals before a text is read has also been used to manipulate reading purpose. Both direct and indirect facilitatory effects of providing study goals have been found on later memory tests for the kinds of information specified in the goals (Frase, 1972, 1975; Rothkopf & Kaplan, 1972). The more specific the goals, the bigger the effect. Of particular interest are the indirect effects found by Frase (1972, 1975). He found that the parts of the text that the subjects would have to process to attain the reading objective were also the parts that were facilitated by the objective.

These educational psychology studies are quite different from text-understanding research in cognitive psychology. The educational psychologists have focused on adjunct learning aids like questions and statements of objectives, whereas the cognitive psychologists have focused on the effects of variations in the text. The cognitive psychologists have concentrated on inferences made during reading and gist memory for what was read, whereas the educational psychologists have concentrated on verbatim memory for low-level details. There is, however, a line of research that has concentrated on verbatim memory and the effects of the kinds of processing subjects do on their later verbatim memory for what they processed. This research falls under the general rubric of "levels of processing."

PROCESSING LEVEL AND MEMORY

There is now substantial evidence showing that "deeper" processing of words yields better memory than "shallow" processing. For example, Craik and Tulving (1975) found that when subjects searched a list of words for one that rhymed with a criterion word, the scanned words were remembered better than if the target was defined as a word in capital letters. Even better memory was obtained if the target word was required to complete a particular sentence. The more "meaningful" the processing, the better the memory.

Thus, both the "mathemagenic activity" research in educational psychology and the "levels of processing" research in cognitive psychology have shown that the purpose for processing information affects later memory for that information. However, the types of purpose used are only a small group from the potential set and more sophisticated purposes are possible.

READING PURPOSE AND INFERENCES

Frederiksen (1975) reported an experiment that compared a sophisticated reading purpose with reading for memory and examined later memory for both stated information and inferences. Subjects read a text describing the characteristics of an imaginary island. Frederiksen used instructions to vary the reading purpose and then examined free recall of the text for reproduction of text statements and intrusion of inferences. One group of subjects read the passage for a later memory test; another group read the passage to propose a solution for the political problem posed in the text.

Frederiksen's results showed that readers' inferential processing, as measured by later false memories, was altered by instructions varying the reading purpose. The experiment reported here also demonstrates an effect of reading purpose on inferences, but it extends Frederiksen's results in several ways. It used a recognition test instead of recall to provide more potential observations of false memories for inferences, texts that included a variety of relations other than the set relations on which Frederiksen focused, a more extensive classification of inferences, and a different set of reading purposes. One group read the texts to evaluate how understandable they were; another group read them in preparation for a memory test; and a third group read them in order to write an essay that would apply each text's main point to an issue related to it.

Inference Classification

To create a classification of inferences, I picked three distinctions that had been previously found useful and seemed likely to distinguish the different reading purposes used in the memory experiment: (1) whether the inference was derivable using only word meanings and the deductive rules of logic (derived inferences) or using knowledge about the real world (elaborative inferences; e.g., Brewer, 1977); (2) whether the related information stated in the text was located together (local inferences) or separately (global inferences; Frase, 1975); and (3) whether making the inference required a few steps or many (Bower et al., 1979).

I illustrate these distinctions using some simple examples, before citing actual inference items used in the experiments. If

> John is taller than Bill and Bill is taller than Steve. In addition, Joe is shorter than Steve and Mark is even shorter than Joe.

then "John is taller than Steve" would be a derived inference of only one step by the transitivity of the relation "taller than." A derived inference of many steps using logical inference rules (transitivity) and word meaning (for taller and shorter) would be "John is taller than Mark." Alternatively, if

> John decided to go to see the doctor. The doctor told him he had the flu and John picked up his medicine on the way out of the office.

then "The doctor prescribed some medicine" is an immediate (i.e., few steps) elaborative inference using real-world knowledge about how patients obtain medicine and follows from the explicit statements in the second sentence of the example. Similarly, the statement "John entered the doctor's office" is an elaborative inference using real-world knowledge about visiting doctor's offices, but inferring it as a link between the two sentences in the example requires several steps.

The criterion I used to classify an inference as local or global is: A local inference had to be deduced from information contained within the same paragraph in the text, whereas a global inference drew upon information separated in the text by at least one paragraph. The Appendix gives as an example one of the texts used in the experiments and Table 20.1 shows some examples of the inferences used.

The first inference example in the table is a global elaborative inference requiring many steps. It is global because the related statements in the text are

> The cognitive aspect is the information-oriented speculative part of the story.

from the second paragraph in the *Science Fiction* text, and

> At least one aspect of a science fiction story is like a computer simulation. Science fiction is the layman's form of computer simulation.

from the last paragraph. The inference is elaborative because it requires knowledge about computers to deduce that the simulation-like aspect of a science fiction story is the cognitive aspect and not the romantic aspect. Combining text information and real-world knowledge to produce the inference item involves several deductive steps.

The last inference example in the table is at the opposite extreme—namely, a locally derived inference requiring only a few steps. The inference is local because the related text information

> In fact, there are two aspects to any story—the romantic aspect and the cognitive aspect.

TABLE 20.1

Given here are examples of the recognition memory-test items for the *Science Fiction* text. The inference items are classified using three dimensions—whether the text statements related to the inferences are close together in the text (local) or far apart (global), whether the inferences can be made using only word meanings and logical inference rules (derived), or whether real-world knowledge must also be invoked (elaborative) and whether the inferences are immediate (take few steps) or involved (take many steps).

A.   Noninference Items
    1.   True
        We might have a science fiction story about a space war.
    2.   False
        The writing style of science fiction writers is generally unsophisticated.
B.   Inference Items
    1.   Global, elaborative, many steps
        The cognitive aspect of a science fiction story is like a computer simulation.
    2.   Global, elaborative, few steps
        The romantic aspect of science fiction keeps the reader's interest, whereas the cognitive aspect predicts the future.
    3.   Global, derived, many steps
        Even the literary establishment has begun to read such authors as Herbert and Niven.
    4.   Global, derived, few steps
        Science fiction is the layman's way of simulating the future.
    5.   Local, elaborative, many steps
        Computer simulation models offer man a way out of his current precarious situation.
    6.   Local, elaborative, few steps
        Science fiction stories that concentrate on the romantic aspect are basically adventure stories.
    7.   Local, derived, many steps
        Because the power that man commands has increased greatly, it is crucial that one be able to figure out the consequences of his actions before he acts.
    8.   Local, derived, few steps
        There are two parts to a science fiction story—the romantic part and the cognitive part.

is in the same paragraph (the second). The inference is derived with few steps because it follows from the minor deduction that if any story has some property, then a specific kind of story must also have that property.

Whether an inference is local or global can be objectively determined by examining the text using my criterion. The derived–elaborative and few–many steps distinctions, however, are more subjective, and subject ratings were therefore collected to validate the intuitive distinction. I gave 42 subjects the two texts and the inference items used on the recognition test in the main experiment reported later. The subjects rated the items on derived–elaborative and few–many steps scales. The subjects' ratings corresponded to my original inference classifications, so it seems justifiable to conclude that the subjects are sensitive to the derived–elaborative and number-of-steps distinctions. Black (1980) gives a detailed report of this preliminary normative study.

READING PURPOSE AND MEMORY EXPERIMENT

In the experiment, the false memories for inferences in addition to stated and totally new items were examined on a recognition test. The false-recognition rate for the inferences was also examined to see if it differed according to the distinctions discussed already. The reading purposes chosen for this experiment were tasks that should have been familiar to the subjects from their academic experiences. They were: (1) rating the comprehensibility of the passages; (2) preparing for a memory test on the passages; and (3) preparing for an essay test that required the use of the main points of the passages. The purposes seemed likely to affect both memory for explicitly stated information and false memory for potentially inferable information.

Method

Subjects

The subjects were 42 volunteer high school students paid for their participation.

Materials

The texts used were two essays. One essay was entitled *Science Fiction* and it gave an argument for the importance of science fiction. This text contained 358 words and the Appendix gives it in its entirety. The other essay was entitled *A New Form of Teaching* and presented an argument for the importance of a particular kind of computer-assisted instruction. This text contained 325 words. A 72-item recognition test was constructed from 24 inference items, 24 trues (i.e., stated in text) and 24 falses (i.e., not stated in text). The 24 inference items for each essay were chosen so that there were three in each of the eight inference categories formed by combining the derived–elaborative, local–global, and few–many steps distinctions. Table 20.1 gives examples of all the types of recognition test items. The trues were actual statements from the text with slight changes in wording. For example, the true item given in Table 20.1 corresponds to the following statement from the text given in the Appendix:

> Hence, for example, we might have a science fiction tale about Earthmen fighting a space war with an alien society.

The falses were statements that might well have been stated in the text but were not; neither were they implied by the text.

Procedure

The subjects were tested in six groups of seven. Each subject was given a booklet containing the two essays, and each group was given different reading instructions as follows.

1. Comprehensibility Ratings. I want you to read and then rate the following two passages on how easy to understand or comprehensible you find them. I want you to use a 1-to-7 scale for the ratings where 1 means obscure and incomprehensible and 7 means very clear and comprehensible. You will have 4 min to complete this task for the two passages.

2. Memory Test. Read these two passages carefully, for I shall test your memory for exactly what is stated later in this experiment. You will have 4 mins to read the two passages.

3. Essay Test. Read each of these two passages carefully trying to get the author's main point. Later I shall ask you to apply the main point of each of these two passages to a related issue. The test will be two short-answer essay questions (one for each passage), where you will have to give not only your answers but also your reasons for making them. You will have 4 min to read the two passages.

After spending 4 min reading the two essays, the subjects spent 20 min on an intervening task. The intervening task involved ordering story statements according to their importance. The materials were unrelated to the two essays. The subjects were then given a booklet containing the recognition-test items for each essay (blocked by essay title) and wrote their confidence ratings by the items in the booklets. The ratings were on a 1-to-7 scale where 1 meant "certain the item had not been read before" and 7 meant "certain that it had been read before." Everyone completed the recognition test in the 20 min allotted.

Results

The recognition-memory confidence ratings for the inference items varied with the reading-purpose instructions. Table 20.2 gives the overall results for the inference, true and false test items. The memory-test instruction subjects were the most confident that they had read the inferences in the text (4.75), the essay-test group was somewhat less confident (4.37), and the comprehension-rating subjects were much less confident (3.89). The overall difference between the three groups is significant, $F'(2, 31) = 16.7$, $p < .001$, with the essay-test group significantly higher than the ratings group, $F'(1, 28) = 8.2$, $p < .01$, and with the memory-test group significantly higher than the essay-test group, $F'(1,$

TABLE 20.2
Mean Recognition-Test Confidence Ratings for True, False, and
Inference Items in the Memory Experiment. A Rating of 1 Means Certain
Did Not Read Statement in Text and a Rating of 7 Means Certain
Did Read Statement

Reading Purpose	True Items	False Items	Inference Items
Rating comprehensibility	4.51	3.30	3.89
Memory test	4.74	3.83	4.75
Essay test	4.55	3.35	4.37
Mean	4.60	3.49	4.34

25) $= 4.75$, $p < .05$. [The statistical test used throughout is the *quasi-F* (F')—appropriate for considering both subjects and inferences as random effects.]

Table 20.2 also gives the inference ratings for the true and false items. The trues received higher confidence ratings than the inferences, $F'(1, 27) = 4.5$, $p < .05$, and the inferences received higher ratings than the falses, $F'(1, 28) = 21.6$, $p < .01$. There was a significant interaction between the true-inference contrast and the reading-purpose instructions, $F'(2, 26) = 10.2$, $p < .01$, due to the true and inference items receiving the same rating in the memory-test group. Although the interaction between the true–false contrast and the reading-purpose was not significant, $F'(2, 29) = 2.12$, $p > .05$, the true–false difference was less for the memory-test group than for the other two groups. The higher rating for the false items in the memory-test group poses a problem for evaluating differences in inference item ratings between the instruction groups. Therefore, all the ratings were converted for the inferences into an adjusted ratio score (R) that equaled $(I - F)/(T - F)$, where I is the inference ratings, F is the false rating, and T is the true rating. For example, the overall R for the comprehensibility-rating group was .49; for the memory-test group, 1.02; and for the essay-test group, .85. Because the adjusted inference scores gave the same pattern of results as the unadjusted scores, only the results of the unadjusted confidence ratings are reported.

Table 20.3 gives the results for the local–global inference distinction. Global inferences received a higher confidence rating than the local ones, $F'(1, 26) = 6.8$, $p < .01$, but there was also an interaction with reading purpose, $F'(2, 30) = 3.5$, $p < .05$. The interaction occurred because the comprehensibility-rating group showed no local–global difference, unlike the other two conditions.

The recognition ratings for the few-step inferences (4.45) was not significantly different from the ratings of the many-step inferences (4.23), $F'(1, 22) = 1.7$, $p > .05$. The interaction between number of steps and reading purpose was also not significant, $F'(2, 24) = 1.2$, $p > .05$.

TABLE 20.3
Mean Recognition-Test Confidence Ratings for Local–Global and
Derived–Elaborative Inference Distinctions in the Memory Experiment.
A Rating of 1 Means Certain Did Not Read Statement in Text and
a Rating of 7 means Certain Did Read Statement

Reading Purpose	Local Inferences	Global Inferences	Derived Inferences	Elaborative Inferences
Rating comprehensibility	3.89	3.89	4.53	3.25
Memory test	4.30	5.20	4.81	4.70
Essay test	4.04	4.70	4.51	4.23
Mean	4.08	4.60	4.62	4.06

Table 20.3 also gives the results for the derived–elaborative inference distinction. The derived inferences received a higher confidence rating than the elaborative inferences, $F'(1, 29) = 12.1$, $p < .01$, but there was also an interaction with reading purpose, $F'(2, 25) = 7.4$, $p < .01$. The interaction occurred because most of the derived superiority was due to the comprehensibility-rating condition.

DISCUSSION

The experiment has shown that although there was little difference overall between the reading-purpose conditions on the true (old) and false (totally new) items contained in the recognition test, there were inference differences. Specifically, the memory-test condition showed the highest false-recognition rate on the inference items and the comprehensibility-rating condition showed the lowest, and the essay-test condition was intermediate between the two extremes (but closer to the memory-test condition). Thus, the "deeper" tasks did not lead to better memory for the stated information in the text, but they did show more inferences than the "shallow" task. However, contrary to expectation, the memory-test condition showed more inferences than the essay-test condition.

The recognition-test results for the inference items were also affected by the local–global and the derived–elaborative inference distinctions, but the few-many inferential steps distinction had no effect. In particular, the comprehensibility-rating condition gave equal recognition confidence ratings to local and global inferences, but the memory-test and essay-test conditions gave higher ratings to the global inferences. Also the comprehensibility-rating condition gave higher confidence ratings to derived than elaborative inferences, whereas the memory-test and essay-test conditions gave them essentially equal ratings. These specific inference results were consistent with the memory-test and essay-test conditions as "deeper" tasks than the comprehensibility-rating condition. Specifically, the memory-test and essay-test conditions exhibited more elaborative and global inferences than the comprehensibility-rating condition. The elaborative–global inference bias is what one would expect from "deeper" processing.

Although it was encouraging to find inference differences in the three reading-purpose conditions, it was disappointing that the memory-test condition showed more inferences of all kinds than the essay-test condition. Perhaps the appropriate conclusion here is not so much that memory tests always elicit more inferences but that this experiment only tested the kinds of inferences favoring the memory-test condition.

In an effort to discover distinguishing characteristics of the essay-test condition, a post hoc analysis was performed on the recognition-test results. I examined the recognition confidence ratings for each item for which the essay-test condition gave significantly higher recognition ratings than the memory-test group. A criterion of at least one point superiority for the essay test (on a 7-point scale) was met by 11 of the 72 recognition items for the *Science Fiction* essay and 8 of the 72 items for the *New Form of Teaching* essay. The items were trues, various kinds of inferences, and falses. Each item related to the main point of its essay, and *all* the recognition test items that related to the main points of the essays were included in the sets.

For example, intuitively the main point of the *Science Fiction* essay is that science fiction can be used to predict the future in the same way that computer simulation can. All the essay-test superiority items for this essay were related to some aspect of this main point. For instance, the first inference item example in Table 20.1 was one of the essay-superiority items: Its mean recognition rating was 3.50 in the comprehensibility condition, 4.00 in the memory condition, and 5.36 in the essay condition. The item directly states the comparison that is the main point of the essay—namely, that the cognitive aspect of a science fiction story is like a computer simulation. Thus it appears that the essay-test subjects focused on the main point of the passage, as their reading-purpose instructions directed but that the inference classification scheme used was not sensitive to this main-point-oriented processing.

Kintsch and van Dijk (1978) and Schank and Abelson (1977) have made a distinction between microstructure and macrostructure in the memory representation for a text. The distinction provides a framework for interpreting these results. The microstructure of a text is the set of propositions in the text together with their pairwise conceptual connections and the implicit propositions inferred to establish those connections. The macrostructure, on the other hand, is a high-level schematic structure that represents the overall structure of the text (e.g., the standard sections in a scientific research report). Intermediate between the two extremes are macropropositions derived by applying generalization rules to the microstructure. In the present case, the text propositions together with the few-steps, derived, and local inferences would form the microstructure; and the many-steps, elaborative, and global inferences would be the intermediate level. However, the macrostructure level was not explicitly examined in the recognition-test distinctions used. What is the macrostructure for these texts? Both texts compare and contrast two concepts. The *Science Fiction* passage compares science fiction with computer simulation and notes their similarities, whereas the *New Form of Teaching* passage contrasts passive and active interaction with computers. Compare-and-contrast is a common expository method (Brooks & Warren, 1972), so it seems to be a good candidate for a macrostructure or text schema.

Now we can use this memory-representation-level framework to interpret the reading-purpose instructions used in the experiment. The subjects reading the texts under the comprehensibility-rating instructions would merely construct a microstructure in memory and evaluate how hard it would be to construct macropropositions and apply a macrostructure. In contrast, the memory-test subjects would devote their processing resources to constructing all three levels of the memory representation. The essay-test subjects, on the other hand, would concentrate most of their processing resources at the macrostructure level. The results of the experiment were consistent with these interpretations of the instructions. In particular, the comprehensibility-rating condition exhibited less global and elaborative inferences than did the other two conditions; that is, the comprehensibility-rating subjects exhibited the microstructure but not the other two memory-representation levels. The memory-test and the essay-test conditions exhibited the global and elaborative inferences associated with the macroproposition level (although less than the memory-test condition), but the essay-test condition gave the highest recognition ratings to the main-point or macrostructure items that emerged in the post hoc analysis.

CONCLUSIONS

The experiment reported here showed that the inferences people make while reading a text are affected by the purpose for which the text is read. The results indicate that any text-understanding theory is incomplete if it specifies a fixed set of inferences to be made as part of understanding a text or if it fails to account for the inferential processing that varies with the reading purpose. This research is an initial demonstration that such variation does occur. Further research is needed to discover specific relationships between reading-purpose and inferential processing. For example, the kinds of reading-purpose instructions that give priority to each of the different memory representation levels and the instructions that accent different kinds of inferred relations within each level—for example, stress causal or referential connections. Reading purpose was shown here to affect later false memory for inferences, but the interpretation of the results predicts that there should be similar effects on reading time. Further research is needed to test this prediction as part of the fruitful exploration of the specific relationships between reading purpose and the inferences made during reading.

ACKNOWLEDGEMENTS

I thank Ernst Rothkopf for his assistance with this research and Philip Barnard for his comments on a previous version of the manuscript. The writing of this chapter was supported by a grant from the Sloan Foundation. The research was conducted during a summer the author spent as a visiting staff member of the Learning and Instruction Research Group, Bell Laboratories, Murray Hill, N.J., U.S.A. Reprints may be obtained from John B. Black, Yale University, Department of Psychology, Box 11A Yale Station, New Haven, Conn. 06520, U.S.A.

APPENDIX

Example of texts used in the experiments.

Science Fiction

In today's complicated world, everything seems to be becoming interconnected with everything else. At the same time, the power that man commands has increased greatly. These factors put mankind in a precarious situation. Thus it is crucial that one be able to figure out the consequences of his/her actions before acting. Computer simulation models have been developed that enable one to combine known information and best guesses in order to predict the future. One way of predicting the future is to create possible worlds and then turn them loose to function for awhile to see what will happen.

It is interesting that at this time a new literary form is coming to the fore. Science fiction's influence has been increasing. More and more people are reading it, and even the literary establishment has begun to read it. Obviously the name *science fiction* has two parts—namely, *science* and *fiction*. In fact, there are two aspects to any story—the romantic aspect and the cognitive aspect. The romantic aspect is the human interest- and action-oriented parts of the story; whereas, the cognitive aspect is the information-oriented speculative part of the story. Hence, for example, we might have a science fiction tale about Earthmen fighting a space war with an alien society. The first aspect of it would be the descriptions of the battles and the love life of the hero; whereas, the second aspect of it would be the descriptions of the future societies, future weapons, and the aliens themselves.

Science fiction stories differ greatly in the relative weightings they give to these two aspects. Herbert's *Dune,* for example, is almost entirely an adventure story. Herbert's stories always concentrate on the romantic aspect. In contrast, Niven's *Ringworld* concentrates on the cognitive aspect. Niven is often refered to as a "hard science" science fiction writer.

At least one aspect of a science fiction story is like a computer simulation. Science fiction is the layman's form of computer simulation. Science fiction's emergence into the limelight at this point in history is an encouraging sign. It almost seems as though people know what they need to be reading.

REFERENCES

Anderson, J. R., & Bower, G. H. *Human associative memory.* Washington, D.C.: V. H. Winston, 1973.

Anderson, R. C., & Biddle, W. B. On asking people questions about what they are reading. In G. H. Bower (Ed.), *The psychology of learning and motivation* (Vol. 9). New York: Academic Press, 1975.

Black, J. B. The effects of reading purpose on memory for text. *Cognitive Science Technical Report,* No. 7, Yale University, 1980.

Black, J. B., & Bern, H. Causal coherence and memory for events in narratives. *Journal of Verbal Learning and Verbal Behavior,* in press.

Bower, G. H., Black, J. B., & Turner, T. J. Scripts in memory for text. *Cognitive Psychology,* 1979, *11,* 177-220.

Bransford, J. D., Barclay, J. R., & Franks, J. J. Sentence memory: A constructive versus interpretive approach. *Cognitive Psychology,* 1972, *3,* 193-209.

Brewer, W. F. Memory for the pragmatic implications of sentences. *Memory & Cognition,* 1977, *5,* 673-678.

Brooks, C., & Warren, R. P. *Modern rhetoric.* New York: Harcourt, Brace & Jovanovich, 1972.

Craik, F. I. M., & Tulving, E. Depth of processing and the retention of words in episodic memory. *Journal of Experimental Psychology: General,* 1975, *104,* 268-294.

de Villiers, P. A. Imagery and theme in recall of connected discourse. *Journal of Experimental Psychology,* 1974, *103,* 263-268.

Frase, L. T. Maintenance and control in the acquisition of knowledge from written materials. In R. O. Freedle & J. B. Carroll (Eds.), *Language comprehension and the acquisition of knowledge.* Washington, D.C.: V. H. Winston, 1972.

Frase, L. T. Prose processing. In G. H. Bower (Ed.), *The psychology of learning and motivation* (Vol. 9). New York: Academic Press, 1975.

Frederiksen, C. H. Effects of context-induced processing operations on semantic information acquired from discourse. *Cognitive Psychology,* 1975, *7,* 371-458.

Haberlandt, K., & Bingham, G. Verbs contribute to the coherence of brief narratives: Reading related and unrelated sentence triples. *Journal of Verbal Learning and Verbal Behavior,* 1978, *17,* 419-425.

Haviland, S. E., & Clark, H. H. What's new? Acquiring new information as a process in comprehension. *Journal of Verbal Learning and Verbal Behavior,* 1974, *13,* 512-521.

Johnson, M. K., Bransford, J. D., & Solomon, S. Memory for tacit implications of sentences. *Journal of Experimental Psychology,* 1973, *98,* 203-205.

Kintsch, W., & van Dijk, T. A. Toward a model of text comprehension and production. *Psychological Review,* 1978, *85,* 363-394.

Rothkopf, E. Z. The concept of mathemagenic activities. *Review of Educational Research*, 1970, *40*, 325-336.

Rothkopf, E. Z., & Kaplan, R. Exploration of the effects of density and specificity of instructional objectives on learning from text. *Journal of Educational Psychology*, 1972, *63*, 295-302.

Schank, R. C., & Abelson, R. P. *Scripts, plans, goals, and understanding*. Hillsdale, N.J.: Lawrence Erlbaum Associates, 1977.

21 Event Schemas, Story Schemas, and Story Grammars

William F. Brewer and Edward H. Lichtenstein
Center for the Study of Reading and Department of Psychology
University of Illinois at Urbana-Champaign, Illinois
U.S.A.

ABSTRACT

The present chapter investigates aspects of an individual's story schema. A theory is proposed relating structural characteristics of narratives to the reader's affective response and to the reader's intuitions about what constitutes a story. Two levels of narrative structure are distinguished: the event structure (the chronological sequence of events) and the discourse structure (the order in which events are presented in the narrative). An experiment was carried out to examine predictions of the story theory. Subjects read differently organized versions of the same event structures (i.e., different discourse structures), rated them for suspense and surprise at four points in the passages, and made judgments about the extent to which the narratives were stories. As predicted by the theory: (1) Different discourse arrangements of the same event structures produced different patterns of affective response. (2) Discourse structures that produced suspense and resolution, or surprise and resolution, were judged to be stories, whereas narratives that did not show these affective patterns were not judged to be stories. The results suggested a reinterpretation of the story grammar literature.

INTRODUCTION

The present study investigates narrative discourse, where narrative is used in a broad sense, to include any discourse that embodies a coherent series of temporal events. In particular, we have attempted to provide an account of the psychological processes that allow individuals to distinguish between narratives that are stories and those that are not; that is, we examined some fundamental aspects of an individual's schema for stories.

STORY GRAMMARS

Most of the recent work on narrative has involved a class of theoretical structures known as story grammars (Mandler & Johnson, 1977; Rumelhart, 1975; Stein & Glenn, 1979; Thorndyke, 1977). These grammars attempt to provide a theoretical account of the structure that causes one sample of discourse to be a coherent story, whereas another arrangement of the same sentences is not a coherent story. Although particular story grammars differ in detail, they all postulate a set of categories that must be included in a story and provide rules that specify the relations between the categories. A fundamental category that is included in all the story grammars is one that accounts for a character's actions in terms of the character's goals and the subgoals necessary to satisfy these goals.

There have been a large number of experiments studying the use of story grammars in the memory and comprehension of text. The story grammars have been able to account for a variety of empirical findings: Text that can be derived from a story grammar is more comprehensible than reoganizations of the text that cannot be derived from a story grammar (Thorndyke, 1977). Information higher in the hierarchical structure is better recalled than information lower in the hierarchy (Thorndyke, 1977) and is more likely to be included in a summary of the story (Rumelhart, 1977). The temporal order of information in text that is consistent with the structure of a story grammar is often better retained than is the order information for text that is not arranged in this fashion (Mandler, 1978; Thorndyke, 1977; Stein & Nezworski, 1978). Overall, these results have been taken to support the position that the structural relations represented in story grammars are used to understand and remember stories.

However, the results of a recent series of experiments by Lichtenstein and Brewer (1980) suggest a reinterpretation of the story grammar work. In that paper we examined subjects' memory for videotaped goal-directed events and for narrative descriptions of these same events. The results supported the hypothesis that, in both cases, the information was interpreted and encoded in terms of a plan schema, the subjects' nonlinguistic knowledge of the structure of goal-directed events. Because our results for *both* observed events and for narratives were similar to the results found in the story grammar experiments, we suggested that most of the findings in the story grammar experiments may not have been due to the structural knowledge that readers have about *stories* but to the fact that the subjects were using their nonlinguistic knowledge of events to organize and recall the event information contained in the narratives.

SCHEMAS FOR STORIES

Although the results of the Lichtenstein and Brewer (1980) study were consistent with those found in the story grammar experiments, it seemed to us that the narratives used in our study (e.g., a dull description of someone setting up a projector) were *not* stories (cf. Black & Wilensky, 1979, for a similar argument). But this reinterpretation of the story grammar literature leads to an interesting problem. If story grammars turn out to be predominantly theories of schemas for the description of events (i.e., narratives), then what are stories? The purpose of this chapter is to investigate the properties of the story schema (the knowledge about the structure of stories that underlies an individual's intuitions about what a story is).

It seems to us that what is missing from the structures provided by event and plan schemas are constructs relating to the emotive effects of stories—the conflict, the suspense (Morgan & Sellner, 1980). The discourse force of stories is to entertain the reader by arousing certain affective states—not simply to transmit information about sequences of events (Brewer, 1980). What we need is a structural theory of stories, one in which the structures are related to the affective states produced in the reader.

In order to develop a theory of stories, it is necessary to make a theoretical distinction between the two levels in narrative—the underlying events and the linguistic presentation of those events in the narrative. This distinction has been a traditional one for those scholars in the humanities who take a structural approach to literature (Chatman, 1978; Erlich, 1980). We refer to these two levels as the *event structure* and the *discourse structure*. In the event structure, events are organized in their temporal sequence in some presumed event world. At this level of analysis, one's understanding of events and of characters' actions might be structured by means of event or plan schemas. In the discourse structure, events are organized in terms of their order of occurrence in the discourse. This distinction between the event and discourse structures provides advantages in theorizing about narratives that is analogous to the advantages that the distinction between abstract structure and surface structure provides for sentences.

When an author is writing a narrative, the resources of the language (tense, adverbs, etc.) and of literary convention (flashbacks, flashforwards, point of view, etc.) make it possible to take the information from the event level and place it in the discourse level in virtually any order desired. However, certain orderings of events in the discourse tend to produce particular affective outcomes (Sternberg, 1978). For example, consider the following *event structure:* (1) BUTLER PUTS POISON IN WINE (2) BUTLER CARRIES WINE TO LORD HIGGINBOTHAM (3) LORD HIGGINBOTHAM DRINKS WINE (4) LORD HIGGINBOTHAM DIES. If an event structure contains an initiating event with a potentially significant outcome, ordering these events in the discourse structure in the same order in which they occur in the event structure will produce suspense. The suspense is created when the reader becomes concerned about the outcome of the events set into motion by the initiating event. Thus, a *discourse structure* designed to produce suspense from this event sequence would be: (1) *The butler put poison in the wine.* (2) *The butler carried the wine to Lord Higginbotham.* (3) *Lord Higginbotham drank the wine.*

The creation of surprise requires a different relationship between the discourse organization and event organization. In order to produce surprise in the reader, the author omits a significant underlying event or expository information from the discourse without letting the reader know that something has been omitted. Then, when something occurs that is a consequence of the missing information, the reader will not have been anticipating it and will be surprised. Thus, a discourse order designed to produce surprise would be: (2) *The butler carried the wine to Lord Higginbotham.* (3) *Lord Higginbotham drank the wine.* (4) *Lord Higginbotham fell over dead.*

The creation of curiosity involves yet a different relation between discourse structure and event structure. In order to produce curiosity in the reader, the author leaves some significant event out of the discourse, but lets the reader know that the information is missing, thus causing the reader to become curious about the omitted events. A discourse structure designed to produce curiosity would be: (4) *Lord Higginbotham fell over dead.* Given only event 4, the reader should be curious about what caused Lord Higginbotham's death; if he was murdered, the reader should be curious about who did it and how; in other words, the reader should be curious about events 1, 2, and 3.

The techniques just discussed all lead to the arousal of affective states in the reader. There are also a number of techniques for reducing these affective states. Resolution of suspense is accomplished by providing the reader with the outcome of the series of events about which the reader has been concerned. Resolution of surprise consists of the reader's reinterpretation of the preceding events in light of the surprising information that had been withheld until that point. Resolution of curiosity consists of providing the reader with information about the earlier events that the reader knows has been withheld.

By using the distinction between the event structure and the discourse structure, it is possible to develop a structural theory of stories that incorporates the affective characteristics that are not accounted for in story grammars. We propose that a story is a narrative in which information about events has been organized in the discourse structure to produce suspense and resolution, surprise and resolution, or curiosity and resolution. To produce suspense, the event structure must contain an initiating event with a potentially significant outcome. A significant outcome is an outcome with important consequences (good or bad) for one or more characters in the narrative.

In the earlier discussion of the discourse organization for suspense stories, we suggested that keeping the discourse order consistent with the underlying event order was an effective way to produce suspense, because this arrangement keeps the reader concerned about the eventual outcome of the event sequence. However, it should also be possible to alter this basic suspense organization in ways that either increase or decrease suspense. Thus, in "foreshadowing," information about a later event is given early in the discourse to increase the reader's concern for the character or to increase the significance of the outcome. On the other hand, if information is given early in the discourse about the eventual outcome of the significant event sequence, this should serve to reduce suspense.

The purpose of the experiment reported in this chapter is to examine some of the predictions of this theory with respect to suspense and surprise. (The predictions relating to curiosity will not be investigated here.) In particular, we test the following hypotheses:

1. Narratives without significant events will not produce suspense.
2. Narratives (containing an initiating event with a significant outcome) organized so that the discourse order matches the event order will produce suspense.
3. Suspense narratives in which the discourse order matches the event order will show a sharp drop in suspense (resolution) at the point in the discourse where information about the outcome is given.
4. Narratives organized to produce suspense and resolution will be stories.
5. Narratives organized so as to produce suspense without resolution will not be stories.
6. Suspense structures modified to give information about the significant outcome early in the discourse will show no suspense.
7. Suspense structures modified to give information about the significant outcome early in the discourse will not be stories.
8. Suspense structures with foreshadowing of significant later events will show heightened suspense.
9. Narrative structures in which an initiating event with a significant outcome is withheld from the discourse structure will produce surprise in the reader, when the outcome of the event occurs in the discourse.
10. Narrative structures organized so as to produce surprise and resolution will be stories.

In order to test these hypotheses, we selected three event sequences of quite different content and then organized these event sequences in ways designed to produce discourse structures with the characteristics needed to test the theory. Next we obtained ratings on the affect produced at various stages in the reading of the narratives to see if these ratings were as predicted by the theory. Finally, we obtained a series of judgments on the structural properties of the narratives, to see if the affective ratings would predict which narratives were judged to be stories.

Method

Materials

Three event structures of different content were developed, and each was organized into a set of six different discourse structures. For each discourse structure a narrative was written that was about two pages long, divided into four segments of about one-third to three-fourths page each. Each segment was printed on a separate page.

Base Narrative.   The base version of each of the three different event structures consisted of a description of a character pursuing some rather routine plans. *The Trip Home* described a man driving home from work, coping with several minor mechanical obstacles. *A Day at the Beach* described a man letting his mind wander as he relaxed on a Hawaiian beach. *The Gardener* described a poor gardener raking up and burning leaves in the yard around a mansion. In all these narratives, some characterization was built in by letting the reader learn something of the character's thoughts, feelings, and background. By the end of the narratives, the characters achieved their goals or finished their plans: The man driving home arrived there; the sunbather walked back to his hotel; and the gardener finished his yard work and drove home.

In the other discourse versions of each narrative, an initiating event and an outcome event were inserted into the event structure. The initiating event was chosen so that the outcome was likely to have significance for the character. Initiating events: In *The Trip Home* a bomb with a 10-min timer was activated in the car as the driver got in; in *A Day at the Beach* an underwater earthquake set off a tidal wave heading for the island; and in *The Gardener* a car speeding past the mansion dumped a litter bag containing a sweepstakes ticket worth $100,000 onto the yard. Outcomes: As the driver closed his house door, the bomb in his car exploded outside; the tidal wave hit the beach, but the character was just out of reach; and the gardener found the ticket.

Suspense Standard.   In this condition, information about all the events in the event structure was given in chronological order in the discourse structure. The initiating event was described on the first page of the narrative and the outcome described on the fourth page.

The other three suspense versions also contained the initiating event on the first page, with the following additions or modifications:

Suspense Foreshadowing.   The events were ordered as just described, except that information concerning a later event, designed to increase concern about the outcome, was also placed on the first page. Thus, readers were forewarned that the car with the bomb would soon be traveling down a dangerous pothole-filled road, that the sunbather would not see the tidal wave coming until it hit the shore, and that the owner of the mansion would come out and notice the cardboard ticket on the lawn.

Suspense Misarranged.   Information concerning the eventual outcome was described on the first page. Readers were told that, because the driver would take the shortcut home, he would be safely inside his home before the bomb exploded; that the sunbather would be safe halfway up a cliff behind the beach when the tidal wave arrived; and that a gust of wind would save the sweepstakes ticket from the fire, so that the gardener would become rich.

In the above three suspense conditions, pages 2 through 4 were identical.

Suspense No Resolution.   This version was exactly like the suspense-standard version except that page 4, which contained the outcome, was omitted.

Surprise.   The initiating event was omitted from page 1. Thus, the passage was exactly like the base narrative for pages 1 to 3. On page 4, the outcome occurred exactly as in the suspense conditions, followed by a description of the omitted initiating event (as described on the first page of the suspense conditions).

Following each segment of each narrative were 7-point rating scales for suspense and surprise. The suspense scale asked the subjects to indicate "to what extent are you now in *Suspense* (concerned about what *will* happen or about the outcome)?" The surprise scale asked the subjects to indicate "in the portion *just read,* to what extent were you *Surprised* by any events or information in the passage?"

At the end of each narrative, there was a page of 7-point rating scales measuring: (1) overall liking; (2) the extent to which the passage was, or was not, a "story" (with scale value 3 defined as "barely a story"); (3) satisfaction with the outcome; (4) how complete the passage seemed; (5) how effectively the information was arranged.

The suspense-standard discourse version of *The Trip Home* is given in the Appendix.

Procedure

Subjects were run individually and in groups. Each subject was given a booklet consisting of an instruction sheet and from 2 to 11 narratives, depending on the time available. The booklets included *from 1 to 3* of the narratives from the present study, along with other passages of similar format from another study. No subject read more than one version from the same content set. Subjects receiving more than one passage from this study did not receive more than one with the same discourse organization (e.g., no more than one suspense foreshadowing). The order of the passages in each booklet was random.

Subjects read the instructions and worked through the booklets at their own pace.

Subjects

The subjects were 103 undergraduates at the University of Illinois. Twenty subjects read each narrative version. For each version, 10 of the subjects were participants from Introductory Psychology or Educational Psychology classes, and 10 were paid undergraduate subjects.

Results

Affective Ratings during Reading

The results on the affective ratings for the six different discourse structures for each of the three event structures are given in Fig. 21.1, 21.2, and 21.3. All predictions were tested with one-tailed t-tests, $p < .05$ unless otherwise noted.

Suspense. The base narratives were lower on the suspense ratings than any of the narratives organized in terms of the theory to produce suspense. For all three content versions, the suspense-standard narratives were significantly higher than their corresponding base narratives on the suspense ratings (averaged across segments 1, 2, and 3). There was also a dramatic drop in the suspense ratings for the suspense-standard narratives on the segment in which the resolution occurred for all three content versions (segment 3 compared to segment 4, $p < .001$). The curves for the suspense-foreshadowing narratives were not significantly different from the corresponding suspense-standard curves. The suspense-misarranged narratives showed significantly lower suspense ratings than the suspense-standard narratives for two of the three content versions (*The Trip Home* not significant) but significantly higher suspense ratings than the base narratives for two of the three content versions (*The Gardener* not significant).

Surprise. For all three content versions, the surprise narratives were not significantly different from the base narratives on the surprise ratings for the average of the first three segments but were significantly higher for the last segment ($p < .001$).

On the whole, the results of the affect rating task supported the theoretical relationships between the major discourse structures and affect. The next section of the results reports the data on the structural judgments to see if they are related to the shapes of the affective curves as predicted by the theory.

Structural Judgments

The mean structural ratings for the different discourse organizations for each content passage are given in Table 21.1. Question 2 was specifically designed to obtain subjects' intuitions about the degree to which a given passage was or was not a "story." For each of the three content versions the base narratives received lower story ratings than any other discourse structure. The means of the base narratives for each of the three content versions was below 3.0 on the story rating scale, where 3.0 had been defined as "barely a story." The means for the suspense-standard narratives on the story ratings were all above 3.0, and they were significantly higher than the corresponding base narratives for all three content versions ($p < .001$). The suspense-no-resolution narratives were significantly below the corresponding suspense-standard narratives on the story ratings for all three content versions, and two of the three content versions were below 3.0 on the story rating scale (the mean for *The Gardener* passage was 3.2). The suspense-no-resolution narratives showed the lowest scores on the completeness

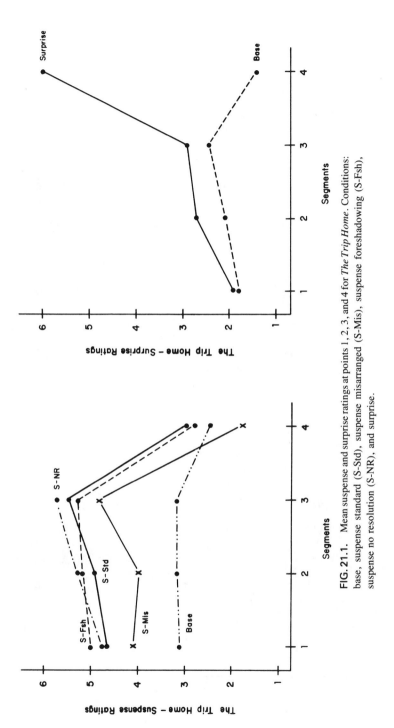

FIG. 21.1. Mean suspense and surprise ratings at points 1, 2, 3, and 4 for *The Trip Home*. Conditions: base, suspense standard (S-Std), suspense misarranged (S-Mis), suspense foreshadowing (S-Fsh), suspense no resolution (S-NR), and surprise.

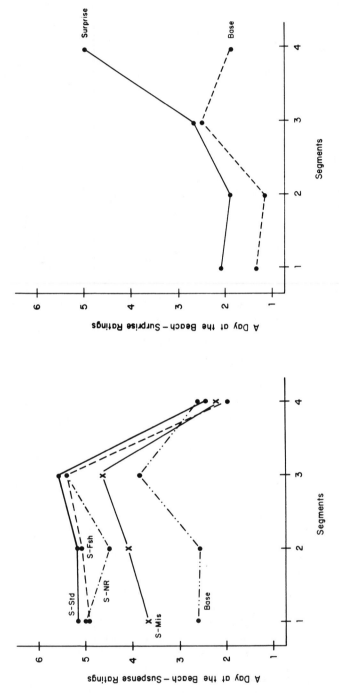

FIG. 21.2. Mean suspense and surprise ratings at points 1, 2, 3, and 4 for *A Day at the Beach*.

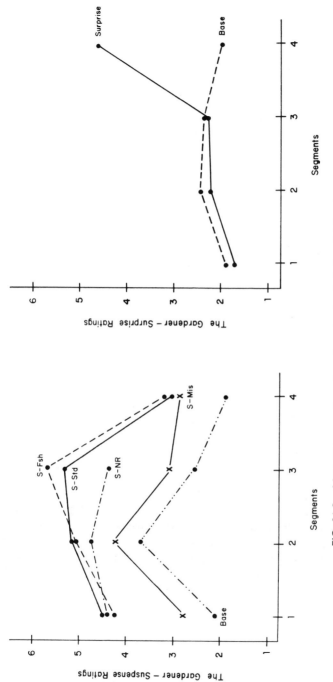

FIG. 21.3.   Mean suspense and surprise ratings at points 1, 2, 3, and 4 for *The Gardener*.

TABLE 21.1
Mean Structural Judgments for the Narratives

The Trip Home

Rating Scales	Base Narrative	Suspense Standard	Suspense Misarranged	Suspense Foreshadowing	Suspense No Resolution	Surprise Narrative
Liking	2.15	4.85	3.65	4.30	3.85	4.30
Story rating	2.45	5.05	4.50	4.45	2.75	4.30
Outcome	2.15	4.90	3.90	4.55	1.60	3.95
Completeness	2.75	4.90	4.95	5.15	1.25	4.35
Arrangement	4.35	5.45	3.10	4.75	5.05	4.25

A Day at the Beach

Rating Scales	Base Narrative	Suspense Standard	Suspense Misarranged	Suspense Foreshadowing	Suspense No Resolution	Surprise Narrative
Liking	3.25	4.50	3.95	4.25	3.50	3.75
Story rating	2.35	4.90	4.25	5.00	2.60	3.90
Outcome	2.10	4.25	3.40	4.25	1.55	3.20
Completeness	2.75	4.65	4.90	4.90	1.30	3.40
Arrangement	4.30	5.05	2.95	5.40	4.75	4.85

The Gardener

Rating Scales	Base Narrative	Suspense Standard	Suspense Misarranged	Suspense Foreshadowing	Suspense No Resolution	Surprise Narrative
Liking	2.40	4.75	3.15	4.45	3.45	4.40
Story rating	2.90	5.10	4.35	5.20	3.20	4.70
Outcome	2.10	5.30	3.75	5.00	1.80	4.25
Completeness	3.40	4.85	4.35	5.10	2.55	4.80
Arrangement	4.20	5.50	2.15	4.95	4.85	5.40

scale for any discourse structure and were significantly lower than those for the suspense-standard narratives for each of the three content versions.

The suspense-misarranged narratives showed significantly lower ratings on the arrangement effectiveness scale than the suspense-standard narratives for each of the three content versions. On the story rating, the means for the suspense-misarranged narratives were below those of the corresponding suspense-standard narratives on all three content versions, but none of the differences were significant. However, on the overall-liking scale, the suspense-misarranged narratives were significantly below the corresponding suspense-standard narratives for two of the three content versions (*A Day at the Beach* not significant). The suspense-foreshadowing narratives were not significantly different from the corresponding suspense-standard narratives on the story scale, the liking scale, or the arrangement effectiveness scale.

All three surprise narratives showed ratings above 3.0 on the story rating scale, ratings that were significantly above those of the corresponding base narratives ($p < .001$).

DISCUSSION

Overall, the results from both the affective rating tasks and the structural judgments provide considerable support for the theory of stories proposed in this chapter.

The base narratives, which did not include an event with a significant outcome for one of the characters, showed low ratings on both suspense and surprise. The suspense discourse structures, which did include a significant event, showed a high suspense curve and then a sharp drop at the point of resolution. The surprise discourse structures showed a sharp spike on the surprise scale when information relating to the outcome of an omitted event occurred in the discourse. Contrary to our predictions, the suspense discourse structures with foreshadowing of future events did not show increased suspense. This may be due to problems with our particular examples. It is difficult to write good instances of foreshadowing, because the author must give some information that will increase the reader's concern about the outcome and yet not give away information about the outcome that will reduce suspense. It is possible that better examples of foreshadowing would show the predicted effect. The misarranged-suspense discourse structures showed a reduction in suspense, although the suspense ratings were not reduced to the level of the base narrative as predicted. Informal questioning of our subjects suggested that it is almost impossible to give the reader enough information about the outcome of a significant event to reduce their concern about the outcome completely. Even when the author gives away some specific details of the outcome, as we did in these narratives, the reader can still find some events to remain concerned about.

The results from the affective ratings suggest that our technique for obtaining data about the subjects' affective responses during reading is successful. Taken as a whole, the data support the part of the theory relating discourse structures to affective response. The suspense-standard, suspense-misarranged, and surprise versions of each set had identical underlying event structures and yet produced quite different types of affective curves. Thus, the differences in these affective responses to the narratives were a function of the differing arrangement of the events in the discourse structures and not a function of the event structure itself. In addition, the overall consistency of the results from the three different content versions (*The Trip Home, A Day at the Beach, The Gardener*) suggests that the theory is not content-specific. The subject matter of these three event structures are very different; yet the theoretically important aspects of the affective curves are very similar across the content domains. These two findings clearly indicate that a theory of stories must include a level of discourse structure that mediates between the event structure and the affective response.

The results from the structural judgment tasks support the part of the theory relating affective response to intuitions about stories. The base narratives were clear cohesive prose, but the subjects' story ratings showed that the subjects did not think these narratives were stories. Suspense narratives without resolutions were also not considered to be stories. However, the corresponding narratives that were organized to produce suspense and resolution as well as surprise and resolution were considered to be stories. The suspense narratives with foreshadowing produced judgments similar to the standard-suspense narratives, as would be expected, because the affect ratings were quite similar.

The misarranged-suspense stories were not significantly below the standard-suspense stories on story rating. This was not as predicted. A possible explanation for this inconsistent finding is that the affective ratings were only moderately reduced by the misarrangement of the discourse, and thus suspense might still have been strong enough to produce the story ratings. In this respect, it is interesting to note that our subjects gave lower enjoyment ratings to the misarranged suspense narratives. They also had no trouble telling that the misarranged narratives were badly told, since all three received ratings on the correct arrangement scale that were significantly lower than the suspense-standard version. These low ratings were not, however, simply due to the fact that the discourse order deviated from the chronological (event structure) order. The discourse organization of the suspense-foreshadowing versions of the stories also deviated from the event order, but these versions received correct arrangement ratings that were not significantly different from the suspense-standard versions.

In the overall pattern of results, the presence or absence of a significant event covaries with the story ratings. Therefore, one could hypothesize that the presence of a significant event and its outcome in a narrative is sufficient to predict the story ratings. Although it is probably true that a suspense discourse structure requires an event with a significant outcome, the fact that the surprise narratives also contained a significant event is an artifact of the requirement for the experimental design to use the same event structure for all the different discourse structures. It seems quite likely that there are surprise discourse structures that would be considered stories that do not contain a significant event. Thus, it seems unwise to adopt the hypothesis that stories are to be defined merely by the presence of a significant event in the event structure.

The present results, taken in conjunction with the findings of Lichtenstein and Brewer (1980), suggest the need for a reinterpretation of the story-grammar approach. The story grammars were developed to be theories of subjects' knowledge about stories; yet they classify most narratives describing goal-directed actions as stories. In contrast, the affective component of the present theory predicts that stories are a particular subclass of the larger set of coherent narratives. For example, both our base narratives and our suspense narratives would conform in many respects to most story grammars because they contain descriptions of goal-directed events, with subgoals, outcomes, etc. However, our subjects classified the base narratives as nonstories and the suspense narratives as stories. Furthermore, to the extent that the surprise and suspense-foreshadowing narratives deviate from the chronological (event structure) order, they may not meet the requirements of a story grammar. Yet, our subjects clearly considered these narratives to be stories. Thus, the present theory tends to partition correctly the class of stories from the larger set of narratives, whereas the story grammars do not.

The present work suggests that there are important theoretical differences among schemas for events, schemas for narratives, and schemas for stories. In our view, *events* must be understood in terms of the underlying event, script, and plan schemas that an individual uses to interpret, comprehend, and recall them. *Narratives* require an additional level of analysis. In addition to the event and plan schemas that are used to understand events, a theory of narratives must include constructs to deal with the structural relationships between the event and discourse levels. Finally, because affective response is primarily a function of the discourse structure rather than of the event structure, a theory of *stories* must include the role of the discourse structure in producing the affective response curves and the relationships between the affective responses and intuitions about stories. In terms of this distinction between types of schemas, it seems to us that theories of comprehension will focus primarily on event schemas and narrative schemas, whereas theories dealing with the entertainment provided by stories will focus on story schemas.

Although this chapter is intended to provide a theoretical framework and methodology for the study of stories, the particular experiments reported here have not examined all aspects of the reader's story schema. For instance, there may be other affective states, such as curiosity and humor, that have related discourse structures that also produce stories. Another important aspect of the reader's overall story schema is genre-specific information about stories. Thus, the reader of classic mystery stories knows that stories of this type will typically involve a brilliant detective, who will solve the crime by the end of the story. A complete theory of story schemas will also have to incorporate this type of genre-specific information. Finally, more experimental work will be necessary to understand how the various aspects of the story schema may be involved in the comprehension, memory, and appreciation of stories.

ACKNOWLEDGMENTS

This research was supported in part by Contract No. HEW-NIE C-400-76-0116. We would like to thank Harry Blanchard for help with materials preparation and Jerry Morgan, Ed Shoben, and Charles Osgood for their comments. Requests for reprints should be sent to William F. Brewer, Department of Psychology, University of Illinois, Psychology Building, Champaign, Ill. 61820.

APPENDIX
THE TRIP HOME: SUSPENSE-STANDARD VERSION

(Page 1)

Sam Levine got into his old VW as the clock on City Hall struck six. Across the street a man waiting in a new Cadillac pushed a button, activating by remote control a 10-minute timer on a bomb hidden in Levine's car.

Sam was tired and dreaded the 20-minute drive home. He had arrived at the office several hours earlier than the rest of his staff. The job of District Attorney was more work than he had thought it would be when he ran for the office. Taking on the Mob in court was a tough, exhausting job.

(Page 2)

Sam turned the key, but nothing happened. "The ignition wire again," he thought, as he got out of his car and opened the hood. Finding a loose ignition wire, he tightened it and got back into the car. This time it started smoothly.

Sam became impatient to get home, so he decided to take the shortcut home. That way he could cut his trip home down to about 10 minutes. He pulled out of traffic, got off the main highway, and drove through town.

(Page 3)

Sam felt a little uneasy as he drove through the busy sections of town. He began daydreaming, thinking about how quiet it would be when he got home. Carol and the girls were visiting the grandparents. Suddenly, his car bounced across a rather deep pothole. Startled, Sam began to pay more attention to his driving, and managed to avoid most of the other holes.

As he got into the quieter section of town, Sam became aware of a noise coming from the front of the car. Wondering what it was, he pulled over to the side, got out, and walked around to the front. He checked the tires, and found that a rock had gotten stuck in the tread of the right tire. He pulled the rock out and got back inside. He looked at his watch—it was 6:09—and started on the last stretch of his trip home.

(Page 4)

As he drove, Sam looked forward to making himself some spinach crepes for supper. No one else liked them, so while the family was away was a good time to make them. Finally arriving home, he stopped the car, got out, and slowly walked up the winding path to the house. He unlocked the door and walked inside.

Just as Sam closed the door behind him, his VW exploded into a fountain of flame. By taking the short-cut home, Sam had thwarted the Mob's attempt to make an out-of-court settlement.

REFERENCES

Black, J. B., & Wilensky, R. An evaluation of story grammars. *Cognitive Science,* 1979, *3,* 213–230.

Brewer, W. F. Literary theory, rhetoric, stylistics: Implications for psychology. In R. J. Spiro, B. C. Bruce, & W. F. Brewer (Eds.), *Theoretical issues in reading comprehension: Perspectives from cognitive psychology, linguistics, artificial intelligence, and education.* Hillsdale, N.J.: Lawrence Erlbaum Associates, 1980.

Chatman, S. *Story and discourse: Narrative structure in fiction and film.* Ithaca, N.Y.: Cornell University Press, 1978.

Erlich, V. *Russian formalism: History-doctrine* (4th ed.). The Hague: Mouton, 1980.

Lichtenstein, E. H., & Brewer, W. F. Memory for goal-directed events. *Cognitive Psychology,* 1980, *12,* 412–445.

Mandler, J. M. A code in the node: The use of a story schema in retrieval. *Discourse Processes,* 1978, *1,* 14–35.

Mandler, J. M., & Johnson, N. S. Remembrance of things parsed: Story structure and recall. *Cognitive Psychology,* 1977, *9,* 111–151.

Morgan, J. L., & Sellner, M. B. Discourse and linguistic theory. In R. J. Spiro, B. C. Bruce, & W. F. Brewer (Eds.), *Theoretical issues in reading comprehension: Perspectives from cognitive psychology, linguistics, artificial intelligence, and education.* Hillsdale, N.J.: Lawrence Erlbaum Associates, 1980.

Rumelhart, D. E. Notes on a schema for stories. In D. G. Bobrow & A. Collins (Eds.), *Representation and understanding: Studies in cognitive science.* New York: Academic Press, 1975.

Rumelhart, D. E. Understanding and summarizing brief stories. In D. LaBerge & J. Samuels (Eds.), *Basic processes in reading and comprehension.* Hillsdale, N.J.: Lawrence Erlbaum Associates, 1977.

Stein, N. L., & Glenn, C. G. An analysis of story comprehension in elementary school children. In R. Freedle (Ed.), *New directions in discourse processing.* Norwood, N.J.: Ablex, 1979.

Stein, N. L., & Nezworski, M. T. The effect of organization and instructional set on story memory. *Discourse Processes,* 1978, *1,* 177–193.

Sternberg, M. *Expositional modes and temporal ordering in fiction.* Baltimore: Johns Hopkins University Press, 1978.

Thorndyke, P. W. Cognitive structures in comprehension and memory of narrative discourse. *Cognitive Psychology,* 1977, *9,* 77–110.

VI
LONGER-TERM MEMORY

22

Encoding and Retrieval Effects in Human Memory: A Partial Review

Fergus I. M. Craik
Erindale College, University of Toronto
Toronto, Ontario
Canada

ABSTRACT

This chapter reviews recent ideas and findings in the encoding of information into memory, the retrieval of information from memory, and the interaction between encoding and retrieval processes. It is a partial review, both in the sense that only a limited area of the field is covered and in the sense that the review is biased toward the author's personal point of view. The topics covered include the effects of processing difficulty on later retention, different types of processing (intraitem and interitem processing), different types of rehearsal (maintenance and elaborative), the effects on encoding of resource withdrawal, different types of retrieval, and the various effects that follow when encoding context is reinstated at retrieval.

INTRODUCTION

Human memory has been studied in a variety of ways and using a variety of methods. These include attempts to verify anecdotal observations by means of controlled experiments, models based on plausible metaphors (e.g., associations between mental elements, the brain as an information-processing device), mathematical models, and computer simulations. None of these approaches has been strikingly successful and some theorists have expressed a degree of pessimism about our lack of progress (Tulving, 1979). My personal preference is to construct a general descriptive model of the processes involved in memory and to use the model, not as a copy of ''reality'' to be confirmed or rejected but as a

guiding set of principles whose precision, limits, and interrelations can be eluci-
dated and clarified through empirical observation.

In an earlier review (Craik, 1979) I took the hopeful position that much recent
work in human memory was converging on an agreed set of ideas. The ideas
concern memory for specific events—episodic memory—and are couched in
general processing terms; they are not the views of one particular theorist but
represent the common ground among several research workers in the area. In
outline, the view states that past experience, in some organized form, serves as
the basis for the perception and interpretation of current stimulus patterns. According to some theorists, the specific analyses carried out on any occasion are
preserved as a record (the "memory trace") of the episode, whereas other
theorists argue that the whole processing system is modified to some extent by
each stimulus pattern and thus the system responds somewhat differently when
the same event recurs. By either view, if the stimulus is common or is expected,
processing is relatively automatic; few analytic operations need be carried out
and the resulting memory trace will be impoverished. Alternatively, if the task or
the material induces extensive elaborate processing, a rich mnemonic record will
be formed and this distinctive trace will be highly discriminable at retrieval. For
retrieval to be effective, retrieval processing must be qualitatively similar to the
processing carried out at input (the encoding specificity principle). In turn,
retrieval processing will be shaped and guided by various forms of context and by
retrieval cues provided by the experimenter. The effectiveness of a specific cue
will depend on its similarity to the encoded trace (a positive feature) but also on
its similarity to other traces that are then said to interfere with successful retrieval
of the wanted event (Craik, 1979, p. 97).

The present chapter updates the previous review and attempts to show how a
number of theoretical and empirical articles that have appeared during the last
2–3 years have confirmed the usefulness of the general processing view of the
human memory system. Personally, I believe that several issues have been
clarified. The reasons for this optimism are discussed in the following sections
dealing with encoding processes, retrieval processes, and their interactions.

ENCODING EFFECTS

Automatic Versus Elaborate Processing

Although it is difficult to group different studies conducted for different reasons
under one neat heading, there is growing evidence that when initial processing is
relatively easy, effortless, and "automatic," subsequent memory for the event is
typically poor; when initial processing is difficult, extensive, or elaborate, on the
other hand, retention is at a relatively high level.

Several recent studies have provided further evidence on the idea that difficult
or extensive initial processing is associated with high levels of performance on a

subsequent retention test. For example, Johnson-Laird, Gibbs, and de Mowbray (1978) had subjects listen to a list of words and classify each of them as belonging or not belonging to the category of substances that are consumable, solid, and natural. The list contained words with all three components (e.g., apple), with two components (e.g., coal), with one component (e.g., sweat) and with none of the components (e.g., paraffin). After the classification task, subjects were unexpectedly asked to recall as many words as possible from the list; it was found that words that shared 0, 1, 2, 3 components were recalled with probabilities .32, .34, .45, and .57, respectively. The authors concluded that some semantic components of a word can be processed without all of them being processed and that the greater the amount of semantic processing, the more likely the word is to be remembered. Semantic processing is a matter of degree, not an all-or-none affair.

A similar general conclusion can be drawn from an experiment carried out by Friedman (1979). She asked subjects to scan pictures of coherent scenes containing both expected objects (e.g., a stove in a kitchen scene) and *unexpected* objects (e.g., a factory chimney stack in a farm scene). In a later recognition memory test, subjects exhibited relatively poor recognition of the expected objects but good recognition of the unexpected objects. They frequently failed to notice missing, new, or changed expected objects, unless the substituted object was itself unexpected (e.g., changing a cow to a hippopotamus in a farm scene). This result was not simply due to longer initial viewing time of unexpected objects because eye movements were recorded and the result held even when viewing times were equated. Friedman argued that the general aspects of the scene provide a schema or ''frame'' for perception and comprehension of detail; if a particular object fits the expectation set up by the schema, it is analyzed in relatively general, global terms. The analysis is sufficient to discriminate the object from quite different objects in a later test but insufficient to discriminate it from other examples of its own class.

Two studies have examined the effects of initial *retrieval* difficulty on subsequent retention of words. Whitten and Leonard (1980) varied the difficulty of initial recognition by giving a multiple-choice test consisting of either 2, 4 or 8 alternatives. In a subsequent unexpected free recall test, performance was related to initial difficulty—the 8-alternative words were best recalled and the 2-alternative words least well recalled, although the effects were not large. In a similar experiment, Bjork and Geiselman (1978) varied the length of a filled delay interval before words were recalled; they found that longer delays before initial retrieval were associated with higher levels on a second recall test (even for items untested in the first recall test) but that initial delay had no effect on subsequent recognition. Apparently, recall and recognition depend on somewhat different initial processing—further evidence on this point is discussed later.

Perhaps the most dramatic example of these demonstrations that difficult initial processing is associated with high levels of retention is provided by the ''generation effect'' (Jacoby, 1978; Slamecka & Graf, 1978). In Slamecka and

Graf's experiments subjects were given related word pairs that were either complete (e.g., rapid–fast, ruby–diamond) or in which the second word of the pair was represented by its initial letter (e.g., rapid–f, ruby–d). Subjects read the complete pairs and generated the response members of the incomplete pairs, having been informed of the rule that linked members of each pair. In several experiments it was shown that response members of the word pairs were substantially better recognized and recalled following the generation condition. The generation phenomenon is very robust—it can be demonstrated easily as a laboratory exercise, for example—and is found under both incidental and intentional learning conditions. Slamecka and Graf leave the explanation of the effect as an open question, but it is certainly tempting to follow Jacoby's (1978) suggestion that generation (or construction) involves conscious problem-solving processes to some degree. ''The idea is that the necessity of construction involves consciousness and engenders arousal in a way that effortless remembering does not; it is this involvement of consciousness and heightened arousal that is responsible for differences in subsequent levels of retention [p. 663].'' Jacoby also suggests that reading may be more automatized than the activity of generating. Through practice, skilled readers have learned to delete unnecessary perceptual operations, and although this deletion is beneficial for the fluency of reading, retention suffers, because deleting operations reduces the event's encoded distinctiveness. In a sense, the necessity to generate even very obvious completions may kick the processing system out of a somewhat automatic mode into a more conscious ''controlled'' mode. The same account might be given of Kolers' (1973) demonstration that reading inverted script is associated with higher retention levels than reading the same script in normal orientation.

Friedman (1979) gives a very similar explanation for the finding that unexpected objects in a scene are better recognized. She suggests that ''subjects might be able to identify expected objects by using automatized encoding procedures that operate on global physical features. In contrast, identification of unexpected objects . . . should generally require more analysis of local visual details [p. 316].'' In the recognition test, subjects did not notice subtle changes to expected objects because only their global features had been encoded. Paradoxically, higher levels of perceptual skill are associated with lower levels of retention of detail (Kolers, 1975).

Is it possible to say more at this stage about these various examples of a relation between difficulty or extensiveness of initial processing and subsequent retention? Tyler, Hertel, McCallum, and Ellis (1979) argued that cognitive effort during encoding is an important determinant of later memory performance. It seems clear indeed that difficulty or effort (indexed, for example, by performance on a secondary task) is typically a correlate of elaborate or extensive processing, but personally I am reluctant to believe that effort as such plays any causative role. To make the point clearer, it is known that if a subject carries out extensive or ''deep'' processing, such operations demand more attentional capacity (Johnston & Heinz, 1978) and probably involve a greater feeling of effort; it is also known that such processing is associated with high levels of retention. In that situation, then, effort will be correlated with memory performance. On the other hand, a difficult task involving "shallow" surface aspects of the stimulus will also involve effort but is much less likely to be associated with good retention (Craik & Tulving, 1975, Exp. 5). Degree of effort, by itself, is unlikely to furnish an explanation of differences in retention.

In summary, whereas the difficulty of a mental task (measured for example by speed or accuracy of performance) and the degree of subjective effort required for the task (measured for example by concurrent task performance) are often correlated positively with subsequent retention, these aspects of initial processing are almost certainly secondary to the extensiveness and qualitative nature of initial processing as predictors of later memory performance. "Difficulty" and "effort" typically signal deep, elaborate, or extensive processing but do not in themselves give rise to high levels of retention.

Different Types of Processing

Over the last few years several investigators have shown that different types of initial processing are optimal for recall and recognition, respectively (Tversky, 1973). More recently G. Mandler (1979) has suggested a distinction between intraitem and interitem processing. Intraitem processing serves an integrative function; it renders items more discriminable from other encoded events and is particularly effective in supporting later recognition memory. Interitem processing serves an elaborative function by promoting associative interconnections between the target item and other information; this type of processing is particularly beneficial for recall. In his 1979 article, Mandler makes a convincing case for the two types of processing. Although he describes them as two dimensions of *organization,* Mandler also points out that the notions of intraitem and interitem processing have much in common with the two types of *rehearsal* postulated by Woodward, Bjork, & Jongeward (1973) and by Craik and Watkins (1973). It might be said that maintenance (or primary) rehearsal enhances intraitem organization and that elaborative (or secondary) rehearsal enhances interitem organization. In fact, recent experimental results (to be discussed later) have strengthened the case for the two types of rehearsal and clarified their characteristics.

In a further article, Mandler (1980) argued that recognition memory is based on two processes—familiarity and retrieval of context. His position is similar to that advanced by Atkinson and Juola (1974). Essentially, Mandler suggested that one operation in a recognition memory task involves a test for familiarity based on intraitem integration. The familiarity judgment is relatively automatic and depends on the similarity of the test item to the encoded item—especially similarity of perceptual features, because the "integration" in question is based heavily (though not exclusively) on perceptual information. Thus, the familiarity effect should be less when modality is switched between presentation and test. If the familiarity test does not yield a clear-cut *yes* or *no* decision or if fuller contextual information is required ("his face is familiar, but where have I seen him before?") information from the second component—retrieval of context—is also evaluated. Retrieval is seen as a more optional, controlled process and in this case recognition performance will depend on the richness of the encoded contextual information and on the ease with which the item can redintegrate that information at test.

Similar theoretical ideas have been advanced independently by Jacoby and Dallas (1981) and by Geiselman and Bjork (1980). In the first experiment to be described (one of a series by Jacoby and Dallas, 1981) the authors presented words to subjects in two successive phases. In the first phase, subjects encoded each word by answering a question about its physical, rhyme, or semantic characteristics following the technique of Craik and Tulving (1975). Each question gave rise either to a positive response (e.g., "rhymes with train?—BRAIN") or to a negative response (e.g., "a religious building?—HAMMER"). Following this first phase, the second phase consisted of either a recognition memory test or a perceptual identification test in which words were exposed tachistoscopically for 35 msec—the subject's task was simply to identify the word. In the identification test both old words (previously encoded in Phase 1) and new words (not seen in Phase 1) were presented. Table 22.1 shows that the "levels" manipulation had the typical effect on recognition memory—a large benefit to deeper processing, with positive responses being associated with higher levels of recognition than negative responses. However, strikingly, the encoding manipulation had no effect whatsoever on perceptual identification—performance levels varied only minimally, between 78% and 83% correct. The task is quite sensitive, however, because nonpresented (new) words were identified on only 65% of the trials. Clearly, the encoding manipulation affects recognition memory but not perceptual identification. On the other hand, a further experiment showed that increasing the number of repetitions of the word in Phase 1 let to improvements in both identification and recognition memory. These results also fit well with recent models of word identification (Broadbent & Broadbent, 1975; Morton, 1969).

Jacoby and Dallas agree with Mandler in postulating two bases for recognition memory. The first they term "perceptual fluency," which is modality-specific and positively affected by prior presentations. Perceptual fluency also acts in perceptual identification and may be said to be based on Mandler's intraitem processing. The second basis is termed "retrieval of study context" and is essentially identical to Mandler's retrieval notion. It seems that perceptual identification is based largely on intraitem encoding, recognition memory is affected by both intraitem and interitem encoding, and recall depends primarily on interitem processing. Both Jacoby and Dallas (1981) and Mandler (1980) point out

TABLE 22.1
Proportions of Words Correct in Recognition Memory and
Perceptual Identification Following Different Types of Encoding at Input
(Jacoby & Dallas, 1981)

	Physical		Rhyme		Semantic		New
	Yes	No	Yes	No	Yes	No	
Recognition memory	51	49	72	54	95	78	
Perceptual identification	78	81	82	80	80	83	65

that the dissociation of factors affecting recognition is similar to the dissociation exhibited by amnesic patients who can judge an item familar (or can carry out some action based on past familiarity) but fail to recognize the item as having occurred before on some particular occasion. Such patients can utilize intraitem encoding (or perceptual fluency) but are unable to retrieve the context in which the event initially occurred.

A second study, by Geiselman and Bjork (1980) also fits well with Mandler's viewpoint. Their experiment was designed to explore the effects of maintenance and elaborative processing on later recognition memory and also to explore the effects of testing items in the same perceptual form as they were presented. Subjects were asked to rehearse word triads for 5, 10, or 15 sec. During the rehearsal interval they simply either repeated the three words over and over (maintenance rehearsal) or constructed meaningful relations, short sentences, etc., using the three words (elaborative rehearsal). An ingenious feature of the study is that subjects were familiarized with a particular speaker's voice and were then required to carry out their rehearsal activities by imagining rehearsal in the speaker's voice. At test, words were presented for recognition either in that same speaker's voice (thereby making the test compatible with the previous rehearsal activities) or in a different speaker's voice.

Figure 22.1 shows that secondary (elaborative) rehearsal led to higher levels of recognition than did primary (maintenance) rehearsal and that longer intervals of elaborative rehearsal were associated with better recognition memory regardless of whether or not the test voice was the same as the voice used during rehearsal. For maintenance rehearsal, on the other hand, compatibility of rehearsal and test voices had a large positive effect; rehearsal duration also had a positive effect on recognition performance for the same voice condition but had no effect when the voices were different.

Several conclusions may be drawn from this very pretty pattern of results. First, it confirms the usefulness of the distinction between maintenance and elaborative processing and confirms Mandler's suggestion that maintenance processing primarily involves perceptually based intraitem encoding. Maintenance processing does not simply increase some generalized "strength" of the memory

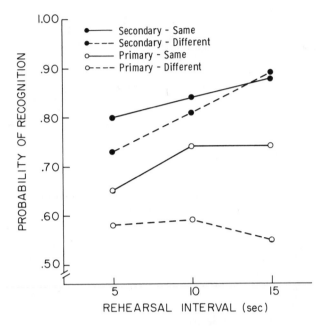

FIG. 22.1. The probability of word recognition as a function of type of rehearsal, comptatibility between rehearsal and test forms, and rehearsal interval (Geiselman & Bjork, 1980).

trace, because its effectiveness depends on the compatibility of input and test forms. Also, it appears that repetition of the same perceptual operations at the time of recognition is less critical when the memory code involves "deep" as opposed to "shallow" information. Maintenance rehearsal *does* have some effect on the system (contrary to Craik & Lockhart's [1972] original suggestion) but it is a qualitative, not a quantitative change. These points are discussed again later in the chapter. Another point made by Geiselman and Bjork's results is that it is the functional encoding that determines later memory performance, not the nominal manner in which the event was presented.

Taken together with some previous results (Woodward, et al., 1973) it now seems possible to conclude with some confidence that two broad categories of input processing or rehearsal may be distinguished. Interitem processing (elaborative or secondary rehearsal) enhances both recall and recognition and serves to integrate an event with its context; this form of processing has no beneficial effect on perceptual identification, however. Intraitem processing (maintenance or primary rehearsal) has little or no effect on recall; it does increase recognition memory performance, if the input and test forms are perceptually compatible, and it also increases perceptual identification.

Maintenance and Elaborative Processing

In the light of these recent developments it may be useful to survey the various studies that have addressed the distinction between maintenance and elaborative processing. Craik and Lockhart (1972) suggested that "same-level" rehearsal should have no beneficial effects on memory performance. In that article they focused primarily on the effects of different forms of rehearsal rather than of spaced repetitions, saying for example: "while PM (primary memory) retention is, thus, equivalent to continued processing, this type of processing merely prolongs an item's high accessibility without leading to formation of a more permanent memory trace. Thus Type 1 (maintenance) processing, that is, repetition of analyses which have already been carried out, may be contrasted with Type II (elaborate) processing which involves deeper analysis of the stimulus. Only this second type of rehearsal should lead to improved memory performance [p. 676]." However, they also suggested that the effects of repeated presentation would depend on whether the repeated stimulus was processed to the same level or encoded differently on its further presentations. Subsequent evidence has borne out Craik and Lockhart's suggestions with regard to *rehearsal* (with certain modifications), but whereas same-level *repetition* has little or no effect at the sensory level (Moray, 1959; Turvey, 1967), it now seems clear that if a word is presented on several different occasions, together with an identical or "same-level" encoding question, its retention is enhanced (Craik & Tulving, 1975; Nelson, 1977). Thus, the notion that memory performance depends only on the deepest level of processing reached is too simple.

With regard to rehearsal, other theorists shared the view that maintenance processing does little to increase retention (Jacoby, 1973; Woodward et al., 1973). The prediction has been confirmed for recall (Craik & Watkins, 1973; Jacoby, 1973; Woodward et al., 1973) but, in the case of recognition, maintenance processing has usually been associated with increments in performance (Glenberg, Smith, & Green, 1977; Woodward et al., 1973). As argued previously, this dissociation between recall and recognition may be attributable to the possibility that only recognition is sensitive to the effects of intraitem (or maintenance) processing.

Recent studies have clarified the effects of maintenance rehearsal. Rundus (1977) developed a technique in which subjects "rehearsed" words for various intervals but thought that they were doing so to prevent them rehearsing numbers to be recalled in the Brown–Peterson task; that is, the words were given as the filler activity in the initial phase, but subjects were then unexpectedly asked to recall them. In this situation there is presumably no motivation to do more than maintain the words over the initial rehearsal interval, and Rundus found that the duration of rehearsal had no effect on recall, although the number of repetitions of a word was positively related to recognition. Glenberg et al. (1977) independently developed the same technique and confirmed that the relatively pure maintenance rehearsal activity found in this situation did not enhance recall but did increase recognition. In further work, Glenberg and Adams (1978) provided further evidence that maintenance rehearsal improves recognition memory and demonstrated that the acoustic–phonemic components of the memory trace are the aspects strengthened by this type of rehearsal. The next important piece of evidence was provided by Geiselman and Bjork (1980) and was discussed earlier—that maintenance rehearsal enhances recognition, but only when the input and test forms are perceptually compatible.

In summary, the distinction between two major types of rehearsal has been well supported by the results of recent empirical studies. It is now clear that maintenance processing does enhance at least certain types of retention—namely recognition memory, provided that the test stimulus is compatible with the mode of initial processing. More broadly, it now seems necessary to postulate two rather different bases for learning, one based on relations among items ("organization," "structure," "interitem processing") and the other based on characteristics of the item itself ("strength," "intraitem integration") (Jacoby, Bartz, & Evans, 1978; G. Mandler, 1979). It is important to note, however that "strength" must always be considered specific to some qualitative dimension. One final point, made both by Craik and Jacoby (1979) and by Glenberg and Adams (1978) is that it is probably a mistake to think of maintenance and elaborative processing as two discrete categories. It is more likely that they represent ends of a continuum—that is, rehearsal can vary from "pure" maintenance, through a mixture of maintenance and elaborative operations, to relatively pure elaborative processing. Glenberg and Adams make the additional point that rehearsal operations will require more cognitive capacity as they tend to the elaborative end of the continuum—a point that fits well with Johnston and Heinz's (1978) analysis of attention.

Effects of Resource Availability

The position argued in this section is that encoding processes require a certain amount of attentional capacity, or "processing resource" to use Norman and Bobrow's (1975) term and that encoding is necessarily altered when insufficient attentional resources are available. The study of how encoding processes change as a function of available resource is an important one because many cases of memory deficit may result from a lack of such resource. Craik and Simon (1980) argued that adult age changes in memory form one such case and that alcoholic intoxication and fatigue may be other examples. They also suggested that these conditions may be mimicked in normal young subjects by having them encode events while also carrying out a second task, that is, under divided attention conditions.

It has been known for some time, for example, that divided attention reduces the secondary memory component, but not the primary memory component, in a free recall task (Murdock, 1965). This pattern of results is also found in older subjects (Craik, 1968) and in intoxicated subjects (Jones, 1973). What is the nature of the memory decrement observed under these conditions? What processes or operations do older or divided-attention subjects fail to carry out? There is now quite good evidence from the literature on age differences in memory that older subjects do not establish adequate interitem relationships when encoding a list of items—that is, there is a failure of organization (Hultsch, 1971a). Also, old subjects are deficient in drawing inferences from text material, although they are not at a disadvantage when remembering the material verbatim (Cohen, 1979; Till & Walsh, 1980). Both of these processing deficits may be characterized as failures to process deeply in the sense used by Craik and Lockhart (1972).

Do the failures to process deeply observed with older people (and possibly under conditions of divided attention) represent an *inability* to carry out deeper processing, or is the deficit better characterized as a processing *inefficiency?* That is, are older people capable of carrying out effective encoding operations, but do not carry them out spontaneously; do they in fact show a production deficiency of the type observed in young children's memory? One way to answer this question is to determine whether the memory deficits under consideration can be reduced by guiding the subject's processing by means of an orienting task. The rationale here is that a semantic orienting task induces a "good" encoding regardless of the subject's intention to learn the material (Craik & Tulving, 1975). Thus, such an orienting task might induce effective encoding operations despite the older person's failure to carry them out under normal learning conditions.

There is now good evidence that semantic orienting tasks do reduce the age differences found in free learning situations. Hultsch (1971b) used the Mandler sorting technique, in which subjects are asked to sort 52 unrelated words into two to seven categories until two identical sorts are achieved, and found that the sorting technique reduced age differences in subsequent recall relative to a free learning condition. White (reported by Craik, 1977) showed that orienting tasks at input combined with recognition tests at retrieval, essentially eliminated age differences. This result was also reported by Perlmutter (1979). Finally, in Till and Walsh's (1980) experiment the age-related failure to draw inferences from sentences was eliminated by the requirement to write a word reflecting the subject's understanding of each sentence. All of these results support the conclusion that older people retain the cognitive ability to process deeply, but they do not do so spontaneously.

What underlies this inefficient pattern of processing? One possibility, based on findings from the child development literature, is that older subjects exhibit a failure in meta-memory; that is, they do not realize what mental operations they ought to carry out in order to remember well. It is well established that younger children's memories are poor (at least in part) because of a failure to utilize efficient strategies during learning and remembering, but it is much less easy to see why older people should forget how to learn and retrieve. It does seem possible, however, that lack of practice at intellectual skills contributes to the age deficit in remembering. The second possibility is that the declining availablity of cognitive resource in older people means that deeper, extensive processing is simply more effortful for them and is gradually abandoned; at an extreme, deeper comprehension may become impossible as cognitive resources dwindle. The similar pattern of results between aging and divided attention favors the argument of reduced resource—it is difficult to believe that divided-attention subjects simply forget how to learn. A recent experiment in my own laboratory studied the retention of 12-word lists following either free learning or a semantic orienting task; subjects performed the task either under conditions of full attention to the word lists or under divided-attention conditions. The results were very similar to those found with age as a variable; there was an interaction between the encoding task and divided attention such that the decrement in retention from full to divided attention was substantially less in the orienting task condition. It seems that one of the first effects of a reduction in processing resources is a failure to switch in adequate encoding operations, although the subject is still capable of carrying them out. The semantic orienting task channels and guides the use of the remaining processing resources more effectively.

All these studies support the idea that semantic processing is less deep and extensive in older people and in subjects learning under divided-attention conditions; however, it is undoubtedly too extreme to argue that *no* semantic processing occurs in these cases. A further series of studies carried out in my lab in conjunction with Jan Rabinowitz and Brian Ackerman shows that memory traces are more general and prototypical in nature under these conditions of curtailed semantic processing. This lack of specificity and distinctiveness is then associated with lower levels of retention (Jacoby & Craik, 1979; Eysenck, 1979).

The conclusion of greater generality of encoding was reached on the basis of comparing the relative effectiveness of different retrieval cues (Simon, 1979). Following Tulving's encoding specificity principle (Tulving & Thomson, 1973), we assume that cue effectiveness reflects the nature of the trace. In one such study, young and old subjects were asked to generate an associate to each of a number of words. At retrieval, either the subject's own generated associate was given as a cue for the original word or the general category label for the word was provided as a cue (e.g., ELEPHANT—subject generates "trunk"; at retrieval, either "trunk" or "4-legged animal" given as cues). For older subjects, the general category cue was about as effective as the contextually specific association, whereas for young subjects the specific association was more effective. The same pattern of results has been obtained using somewhat different paradigms. Our interpretation of the finding is that older subjects encode general global features of events much as younger subjects do; thus general cues are equally effective for young and old. However, only younger subjects make full use of the specific context to form a specific, distinctive trace, and this difference shows up in the higher recall levels obtained with young subjects and contextually specific cues. The conclusion that subjects encode more generally under certain circumstances is also borne out by findings from other labs that both older subjects (Rankin & Kausler, 1979) and subjects under divided attention conditions (Mandler & Worden, 1973) make many more false alarms in a recognition task to words similar in meaning to the target words.

Interestingly, the pattern of encoding changes under conditions of reduced attentional resource is quite similar to the pattern observed when perceived events are highly expected (Friedman, 1979). In both cases, general, global aspects of the event are processed, but specific details are not. It seems possible that general features are encoded relatively automatically but that specific and contextual aspects require fuller attention and greater effort. Such specific detail may be unnecessary (in the case of expected events) or difficult (when processing resources are diminished) to encode, and the result is poorer episodic memory for the event. Clearly this account is speculative, but the evidence for it is accumulating and it provides a useful focus for further research on various types of memory impairment.

RETRIEVAL EFFECTS

Types of Retrieval

There is growing agreement that the principal requirement for successful remembering is that the mental operations carried out at the time of retrieval match those carried out when the event in question was initially encoded. This notion has been expressed both in terms of repetition of the encoding operations themselves (Kolers, 1973) and in terms of a sufficient overlap of information between the products of input and retrieval processes (Tulving & Watkins, 1975). Tulving's views have led to the formulation of the encoding specificity principle (Tulving & Thomson, 1973). Because it is well established that encoding processes vary qualitatively, it is thus equally necessary to study qualitative variations in retrieval processes. Just as encoding processes can be described as varying in modality, depth, and extensiveness, so retrieval processes can also be described, although fewer studies have focused on retrieval operations up to the present time.

One question that has received some recent attention is the extent to which the retrieval operations used in recall and in recognition are similar or different. Over the last few years, several theorists have converged on the position that the *processes* involved in recall and recognition are very similar but that the *information* utilized is different in the two situations. On the latter point, Flexser and

Tulving (1978) have shown that when both recognition and recall tests are carried out on a list of word pairs, those response items that can be recalled are recognized very little better than those that cannot be recalled. Recallability does not predict recognizability in the paired–associated situation, a finding that strongly suggests the independence of the information on which the two types of retention test are based. This conclusion can be interpreted in various ways. One possibility is that an encoded event may be thought of as containing information relevant to the central item plus information relevant to the encoding context. In a recall test some contextual information is re-presented and the system must "find" the item, whereas in a recognition test information about the central item is re-presented and the system must retrieve contextual information. In both cases information about the encoded item-plus-context must be reactivated but by different routes. Alternatively, the independence of recall and recognition can be interpreted as evidence confirming the notion that recall performance is based largely on interitem organization, whereas recognition utilizes intraitem (familiarity) information as well as requiring retrieval of context (G. Mandler, 1979, 1980).

In terms of the processes involved there has been some debate on the role of generative or reconstuctive processes in retrieval. Tulving has consistently denied the usefulness of generative processes in recall (Tulving, 1976), although Mandler and his colleagues have made the case for generation being a useful auxiliary strategy (Rabinowitz, Mandler, & Patterson, 1977). In any event, a distinction can probably be drawn between blind generation of possible items that are then subjected to recognition procedures and "reconstruction" guided by feelings of familiarity toward successful remembering of the sought-for event. That is, schema-driven reconstructive processes can interact with memory trace information so that both sources of information contribute to remembering, in exactly the same way as schematic information interacts with incoming sense data during the course of perceiving (Lockhart, Craik, & Jacoby, 1976; J. Mandler, 1978).

Hasher and Griffin (1978) drew the distinction between reconstruction and reproduction in recall. They suggested that subjects can adopt either a reconstructive or a reproductive strategy at retrieval—the former relies heavily on accumulated general knowledge of the situation, whereas the latter involves a more direct readout of episodic trace information. In their experiment, subjects read a prose passage and recalled it after a 5-min, 2-day, or 1-week interval. The passages were ambiguous in that they could apply to either of two very different situations (e.g., one passage about a voyage was entitled "Columbus discovers a new world" or "First trip to the moon"). The idea was that the title provided general thematic information that would influence both encoding and retrieval of the passage. The major manipulation was to present either the same title or the alternative title at the time of retrieval, with the idea that when the same title was presented, the subject would indulge in much reconstructive, thematic recall and would rely heavily on his or her past knowledge of the situation as opposed to the

TABLE 22.2
Proportions of Idea Units Recalled as a Function of
Experimental Condition and Retention Interval
(Hasher & Griffin, 1978)

	Retention Inverval		
	5-min	2-day	1-week
Same title	.34	.17	.15
Different title	.35	.31	.26

verbatim details of the passage as presented. On the other hand, it was postulated that when the title was changed at recall, the subject would rely more on reproductive retrieval, make fewer thematic intrusions, and (critically) would actually recall more of the original passage. This last counterintuitive prediction is based on the idea that because subjects cannot rely on general thematic knowledge, they will be forced to heighten the effort put into their retrieval processing. The main results of Hasher and Griffin's (1978) experiment are shown in Table 22.2. They demonstrate the predicted effect very clearly; the different-title condition gave rise to a greater number of idea units correctly recalled, especially at the longest retention interval. In addition, the same-title group produced an average of 3.0 intrusion errors related to the theme of the passage, whereas the different-title group produced an average of only 0.5 intrusions relevant to the first-title theme and 0.3 intrusions relevant to the second-title theme. Reproductive and reconstructive modes of retrieval appear to differ in the extent to which they involve schematic knowledge; there is clearly a parallel here to bottom–up (or data driven) and top–down (or schema driven) processing in perception.

   In summary, relatively few studies have been carried out so far in which the quality or amount of retrieval processing is varied. The topic does appear to be a fruitful one, however, especially when the parallel to input processing is considered. What are the effects of resource withdrawal at retrieval, for example? It seems quite possible that some retrieval operations are relatively automatic whereas others require more conscious effort and cognitive resource (Jacoby & Dallas, 1981; G. Mandler, 1980).

ENCODING-RETRIEVAL INTERACTIONS

Context Effects

Another area in which substantial recent progress has been made is in the understanding of the effects of context on remembering—in particular, the effects of similarity between encoding and retrieval contexts. Several different factors appear to be operating in the area. First, a context can bias the precise way in which an item is encoded. Given the encoding specificity principle, it follows that if the same context is present at the time of the retention test, a similar encoding will again be induced, and the probability of remembering will be high. This effect is clearly seen in studies of recognition memory, both in situations where the sense of a word can be grossly altered by context (traffic JAM versus strawberry JAM) as in the experiments by Light and Carter-Sobell (1970) and also in situations where the exact sense of a word can be more subtly changed by its semantic context (train–BLACK versus white–BLACK) as in the studies by Tulving and Thomson (1973).

Do other context effects operate in the same way? It seems that they do not, because a number of researchers have now pointed out that reinstatement of various types of context affect recall but not recognition. For example, Godden and Baddeley (1975) showed that divers recalled a list of words best when they recalled them in the same environment as they had learned them (i.e., underwater or on dry land). However, similarity of the environment had no effect on recognition memory of the words (Godden & Baddeley, 1980). Similarly, Smith, Glenberg, and Bjork (1978) found that reinstating the physical learning environment had a large positive effect on free recall, a smaller effect on cued recall, and no effect on recognition memory. In a useful article, Eich (1980) restored a good deal of order to the chaotic literature on state-dependent learning effects using drugs, by showing that positive effects of the same drug state are found in recall but are generally absent in recognition. There is general agreement that the subject relies less on external cues in recognition memory; retrieval processes are sufficiently guided by the target item itself to give rise to an adequate overlap of information between the memory trace and the test item (although this explanation is not wholly satisfactory—when recognition is not perfect, why does the similar environment not give at least some help?) How exactly is recall helped by the same environment or drug state? Recall appears to depend more heavily on subject-initiated reconstructive activities and it may be that these operations are heavily influenced by context. At this point the phenomenon is clearly established but the explanations are weak.

A third situation in which context affects retention occurs in the Geiselman and Bjork (1980) experiment described earlier in the chapter. They suggested that primary rehearsal serves to strengthen the association between an item and the "intraitem situational context," that is, the physical properties of the stimulus package. Thus, if a word is re-presented for recognition in the same modality, same typescript, or same voice, recognition performance will be enhanced. This analysis makes it unnecessary to postulate long-decaying echoes or icons to account for the beneficial effects of repeated voices or modalities (Craik & Kirsner, 1974). Instead, it can be argued that if the voice, orthography, or other perceptual aspects of the stimulus form part of the event's encoding, then reinstatment of the same physical package will increase the match between test stimulus and trace, and thus lead to a higher probability of recognition—even if recognition takes place a considerable time later. It is possible that "participation in a psychological experiment" may serve as a context in this sense. Jacoby and

Dallas (1981) found that presentation of a word facilitated its perceptual recognition 24 hr later. It is implausible to talk of "activation" persisting for this length of time but just conceivable that the general experimental context serves to facilitate performance in much the same way as does repetition of voice or orthography (Kolers, 1975).

Two further interesting results will be described in conclusion. Smith (1979) found that recall was enhanced when subjects were instructed to imagine the original learning environment. He points to the important practical consequences of this finding. Bower, Monteiro, and Gilligan (1978) reported the first of a series of studies investigating the effects of mood changes on remembering. They found a state-dependent effect for mood, but only in a situation where different words served to distinguish one set of learned materials from another. The authors suggested that the discriminable moods acted rather like a peg-word mnemonic to reduce interference and confer distinctiveness on the events to be remembered.

In general, these findings and speculations on the effect of context are rather satisfying because they are interesting theoretically, are important practically, and extend our commonsense knowledge that reinstatement of context is a useful aid to remembering.

CONCLUSIONS

In summary, the general view that memory can be understood in terms of encoding processes, retrieval processes, and their interrelations has proved of continuing usefulness over the past few years. Although many researchers clearly feel uncomfortable with something as vague as a general framework to guide thinking and experimentation, the fact is that this approach has been successful in generating new empirical phenomena (Geiselman & Bjork, 1980; Jacoby & Dallas, 1981; Slamecka & Graf, 1978) and also new theoretical formulations (Jacoby & Dallas, 1981; Johnston & Heinz, 1978; Mandler, 1980). A good example of how theory and experiment can interact to clarify a specific issue is the work on maintenance and elaborative processing. Empirical work yielded the puzzling finding that maintenance rehearsal did not enhance recall but did enhance recognition; the area has been greatly clarified by the recent work of Geiselman and Bjork, Jacoby and Dallas, and G. Mandler, and it is now possible to conclude that maintenance rehearsal functions to integrate an item with its perceptual features and that recognition is enhanced provided the item is re-presented in the same physical form. A further application of the general processing theory of memory is to memory deficits (Craik & Simon, 1980; Jacoby & Dallas, 1981), and it seems likely that this topic will be an important one in the next few years.

A general processing framework for memory is clearly not so elegant or so rigorous as mathematical modeling or computer simulation, but ultimately the various approaches to the study of memory must be judged more or less successful not as intellectual exercises in their own right but in terms of their success in advancing our understanding of phenomena in the real world. In my view, the general processing framework has evolved and been strengthened by recent work; it continues to provide useful guidelines for further research.

ACKNOWLEDGMENTS

Preparation of this chapter was facilitated by a grant from the Natural Sciences and Engineering Research Council of Canada. I am very grateful to the following colleagues for their helpful comments on an earlier draft: Michael Eysenck, Graham Hitch, Larry Jacoby, Raymond Nickerson, and Jan Rabinowitz.

REFERENCES

Atkinson, R. C., & Juola, J. F. Search and decision processes in recognition memory. In R. C. Atkinson, D. H. Krantz & P. Suppes (Eds.), *Contemporary development in mathematical psychology*. San Francisco: W. H. Freeman, 1974.

Bjork, R. E., & Geiselman, R. E. Constituent processes in the differentiation of items in memory. *Journal of Experimental Psychology: Human Learning and Memory*, 1978, *4*, 347–361.

Bower, G. H., Monteiro, K. P., & Gilligan, S. G. Emotional mood as a context for learning and recall. *Journal of Verbal Learning and Verbal Behavior*, 1978, *17*, 573–585.

Broadbent, D. E., & Broadbent, M. H. P. Some further data concerning the word frequency effect. *Journal of Experimental Psychology: General*, 1975, *104*, 297–308.

Cohen, G. Language comprehension in old age. *Cognitive Psychology*, 1979, *11*, 412–429.

Craik, F. I. M. Two components in free recall. *Journal of Verbal Learning and Verbal Behavior*, 1968, *7*, 996–1004.

Craik, F. I. M. Age differences in memory. In J. E. Birren & K. W. Schaie (Eds.), *The handbook of the psychology of aging*. New York: Van Nostrand Reinhold, 1977.

Craik, F. I. M. Human memory. *Annual Review of Psychology*, 1979, *30*, 63–102.

Craik, F. I. M., & Jacoby, L. L. Elaboration and distinctiveness in episodic memory. In L.-G. Nilsson (Ed.), *Perspectives on memory research*. Hillsdale, N.J.: Lawrence Erlbaum Associates, 1979.

Craik, F. I. M., & Kirsner, K. The effect of speaker's voice on word recognition. *Quarterly Journal of Experimental Psychology*, 1974, *26*, 274–284.

Craik, F. I. M., & Lockhart, R. S. Levels of processing: A framework for memory research. *Journal of Verbal Learning and Verbal Behavior*, 1972, *11*, 671–684.

Craik, F. I. M., & Simon, E. Age differences in memory: The role of attention and depth of processing. In L. W. Poon, J. L. Fozard, L. S. Cermak, D. Arenberg, & L. W. Thompson (Eds), *New directions for memory and aging*. Hillsdale, N.J.: Lawrence Erlbaum Associates, 1980.

Craik, F. I. M., & Tulving, E. Depth of processing and the retention of words in episodic memory. *Journal of Experimental Psychology: General*, 1975, *104*, 268–294.

Craik, F. I. M., & Watkins, M. J. The role of rehearsal in short-term memory. *Journal of Verbal Learning and Verbal Behavior*, 1973, *12*, 599–607.

Eich, J. E. The cue-dependent nature of state-dependent retrieval. *Memory and Cognition*, 1980, *8*, 157–173.

Eysenck, M. W. Depth, elaboration, and distinctiveness. In L. S. Cermak & F. I. M. Craik (Eds.), *Levels of processing in human memory*. Hillsdale, N.J.: Lawrence Erlbaum Associates, 1979.

Flexser, A. J., & Tulving, E. Retrieval independence in recognition and recall. *Psychological Review*, 1978, *85*, 153-171.

Friedman, A. Framing pictures: The role of knowledge in automatized encoding and memory for gist. *Journal of Experimental Psychology: General*, 1979, *108*, 316-355.

Geiselman, R. E., & Bjork, R. A. Primary versus secondary rehearsal in imagined voices: Differential effects on recognition. *Cognitive Psychology*, 1980, *12*, 188-205.

Glenberg, A., & Adams, F. Type 1 rehearsal and recognition. *Journal of Verbal Learning and Verbal Behavior*, 1978, *17*, 455-463.

Glenberg, A., Smith, S. M., & Green, C. Type 1 rehearsal: Maintenance and more. *Journal of Verbal Learning and Verbal Behavior*, 1977, *16*, 339-352.

Godden, D. R., & Baddeley, A. D. Context-dependent memory in two natural environments: on land and underwater. *British Journal of Psychology*, 1975, *66*, 325-332.

Godden, D. R., & Baddeley, A. D. When does context influence recognition memory? *British Journal of Psychology*, 1980, *71*, 99-104.

Hasher, L., & Griffin, M. Reconstructive and reproductive processes in memory. *Journal of Experimental Psychology: Human Learning and Memory*, 1978, *4*, 318-330.

Hultsch, D. E. Organization and memory in adulthood. *Human Development*, 1971, *14*, 16-29.(a)

Hultsch, D. E. Adult age differences in free classification and free recall. *Developmental Psychology*, 1971, *4*, 338-342.(b)

Jacoby, L. L. Encoding processes, rehearsal, and recall requirements. *Journal of Verbal Learning and Verbal Behavior*, 1973, *12*, 302-310.

Jacoby, L. L. On interpreting the effects of repetition: Solving a problem versus remembering a solution. *Journal of Verbal Learning and Verbal Behavior*, 1978, *17*, 649-667.

Jacoby, L. L., Bartz, W. H., & Evans, J. D. A functional approach to levels of processing. *Journal of Experimental Psychology: Human Learning and Memory*, 1978, *4*, 331-346.

Jacoby, L. L., & Craik, F. I. M. Effects of elaboration of processing at encoding and retrieval. In L. S. Cermak & F. I. M. Craik (Eds.), *Levels of processing in human memory*. Hillsdale, N.J.: Lawrence Erlbaum Associates, 1979.

Jacoby, L. L., & Dallas, M. On the relationship between autobiographical memory and perceptual learning. *Journal of Experimental Psychology: General*, 1981, in press.

Johnson-Laird, P. N., Gibbs, G., & de Mowbray, J. Meaning, amount of processing and memory for words. *Memory and Cognition*, 1978, *6*, 372-375.

Johnston, W. A., & Heinz, S. P. Flexibility and capacity demands of attention. *Journal of Experimental Psychology: General*, 1978, *107*, 420-435.

Jones, B. M. Memory impairment on the ascending and descending limbs of the blood alcohol curve. *Journal of Abnormal Psychology*, 1973, *82*, 24-32.

Kolers, P. A. Remembering operations. *Memory and Cognition*, 1973, *1*, 347-335.

Kolers, P. A. Memorial consequences of automatized encoding. *Journal of Experimental Psychology: Human Learning and Memory*, 1975, *1*, 689-701.

Light, L. L., & Carter-Sobell, L. Effects of changed semantic context on recognition memory. *Journal of Verbal Learning and Verbal Behavior*, 1970, *9*, 1-11.

Lockhart, R. S., Craik, F. I. M., & Jacoby, L. L. Depth of processing, recognition and recall: Some aspects of a general memory system. In J. Brown (Ed.), *Recall and recognition*. London: Wiley, 1976.

Mandler, G. Organization and repetition: An extension of organizational principles with special reference to rote learning. In L.-G. Nilsson (Ed.), *Perspectives on memory research*. Hillsdale, N.J.: Lawrence Erlbaum Associates, 1979.

Mandler, G. Recognizing: The judgement of previous occurrence. *Psychological Review*, 1980, *98*, 252-271.

Mandler, G., & Worden, P. E. Semantic processing without permanent storage. *Journal of Experimental Psychology*, 1973, *100*, 277-283.

Mandler, J. M. A code in the node: The use of a story schema in retrieval. *Discourse Processes,* 1978, 1, 14–35.

Moray, N. Attention in dichotic listening: Affective cues and the influence of instructions. *Quarterly Journal of Experimental Psychology,* 1959, 11, 56–60.

Morton, J. Interaction of information in word recognition. *Psychological Review,* 1969, 76, 165–178.

Murdock, B. B., Jr. Effects of a subsidiary task on short-term memory. *British Journal of Psychology,* 1965, 56, 413–419.

Nelson, T. O. Repetition and depth of processing. *Journal of Verbal Learning and Verbal Behavior,* 1977, 16, 151–172.

Norman, D. A., & Bobrow, D. G. On data-limited and resource-limited processes. *Cognitive Psychology,* 1975, 7, 44–64.

Perlmutter, M. Age differences in adults' free recall, cued recall and recognition. *Journal of Gerontology,* 1979, 35, 533–539.

Rabinowitz, J. C., Mandler, G., & Patterson, K. E. Determinants of recognition and recall: Accessibility and generation. *Journal of Experimental Psychology: General,* 1977, 196, 302–329.

Rankin, J. L., & Kausler, D. M. Adult age differences in false recognitions. *Journal of Gerontology,* 1979, 34, 58–65.

Rundus, D. Maintenance rehearsal and single-level processing. *Journal of Verbal Learning and Verbal Behavior,* 1977, 16, 665–681.

Simon, E. Depth and elaboration of processing in relation to age. *Journal of Experimental Psychology: Human Learning and Memory,* 1979, 5, 115–124.

Slamecka, N. J., & Graf, P. The generation effect: Delineation of a phenomenon. *Journal of Experimental Psychology: Human Learning and Memory,* 1978, 4, 592–604.

Smith, S. E. Remembering in and out of context. *Journal of Experimental Psychology: Human Learning and Memory,* 1979, 5, 460–471.

Smith, S. M., Glenberg, A., & Bjork, R. A. Environmental context and human memory. *Memory and Cognition,* 1978, 6, 342–353.

Till, R. E., & Walsh, D. A. Encoding and retrieval factors in adult memory for implicational sentences. *Journal of Verbal Learning and Verbal Behavior,* 1980, 19, 1–16.

Tulving, E. Ecphoric processes in recall and recognition. In J. Brown (Ed.), *Recall and recognition.* London: Wiley, 1976.

Tulving, E. Memory research: What kind of progress? In L.-G. Nilsson (Ed.), *Perspectives on memory research.* Hillsdale, N.J.: Lawrence Erlbaum Associates, 1979.

Tulving, E., & Thomson, D. M. Encoding specificity and retrieval processes in episodic memory. *Psychological Review,* 1973, 80, 352–373.

Tulving, E., & Watkins, M. J. Structure of memory traces. *Psychological Review,* 1975, 83, 261–275.

Turvey, M. T. Repetition and the preperceptual information store. *Journal of Experimental Psychology,* 1967, 74, 289–293.

Tversky, B. Encoding processes in recognition and recall. *Cognitive Psychology,* 1973, 5, 275–287.

Tyler, S. W., Hertel, P. T., McCallum, M. C., & Ellis, H. C. Cognitive effort and memory. *Journal of Experimental Psychology: Human Learning and Memory,* 1979, 5, 607–617.

Whitten, W. B., II, & Leonard, J. M. Learning from tests: Facilitation of delayed recall by initial recognition alternatives. *Journal of Experimental Psychology: Human Learning and Memory,* 1980, 6, 127–134.

Woodward, A. E., Bjork, R. A., & Jongeward, R. H., Jr. Recall and recognition as a function of primary rehearsal. *Journal of Verbal Learning and Verbal Behavior,* 1973, 12, 608–612.

23 Order Effects in Recall

Jeroen G. W. Raaijmakers
University of Nijmegen
Nijmegen, The Netherlands

Richard M. Shiffrin
Indiana University
Bloomington, Indiana
U.S.A.

ABSTRACT

An experiment combining free (noncued) and cued recall of lists of single words and paired associates is described. List-length effects were observed in both free and cued recall, contrary to conclusions drawn by Murdock (1967). It was found that a prior free recall test had a negative effect on subsequent cued recall, whereas no such effect was observed in free recall of single words. Moreover, the probability of recall for paired associates showed a small decrease as a function of output position. These results are analyzed from the point of view of the search theory for retrieval from memory proposed by Raaijmakers and Shiffrin (1981). A model for these types of experiments based on this theory is described. The model was found to be able to handle all the major findings of this experiment. The effects are interpreted as a consequence of the role of contextual retrieval cues in both cued and noncued recall.

INTRODUCTION

In this chapter we describe and analyze a number of order effects in recall from the point of view of our recently proposed search theory for retrieval from long-term memory (Raaijmakers, 1979; Raaijmakers & Shiffrin, 1980, 1981).

We make use of the theory to predict simultaneously free recall and single-trial paired-associate recall.

Our theory combines elements of probabilistic search theory (Shiffrin, 1970) with elements of associative network theories (Anderson, 1972; Anderson & Bower, 1973). It posits cue-dependent probabilistic search of an associative long-term memory network and is denoted SAM, for *S*earch of *A*ssociative *M*emory. Given the length of this chapter, only a brief sketch of the theory can be given. For more details the reader is referred to Raaijmakers and Shiffrin (1981).

It is assumed that during study of a list of items episodic images consisting of item and context information are stored in LTS. Item information is that part of the information in the stored image that refers to the item as defined by the experimenter. For example, if the experimenter presents a list of words, the item information would refer to that information that enables the subject to produce the ''name'' of the encoded word. Context information refers to all other information stored in the image (i.e., temporal and situational features that might also be present in short-term store at a given time, including environmental details, physical sensations, emotional feelings, and all thought processes not directly relevant to response production). These episodic features are interconnected within an image and are also associated to other images.

Memory retrieval is cue-dependent: Which image is elicited from memory is determined by the probe cues utilized at that moment (Tulving, 1974). It is therefore convenient (if one is mainly interested in retrieval) to specify directly the relationships between the probe cues and the memory images. This is accomplished by defining a *retrieval structure*. The retrieval structure gives the strength of relationship between each possible probe cue and each possible image. Note that the retrieval structure is a simplifying device; it gives overall directional strengths but ignores details such as the kind of association or relation involved. The retrieval structure is designed to capture those aspects of the storage structure (which may be more complex than the retrieval structure) that are important for retrieval. The degree to which an image in memory is associated to the set of probe cues, in comparison with the degree to which other images are associated to the set of probe cues, determines the probability that that item will be selected at that moment in the search.

As in Shiffrin (1970), retrieval is assumed to consist of two phases: *sampling* and *recovery*. At each step of the search process, a set of cues is used as a probe of long-term store. From the briefly activated set of information a single image is sampled. The probability of sampling a particular image is a function of the strength of association between the probe cues and that image [denoted by $S(Q_j, I_i)$]. Specifically, the probability of sampling image I_i using a set of probe cues, $Q_1, \ldots, Q_m$, is given by the following equation:

$$P_S(I_i|Q_1, \ldots, Q_m) = \frac{\prod_{j=1}^{m} S(Q_j, I_i)^{w_j}}{\sum_{k=1}^{N} \prod_{j=1}^{m} S(Q_j, I_k)^{w_j}} \tag{1}$$

The w_j in the right-hand expression are weights assigned to the different cues representing their relative saliency. In what follows we assume all these weights to be 1.0.

This equation incorporates the key assumption of the present approach. The strengths to the different cues are multiplied and the ratio rule (Luce, 1959) is applied to the products. This multiplicative feature allows focusing of the search. The images most likely to be sampled are those that are associated strongly to all cues rather than to just one. The sampled image tends to come from the intersection of the sets of images strongly associated to each cue separately.

When an image is sampled, its features will tend to become activated. It is assumed that the stronger the associative strength between the selected image and the probe cues, the larger will be the proportion of image elements that will be activated and made available to the subject's evaluation and decision-making mechanisms. This process is termed *recovery*. It is assumed that the set of activated image elements is determined largely by the set of probe cues used; furthermore, we propose that over the short time period of a single memory search these sets will not change appreciably. Thus, if a given set of probe cues samples a particular image twice during retrieval, we assume that roughly the same elements will be activated on both occasions. The following implication results: If recovery succeeds on one occasion for a given set of probe cues, it will succeed on all other occasions, and conversely.

In recall tasks the subject has to generate the "name" of the item encoded in the selected image. The following equation gives the probability of recovering enough information to give correctly the name encoded in the image newly sampled by probe cues Q_1 to Q_m:

$$P_R(I_i | Q_1, \ldots, Q_m) = 1 - \exp\left[- \sum_{j=1}^{m} w_j S(Q_j, I_i) \right] \qquad (2)$$

In essence, this recovery rule transforms the summed associative strengths to a number between 0 and 1. Note that both the sampling and the recovery rule are natural extensions of the rules proposed by Shiffrin (1970). Memory search consists of a series of retrieval attempts, each consisting of a sampling and a recovery phase. This search goes on until a stopping criterion based on the number of failures is reached.

This theory has been applied with considerable success to a variety of results in single-trial free recall. Among others, the model predicts the effects of list length and presentation time, interresponse times, cued and noncued recall of categorized lists, and the part-list cuing effect. Most of these results are reported in Raaijmakers and Shiffrin (1980).

Although this model was originally developed to handle data from free recall experiments, it contains all the ingredients necessary to predict paired-associate recall. It would therefore be of some value to see whether the model is able to handle the results when free recall and paired-associate recall are mixed in a single study. Moreover, there is a suggestion in the literature (Murdock, 1967) that some results may be different in single-trial paired-associate recall compared to single-trial free recall, in particular, the list-length effect. On the basis of his results, Murdock (1967; see also Murdock, 1974, p. 99) concluded that the asymptotic probability of recall did not depend on list length. This result, which is in agreement with his fluctuation model, is rather surprising from our point of view. In our framework, list-length effects are due to the assumption that retrieval involves a sampling-with-replacement process in which contextual retrieval cues corresponding to the list context are used. Because such context cues would be expected to be used in paired-associate recall as well as in free recall, we would predict a list-length effect in single-trial paired-associate recall. It should be noted, however, that Murdock (1967) based his conclusion on somewhat indirect evidence (viz., a correspondence between the slope of the function relating list length to number of pairs recalled and the asymptotic probability of recall as found in probe paired-associate studies). In this way, Murdock attempted to circumvent the problem of concluding the existence of a list-length effect simply because of the inclusion of short-term memory recall (which would give the smaller list lengths an advantage irrespective of the asymptotic level of recall). It is not clear, however, what the results would have been if recall from short-term memory had been eliminated experimentally (e.g., by a distractor task).

In this chapter, we discuss the results of an experiment designed to show: (1) the role of contextual associations in cued and noncued recall; and (2) the influence of strengthening of the contextual associations for one group of items on the retrieval of other items. In this experiment subjects were presented lists of items composed of single words only (as in the usual free recall paradigm), pairs of words only (as in paired-associate studies), or both single words and pairs. The recall test consisted of a noncued (free) recall test for the single words on the list and/or a cued (paired-associate) recall test for the paired words. We are especially interested in the possible effects of a prior cued (noncued) recall test on a subsequent noncued (cued) test. We also discuss an application of the SAM theory for retrieval from long-term memory to the results of this experiment.

Method

Design

There were 10 conditions in this experiment differing in the number of single words (denoted by FR) and the number of pairs (denoted by PA) on a list. A single-trial procedure was used, so each list was studied only once. The 10 conditions were:

Number of PA items:	0	0	0	5	5	5	15	15	15	30
Number of FR items:	10	30	40	0	10	30	0	10	30	0

(Note that the number of PA items is given in terms of the number of pairs; the number of words is therefore given by twice this number.) PA items and FR items were not presented in a blocked fashion but were randomly mixed on a list. A Latin square design with 10 groups of subjects was used. Each group was given only one list in each condition. For each condition, half the subjects were tested first on the PA items (cued testing) and the other subjects were tested first on the FR items (noncued testing). Subjects were not told before study of the list which items would be tested first.

The words were presented visually, a single word for 2 sec, a pair for 4 sec. PA items were tested either in a forward or in a backward manner: If the pair was A–B, it was tested either as A–? or as ?–B. Only four-fifths of all PA items were tested in this immediate test; the remaining items were tested only at an end-of-session test (the results of which will not be reported in this chapter).

Materials

Each list for a given group of subjects consisted of a random selection from a master list of 600 monosyllabic English nouns. No word was presented more than once in any of the lists. An additional practice list was constructed consisting of five pairs and five single words. The same practice list was used for all groups of subjects.

Subjects

The subjects were 79 undergraduates at Indiana University. They were given introductory psychology course credit for their participation in the experiment. Due to the fact that some subjects did not complete the experiment and due to experimenter error, not all the results are based on 79 subjects; all results are, however, based on at least 69 subjects. Subjects were tested in groups of approximately 8 subjects each.

Procedure

Subjects were given instructions regarding the nature of the lists and the type of tests that would be given. They were asked to allot an equal amount of effort to studying each word. The instructions emphasized that they should try to link together the two members of a word pair into a single unit, by forming a mental image or by using some kind of verbal code. After presentation of the list a 20-sec arithmetic task was given to eliminate short-term effects. A written recall procedure was used. There were two types of tests, one for single words only and one for pairs only. Single words were tested using a 2-min free recall testing procedure; paired words were tested with a paired-associate testing procedure. In this case the subjects had 4 sec to write down their answer. The next list was always presented within a minute of the previous list being tested.

Results

Figure 23.1 shows the effect of list length on recall of the PA items and the FR items. These data are averaged over order of testing and over testing with the A member and with the B member of the A–B pair. It is evident that the results are

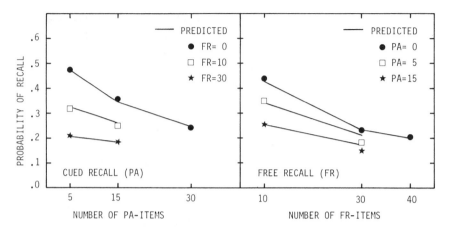

FIG. 23.1. Observed and predicted probabilities of recall for cued and noncued recall as a function of the number of single words (FR) and the number of word pairs (PA) on the list.

quite consistent. In free recall testing the probability of recall decreases not only as a function of the number of FR items but also as a function of the number of PA items on the list. A similar list-length effect is observed for the PA items, and again the probability of recall decreases when other items are mixed in the list. It should be noted that these list-length effects take place even though recall is directed specifically to either FR or PA items. Note that the list-length effect in single-trial paired-associate recall is of about the same magnitude as the list-length effect observed in single-trial free recall, contrary to the conclusions of Murdock (1967).

Figure 23.2 shows the effects of order of testing on the probability of recall in the case of mixed lists. The main result to note here is that noncued recall of the FR items is only slightly reduced by a prior cued test of the PA items. On the other hand, cued recall of PA items is considerably reduced by a prior free recall test of FR items. Overall, the probability of recall for PA items when they are tested first is .271; and when they are tested second, .189. For FR items the overall probability of recall when free recall testing is first is .211 and .191 when second.

Some additional findings are of interest. We did not find a systematic difference between forward and backward recall (the overall probability of forward recall was .255, that of backward recall .286). This result replicated earlier findings (Murdock, 1974, p. 127). Neither did we find a primacy effect for the PA items (see Fig. 23.3), also replicating earlier findings. Note that the fact that we did not find an effect of serial presentation position for the PA items also eliminates one uninteresting explanation of the differential order of testing effect, namely that this differential effect is due to differential output delays. Such a hypothesis would have to predict a lower probability of recall for the items presented earlier in the list. Figure 23.4 shows the probability of recall for PA

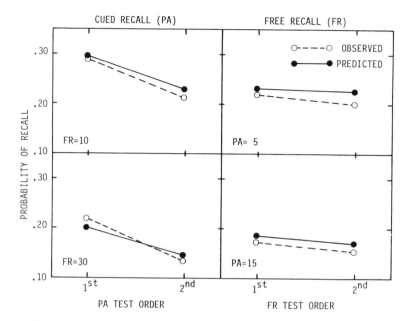

FIG. 23.2. Observed and predicted effect of order of testing on cued and non-cued recall, partitioned according to the number of items of the other type.

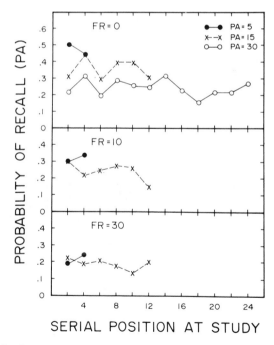

FIG. 23.3. Probability of recall for PA items as a function of serial presentation position (within the class of PA items). Each point is the mean of two successive serial positions.

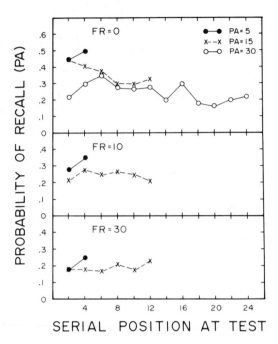

FIG. 23.4. Probability of recall for PA items as a function of output position. Each point is the mean of two successive positions.

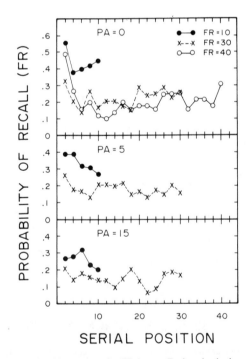

FIG. 23.5. Serial position curves for FR items. Each point is the mean of two successive serial positions (within the class of FR items).

410

items as a function of test position. There does not seem to be a systematic effect of test position, contrary to what would seem to be predicted by our model.

Serial position curves for the FR items are shown in Fig. 23.5. In this case a primacy effect is obtained but it seems somewhat reduced for the mixed lists. This might indicate that a subject stops rehearsing the FR items when a pair is presented for study.

In the following section we apply a model based on the SAM theory for retrieval to the results of this experiment.

APPLICATION OF THE SAM THEORY

It is assumed that the two members of a PA item are associated during study to each other and to the context. FR items (single words) are associated to other FR items that are simultaneously present in STS and to the context. The retrieval structure (Raaijmakers & Shiffrin, 1981) contains associative strengths between a general context cue and the images on the lists and between item cues and those images. These associative strengths are assumed to depend on the length of time that an item (or a pair of items) is rehearsed in STS. It is assumed that all items not rehearsed together in STS have a common residual interitem association value, denoted by d.

Because we are not primarily interested in the particular rehearsal strategy adopted by the subject but only in the long-term retrieval processes, we have decided to let our rehearsal assumptions be shaped by the observed data. The data of the experiment just described suggest that a subject stops rehearsing any of the items in the buffer upon presentation of a new PA item and that PA items are deleted from the buffer upon presentation of a new item (either PA or FR). These assumptions are consistent with the observation that there is no primacy effect for the PA items (each PA item is studied equally long) and that the primacy effect for the FR items decreases with the number of PA items on the list (see Fig. 23.3 and 23.5).

Thus, each PA item (a pair of words) clears the buffer, and each FR item clears the buffer of PA items but adds to any FR items in the buffer (up to the buffer size, r; then one of the previous buffer members is deleted). The two members of a PA item build up item-to-context strength (parameter = a_{PA}) and interitem strength (parameter = b_{PA}) as a function of rehearsal time (always 4 sec in this case). An FR item builds up item-to-context strength (parameter = a_{FR}) and interitem strength (parameter = b_{FR}) as a function, respectively, of rehearsal time, and of joint rehearsal time. It is assumed that the amount of information stored in LTS depends inversely on the number of items in the buffer (Atkinson & Shiffrin, 1968, p. 180): If there are m individual words in the buffer together for t sec, the rehearsal time for any word, or any pair of words, is in each case equal to t/m.

For noncued testing (i.e., free recall), the same model was used as described in Raaijmakers and Shiffrin (1981). The search process is conceived as a series of retrieval attempts, each retrieval attempt consisting of a sampling and a recovery phase. Search goes on until a criterion of KMAX total failures (failures to recall a new FR item) is reached. The subject starts by using the general context cue, representing the context during study of that particular list, to sample from the images that are associated to that cue (Equation 1 is used with all weights equal to 1.0). When a particular image has been sampled, the "name" of that item has to be recovered. It is assumed throughout that recovery will not succeed if this particular image has already been sampled (unsuccessfully) by each of the present cues, either alone or in some combination (Raaijmakers & Shiffrin, 1981). Otherwise, the recovery rule of Equation 2 is applied. During free recall testing, retrieval of a PA item or an already recalled item is considered a failure. Upon a failure, context sampling is tried again, unless the total failure criterion has been reached.

After successful recovery, the recalled word is used as a retrieval cue along with context. If this probe set does not lead to recall of new items (i.e., if a criterion of LMAX failures with this probe set is reached), then the subject switches back to context as the only cue.

It is assumed that learning takes place during retrieval. To be precise, the relevant associative strengths are incremented upon successful retrieval of an item. The context strength is incremented by e_{FR} and the interitem strength by f_{FR} (if an item was used as a retrieval cue). As in previous applications, the strength of an item cue to its own image was, somewhat arbitrarily, set equal to that item's context strength (and the increment was set equal to the context increment). When KMAX is reached, a rechecking process was assumed in which each of the recalled items is used as a retrieval cue in a last attempt at recall of additional items. Finally, it should be noted that it was assumed that any sampled and recovered item could be classified correctly as to type (PA or FR) because intrusions of PA items in free recall were very rare (and similarly for intrusions of FR items in cued recall).

In cued testing, it was assumed that each sample is made with both context and the provided item cue and that search ceases when a criterion of LPAMAX failures is reached (because only 4 sec were provided for recall, this parameter was arbitrarily set to 1). As in noncued recall, the strengths to the probe cues are incremented upon successful retrieval. The increment in the context strength is denoted by e_{PA}. Because in this particular case a PA item cue will never be used again as a retrieval cue (neither in cued nor in noncued recall), it follows that the value of the increment in the interitem associative strength for the two members of a PA item is irrelevant to our predictions, so this parameter (f_{PA}) is not used in this application.

Only a limited parameter search was carried out, based on a Monte Carlo procedure. An adequate fit was obtained for the following values: KMAX = 30; LMAX = 4; LPAMAX = 1; r = 4; a_{FR} = .315; a_{PA} = .16; b_{FR} = .305; b_{PA}

$= .58; d = .029; e_{FR} = f_{FR} = 2.90; e_{PA} = .90$. The major predictions are shown in Fig. 23.1 and 23.2. The model handles these data quite well.

The list-length effects shown in Fig. 23.1 can be explained by the assumption that all items are associated to the same context and that contextual associations are used in both cued and noncued recall. The list-length effect in cued recall is a result of the assumption that the item cue is not only associated to the target image but also (residually) to all other images. The product of associative strengths to the context cue and to the item cue (and thus the sampling probability) is therefore not zero for these other images. Increasing the number of items (both PA and FR) on the list increases the size of the search set, the set of images with nonzero sampling probabilities. Such an increase in the size of the search set leads to a decrease in the sampling probability for any particular item: The denominator of Equation 1 becomes larger, and hence the sampling probability for a particular image, lower (because the numerator does not change).

The order of testing effect is predicted because the increment in context strength for FR items is relatively large compared to the stored context strength of the PA items, whereas the increment in PA context strength is much smaller relative to the context strength of the FR items. Thus, the magnitude of the list-length effects and the effects of order of testing are determined by the relative strengths of the contextual associations (because these contextual associations determine the sampling probabilities of "irrelevant" items).

It was mentioned previously that our model predicts an effect of output order on the probability of recall of PA items. The interfering effect of other list items in cued recall is a function of the total strength of the contextual associations of these other items. Because it is assumed that the contextual associative strengths are incremented upon recall of an item, it follows that the more items have been recalled, the larger the interference. Figure 23.6 gives the observed and predicted

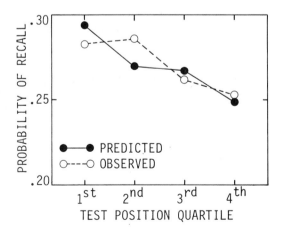

FIG. 23.6. Observed and predicted probability of recall for PA items, for all list types lumped together, as a function of test quartile.

probabilities of recall for PA items for successive quartiles, averaged over all lists. The effects are indeed predicted to be quite small. Therefore, the observation that no consistent effect of output order was evident in Fig. 23.4 does not contradict the present model. In fact, it is a strong point in favor of the model that it predicts small effects when they are small (or not significant) and large effects when they are indeed large (as in other studies not reported here).

FINAL COMMENTS

It was shown that a model based on the SAM theory for retrieval from long-term memory was able to predict the data of the present experiment. The model predicted a list-length effect in cued recall, a negative effect of prior noncued recall on subsequent cued recall, and an effect of output order in cued recall.

The list-length effect was contrary to the conclusions drawn by Murdock (1967). It should be noted, however, that similar effects are evident in cued recall of categorized lists (Tulving & Pearlstone, 1966). Moreover, in follow-up experiments we have found similar (or even larger) effects (for a first report, see Raaijmakers, 1979). The differential order-of-testing effect has also been replicated in other experiments. Moreover, it is interesting to note that it was also present in the well-known Tulving and Pearlstone experiment on cued and noncued recall of categorized lists (Tulving & Pearlstone, 1966, Fig. 1), although this was subsequently ignored. The effect of output position in cued recall is of course similar to the corresponding effect in cued recall of categorized lists observed by Smith (1971) and Roediger (1973), among others. Roediger and Schmidt (1980) report a similar effect of test order in paired-associate recall.

Taken together, these results imply that, in both cued and noncued recall, contextual as well as interitem associations are used in retrieval. Moreover, the fact that a system developed for free recall is able to handle so accurately these various results is, in our opinion, a strong point in favor of the SAM theory for retrieval.

Finally, it should be noted that in this particular application we have assumed that a PA item (A–B) is stored as two separate images with a strong interitem strength. It is of some importance that equally good fits are obtained with a model that assumes that a PA item is stored as a single image (of course with somewhat different parameter values). This latter model would correspond to a redintegrative view of paired-associate retrieval (see the ''fragmentation'' model of Jones, 1976, for comparison). So, in this kind of experiment these two types of models cannot be discriminated. We have found, however, that in other types of experiment, carried out by Al White at Indiana University, where triples instead of pairs are interassociated during study, the second, redintegrative, type of model is clearly superior.

ACKNOWLEDGMENTS

This research was supported in part by a fellowship from the Netherlands Organization for the Advancement of Pure Research (Z.W.O.) to the first author, and Public Health Service Grant 12717 and National Science Foundation Grant BNS-77-00156 to the second author. We gratefully acknowledge the help of Gary Gillund, who assisted us in various ways during the development of this work.

REFERENCES

Anderson, J. R. FRAN: A simulation model of free recall. In G. H. Bower (Ed.), *The psychology of learning and motivation: Advances in research and theory* (Vol. 5). New York: Academic Press, 1972.

Anderson, J. R., & Bower, G. H. *Human associative memory*. Washington, D.C.: V. H. Winston, 1973.

Atkinson, R. C., & Shiffrin, R. M. Human memory: A proposed system and its control processes. In K. W. Spence & J. T. Spence (Eds.), *The psychology of learning and motivation: Advances in research and theory* (Vol. 2). New York: Academic Press, 1968.

Jones, G. V. A fragmentation hypothesis of memory: Cued recall of pictures and of sequential position. *Journal of Experimental Psychology: General*, 1976, *105*, 277–293.

Luce, R. D. *Individual choice behavior: A theoretical analysis*. New York: Wiley, 1959.

Murdock, B. B., Jr. A fixed-point model for short-term memory. *Journal of Mathematical Psychology*, 1967, *4*, 501–506.

Murdock, B. B., Jr. *Human memory: Theory and data*. Hillsdale, N.J.: Lawrence Erlbaum Associates, 1974.

Raaijmakers, J. G. W. *Retrieval from long-term store: A general theory and mathematical models*. Doctoral dissertation, University of Nijmegen, Nijmegen, The Netherlands, 1979.

Raaijmakers, J. G. W., & Shiffrin, R. M. SAM: A theory of probabilistic search of associative memory. In G. H. Bower (Ed.), *The psychology of learning and motivation: Advances in research and theory* (Vol. 14). New York: Academic Press, 1980.

Raaijmakers, J. G. W., & Shiffrin, R. M. Search of associative memory. *Psychological Review*, 1981.

Roediger, H. L. Inhibition in recall from cueing with recall targets. *Journal of Verbal Learning and Verbal Behavior*, 1973, *12*, 644–657.

Roediger, H. L., & Schmidt, S. R. Output interference in the recall of categorized and paired-associate lists. *Journal of Experimental Psychology: Human Learning and Memory*, 1980, *6*, 91–105.

Shiffrin, R. M. Memory search. In D. A. Norman (Ed.), *Models of human memory*. New York: Academic Press, 1970.

Smith, A. D. Output interference and organized recall from long-term memory. *Journal of Verbal Learning and Verbal Behavior*, 1971, *10*, 400–408.

Tulving, E. Cue-dependent forgetting. *American Scientist*, 1974, *62*, 74–82.

Tulving, E., & Pearlstone, Z. Availability versus accessibility of information in memory for words. *Journal of Verbal Learning and Verbal Behavior*, 1966, *5*, 381–391.

24

Mentalmorphosis: Alterations in Memory Produced by the Mental Bonding of New Information to Old

Elizabeth F. Loftus
University of Washington
Seattle, Washington
U.S.A.

ABSTRACT

After an event has occurred, postevent information can be introduced into a person's recollection, sometimes supplementing the previously acquired memory and sometimes altering it. The attachment of new information to an earlier memory, called *mental bonding,* is proposed to occur relatively automatically, unless the information is tagged as being inappropriate. Mental bonding is enhanced when postevent information contains complex rather than simple presuppositions, possibly because the complex version causes attention to be diverted away from the critical information making it less likely that a person will resist its influence. Mental bonding is also influenced by the amount of attention paid to the original event. A simple probabilistic model that relates the likelihood of suggestible behavior to two processes—comprehension of the postevent information and acceptance of its content—can aid in the understanding of variables that influence the degree of mental bonding.

INTRODUCTION

After a person has witnessed an event, say, a crime, an accident, or even a more ordinary event, new information can come to that person's attention. Numerous experiments have shown that this new information can become incorporated into memory, supplementing or altering the original memory.

An experiment in which subjects are presented with a film of a complex event and immediately afterward are asked a series of questions is representative of the

417

paradigm we have used to study the incorporation of new information into memory. (See Loftus, 1979, for a review.) Typically, some of the questions are designed to present misleading information—that is, to suggest the existence of an object that did not in fact exist. Thus, in one study we asked some subjects who had just watched a film of an automobile accident, ''How fast was the white sports car going when it passed the barn while traveling along the country road?'' whereas no barn existed. Other subjects were asked a control question, such as ''How fast was the white sports car going while traveling along the country road?'' All subjects were later asked whether they had seen a barn.

We found that the misleading questions increased by a factor of six the likelihood that the subjects would later report having seen the nonexistent barn. We advanced the argument that the questions are effective because they contain information—in this case false information—that becomes integrated into the person's recollection of the event, thereby supplementing that memory.

In other studies, we have shown that new information can do more than simply supplement a recollection: It can occasionally alter, or transform, a recollection. Thus, in one study, subjects saw a series of color slides depicting successive stages in an accident involving an automobile and a pedestrian. In the midst of the series, the auto, a red Datsun, was seen traveling along a side street toward an intersection at which there was a stop sign for half of the subjects and a yield sign for the remaining subjects. Some subjects then received a question containing a piece of misinformation: For example, the question ''Did another car pass the red Datsun while it was stopped at the stop sign?'' contains a piece of misinformation when it is asked of subjects who actually saw the yield sign. And, finally, subjects were tested for their recollection of the sign. Depending on the time intervals that occurred between the slides, the intervening questions, and the final recollection, up to 80% of the subjects indicated that their recollections were influenced by the misinformation.

These experiments, along with many others using similar procedures, indicate that false information can be introduced into a person's recollection, whether that recollection is measured by a recall or a recognition procedure. Further, the information can supplement the previously acquired memory (as in the case of the barn) or it can actually transform it (as in the case of the stop sign/yield sign). For purposes of the present chapter, we combine these two outcomes and say that postevent information has been *bonded* to the original memory.

MENTAL BONDING

People vary in suggestibility, meaning the extent to which they will modify their recollections of an event in light of later information. When people have witnessed a complex event and are subsequently exposed to misleading suggestions about that event, some will modify their recollections a great deal, whereas others change only slightly or not at all (Loftus, 1977). Furthermore, there are situational variables that lend themselves to maximal rather than minimal modification. One purpose of the present chapter is to explore some hypotheses about the maximal conditions for bonding of postevent information to occur.

One hypothesis about postevent information is that it will be stored in memory where related information is already stored. The bonding of postevent information may occur relatively automatically, unless the postevent information is tagged as being inappropriate.

What Does It Mean to Tag Something Inappropriate?

People can prevent the bonding of postevent information. For example, in one study subjects were exposed to a piece of false information that blatantly contradicted a clearly perceived detail. After viewing a series of slides in which a thief stole a bright red wallet, subjects read a version of the incident ostensibly written by another witness who referred to the wallet as dark brown. Later when subjects were asked for their recollection of the wallet, all insisted it was red and not brown. Furthermore, those subjects who were given the blatant false suggestion tended to be more resistant to other misleading suggestions to which they might ordinarily fall prey (Loftus, 1979). In a related study (Dritsas & Hamilton, 1977), subjects showed less bonding of postevent information when it contradicted a salient and central object than when it contradicted a peripheral object. In a final study (Dodd & Bradshaw, 1980), subjects resisted misleading postevent information from a biased source even though that same information attributed to a neutral source became bonded into memory. Taken together, these studies indicate that subjects will use information in memory as well as postevent facts to tag incoming information as inappropriate.

What Does It Mean to Process Automatically?

Several investigators have advanced the notion that humans can automatically encode certain kinds of stimuli into memory. Typically they have referred to well-learned, highly familiar stimuli, like the letters of the alphabet: The idea is that these can become encoded into memory without the involvement of attention and without reducing the ability to process other signals (Keele, 1973; Laberge & Samuels, 1974; Posner & Rogers, 1978; Shiffrin & Schneider, 1977). Although many researchers believe that some stimuli may not require the active attention of a person in order to become incorporated into memory, others believe that even in these "automatic" cases some attention is being allocated by subjects to the critical stimuli (Ogden, Martin & Paap, 1980). Allocation of attention is thought to be largely under the control of subjects' strategies and is based on subjects' expectancies about the task. Skilled performers develop ways of allocating attention optimally so that processing capacity devoted to certain kinds of stimuli is at a minimum but sufficient for encoding. Once this is accomplished, concurrent mental activity can proceed in a state of shared attention (Sperling & Melchner,

1978). Thus, there is precedent for the notion that information can be incorporated into memory with a minimal amount of attention devoted to it—almost automatically.

We can apply these ideas about quasiautomatic processing to a situation in which a subject sees a complex event and then is introduced to postevent information about that event. If the postevent information is attended to and scrutinized, it can be tagged as inappropriate and bonding is then prevented. But what if attention is diverted? Obviously if attention is completely diverted, the postevent information will not be processed, and thus bonding cannot occur. But suppose attention is partially diverted such that a minimal amount is devoted to the critical piece of misinformation—enough so that it is processed but not so much that it is scrutinized. This may be optimal for bonding.

In previous experiments we may have stumbled—almost by accident—upon an optimal procedure for inducing bonding. Recall the structure of the questions that we used to introduce misinformation. In one study, the question was:

1. How fast was the white sports car going when it passed the barn while traveling along the country road?

In another study the question was:

2. Did another car pass the red Datsun while it was stopped at the stop sign?

In both cases, the questions are rather complex, and the misleading information is embedded in a clause. In both cases, the question focuses the respondent on some aspect of the situation that is irrelevant to the misleading detail. In one case, the respondent is focused on the speed of the white sports car, whereas in the second case the respondent is concentrating on whether another car passed the red Datsun at some point in time. Put another way, the misinformation in both cases is presupposed in a peripheral part of the question, while attention is devoted to a more central part of the question. Does the complex wording of these questions contribute to the bonding that we observe? One hypothesis is that these questions may be effective because they draw attention away from the critical detail, focusing it elsewhere in the question. When reduced attention is devoted to that critical detail, subjects may not scrutinize it at the time they process it, but it may still be encoded into memory. Without the diversion, additional attention may be applied to that critical detail, and it might be easier for some subjects to tag it as something that was not really noticed by them. The likelihood of its incorporation into memory would consequently be reduced. Thus, the complex questions may be especially suited for inducing bonding of postevent information.

Later in the chapter, we consider the role of attention on the witnessed event itself. And, finally, we suggest a new way of viewing the malleability of memory in terms of the components that enter into mental bonding.

QUESTION COMPLEXITY

In a recent doctoral dissertation, Kenneth Johnson (1979) examined variations in question wording and the extent to which these influenced the likelihood that a piece of misinformation would later be recalled erroneously by a subject. In his Experiment 4, Johnson used questions containing two kinds of presuppositions, which he referred to as linguistic and logical presuppositions. Although the precise distinction between these two kinds of presuppositions is somewhat complex and tangential to the main purpose of this chapter, his questions containing logical presuppositions were invariably longer and more complex than the questions containing linguistic presuppositions. Compare these two ways of presupposing the existence of a "loans" sign:

1. Was the "loans" sign knocked off a desk by a robber?
2. Was the woman, who was sitting at the desk with the "loans" sign, biting her fingernails?

Compare these two ways of presupposing the existence of luggage racks on the getaway car:

1. Were the luggage racks on the getaway car holding a large carton?
2. Was the station wagon, which was equipped with luggage racks, carrying a large carton?

In the shorter and simpler version of these questions, the linguistic presupposition is accomplished by the definite reference of the article *the*. The critical object is, in each case, part of the focus of the question. In the complex version of the questions, the logical presupposition is introduced via a restrictive relative clause. The misinformation in this case is not part of the focus of the question. In fact the relative clause, and the embedded item, can virtually be ignored and the question can still be answered.

Johnson's 156 subjects participated in an experiment in which they viewed a series of slides, answered an intervening questionnaire, and then took a final test for their memory for the details of the slides. The intervening questionnaire included some critical questions that were designed to contain either simple or complex presuppositions.

The Witnessed Event

The participants viewed a narrated slide show of a bank robbery. The slides consisted of 12 line drawings depicting various scenes from a bank robbery. The jointed scenes were made comprehensible with the addition of narration by a presumed witness. For example, while watching the first slide, the subjects heard: "I had just arrived at the bank. I needed some money for lunch. There were a lot of people. I had to wait a long time, as usual. One man bought a lot of traveler's checks; another brought in a bag of dimes and quarters from his vending machine.'' The slides were projected for approximately 10 sec to 15 sec, the length of time it took to present the accompanying narration.

Two different versions of each slide were used; one contained a critical object such as a ''loans'' sign, whereas the other did not. Half of the slides shown to each subject did not contain the central object.

The Intervening Questionnaire

After watching the slides, subjects spent 15–20 min writing a summary of the main points of the event. They then filled out an intervening questionnaire that contained the critical questions. Finally, they returned one day later to answer direct questions about 12 critical items. These questions took the form ''Did you see the 'loans' sign?''

In addition to the two experimental conditions in which subjects received either simple or complex presuppositions in the questionnaire, two control conditions were used. In one control, named the *delayed question control,* subjects received no mention of the critical object at any earlier time. In the other control, the *repeated question control,* subjects received a question of the form ''Was there a clock?'' one day later. This second control was included for the following reason. It is possible that any increase in false positives due to the presuppositions is wholly due to the object having been mentioned in the earlier session. If an earlier question merely asks about a critical object, say a clock, instead of presupposing it, subjects might later say to themselves ''I remember something about a clock, so I guess I must have seen one.'' If this were the case, then merely asking about a nonexistent object could increase the tendency to report the existence of that object at some later time, obviating the need for fancy questions, complex or otherwise, containing false presuppositions.

The Final Questionnaire

The final questionnaire given one day later contained direct questions about the critical objects worded with ''Did you see.'' The instructions to the subjects emphasized that subjects were to rely on their own memory.

Results

The proportion of incorrect *yes* responses to direct questions on the second questionnaire is presented in Table 24.1. As seen, subjects were most likely to indicate erroneously that they had seen a particular detail when that detail had been embedded in a complex question.

Johnson himself noted that there was one item that received an unusually large number of false positives (.69) in the delayed question control condition; it

TABLE 24.1
Proportion of *Yes* Responses to Direct Questions
about Absent Items as a Function of Type of
Intervening Information
(Adapted from Johnson, 1979)

Delayed Question Control	Repeated Question Control	Simple Presupposition	Complex Presupposition
.16	.18	.20	.28

concerned children looking in the bank window. When this problematic item is removed from the tabulations, the difference between the delayed question control and the complex presupposition becomes even larger (.11 versus .28) with the other two proportions again being intermediate.

The difference in proportion of *yes* responses between the two extreme conditions was relatively small in Johnson's experiment. Subjects asked the questions containing complex presuppositions indicated they had seen the nonexistent object 28% of the time, only 12% more often than the delayed question control. This may have been due, in part, to the instruction given to subjects just prior to their receiving the intervening questionnaire. Those instructions were as follows: "The following questions are drawn, in part, from the account of another person who witnessed the robbery, and they may mention some aspects or events of the robbery that were not reported by the witness who narrated the slides. Answer the questions based on your knowledge of the robbery from the slides that you viewed, or if a question is about something the narrator said, on the basis of what she reported."

It is possible that this instruction "alerted" the subjects to watch for those aspects of the robbery that were new. If this were the case, subjects may have paid more attention to the new items than they might have ordinarily done. Furthermore, the intervening questionnaire attempted to mislead subjects about multiple nonexistent items. Subjects could have "caught on" to the manipulation and subsequently responded differently than they might have ordinarily responded. These considerations, in part, motivated a follow-up experiment on complexity effects.

Further Complexity Effects

The follow-up experiment attempted to replicate Johnson's finding using different subjects and materials and correcting some of the problems noted previously. In this experiment, subjects were asked only one critical question that contained a piece of misinformation, in order to minimize the chances that subjects would become suspicious about the presence of misleading details. In this study, too, subjects were later asked whether they had actually seen various objects, including the critical one. And, finally, they were tested for their memory for the intervening questions—something Johnson had not done.

The study addressed an additional question: To what extent would subjects *remember* having *read* about the misinformation on their intervening questionnaire? Would memory be different depending on whether the information was introduced via a complex versus a simple presupposition? The idea that subjects will focus differently on different parts of an assertion of a question is not new (Clark & Clark, 1977). If the critical misinformation is introduced via a simple presupposition, it tends to be the object of focus. It may be remembered better because it plays an active, salient role. Such a finding would ordinarily not be surprising, but in the present context subjects appear to be less likely to think that they have seen the objects introduced via simple presuppositions. If they were simultaneously more likely to remember that they had read about the object, this contrast would be interesting.

The subjects in this study were 147 students who were enrolled in an undergraduate psychology course. During an ordinary class period, two men abruptly came into the classroom. One of them stood by the door while the other interrupted the class to pick up a book that he had left on a table in the front. The taller one had a brief argument with the professor and both of them left. About 40 min later, the students were given a questionnaire designed to test their memory for the incident. The questionnaire contained 15 questions, the tenth of which was critical. For each question the subject responded by checking a space for yes, no, or I don't know. Unbeknown to the subjects, two versions of question 10 were constructed, both of which falsely presupposed that the intruder had a moustache.

1. Was the moustache worn by the tall intruder light or dark brown?
2. Did the intruder who was tall and had a moustache say anything to the professor?

One-third of the subjects were asked the question with the simple presupposition; one-third were asked the question with a complex presupposition; and the remaining third were asked a control question about the tall intruder's eyebrows.

One day later, the subjects were given an additional questionnaire that contained 10 new questions of the form "did you see?" The ninth question asked whether or not the subjects had seen a moustache on the tall intruder.

Only 4% of the subjects in the control condition claimed to have seen a moustache on the intruder. When the moustache had been mentioned via a simple presupposition, that percentage rose to 26%, $z = 3.05$, $p < .001$. When the moustache had been mentioned via a complex presupposition, the percentage falsely saying *yes* was even higher: 39%. The difference between simple and complex was marginally different, $z = 1.44$, $.10 > p > .05$, one-tailed.

The final result concerned memory for what was mentioned on the initial questionnaire. Almost none of the control subjects (1%) incorrectly claimed to have read about the moustache on their questionnaire. However, many of the other subjects correctly remembered the mention of the moustache: 20% of the subjects who had been given the simple presupposition definitely remembered the moustache being mentioned, whereas only 8% of those given the complex presupposition definitely remembered reading about the moustache, $z = 1.71$, $p < .05$, one-tailed.

These results, in conjunction with those of Johnson (1979), suggest that misinformation embedded in more complex questions is likely to have a greater effect on memory than that same information conveyed in simpler questions. The complex question seems to work because it focuses the subject's attention on something other than the critical information.

Further evidence that subjects do not pay as much attention to the critical object when it is deeply embedded comes from the final memory test: Subjects were less likely to remember having read about the critical object when it appeared as a complex rather than a simple presupposition.

In all fairness, it should be mentioned that there are other explanations for why the questions containing complex presuppositions are better able to mislead subjects into thinking they had seen nonexistent objects. The first possibility (suggested by P. Rabbitt) is that the complex questions contain more details, and consequently they may provide a better "match" with the original representation in memory. A second possibility (suggested by S. Sternberg) is that the complex questions convey a stronger "belief" that the nonexistent object did in fact exist. To test the "stronger belief" explanation, we presented a group of 40 new subjects with a brief description of a scenario in which two men disrupt a classroom. The subjects were also told that one witness to the scenario, Witness 1, was given the job of gathering information from other witnesses about what had happened. The subjects saw the list of questions that Witness 1 had asked the others. This list included either question 1 (containing the simple presupposition) or question 2 (containing the complex presupposition) regarding the moustache. Finally, the subjects were asked to indicate how confident they were that Witness 1 believed that various items had actually happened. For example, how confident were they that Witness 1 believed that there were two intruders, that the short intruder wore a jacket, that the short intruder spoke to the professor, and that the tall intruder had a moustache. The subjects indicated their confidence in each item using a 7-point scale, where 7 represented very confident and 1 represented not at all confident.

The results showed that subjects felt that Witness 1 was more confident that "the tall intruder had a moustache" when Witness 1 asked the question using the complex presupposition rather than the simple presupposition [5.5 versus 3.8, $t(38) = 2.63$, $p < .02$]. Thus, it is plausible that the complex questions have a greater impact in part because they convey a stronger belief in the existence of the critical object. How much of their impact is due to this quality rather than the diverting of attention remains a matter for further research.

When conducting further research on the role of attention, it should be kept in mind that the relationship between amount of attention devoted to the critical postevent information and amount of bonding is not a simple one. Too little attention and the critical information is not even processed; too much attention and it is scrutinized and possibly rejected. Finding the optimal middle group will not be simple, because it must be remembered that two distinct elements enter into a person's willingness to accept misleading information. First the person must comprehend the information and then he must accept it. Before developing a formulation that takes account of these two elements, consider a related topic, that of attention to the witnessed event itself.

ATTENTION TO THE WITNESSED EVENT

To reiterate, people vary in terms of the ease with which postevent information becomes bonded into memory. Consider the question of whether there is a relationship between the accuracy of a person's immediate report of the details of an incident (which presumably reflects attention to the incident) and subsequent susceptibility to suggestion. A reasonable hypothesis is that those subjects who are less accurate about an episode would tend to be more influenceable. This could occur if persons who are poor at perceiving and recalling the details of a complex event are also more likely to welcome suggestive information from any source to fill in the gaps in memory. If this were the case, we might find that those low in accuracy would be more receptive to suggestion. Conversely, persons high in accuracy might possess the superior cognitive capacities that permit them to resist incorrect information successfully, particularly when it conflicts with what is stored in memory. A negative correlation between the overall accuracy and suggestibility would be predicted.

On the other hand, if we take into account both of the two elements that enter into a person's willingness to accept misleading information, comprehension, and acceptance, we might make a different prediction. Perhaps inaccurate persons are also inattentive in general and would have relatively more difficulty comprehending intervening suggestive information. They might be influenced by it relatively little. Attentive people might be correspondingly more influenced. In this case, a positive correlation between overall accuracy and suggestibility would be predicted.

In a recent experiment (Powers, Andriks, & Loftus, 1979), subjects looked at a series of slides depicting a wallet-snatching incident. Then they took a test designed to measure their attentiveness to or accuracy for the details of the incident. Following this, they read a version of the incident that for some of them contained misleading information about certain objects in the series of slides. Finally, a test was administered to measure the extent to which the misleading information was incorporated into the subjects' recollections. The relationship between accuracy and suggestibility was computed using data from 25 experimental subjects. The equation of the best fitting regression line is: $S = -.63 + .13A$, where S is the suggestibility score and A the accuracy score. The correlation between the two sets of scores was .348, which did not reach significance. The positive correlation indicates that subjects with higher accuracy scores tended to receive slightly *higher,* albeit not significantly, suggestibility scores.

Despite the lack of relationship between *overall* accuracy and suggestibility, these investigators found a relationship between accuracy on a *specific* item and a person's ability to resist suggestive influences about that item. For example, if a subject accurately indicated that the object that the victim's friend was carrying was a notebook (rather than an umbrella or some other object), a misleading description of its color was less likely to be accepted than if the object had not been noticed in the first place. By contrast, if the item was not originally recalled on the accuracy questionnaire, it was relatively easier to convince the subject of both the existence of the object and the properties suggestively ascribed to it. Put another way, a person who, overall, is more accurate about objects that existed in a complex event is not necessarily better able to resist misleading suggestions about those objects. Yet, a person who is accurate about some specific object is better able to resist a misleading suggestion about that particular object. At first this seems paradoxical. Surely if the subjects had been given an inordinately long time to look at the scene, thereby producing accuracy scores of 100%, it would be quite difficult to entice them to accept a misleading suggestion about some item. No amount of coaxing or clever manipulation should convince a rational reader that the paper on which this article is printed is pink rather than white. Is it possible that overall accuracy and suggestibility are unrelated *across* subjects but negatively related *within* a subject? This question is addressed in the following experiment, in which event presentation time is the major independent variable.

Method

Subjects.   Eight females participated in this study. Each received the sum of $5.00 for completing two 2-hr sessions.

Procedure

Subjects were run in groups. Each was told that she was to see a series of slides and would be asked a few questions about the slides. The overall procedure included four major phases on day 1: (1) viewing the slides; (2) filling out an "accuracy" questionnaire; (3) reading a "suggestibility" paragraph; (4) taking a final test. Three days later the subjects returned for a second session. At this time they saw a different set of slides and completed phases 2, 3, and 4 with respect to these slides. Subjects saw one set of slides at a 5-sec rate, and the slides in the second set were viewed for 20 sec each. Half of the subjects got the fast rate of presentation first; the other half began with the slower rate.

Day 1

1. The Slides.   A sequence of 24 slides depicting a wallet-snatching incident in a small town was shown to the subjects. The slide sequence opens with a young woman walking down a busy street. The remaining slides show her meeting a friend for a brief chat, being bumped by a "thief" who steals her wallet, and later being told about the theft. (See Fig. 24.1 for a sample slide.)

2. The Accuracy Questionnaire.   After a short filler activity in which subjects looked at a color chart and provided names for various colors, the subjects filled out a questionnaire designed to determine accuracy. The questionnaire consisted of 30 items that addressed diverse details of the wallet-snatching incident. The 30 items were declarative sentences requiring a phrase or word to be completed. To complete these sentences, a five-alternative multiple-choice test was given. For example, one question was "The victim's friend was carrying _____. (1) a newspaper; (2) a shopping bag; (3) a notebook; (4) an umbrella; (5) none of the above." For each item, the subjects indicated their confidence in their answers using a 3-point rating scale where 1 indicated that the subject was guessing and 3 indicated high confidence. After completing the questionnaire, a filler activity was performed.

3. Suggestibility Paragraphs.   Having completed the filler activity, all subjects were given a "suggestibility" narrative to read. The narrative was allegedly written by a professor who had seen the slides for 30 sec each. To conceal the purpose of this task, the subjects were asked to rate the narrative on certain attributes such as clarity of writing. The narrative contained erroneous information about four critical items. For example, the victim's friend actually carried a green notebook, but the narrative erroneously called it a blue notebook. After rating the narrative, the subjects completed a 10-min filler activity and then were given a final test on the details of the slides.

4. The Final Test.   The final test contained 20 items. The items were declarative sentences lacking a phrase or word. These were to be completed with one of the three choices listed with it.

Day 4

Three days later, the subjects returned for a second session. At this time they viewed a different set of 24 slides, filled out a 30-item accuracy questionnaire, read a suggestibility paragraph, and took a final test. To reiterate, those subjects who had viewed the previous slide set at the 5-sec rate looked at the current set for 20 sec each, whereas those who had previously viewed slides for 20 sec each now looked at the current set for 5 sec each.

FIG. 24.1.   One black and white version of a photograph that was among the 24 color slides depicting a wallet-snatching incident shown to subjects in the experiment concerning the relationship between accuracy and suggestibility.

Results

For each subject we obtained several scores for the incident viewed at the 5-sec rate. We obtained an overall accuracy score that ranged from 0% to 100%, depending on how many of the 30 items a person answered correctly. In addition, we obtained a suggestibility score ranging from 0 to 4, depending on how many of the "suggested responses" a person gave on the final test. For the incident viewed at the 20-sec rate, these same two scores were calculated. Thus, each

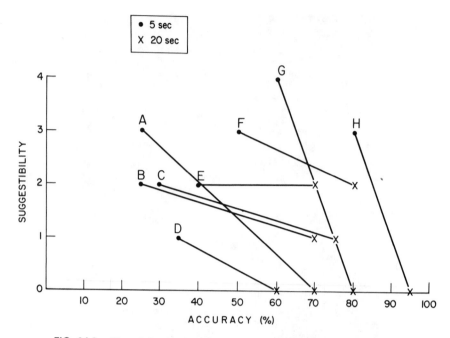

FIG. 24.2. The relationship between accuracy and suggestibility, for subjects who viewed one incident at 5 sec per slide and another at 20 sec per slide. The letters represented individual subjects. Higher scores indicate greater suggestibility.

subject provided two data points for the graph shown in Fig. 24.2. As seen, for seven out of eight subjects, when given more time with each slide, accuracy rose and suggestibility dropped. This is significant by a sign test. When one looks across subjects within a given presentation rate, accuracy and suggestibility do not appear to be systematically related to one another.

DISCUSSION

The major result to emerge from this study is that when subjects viewed a complex incident, accuracy across subjects was not related to suggestibility. However, giving an individual more time to view the initial incident resulted in a higher overall accuracy score and lower suggestibility, indicating that, within an individual, accuracy and suggestibility are related to one another. Witnesses can look over an entire scene, but unless they devote sufficient processing to a critical detail, they will not be resistant to postevent suggestions about that detail.

The results of this study lend further support to the notion that subjects can use information stored in memory to tag postevent suggestions as being inappropriate. The critical detail must have been noticed in order for it to be useful in this capacity.

THE COMPONENTS OF MENTAL BONDING

Progress in understanding the circumstances under which memories can be altered has much to gain from a look back to earlier work on the related subject of susceptibility to social influence. In this domain, several investigators have advanced thoughtful formulations, most notably McGuire (1968) and Wyer (1974).

McGuire (1968) offered six principles underlying influenceability. One of these, the *mediational* principle, went as follows. Opinion change is not a direct response but the net outcome of a chain of behavioral steps. As a minimum it requires: (1) adequate reception (through attention and comprehension) of the persuasive message; and (2) yielding to what is comprehended. In his view, the mediational role of reception is often overlooked, whereas that of yielding is overemphasized. Although each of the two behavioral steps (receptivity to the content of the persuasive message and tendency to yield to what is received) is positively related to influenceability, the relation of any given personality or situational variable to one of these steps is often quite different from its relationship to the other. Hence its net relationship to the resultant influenceability can be complex and even nonmonotonic. Wyer (1974) extended these ideas, and the current formulation borrows heavily from both sources. This framework allows us to describe and interpret the role of attention as well as many other variables in the memory change domain.

In the memory change domain, there are three important stages to be distinguished: First, the subject views the event; second, there is exposure to some misleading information; third, the subject is tested to determine the extent to which the recollection has been modified by the misleading information. Before new information can become incorporated into a person's memory, it must first be encoded or comprehended and then must be accepted. Only then will suggestible behavior be evident at the time of the final test. A simple probabilistic model of the factors that determine the likelihood that one will be suggestible in a given situation can be constructed.

A model adapted from one that has worked reasonably well in the social influence research is given by Equation 1:

$$P_S = P_C P_A \qquad (1)$$

where P_S is the probability that a subject exhibits suggestible behavior about a given event; P_C is the probability of comprehending the postevent information; and P_A is the probability that the postevent information is accepted as valid. Equation 1 implies that two factors, one of which affects the comprehensibility of the new information and the other of which affects the likelihood that it will be accepted, will have multiplicative or interactive effects upon the likelihood that a subject will exhibit suggestible behavior. According to this formulation, various situational and individual difference variables will affect suggestibility because of their influence upon either one of the components of Equation 1. Often, however, a single factor may have a different effect upon comprehension and acceptance. For example, P_C may increase with factors such as the general attentiveness of an individual or the amount of attention devoted to postevent information, whereas P_A decreases. Precisely what effect a change in one of these variables is likely to have on the suggestibility will be difficult to predict unless the initial values of P_C and P_A are known.

For example, take three witnesses, A, B, and C, who differ in their general attentiveness or ability to view an event and answer accurately about it. Say that Witness A, of moderate ability, has a moderate likelihood of comprehending a piece of new information and accepting it, say, $P_C = P_A = .5$. Then, from Equation 1, $P_S = .25$. Compare this to Witness B, who has greater ability. In this case, the probability of comprehending the new information might be higher (say $P_C = .8$), whereas the probability of accepting it might be lower (say $P_A = .2$). In this case, $P_S = .16$. Thus, a person with increased ability would seem to be less suggestible. On the other hand, take Witness C, a person of low ability, for whom the probability of comprehending new information might be low (say $P_C = .2$), whereas the probability of accepting it might be quite high (say $P_A = .8$). Again, from Equation 1, $P_S = .16$. According to this analysis, then, subjects of great ability and those of little ability will both exhibit less suggestible behavior after misleading information than will moderately able subjects. Averaging across these subjects might lead to the conclusion that this particular ability had no effect on suggestibility.

But, consider what happens when these individuals are all given more time to view the initial event upon which they will later be tested. Increasing the time to view the event should have no effect on the probability that some postevent information is comprehended by the subject. However, increasing the time should have a substantial effect on the likelihood that the information is accepted. With more time, more details can be encoded in memory, and these can be used to refute the misleading information, lowering the probability of its acceptance. The result will be a decrease in the probability that the subject will exhibit suggestible behavior.

The relationship between overall ability to report the details of an incident accurately and overall susceptibility to suggestive information is not as simple as one might first suspect. However, when the suggestible behavior is analyzed in terms of two processes, the comprehension of the suggested information and the acceptance of its content, the relationship between accuracy and suggestibility can be understood and predicted.

This formulation is also useful for understanding the impact of changes in the amount of attention devoted to the postevent information itself rather than to the witnessed event or to the witness's ability. Take three witnesses of equal ability and suggestibility. If Witness *A* pays almost no attention to a piece of postevent information, the probability of comprehending the information would be low, and consequently the probability of its being bonded to memory would be low. If Witness *B* pays a great deal of attention to a piece of postevent information, the chances may be enhanced that this scrutiny will lead to the rejection of that information. With moderate attention, Witness *C* may exhibit the greatest degree of bonding. Within this middle range much variation is possible. Whether one sees increased or decreased bonding with increases in attention to postevent information will depend where on this nonmomotonic function one began.

The formulation advanced here can be extended to explore the impact of any situational or individual difference variables on suggestibility. For example, the degree of mental bonding has been shown to depend on these factors among others: The interval between the event and the postevent information, whether the witness consciously thinks about the event prior to the postevent manipulation and whether the postevent information is plausible or implausible (all reviewed in Loftus, 1979). Furthermore, bonding depends on whether the postevent information contradicts a central versus a peripheral witnessed detail (Dritsas & Hamilton, 1977) and whether the postevent information comes from a biased or neutral source (Dodd & Bradshaw, 1980). On the other hand, numerous factors have failed to influence the degree of mental bonding (e.g., intelligence) (Powers et al., 1979). A careful look at the extent to which these independent variables separately affect the components of comprehension and acceptance will help us understand these complex relationships and predict future ones.

ACKNOWLEDGMENTS

The National Science Foundation generously supported this research. Portions of these ideas were developed while the author was a fellow at the Center for Advanced Study in the Behavioral Sciences during the year 1978–1979. I am indebted to Bob Weber and Bob Wyer for valuable discussions.

REFERENCES

Clark, H. H., & Clark, E. V. *Psychology and language.* New York: Harcourt Brace Jovanovich, 1977.

Dodd, D. H., & Bradshaw, J. M. Leading questions and memory: Pragmatic constraints. *Journal of Verbal Learning and Verbal Behavior,* 1980, *19,* 695–704.

Dritsas, W. J., & Hamilton, V. L. Evidence about evidence: Effects of presuppositions, item salience, stress, and perceiver set on accident recall. Unpublished manuscript, University of Michigan, 1977.

Johnson, K. A. *The leading question: Isn't there an effect?* Unpublished doctoral dissertation, University of Washington, Seattle, 1979.

Keele, S. W. *Attention and human performance*. Pacific Palisades, Calif.: Goodyear, 1973.

Laberge, D., & Samuels, S. J. Toward a theory of automatic information processing in reading. *Cognitive Psychology*, 1974, *103*, 97–106.

Loftus, E. F. Shifting human color memory. *Memory and Cognition*, 1977, *5*, 696–699.

Loftus, E. F. *Eyewitness testimony*. Cambridge, Mass.: Harvard University Press, 1979.

McGuire, W. J. Personality and susceptibility to social influence. In E. F. Borgatta & W. W. Lambert (Eds.), *Handbook of personality theory and research*. Chicago: Rand McNally, 1968.

Ogden, W. C., Martin, D. W., & Paap, K. R. Processing demands of encoding: What does secondary task performance reflect? *Journal of Experimental Psychology: Human Perception and Performance*, 1980, *6*, 355–367.

Powers, P. A., Andriks, J. L., & Loftus, E. F. Eyewitness accounts of females and males. *Journal of Applied Psychology*, 1979, *64*, 339–347.

Posner, M. I., & Rogers, M. G. K. Chronometric analysis of abstraction and recognition. In W. K. Estes (Ed.), *Handbook of learning and cognitive processes* (Vol. 5): *Human information processing*. Hillsdale, N.J.: Lawrence Erlbaum Associates, 1978.

Shiffrin, R. M., & Schneider, W. Controlled and automatic human information processing. II. Perceptual learning, automatic attending, and a general theory. *Psychological Review*, 1977, *84*, 127–190.

Sperling, G., & Melchner, M. J. The attention operating characteristic: Examples from visual search. *Science*, 1978, *202*, 315–318.

Wyer, R. S. *Cognitive organization and change: An information processing approach*. Hillsdale, N.J.: Lawrence Erlbaum Associates, 1974.

VII

SEQUENCING OF MOVEMENTS

25 Contrasting Perspectives on Order and Regulation in Movement

J. A. Scott Kelso
Haskins Laboratories, New Haven, Connecticut
and
Departments of Psychology and Biobehavioral Sciences
University of Connecticut,
Storrs, Connecticut
U.S.A.

ABSTRACT

Current theorizing in movement control explains order and regulation in terms of central programs or the reference levels of closed-loop servomechanisms. Specifically, the order and regulation observed results from a priori prescriptions, and the devices responsible are conceptually separate from that which they regulate. Neither theory adequately addresses how the free variables of the system are regulated (Bernstein's [1967] degrees of freedom problem). In the alternative perspective, promoted here, order and regulation are seen as a posteriori emergent consequences of the dynamical behavior of the system. In this view, solutions to the degrees of freedom problem may lie in the principles of Iberall's (1977) Homeokinetic Physics, which characterizes biological systems as ensembles of nonlinear, limit cycle oscillators, coupled and mutually entrained at all levels. Homeokinetics provides a secure basis for recent developments in neuroscience and offers an alternative rationale for some relevant facts in movement control and coordination.

INTRODUCTION

Actions must be precisely ordered spatially and temporally. But how is such order to be understood? One popular account uses the computer, "machine" analogy where order originates from a central program that elicits instructions to

437

select the correct muscles and contract and relax them at the right time. Much of the data concerning movement control and coordination can be given a reading in this terminology. Evidence on a variety of sequencing skills—laboratory and real life—is to be found in an excellent review by Keele (1980). In the early part of this chapter I consider some of the data on movement sequencing from a program perspective. Despite the appeal of conventional "programming" explanations, I argue later that such accounts are not necessary to represent order and regulation in natural systems. Rather, I promote an alternative view—already elaborated in several recent papers (Kelso, Holt, Kugler, & Turvey, 1980; Kelso, Tuller, & Harris, in press; Kugler, Kelso, & Turvey, 1980; in press)—that natural systems are composed of ensembles of coupled and mutually entrained oscillators and that spatiotemporal order is a *consequence* of this fact. This latter view, grounded jointly in the newly emerging theories of homeokinetics (Iberall, 1977; Iberall & Soodak, 1978; Yates, 1980, in press; Yates & Iberall, 1973) and "dynamic patterns" (Fentress, 1978; Katchalsky, Rowland, & Blumenthal, 1974; Szentagothai, 1978), contrasts deeply with the programming conception in which there exists an a priori prescription *independent of* and *casually antecedent to systemic behavior*. Instead, order is seen as an emergent property, as an a posteriori fact, dependent on the dynamical behavior of the system.

This apparently exotic claim is not completely new. Many have considered the need for a rhythmical (oscillatory) organization to account for the multitude of overlapping and closely patterned neuromuscular events when an animal acts (Lashley, 1951; Lenneberg, 1967; Martin, 1972). Indeed the evidence for endogenous neural networks capable of rhythmical patterns in vertebrates and invertebrates is virtually unassailable (Davis, 1976; Miles & Evarts, 1979; Stein, 1978) and maybe the rhythmic structure for biological systems should even be considered a principle (Aschoff, 1979). What is new here is that spatiotemporal order can be seated in the principles of physical biology and in the language of dynamics. If this view is correct, there may be no need to introduce the special mechanisms of modern control theory (algorithms, reference levels, comparators, error correction mechanisms, and so on) to explain order and regulation. Such notions may be obviated by a dynamic scheme in which internal states are a consequence of the interaction of nonlinear, limit cycle oscillators called "thermodynamic engines" (Soodak & Iberall, 1978). Cyclical behavior then does not originate in special biological mechanisms but rather is a general physical property of systems undergoing energy flux.

To anticipate somewhat, we note with Fentress (1978), that the concept of order is fundamental to the description and interpretation of behavior. A central theme in the neurophysiological and behavioral analyses of movement is that levels of order can be ranked hierarchically (Keele & Summers, 1976). A major question for this view is how levels of order relate to and influence each other. Our perspective offers a possible answer by advocating a set of principles consistent with contemporary physical theory that are *level-independent*.

ORDER AND REGULATION IN MOVEMENT:
A CONVENTIONAL PERSPECTIVE

Motor Programs: Definitions and Issues

From an early and influential definition as a set of prestructured commands organized prior to movement and run off uninfluenced by peripheral feedback (Keele, 1968), the concept of central program to explain spatiotemporal order has undergone revision. In part, there was confusion regarding the role of peripheral information. The program concept was only thought viable when peripheral inputs were: (1) effectively removed by sensory deafferentation; or (2) not employed (e.g., so-called ballistic movements). These are too stringent criteria for many investigators, who doubt the complete effectiveness of the classical preparation for removing sensory information from limbs (dorsal rhizotomy) and given the discovery of putative feedback circuits with rapid loop times (Kelso & Stelmach, 1976; Smith, 1978).

However, the notion of a central representation of a skill that can lead to patterned movement is still retained, and the issue—at least concerning the role of peripheral information—is when and how such information is used. Thus, there is no necessary dichotomy between so-called "program" and "feedback-based" control notions even though some may wish to retain it (Adams, 1977). Programming theorists no longer address the question of whether motor programs exist or not; rather they assume some type of planning occurs before movement execution. It is to problems concerning the structure and composition of such motor programs that much of current research is directed.

The Abstract Nature of "Programs"

The early definition of program as a series of prestructured motor commands specifying spatiotemporal messages to the muscles received heavy criticism not only because of its default basis [How else can a skilled pianist perform so quickly? (Lashley, 1951) or how else can an animal move without feedback? (Taub, 1976)], but also because it implied a separate program for every different movement an individual could produce. Concern has been voiced about the so-called "storage" problem that such a view creates—although no limits to CNS storage have ever been demonstrated. Nevertheless programming theorists have pursued parsimony and attempted to avoid the putative storage problem by revising the notion of a program. They have, as it were, pushed the program further back in the head. In one view, the program is considered a *generalized* entity (Schmidt, 1980). In another, the program is considered an abstract representation of a muscle sequence elaborated into its more specific components as information descends the hierarchy (Keele, 1980). Both views agree that parameters can be specified at lower levels without changing the abstract structure of the program. For example, the same program executes throws of different distances.

Or one can use the same program with different sets of muscles. Thus, one's handwriting does not lose its individuality when one writes on a blackboard (Merton, 1972). Also, Raibert (1977) has demonstrated that the handwriting pattern is preserved even when the particular muscular system employed (e.g., the foot) has never previously performed such an activity.

Similarly, there is much evidence that talkers can spontaneously adjust the movement patterns of their articulators in spite of various types of disruption and still produce highly intelligible acoustic output (Kelso, Holt, Kugler, & Turvey, 1980; MacNeilage, 1970). The talking pipe smoker is a good example, but there are formal demonstrations showing that subjects can produce—*in their first attempt*—steady state vowels with the jaw fixed by a bite block without the need for acoustic feedback (as evidenced by "normal" formant patterns in the first glottal pitch pulse, Lindblom & Sundberg, 1971) and even when propriocep-tive information is drastically reduced (Kelso & Tuller, in preparation; Lindblom, Lubker, & Gay, 1979).

Should we attribute this creative or generative ability under novel contextual conditions in speech as different in kind from the ability to write intelligibly with the big toe? Perhaps not. A dominant feature in both activities is the preservation of certain relationships that maintain the essential character of the activity in spite of changes in values of particular dimensions. This suggests similarities in prin-ciple (see pp. 444–448).

The Parameters in the Program

The notion that the motor program undergoes progressive elaboration from some abstract, nonmotoric level (specifying the actor's goals) to a level specifying the parameters defining the spatiotemporal course of the movement has led to con-sideration of the contents and construction of such programs.

To answer such questions, reaction time has been used to index the amount of central preparation required for particular features of the upcoming movement. Thus, if a motor program is prepared in advance, preparation time should be a reflection of the upcoming movement's complexity. However, if no prior prepa-ration takes place, that is, if the movement essentially unfolded with feedback triggering each response component, complex movements should take no more time to prepare than simple ones. Considerable evidence appears to favor the former proposition in both simple and choice reaction-time paradigms (Klapp, this volume).

Unfortunately, much of the data linking reaction time to features of upcoming movements is equivocal. Excluding one or two robust results, for example, that reaction time increases as a function of the number of segments in a sequence (Henry, 1980), agreement across experiments is unimpressive. Often experi-ments examining effects of the *same* parameter on RT produce opposite results. It seems that one could choose *any* aspect of an upcoming movement and relate it to RT if one constrained the experiment appropriately.

Models relating movement parameters to reaction time often fail to recognize that task-defined parameters (such as arm, direction, and extent) may be quite different from those *used* by the motor control system (Goodman & Kelso, 1980; Rosenbaum, 1980). For instance, distance or extent of movement is not, as Keele (1980) points out, in the language of muscles but instead is a consequence of the muscular forces that accelerate and decelerate the limb. For reasons given shortly, the evaluation of programming effects on kinematic variables may be quite inappropriate: Kinematic measures are, after all, only the result of the system's dynamic parameters. Let us pursue the dynamic theme in more detail and attempt to show why, in the long run, it may offer significant insights into the coordination and control of movement.

CONTRASTING ORIENTATIONS ON ORDER

A Priori Versus A Posteriori

A major problem for the program conception of spatiotemporal order, already highlighted, is that the putative transfer function between higher, mental entities (algorithms, perceptual traces, templates, etc.) and the language of the skeletomotor apparatus is simply ignored (for exceptions, see Raibert, 1977, & Saltzman, 1979). The brain as the source of signals for coordination and control is held conceptually separate from the putative recipient of such messages, the high-power energy-converting muscular system. Such notions, as emphasized by Yates, Marsh, and Iberall (1972), attempt to account for the small signal, information aspects of the system but undervalue the equally important energy-converting machinery (the power fluxes). Yet a viable analysis of motor activity (and living systems) must embrace—and understand—the mutuality between informational and power processes. Since Lashley's (1951) paper on serial order, it has been assumed that this coupling involves some type of translation step: "The *translation* from the spatial distribution of memory traces to temporal sequence seems to be *a fundamental problem of serial order* [p. 128]."

In short, the contents of the so-called program are discrete, timeless, and context-free; yet the characteristics of activity are continuous, dynamic, and context-sensitive. In modern theories of movement control, Lashley's problem is circumvented by simply assuming the existence of a "between thing" (Dewey & Bentley, 1948), for example, a translation mechanism, that will map a static, timeless representation into a four-dimensional dynamic action that emerges in real time (see Fowler, Rubin, Remez, & Turvey, 1980 for further discussion).

We have argued elsewhere that the need for "between things" may be obviated once the causal and logical support for behavioral phenomena is better understood (Kugler, Kelso, & Turvey, 1980, in press; Shaw & Turvey, in press). For present purposes, some examples illustrating the "emergent" perspective may be more appropriate. Consider an artifact well-known to researchers of movement, namely, the cybernetic closed-loop system (Adams, 1977; Powers, 1978). In such a system, a template or reference level compares the input it receives to its own value. Based on this comparison, orders go to an effector system to eliminate possible error, thus assuring the stability of the system. Reference levels or "set points" feature heavily in explanations of biological systems, but how does a given reference level attain its constancy? An infinite regress results from the claim that a referent signal at one level is simply the output of another, higher-order servomechanism. A better claim, we would argue (see following) is that constancy in biological systems is an emergent and distributed property (a steady state operating condition) of physical processes. To buttress this view, consider an activity whose regulation has long been thought to rely on a system of set points.

The Message from Temperature Regulation

Temperature regulation shares many of the problems of order and regulation common to other systems. A dominant view is that the reference level for temperature regulation resides in the thermosensitive cells of the preoptic area of hypothalamus (Satinoff, 1978, for review). Given this, to understand thermoregulation is: (1) to determine what extra hypothalamic factors input to the reference signal (i.e., inform the animal of the state of the body temperature); and (2) to work out the controller equations for the effectors and how they react to the direction and magnitude of the error signal. But the situation is not quite that simple. Findings showing different thermoregulatory responses when different parts of the nervous system are lesioned or heated with thermal probes have led to the conclusion that the orderly sequence of thermoregulatory behaviors in response to thermal stress results from a system with not one but *multiple* set points arranged in hierarchical fashion (Satinoff, 1978).

There are, however, empirical grounds for suspecting the validity of the set-point concept. According to Snellen (1972; Mitchell, Snellen, & Adkins, 1970), there is no such thing as an anatomical structure providing a reference signal to the integrating centers of the thermoregulatory system. When other (physical) factors are considered such as the regional distribution of blood flow, what is called "set point" is the input–output relationship between the heat lost and heat produced by the system. When the net balance between these factors is altered (e.g., by exercise), the so-called set point undergoes a shift. Here, set point is an *emergent and distributed* property (a steady state operating condition) *of physical processes involved in local heat balance.*

Similarly Werner (1977) has shown that heat-flow equations for all local body coordinates result in two kinds of characteristic function. The first, a "controller" characteristic of negative slope, is the dependence of metabolism, U, on core temperature, T_c, all other variables held constant. This relationship may be altered ("tuned") by the onset of exercise or the intake of pyrogenic agents. The second, a steady state positive slope function of the "passive" system, is the effect of metabolic rates on core temperature via heat-transport processes. This function is tunable by ambient air conditions such as humidity or air temperature. The common point between the functions *for any given body part* defines the steady state temperature of the system. Thus, as Werner (1977) emphasizes, "neither a reference signal nor a comparison of neuronal signals with different temperature coefficients is necessary, as the reached steady state is the only one which is possible under the assumed conditions [p. 95]."

The message from Snellen and Werner is clear: Core temperature is an a posteriori fact of the system, not an a priori reference signal imposed *on* or prescribed *for* the system. More generally, when the complementary components of the system are fully explored and understood, there may be no need to posit a special regulator or even a set hierarchically arranged to account for a system's conservation of a certain value.

Once Again the Mass–Spring (Oscillatory System) Story

Just as the concept of set point in thermoregulation is best viewed as an emergent and distributed physical property of the system, so it is, if recent evidence be a guide, that the plan for an act is an effective organization of the muscles that is *concomitant* with, not a precursor to, the activity (Fowler, 1977). Kinematic details and discrete movement segments that repeat in a particular order are a posteriori facts of a systemic organization; there is no reason to believe that they are symbolically represented anywhere (Fitch & Turvey, 1978; Fowler et al., 1980; Kugler et al., 1980).

The strongest evidence for this position comes from work on limb localization in monkeys and humans (Bizzi, 1980, Kelso, Holt, Kugler & Turvey, 1980) showing that a steady state equilibrium position of the limb can be attained despite: (1) changes in initial conditions (Fel'dman, 1966; Kelso, 1977); (2) unexpected and abrupt load disturbances applied during the movement trajectory (Kelso & Holt, 1980; Polit & Bizzi, 1978); and (3) both (1) and (2) when monkeys undergo dorsal rhizotomy (Polit & Bizzi, 1978) and humans are reversibly anesthetized (Kelso, 1977; Kelso & Holt, 1980) or the joint capsule is surgically removed (Kelso, Holt, & Flatt, 1980).

The most (neuro)economical explanation of these data is that the limb behaves qualitatively similar to a nonlinear oscillatory system, in which the steady state position of the limb (its equifinality characteristic) is determined by the dynamic parameters (mass, stiffness, damping) of the system. Hollerbach (1980) has extended the mass–spring model by showing that cursive handwriting may be produced by coupled oscillations of horizontal and vertical joints of the wrist–hand linkage. Modulating the oscillation at particular times in the cycle and with specific phase and amplitude changes pemits the transformation of one basic pattern of shapes into another. For example, amplitude modulation of the vertical spring–mass oscillator can yield different letter heights. Also, some of the stylistic constraints imposed by slant constancy and letter shaping can be satisfied by assuming a variable stiffness setting of agonist–antagonist muscle pairs (Hollerbach, 1980).

The important points to emphasize from recent work on limb localization and handwriting skill are twofold: First, the many kinematic details that we observe in movement do not require individual specification. Second, and relatedly, it cannot be said that an oscillatory system such as a mass–spring embodies a (symbolic) representation of kinematic events. To the contrary, *kinematic details are consequences of underlying oscillatory processes and are determined by them.*

Summary

Here we have contrasted two views of order and regulation in movement. In the more popular, conventional view, order and regulation result from central programs (following the computer metaphor) or reference levels (following the cybernetical, closed-loop device). More precisely, the orderliness of movement results from explicit a priori prescriptions. Moreover, the devices responsible for the orderliness are separate from that which they regulate and hence require a mediary or translation mechanism. In the alternative perspective, insights gained from thermoregulation and posturing of limbs suggest that order and regulation are a posteriori consequences of the dynamical behavior of the system. This latter view envisions coordination and control as an emergent characteristic of the system. Priority is not given to the *order* grain of analysis (as in the programming account); rather the emphasis is on the mutuality of components and an explication of the systematic *relations* holding among variables, when humans and animals perform activity. We now turn to the identification of systematicities in movement behavior and to a rationalization of those systematicities.

THE RELATIONAL INVARIANTS APPROACH OR WHAT IS THE DESIGN LOGIC OF THE MOTOR SYSTEM?

In rationalizing relations observed in systematic behavior we observe invariances which give us important clues about the design logic of the system (Yates, in press).

It was Bernstein (1967) perhaps who first presented logical argument against conventional assumptions that the many free variables of the skeletomuscular system are individually controlled. He argued that variables are organized into larger units called "synergies" (Gurfinkel, Kots, Paltsev, & Feldman, 1971), "collectives" (Gelfand, Gurfinkel, Tsetlin, & Shik, 1971), or "coordinative structures" (Easton, 1972; Turvey, 1977). Within a muscle collective, the values of component variables are mutually dependent or constraining and hence can be regulated in a unitary way.

Coordinative structures are units of action that are not restricted to a set of muscles having fixed actions at a joint, nor are they limited to inborn reflexes (Easton, 1972). Rather coordinative structures connote the use of muscles in a behavioral situation: They are marshalled temporarily and expressly for the purpose of accomplishing particular acts (Boylls, 1975; Fitch & Turvey, 1978).

A major way of uncovering these "significant units" (Greene, 1972) is to alter the metrics of the activity (speed it up, do it more forcefully). In this way, it is possible to observe which variables are modified and which variables, or relations among variables, remain unchanged. Note that changing the metrical properties of an act could obscure its basic form by altering properties of individual components that might otherwise remain stable. Alternatively, these changes may index the major ways that invariance can be observed: Some variables must change but others must remain the same if the structure of the act is to be preserved and if a given pattern is to be categorized as an instance of the same act.

Note that the previous criteria are exactly those applied to the identification of motor programs. In contrast to some of the programming approaches discussed on pp. 440–441, which consider the preparatory period before an act is initiated, this approach seeks out invariant properties of the space–time pattern during the act itself. However, the systematic features (kinematic, electromyographic) of acts observed in such experiments may be rationalized on quite different grounds than those of motor programming.

A dominant idea about so-called programs is that they should be "playable" at different speeds without disrupting their internal structure; that is, certain preferred stable relationships among muscles will be preserved in spite of instabilities that are created by scaling up on rate. Consider the hypothetical motor activity shown in Fig. 25.1. Although muscle activities are illustrated, the basic idea can also be applied to kinematic and discrete events such as typing and piano playing. The crucial feature in Fig. 25.1 is that the *relationships among muscles are preserved* over changes in rate. The absolute duration of the activity changes and the amplitudes and durations (within limits) of individual muscle events can change without disrupting the overall pattern.

This is exactly what is observed, of course, in locomotion. For example, Grillner and Zangger (1975) compared the relative phase position of seven hindlimb muscles in normal and deafferented cats. The same timing of muscles in relation to each other was generally observed in both preparations. Similarly, when lobsters (MacMillan, 1975) and humans (Madeiros, 1978) walk at different speeds, there is considerable variability in the onsets and durations of EMG bursts but the overall phase relationships among different muscles are preserved.

HYPOTHETICAL MOTOR ACTIVITY PERFORMED AT DIFFERENT RATES
A 'RELATIONAL INVARIANTS' APPROACH

A. RATE 1

$$\text{PHASE POSITION} = \frac{\text{LATENCY } B, A}{\text{PERIOD } A}$$

$$= \frac{x}{y} \text{ msec}$$

$$= k$$

B. RATE 2 'faster than' RATE 1

$$\text{PHASE POSITION} = \frac{x_1}{y_1} \text{ msec}$$

$$= k$$

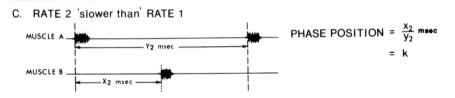

C. RATE 2 'slower than' RATE 1

$$\text{PHASE POSITION} = \frac{x_2}{y_2} \text{ msec}$$

$$= k$$

FIG. 25.1. A diagram illustrating the preservation of relative timing among muscles across various rates of movement.

In addition, pulling or carrying a weight leads to a reduction in variability but does not alter noticeably the timing relationships among muscles.

Changes in the speed of locomotion are known to be accomplished by distributing more force into the support or stance phase of the cycle. The duration of this phase decreases as an animal speeds up but the duration of the transfer phase changes very little in comparison (in this way, more distance is covered per unit time). What is significant is that increases in propulsive force during the stance phase do not disrupt the *relative timing* among linked extensor muscles, even though the absolute duration changes considerably. Force and relative timing, within limits, appear to be independent properties of coordination.

Can the feature of relative timing as an invariant characteristic of locomotion be extended to other motor activities? Increasing evidence suggests the affirmative on both micro and macro scales of motor behavior. At a micro level, consider the phenomenon of physiological tremor, a low-amplitude oscillation (around 10 Hz) that occurs in an extremity when muscles are tonically activated to maintain a fixed posture. Imagine that, as one is measuring the tremor of the finger (specifically the first dorsal interosseus muscle), subjects are instructed to produce a variety of force outputs to correspond to a voltmeter display. Significantly, tremor rate or frequency remains stable with variations in force, but tremor amplitude systematically increases with rising force (up to 7 kg; Freund & Dietz, 1978, Fig. 3).

At a more macro level, that of discrete ballistic movements, Freund and Büdingen (1978) had subjects produce isometric or isotonic movements as fast as possible under self-defined conditions and conditions in which a target force or angle was specified visually to the subject. Under all conditions, the rise time of voluntary contraction was constant no matter how strong the contraction was or how far the limb had to move. According to Freund and Büdingen (1978) "the independence of the time of contraction of skeletal muscles from the final force level or angle of movement is regarded as a necessary condition for the synchrony of synergistic action [p. 2]."

We might suppose that the preservation of constant timing relationships in these simple activities maintains the unity of the act and metrical changes allow for flexibility. This seems to be the case in more complicated and less "stereotyped" skills like typing, handwriting, and piano playing. Terzuolo and Viviani (1979) had experienced typists (speeds over 80 words per minute) type the same words in a variety of contexts. Even though the overall durations for the word are different (up to 60% in some cases), *the ratio between times of occurrence of each letter pair is constant.* When the individual word data are in turn expanded or contracted to approximate the average duration, the resulting pattern is highly invariant. [Also, if loads are added to the fingers during typing (up to 3 times the mass of the fingers), absolute but not relative timing is affected (Terzuolo & Viviani, 1979)].

A similar situation occurs in handwriting when individuals vary writing speed without altering movement amplitude (Viviani & Terzuolo, 1980). When the tangential velocity records are ranked and scaled (as in typing), velocity changes so as to leave invariant the time of occurrence of major features. Relative timing can even be preserved over changes in forces applied to the limbs when they are performing different spatial tasks (Kelso, Southard, & Goodman, 1979). Moreover in piano playing (Shaffer, 1980) the right hand carrying the melody plays with more "weight" than the left, and gradual and sudden changes in both limbs can be made independently without disrupting timing (although in piano playing timing is built-in to accommodate the structure of the music).

The similarities across a wide number of laboratory and real-life activities suggest strongly that certain variables (called nonessential by Gelfand and Tsetlin, 1962) can produce scalar changes in muscles and kinematic patterns without destroying the structure or topological properties of the act. Significantly this design applies to systems whose structural features are vastly different.[1] Consider the systems for speaking and manual activity. Subjects can easily coordinate

---

[1]Note that nothing has been said about mechanism here; an enterprise that is probably premature and maybe even misguided. The physicist Bohm (1969) points out, for example, how strange it is that biology and psychology are moving closer to mechanism while physics (especially quantum theory) focuses on systems of interlocking dimensions not unitary mechanisms.

speaking and moving when asked to produce cyclical movements of the right index finger while simultaneously uttering a string of identical syllables. Now imagine that the subject is instructed to vary the stress of alternate syllables in a strong–weak manner (phonetically, /'stak, stak, 'stak, stak . . . /) while maintaining amplitude and frequency of finger movement constant. Finger movements are modulated, in spite of instructions not to do so, so as to conform to the stress of speaking; that is, longer finger movements accompany stressed syllables, and shorter finger movements accompany unstressed syllables. This is not a consequence of the speech system "driving" the motor system. A parallel experiment required subjects to keep stress of speaking constant but to vary the extent of finger movement (i.e., alternating long and short excursions). In many cases, the change in amplitude of finger movement was accompanied by a change in the pattern of syllable production. Longer movements were associated with syllables of higher amplitude and shorter movements with syllables of lower amplitude (Kelso, Tuller, & Harris, in press).

In concluding this section, we should first emphasize that the speech–limb coordination experiments demonstrate mutuality rather than competition between speaking and manual performance. Second, and perhaps more important for this discussion, activities that require coupling among very dissimilar anatomical systems seem to operate on the same principles as activities such as walking, handwriting, and coordinating the limbs in typing and piano playing. In short, when an individual speaks and moves at the same time, the degrees of freedom are constrained such that the parameterization is over the total unit. The ubiquitous feature characterizing all the motor behaviors discussed, from physiological tremor to coordinating the limbs with speaking, is the independence of the force or power expressed by the muscle collective and the relative timing of activities (electromyographic and kinematic) within that collective. The available data suggest that the motor system has a preferred mode of operation: where possible, scale up on power but keep timing constant. The invariance in timing relations and the flexibility attained by adjusting control parameters hints strongly of a design logic. A first pass at rationalizing the logic on principled grounds follows.

ORDER AND REGULATION IN MOVEMENT: A DYNAMICAL PERSPECTIVE

Programming theorists have found it difficult to rationalize the presence of timing constraints as a major characteristic of coordinated activity without proposing a muscle selector and a clock whose "ticks" define when muscles will actuate or not (Rosenbaum & Patashnik, 1980). But dynamics—the physics of motion and change—offers an alternative in terms of physical principles. To anticipate, the physics of systems undergoing energy flux *defines* living things as rhythmic and time-locked. More important, no *new* mechanisms need to be introduced to account for this fact (Morowitz, 1979).

Homeokinetics

In the past, dynamics has not been considered particularly appropriate for an analysis of biological systems because it has dealt almost exclusively with linear conservative systems. Consider, for example, simple mechanical systems such as a mass–spring, where the equation of motion describes a trajectory toward an equilibrium state. Such a linear system is represented by a second-order differential equation:

$$m\ddot{x} + c\dot{x} + kx = 0 \tag{1}$$

In Equation 1, oscillatory motion will decay in proportion to the magnitude of the viscous (frictional) term (c). All this is predicated on the second law of thermodynamics—time flows in the direction of entropy. Yet living systems are characterized by sustained motion and persistence; as Schröedinger (1945) first remarked, living systems "accumulate negentropy." Living systems are not statically stable; they maintain their form and function by virtue of their *dynamic stability*.

But how can sustained motion be assured without violating thermodynamic law? Consider again the familiar mass–spring equation, but this time with a forcing function (e):

$$m\ddot{x} + c\dot{x} + kx = e \tag{2}$$

Obviously it is not enough that a forcing function, e, be supplied to the system described in Equation 2; it must also be supplied at the right place and time in the oscillation. To guarantee persistence (and to satisfy thermodynamic strictures) the forcing function must exactly offset the energy lost in each cycle. Real systems meet this requirement by including a function, called an *escapement*, to overcome dissipative losses. The escapement constitutes a nonlinear element that taps the source of potential energy (as long as it lasts) to overcome local thermodynamic losses. Thus a pulse or "squirt" of energy is released via the escapement such that, averaged over cycles, the left-hand side of Equation 2 equals the right-hand side and sustained motion is thereby assured.

This brief analysis (for more details, see Andronov & Chaiken, 1949; Iberall, 1975; Kelso, Holt, Rubin, & Kugler, 1980; Kugler, Kelso, & Turvey, 1980, in press; Yates & Iberall, 1973) draws our attention to some fundamentally important concepts: First, stability in the system can only be established and maintained if work is performed; second, work is accomplished by the flow of energy from a high source of potential energy to a lower potential energy "sink." This continuous flow of energy through a system and the ability to do work distinguishes open, irreversible systems (which exchange energy with their surrounds) from the isolated closed systems of classical reversible thermodynamics that tend to run down toward a disordered state. Energy flow then can give rise to order in a system and, for a system to maintain order, energy flow must be continuous (Morowitz, 1979). Third, and perhaps most significant, for an account of the timing constraints we observe in movement is Morowitz's (1979) main theorem: *The flow of energy from a source to a sink will lead to at least one cycle in the system.*

It has long been recognized that cyclicity lies at the very heart of biological functioning. A quote by Goodwin (1970) captures the message perfectly: "Oscillatory behavior is the fundamental dynamic mode of living, self-producing systems as we know them at and above the cellular level. The oscillation is not imposed by the environment; nor is it incidental to the living process. It is central to the organization [p. 8]." But, as emphasized here, cyclicity is not some epiphenomenal property of biological systems. It is central because the only known stability for systems that degrade free energy (as do all natural systems) is a *dynamic stability* necessarily consisting of periodicities or repeated motions (Yates, Marsh, & Iberall, 1972).

Cyclicity, as we have noted, is a nonlinear phenomenon. In effect the escapement is a nonlinear element that can make up for local thermodynamic losses and sustain oscillatory behavior. Such cycles are called *limit cycles* because they are capable of returning to a stable mode regardless of disturbances that speed up or slow down the cycle. Self-organizing, autonomous systems become viable, it is thought, when many cyclical processes become entrained. The latter *homeokinetic* scheme denotes systemic behavior as established by an ensemble of nonlinear oscillators that are entrained into a coherent harmonic configuration (Iberall, 1978; Soodak & Iberall, 1978). For homeokinetics, limit cycle entrainment ensures a solution to the degrees of freedom problem of movement control.

The features of coordinated movement identified in the previous section can now be rationalized on grounds other than motor programs. Coordinative structures, we suspect, *are* nonlinear oscillators of the limit cycle type, whose design necessarily guarantees that the timing and duration of "squirts" of energy will be independent of their magnitude within a fixed time frame (a period of oscillation, see Kugler, et al., 1980). Referring back to Equation 2, the magnitude of the forcing function will be some proportion of the potential energy available, but the forcing function itself is not dependent on time (Iberall, 1975; Yates & Iberall, 1973). Nonconservative, nonlinear oscillators are truly *autonomous* devices in a formal mathematical sense; time is nowhere represented in such systems (Andronov & Chaiken, 1949) and energy is provided in a "timeless" manner.

Perhaps the example that best captures the autonomous self-organizing nature of coordinative structures comes from Orlovskii's (1972) study of mesencephalic locomotion. Stimulation of the hind-limb areas of Red and Dieters nuclei in a stationary cat energizes the flexor and extensor synergies that correspond to the locomotory swing and stance phases, respectively. During induced locomotion, however, continuous stimulation of one site or the other has an effect *only when the respective synergies are actually involved in the step cycle.* Supraspinal influences (the energy supply) are only tapped in accordance with the basic oscillator design of the spinal circuitry. It is the latter that determines *when* the system receives its pulse of energy as well as the *duration* of the pulse (see Boylls', 1975, discussion of spinal "slots").

Elsewhere we have shown that several important aspects of movement control result from a nonlinear limit cycle design. All the studies showing equifinality following limb perturbations can be given a reading in these terms (see pp. 443–444; also Fowler et al., 1980; Kelso & Holt, 1980; Kelso, Holt & Flatt, 1980; Schmidt, 1980). In addition, limit cycle oscillators have the entrainment property—already mentioned—that simple oscillatory systems such as a mass-spring do not possess. Entrainment is the chief mode of cooperation among self-sustaining oscillators and can take several forms. *Mutual entrainment* occurs when oscillators with similar but nonidentical frequencies interact such that both adopt an intermediate frequency (for examples, see Kelso et al., 1980; also von Holst's, 1973, "magnet effect"). *Harmonic entrainment* is that form of interaction that results when one oscillator adopts a frequency that is an integer multiple of another to which it is coupled (for examples of moving two limbs at different rhythms, see von Holst, 1973, and Kelso et al., 1980). These effects are omnipresent even in tasks that require the use of different structural systems. Individuals who are instructed to speak at a different rate than hand movement (and vice versa) either perform both activities synchronously or make one a subharmonic of the other (see Kelso et al., in press). In sum, entrainment is an emergent property of the interaction of nonlinear oscillatory systems; it is a self-organizing process in the sense that a collection of mutually entrained oscillators functions in a unitary way. The existence of timing constraints in many actions, we suspect, is not pernicious and accountable for by increasingly elaborate motor programs. In contrast, cyclicity is a necessary consequence of the physics of living systems (homeokinetics). Without timing constraints like entrainment, I suspect there could be no temporal resolution of the many simultaneous processes that occur when animals move.

CONCLUDING REMARKS

Homeokinetics characterizes biological systems as ensembles of nonlinear, limit cycle oscillators coupled and mutually entrained at all levels of organization. The appropriate (physical) image, as Yates (in press) points out, is one of multiple oscillators, not keeping time particularly well but weakly coupled in such a way that the ensemble is characterized by multiple rhythms, some timed quite precisely (as in some of the experiments mentioned earlier). The regulated state of the system in the homeokinetic view is defined by the operating conditions of interacting limit cycles, not by the reference levels, comparators, or error-detecting mechanisms of cybernetical devices.

This latter perspective—though largely unacknowledged by neuroscience—nevertheless interfaces perfectly with recent developments in that discipline.

Delcomyn (1980), for instance, in an exhaustive review of the neural basis for rhythmic behavior, identifies as new and "fundamentally important problems in neuroscience" precisely what we have considered here, namely the significance of oscillation and how oscillators interact to effect coordination between different parts of an animal (see Delcomyn, 1980, p. 497). According to the present perspective, oscillatory processes are pervasive in biology because living systems are members of a class of physical systems that are open to flux of energy and matter. Cyclicity or oscillation is an inevitable consequence of this fact (Turvey, Kelso, & Kugler, 1980).

Although many motor behaviors exhibit limit cycle properties (and may even be predictable by them), limit cycles per se do not have first-order status in explaining those behaviors. As pointed out at the beginning of this chapter, in order to observe spectrally distributed limit cycle regimes, certain necessary conditions must be present.

For new spatial and temporal organizations to emerge from previously existing steady states, the following constitute essential conditions (Iberall, 1977, 1978; Katchalsky et al., 1974; Kugler et al., 1980; Prigogine & Nicolis, 1971; Yates, 1980):

1. The presence of a large number of stochastically fluctuating elements—a many degree of freedom system.
2. Interactions between elements of a nonlinear kind.
3. A scale change such that nonlinear interactions are amplified.
4. Free energy should be dissipated by the system.

One of the best examples illustrating the application of these conditions to biological phenomena comes from work on termite architecture (Prigogine & Nicholis, 1971; see also Kugler, Shaw, & Turvey, in press). A careful analysis reveals that the elaborate walls, pillars, and arches constructed by a congregation of termites can be explained in terms of physical conditions that generate "dissipative structures"—spatially structured steady states or time-dependent limit cycle regimes that require a continuous flow of matter and energy for their formation and maintenance. Termites, it seems, do not possess a program for arch building that is isomorphic with the product of this behavior. Similarly, with respect to movement, many of the changes that occur when animals change gait may be explained without requiring the selection of a new program for each. Scale changes and nonlinearities in the system generate "phase transitions" and are capable of driving the system to qualitatively new spatiotemporal patterns that are formed and maintained by degrading free energy.

In this chapter I have tried to show by reason and by example that certain biological phenomena such as the preservation of a stable temperature or the acquiring of desired limit postures (pp. 442–444) may be explainable in terms other than programs or servomechanisms. This "other" explanation has its foundations in the contemporary physical theories of homeokinetics and dissipa-tive structures (or dynamic patterns). The orderliness of systemic behavior in the physical view is not due to an isomorphic prescription *for* the system but is an a posteriori fact *of* the system—a necessary consequence of selective constraints and physical law. It is worth noting that certain eminent neurophysiologists have become sensitive to the fact that the neural networks of the brain and related structures offer all the requisite architectural conditions for the emergence of dynamic patterns (Katchalsky et al., 1974; Llinas & Iberall, 1977; Szentagothai, 1978).

Of course, the goal of the present chapter has been to show in a very prelimi-nary way what Yates (in press) suggests life itself shows, that is, how much action can emerge from some relatively primitive arrangements given the pres-ence of a nonlinearity or two. Contemporary physical theory offers a dynamic vocabulary and gives due credit to the intrinsic relationship between plant pro-cesses and the small signal, communication aspects of the system. It promises to provide an accurate description of the mechanisms of emergence, of qualitative change in behaviors that cannot be understood with reference to quantitatively known component processes. Above all, it offers a principled account of how a system's internal degrees of freedom are regulated: Bernstein's (1967) problem. Perhaps it is not too early, then, to consider contemporary physics as a serious alternative to the vocabulary of formal machines that invests in the program the very phenomena that a theory of movement has to explain.

ACKNOWLEDGMENTS

I am indebted to my colleagues Michael Turvey and Peter Kugler for the many discussions they have shared with me. I also thank Michael Turvey for an extensive critique on an earlier version and John Long, Alan Wing, and Jean Requin for very helpful comments. Preparation of this chapter and some of the research reported herein was supported by Grants NS 13617 and AM 25814 from the National Institute of Health.

REFERENCES

Adams, J. A. Feedback theory of how joint receptors regulate the timing and positioning of a limb. *Psychological Review, 1977, 84,* 504-523.

Andronov, A., & Chaiken, C. E. *Theory of oscillations.* Princeton, N.J.: Princeton University Press, 1949.

Aschoff, J. Circadian rhythms: General features and endocrinological aspects. In D. Krieger (Ed.), *Endocrine rhythms.* New York: Raven Press, 1979.

Bernstein, N. A. *The coordination and regulation of movements.* London: Pergamon Press, 1967.

Bizzi, E. Central and peripheral mechanisms in motor control. In G. E. Stelmach & J. Requin (Eds.), *Tutorials in motor behavior.* Amsterdam: North-Holland, 1980.

Bohm, D. Some remarks on the notion of order. In C. H. Waddington (Ed.), *Towards a theoretical biology* (Vol. 2). Chicago: Aldine Pub., 1969.

Boylls, C. C. A theory of cerebellar function with applications to locomotion. II. The relation of anterior lobe climbing fiber function to locomotion behavior in the cat. *COINS Technical Report 76-1*, Department of Computer and Information Sciences, University of Massachusetts, 1975.

Davis, J. Organizational concepts in the central motor networks of invertebrates. In R. M. Herman, S. Grillner, P. S. G. Stein, & D. G. Stuart (Eds.), *Neural control of locomotion*. New York: Plenum, 1976.

Delcomyn, F. Neural basis of rhythmic behavior in animals. *Science*, 1980, *210*, 492–498.

Dewey, J., & Bentley, A. F. *Knowing and the known*. Boston: Benion, 1948.

Easton, T. A. On the normal use of reflexes. *American Scientist*, 1972, *60*, 591–599.

Fel'dman, A. G. Functional tuning of the nervous system with control of movement or maintenance of a steady posture. III. Mechanographic analysis of execution by man of the simplest motor tasks. *Biophysics*, 1966, *11*, 766–775.

Fentress, J. C. *Order in ontogeny: Relational dynamics*. Paper given at the Interdisciplinary Study of Behavioral Development, Bielefeld, Germany, March, 1978.

Fitch, H., & Turvey, M. T. On the control of activity: Some remarks from an ecological point of view. In D. Landers & R. Christina (Eds.), *Psychology of motor behavior and sport*. Urbana, Ill.: Human Kinetics, 1978.

Fowler, C. *Timing control in speech production*. Bloomington, Ind.: Indiana University Linguistics Club, 1977.

Fowler, C. A., Rubin, P., Remez, R. E., & Turvey, M. T. Implications for speech production of a general theory of action. In B. Butterworth (Ed.), *Language production*. New York: Academic Press, 1980.

Freund, H. J., & Büdingen, H. J. The relationship between speed and amplitude of the fastest voluntary contractions of human arm muscles. *Experimental Brain Research*, 1978, *31*, 1–12.

Freund, H. J., & Dietz, V. The relationship between physiological and pathological tremor. In J. E. Desmedt (Ed.), *Physiological tremor, pathological tremors and clonus*. Basel: S. Karger, 1978.

Gelfand, I. M., Gurfinkel, V. S., Tsetlin, M. L., & Shik, M. L. Some problems in the analysis of movements. In I. M. Gelfand (Ed.), *Models of the structural and functional organization of certain biological systems*. Cambridge: MIT Press, 1971.

Gelfand, I. M., & Tsetlin, M. L. Some methods of control for complex systems. *Russian Mathematical Surveys*, 1962, *17*, 95–116.

Goodman, D., & Kelso, J. A. S. Are movements prepared in parts? Not under compatible (naturalized) conditions. *Journal of Experimental Psychology: General*, 1980, *109*, 475–495.

Goodwin, B. Biological stability. In C. H. Waddington (Ed.), *Towards a theoretical biology*. Chicago: Aldine Pub., 1970.

Greene, P. H. Problems of organization of motor systems. In R. Rosen & F. Snell (Eds.), *Progress in theoretical biology* (Vol. 2). New York: Academic Press, 1972.

Grillner, S., & Zangger, P. How detailed is the central pattern generation for locomotion. *Brain Research*, 1975, *88*, 367–371.

Gurfinkel, V. S., Kots, Ya. M., Paltsev, E. I., & Feldman, A. G. The compensation of respiratory disturbances of the erect posture of man as an example of the organization of interarticulatory organization. In I. M. Gelfand (Ed.), *Models of the structural-functional organization of certain biological systems*. Cambridge, Mass.: MIT Press, 1971.

Henry, F. M. Use of simple reaction time in motor programming studies: A reply to Klatt, Wyatt and Lingo. *Journal of Motor Behavior*, 1980, *12*, 163–168.

Hollerbach, J. M. *An oscillation theory of handwriting*. MIT: Artificial Intelligence Laboratory, 1980.

Iberall, A. S. On nature, man and society: A basis for scientific modelling. *Annals of Biomedical Engineering*, 1975, *3*, 344–385.

Iberall, A. S. A field and circuit thermodynamics for integrative physiology: I. Introduction to general notion. *American Journal of Physiology/Reg., Integ. Comp. Physiology*, 1977, *2*, R171–R180.

Iberall, A. S. A field and circuit thermodynamics for integrative physiology: II. Power and communicational spectroscopy in biology. *American Journal of Physiology/Reg., Integrative Comp. Physiology,* 1978, *3,* R3–R19.

Iberall, A. S., & Soodak, H. Physical basis for complex systems—Some propositions relating levels of organization. *Collective Phenomena,* 1978, *3,* 9–24.

Katchalsky, A. K., Rowland, V., & Blumenthal, R. Dynamic patterns of brain cell assemblies. *Neurosciences Research Program Bulletin,* 1974, *12,* 1–181.

Keele, S. W. Movement control in skilled motor performance. *Psychological Bulletin,* 1968, *70,* 387–403.

Keele, S. W. Behavioral analysis of motor control. In V. Brooks (Ed.), *Handbook of physiology, motor control volume.* Washington, D.C.: American Physiological Society, 1980.

Keele, S. W., & Summers, J. The structure of motor programs. In G. E. Stelmach (Ed.), *Motor control: Issues and trends.* New York: Academic Press, 1976.

Kelso, J. A. S. Motor control mechanisms underlying human movement reproduction. *Journal of Experimental Psychology,* 1977, *3,* 529–543.

Kelso, J. A. S., & Holt, K. G. Exploring a vibratory systems account of human movement production. *Journal of Neurophysiology,* 1980, *43,* 1183–1196.

Kelso, J. A. S., Holt, K. G., & Flatt, A. E. The role of proprioception in the perception and control of human movement: Towards a theoretical reassessment. *Perception & Psychophysics,* 1980, *28,* 45–52.

Kelso, J. A. S., Holt, K. G., Kugler, P. N., & Turvey, M. T. On the concept of coordinative structure as dissipative structure. II. Empirical lines of convergence. In G. E. Stelmach & J. Requin (Eds.), *Tutorials in motor behavior,* Amsterdam: North-Holland, 1980.

Kelso, J. A. S., Holt, K. G., Rubin, P., & Kugler, P. N. Patterns of human interlimb coordination emerge from the properties of non-linear oscillators. Manuscript submitted, Oct., 1980.

Kelso, J. A. S., Southard, D. L., & Goodman, D. On the nature of human interlimb coordination. *Science,* 1979, *203,* 1029–1031.

Kelso, J. A. S., & Stelmach, G. E. Central and peripheral mechanisms in motor control. In G. E. Stelmach (Ed.), *Motor control: Issues and trends.* New York: Academic Press, 1976.

Kelso, J. A. S., & Tuller, B. H. Manuscript in preparation.

Kelso, J. A. S., Tuller, B. H., & Harris, K. S. A 'dynamic pattern' perspective on the control and coordination of movement. In P. MacNeilage (Ed.), *Motor control of speech production.* Springer Verlag. In press.

Kugler, P. N., Kelso, J. A. S., & Turvey, M. T. On the concept of coordinative structure as dissipative structure. I. Theoretical lines of convergence. In G. E. Stelmach & J. Requin (Eds.), *Tutorials in motor behavior.* Amsterdam: North Holland, 1980.

Kugler, P. N., Kelso, J. A. S., & Turvey, M. T. On the control and coordination of naturally developing systems. In J. A. S. Kelso & J. E. Clark (Eds.), *The development of movement control and coordination.* New York: John Wiley, in press.

Kugler, P. N., Shaw, R., & Turvey, M. T. Is the "cognitive penetrability" criterion invalidated by contemporary physics? *The Behavioral and Brain Sciences,* in press.

Lashley, K. S. The problem of serial order in behavior. In L. A. Jeffress (Ed.), *Cerebral mechanisms in behavior.* New York: Wiley, 1951.

Lenneberg, E. H. *Biological foundations of language.* New York: Wiley, 1967.

Lindblom, B., Lubker, J., & Gay, T. Formant frequencies of some fixed mandible vowels and a model of speech motor programming by predictive simulation. *Journal of Phonetics,* 1979, *7,* 147–162.

Lindblom, B., & Sundberg, J. Acoustical consequences of lip, tongue, jaw and larynx movement. *Journal of the Acoustical Society of America,* 1971, *50,* 1166–1179.

Llinas, R. R., & Iberall, A. A global model of neuronal command-control systems. *Biosystems,* 1977, *8,* 233–235.

Macmillan, D. L. A physiological analysis of walking in the American lobster. *Philosophical Transactions of the Royal Society of London*, 1975, *270B*, 1–59.

MacNeilage, P. The motor control of serial ordering in speech. *Psychological Review*, 1970, *77*, 182–196.

Madeiros, J. M. *Investigation of neuronal mechanisms underlying human locomotion: An EMG analysis.* Unpublished doctoral dissertation, University of Iowa, 1978.

Martin, J. G. Rhythmic (hierarchical) versus serial structure in speech and other behavior. *Psychological Review*, 1972, *79*, 487–509.

Merton, P. A. How we control the contraction of our muscles. *Scientific American*, 1972, *226*, 30–37.

Miles, F. A., & Evarts, E. V. Concepts of motor organization. *Annual Reviews of Psychology*, 1979, *30*, 327–362.

Mitchell, D., Snellen, J. W., & Adkins, J. R. Thermoregulation during fever: Change in setpoint or change in gain. *Pflugers Archivěs*, 1970, *321*, 293.

Morowitz, H. J. *Energy flow in biology.* Woodbridge, Conn.: Ox Bow Press, 1979.

Orlovskii, G. N. The effect of different descending systems on flexion and extensor activity during locomotion. *Brain Research*, 1972, *40*, 359–371.

Polit, A., & Bizzi, E. Processes controlling arm movements in monkeys. *Science*, 1978, *201*, 1235–1237.

Powers, W. T. Quantitative analysis of purposive systems: Some spadework at the foundations of scientific psychology. *Psychological Review*, 1978, *85*, 417–435.

Prigogine, I., & Nicolis, G. Biological order, structure and instabilities. *Quarterly Review of Biophysics*, 1971, *4*, 107–148.

Raibert, M. *Motor control and learning by the state space model.* MIT: Artificial Intelligence Laboratory, 1977.

Rosenbaum, D. A. Human movement initiation: Specification of arm, direction and extent. *Journal of Experimental Psychology: General*, 1980, *109*, 444–474.

Rosenbaum, D. A., & Patashnik, O. Time to time in the human motor system. In R. S. Nickerson (Ed.), *Attention and performance VIII.* Hillsdale, N.J.: Lawrence Erlbaum Associates, 1980.

Saltzman, E. Levels of sensorimotor representation. *Journal of Mathematical Psychology*, 1979, *20*, 92–163.

Satinoff, E. Neural organization and evolution of thermal regulation in mammals. *Science*, 1978, *201*, 16–22.

Schmidt, R. A. On the theoretical status of time in motor program representations. In G. E. Stelmach & J. Requin (Eds.), *Tutorials in motor behavior.* Amsterdam: North Holland, 1980.

Schröedinger, E. *What is life?* London and New York: Cambridge University Press, 1945.

Shaffer, L. H. Analyzing piano performance: A study of concert pianists. In G. E. Stelmach & J. Requin (Eds.), *Tutorials in motor behavior.* Amsterdam: North Holland, 1980.

Shaw, R., & Turvey, M. T. Coalitions as models for ecosystems: A realist perspective on perceptual organization. In M. Kubovy & J. Pomerantz (Eds.), *Perceptual organization.* Hillsdale, N.J.: Lawrence Erlbaum Associates, in press.

Smith, J. S. Sensorimotor integration during motor programming. In G. E. Stelmach (Ed.), *Information processing in motor learning and control.* New York: Academic Press, 1978.

Snellen, J. W. Setpoint in exercise. In J. Bligh & R. Moore (Eds.), *Essays on temperature regulation.* Amsterdam: North-Holland, 1972.

Soodak, H., & Iberall, A. S. Homeokinetics: A physical science for complex systems. *Science*, 1978, *201*, 579–582.

Stein, P. S. G. Motor systems with specific reference to the control of locomotion. *Annual Review of neuroscience*, 1978, *1*, 61–81.

Szentagothai, J. A false alternative: Commentary on Pucetti and Dykes: Sensory cortex and the mind-brain problem. *The Behavioral and Brain Sciences*, 1978, *3*, 367–368.

Taub, E. Movement in non-human primates deprived of somatosensory feedback. *Exercise and Sport Science Reviews,* 1976, *4,* 335–374.

Terzuolo, C., & Viviani, P. About the central representation of learned motor patterns. In R. Talbot & D. R. Humphrey (Eds.), *Posture and movement.* New York: Raven Press, 1979.

Turvey, M. T. Preliminaries to a theory of action with reference to vision. In R. Shaw & J. Bransford (Eds.), *Perceiving, acting and knowing: Toward an ecological psychology.* Hillsdale, N.J.: Lawrence Erlbaum Associates, 1977.

Turvey, M. T., Kelso, J. A. S., & Kugler, P. N. A physical, rather than a biological basis for oscillatory processes. Manuscript submitted, Nov., 1980.

Viviani, P., & Terzuolo, C. Space-time invariance in learned motor skills. In G. E. Stelmach & J. Requin (Eds.), *Tutorials in motor behavior.* Amsterdam: North-Holland, 1980.

von Holst, E. *The behavioral physiology of animals and man.* Coral Gables, Fla.: University of Miami Press, 1973.

Werner, J. Mathematical treatment of structure and function of the human thermoregulatory system. *Biological Cybernetics,* 1977, *25,* 93–101.

Yates, F. E. Physical causality and brain theories. *American Journal of Physiology,* 1980, *238,* R277–R290.

Yates, F. E. Physical biology: A basis for modeling living systems. *Journal of Cybernetics and Information Science,* in press.

Yates, F. E., & Iberall, A. S. Temporal and hierarchical organization in biosystems. In J. Urquart & F. E. Yates (Eds.), *Temporal aspects of therapeutics.* New York: Plenum, 1973.

Yates, F. E., Marsh, D. J., & Iberall, A. S. Integration of the whole organism: A foundation for a theoretical biology. In J. A. Behnke (Ed.), *Challenging biological problems: Directions towards their solution.* New York: Oxford University Press, 1972, 110–132.

26

Buffer Storage of Programmed Articulation and Articulatory Loop: Two Names for the Same Mechanism or Two Distinct Components of Short-Term Memory?

Stuart T. Klapp, David M. Greim, and Elizabeth A. Marshburn
California State University, Hayward
Hayward, California, U.S.A.

ABSTRACT

Choice reaction time (RT) prior to pronunciation increases as a function of the number of syllables to be articulated, suggesting that articulation must be programmed prior to speech. However, when the item to be pronounced is precued before the response signal, simple RT is relatively independent of the number of syllables. Apparently, subjects can program the articulation in advance of the simple RT interval, holding the programmed representation in buffer storage until the response is required. Experiment 1 showed that simple RT was independent of the number of syllables, even if irrelevant unvoiced articulation was required between the precue and the response signal. Thus, irrelevant articulation does not suppress formation of buffer storage. By contrast, irrelevant unvoiced articulation disrupted immediate serial recall in Experiment 2, suggesting suppression of the "articulatory loop" component of short-term memory. Because irrelevant articulation suppresses articulatory loop but not buffer storage, we conclude that these are distinct systems of memory. Experiment 2 also showed that relevant auditory input can overcome the otherwise disruptive effect of irrelevant articulation in immediate recall. Therefore, the articulatory loop may be auditory in nature. A three-component model of short-term memory is proposed involving an auditory store (replacing articulatory loop), an articulatory buffer storage, and central executive.

INTRODUCTION

Two diverse traditions share the assumption that articulation (or other motor action) is represented in a component of short-term memory (STM). The "articulatory loop" notion developed from the study of immediate recall of verbal

459

materials. The "buffer storage" notion developed from reaction time (RT) analysis of programming articulatory (and other) responses. The present experiments address the issue of whether a common mechanism can account for the findings from these two paradigms.

The articulatory loop concept originated from the observation that immediate recall is greatly reduced when irrelevant articulation is required during visual presentation of the items (Crowder, 1978; Levy, 1971). The loss in recall is attributed to suppression of the formation of one component of STM (articulatory loop), when the relevant items cannot be articulated at input. When the articulatory loop is present, the number of items recalled is smaller if the items are ones that take longer to pronounce, suggesting that only a limited duration of speech articulation can be retained in the articulatory loop. This "word-length effect" disappears with visual presentation and articulatory suppression (irrelevant articulation), consistent with the view that the manipulation eliminates the articulatory loop (Baddeley, Thomson, & Buchanan, 1975). Another effect, diagnostic of the articulatory loop, is the articulatory–acoustic confusability effect, in which visually presented items having articulatory features in common are recalled more poorly than are items that have distinct sounds and articulations (Conrad & Hull, 1964). The effect, like the word-length effect, vanishes when articulation is suppressed with visual input (Peterson & Johnson, 1971). An essential feature of Baddeley's notion of "articulatory loop" (Baddeley, 1978) is that it is only one component of STM. The other component, "central executive" represents the system which is also involved in verbal reasoning.

The notion of buffer storage (Klapp, 1976) was inferred from a pattern of results obtained in experiments measuring RT as a function of the nature of the muscular (including articulatory) response to follow. First consider choice RT, a procedure in which the stimulus marking the beginning of the RT interval informs the subject which of a set of possible responses is required on a particular trial. Choice RT has been found to depend on the nature of the response in general and on the number of syllables to be articulated in particular. By contrast, in the simple RT procedure the response to be made on the particular trial is identified in advance of the imperative stimulus marking the beginning of the simple RT interval. Thus, the imperative stimulus informs the subject that he should respond as quickly as possible by producing the response that has been identified earlier. The general finding is an interaction such that simple RT is relatively independent of response parameters, such as syllable count, which influence choice RT.

This interaction has been reported for the responses of: (1) key presses of varying temporal duration (Klapp, 1977a; Klapp, Wyatt, & Lingo, 1974),[1] (2)

---

[1]The key press paradigm has been shown to be sensitive to the tolerance on duration feedback in an unexplained manner (Kerr, 1979; Klapp & Greim, in press). Therefore, these results must be interpreted with great caution.

single compared to longer duration two-component key presses (Jagacinski, Shulman, & Burke, 1980); (3) short-amplitude-aimed movements varying in required accuracy and in duration (Glencross & Gould, 1979; Klapp & Greim, 1979); and (4) articulation of speech varying in syllables (Eriksen, Pollack, & Montague, 1970; Klapp, 1974; Klapp, Anderson, & Berrian, 1973). Some workers, by contrast, have reported effects of response duration on simple RT as well as choice RT. This issue has been discussed in detail elsewhere (Klapp, Abbott, Coffman, Greim, Snider, & Young, 1979; Klapp et al., 1974; Sternberg, Monsell, Knoll, & Wright, 1978). It is our view that, with proper controls and proper motivation of subjects to use the precue signal of the simple RT proce- dure, the effect of response duration is primarily in choice RT and vanishes or is very small in simple RT. The present Experiment 1 included a replication of the interaction for speech articulation.

To interpret the choice RT results, note that the response is varied (e.g., number of syllables), not decision factors (e.g., number of alternative responses or response probability). Furthermore, care is taken to ensure that stimuli are balanced with respect to required responses (Klapp et al., 1974) or that control data are recorded to ensure that the time required to perceive the stimuli is constant (Klapp et al., 1973) or that sets of stimuli are used that would make a perceptual interpretation implausible (e.g., Experiment 1 here). Having elimi- nated perception and decision interpretations, next observe that the responses are highly learned (e.g., speaking common words or numbers), so that the effects cannot be attributed to the "invention" of novel responses. Our interpretation is that responses are stored in long-term memory in a representation that cannot be used to control motor movements until it is transformed. The transformation, or programming, is the component of choice RT that varies as a function of the response. For a recent review of this and related research, see Keele (in press) or Klapp (1977b).

Longer RT prior to longer and more complex motor responses appears for choice RT in which the response to be made is signaled by the stimulus that marks the beginning of the RT interval. The subject cannot program his response prior to this signal because he has not been informed which response to make on that particular trial. Therefore, programming must occur during the choice RT interval. By contrast, in the simple RT procedure the response is precued before the signal that marks the onset of the RT interval. Therefore, the subject might be able to program the response before the simple RT interval. However, if the time of occurrence of the imperative stimulus is randomized, the subject cannot post- pone programming until just prior to the imperative stimulus. Rather, the subject must program in advance and then hold the response program in memory (buffer storage) until the imperative stimulus occurs. Thus, we can account for the reduction of the effect of response parameters for simple RT, if we assume that advance programming occurs and that buffer storage is available.

In summary, articulatory loop and buffer storage both assume a component of STM that involves memory for speech articulation. Might the two systems represent an identical mechanism studied within two different experimental traditions? The present experiments address this issue.

EXPERIMENT 1

In Experiment 1 the simple-choice RT and irrelevant articulation manipulations were combined. Reaction time was measured as a function of the number of syllables to be articulated under three conditions: choice RT, simple RT, and simple RT plus irrelevant articulation from a time prior to the precue until the imperative stimulus. The choice and simple RT conditions represent a replication and reference. The critical condition is simple RT plus irrelevant articulation. Irrelevant articulation reduces immediate recall from STM. This is attributed to suppression of the formation of the articulatory loop. If the articulatory loop and output buffer represent the same mechanism, then irrelevant articulation should also suppress formation of the buffer storage. If there is no buffer storage, programming would occur in the simple RT interval. Therefore, the single process view of articulatory loop and buffer storage predicts that simple RT accompanied by irrelevant articulation would depend on the number of syllables to be pronounced.

Method

To-Be-Pronounced Stimuli.   Two sets of to-be-pronounced stimuli were used. The first set comprised two-digit numbers ending in 4, 6, or 7 (e.g., 26). These were to be pronounced as *twenty-six* rather than *two-six*. Numbers ending in 7 (e.g., 27) involve four syllables, but the other numbers (e.g., 24, 26) involve only three syllables. (Note that 7 is the only multisyllable number.) The three terminal digits (4, 6, or 7) were combined with initial digits of 2, 3, 5, 8, or 9 to yield 15 two-digit numbers. These particular initial digits were selected to avoid teens and repeating digits (e.g., 66). The use of two-digit numbers permits the initial vocalization sound to be balanced across syllables (as in the set 34, 36, and 37) so that sensitivity of the voice-activated apparatus to different initial sounds cannot affect the results. The numbers also avoid the problem of confounding decades (e.g., 30) with syllables (Henderson, Coltheart, & Woodhouse, 1973), because decades were not employed. An effect of number of syllables on choice RT, but no effect for simple RT, has been reported previously for these particular stimuli (Klapp, 1974).

The second set of to-be-pronounced stimuli were the single digits and single letters 4, 6, 7, T, A, W. The stimuli 4, 6, T, and A involve only one syllable, compared to two syllables for 7 and three for W. (Note that W is the only multisyllable letter.) The stimuli were used so that the results obtained would generalize beyond the particular case of two-digit numbers, although the second set of stimuli does not match initial sounds.

Each subject was tested for a 90-trial block using the two-digit numbers (i.e., 30 trials for each terminating digit) and for a 96-trial block with the single-digit single-letter set (i.e., 16 trials for each stimulus). Within each stimulus set, all possible stimuli were presented in random order. The stimuli were then reordered and presented again for 6 repetitions for two-digit numbers or 16 repetitions for the single stimuli. The order in which the two-digit-number block and the single-digit, single-letter block of trials appeared was balanced across subjects. In addition to these scored trials, each set of stimuli was introduced by approximately 20 practice trials.

Trial Sequence.   Each trial of the *choice* condition began with the presentation of the word ALERT, which remained visible for 500 msec on the CRT display, 1° high, at a viewing distance of 60 cm. There followed a blank interval between 300 msec and 450 msec, determined randomly. The stimulus letter or number was then displayed, and the RT clock started. Subjects pronounced the stimulus as quickly as possible after it appeared. Upon detection of the first emitted sound, the RT clock stopped and the stimulus was removed. After an intertrial interval of 2.5 sec (two-digit) or 4.0 sec (single stimulus), the events were repeated. Subjects were instructed to inhale when the alert signal appeared in order to be ready to respond when the stimulus appeared. The rate of presentation permitted a comfortable rate of breathing.

Each trial of the *simple* condition began with the presentation of the stimulus letter or number for 250 msec. Then the CRT was blanked for an interval between 500 msec and 650 msec, determined randomly. Next the word ''GO'' appeared and the RT clock was started. The subject was to plan the response after the number or letter appeared, but withhold responding until the GO appeared. Then the response was to be as soon as possible. Upon detection of the first emitted sound the RT clock stopped and the display was cleared. The intertrial interval and breathing instructions were the same as for the choice condition.

Each trial of the *simple with articulation* condition began with the presentation of the symbol * for 150 msec, indicating that the subject should inhale and then start to articulate silently the syllable ''La'' repeatedly. After a 500-msec blank interval, the letter or number stimulus was displayed for 250 msec. A blank interval of from 500 msec to 650 msec followed, determined randomly, during which the subject continued articulation of La silently and also prepared to pronounce the letter and number stimulus (if possible). Then the word GO appeared and the RT clock was started. The subject stopped silent articulation of La and pronounced the number or letter aloud as soon as possible. The first sound from the response stopped the RT clock and cleared the display. The intertrial interval was the same as for the other conditions. The use of the * signal prior to presentation of the to-be-spoken stimulus was to assure that the La pronunciation would be started and continue during the stimulus presentation. Pilot work indicated that subjects tended to delay starting the La articulation, if instructed to begin when the letter or number appeared. Because any such delay could be used to form the buffer storage, we wanted to ensure that the articulation was well underway before stimulus presentation.

Subjects.   Subjects were assigned to one of the three conditions (choice, simple, simple with articulation) in sequence as they reported for the experiment, 10 subjects per condition. The 30 subjects were students in Introductory Psychology at California State University, Hayward, who participated as one option of a course requirement. Two subjects were replaced before completing their session for failing to follow directions.

Data Reduction.   All trials in which RT was greater than 750 msec or on which a response was detected prior to the appropriate stimulus were rejected. Then, for each subject the mean RT for the remaining trials was computed for each condition. The analysis reported is based on these means.

Results and Discussion

Rejected Trials.   Less than 0.25% of the trials in the choice condition were rejected. By contrast, 7.4% of the trials in the other conditions (simple and simple plus articulation) were rejected, primarily due to anticipations. Note that anticipation was possible only in these conditions. The rate of rejected trials did not differ markedly between the two simple conditions nor among the stimulus types.

Reaction-Time Overall.   Mean RT data appear in Table 26.1. Although RT differed among the three stimulus sets, $F(2, 54) = 8.2$, $p < .001$, the pattern of results was the same for each stimulus set, with no significant interaction, $F(1, 27) = 1.3$, $p > .20$. Therefore, the data were collapsed across stimulus sets for the remaining analyses. Performance differed among conditions (choice, simple, simple plus articulation), $F(2, 27) = 10.3$, $p < .001$, and as a function of syllables, $F(1, 27) = 9.9$, $p < .005$. The condition and syllable variables interacted, $F(2, 27) = 13.6$, $p < .001$. Thus a further breakdown of results by condition is justified.

Choice RT Replication.   In the choice condition, RT was longer when more syllables were to be articulated, $F(1, 9) = 27.2$, $p < .001$. For each type of stimulus, choice RT was longer for the multiple-syllable items (e.g., those involving W or 7). It is important to note that the relation between choice RT and syllables cannot be given a perceptual interpretation in which the subject is assumed to require more time to perceive more syllables. Perceptual theories (e.g., Spoehr & Smith, 1973) hold that, for words, the letters are grouped into syllables and then each syllable group is perceived independently. Note, however, that for numbers and letters the syllables do not appear in a lexigraphic presentation so that this type of perceptual theory cannot hold. Furthermore, Klapp et al. (1973) showed that perception time was independent of syllable

TABLE 26.1
Reaction Time (msec) as Function of Syllables To Be Pronounced and
Condition for Experiment 1; Results for Three Sets of Stimuli Are Displayed

Two-Digit Numbers Terminating in Specified Digit

	Three Syllables			Four Syllables
Condition	4	6	Mean of 4 and 6	7
Choice	355	371	363	377
Simple	268	272	270	269
Simple + articulation	327	320	324	323

One-Digit Numbers

	One Syllable			Two Syllables
Condition	4	6	Mean of 4 and 6	7
Choice	389	413	401	422
Simple	269	288	279	282
Simple + articulation	323	338	330	331

Single Letters

	One Syllable			Three Syllables
Condition	T	A	Mean of T and A	W
Choice	356	360	358	395
Simple	274	256	265	253
Simple + articulation	318	293	305	307

count for a set of words for which choice RT prior to pronunciation depended on the number of syllables to be pronounced. Because the perceptual interpretation is not valid, the relation between choice RT and syllables seems to require a response-programming interpretation.

Choice-Simple by Syllable Interaction. By contrast to the relation between number of syllables and choice RT, number of syllables did not affect simple RT, $F(1, 9) = 1.2$, $p > .20$. The difference in role of syllables for choice and simple RT was confirmed by a significant interaction of choice versus simple condition by syllables, $F(1, 18) = 26.1$, $p < .001$. As noted previously, buffer storage is inferred from this interaction, which replicates a previous report for the two-digit number stimuli (Klapp, 1974) and extends the result to single-digit numbers and single letters. A similar interaction has been reported for pronouncing words

(Klapp et al., 1973) and for other responses (see the Introduction). Choice RT was also reliably longer than simple RT, $F(1, 18) = 50.5$, $p < .001$.

Irrelevant Articulation—Simple RT.   Of critical importance for the present analysis is the simple plus articulation condition. If irrelevant articulation suppresses formation of the buffer storage, then subjects would be obligated to program the response during the simple RT interval (after irrelevant articulation had terminated). If this were the case, then RT should depend on the number of syllables to be pronounced as in the choice RT procedure. If, on the other hand, responses can be programmed and stored in the buffer storage, then RT should be independent of syllables as in the simple RT procedure. As is evident in Table 26.1, the results confirm the latter prediction. There was no effect of syllables on RT in the simple plus articulation condition, $F(1, 9) < 1$, and the effect of syllables interacted significantly comparing the choice and simple plus articulation conditions, $F(1, 18) = 13.7$, $p < .005$. We conclude that irrelevant unvoiced articulation does not suppress formation of the buffer storage.

Overall RT in the simple plus articulation condition tended to be longer than in simple without articulation, $F(1, 18) = 3.2$, $.05 < p < .10$. The long RT with articulation might reflect the necessity to stop silent articulation prior to emitting the response. If this is correct, it could be taken as support for the premise that subjects maintain silent articulation until the GO stimulus. We tried to encourage this both by instruction and by making the time of occurrence of the GO stimulus uncertain. Of course, the interpretation of Experiment 1 would not hold if subjects were to interrupt silent articulation before the GO signal in order to program the relevant response.

EXPERIMENT 2

Experiment 1 showed that unvoiced articulation did not suppress formation of the buffer storage. Experiment 2 attempted to demonstrate that unvoiced irrelevant articulation, as well as the customary voiced irrelevant articulation, disrupts immediate recall. This is necessary if we are to conclude that buffer storage and articulatory loop are distinct mechanisms, because they are affected differently by irrelevant articulation.

A second aspect of Experiment 2 explored the possibility that the articulatory loop may be auditory rather than articulatory. To study this possibility the articulation variable (relevant versus irrelevant) was crossed with several types of auditory input. The subject-voiced condition involved a voiced articulation at input. The remaining conditions involved silent (unvoiced) articulation but different types of external auditory input: relevant digit, irrelevant (La La La), and none.

Method

Task.   The subject's task on each trial was to write eight digits in the correct order immediately after presentation. For each trial, eight different digits were presented in random order using the digits 1–9 with omission of the two-syllable digit 7. The digits were presented successively for 300 msec each with an interdigit interval of 100 msec, except that after the third and seventh digit the interdigit interval was increased to 500 msec. The temporal pattern may be thought of as an American telephone number (with pause) followed by one additional pause and one additional digit. Pilot work (Wilkes, Lloyd, & Simpson, 1972) indicated poor recall without a rhythmic pattern and that many subjects imposed their own rhythm if none was present. We preferred to control this patterning rather than to allow it to vary between subjects.

Trial Sequence.   Each trial began with an identification such as "TRIAL 5" displayed for 1 sec. After a 1-sec delay, the eight digits were displayed as described previously. An asterisk (*) was then displayed for 500 msec indicating that the digits were completed and the subject was to write the digits in the answer booklet. The subject signaled when finished, and the experimenter caused the program to continue with display of the word "ANSWER," followed by the correct string of digits. The display remained for 7.5 sec followed by a 2.5-sec interval in which the screen was blank prior to starting the next trial.

Auditory Input.   Under conditions involving auditory input, the numbers or syllables La, La, . . . were spoken over an intercommunication device by the experimenter. The sound volume was fairly loud but comfortable. The experimenter had a CRT display that presented the numbers in the same manner as seen by the subject and that also presented the entire digit string in advance. The experimenter used this to anticipate each digit prior to its sequential presentation in order to pronounce the digits with minimal lag after visual presentation.

Design.   Each of the eight subjects was tested in all eight conditions of the experiment as defined in Table 26.2. The order of testing was balanced across subjects. Each condition was represented by an unscored practice trial followed by 25 scored trials. Each subject was tested in two 1-hr sessions on separate days, with four conditions tested on each day. Prior to these two scored sessions, there was a 1-hr practice session in which eight trials per condition were presented for all conditions.

Subjects.   The eight subjects were from the same population as in Experiment 1, except that only female subjects were tested. This was because the experimenter was female, and a match between the voice of experimenter and subject was desired.

Scoring.   Responses were scored in three different ways: (1) proportion of trials completely correct (all digits in correct order); (2) number of digits in the correct serial position. This method gives credit for single isolated digits in

TABLE 26.2
Immediate Serial Recall as a Function of Input Articulation and Audition for
Experiment 2; results of Three Scoring Methods Are Displayed

Proportion of Trials Completely Correct

			Unvoiced Articulation	
Input Articulation	*Voiced Articulation*	*No Audition*	*Relevant Audition*	*Irrelevant Audition*
Relevant	.70	.63	.70	.46
Irrelevant	.13	.29	.72	.22

Number of Digits in Correct Serial Position (8 possible)

			Unvoiced Articulation	
Input Articulation	*Voiced Articulation*	*No Audition*	*Relevant Audition*	*Irrelevant Audition*
Relevant	7.32	7.15	7.34	6.54
Irrelevant	4.5	5.44	7.38	5.39

Number of Digits in Correct Runs (eight possible)

			Unvoiced Articulation	
Input Articulation	*Voiced Articulation*	*No Audition*	*Relevant Audition*	*Irrelevant Audition*
Relevant	7.23	7.07	7.28	6.44
Irrelevant	4.16	5.14	7.32	5.15

correct serial position and hence may inflate scores somewhat; and (3) number of digits appearing in strings of two or more in correct order. When more than one string appeared, the lengths of the strings were added for the total score.

Results and Discussion

The details of the serial position effect and of interactions involving serial positions do not change the picture compared to an overall analysis collapsed across serial position. Therefore, only overall data are presented. As indicated in Table 26.2, the pattern of results was very similar for the three scoring methods. Only those findings that held for all methods of scoring are described, and the F ratios from the scoring method yielding the lowest (most conservative) ratio are re-ported. Data from the first scoring method are noted in the narrative to identify some of the comparisons. Performance varied as a function of audition, $F(3, 21)$ = 29.5, $p < .001$, and of articulation relevance, $F(1, 7) = 24.5$, $p < .005$. Because these variables interacted, $F(3, 21) = 23.9$, $p < .001$, a detailed break-down is justified.

First, consider unvoiced articulation with no auditory input. Recall was lower with irrelevant articulation (.29) than with relevant articulation (.63), $F(1, 7) =$ 14.3, $p < .01$. This extends previous findings for voiced irrelevant articulation to the case of unvoiced articulation. Experiment 1 showed that irrelevant unvoiced articulation did *not* eliminate the buffer storage inferred from RT results. By contrast, irrelevant unvoiced articulation *did* reduce recall presumed to be from the articulatory loop (Experiment 2).

Next, consider the voiced articulation condition. Consistent with previous reports, recall was sharply reduced when irrelevant voiced articulation was re-quired at input (.13 versus .70), $F(1, 7) = 66.8$, $p < .001$. The effect of relevant versus irrelevant articulation was more pronounced with voiced than with silent articulation, $F(1, 7) = 11.7$, $p < .025$. Because the addition of subject-produced auditory input to accompany articulation increased the effect of type of articula-tion, we conclude that auditory storage plays an important role in the so-called articulatory loop.

The results with experimenter-produced auditory input (and unvoiced articula-tion by the subject) also support the importance of auditory storage. There was no hint that recall was less with irrelevant articulation (.72) compared to relevant articulation (.70), when the relevant auditory input was provided by the experi-menter. Thus, articulation relevance and auditory input (none versus relevant) interact strongly, $F(1, 7) = 14.7$, $p < .01$, indicating that providing relevant audition overcomes the effect of articulation relevance. An even more striking confirmation of the dominance of auditory over articulatory manipulations may be seen from the conditions in which the manipulations were in conflict. Recall was better with relevant audition but irrelevant articulation (.72) than with irrele-vant audition supported by relevant articulation (.46), $F(1, 7) = 7.75$, $p < .05$.

These results are inconsistent with the view that the articulatory loop is actu-ally articulatory because of the dominance of auditory over articulation factors in determining recall. One model that would account for these results would assume independent articulatory and auditory components of STM with auditory domi-nant. Another model, which we prefer, assumes only a single auditory memory together with the premise that articulation involves the equivalent of a weak auditory image that can enter auditory memory. The later premise is needed to account for the effect of the relevance of unvoiced articulation in the no audition and irrelevant audition conditions. Because the auditory image produced by articulation is assumed to be weaker than that produced by auditory input, the model would also account for the dominance of audition. An appealing way to account for this weak auditory image is based on ideomotor theory (Greenwald, 1970) that assumes that responses such as articulation are initiated by an image of the sensory feedback that the response will produce.

GENERAL DISCUSSION

Irrelevant unvoiced articulation at input reduced immediate recall (Experiment 2), presumably by suppressing *formation* of the articulatory loop component of STM. By contrast, we conclude that irrelevant articulation does not disrupt *formation* of buffer storage because simple RT remained independent of syllables even with irrelevant articulation (Experiment 1). Because formation of buffer storage and articulatory loop are differentially influenced by irrelevant articulation, we conclude that these must be different STM mechanisms.

However, if one assumes that irrelevant articulation enters memory and competes for limited storage capacity rather than suppressing the formation of a form of memory, one can account for the difference between Experiments 1 and 2 without the need to conclude that buffer storage and articulatory loop are different mechanisms. Experiment 1 might be viewed as having low loading of memory (at most a two-digit number plus the irrelevant La La), in contrast to much greater loading in Experiment 2 (eight items plus La La). By this view, the addition of the loading due to irrelevant articulation is disruptive in Experiment 2 due to overloading of STM. The plausibility of this alternative formulation depends on accepting the premise that the irrelevant articulation at input becomes a memory component rather than acting to suppress memory formation. We prefer the suppression interpretation because the irrelevant La La contains little information and need not be recalled. Furthermore, reduction of recall with irrelevant articulation occurs only when there is no auditory presentation (Experiment 2). If it were the case that irrelevant articulation enters and loads memory, then irrelevant articulation should have the same disruptive effect regardless of auditory input. Similarly, Baddeley et al. (1975, Exp. 8) report that irrelevant input articulation eliminated the word-length effect only for visual input and not for auditory input, from which they conclude that irrelevant articulation "... inhibits the translation of visual material into a phonemic code [p. 586]," that is, that it suppresses input rather than loads memory. Therefore, there is substantial reason to doubt the memory-loading premise of the alternative interpretation of our results.

A converging approach to demonstrate independence of articulatory loop and buffer storage would be manipulation of simple versus choice RT procedure factorially with the number of items in a concurrent memory load task. If articulatory loop and buffer storage are the same, then there should be an interaction such that increasing memory load would interfere with simple RT (for which buffer storage is required) more than it does with choice RT (for which no buffer storage is required), provided that the memory load is sufficient to require use of the articulatory loop. Logan (1980) reported either no interaction (Exp. 1 and 2) or an interaction in the opposite sense to that predicted by the same process view (Exp. 3). Similarly Sternberg et al. (1978) report that loading STM does not influence simple RT. We can take these data as converging support for the position that articulatory loop and buffer storage represent different memory systems.

The results of Experiment 2 indicate that the articulatory loop is not articulatory and may, in fact, be auditory. This is consistent with the major conclusion that buffer storage of articulatory commands is not to be identified with the articulatory loop. The present analysis, together with that of Baddeley (1978), suggests that there may be at least three components of STM: (1) an articulatory buffer storage; (2) an auditory storage identified as "articulatory loop" (Baddeley, 1978), "echoic persistence" (Watkins & Watkins, 1980) or acoustic storage (Crowder, 1978); and (3) central executive the processing space for mental operations.

ACKNOWLEDGMENTS

The authors wish to thank Joanne Woolf-Toback for assistance in gathering the data of Experiment 1 and Gregory Messer and George Eggleton for assistance with the equipment.

REFERENCES

Baddeley, A. D. The trouble with levels: A re-examination of Craik and Lockhart's framework for memory research. *Psychological Review*, 1978, *85*, 139–152.

Baddeley, A. D., Thomson, N., & Buchanan, M. Word length and the structures of short-term memory. *Journal of Verbal Learning and Verbal Behavior*, 1975, *14*, 575–589.

Conrad, R., & Hull, A. J. Information, acoustic confusions, and memory span. *British Journal of Psychology*, 1964, *55*, 429–432.

Crowder, R. G. Audition and speech coding in short-term memory: A tutorial review. In J. Requin (Ed.), *Attention and performance VII*. Hillsdale, N.J.: Lawrence Erlbaum Associates, 1978.

Eriksen, C. W., Pollack, M. D., & Montague, W. E. Implicit speech: Mechanism in perceptual encoding? *Journal of Experimental Psychology*, 1970, *84*, 502–507.

Glencross, D. J., & Gould, J. H. The planning of precision movements. *Journal of Motor Behavior*, 1979, *11*, 1–9.

Greenwald, A. G. Sensory feedback mechanisms in performance control: With special reference to the ideo-motor mechanism. *Psychological Review*, 1970, *77*, 73–99.

Henderson, L., Coltheart, M., & Woodhouse, D. Failure to find a syllabic effect in number naming. *Memory & Cognition*, 1973, *1*, 304–306.

Jagacinski, R. J., Shulman, G., & Burke, M. W. Motor programming and alerting. *Journal of Human Movement Studies*, 1980, *6*, 151–164.

Keele, S. W. Behavioral analysis of movement. In V. Brooks (Ed.), *Handbook of physiology*, Bethesda, Md., American Physiological Society, in press.

Kerr, B. Is reaction time different for long and short response durations in simple and choice conditions? *Journal of Motor Behavior*, 1979, *11*, 269–274.

Klapp, S. T. Syllable-dependent pronunciation latencies in number naming: A replication. *Journal of Experimental Psychology*, 1974, *102*, 1138–1140.

Klapp, S. T. Short-term memory as a response preparation state. *Memory & Cognition*, 1976, *4*, 721–729.

Klapp, S. T. Response programming, as assessed by reaction time, does not establish commands for particular muscles. *Journal of Motor Behavior*, 1977, *9*, 301–312. (a)

Klapp, S. T. Reaction time analysis of programmed control. *Exercise and Sports Sciences Reviews*, 1977, *5*, 231–253. (b)

Klapp, S., Abbott, J., Coffman, K., Greim, D., Snider, R., & Young, F. Simple and choice reaction time methods in the study of motor programming. *Journal of Motor Behavior*, 1979, *11*, 91–101.

Klapp, S. T., Anderson, W. G., & Berrian, R. W. Implicit speech in reading, reconsidered. *Journal of Experimental Psychology*, 1973, *100*, 368–374.

Klapp, S. T., & Greim, D. Programmed control of aimed movements revisited: The role of target visibility and symmetry. *Journal of Experimental Psychology: Human Perception and Performance*, 1979, *5*, 509–521.

Klapp, S. T., & Greim, D. M. Technical considerations regarding the short (dit)-long (dah) key press paradigm. *Journal of Motor Behavior*, in press.

Klapp, S. T., Wyatt, E. P., & Lingo, W. M. Response programming in simple and choice reactions. *Journal of Motor Behavior*, 1974, *6*, 263–271.

Levy, B. A. Role of articulation in auditory and visual short-term memory. *Journal of Verbal Learning and Verbal Behavior*, 1971, *10*, 123–132.

Logan, G. D. Short-term memory demands of reaction-time tasks that differ in complexity. *Journal of Experimental Psychology: Human Perception and Performance*, 1980, *6*, 375–389.

Peterson, L. R., & Johnson, S. T. Some effects of minimizing articulation on short-term retention. *Journal of Verbal Learning and Verbal Behavior*, 1971, *10*, 346–354.

Spoehr, K. T., & Smith, E. E. The role of syllables in perceptual processing. *Cognitive Psychology*, 1973, *5*, 71–89.

Sternberg, S., Monsell, S., Knoll, R. L., & Wright, C. E. The latency and duration of rapid movement sequences: Comparisons of speech and typewriting. In G. E. Stelmach (Ed.), *Information processing in motor control and learning*. New York: Academic Press, 1978.

Watkins, O. C., & Watkins, M. J. The modality effect and echoic persistence. *Journal of Experimental Psychology: General*, 1980, *109*, 251–278.

Wilkes, A. L., Lloyd, P., & Simpson, I. Pause measures during reading and recall in serial list learning. *Quarterly Journal of Experimental Psychology*, 1972, *24*, 48–54.

27 Programmed Aftereffects Following Simple Patterned Movements of the Eyes and Limbs

Brian Craske
Memorial University of Newfoundland
St. John's, Newfoundland
Canada

ABSTRACT

Experiments are reported which use as treatment large, horizontal or vertical, voluntary, periodic saccades, with fixation periods after each movement of between 1 and 16 sec. Following 20 cycles of such treatment, the resting position of the eyes in the dark exhibits involuntary decaying oscillation along the axis of the original movement. This is called a *programmed aftereffect* (programmed AE). Simultaneous, independent programmed AEs can occur along orthogonal axes of eye movement; these oscillations are vector summed and cause the eye to trace out a Lissajous figure.

It is likewise shown that periodic movements of the arm that are associated with pushing against restraint at the end of each swing or periodic voluntary efforts to move the arm in opposing directions with no concurrent movement both lead to involuntary oscillations of the arm. Effortful periodic movements of other parts of the body are also shown to produce involuntary programmed AEs. Similar movements of the arm in which effort is minimized yield no AEs: Movement alone is not a sufficient condition for their generation. It is suggested that these programmed AEs come about as a result of coding the temporal course of the effort expended in the initial performance, the decaying effort programs yielding the observed movements. The well known post-contraction phenomenon is argued to be one of the class of programmed AEs.

INTRODUCTION

It is commonplace to argue that much of our behavior can be considered to result from programs: plans for behavior that are stored and that can generate meaningful sequential action (Keele, 1968; Miller, Galanter, & Pribram, 1960;

Turvey, 1977). In particular, this is true for situations involving high levels of predictability. Although the evidence supporting the existence of programming in motor control may not be in dispute (Stelmach, 1976), what is stored is still a matter for debate. Certainly, however, in order for the performer to formulate commands that accurately carry out a repetitive action, it is essential that the dynamic characteristics of the limb be taken into account. This is to argue that the *force* requirements of action have to be encoded and be part of or associated with any controlling program. In conjunction with the necessity for timing, a part of the answer to the problem of what is stored is suggested to be a code that temporally organizes the *sequence of forces* utilized in the execution of the skilled act. Data to be reported in this chapter bear directly on this question. There is some evidence for the existence of central utilization of force information (Evarts, 1967; Pribram, 1971; Turvey, 1977).

Excluded from this discussion is that class of acts that, when directed to a given end, can be carried out in an indefinitely large number of ways. Actions of this kind would seem to be based on abstractions and need not be carried out as a result of the dispatch of a narrowly defined, previously encoded program. The skills on which this chapter focuses are highly specific. They were termed "closed skills" by Poulton (1957) and require a set movement pattern. Here the performer attempts to produce a template or model act under constant operational conditions. In conjunction with this, I want to introduce the topic of aftereffects (AEs) displayed by motor systems. It is clear from the literature that such AEs have played no significant role in the development of theory or paradigm in the study of the acquisition and production of skilled performance. This may not be puzzling, for a list of commonly accepted motor AEs cannot readily be drawn up. It is not clear, however, whether this is because there are few to be found or whether the lack of interest in the approach has ignored or not uncovered them. Indeed, I wish to argue that there are AEs of action or effort, and if sought they will be found.

The importance of AEs may be adduced by reference to the area of perception, which has traditionally used the AE as a phenomenon from which inferences about underlying processes and mechanisms can be drawn. In the same way, the mechanisms underlying skilled performance may well open themselves to inspection, if we take a closer look at AEs that may follow certain kinds of motor behavior.

Anecdotal, but nonetheless important, support for the notion of motor AEs is given by the syndrome of "land sickness," which can follow sea voyages. Previously, the seaman had to expend effort to adjust to the motions imposed on his body by the ship; subsequently there is perceived instability of terra firma. This may be redescribed as an experienced periodic AE.

In the same vein, it has recently been shown (Lackner & Graybiel, 1980) that after a sequence of parabolic maneuvers that produce periods of sub-G and supra-G, AEs occur that are less intense but similar to the original sensations.

This occurs even though the subject is on the ground. I argue that these observations are the result of the organization of *effort programs* that yield patterns of innervation to counteract the imposed motion. Thus, adapting the ideas of Kots, Krinskiy, Naydin, and Shik (1971), effort patterns are assembled and preprogrammed for a particular motor task. Gelfand, Gurfinkel, and Tsetlin (1971) have argued that such patterns of control tend to minimize the effects of perturbations, which could potentially degrade coordinated response. Nashner (1977) has indeed provided evidence that imposed sway (and thus coordinated efforts to overcome it) can bring about preprogrammed responses in functionally related leg and trunk muscles.

My argument, then, is that both land sickness and AEs related to flight maneuvers are the consequence of continuing centrally organized programs that, presumably, assist in the primary task. Thus the AE, the involuntary continuation of effort, whether unidirectional or multidirectional, has particular directional qualities characteristic of the treatment.

The experiments that follow are reported in historical order, and it will be noticed that the emphasis on effort is not reflected in the earlier experiments. The role of effort was made manifest in the later experiments on arms.

INITIAL EXPERIMENTS ON EYES

The AE on the Resting Position of the Eyes in the Dark of Horizontal (Left–Middle) or Vertical (Middle–Up) Movements

Introduction. The resting position has been used as an index of oculomotor function (Craske, Crawshaw, & Heron, 1975). The task requires S to let the eyes position themselves in the dark rather than requiring a judgment of visual direction. The operational definition used by Craske et al. defined resting position to be, "that position which the eyes are observed to take up when attempts at voluntary positioning are suspended, and a homogeneous field is viewed." This technique has shown itself to be a sensitive indicator of oculomotor disturbance.

Subjects. The primary subject was the author, and it is his results that are presented. Other subjects have been tested, however (see final paragraph of the following Results, p. 476).

Method and Procedure. The subject sat in a totally dark room with head position maintained by a dental impression. The right eye was flooded with infra-red light filtered to be completely invisible. The movements of the eye could be recorded by infra-red TV, and the magnified image ($\times 10$) could be viewed outside the room.

The experimental treatment required S to move his eyes between two microlights mounted 1.5 m distant from the eye. For the horizontal treatment, the lights were straight ahead of the left eye and 45° to its left. A given treatment had S fixate each light in turn for one of 1, 2, 4, 8, or 16 sec, with a given epoch being chosen at random. An experimental session was in three parts. First there was a 60 sec pre-treatment (control) period, during which S sat in the dark, allowing the eyes to position themselves. This was followed by 20 cycles of left–right eye movement at a pre-selected frequency. This was dictated to S by the switching rate of the fixation lights. Immediately the treatment was concluded (Ss eyes in the central position), the fixation light was extinguished, and S sat in the dark allowing the eyes to position themselves. The post-treatment period continued until E halted the session (when there were no observable AEs).

The figures were derived from video tape recordings of the eye movements. The playback was viewed on the surface of a digitizing tablet and the luminous point of its cursor was moved with an obvious mark on the iris. This technique is adequate in this situation only because the eye moves smoothly and slowly: The method undoubtedly has sufficient fidelity to show the general nature of the phenomenon.

Results.   Results for the author's eye, which are typical of a large number of sessions, are discussed here and shown in Fig. 27.1. During the control period that preceded each treatment, eye position remains fairly constant, with a non-periodic range of movement of about 4° along both axes. The left panel of Fig. 27.1 shows the last 40 sec of a 4-sec treatment period, which is followed by an AE that lasted for 90 sec. As the oscillation dies away, its period decreases. Also, it is superimposed upon a drift in mean position of the eye from the direction of previous maximal effort (left) toward the straight ahead. The AE consequent upon a vertical (middle–up) treatment is along a vertical axis but otherwise displays the same characteristics as the horizontal AE. The AEs consist mainly of smooth movements, although occasionally low amplitude saccades do occur.

The subject can voluntarily inhibit the oscillatory AE by "fixed staring" in the dark. The eye is not as stable as it would be in a control condition, however, exhibiting a large number of low-amplitude saccades. It was also noted that continuing inhibition does not result from brief interruption of the AE by voluntary fixation. In about half the cases, the period of the waveform decreases as it decays. The remainder show little change in period. However, the duration of the first cycle of the AE is considerably longer than the cycle time of the treatment.

The time constant of the envelope of the decaying oscillation is of interest and, with treatment periods of 2, 4, 8, 16, and 32 sec, time constants of the AEs were 40, 50.7, 57.4, 116.5, 135.0 sec, respectively. No other S has been exposed to the whole treatment sequence a sufficiently large number of times to present other data. It must be noted that similar horizontal and vertical AEs resulting from these treatment periods have been observed consistently for two research assistants, likewise, for single-treatment sessions for other subjects over the last 2 years.

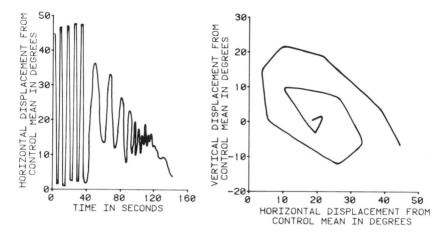

FIG. 27.1. Disturbance of the resting position of the author's eye. Left Panel: After 20 cycles of 45° left–middle excursion of the eye (last 5 cycles of treatment shown). This is followed by involuntary, horizontal oscillatory eye movements. Right Panel: Bi-dimensional AE subsequent to 20 cycles of left–middle–up treatment using 4-sec fixation.

The AEs on the Resting Position of Bidirectional (Left–Middle–Up) Movements

Introduction.   If the visual system can store both vertical and horizontal movement patterns, are they independent of each other? The appropriate experiment is to provide a treatment that, if it leads to independent AEs, allows prediction of the resultant eye movement. Clearly, if the globe is driven by two damped orthogonal oscillatory functions, we should observe two-dimensional AEs diminishing with time, the path depending on the phase relation of the pair of oscillations. In fact, as the following figures show, a number of eye-movement paths may result. However, they may be considered as linked Lissajous figures.

Results.   The right panel of Fig. 27.1 shows the AE for the author. The vertical and horizontal eye-movement controllers release oscillatory AEs but not patterned as the original, where the cycle on one channel follows the cycle on the other. Here, and for all Ss observed, they are released *simultaneously and independently;* for this subject they stay phased locked, but 90° out of phase for about 1½ cycles.

Figure 27.2 shows the AE given by a sample of 2 from 22 Ss in which S is allowed to "track" a small bright afterimage, produced at the end of 20 cycles of left–middle–up treatment by E triggering a flashtube with a circular aperture that was coincident with the final fixation point. We know that there is no eye movement resulting from the foveal AE during fixation in the dark for the normal

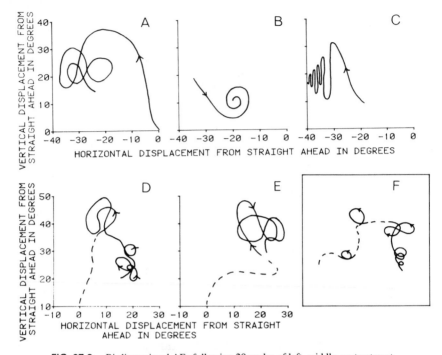

FIG. 27.2.   Bi-dimensional AEs following 20 cycles of left–middle–up treatment sequences. *Top row:* After 2-sec fixation at each point S 4 tracks an afterimage during the AE. Panel A: The first 18 sec shows interlinked Lissajous figures in which the frequency on *Y* is approximately twice that on *X*. Panel B: Next 5 sec; phase relationships stay constant and amplitudes on *X*- and *Y*-axes covary. Panel C: The final 15 sec shows strong vertical AEs associated with leftward drift. Discontinuities between figures are due to blinking. Minus on *X*-axis indicates position to S's left. *Bottom row:* S 14. Panel D: AE following 1-sec fixation at each point. Panel E: Following 2-sec fixation at each point. Panel F: Perceived autokinesis as AK occurred subsequent to 40 cycles of left–middle–up treatment with 1-sec fixations. Major circle diameters estimated to be 2 in.

S (Mack & Bachant, 1969), whereas the above figures show large sweeping movements and Lissajous figures.

In Fig. 27.2, Panels A, B, and C (S 4) consist of one single AE displayed in three parts. The AEs show the components exhibiting shifting phase relations and amplitudes in both the horizontal and vertical channels. In Fig. 27.2, Panels D and E (S 14) show similar Lissajous AEs that resulted from two different treatment rates.

The Use of Autokinesis

Following the treatment conditions so far mentioned, a few Ss, while steadily fixating, would experience autokinetic effects of predictable pattern (as indeed did the S whose casual comment initiated all these experiments). The perceived movement was drawn during the AK trial or on its conclusion. In Fig. 27.2, Panel F shows one such drawing as executed by S 14 after bi-dimensional treatment. The voluntary activity of fixating, however, seems to obliterate or eliminate the periodic AE for many subjects, so this technique was considered too insensitive to pursue.

EXPERIMENTS ON ARMS

The AE Following Horizontal Abduction and Adduction of the Arm with and without Accompanying Effort

Introduction.   Thus far we can see that short sequences of periodic movement can lead to motor AEs. The idea that effort may be a powerful factor has been mentioned in the Introduction. On considering land sickness, it occurred to me that a simulation of the shipboard experience might be to thrust oneself from side to side in a periodic fashion: This was tried around the laboratory. Using the leg muscles, the upper body was thrust to left and right against restraints (a door and adjacent wall). After 20 cycles, at about 2 sec/cycle, the door was opened, S stepped away from the wall and shut his eyes. With feet together, S continued, involuntarily, to rock gently from side to side. This would seem to be a periodic AE of effort, for very little movement was involved in the treatment, far less than exhibited in the AE. This firmly points to the idea that the AEs so far observed are likely to be more general in nature.

Method.   Twenty volunteer Ss were used. The S had to lie prone on a padded table that had been cut away around the left shoulder. His left arm hung vertically, and could be abducted and adducted through the transverse plane over plus or minus 15° to end stops at wrist height against which he could press hard. His right hand gripped a convenient handhold that helped to stop the body being rolled about. The arm swung in front of an angular scale, point of origin the shoulder. All movements were videotaped. Movements of better than 0.25° could be detected.

Procedure.   The experiment was in two parts. The control procedure required the blindfolded S to swing his left arm back and forth through 30°, for 20 cycles, keeping the arm resting *gently* against each end-stop for 2 sec. The arm moved according to tape-recorded commands. When this control procedure had ended, S let his arm hang and avoided voluntary movements. Any arm movements were recorded.

The treatment was carried out after the control. This order was adopted, for were there to be any carryover effects, more bias would be likely to accrue with the order experimental/control rather than the reverse. The treatment consisted of the same sequence of events as the control, with one exception. During the 2-sec pauses at the end of each swing, S pressed *strongly* against the restraint. How hard to press had previously been practiced. He was aiming to match an exerted

TABLE 27.1
Basic Measures of the Programmed AE (20 Subjects)

		Control	Experimental
Amplitude of first oscillation (degrees)			
	$\bar{X}$	1.83	8.60
	s	3.62	7.40
Number of cycles in 371 sec			
	$\bar{X}$	1.51	11.17[a]
	s	4.17	15.39[a]
Duration of AE (sec)			
	$\bar{X}$	21	142
	s	38	107
Percentage of Ss showing oscillatory AE		25	85

[a] One outlier not included in these figures. Number of cycles was 193.

TABLE 27.2
Number of Subjects Who Showed Each Type of
Oscillatory Pattern (20 Subjects)

	Control	Experimental
Oscillation	5	17
No oscillation	15	3
Subsultive movements[a]	12	15

[a] These seem to be random and occur in both oscillation and no-oscillation groups.

pressure equivalent to a static load of 4.5 kg. No measurements relating to amount of effort were taken during the treatment.

Results. We wish to determine whether motor AEs occur and, if so, whether they occur as a result of periodic *movement* (with a very low level of end-point effort). This is to be compared with any AEs resulting from *identical movements with high levels of end-point effort*. Subjects performed as indicated in Table 27.1, with all oscillations in the plane of previous movement. Table 27.2 shows the pattern of oscillation observed. The left panel of Fig. 27.3 shows the results in both conditions for S 16. These data are typical, although periods, amplitudes, and duration of AE vary enormously across Ss. Thus, the post-control session (movement only) exhibits little or no AE, whereas the post-treatment (movement plus effort) shows damped oscillation, asymmetrical about the zero (straight down) position.

The implication of these results is that the AE does not arise from a program concerned only with a previous pattern of movement, although the AEs are themselves sequences of movements. However, during the treatment, the brain may set up *effort programs*. Effort is a force concept, hence effort has magnitude

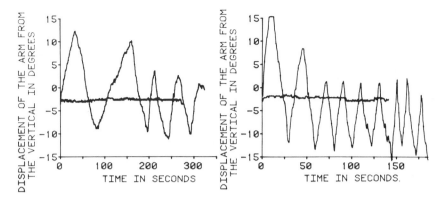

FIG. 27.3. Programmed AE for the left arm. Left Panel: After 20 cycles swinging through 30° and exerting effort for 2 sec in the direction of previous swing at the end of each movement. Center trace shows arm position subsequent to similar treatment with no effort. The full AE continues for 342 sec (S 16). Right Panel: After 20 cycles of periodic back and forth effort with no movement allowed (2 sec in each direction). Center trace shows arm position subsequent to control condition (no effort). AE continues for 495 sec (S 2). Zeros on Y-axes are set by plumbline.

and direction; effort programs may thus underlie the AE, and movement as such may not be relevant.

AEs Following Periodic Effort

Method.   The previous reasoning led to the following experiment, similar in essence to the first. Ten Ss were used. Here the control period was 40 sec during which the arm hung down; this was followed by the treatment of 20 cycles in which the arm hung in the same position, and S strained back and forth for 2 sec in each direction. The arm was firmly clamped and not allowed to move in either condition. At the end of each condition, the clamps were immediately removed, and the AE recorded.

Results.   These were unequivocal. After the experimental treatment, all Ss showed oscillation of the arm, in the plane of the previous strain (Fig. 27.3, right panel; S 2 is typical). Table 27.3 shows the pattern of oscillation observed in this condition. There was no AE following the control.

RELATED OBSERVATIONS

It is clear that periodic motor AEs exist, both in the oculomotor system and in the motor system controlling the upper limbs. These results indicate that a sufficient condition for the occurrence of these AEs is prior, periodically occurring effort.

TABLE 27.3
Basic Measures of the Programmed AE When Subjects Strained
without Movement (10 Subjects)

		Control	Experimental
Amplitude of first oscillation (degrees)			
	$\overline{X}$	0	7.90
	$\tilde{s}$	0	9.54
Number of cycles in 242 sec			
	$\overline{X}$	0	13.69[a]
	$\tilde{s}$	0	16.09
Duration of AE (seconds)			
	$\overline{X}$	0	179
	$\tilde{s}$	0	128
Percentage of S's showing oscillatory AE		0	100

[a] One outlier not included in these figures. Number of cycles was 198.

It follows that movement as such is neither a necessary nor a sufficient condition for the assembly of these AEs. The demonstration of body sway after rhythmic leaning suggests that the AE is an even more general effect. Other simple demonstrations and observations confirm this. I asked an international race walker (who is also a psychologist) to observe any motor AEs immediately on stopping a training walk. Specifically, he was asked to look straight forward while standing still on one extended leg, while the other (the right) merely hung from the hip. "I sensed nothing," he said, "until I started to topple forward. I found that the right leg had lifted and moved forward, which caused me to overbalance. Furthermore, after I put the right leg on the ground, the left proceeded to execute the same involuntary maneuver."

Other predictable and easily demonstrated programmed AEs should be mentioned. Two-dimensional circling (Lissajous) AEs can be produced in an arm by straining in orthogonal directions for 20 cycles. Thus, with the arm hanging to the side, S grasps an immovable object and periodically strains forward, backward, right and left, without moving the wrist. The AE shows up by letting the arm hang free, close to the treatment position.

The tongue will give a circular AE if, in the same way, it is pressed to left, right, up, and down, on convenient parts of the mouth (I used .5 sec in each position). The AE is best observed if the mouth is opened into an O and tip of the tongue protruded no further than the plane of the teeth. For the simple left–right condition the cycle time of my tongue was 25 sec during the AE. Clearly the AEs do not have temporal characteristics that are directly related to those of the treatment. If the experimental condition were prolonged, would the frequency of AE and treatment eventually match? The movements seemed to for the race walker, but the frequency did not. An interesting question arises from this. Is it momentum that carries the runner well past the tape, or is it comfortable or convenient to let the motor AE run down after such maximal efforts?

DISCUSSION

The main findings are that simple periodic movements, or more specifically, periodic efforts, can lead to slow, involuntary, periodic motor AEs in the eyes or limbs. The period of the AE is complexly related to the period of treatment for a given S, and the pattern of the AE is predictable and restricted to the dimensions used in the treatment.

The bi-directional treatment and its AE raises an important question. It might be expected that if the former were left, right, up, down, left, and so on, then so should be the latter; yet this is not so for the eyes (Fig. 27.1, right panel, and Fig. 27.2), nor was it so in the examples for the arm or tongue. The AE takes the form of a distorted Lissajous figure. This clearly demonstrates that two orthogonal channels are releasing oscillatory AEs simultaneously at the end of the treatment. Here we observe sequential input, followed by simultaneous release of AEs in a pattern that preserves the characteristics of each individual channel. This strongly suggests that the two orthogonal channels are independently controlled. This conclusion lends credence to the view that a study of AEs can lead to insights into the organization of the underlying mechanisms.

I have called these positive, motor AEs programmed AEs on logical grounds. In terms of behavior, a program is the coded set of instructions that plans a sequence of actions. Here, the AEs are bi-directional or multi-directional movements, and are clearly controlled (as opposed to freely swinging, or reflecting decaying offsets). An instruction set, at some level, must be involved.

I would like to suggest that a limiting case of a programmed AE is the after-contraction phenomenon (Sapirstein, Herman, & Wallace, 1937). Here the treatment is unidirectional, and the AE is normally reported to be a movement in the direction of previous strain. However, closer observation of the after-contraction phenomenon reveals that *it too is oscillatory* (the agonist contracts, relaxes, contracts again, . . .).

Also supporting the idea that after-contraction is part of the class of programmed AEs is the finding of Hick (1953), who showed that, when attempting to produce previously learned forces, an after-contraction is not superimposed on antagonist contractions. This indicates that the mechanism controlling the AE in one direction is *independent* of that controlling the other. This is consistent with the view that at some level the process of the programmed AE reported here is organized by two or more independent controlling mechanisms. If there is independence, then the lack of phase locking, which so often occurs in the bi-directional case, is to be expected, for the different channels may be differentially affected or be organized slightly differently. For the eyes, the overall results are consonant with the view of Bahill and Stark (1975), who report that the horizontal and vertical eye-movement channels can show independence.

In support of the results in general, there is one report in the oculomotor literature that appears to be an unnoticed programmed AE. Heywood and Churcher (1971) reported experiments on eye movements and the afterimage.

They appear to have required their subjects to track in the dark an imaginary pendulum for about 30 sec. This was carried out, producing periodic, saccadic eye movements of amplitude between 20 and 60°. Soon after this was completed, S was given an afterimage and was told to "track it if it moves." Their Ss showed relatively smooth oscillations of the eyes similar to Fig. 27.3. Here we have an independent observation of what I call a programmed AE. It has the same properties, insofar as the eye movements of the AE are smooth, whereas those of the treatment are saccadic.

For the eyes, the characteristic difference in type of movement of treatment and AE deserves some mention. Although the control systems for saccadic and smooth movement are known to be separate (Rashbass, 1960), the previous finding provides no embarassment, for I argue that it is not *movement* but *effort* that is important in the genesis of programmed AEs. So it seems not unreasonable to assume that the coding and programming takes place at a location different from that of the movement controllers.

Mention should be made of results that show some similarity to programmed AEs. Rosenbaum's (1977) data lends general support to mine in sharing the inference about the existence of pattern controllers in motor systems. Collewijn (1979) showed post-oscillatory eye-movement AEs subsequent to vestibulo ocular reflex in rabbit. Cohen, Matsuo, & Raphan (1977) have reported optokinetic afternystagmus. The overlap between these effects and programmed AEs remains to be investigated.

There seems no clear relationship between programmed AEs and the oscillation of the eyes reported by Craske and Templeton (1968) or those of Ten Doesschate (1954). However, it must be evident that oscillation of the eye seems to occur with some readiness. In general, it is possible for any of the treatment conditions described to drive a potentially oscillatory system, whether eye or limb: forced oscillation of a self-oscillator.

In conclusion, these data suggest that, for mobile parts of the body, periodic effort is stored as an effort program. This may subsequently be observed as a programmed AE. These simple oscillatory motor behaviors may reflect fundamental building blocks of motor movement and control. Analysis of the relationship between the characteristics of imposed periodic effort and programmed AEs may provide a fruitful approach to understanding the rules by which the brain assembles motor programs.

ACKNOWLEDGMENTS

This research was supported by the Natural Sciences & Engineering Research Council Canada Grant A0268. I am indebted to Daksha Acharaya, Janet Craske, and Joan Lawrence for their help with this work.

REFERENCES

Bahill, A. T., & Stark, L. Neurological control of horizontal and vertical components of oblique saccadic eye movements. *Mathematical Biosciences,* 1975, *27,* 287-298.

Cohen, B., Matsuo, V., & Raphan, T. Quantitative analysis of the velocity characteristics of optokinetic nystagmus and optokinetic after nystagmus. *Journal of Physiology,* 1977, *270,* 321-344.

Collewijn, H. The modifiability of the adult vestibulo-ocular reflex. *Trends in Neurosciences,* 1979, *2,* 98-102.

Craske, B., Crawshaw, M., & Heron, P. A. Disturbance of the oculomotor system due to lateral fixation. *Quarterly Journal of Experimental Psychology,* 1975, *27,* 459-465.

Craske, B., & Templeton, W. B. Prolonged oscillation of the eyes induced by conflicting position input. *Journal of Experimental Psychology,* 1968, *76,* 287-393.

Evarts, E. V. Representation of movements and muscles by pyramidal tract neurons of the precentral motor cortex. In M. D. Yahr & D. P. Purpura (Eds.), *Neurophysiological basis of normal and abnormal motor activities.* New York: Raven Press, 1967.

Gelfand, I. M., Gurfinkel, V. S., & Tsetlin, M. L. Problems in the analysis of movements: In I. M. Gelfand, V. S. Gurfinkel, S. V. Fomin, & M. L. Tsetlin (Eds.), *Models of the structural functional organization of certain biological systems.* Cambridge, Mass.: MIT Press, 1971.

Heywood, J., & Churcher, J. Eye movements and the after-image—I. Tracing the afterimage. *Vision Research,* 1971, *11,* 1163-1168.

Hick, W. E. Some features of the after contraction phenomenon. *Quarterly Journal of Experimental Psychology,* 1953, *5,* 166-170.

Keele, S. W. Movement control in skilled motor performance. *Psychological Bulletin,* 1968, *70,* 387-403.

Kots, Ya. M., Krinskiy, V. I., Naydin, V. L., & Shik, M. T. The control of movements of the joints and kinesthetic afferentation. In I. M. Gelfand, V. S. Gurfinkel, S. V. Fomin & M. L. Tsetlin (Eds.), *Models of the structural functional organization of certain biological systems.* Cambridge, Mass.: MIT Press, 1971.

Lackner, J. R., & Graybiel, A. Visual and postural aftereffects following parabolic flight. *Aviation, Space and Environmental Medicine,* 1980, *51,* 230-233.

Mack, A., & Bachant, J. Perceived movement of the afterimage during eye movements. *Perception & Psychophysics,* 1969, *6,* 379-384.

Miller, G. A., Galanter, E. G., & Pribram, K. H. *Plans and the structure of behavior.* New York: Holt, 1960.

Nashner, T. M. Fixed patterns of rapid postural responses among leg muscles during stance. *Experimental Brain Research,* 1977, *30,* 13-24.

Poulton, E. C. On prediction in skilled movements. *Psychological Bulletin,* 1957, *54,* 467-479.

Pribram, K. H. *Languages of the brain: Experimental paradoxes and principles in neuropsychology.* Englewood Cliffs, N.J.: Prentice-Hall, 1971.

Rashbass, C. New method for recording eye movements. *Journal of the Optical Society of America,* 1960, *50,* 642-644.

Rosenbaum, D. A. Selective adaptation of 'command neurons' in the human motor system. *Neuropsychologia,* 1977, *15,* 81-91.

Sapirstein, M. R., Herman, R. C., & Wallace, G. B. A study of aftercontraction. *American Journal of Physiology,* 1937, *119,* 549-556.

Stelmach, G. E. (Ed.). *Motor control: Issues and trends.* New York: Academic Press, 1976.

Ten Doesschate, J. A new form of physiological nystagmus. *Opthalmologica,* 1954, *127,* 66-73.

Turvey, M. T. Preliminaries to a theory of action with reference to vision. In R. Shaw & J. Bransford (Eds.), *Perceiving, acting and knowing.* Hillsdale, N.J.: Lawrence Erlbaum Associates, 1977.

28 Action Sequencing and Lateralized Cerebral Damage: Evidence for Asymmetries in Control

Eric A. Roy
Department of Kinesiology
University of Waterloo
Waterloo, Ontario

Department of Rehabilitative Medicine
University of Toronto
Toronto, Ontario
Canada

ABSTRACT

Patients with left-hemisphere damage (both aphasic and nonaphasic) and patients with right-hemisphere damage attempted to learn an action sequence involving four responses. Fewer of the left-hemisphere patients learned the task and those who did took significantly longer than the right-hemisphere patients. The learning deficit was associated with an increased tendency to make both perseverative and sequencing errors. Qualitative analyses suggested the left-hemisphere patients made more complex and repetitive sequencing errors than did the right-hemisphere patients. The increased propensity to perseverate actions suggested a difficulty in making transitions between actions in the sequence. Support for the idea that the left-hemisphere programs action transitions was provided by additional analysis, involving response time and other motor performance measures. Although the learning deficit in the left-hemisphere patients appeared largely due to response-related processes, there was also some suggestion of a verbal/conceptual component.

INTRODUCTION

Neural and behavioral processes involved in the control of motor responses have been a major recent concern of research in the movement sciences (Stelmach, 1978). Part of this work involves cerebral hemispheric asymmetries in motor control processes, which have been studied using a wide variety of tasks in both normal (Todor & Doane, 1978) and brain-damaged populations (Kimura, 1977; Roy, 1978; Wyke, 1971). The concern of this chapter is with movement disorders associated with lateralized cerebral brain damage, particularly to the left hemisphere.

Much research has shown that left-hemisphere damage is associated with deficits on both manual (Kimura, 1977; Kimura & Archibald, 1974; Roy & Elfeki, 1979; Wyke, 1971) and oral (Mateer, 1978) tasks. However, the nature of the motor control exerted by the left hemisphere is not clear. The left hemisphere may be important in the control of sequential motor acts requiring a number of responses in space over time. Patients with left-hemisphere damage incurred a greater number of sequencing errors in such tasks than did right-hemisphere patients (Kimura & Archibald, 1974; Roy & Elfeki, 1979). However, an alternative view is possible (Kimura, 1977, 1979). In performing a movement task requiring either successive changes in limb posture (Kimura, 1977) or in tongue positions (Mateer, 1978), perseverations rather than sequencing errors were found to be the principal type of error which distinguished left- from right-hemisphere patients. Perseverations involve the repetition of a preceding movement or action and might be interpreted as the result of difficulty in making transitions from one posture or position to another. In essence, this is Kimura's view. The left hemisphere is not important for the control of sequencing per se; rather, it exerts a control over an effector (limb or tongue) in transitions between positions and/or postures.

A number of aspects of Kimura's position remain to be clarified. First, although she found that left- and right-hemisphere patients made about the same *number* of sequencing errors, no consideration was given to the *nature* of these errors. Qualitative analyses of performance have helped delineate disorders in aphasia (Lesser, 1978) and may also be useful in the study of movement sequencing disorders. The nature of sequencing errors may be evaluated in a number of ways: Complexity, repetitive versus nonrepetitive errors, and the pattern of substitutions are ones considered here.

Second, the nature of perseveration requires clarification. Are perseverations evenly distributed across all positions in the sequence? How often are actions perseverated? If, for example, patients do have difficulty in changing from one posture or position to another, they might very seldom progress beyond the posture or action performed initially. Such information was not available from Kimura's analysis but is provided here.

A final point concerns the role of perceptual factors in performance. In Kimura's task, the response modules provided perceptual cues as to what action might be performed on each. What might happen to performance differences between left- and right-hemisphere patients in the absence of such cues when the patient must depend on memory (response) processes? In this experiment, an attempt is made to dissociate perceptual from response (memory) processes in the performance of action sequences. The dissociation between acquisition and retention factors in learning may provide a clearer definition of the learning deficit in left-hemisphere patients.

In sum, there are a number of unresolved questions as to hemispheric differences and the nature of control processes involved in performing action sequences. The experiment reported here is the first in a series that investigates these questions.

Method

Thirty-two hemiparetic patients with lateralized cerebral damage (vascular in origin) served as subjects (see Table 28.1). Lateralization of the lesion was confirmed by conventional brain scan, CTT scan, or EEG. All patients were assessed on a shortened version of the Halstead–Wepman aphasia screening test (Halstead & Wepman, 1959) to assess the presence of speech/language deficits. Those patients who were found to have some degree of deficit (only left-hemisphere patients) were examined on the Boston Aphasia Battery (Goodglass & Kaplan, 1972). Those classified as aphasic were found to have both expressive and receptive deficits, with the expressive deficits more marked.

The left-hemisphere patients were older than the right-hemisphere patients, but the difference was not significant. They also scored lower on the Raven's

TABLE 28.1
Information Regarding Patients

Patient[a] Group	Age (Years)	Number of Each Sex		Raven's[a] Matrices Score	Time since Brain Damage (Months)
		M	F		
Left nonaphasic	57.84	7	5	18.67	10
Left aphasic	60.28	3	5	16.83	11
Right	51.34	4	8	23.67	8

[a] There were no significant differences between groups on any of these variables.

[b] Raven's colored progressive matrices (Raven, 1965).

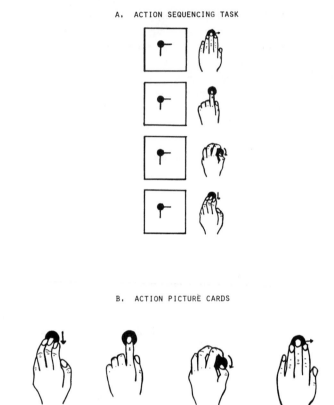

FIG. 28.1.   The apparatus and action–picture cards.

Matrices Test (Raven, 1965), a measure of nonverbal reasoning, but again the difference was not reliable. All patients were self-professed right handers prior to the trauma; during testing they used the nonparetic arm (i.e., the one ipsilateral to the damaged hemisphere).[1]

The apparatus (Fig. 28.1a) consisted of a vertical array of response modules. In each was a knob that the subject moved with his fingers in different action patterns indicated by a series of cards (Fig. 28.1b). For patients using the left

---

[1]One important rival hypothesis to the one proposed (i.e., that differences are associated with the lateralization of the brain lesion) is that the left and right groups differ because of factors due to handedness. Because all patients were right-handed, the left-hemisphere group may have performed differently because they used their left (nonpreferred) hand. Preliminary tests on age-matched control (nonbrain damaged) patients indicates no consistent hand effects either in terms of time or errors.

hand (left hemisphere), the cards were placed to the right of the response modules. They were placed to the left for those using the right hand. There were telegraph keys at either end of the response board. Depression of the key closest to the subject started a timer (beginning of the sequence); the clock was stopped when the key farthest from the subject was depressed (end of the sequence). In this way, the time taken to complete the response was measured.

Patients were first taught what action corresponded to each of the action pictures. This was done in two steps. First, each picture–action combination was shown twice so as to familiarize the patient with them. Then, a series of learning trials was administered in which the pictures were shown successively in a random order; the patient performed the action that was associated with each picture; he was corrected, if an error was made. The learning trials continued until the patient achieved five consecutive correct trials for each picture–action combination.

Following the learning phase, the patient performed the sequencing task. Each trial involved a *perceptual* phase and a *memory* phase. In the perceptual phase, the patient performed the sequence according to the order indicated by the array of action–picture cards. If the patient performed the action sequence correctly, the action cards were immediately removed and the patient performed the sequence from memory (memory phase). Because the emphasis was on learning the action sequence, the same order of action cards was used on each trial (pull, turn, point, slide). The learning criterion for the sequence was the correct performance of 5 consecutive *memory* trials. A maximum of 24 trials was allowed.

Performance was also assessed on a test of limb praxis, a single finger-tapping test, and a test of movement time on the sequencing board. The *limb praxis test* involved performing a series of gestures involving both limb actions (salute, throw a kiss, wave goodbye, hitchhike, make a fist), and facial actions (wrinkle nose, smile, lick upper lip, whistle, frown) and demonstrating how to use common objects without actually holding them (toothbrush, comb, razor/lipstick, hammer, screwdriver). A score of 2 was given if the patient performed correctly on command, 1 if he performed correctly on imitation, and 0 otherwise. A maximum score of 10 was possible on each of the three subtests making a possible 30 overall.

The *finger-tapping test* involved the patient tapping a telegraph key as many times as possible in a 30-sec interval. Each key depression was recorded on an electronic counter. Three trials were given and the average used in the analysis.

The *movement-time test* involved the patient moving his hand from the bottom to the top telegraph key, touching each response module knob on the way with his extended index finger (i.e., the point action). The resulting movement time reflected the time taken to traverse the board as quickly as possible. The time measure was used to help interpret group differences on the response time for action sequencing.

TABLE 28.2
Pattern of Errors in Perceptual and Memory Phases of Trials

		Perceptual Phase			Memory Phase		
	Patient Group	Proportion of Patients	Errors/Trial	Proportion of Total Error	Proportion of Patients	Errors/Trial	Proportion of Total Error
Position	LNA	1.000	.201	48.905	1.000	.558	62.769
	LA	.888[a]	.796	50.252	1.000	.733	35.461
	R	.588	.029	60.417	.667	.458	65.430
Order	LNA	1.000	.162	39.416	1.000	.291	32.731
	LA	.888	.375	23.674	1.000	.337	16.299
	R	.588	.019	39.583	.667	.236	33.711
Perseveration	LNA	.333	.038	9.246	.500	.018	2.020
	LA	.750	.414	26.074	.667	.996	48.229
	R	.000	.000	.000	.250	.008	1.139
Omission	LNA	.333	.010	2.433	.333	.020	2.250
	LA	.125	.000	.000	.333	.001	.001
	R	.000	.000	.000	.333	.008	1.140

[a] Means spanned by brackets were not significantly different using Mann–Whitney U tests ($p < .05$).

Results

Learning was assessed by the number of trials taken to perform 10 consecutive memory trials. Performance was assessed using variables related to response time (correct trials), accuracy (proportion correct trials and total number of errors), and errors. Several types of errors were assessed: *sequencing* errors, which involved position and order errors (relative position); *perseveration* errors, which involved repeating an action (which was correct) at one or more successive positions; and *omission* errors, which occurred when the patient omitted an action at a position in the sequence. The errors were tabulated so that they would be mutually exclusive and they were evaluated in three ways (see Tables 28.2 and 28.3). In addition, qualitative analyses were also performed. For sequencing errors, these involved complexity, repetitiveness, and substitutions.[2] For perseverations, analysis involved the number of perseverations originating from each of the first three positions in the sequence and the number of times an action was repeated.

---

[2]Complexity refers to the number of position/order errors. A simple sequencing error was one in which only one position and one order error occurred. All other combinations were considered complex. A repetitive sequencing error is one in which an action is repeated at a position following the subsequent one. With regard to substitutions, the sequencing task was designed such that three of the actions, slide, pull, and twist, are very similar in terms of the hand postures and the muscle groups

TABLE 28.3
Nature of Sequencing Errors in Perceptual and Memory Phases of Trials

Phase	Patient Group	Complexity		Type		Substitutions	
		Complex	Simple	Repetitive	Nonrepetitive	Related	Unrelated
Perceptual	LNA	0(0)[a]	28(100)	28(100)	0(0)	28(100)	0(0)
	LA	18(82)[b]	4(18)	20(91)	2(9)	34(45)	42(55)
	R	0(0)	4(100)	4(100)	0(0)	4(100)	0(0)
Memory	LNA	24(66)[b]	12(34)	20(56)	16(44)	70(85)	12(15)
	LA	16(73)	6(27)	20(91)	2(9)	36(48)	40(52)
	R	16(40)	24(60)	4(13)	28(87)	28(83)	6(17)

[a] Number in parentheses denotes percentage.
[b] Cells spanned by brackets were not significantly different using χ^2 tests ($p < .05$).

Due to large differences in variance among the groups, nonparametric statistical tests were predominantly used in analyzing these data (Kruskal–Wallis analysis of variance tests, Mann–Whitney U tests, and X^2 tests). In general, only significant results ($p < .05$) are described here. Results of significance tests on group differences are provided in Tables 28.2 and 28.3.

Learning

Using the criterion of 5 consecutive memory trials, the right-hemisphere patients took significantly fewer trials (12.25) to learn the task than did the left aphasics (21.50) or nonaphasics (18.00). Eighty-three percent of the right-hemisphere patients learned the task, whereas only 30% of the left nonaphasics and only 37% of the left aphasics did so. Learning was also measured using a more lax criterion, related to the perceptual trials (i.e., 5 consecutive correct trials in the perceptual phase). The left aphasic patients took significantly more trials (20.75) to learn the task than either the left nonaphasics (12.33) or the right-hemisphere patients (10.25). By the lax criterion, 100% of both the left nonaphasics and the right-hemisphere patients learned the task. Only 37% of the aphasics did so, however.

employed; the fourth, point, is quite dissimilar to the other three in this regard. When patients make an error, they might substitute an action that is similar to the one that should have been performed or one that is unrelated. Some idea of the patient's knowledge of the action categories would seem to be afforded by examining the pattern of substitutions made (Bousfield & Bousfield, 1966; Tulving, 1968). If the patient has (or acquires) a knowledge of the imposed categorization of actions, one would tend to see a larger number of substitutions involving similar than dissimilar actions; that is, their errors are constrained by their knowledge of the actions. If, however, the patients do not understand the actions involved, their errors would tend to be less constrained by this inherent similarity, thus resulting in a random pattern of substitutions.

Performance on Perceptual Phase of Trials

Accuracy. Analysis of the proportion of correct trials revealed that the left aphasics made significantly fewer correct trials (37%) than either the left nonaphasics (80%) or the right-hemisphere patients (82%). Analysis of the other measure of overall performance accuracy, the total errors patients made on incorrect trials, revealed that both the left aphasics (1.58), and left nonaphasics (.411) made significantly more errors per trial than did the right-hemisphere group (.048).

Errors. For sequencing errors (Table 28.2), the proportion of left nonaphasics making errors was significantly greater than that for the right-hemisphere patients. Analysis of the number of sequencing errors per trial revealed that both the left-hemisphere groups made significantly more sequencing errors per trial than the right-hemisphere group.

A close examination of the nature of sequencing errors (see Table 28.3) revealed some interesting differences among the groups. From the standpoint of complexity it is apparent that the left nonaphasics and right-hemisphere patients both make predominantly simple sequencing errors (i.e., errors involving one position and one order error). Left aphasics, on the other hand, make a substantial proportion of complex sequencing errors (i.e., errors involving more than one position/order error). Although all groups tended to make repetitive-type sequencing errors, analyses of the nature of substitutions revealed that the left nonaphasics and right-hemisphere patients tended to substitute actions similar to the action that should have been performed. The pattern of substitutions here was significantly different than chance (50% in each category) in both groups. Left aphasics, on the other hand, made significantly fewer related substitutions. The pattern here was not different from chance.

Perseverations were similarly analyzed. They occurred more frequently in the left-hemisphere patients (see Table 28.2). These patients also made significantly more perseverations per trial, and perseverations contributed significantly more to total error than for the right-hemisphere patients.

Further analysis revealed that perseverations were fairly evenly distributed across positions with 12 at position 1 and 9 at positions 2 and 3. Also the left nonaphasics tended to perseverate an action only once (4 actions repeated once), whereas the aphasics made a substantial number of perseverations in which the action was repeated more than once (14 repeated once; 10 repeated twice; 2 repeated three times). This suggests that the quantitative difference between the groups in the number of perseverations is related to a difference in the nature of perseverations.

Response time. Response time for the left-hemisphere groups (nonaphasics, 11.45 sec; aphasics, 13.49 sec) was longer than that for the right-hemisphere group (9.67 sec). A Kruskal–Wallis analysis of variance revealed that these differences were almost significant, $F(2) = 4.76$, $p < .08$.

Performance on the Memory Phase of Trials

Accuracy. Analysis of the proportion of correct trials revealed differences among the groups that were also almost significant, $F(2) = 4.78$, $p < .08$. Analysis of the total errors made on incorrect trials indicated that the right-hemisphere patients made significantly fewer errors per trial than the other two groups (Table 28.2).

Errors. Although there were no differences among the groups regarding the number of sequencing errors per trial (Table 28.2), further analysis (Table 28.3) showed some interesting patterns that paralleled those observed in the perceptual phase of the trial. The right-hemisphere group made a significantly lower proportion of complex errors than did either of the other groups. The left groups made a significantly higher proportion of repetitive errors than did the right group. Finally, analysis of substitutions revealed that the left aphasics made a significantly lower proportion of related substitutions than the other groups. The pattern of substitutions in this group was not significantly different from chance, although that in the other two groups was.

Examination of the pattern of substitutions made in the unrelated category showed an unexpected result in that the left-hemisphere patients (left aphasics, 25%; left nonaphasics, 10%) made a much higher proportion of substitutions involving the point/pull actions than did the right-hemisphere patients (3%). These substitutions are important in that they suggest patients may have employed verbal mediation (see following Discussion section).

Analysis of perseverations showed the left aphasics to have made significantly more perseverations per trial than the other groups. Also, perseverations accounted for significantly more of the total error for the left aphasics than for the other two groups. Further analysis of perseverations showed them to be distributed fairly evenly across the first three positions, with six at position 1 and nine at positions 2 and 3. The pattern of those actions that were repeated indicated that both the right-hemisphere patients (two actions repeated once) and the left nonaphasics (eight actions repeated once) tended to perseverate actions only once. The left aphasics, on the other hand, made a substantial number of higher-order perseverations, in which actions were repeated more than once (eight repeated once, five repeated twice, and one repeated three times). These observations parallel those from the perceptual phase.

Response Time. The left-hemisphere patients demonstrated longer response times (aphasics, 12.92 sec; nonaphasics, 14.26 sec) than did the right-hemisphere group (10.17 sec). These differences were almost significant, $F(2) = 4.68$, $p < .07$.

Performance on Related Tasks

On the apraxia test the left aphasics achieved a significantly lower score (14.38) than did either the left nonaphasics (29.00) or the right-hemisphere patients (28.18). Finally, performance on the movement-time test demonstrated that the left aphasics (5.24 sec) moved more slowly than the left nonaphasics (5.01 sec) or the right-hemisphere patients (5.14 sec). On the finger-tapping test, the left aphasics tended to make less taps (22.13) than did the other groups (nonaphasics, 29.00; right hemisphere, 28.42). The differences on these latter two tests were not significant.

DISCUSSION

In general, these findings corroborate and extend those reported by Kimura (1977). First, the left-hemisphere patients here have more difficulty learning the action sequence. The data suggest, however, that there may be differences between the left-hemisphere groups in the nature of the learning deficit. The nonaphasics were unable to learn the sequence, because they could not remember the requisite sequence of responses. The deficit in the aphasics, on the other hand, seems associated more with a disorder in acquisition. These patients seem no better able to generate the required number of correct action sequences in the perceptual phase than in the memory phase.[3]

Second, perseverations were more frequent in the left-hemisphere groups in accord with Kimura (1977). In addition, however, it appears that these perseverations did not begin only from the first position in the sequence. Rather, they seem to be fairly evenly distributed across positions. Apparently, then, although these patients do have difficulty in changing from one position or posture to another, they do seem able to effect such changes, as perseverations sometimes do not occur until the third position in the sequence. Further, perseverations seem to be qualitatively different in the aphasic group. In both the nonaphasic and the right-damaged groups, patients repeated an action only once. The aphasics, however, tended to repeat actions more than once (i.e., they made many more higher-order perseverations).[4]

---

[3]The left-hemisphere patients' poor performance could have been due to their forgetting the action picture contingencies. All but one of the patients in each of the left nonaphasic and right-hemisphere groups who participated in the experiment were retested (3 months after original testing) at learning these contingencies using the procedure outlined previously (p. ■■■). After learning to criterion the patients were allowed to engage in their normal activities for a period equivalent to the longest time (25 min) involved in learning the action sequence during the experiment. Following this delay the patients were tested on their memory for these action–picture associations. Three trials were given for each. All the patients achieved greater than 87% accuracy. These findings suggest that the errors encountered by the left-hemisphere patients in learning the sequence of actions were probably not due to differential memory loss for the individual action–picture contingencies.

[4]Evidence that perseverations may involve response-related processes comes from comparing performance in this action task to that in a comparable task. In this task the same sequence of action picture cards was used. In this case, however, the patients had to match the sequence of picture cards with a sequence of action–word cards rather than with a sequence of actions as done in the task described in this experiment. There were four piles of action–word cards, each displaying the action

The notion that left-hemisphere damage is associated with a difficulty in making postural changes seemed exemplified in performance on correct trials (as measured by response time). The response-time difference between the left- and right-hemisphere groups in the sequencing task appears to be due to transitions between actions or postures, given no group differences on the control movement-time task, in which an action (pointing) was repeated. It would seem that the left-hemisphere patients take longer to make these transitions than do the right-hemisphere patients. Such an interpretation is consistent with the analysis of errors, which indicated an increased difficulty for the left-hemisphere patients to make transitions between actions in a sequence. It would make sense that these patients should also take longer to make transitions between actions on correct trials. More careful analyses, using measures reflecting both response organization (e.g., reaction time) and execution processes would reveal the extent to which these response times actually do reflect interresponse transition times (Sternberg, Monsell, Knoll & Wright, 1978).

Finally, there is strong support for the notion that the effect of left-hemisphere damage is most marked if a *number of different* responses are made (i.e., the action sequencing task). Finger tapping, which requires the repetition of the same response, did not discriminate between the groups. Likewise, on the apraxia test, the majority of left-hemisphere patients (18 out of 20) were able to perform the single gesture or action appropriately under conditions (i.e., imitation) comparable to those employed in the action sequencing task.

Although these data generally corroborate those of Kimura (1977), there is one important difference. It appears that the left- and right-hemisphere groups here do differ with regard to sequencing errors. First, the left-hemisphere patients tended to make complex sequencing errors, whereas the right-hemisphere patients made simple errors. Thus, the left-hemisphere patients appear to have a qualitatively more pronounced deficit in the sequential organization of action. Second, the left-hemisphere patients tended to make more repetitive-type sequencing errors. This may relate to the increased propensity for these left-hemisphere patients to perseverate. Both types of errors may reflect the difficulty in making postural/action transitions.

Finally, another view of the nature of sequencing errors is afforded by examining the pattern of substitutions. Comparisons of related versus unrelated substitutions indicated that those made by the nonaphasics and the right-hemisphere

---

word (e.g., pull). Because each pile had four cards in it, it might be possible for the patient to select from one pile (action word) more than once. In this action–word task, although all the patients made sequencing errors, no perseverations were made, not even by the aphasics. This suggests that the perseverations observed in the action sequencing task are probably not due to higher cognitive or verbal processes. Had there been some such component, one might have expected perseveration of the action words in the task just described; that is, if the patients perseverated because of the persistance of the *idea* of an action, then one would probably have seen perseverations in the action–word task where this ideational aspect predominates.

patients were constrained by the inherent similarity of the actions involved; most were in the related category. Those made by the aphasics, however, were not so constrained. This suggests that the nonaphasics and the right-hemisphere patients have a knowledge of the actions required. The aphasics, on the other hand, do not seem to have as clear an understanding of the categories of action involved (see Footnote 2, p. 492). Poorer knowledge might have led to increased difficulty in learning the event–event and/or event–position contingencies, which define the sequence. More work is necessary, however, before any meaningful interpretation can be made of the relationship between knowledge of the actions involved in a sequence and performance of that action sequence.

The other interesting observation, with regard to substitutions, was that the left–hemisphere patients confused the actions "point" and "pull" more frequently than did those with right-hemisphere damage. The actions were not similar in terms of the initial postures or the movements involved. They were, however, similar from a linguistic standpoint, having the same initial phoneme. The substitutions, then, may have occurred because of the similarity between the verbal labels describing the actions. This suggests some form of verbal mediation process may have been involved in performing the task. Anecdotal evidence supports the role of verbal mediation in that, for all the right-hemisphere patients and several of the left nonaphasics, spontaneous verbalizations involving the words describing the actions accompanied their actions. Some of the difficulty these left-hemisphere patients had in learning this task, then, may have resulted from a deficit in mediating action through language (Luria, 1966). There is considerable evidence to support the importance of verbal mediation in the early stages of learning a novel motor task such as the one used in this experiment (Adams, 1971). Patients with damage in and/or adjacent to neural centers subserving language might have difficulty in using verbal mediation.

Contrary to Kimura's (1977) findings, then, these data suggest that it is possible to discriminate between the left- and right-hemisphere groups in terms of sequencing errors. When an analysis of the *nature* rather than the *number* of errors is made, discrimination between the groups is possible, both in terms of the severity (i.e., complexity) and the character (i.e., repetitions and substitutions) of the sequencing disorder.

Much is still to be discovered about the nature of control exerted by the left hemisphere. What is the mechanism underlying the left-hemisphere patient's tendency to perseverate? (See Kimura, 1977, for one explanation.) Can control be understood in terms of current theories of serial order in behavior (Shaffer, 1976; Summers, 1975)? Although left-hemisphere damage is associated with a difficulty in changing postures in a movement sequence, understanding the categories of actions involved and regulating the action sequence through language may also be affected. Much careful consideration should be given to these apparently conceptual/cognitive disorders. In addition, more detailed analyses must be carried out on the production of action sequences. Although emphasis in this experiment was placed on the identity and order of elements (action) in a sequence of actions, temporal factors should also be evaluated because the relative timing (phasing) of movements in a sequence have been shown to be important in the representation and the programming of action sequences (Glencross, 1980). Finally, patients with lateralized damage but without hemiparesis should be examined on this action sequencing task to determine the extent of bilateral impairment.

ACKNOWLEDGMENTS

Funding for this research was provided by grants from the Medical Research Council, from the National Science and Engineering Research Council, and from the University of Waterloo Research Subcommittee. I would like to express my appreciation to the Medical Advisory Boards of the Kitchener–Waterloo Hospital and the Queen Elizabeth Hospital for permission to examine patients. Also, thanks to Miss Rosemary Roderick for her help in testing patients and in doing preliminary analyses of the data. Her diligence and insightfulness were invaluable in this project.

REFERENCES

Adams, J. A. A closed-loop theory of motor learning. *Journal of Motor Behavior,* 1971, *3,* 111–149.

Bousfield, A. K., & Bousfield, W. A. Measurement of clustering and of sequential dependencies in related free recall. *Psychological Reports,* 1966, *19,* 935–942.

Glencross, D. J. Response planning and the organization of speed movements. In R. Nickerson (Ed.), *Attention and performance VIII.* Hillsdale, N.J.: Lawrence Erlbaum Associates, 1980.

Goodglass, H., & Kaplan, E. *Assessment of aphasia and related disorders.* Philadelphia: Lea and Febiger, 1972.

Halstead, W. C., & Wepman, J. M. The Halstead-Wepman aphasia screening test. *Journal of Speech and Hearing Disorders,* 1959, *14,* 9–15.

Kimura, D. Acquisition of a motor skill after left hemisphere damage. *Brain,* 1977, *100,* 527–542.

Kimura, D. Neuromotor mechanisms in the evolution of human communication. In H. D. Steklis & J. J. Raleigh (Eds.), *Neurobiology of social communication in primates.* New York: Academic Press, 1979.

Kimura, D., & Archibald, Y. Motor functions of the left hemisphere. *Brain,* 1974, *97,* 337–350.

Lesser, R. *Linguistic investigations of aphasia.* London: Arnold Pub., 1978.

Luria, A. R. *Higher cortical functions in man.* New York: Basic Books, 1966.

Mateer, C. Impairments of nonverbal oral movements after left hemisphere damage: A follow-up analysis of errors. *Brain and Language,* 1978, *6,* 334–341.

Raven, J. C. *The coloured progressive matrices.* London: Lewis, 1965.

Roy, E. A. Apraxia: A new look at an old syndrome. *Journal of Human Movement Studies,* 1978, *4,* 191–210.

Roy, E. A., & Elfeki, G. Hemispheric asymmetries in a finger sequencing task. In G. D. Roberts & K. Newell (Eds.), *Psychology of motor behavior and sport—1978.* Champaign-Urbana, Ill.: Human Kinetics Pub., 1979.

Shaffer, L. H. Intention and performance. *Psychological Review,* 1976, *83,* 375–393.

Stelmach, G. (Ed.). *Information processing in motor control and learning.* New York: Academic Press, 1978.

Sternberg, S., Monsell, S., Knoll, R. L., & Wright, C. E. The timing of rapid movement sequences. In G. E. Stelmach (Ed.), *Information processing in motor control and learning.* New York: Academic Press, 1978.

Summers, J. The role of timing in motor program representation. *Journal of Motor Behavior,* 1975, *7,* 229–249.

Todor, J., & Doane, T. Handedness and hemispheric asymmetry in the control of movement. *Journal of Motor Behavior,* 1978, *10,* 295–300.

Tulving, E. Theoretical issues in free recall. In T. R. Dixon & D. L. Horton (Eds.), *Verbal behavior and general behavior theory.* Englewood Cliffs, N.J.: Prentice-Hall, 1968.

Wyke, M. The effects of brain lesions on the learning of a bimanual coordination task. *Cortex,* 1971, *7,* 59–72.

VIII

PRODUCTION OF SPEECH

29

The Production of Speech: Development and Dissolution of Motoric and Premotoric Processes

Peter F. MacNeilage, Judith A. Hutchinson, and Sarah A. Lasater
University of Texas at Austin
Austin, Texas
U.S.A.

ABSTRACT

We present the hypothesis that consonantal production preferences in prelinguistic babbling and the relative frequencies of consonants in adult languages reflect difficulty at a terminal motoric stage of speech production. On the other hand, the lack of preferences in consonantal substitution errors of normal adults suggests a premotoric locus for the errors. When viewed in the context of other symptoms, the consonant production preferences we observed in aphasic speech errors, including consonantal substitutions, may have two sources: a motoric source most prominent in anterior aphasics and a source related to premotoric lexical confusions, most prominent in posterior aphasics.

INTRODUCTION

The original purpose of this chapter was to provide a comprehensive view of the topic of speech production. But as work proceeded toward that end, it became focused on the general but not global topic indicated in the title. Readers wishing for a more comprehensive review are referred to recent review papers by one of us (MacNeilage, 1980a, 1980b); other reviews by Kent (1976), Perkell (1980), and Fowler, Rubin, Remez, and Turvey (1980); and symposia 1, 2, 3, 5, 6, and 7 in Volume II of the *Proceedings of the 9th International Congress of Phonetic Sciences* (see reference to Ohala, 1979b). The present chapter, however, draws on a number of the issues raised in these reviews and treats in detail some of them.

The standard view of speech production is that there are two relatively independent terminal stages in the process (Kent, 1976). There is a *premotoric* stage of selection and sequencing of speech segments (i.e., consonants and vowels) and a final stage of direct *motoric* control. The most compelling evidence for the existence of the premotoric stage is the presence of speech errors in which two segments, sometimes several words away from each other, are permuted in an otherwise correct sequence (MacKay, 1970). This suggests that some mechanism, which may go wrong, must be responsible for sequencing segments. The independence of this stage from the motoric control stage is indicated by the fact that the segments are correctly produced in their new context, even though the new context typically demands different articulator movements from those demanded by the correct context. This is taken to mean that the movements for production of segments are planned *after* the order of segments has been assigned (MacNeilage, 1980a).

This two-stage view has been most explored for normal adult speech production. In this chapter we explore the extent to which this view can be extended to the domains of infant speech and aphasic speech. The chapter has two main parts. First, we note the presence in prespeech babbling of a very well-defined hierarchy of consonant production preferences, apparently related to production difficulty and obviously associated with the motoric stage of production in that they predate the establishment of the premotoric stage. Second, we consider the extent to which related production preferences are observable in the errors of various types of aphasics, in an attempt to define the role of the motoric stage of production in these disorders.

MOTORIC DEVELOPMENT: CONSONANT PRODUCTION PREFERENCES

The first point at which infants begin to produce truly speech-like sounds is at the onset of the so-called babbling stage. This occurs at about 7 months of age, several months before the infant utters the first meaningful word of his subsequent adult repertoire. Babbling is a term that denotes a child's tendency to alternate between a relatively open (vowel-like) and relatively closed (consonant-like) state of the vocal tract, with rather strict speech-like timing of the sequence of gestures. Here, and in subsequent discussion, we concentrate on consonant production.

Locke (1980) summarizes three studies of babbling of infants in English-speaking environments (Fisichelli, 1950; Irwin, 1947; Pierce & Hanna, 1974). All the studies were based on broad phonetic transcription of the infant vocalizations. This is a rather rough means of characterizing vocalization, with a number

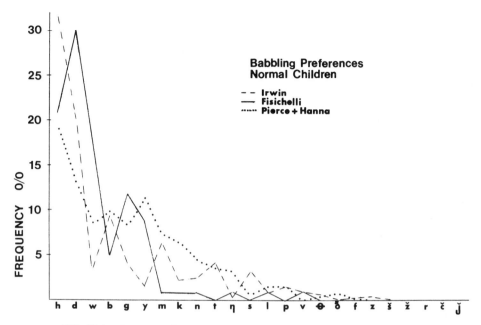

FIG. 29.1.   Summary of the percentages of various consonants produced in babbling.

of methodological problems (Johnson & Bush, 1971; Oller & Eilers, 1975). Despite such problems, there is a good deal of agreement among the three studies. This can be seen from Fig. 29.1. There is a definite hierarchy of prefer- ence. Stop consonants, nasals, and glides are favored over fricatives, affricates, and liquids. (An example of a stop consonant in English is *b*; a nasal, *m*; a glide, *w*; a fricative, *f*; an affricate, *ch*; a liquid, *r*.) This hierarchy appears to result from the relative difficulty of production of different consonants.

An indication that these preferences are indeed determined by *production* constraints and not strongly influenced by perceptual experience within the lan- guage community comes from a number of studies of babbling in deaf infants. Figure 29.2, again adapted from Locke, compares an average from five studies of groups of deaf children ranging from 5 months to 5 years of age, with the average of three normal babbling studies shown earlier. The patterns for these five groups are analogous to the patterns we have seen earlier, in that the most preferred consonants cluster on the left-hand side of the graph (Locke, 1980, discusses the interesting tendency for deaf subjects to prefer especially the bila- bials *b* and *m*).

A further indication that these preferences are not perceptually based comes from studies of babbling in other language communities that have different adult consonant inventories. Locke has made a summary of four babbling studies in the

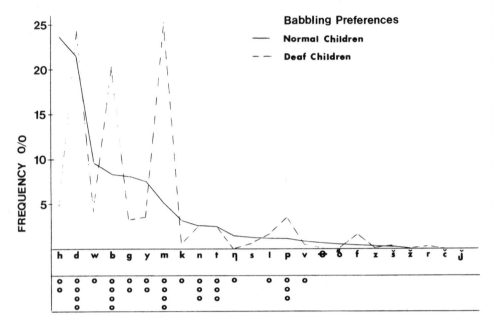

FIG. 29.2. A comparison of average consonantal babbling frequencies of normal children (from Fig. 29.1) and average frequencies from five studies of deaf children. The dots at the bottom indicate the number of times each consonant was noted in four studies of babbling in non-English language environments.

Mayan, Luo, Thai and Japanese language communities. A dot at the bottom of Fig. 29.2 indicates that the consonant occurs in the babbling inventory of one of these languages. The patterns shown here are similar from language to language and similar to that shown by English babblers, in that most of the dots fall on the left side of the figure.

It is obvious that the claim of a hierarchy of production difficulty is based on a circular argument. *Presently* we have no definition of difficulty independent of the observed preferences. However, as we argue in the following, we do believe that it is in principle possible to develop an independent definition.

One of the most significant developments in the study of child language in the last few years is the realization that the sound patterns of the child's first few words strongly reflect the sound patterns of babbling (Cruttenden, 1970; Menyuk, 1968; Oller, Wieman, Doyle, & Ross, 1976). This is true both in terms of phonotactic (sound sequence) patterns and in choice of inventory of sounds. The main phonotactic pattern, as in babbling, is the consonant–vowel sequence, often reduplicated. Final consonants are rare, as are consonant clusters. Consonant inventories tend to include stops, nasals, and glides and to exclude fricatives, affricates, and liquids. In fact, the commonality between early speech sounds and babbling sounds is so great as to encourage Locke to talk of the child's first few words in terms of sound "maintenance" rather than in terms of the more standard term "acquisition" (Locke, 1980).

Linguists have long known that the sounds that are most favored in the child's first words tend also to be most favored in the world's languages. For example, the voiceless unaspirated consonants (e.g., English *b, d* and *g,* which are the most frequently present single subset of consonants in the babbling studies) are widely considered to be the only type of stop consonant present in all languages. In addition, every language shares the child's preference by having at least one nasal consonant in the inventory (Ferguson, 1963). On the other hand, fricatives, not favored by children, are absent in some languages (Wurm, 1971).

Linguists have formalized these tendencies in terms of the concept of "markedness." Sounds termed *unmarked* tend to occur earlier in child speech and more frequently in the world's languages than sounds called *marked.* In fact Jakobson hypothesized a fixed universal order of acquisition of contrasts between sounds in terms of their markedness. In his extremely influential monograph entitled *Child Language, Aphasia and Phonological Universals* (title translated from German), first published in 1941 (Jakobson, 1968), he made the claim that this proposed hierarchical order was a formal property of language. He emphasized strongly that the sounds of the first few words are selected solely on the basis of their linguistic sign function. Thus, at the point where a child begins to develop a set of distinct signs for language purposes, he/she chooses sounds that maximize distinctiveness. In Jakobson's opinion, the choices are made for reasons totally unrelated to facts about the babbling repertoire, such as consonant preferences. In his own words, in contrast to the sign function of early speech sounds, "The question of the prelanguage babbling proves to be, on the contrary, one of external phonetics, predominantly articulatory in nature . . . [p. 27]". However, as we have noted, the early sounds of speech *are* the sounds most favored in babbling, and there is no evidence for a choice of first sounds on a basis other than babbling preferences. Yet Jakobson and others have, by a circular procedure (Ohala, 1979a), elevated the notion of markedness, which is largely defined in terms of speech sound (babbling) preferences, to the status of a *linguistic* concept *explaining* the sound preferences. This circular reasoning has profound implications for modern linguistic theory, in which extensive use has been made of the markedness concept as an abstract underlying *linguistic* property of sound units although the existence of such a property at the linguistic level was never adequately motivated. Considering that the sound *preferences* predate language and cannot be adequately motivated on a linguistic basis, we wish to place them where they belong—in the domain of speech motor control. As we noted earlier, this also involves circularity. We cannot *presently* define difficulty independent of preferences. But we do believe that the hypothesis is in principle testable, whereas a linguistically defined concept of markedness is not.

A start may be made toward testing the difficulty hypothesis by pursuing an aspect of Fitts' law (Fitts, 1954), which claims that slower movements are made toward smaller targets. Thus, in a time-limited situation such as speech, attaining smaller targets may be more difficult. Fricatives require more precise articulator positioning than stops, and articulator movements toward them are slower (Kuehn & Moll, 1976).

Thus, in our view, the motor control possibilities of the infant vocal tract constrain a child's speech sound output, determining the success with which various speech sounds can be produced. Languages *do* tend to include some sounds that are relatively difficult for children to produce, but this may be necessary in order to obtain a sound repertoire large enough to differentiate between members of the enormously large set of words each language possesses.

PREMOTORIC DEVELOPMENT

When a child begins to babble, the entire control structure for his/her acts (beyond his/her motivation to produce them) is probably motoric in nature; that is, it has to do solely with control of actual movements. A reduplicated CV utterance such as "dadada" may involve no more cognitive superstructure than the repeated manual banging that a young child enjoys. But a month or two after beginning to babble, a child enters the "variegated babbling stage" (Oller, 1980), meaning that he/she begins to put more than one type of consonant or vowel in a single continuous utterance (e.g., "yabadi"). The development of a sound choice procedure, independent of the movements themselves, is suggested by these kinds of behaviors. Later, when a child begins to approximate adult words, a cognitive superstructure *must* be placed on the motoric structure. The child must have an internal representation including a semantic representation (broadly defined) and a routine for proceeding from semantic to motoric levels.

A number of writers have suggested that the speech-related aspect of the plan of early words is initially holistic in nature and does not involve separate representation of individual speech segments (Ferguson & Farwell, 1975; Menn, 1978). Perhaps the best evidence for this claim is the existence of what have been called "progressive phonological idioms" (Moskowitz, 1970), words which are pronounced much better than other words which have similar adult models. The most famous example of this is the first word of Hildegard Leopold (Leopold, 1947), the word "pretty." This was pronounced more or less correctly and was much more complex in form than several later words, which called for some of the same sounds. As we noted earlier, consonant clusters (*pr*) and liquids (*r*) are not typically included in early utterances. Further evidence for an initial whole-word stage includes the observation that a child will produce a certain sound in one word but not in another, even though the immediate environment of the sound is the same in both words. For example, he may produce a *d* in "dummy" but say "guck" for "duck," though the environment of the d, namely the following vowel, is the same in both cases. In a related instance, a correct sound may be produced consistently in one word but inconsistently in another word with the same environment. In addition, instances where a child appears to avoid saying a word with which he/she is quite familiar but which contains a sound he/she cannot produce, could be taken as evidence of a holistic representation.

There is some evidence that a child proceeds gradually from this holistic stage to a stage where there is a separate premotor representation of individual sounds. Again the case of phonological idioms is often cited in this regard. There are a number of recorded instances in which phonological idioms are demolished, resulting in an actual deterioration of output forms. For example, Hildegard, after producing "pretty" for a year, began to say "pity," bringing the word into correspondence with her other words, in which r was omitted. A month later, she departed further from her initially correct form, saying "biddy," again in correspondence with rules of word formation she was using elsewhere in her vocabulary (Ingram, 1974).

The question we wish to raise about the development of this premotor stage is: Are consonantal production preferences in any sense *represented* in that stage? To our knowledge, nobody has presented a compelling reason why they should be (although Perkell, 1980, has argued that they should be). If we are correct in assuming such preferences represent purely motoric constraints on the production system, then a premotoric stage of organization would not necessarily be influenced by them. Given our present lack of knowledge of the child's speech production process, we cannot evaluate this question at the moment. But the question *has* been asked for adult speech. Shattuck-Hufnagel and Klatt (1979) have considered the role of consonantal production preferences in two corpora of adult speech errors: the MIT corpus of 1620 consonant substitution errors and the UCLA corpus (Fromkin, 1971) containing 1552 errors (updated by Goldstein, 1977). They considered the question from the point of view of markedness theory. They noted that markedness effects would be revealed by a tendency for more marked consonants to be replaced by more unmarked consonants in substitution errors. (In our terms this would mean replacement of motorically more difficult consonants with motorically less difficult ones). They reasoned that if this was occurring, there would be a systematic imbalance between the row totals of a confusion matrix, indicating frequency of each consonant as a target of a substitution, and the column totals, indicating frequency of each consonant as an intrusion (substituion). A chi-square analysis of the relation between row totals and column totals did show a highly significant value ($p < .001$). But an analysis of individual consonants showed that the significance could be attributed solely to a tendency in two target consonants with alveolar place of articulation to be replaced by consonants with a palatal articulation (/s/ → /š/, /č/; /t/ → /č/). This trend was in the opposite direction to that expected from a markedness hypothesis, as the palatal consonants are considered *more* marked than alveolars. Similar results were found in both the MIT corpus and UCLA corpus. Apparently, markedness (consonantal difficulty) is not a variable in the generation of consonantal errors by normal adult subjects. This result is consistent with our hypothesis that consonantal preferences are entirely motorically based and that the stage(s) of speech production in which segmental errors are generated is a premotor stage.

An alternative interpretation of the previous result is that, for adults, consonants do not differ in difficulty. We cannot rule out this interpretation. Nevertheless we wish to retain, at least for the moment, the hypothesis that consonantal production preferences relate to difficulty because it can serve, in a sense, as a guide in the investigation of aphasic speech. We evaluate the possibility that consonant production preferences are an indicant of motoric involvement in aphasic speech by analyzing aphasic speech errors and considering any preferences we observe in the context of other knowledge of aphasic speech.

APHASIC SPEECH: CONSONANT PRODUCTION PREFERENCES

Before we begin this analysis, let us broaden the conception of consonantal production preferences to some extent. We have noted that these preferences are reflected in the sound patterns of the world's languages in terms of the items in the sound inventories of languages. But it is also likely that the preferences are reflected in the relative frequencies with which the various sounds in the inventory are used. For example, a rank correlation between the mean frequencies of consonants in the three babbling studies reviewed earlier and the frequencies of use of consonants in word-initial position in English (Denes, 1963) gives a value of .76. The traditional interpretation of such a coefficient is that somewhat over 50% of the sources of variance in the two lists are held in common between the two lists. Thus, consonant frequency in the adult language may to some extent serve as an indicant of consonant difficulty. In the following analysis, we have considered the relation between aphasic errors and both babbling frequencies and adult consonant frequencies. The adult consonant frequencies have one advantage that the babbling frequencies lack: They can be used to evaluate word-final consonant errors and overall errors in cases where word-initial and word-final consonant errors were not differentiated. Babbling frequencies are best confined to evaluation of initial consonants, because consonants in babbling are mostly initial consonants; and as a child develops speech, his/her hierarchy of preference for final consonants is quite different from his/her hierarchy for initial consonants. This latter hierarchy has not been documented to the extent that we could use it to evaluate aphasic errors.

There have been a large number of studies of speech production in aphasics using phonetic transcription of consonants. We concentrate here on a reanalysis of the results of three studies that have presented detailed data on a large number of consonants produced by a number of subjects (Burns & Canter, 1977; Johns & Darley, 1970; Trost & Canter, 1974). (In the case of the Burns and Canter and Trost and Canter studies, the most detailed data is available in the doctoral dissertations of Burns, 1975, and Trost, 1970. For a more general view of the literature on aphasic speech production, see Lesser, 1978.) Two major groups of a phasic patients were investigated in these studies: (1) anterior aphasics: patients with damage to the left hemisphere, primarily anterior to the Rolandic fissure, in the frontal lobe (Mohr, 1976); (2) posterior aphasics: patients with damage primarily posterior to the Rolandic fissure in the parietal and/or temporal lobes. The anterior aphasics are most often called *Broca's aphasics*. These patients are nonfluent in the sense that their typical utterance length is abnormally short. They are typically agrammatic (i.e., they have difficulty with inflections and closed-class morphemes). Their speech is effortful, with many segmental errors of substitution or distortion. Nevertheless, they have no muscle weakness or other signs of direct motor damage. Their comprehension is typically much better than their production. Some writers, such as Johns and Darley, consider that anterior cortical damage can give rise to a specific syndrome of speech motor disturbance independent of other symptoms, which they term "apraxia of speech." This is typically described metaphorically as a disorder of "programming" of speech gestures. Both the Johns and Darley and the Trost and Canter studies were concerned particularly with this disorder.

Burns and Canter studied two groups of posterior aphasics: Conduction aphasics and Wernicke's aphasics. Conduction aphasics are described as haltingly fluent. Stretches of normal speech are interspersed with breakdowns in which a word or words cannot be pronounced correctly. The most typical errors are consonantal substitutions often called literal or phonemic paraphasias. Most difficulty is encountered with repetition. Comprehension is typically moderate to good. Damage in these patients usually centers on the supramarginal gyrus region around the posterior termination of the Sylvian fissure (Green & Howes, 1977).

Wernicke's aphasics speak fluently but with paragrammatic (semantically empty) speech. They make frequent phonemic paraphasias but also make verbal (semantic) paraphasias (production of incorrect but related words) and produce neologisms. Their comprehension is severely impaired. Damage typically centers on the superior temporal gyrus (Bogen & Bogen, 1976).

There is good agreement in the literature that some consonants are more difficult than others in anterior aphasics, though difficulty is defined in different ways. A number of studies have noted that more errors tend to occur on affricates and fricatives than on other consonants (Shankweiler & Harris, 1966). In addition Blumstein (1973) and Marquardt, Rinehart, and Peterson (1979) have observed a tendency toward substitution of unmarked for marked consonants in substitution errors. However, it is important to note that these patterns are not consistently observed across repeated attempts of an individual patient to produce a particular word but only show up in large bodies of data. Variability in repeated unsuccessful attempts at consonant production is the rule, so there is seldom any obvious evidence that a subject is *choosing* an easier sound at a premotor level.

There is good consensus that consonant production difficulty is not a factor in posterior aphasics. The relative fluency of their speech and the absence of obvious difficulty with individual consonants contributes to this impression. In addition, although anterior aphasics often produce *distortions,* which are obviously motorically inadequate attempts at a segment, posterior aphasics rarely do. Their errors most often seem to be substitutions, apparently reflecting inadequate choice or sequencing of segments rather than inadequate motoric performance. However, Blumstein (1973) has observed tendencies to substitute unmarked for marked consonants in both Wernicke's and Conduction aphasic subgroups, though the effect did not reach statistical significance in the Conduction aphasics. This is an anomalous result from the point of view of other studies of posterior aphasics, if one believes that markedness effects are motoric difficulty effects. It is also anomalous considering the fact that posterior aphasic substitution errors are superficially quite similar to normal substitution errors of the kind examined by Shattuck-Hufnagel and Klatt but that their study showed no markedness effects. Consequently, one of our main concerns in the following analysis of aphasic errors is to either replicate or disconfirm Blumstein's results for posterior aphasics.

The three studies of aphasic speech that we are about to consider in detail all involved production of monosyllabic words, either read or repeated. The word lists were all phonetically balanced; that is, with minor exceptions, each consonant was presented as a stimulus an equal number of times. Therefore any consonantal frequency effects we observe are not an artifact of the composition of the stimulus material.

Before examining the results of these studies, let us consider the question of how the results might be interpreted in terms of the difficulty hypothesis as we are proposing it. First, regarding the total number of errors made on each consonant, it seems logical to assume that the more errors made, the more difficult the consonant. Thus, if we are correct in assuming that consonants more frequent in babbling and adult inventories are easier, then we would expect a negative correlation between frequency of the consonant in both babbling and adult speech on the one hand and error frequency on the other. Second, consider the main subclass of aphasic errors, the so-called substitution errors. Again, it seems logical to assume that the more frequently a consonant is subject to error in a substitution, or, in other words, is a *target* for a substitution, the more difficult this consonant is to produce. Thus, we would again expect a negative correlation between our consonant frequency indices and target frequencies of consonants. Now, consider the expectation for the consonant that is substituted, that is, the *intrusion* consonant. In this case, it appears logical that the frequency with which

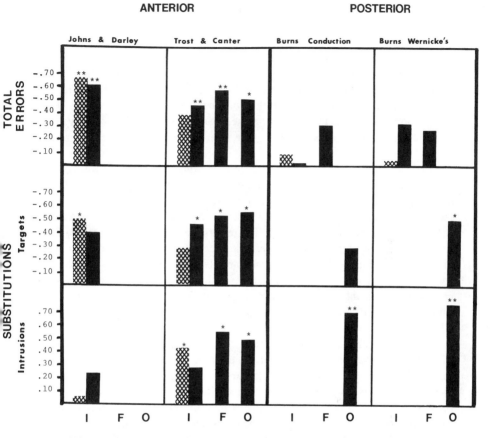

FIG. 29.3. Summary of rank correlation coefficients between aphasic consonant errors and two indices of consonant production preferences. Correlations with babbling frequencies of initial consonants—crosshatched bars; correlations with adult consonant frequencies—solid bars. I = initial consonants, F = final consonants and O = overall consonant frequencies. * indicates $p < .05$; ** indicates $p < .01$.

a consonant intrudes would be *positively* correlated with its normal frequency. Easier consonants would tend to replace more difficult ones. We believe that *all* these results would be obtained if a difficulty factor were operating. In our view, the difficulty factor, being at the terminal stage of speech production, should act as a funneling point for speech production output, and all production should be subject to its influence.

The results of a rank correlation analysis of the relation between consonant errors in the three studies and babbling and adult frequencies are shown in Fig. 29.3. Our analysis is based on a total of 1039 substitution errors: 458 from Trost and Canter (1974), 192 from Johns and Darley (1970), and 389 from Burns and Canter (1977). The results of the correlation analysis are complicated by the fact that separate analyses of initial and final consonants were not available for targets or intrusions in the Conduction and Wernicke's groups. Therefore, only results for overall frequencies (labeled O) were analyzed in these groups. In addition, the Johns and Darley study involved initial consonants only. Babbling frequencies were used to evaluate only initial consonants (labeled I). Results of *these* comparisons are given in the crosshatched bar graphs. Significance levels are indicated by asterisks over the bars. One asterisk means $p < .05$, two mean $p < .01$.

Note first that every single result goes in the direction required for the difficulty hypothesis. Correlations with total errors and with targets are uniformly negative and correlations with intrusions are uniformly positive. No obvious pattern of relations between the correlations with babbling and the correlations with adult frequencies is observable. The results for all four groups are consistent with the difficulty hypothesis. Nevertheless correlations are uniformly low for the posterior aphasics on total error and are also low for intrusions in the Johns and Darley group and low for targets in the Conduction group. No error condition results in significant correlations for all groups. Thus, although the results are supportive of a difficulty hypothesis, they are certainly not strongly supportive in all cases.

These results are consistent with Blumstein's finding of a markedness effect in consonantal substitution patterns for all three of her aphasic groups: Broca's, Conduction, and Wernicke's. As targets are negatively correlated with frequency in the present results and intrusions are positively correlated with frequency, substitutions tend to be in the direction of more frequent (less marked) consonants. Blumstein concluded that such results show that *linguistic* factors play a common role in all types of aphasia. But we have contended that consonantal preferences are *nonlinguistic* because they are prelinguistic in developmental terms. Must we therefore conclude, in terms of our own hypothesis, that *motoric* effects are operating in all three types of aphasia? Further consideration suggests that much more is involved in interpretation of these results than a simple choice between the two hypotheses.

First it is important to note that the procedures for assigning patients to particular categories of aphasia involve multiple criteria, only a few of which pertain directly to segmental production abilities. The criteria are typically not highly correlated with each other, because aphasic syndromes are not discrete. Even patients with confirmed posterior lesions and many of the symptoms of posterior aphasia may have relatively low segmental production abilities. Thus motoric difficulty could affect data from *groups* of posterior aphasics even though it is not commonly great enough to be included in a generalized symptom description of posterior aphasic syndromes.

To our knowledge, the two studies by Blumstein and others (Blumstein, Cooper, Goodglass, Stallender, & Gottlieb, 1980; Blumstein, Cooper, Zurif, &

Caramazza, 1977) are the only objective (instrumental) comparative studies of phonetic aspects of production in different aphasic groups. Both studies provide support for this contention. In studying voice onset time (VOT) of initial stop consonants in groups of Broca's, Conduction, and Wernicke's aphasics they found phonetic (motoric) errors not only in Broca's aphasics but in Conduction and Wernicke's aphasics as well. Phonetic errors were defined as productions of consonants with VOTs intermediate between those typical of normal voiced and voiceless consonants. But only within the Broca's aphasic group did *all* subjects make such errors. Phonemic errors were defined by VOTs with values within the normal range of the consonant opposite in voicing to the one intended. In all three groups, there were *some* subjects that made more phonetic errors than phonemic errors, but this was most often true of Broca's aphasics. One finding was specific to Broca's aphasics and, according to Blumstein et al. (1980), indicative of a "pervasive phonetic disorder [p. 164]." In this group, even responses that were technically "correct" (i.e., within the normal range of VOTs for the intended consonant) had an overall distribution quite different from that observed in normal subjects, suggesting that even these responses were variable in terms of motoric control.

The picture that emerges from these two studies is that phonetic errors occur in all three groups of aphasics but are more typical and widespread in anterior (Broca's) aphasics. Suppose now that these errors tend toward the production of motorically easier consonants. Then, in phonetic transcription studies of the kind we have been examining, some of these errors would be classified as substitutions of motorically easier consonants, thus contributing to the consonant production preferences we observed.

But do phonetic errors tend toward the production of motorically easier consonants? Most attention has been given to this question in the case of initial stop consonants. Two studies of anterior aphasics have reported a tendency for voiceless stop consonant VOTs to move toward values for the corresponding voiced stops (Freeman, Sands, & Harris, 1977; Dibrell, 1978). But this trend was not suggested by the substitution data of the two studies analyzed here; that is, there was no strong trend for voiceless-to-voiced substitutions to exceed voiced-to-voiceless substitutions. On the other hand, one aspect of the Trost and Canter data *was* found to be strongly supportive of the possibility of motoric distortions producing easier consonants. This involved final stop consonants. Children learn to produce final voiceless consonants before final voiced consonants. Furthermore, final voiceless consonants outnumber final voiced consonants in the world's languages and sound changes in the direction of devoicing of final consonants are well-known. Thus, presumably a difficulty factor is operating here at the motoric level. A tabulation of final stop consonant substitutions in the Trost and Canter data reveals 27 occasions when a voiceless consonant was "substituted" for a voiced consonant but *no* examples of the reverse event. Unfortunately, the same situation could not be evaluated in the other groups because data on final consonant substitutions were not available.

From the evidence presented here, it is at least a possibility that some apparent substitutions produced by aphasics are in fact motorically based distortions undetected as such by the phonetic transcribers and that difficulty-related factors may contribute to the consonant production preferences in their substitution data. This line of reasoning could account for the finding of consonantal production preferences in the error patterns of posterior aphasics as well as anterior aphasics. But it cannot account for the fact that the effects we found were approximately as great for posterior aphasics as for anterior aphasics. No one would dispute the fact that segmental production difficulties are greater in anterior than in posterior aphasics. However, it is possible that a second factor, nonmotoric in nature, is contributing to the observed pattern of correlation coefficients and that its contribution to the posterior aphasic results is greater than to the anterior results. This factor can be termed a lexical confusion factor and would give rise to interference effects on consonant choice at a premotor level. It seems likely that lexical interference effects are more common in posterior aphasics than in anterior aphasics (Lesser, 1978). Some of the consonant production preference effects that we observed could simply follow from the fact that lexical items are the vehicle for consonant frequency effects in the language; that is, the more frequent a consonant is in the language, the more likely it is to be present in an interfering lexical item and to intrude in a consonant substitution. The negative correlation of targets with frequency could be a statistical resultant of the fact that consonants less frequent in the language are more likely to have consonants other than themselves intruding on them. To take a simple example, perhaps a consonant that accounts for 8% of all consonantal occurrences in the language would face intrusion of other consonants 92% of the time, but a consonant with a 1% frequency would face foreign intrusion 99% of the time.

We do not wish to imply that motoric difficulty and lexical confusion factors are the only variables operating in the production of aphasic consonant errors. The most prominent attempts to model the speech production process at the segmental level (the level of vowels and consonants) involve a scanning of lexical items to obtain a segmental representation, following which the individual segments are serially ordered. Motoric processes then follow (Shaffer, 1976; Shattuck-Hufnagel, 1979). These scanning and ordering operations are thought to occur between the lexical selection and the motoric stages and to be responsible for consonantal substitution errors in normal adults. It appears likely that anterior and posterior aphasics all have difficulties with these operations and many of the errors in the three studies we have analyzed may be due to them. But as we indicated earlier, we do not believe that these difficulties are reflected in consonant production preferences.

In summary, there may be two factors—a motoric difficulty effect and a premotoric lexical confusion effect—contributing to the observed consonant production preferences of aphasics, in a manner illustrated schematically in Fig. 29.4. This view, although speculative, has the desirable property of preserving

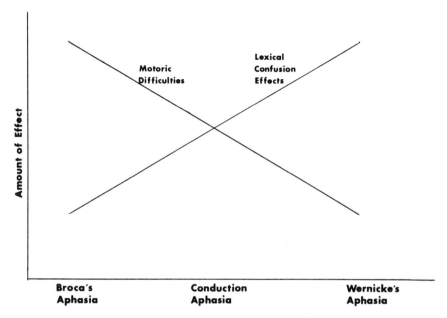

FIG. 29.4.   Schematic view of possible relative roles of motoric difficulties and lexical confusion effects in consonant errors in aphasics.

an apparently necessary distinction between motoric and premotoric processes in speech production. It also respects the fact that aphasic syndromes cannot be expected to be discrete and independent. Finally, the contributions of both motoric and lexical intrusion factors can be tested, making the view preferable to a markedness hypothesis, which attributes the consonant preferences to a formal property of linguistic codes.

ACKNOWLEDGMENT

This chapter was prepared with the support of Grant NS 15336 from the National Institute of Neurological and Communicative Disorder and Stroke.

REFERENCES

Blumstein, S. A. *A phonological investigation of aphasic speech.* The Hague: Mouton, 1973.
Blumstein, S. A., Cooper, W. E., Goodglass, H., Stallender, S., & Gottlieb, J. Production deficits in aphasia: A voice-onset time analysis. *Brain and Language,* 1980, *9,* 153–170.
Blumstein, S. A., Cooper, W. E., Zurif, E. B., & Caramazza, A. The perception and production of voice-onset time in aphasia. *Neuropsychologia,* 1977, *15,* 371–383.
Bogen, J. E., & Bogen, G. M. Wernicke's region—Where is it? In S. R. Harnad, H. D. Stelkis, &

J. Lancaster (Eds.), *Origins and evolution of language and speech*. New York: The New York Academy of Sciences, 1976.

Burns, M. *Phonemic behavior of aphasic patients with posterior cerebral lesions.* Unpublished doctoral dissertation, Northwestern University, 1975.

Burns, M., & Canter, G. Phonemic behavior of aphasic patients with posterior cerebral lesions. *Brain and Language,* 1977, *4,* 492–507.

Cruttenden, A. A phonetic study of babbling. *British Journal of Disorders of Communication,* 1970, *5,* 110–118.

Denes, P. B. On the statistics of spoken English. *Journal of the Acoustical Society of America,* 1963, *35,* 892–904.

Dibrell, J. *Voice-onset time perception and production of initial stop cognates in apraxia of speech.* Unpublished doctoral dissertation, University of Texas at Austin, 1978.

Ferguson, C. A. Assumptions about nasals: A sample study in phonological universals. In J. Greenberg (Ed.), *Universals of language.* Cambridge, Mass.: MIT Press, 1963.

Ferguson, C. A., & Farwell, C. B. Words and sounds in early language acquisition: English initial consonants in the first 50 words. *Language,* 1975, *51,* 419–439.

Fisichelli, R. M. *An experimental study of the speech development of institutionalized infants.* Unpublished doctoral dissertation, Fordham University, 1950.

Fitts, P. M. The information capacity of the human motor system in controlling the amplitude of movement. *Journal of Experimental Psychology,* 1954, *47,* 381–391.

Fowler, C. A., Rubin, P., Remez, R. E., & Turvey, M. T. Implications for speech production of a general theory of action. In B. Butterworth (Ed.), *Language production.* London: Academic Press, 1980.

Freeman, F., Sands, E. S., & Harris, K. S. Temporal coordination of phonation and articulation in a case of verbal apraxia: A voice-onset time study. Haskins laboratories: *Status Report on Speech Research,* 1977, *51/52,* 47–53.

Fromkin, V. The non-anomalous nature of anomalous utterances. *Language,* 1971, *47,* 27–52.

Goldstein, L. *Categorical features in speech perception and production.* Paper presented at the 12th International Congress of Linguists, Vienna, Austria, September, 1977.

Green, E., & Howes, D. The nature of conduction aphasia: A study of anatomic and clinical features and of underlying mechanisms. In H. Whitaker & H. A. Whitaker (Eds.), *Studies in neurolinguistics* (Vol. 3). New York: Academic Press, 1977.

Ingram, D. Phonological rules in young children. *Journal of Child Language,* 1974, *1,* 49–64.

Irwin, O. C. Infant speech: Consonantal sounds according to place of articulation. *Journal of Speech Disorders,* 1947, *12,* 397–401.

Jakobson, R. *Child language, aphasia and phonological universals.* The Hague: Mouton, 1968.

Johns, D., & Darley, F. Phonemic variability in apraxia of speech. *Journal of Speech and Hearing Research,* 1970, *13,* 556–583.

Johnson, C. E., & Bush, C. N. A note on transcribing the speech of young children. *Stanford University Papers and Reports on Child Language Development,* 1971, *3,* 95–100.

Kent, R. D. Models of speech production. In N. J. Lass (Ed.), *Contemporary issues in experimental phonetics.* New York: Academic Press, 1976.

Kuehn, D. P., & Moll, K. L. A cineradiographic study of VC and CV articulatory velocities. *Journal of Phonetics,* 1976, *4,* 303–320.

Leopold, W. *Speech development of a bilingual child: A linguist's record* (Vol. 2: Sound learning in the first two years). Evanston, Ill.: Northwestern University Press, 1947.

Lesser, R. Linguistic investigation of aphasia. In D. Crystal (Ed.), *Studies in language disability and remediation* (Vol. 4). London: Arnold Pub., 1978.

Locke, J. L. *Mechanisms of phonological development in children: Maintenance, learning and loss.* Paper presented at the 16th regional meeting of the Chicago Linguistics Society, Chicago, April, 1980.

MacKay, D. Spoonerisms: The structure of errors in the serial order of speech. *Neuropsychologia*, 1970, *8*, 823-350.

MacNeilage, P. F. Distinctive properties of speech motor control. In G. E. Stelmach & J. Requin (Eds.), *Tutorials in motor behavior*. Amsterdam: North-Holland Pub., 1980. (a)

MacNeilage, P. F. Speech production. *Language and speech*, 1980, *23*, 3-23. (b)

Marquardt, T., Rinehart, J., & Peterson, H. Markedness analysis of phonemic substitution errors in apraxia of speech. *Journal of Communication Disorders*, 1979, *12*, 481-494.

Menn, L. *Pattern, control, and contrast in beginning speech: A case study in the development of word form and word function*. Bloomington, Ind.: Indiana University Linguistics Club, 1978.

Menyuk, P. The role of distinctive features in children's acquisition of phonology. *Journal of Speech and Hearing Research*, 1968, *11*, 138-146.

Mohr, J. P. Broca's area and Broca's aphasia. In H. Whitaker & H. A. Whitaker (Eds.), *Studies in neurolinguistics* (Vol. 1). New York: Academic Press, 1976.

Moskowitz, A. I. The two-year-old stage in the acquisition of phonology. *Language*, 1970, *46*, 426-441.

Ohala, J. J. The contribution of acoustic phonetics to phonology. In B. Lindblom & S. Öhman (Eds.), *Frontiers of speech communication research*. London: Academic Press, 1979. (a)

Ohala, J. J. Universals of labial velars and de Saussure's chess analogy. *Proceedings of the Ninth International Congress of Phonetic Sciences* (Vol. 2). Copenhagen: Institute of Phonetics, University of Copenhagen, 1979. (b)

Oller, D. K. The emergence of the sounds of speech in infancy. In G. Yeni-Komshian, J. Kavanagh, & C. Ferguson (Eds.), *Child phonology, perception and production*. New York: Academic Press, 1980.

Oller, D. K., & Eilers, R. E. Phonetic expectation and transcription validity. *Phonetica*, 1975, *31*, 288-304.

Oller, D. K., Wieman, L. A., Doyle, W. J., & Ross, C. Infant babbling and speech. *Journal of Child Language*, 1976, *3*, 11.

Perkell, J. S. Phonetic features and the physiology of speech production. In B. Butterworth (Ed.), *Language production: Speech and talk* (Vol. 1). London: Academic Press, 1980.

Pierce, J. E., & Hanna, I. V. *The development of a phonological system in English-speaking American children*. Portland, Ore.: HaPi Press, 1974.

Shaffer, L. H. Intention and performance. *Psychological Review*, 1976, *83*, 375-393.

Shankweiler, D., & Harris, K. S. An experimental approach to the problem of articulation in aphasia. *Cortex*, 1966, *2*, 277-292.

Shattuck-Hufnagel, S. Speech errors as evidence for a serial-ordering mechanism in sentence production. In W. E. Cooper & E. C. T. Walker (Eds.), *Sentence processing: Psycholinguistics studies presented to Merrill Garrett*. Hillsdale, N.J.: Lawrence Erlbaum Associates, 1979.

Shattuck-Hufnagel, S., & Klatt, D. H. The limited use of distinctive features and markedness in speech production: Evidence from speech error data. *Journal of Verbal Learning and Verbal Behavior*, 1979, *18*, 41-55.

Trost, J. E. *A descriptive study of verbal apraxia in patients with Broca's aphasia*. Unpublished doctoral dissertation, Northwestern University, 1970.

Trost, J. E., & Canter, G. Apraxia of speech in patients with Broca's aphasia: A study of phoneme production accuracy and error patterns. *Brain and Language*, 1974, *1*, 63-80.

Wurm, S. A. Classifications of Australian languages. In T. A. Sebeok (Ed.), *Current trends in linguistics* (Vol. 8). The Hague: Mouton, 1971.

30

Natural Measurement Criteria for Speech: The Anisochrony Illusion

Carol A. Fowler and Louis G. Tassinary
Dartmouth College, Hanover, New Hampshire
and
Haskins Laboratories, New Haven, Connecticut
U.S.A.

ABSTRACT

When talkers are asked to produce isochronous sequences of monosyllables, they fail in systematic ways, as measured by conventional syllable onset–onset intervals. Listeners, however, hear these attempts as isochronous and hear sequences with equal onset–onset intervals as anisochronous. The agreement between talkers and listeners and the discrepancy between their results and conventional measurements are apparently symptomatic either of a symmetrical production–perception illusion or of systematic measurement error. We examine the second possibility, establishing, in the light of information in the phonetics literature, that the demarcation of syllable onset is flawed if it is intended to mark acoustic reflections of articulatory onset. Moreover, it is flawed in systematic ways that explain many of the talkers' apparent deviations from isochrony. Next we attempt to identify what talkers align temporally in isochronous productions and show that it is a syllable-internal event (as other investigators have also recognized), and not syllable onset. The syllable-internal event appears to be an acoustic reflection of vowel production.

INTRODUCTION

A sequence of spoken digits with isochronous acoustic energy onsets[1] does not sound evenly timed to listeners. Moreover, when listeners are asked to adjust the intervals between a pair of alternating digits until the sequence sounds isochron-

---

[1]We use awkward locutions such as "acoustic energy onset" or, worse yet, "durations of acoustic energy prior to the measured onset of the vowel" ("prevocalic acoustic duration," for short)

ous, they introduce systematic departures from measured isochrony (Morton, Marcus, & Frankish, 1976). Talkers behave compatibly. When asked to utter an isochronous sequence of uniformly stressed monosyllables differing in initial consonant, they generate sequences that, by conventional acoustic measures, are not evenly timed. However, they reproduce just the departures from measured isochrony that listeners require in order to hear even timing (Fowler, 1979). These departures are characterized by a strong positive relationship between onset–onset intervals among syllables and durations of acoustic energy preceding the measured vowel onset in the initial monosyllables of the intervals.

This cluster of findings is interesting in revealing both a close agreement between listener judgments and talker behavior and a clear discrepancy between measures of these behaviors and measures of the acoustic signal. One explanation for the discrepancy ascribes it to an illusion characteristic of language users both as listeners and as talkers. An alternative explanation ascribes it, complementarily, to systematic failures of conventional measures to reflect the natural constituency of the acoustic speech signal. The first explanation is compatible with accounts of a related phenomenon observed when listeners judge sentence timing. Several studies have found that listeners hear interstress intervals in more-or-less naturally produced sentences as isochronous, even when the intervals depart markedly from measured isochrony. Because this apparent insensitivity to anisochrony is absent when nonspeech intervals are judged, investigators ascribe the judgments to an illusion peculiar to speech (Darwin & Donovan, in press; Lehiste, 1973).

Some reason to doubt this account, at least in its application to the less natural sequences of Morton et al. (1976) or of Fowler (1979), is provided by a study of articulatory timing. Tuller and Fowler (1980) obtained concurrent acoustic and electromyographic records during productions of stressed sequences of monosyllables that talkers had intended to be isochronous. In the study, muscle activity underlying production both of consonants and of vowels was isochronous despite substantial measured acoustic anisochrony. Apparently then, talkers followed instructions to produce even timing by regulating articulatory timing, and their impressions of isochrony were not illusory. Given the close agreement between talkers and listeners regarding isochrony, it is likely that listener judgments of isochrony in the studies of Fowler and Morton et al. are based on acoustic reflections of articulatory timing.

If the acoustic signal does reflect articulatory timing in such a way that listeners can detect it, then we must ask why our acoustic measures do not reflect it accurately. In fact, the reason can be discovered in the phonetics literature

---

to describe parts of the acoustic signal. In the isochrony literature, the more convenient terms, "sound onset" or "phonetic-segment onset" have been used as if they were coextensive with "acoustic energy onset." Likewise, "consonant duration" is used as if it were coextensive with "prevocalic acoustic duration" in a CV syllable. However, a major point we hope to make is that the terms are not coextensive. Because it is critical to keep the referents of these terms separate, it is necessary to keep the terminology distinct at the cost of some elegance.

(Fant, 1962; Lisker, 1957). Fundamentally, it is that the criteria for partitioning the acoustic signal into consonants, vowels, and intersyllable intervals used in the isochrony literature violate a natural partitioning of the acoustic signal into those units in two major ways. First, they equate onsets of acoustic energy for a phonetic segment with the phonetic-segment onset itself; second, they ignore the fact of coarticulation among neighboring segments. The research just cited highlights the first of these errors of measurement, as we explain now, and the results of the experiment we report in the following suggest the second.

Phonetic Segment Onsets

The criterion for syllable onset used in our previous studies and in those of Morton et al. (1976) and Lehiste (1973) was the onset of acoustic energy for the syllable-initial segment. Intuitively, there is no more reasonable criterion than this because it represents the first visible evidence of syllable onset in a spectrographic or oscillographic display. However, the criterion is flawed as a measure of *articulatory* onset and hence as a measure of phonetic-segment onset for a talker, because it leads the measurer to designate as onset different phases in the production of different manner classes of consonant.[2] In effect, this measurement criterion implies that, for a talker, achieving isochrony requires certain anisochronies of articulation to line up the release phases of oral stops with the closure phases of other syllable-initial segments. In our production experiment just described, talkers did not behave this way. Instead, they more closely aligned closing phase with closing phase, closure with closure, and release with release. Nor would there be any point in a talker's regulating the acoustic-energy onsets of stops in view of the finding that perceivers require evidence of a closure interval (silence in the studies that have investigated the phenomenon) in order to hear later acoustic evidence of release as a stop consonant (Dorman, Raphael, & Liberman, 1979; Liberman & Pisoni, 1977). These observations support fairly strongly the second proposed interpretation of the discrepancy between speaker/listener behavior and acoustic measures. The discrepancy is due to an optical illusion, so to speak, of the measurers rather than to an acoustic illusion of the speaker-listeners.

Vowel Onsets

Although the study of Tuller and Fowler (1980) revealed articulatory isochrony in utterances with measured acoustic anisochrony, it failed to isolate a particular phonetic segment or any other aspect of the syllable as a possible focus of the

---

[2]Consonants are produced in three broad phases: a closing phase during which an articulator approaches a point of constriction, a closure interval during which the constriction is maintained, and a release phase. The acoustic energy onsets of segments other than oral stops occur at or near the onsets of the closure intervals. But the acoustic energy onsets of syllable-initial oral stops occur at stop release.

talker's timing strategies. An obvious proposal is that the talker intends to initiate the production of syllables at temporally equidistant intervals under isochrony instructions. Our experiment tests this proposal but, before describing the test, we should explain why we expected to *disconfirm* the hypothesis and why we entertained a different one—namely that vowels would be evenly timed under conditions in which the initial segments of a syllable would not.

Our alternative hypothesis was based on the following set of observations:

1. Some investigators have proposed that listeners refer to a syllable-internal location when they make isochrony judgments (Morton et al., 1976). The critical location shifts inward from the measured onset of the syllable as the duration of the prevocalic acoustic signal increases. This hypothesis explains the listener's isochrony judgments equally as well as one assuming that it is the articulatory-syllable onsets to which the listener attends. It has the added advantage of generalizing to some other findings. In particular, listeners' taps to stressed syllables in naturally produced sentences are syllable-internal (Allen, 1972) and Swedish talkers, producing iambic disyllables, align the stressed syllable such that the pulse is syllable-internal (Rapp, 1971).

2. The syllable-internal event has been identified by some investigators with the stress beat of a syllable (Rapp, 1971; Allen, 1972). Allen's conclusion is based on his finding that taps to unstressed syllables have a far less consistent locus than taps to stressed syllables. In Rapp's study, Swedish talkers producing a disyllable in time to a pulse aligned the stressed syllable with the pulse, skipping over the unstressed syllable (Rapp, 1971). Our own studies have included only uniformly stressed syllables and, therefore, cannot in themselves be taken to address the phenomenon of stress. However, in relevant respects, our findings and those of Morton et al. (1976) are compatible with Allen's using spontaneously generated sentences and Rapp's using iambic disyllables. Apparently, phonetic-segmental sources of departure from measured isochrony are not strongly affected by the presence or absence of unstressed syllables in the utterance.

3. Stress is fundamentally a property of a vowel and is not a property of syllable-initial consonants. Linguistic rules of stress placement select syllables for stressing based only on properties of the syllable "rhyme" (that is the vowel and any syllable-final consonants). The syllable "onset" (any prevocalic consonants) is irrelevant in all the dozen or so languages that have been studied in detail (Prince, 1980). In some languages, only the vowel is relevant (Hayes, 1980); in none is the vowel irrelevant.

Based on these considerations, we expected that a study separating the articulation of syllable onset and rhyme would reveal the rhyme as the focus of a talker's timing strategies. A natural hypothesis is that vowel onsets would be regulated by talkers—a hypothesis consistent with the outcome of Tuller and

Fowler (1980). This does not mean that the regulated event would coincide with the conventionally measured vowel onset, however. Instead, due to anticipatory coarticulation of a vowel with a consonant in a CV (Carney & Moll, 1971; Gay, 1977; Ohman, 1966), it should precede the measured vowel onset in any syllable beginning with a consonant.

The experiment had as its major aim to test the hypothesis that talkers regulate the onset of a syllable-initial segment against a hypothesis that they regulate a syllable-internal event. A second aim was to generate information enabling localization of any regulated event if it were to be syllable-internal.

EXPERIMENT

The first intent of the experiment was addressed by designing two types of utterance. One utterance type included the monosyllable /ad/ produced in alternation with rhyming consonant-initial syllables. For continuant consonants, using conventional acoustic measures, we would expect isochrony or near isochrony if the talker regulates the syllable-initial segments of these syllables but not if he or she regulates a syllable-internal event that shifts in relation to the measured syllable onset with different initial segments. The same logic may be applied to utterances of the second type, in which initial consonants are the same across syllables in the utterance, but the size of a prevocalic cluster is varied (e.g., /sad strad . . . /).

The second aim of the study, to locate and identify any syllable-internal event that might be regulated, was addressed by replicating Rapp's procedure in which talkers produce syllables to a metronome.

Method

Subjects. Subjects were three graduate students, two male and one female, enrolled at Dartmouth College. All three are native English speakers.

Stimuli and Materials. We created 33 unique utterances, each a seven-syllable nonsense sentence. As in earlier studies, the monosyllables in the sentences all rhymed with /ad/ but differed in initial consonant or cluster. The orthographic (rather than phonetic) spellings of the sentences were printed in uppercase primer type on 5 × 8 index cards.

Each nonsense sentence was either "homogeneous" or "alternating" in composition. Homogeneous sentences were composed of the same monosyllable repeated seven times (e.g., MOD MOD MOD MOD MOD MOD MOD). Nine were generated from the monosyllables: /ad/, /bad/, /dad/, /fad/, /mad/, /nad/, /pad/, /sad/, and /tad/. Alternating utterances were composed of two different nonsense syllables in alternation. Twenty-four alternating sentences were generated, including: (1) each single-consonant monosyllable alternating with /ad/

(e.g., /sad ad . . . /), plus its mirror reversal (e.g., /ad sad . . . /); and (2) all the following: /strad stad . . . /, /strad sad . . . /, /stad sad . . . /, and /trad tad . . . /, and their mirror reversals.

Two copies of each alternating sentence and four copies of each homogeneous sentence were made. The 84 stimulus cards were split into four groups of 21 with the constraint that groups 2 and 4 and groups 1 and 3 together contained one copy of each alternating sentence and two copies of each homogeneous sentence. Sentences within each group were randomly ordered and this ordering was maintained for all subjects. The groups of 21 sentences were arranged in different pseudorandom orders for each subject with the constraint that either groups 1 and 3 or groups 2 and 4 appear in either of the middle two positions.

Procedure.   Subjects were instructed to read aloud the sentence on each stimulus card in as rhythmic a fashion as they could, stressing every syllable. "Rhythmic" was defined as onset–onset isochrony. They were asked to repeat each sentence until they felt they had succeeded. All of their productions, practice and final, were recorded, but only the last version of each sentence was used in the analysis.

When the 84 nonmetronome trials were completed, the subject was asked to repeat the procedure with the help of a metronome. The subject listened to the metronome and adjusted it to a comfortable speaking rate. The instructions were the same as before only this time the subject was told to "say each syllable on the beat."

Measurements.   Spectrograms were made from the recorded sentences generated on trials 22–63 during both phases of the experiment (84 per subject). To avoid obscuring the rhythmicity effects by utterance-initial and -final lengthening (Lindblom & Rapp, 1973; Klatt, 1976) all measurements were confined to intervals including syllables 2 through 6. The low-amplitude frication of /f/ in /fad/ proved difficult to see on many spectrograms. Therefore we did not make measurements on utterances including that syllable.

The measurement criteria adopted for all the intervals measured were as follows:

1. Acoustic onset: The onset was defined as the onset of frication in fricative-initial syllables, the initial release burst in stop-initial syllables, and the onset of nasal resonance in /nad/ and /mad/. Finally, for the syllable /ad/, the glottal stop (if any) served as onset; otherwise, the prevocalic acoustic onset and the acoustic vowel onset were the same.

2. Acoustic vowel onset: For all the syllables, with the exception of /strad/ and /trad/, the vowel onset was the point where the glottally excited, full formant pattern was first evident. For /strad/ and /trad/ the vowel onset was measured as the start of the rising third formant. When this was not observed, the point at which the third formant approximated that of the alternate syllable in both frequency and amplitude was used.

3. Syllable offset: For all the syllables this was taken to be the offset of regular glottal pulsing. The final /d/ release was not used due to the infrequent acoustic evidence of its occurrence.

Results

The measurements made on each syllable type were averaged across its repetitions. This resulted in 11 numbers per subject for each measure (i.e., one number for each syllable type).[3]

Analysis of Nonmetronome Utterances.   As a check that subjects were able to produce the homogeneous utterances in a stress-timed rhythm, absolute mean differences in syllable onset asynchrony (SOA) were calculated. This involved averaging the odd SOAs—that is, the onset–onset intervals between syllables 2 and 3 and between syllables 4 and 5—and the even SOAs and taking the absolute value of the difference between odd and even intervals. A mean difference score was derived by averaging across all tokens of a given utterance. The mean deviations from isochrony ranged between 3 msec and 31 msec with a mean deviation of 15 msec.

In contrast to this are the corresponding values for the alternating utterances. In these utterances, odd and even SOAs are different in that their initial and final consonants are reversed with respect to one another. Here the mean deviations from isochrony ranged between 21 msec and 187 msec with an average of 62 msec. Figure 30.1 plots this difference in SOA as a function of differences in the durations of acoustic energy prior to the measured onsets of the vowels (henceforth, "prevocalic acoustic durations"). The figure reveals a linear relationship between these two measures ($r = .88$, $p < .001$). All three subjects showed a relationship of approximately this magnitude. This is similar to the relationship reported in Fowler (1979), but in the present data it is shown to hold even for alternating utterances with identical syllable-initial consonants. If talkers were regulating articulatory syllable onsets, these anisochronies, as well as those of the continuant-vowel alternating utterances, would not be expected.

Analysis of Metronome Utterances.   As for the nonmetronome utterances, the relationship between SOA differences and differences in prevocalic acoustic

---

[3]Our criterion for overall agreement was based on a comparison of the matrices of intercorrelations among measures for each subject. We counted as an agreement among subjects any instance in which the correlations between a pair of measures were uniformly nonsignificant or were uniformly significant and compatible in sign. We used the obtained frequencies of nonsignificant outcomes and of significant positive and negative correlations to compute the probability of an agreement. That is, we asked, given the obtained probabilities of each outcome for each subject, what is the probability that across subjects the outcomes would assort themselves as they did into 16 agreements and 7 disagreements or into any combination more extreme than this. The computed probability is vanishingly small. Only one of the seven disagreements was due to significant correlations differing in sign.

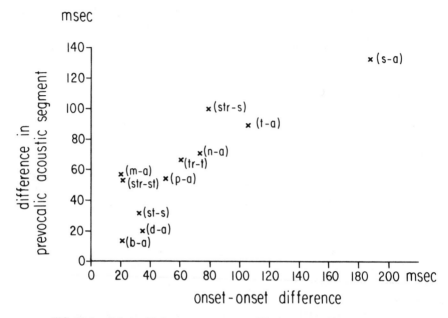

FIG. 30.1. Relationship between onset–onset differences and differences in prevocalic acoustic durations of syllables in alternating utterances.

duration in the metronome utterances is linear ($r = .91$, $p < .001$). Again, the
relationship was characteristic of all three talkers. The mean deviations from
isochrony ranged from 10 msec to 209 msec, averaging 73 msec.

Figure 30.2 represents the relationship of the metronome pulse to certain
intervals within and across syllables. In the figure, the vertical line at zero on the
horizontal axis represents the metronome pulse. The different syllable-initial
consonants or clusters are listed on the vertical axis. Reading from left to right,
points in the figure represent, respectively, the vowel offset of the preceding
syllable, the prevocalic acoustic onset of the syllable, the acoustically defined
vowel onset, and the vowel offset. These measures are collapsed over talkers and
over homogeneous and alternating utterances. The numbered horizontal lines
represent intervals that we discuss.

The figure closely resembles Rapp's (1971) Fig. I-B-6 of disyllables produced
repeatedly to a metronome by native Swedish speakers. One notable outcome,
also evident in Rapp's data, is the locus of the metronome pulse, which tends *not*
to coincide with the boundary of any acoustic segment. In itself, this does not
rule out acoustic segments as critically timed events in isochronous speech,
because we cannot be sure that the pulse location overlays a critical locus of
timing control in the syllable. For some perhaps psychoacoustic reason, the pulse
might be consistently offset from such a locus. However, even if it were, the
figure makes clear that no shift forward or back would cause the pulse to coincide

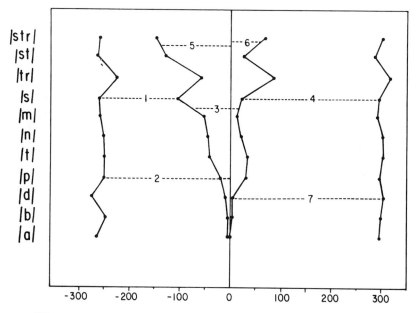

FIG. 30.2. Syllables of the experiment averaged around the metronome pulse. The pulse is the vertical line at zero on the horizontal axis. Along the vertical axis are the different syllable-initial consonants or clusters arranged approximately according to measured duration. Measure 1: intersyllable interval; Measure 2: preceding syllable offset to pulse; Measure 3: prevocalic segment duration; Measure 4: acoustically defined vowel duration; Measure 5: prevocalic acoustic onset to pulse; Measure 6: pulse to measured vowel onset; Measure 7: pulse to measured vowel offset.

consistently with any acoustic-segment boundary except the vowel offsets 260 msec to 300 msec away. Thus, to the extent that we expect to find a particular locus of temporal control in the talker's isochronous productions, the event probably is not coincident with any conventionally measured acoustic segment.[4]

In view of these considerations, the most conservative way to make use of the metronome pulse is in aligning the different syllables with respect to each other as we have done in the figure. From this alignment, several relationships among measures are apparent. In particular, several measures appear to vary systematically with changes in syllable-initial segment and segment duration. As the prevocalic acoustic duration (measure 3) increases, the metronome pulse falls progressively inward from the acoustically defined syllable onset (measure 5) and progressively back from the acoustically defined vowel onset (measure 6).

---

[4]There is also the possibility that there is no special locus of timing control. Isochrony among syllables may be achieved by cyclic articulations in which no one part of the cycle is special. We consider this possibility in Discussion, p. 532.

Separate planned comparisons show that the effect of syllable type, ordered according to measure 3, on measures 5 and 6 is linear, $F(1, 20) = 193.3$, $p < .001$, and $F(1, 20) = 35.2$, $p < .001$, respectively. For its part, measured vowel duration (measure 4) decreases with increases in prevocalic-segment duration. Compression of a vowel in the context of a preceding or following consonant or cluster is commonly reported in the literature (Rapp, 1971; Lehiste, 1970). Vowel duration also is linearly related to syllable type ordered by prevocalic segment duration, $F(1, 20) = 78.172$, $p < .001$. It is interesting that both the vowel's compression and the decrease in preceding vowel offset to syllable onset (measure 1) are just complemented by increases in measures 5 and 6 so that the intervals from preceding vowel offset to pulse (measure 2) and pulse to vowel offset (measure 7) remain invariant across changes in syllable-initial consonant. Planned comparisons on these measures yield F values less than 1. (Planned comparisons performed on the data of individual subjects also failed to reach significance.)

Discussion

The results of the study allow us to reject the hypothesis that talkers regulate articulatory syllable onsets when instructed to produce isochronous sequences. Systematic departures from measured acoustic isochrony were observed for alternating pairs of syllables beginning with the same consonant and for alternating syllables with initial continuant consonants and vowels.

However, isochrony was observed for vowel offsets, implicating the vowel as a regulated segment.[5] This does not necessarily imply that a talker's strategy for producing isochronous monosyllables is one of timing vowel offsets. If vowel offsets are isochronous, so are any points temporally equidistant from the offset. The offset was simply a point that we were able to identify consistently. It may or may not be significant in talking and listening.

In fact, we tend to discount the offset as a likely focus of regulation for two reasons. First it is implausible a priori, particularly in view of the linguistic theories of prosody cited earlier. In these theories, the syllable rhyme, consisting of vowel and postvocalic consonants, is central to explanations of metrical structure in speech. The vowel offset breaks up the rhyme and groups the vowel with the prevocalic consonants, which have no role in explanations of prosody.

---

[5]Given that the criterion for vowel offset was termination of voicing signaling closure for the following /d/, it is possible that this location in the syllable does not correspond to vowel offset for a talker or listener, who may be sensitive to the carryover coarticulation between vowel and final consonant. However, because the final consonant was invariably /d/ and the vowel /a/, the extent of carryover coarticulation should be invariant over syllables. Therefore, the measured vowel offset should be temporally equidistant from the true offset and the fact remains that vowel offsets were isochronous in these productions.

A second reason for discounting the vowel offset as a regulated event is that the metronome pulse fell about as far as possible from the vowel offsets. It was not even the case that the pulse was midway between offsets. Rather it consistently followed an offset by about 260 msec and preceded the next one by 300 msec.

A different proposal is that vowels are produced invariantly and cyclically in these sequences and may or may not have a focal regulatory locus such as vowel onset or offset. It may seem as if this account is somewhat infirmed by the measured shortening of the vowel (measure 4) in the context of long prevocalic acoustic segments. However, as noted earlier, the articulatory onsets of vowels occur within the production of preceding consonants so that their produced extent exceeds their conventionally measured extent. For this anticipatory coarticulation to explain the vowel shortening as apparent—that is, as unaccompanied by an articulatory decrease in vowel duration—it would be necessary for more of a vowel's produced extent to coarticulate with consonants and clusters having longer measured durations.

The speech production literature does not offer either confirming or disconfirming evidence on this point. However, bringing what evidence there is together with a pair of assumptions entailed by the current proposal, we can reproduce the major findings of our study. The evidence concerns timing of the different phases of consonant production and the relative timing of consonants and vowels in CV syllables. It is most complete for voiced and voiceless stops and fricatives, so our description is confined to these segments. The relevant findings from the literature are first that time to closure for voiceless stops is less than for a voiced stop (Chen, 1970). In a VCV this difference is counteracted by differences in closure duration, where voiceless stops have longer closure intervals. However, in syllable-initial position, the closure intervals are equal (Stathopoulos & Weismer, 1979). This implies that voiceless stops will have acoustic consequences relatively sooner after articulatory onset than voiced stops. This is verified in a study of vocal reaction time for CVs (Fowler, 1979) where latency for voiced stops was 358 msec and that for voiceless stops, 340 msec. The direction of difference was consistent across the three voiced-voiceless pairs and significant across the group of five subjects.

There is some evidence that, intervocalically, fricatives have a generally slower closing velocity than stops (see MacNeilage & Ladefoged, 1976, for a review), but the difference apparently is absent in syllable-initial position (Kuehn & Moll, 1976). In any event, fricatives will have acoustic consequences near the beginning of their closure phases and hence, compared to stops, a relatively short time after their articulatory onsets. This difference too is reflected in the vocal reaction time for fricatives relative to stops (Fowler, 1979).

The literature on coarticulation in CVs (in fact, generally, in VCVs) shows evidence of vowel initiation during the closing phase of voiced stops (Ohman,

1966) and fricatives (Carney & Moll, 1971) but at the onset of the closure interval for voiceless stops (Gay, 1977).

All of these facts may be accommodated in Fig. 30.2 if we suppose that consonants in CVs (but not CCVs or CCCVs) are uniformly initiated say, 175–200 msec prior to the metronome pulse and that vowels are invariantly initiated 50–75 msec later. Initial consonants in cluster-vowel syllables must be initiated relatively earlier than those in CVs. Thus, the proposal that vowels are generated cyclically in these productions is compatible with known facts of consonant timing and CV coarticulation and is not infirmed by the occurrence of measured vowel compression.

A remaining issue to consider is whether or not vowels have a focal regulatory locus. As we pointed out in Footnote 4 (p. 529), there need not be any special regulatory focus in the cycle. However, if there is none, we have no way to account for the consistent alignment of the syllables with the metronome pulse. Yet the alignment characteristic of the composite shown in Fig. 30.2 was characteristic of each talker.

Possible explanations for the location of the metronome pulse—and also, we think for the stress beat—would invoke a suprasegmental marker such as an intensity peak or a pitch indicator. We have ruled out most intensity-based explanations by showing that listeners make the same pattern of isochrony judgments to syllable sequences having undergone infinite peak clipping as to sequences with a normal intensity contour (Tuller & Fowler, 1981; see also Morton et al., 1976). Examinations of the syllables used in our studies have not revealed any pitch marker corresponding to the metronome-pulse location or to any point temporally equidistant to it.

An alternative is suggested by the finding that for all three talkers, the metronome pulse fell directly on the vowel's measured acoustic onset (within ±6 msec) in the syllable /ad/. This suggests a possible alignment of the metronome pulse with achievement of the vowel's target vocal-tract shape, a proposal that later studies will test.

In our view, the hypothesis to pursue is that vowels are rhythmically timed in sequences of monosyllables believed by talkers and listeners to be isochronous. We have attempted to obtain evidence that the metronome pulse marks a perceived correlate of the vowel by obtaining measures of perceived relative vowel duration in syllables having different initial consonants. If the metronome pulse does mark a vowel correlate for talkers and listeners, then vowels of the same measured duration should seem relatively longer in the syllable /sad/, say, than in /ad/. We tested this (Fowler & Tassinary, in preparation) using a procedure developed by Raphael (1972). He showed that voicing of a final consonant may be cued by preceding vowel duration—a long-duration vowel cuing final voicing. We used the syllables /sad/, /mad/, /bad/, and /ad/ produced by the three talkers of the present study. From each syllable, we constructed a continuum of 10 different measured vowel durations by removing pitch pulses from each

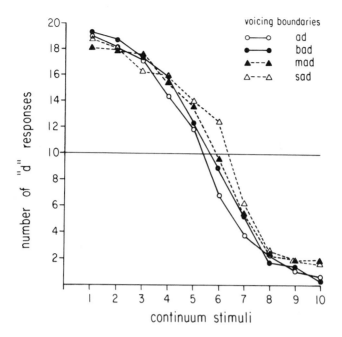

FIG. 30.3. Labeling functions for the four vowel-duration continua: /ɑd/, /bɑd/, /mɑd/, and /sɑd/ collapsed over two talkers (Fowler and Tassinary, in preparation).

vowel's steady states. Subjects were asked to label the final consonant of each syllable as /d/ or /t/. The hypothesis was that subjects would resist hearing /t/ increasingly in the series: /ɑd/, /bɑd/, /mɑd/, and /sɑd/ compatible with the increasing metronome precession of the measured vowel onset in the series (see Fig. 30.2).

Figure 30.3 shows the outcome for two of the three talkers. Listeners were unable to label the final consonants of syllables spoken by the third talker consistently enough to enable us to use their responses. Although the effects on syllables of the remaining talkers were smaller than those predicted based on the metronome precession of the measured vowel onset, the ordinal relationships among the labeling curves are exactly as predicted, $F(1, 3) = 21.6$, $p = .02$, according to a planned comparison.

Together with the results of the metronome study, these results suggest that the vowel onset, as it is generally located in a spectrographic display, has no particular status in perceiving or producing isochronous speech. Except for its salience in displays of speech, it is not surprising that it has no special status, because it does not correspond to an occasion when a phonetic segment begins or reaches its articulatory target. It corresponds only to a point in time when a consonant ceases to predominate in its effects on the acoustic signal visibly displayed. The best evidence we have now suggests that an acoustic measure of intersyllable interval that provides the most natural measure of syllable timing for talkers and listeners will be one time-locked to vowel production.

ACKNOWLEDGMENTS

The research reported here was supported by NINCDS Grant NS 13617 and NIH Grant HD 01994 to Haskins Laboratories and by Biomedical Research Support Grant RR 05392 from the National Institute of Health to Dartmouth College. We thank Scott Orr, Angelo Strenta, and Kathy Vaughan for their patient participation as talkers in the experiment and George Wolford for advice on analysis and for reviewing an earlier version of the manuscript.

REFERENCES

Allen, G. The location of rhythmic stress beats in English: An experimental study, I. *Language and Speech*, 1972, *15*, 72–100.

Carney, P., & Moll, K. A cinefluorographic investigation of fricative consonant-vowel coarticulation. *Phonetica*, 1971, *23*, 193–202.

Chen, M. Vowel length variation as a function of the voicing of the consonant environment. *Phonetica*, 1970, *22*, 129–159.

Darwin, C., & Donovan, A. Perceptual studies of speech rhythm: Isochrony and intonation. In J. C. Simon (Ed.), *Language generation and understanding*, in press.

Dorman, M., Raphael, L., & Liberman, A. Some experiments on the sound of silence in phonetic perception. *Haskins Laboratories Status Reports on Speech Research*, 1979, *SR-58*, 105–137.

Fant, G. Descriptive analysis of the acoustic aspect of speech. *Logos*, 1962, *5*, 3–17.

Fowler, C. A. "Perceptual centers" in speech production and perception. *Perception & Psychophysics*, 1979, *25*, 375–388.

Fowler, C., & Tassinary, L. Manuscript in preparation.

Gay, T. Articulatory movements in VCV sequences. *Journal of the Acoustical Society of America*, 1977, *62*, 183–193.

Hayes, B. *A metrical theory of stress rules*. Unpublished doctoral dissertation, Massachusetts Institute of Technology, 1980.

Klatt, D. Linguistic uses of segment duration in English: Acoustic and perceptual evidence. *Journal of the Acoustical Society of America*, 1976, *59*, 1208–1221.

Kuehn, D., & Moll, K. A cineradiographic study of VC and CV articulatory velocities. *Journal of Phonetics*, 1976, *4*, 303–320.

Lehiste, I. *Suprasegmentals*. Cambridge, Mass: MIT Press, 1970.

Lehiste, I. Rhythmic units and syntactic units in production and perception. *Journal of the Acoustical Society of America*, 1973, *51*, 2018–2024.

Liberman, A., & Pisoni, D. Evidence for a special speech processing subsystem in the human. In T. Bullock (Ed.), *Recognition of complex acoustic signals*. Berlin: Dahlem Konferenzen, 1977.

Lindblom, B., & Rapp, K. Some temporal regularities of spoken Swedish. *Papers in Linguistics from the University of Stockholm*, 1973, *21*, 1–59.

Lisker, L. Linguistic segments, acoustic segments and synthetic speech. *Language*, 1957, *33*, 370–374.

MacNeilage, P., & Ladefoged, P. The production of speech and language. In E. C. Carterette & M. P. Friedman (Eds.), *Handbook of perception* (Vol. 7). New York: Academic Press, 1976.

Morton, J., Marcus, S., & Frankish, C. Perceptual centers. *Psychological Review*, 1976, *83*, 405-408.

Ohman, S. Coarticulation in VCV utterances: Spectrographic measurements. *Journal of the Acoustical Society of America*, 1966, *39*, 151-168.

Prince, A. A metrical theory for Estonian quantity. *Linguistic Inquiry*, 1980, *11*, 511-562.

Raphael, L. Preceding vowel duration as a cue to the perception of the voicing characteristic of word-final consonants in American English. *Journal of the Acoustical Society of America*, 1972, *51*, 1296-1303.

Rapp, K. A study of syllable-timing. *Papers in Linguistics from the University of Stockholm*, 1971, *8*, 14-19.

Stathopoulos, E., & Weismer, G. The duration of stop consonants. In J. Wolf & D. H. Klatt (Eds.), *Speech Communication Papers*. New York: Acoustical Society of America, 1979.

Tuller, B., & Fowler, C. A. Some articulatory correlates of perceptual isochrony. *Perception & Psychophysics*, 1980, *27*, 277-283.

Tuller, B., & Fowler, C. The contribution of amplitude to the perception of isochrony. *Haskins Laboratories Status Reports on Speech Research*, 1981, *SR-65*, 245-250.

31

Planning Speech: Studies in Choice Reaction Time

William E. Cooper and Susan F. Ehrlich
Harvard University
Cambridge, Massachusetts
U.S.A.

ABSTRACT

Experiments are reported in which the response latency to produce one of two possible sentences was measured. On each trial, the two sentences were identical except for one or two contrasting words. When two words were contrasted, they either preceded or straddled a clause boundary. The time taken to memorize the sentences increased with the number of words contrasted, generalizing a result found in an earlier study using pairs of noun phrases. Response latency increased with the number of contrasted words, regardless of whether both words appeared within the first clause. The results provided evidence for prearticulation planning of at least some content within both clauses of two-clause utterances.

INTRODUCTION

This chapter concerns the operations performed by a speaker both to access information stored in memory and to integrate the information into an utterance. Of primary interest are operations that occur prior to the initiation of articulation. Very little is known about such prearticulation planning, largely because it is difficult to devise experimental procedures that can influence the memory representations of the speaker, prior to initiating speech.

Some attempts have been made to observe sentence planning by having subjects memorize sentences and produce them on cue. Johnson (1966), for example, asked subjects to memorize associations between sentences and numbers. The subjects produced one of four possible sentences given a number as a prompt. Response latencies were longer for more complex sentences, defined in terms of the number of left branches contained in a syntactic analysis. Although these results provide useful information about the demand put on the speaker when programming the execution of a particular structure, the method cannot tap the operations used to extract the set of information needed for a particular utterance from a complex memory store.

In a simple reaction-time task, Sternberg, Monsell, Knoll, and Wright (1978) showed that the time to initiate speech is directly proportional to the number of items to be spoken. In a typical experiment, subjects were instructed to utter a prespecified array of words denoting numbers or days of the week, and the time to initiate speech increased by about 10 msec with the addition of each word to be uttered. From these results, it was suggested that the speaker needs to store all words in an articulatory output buffer prior to the initiation of speech, at least under the conditions of considerable practice and time pressure as in these experiments. The simple reaction-time task seems well suited to examining the nature of an articulatory buffer, but again it does not provide much opportunity for engaging high-order operations involved in the integration of information stored in memory.

There is one study in which an attempt was made to influence the memory representation of the speaker while holding constant the utterance that the subject produced. Tannenbaum and Williams (1968) asked speakers to describe pictures using either active or passive sentences. Each picture was preceded by a written context that focused on either the subject or the object of the action depicted in the picture. The results showed that the response latencies to produce active sentences were significantly faster when the prior context focused on the subject versus the object of the picture, with converse results obtained for passive sentences. Contextual focus clearly influenced the operations used to generate particular structures.

In this chapter, an alternative means of affecting the memory representation of the speaker is examined. We attempt to show that a complex memory representation can be induced by asking the subject to memorize two related sentences. Evidence for the use of this type of representation has been presented by Ehrlich and Cooper (Manuscript submitted for publication). In that study, subjects were asked to memorize two visually presented phrases on each trial and to press a button when both phrases had been memorized to the subjects' satisfaction. Both memorization times and response latencies to produce one of the two phrases from a cue were recorded. Example phrase pairs follow, with the contrasted words underlined (no underlining was used in the experiment itself).

ONE WORD CONTRASTED

T	A casino with a gift shop in the	basement	(Modifies PP)
		city	(Modifies subject)

| B | A casino with a <u>snack bar</u> in the | basement | (Modifies PP) |
| | | city | (Modifies subject) |

TWO WORDS CONTRASTED

T	A <u>casino</u> with a gift shop in the	basement	(Modifies PP)
		city	(Modifies subject)
B	A <u>museum</u> with a gift shop in the	lobby	(Modifies PP)
		country	(Modifies subject)

THREE WORDS CONTRASTED

T	A <u>casino</u> with a <u>gift shop</u> in the	basement	(Modifies PP)
		city	(Modifies subject)
B	A <u>museum</u> with a <u>snack bar</u> in the	lobby	(Modifies PP)
		country	(Modifies subject)

On any given trial, the phrases memorized by the subject were identical, contrasting by a single noun, contrasting by two nouns, or contrasting by all three nouns. The location of the contrasting words was varied to include all eight permutations. A second independent variable, varied orthogonally, involved whether the last prepositional phrase of both strings modified the head noun or the immediately preceding prepositional phrase.

The processes required by this task are engaged in the real world when a speaker maintains a stored memory for a carrier phrase and variable words to be inserted. Consider, for example, the case in which a broadcaster is about to declare the winner and runner-up of a horse race, along with the associated prizes awarded to each. The carrier phrase might be "a earns the winner's prize of x" and "b earns the runner-up prize of y." Paralleling our procedure, the two sentences differ from one another by two contrasting words, and the broadcaster must take care to associate the correct contrasting words (e.g., *Golden Eagle, $10,000,* and *Runaway, $5,000*) with the appropriate carrier.

The results showed that both memorization times and response latencies increased with the number of words contrasted between the phrases. On the other hand, neither the memorization times nor response latencies differed significantly for the different types of syntactic structure or for different locations of the contrasted words. The mean memorization times and response latencies, collapsed over locations and structures, are presented in Fig. 31.1. Speakers committed errors (including improper phrase selection, word substitutions and deletions, or lengthy mid-sentence pauses) on about 4% of the trials, and an examination of these errors across conditions showed no evidence of a speed–accuracy tradeoff.

The results for memorization times supported the notion that, in this task, subjects form a complex memory representation for the two phrases on each trial.

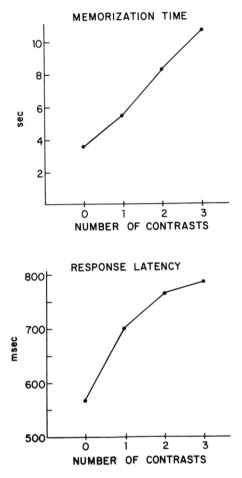

FIG. 31.1.   Mean memorization time and response latency for Experiment 1 (Ehrlich & Cooper, Manuscript submitted for publication).

Because memorization times increased substantially as a function of the number of contrasting words, with the total number of words in each phrase held constant, it can be inferred that subjects spent much of the time in memorizing the contrasted words. Subjects' intuitions, as determined in postexperiment interviews, were in agreement with this inference. Some subjects reported that they first read the top phrase, then scanned the bottom phrase for any contrasting words, and thereafter devoted most of the memorization phase to memorizing the contrasted words, along with their top versus bottom locations.

   Post hoc analysis showed that response latencies differed significantly for conditions with 0, 1, and 2 contrasts. The difference between conditions with 2 versus 3 contrasts did not reach significance. The fact that latencies increased with the number of contrasted words suggested that an increment of processing time was required to isolate each word that was particular to the cued phrase and to integrate that word with the other words that were held in common between the phrases. Thus, these results were considered to be evidence for preproduction planning. Alternatively, the differences in response latencies might indicate that the time needed to locate the first word of the cued phrase increased with the load on short-term memory (STM) (Sternberg, 1969). Theoretically, the subject is only required to choose between one of two alternatives for the first word, in the cases where the initial words are contrasted. However, it remains a possibility that the load on STM may influence such binary decisions (Drewnowski, 1980).

The argument that increases in response latency are attributable to the number of items stored in STM, however, seems inconsistent with the latency effects observed when the first word is held constant between the phrases. In such cases, no cue-dependent decision about the first word is called for, and it seems likely that subjects would be "set" to produce that first word, prior to the cue. If so, increases in reaction time with number of contrasts at the ends of the phrases provide clear evidence of preproduction processing time related to the contrasts to be produced after the first word.

In a second experiment (Ehrlich & Cooper, submitted for publication), we examined the influence of modifying relationships between the contrasted items on both memorization time and response latency. At the outset, we hypothesized that, when two words are contrasted between the phrases, it should be easier for the speaker to memorize and produce one of the phrases when the two contrasting words bear a modifying relationship to one another than when they do not. The sentences of the first experiment may well have failed to reveal a structural effect because of inconsistently varying semantic relationships between modifier and modifiee. In the second experiment, we intentionally covaried the syntactic and semantic relationships between the contrasted words in order to determine whether, together, these relationships would influence memorization times and response latencies.

Example sentence materials for that experiment are illustrated in the following. Each sentence pair contained two contrasted words, appearing either as the first and third nouns or as the second and third nouns. For each of these types, the prepositional phrase including the third noun modified either the prepositional phrase containing the second noun or the head noun phrase.

FIRST AND THIRD WORDS CONTRASTED
LAST PP MODIFIES PRECEDING PP

T   A marble for the boy with a suntan

B   A letter for the boy with a crew cut

LAST PP MODIFIES SUBJECT *

T   A <u>marble</u> for the boy in the <u>toy box</u>

B   A <u>letter</u> for the boy in the <u>mailbox</u>

SECOND AND THIRD WORDS CONTRASTED

LAST PP MODIFIES PRECEDING PP *

T   A note from the <u>principal</u> of the <u>school</u>

B   A note from the <u>architect</u> of the <u>house</u>

LAST PP MODIFIES SUBJECT

T   A note from the <u>principal</u> on the <u>door</u>

B   A note from the <u>architect</u> on the <u>car</u>

*Indicates contrasts having modifying relationship.

The results showed, as predicted, that memorization times were significantly shorter when the contrasting words were related to one another via a modifying link (see Fig. 31.2). Decreased memorization time for related words may have resulted from the fact that subjects did not have to resort to the creation of associations between unrelated words, in order to keep the top versus bottom pairs from being confused.

The response latencies were also shorter when the contrasting words were related to each other but only for the phrases with contrasts between the first and third nouns. If subjects are indeed attempting to "locate" in some sense the appropriate contrasted information during the response latency interval, the advantage of the relationship may be that it provides a strong link between the words that must be integrated. This advantage reveals itself primarily when the speaker must insert two key words separated from one another by intervening common material, taxing the speaker's ability to keep track of the correct pair of key words.

The results of these experiments seem to provide evidence that the integration of information stored in memory occurs prior to the initiation of articulation, when a prompt designates which of two possible utterances should be produced. Under more natural conditions a prompt could be generated in the course of conversation or by some internal thought process.

The nature of the integration process is open to question. Speakers may access contrasting information that is stored independently from the common information and "move" that information into the frame provided by the common information. Alternatively, response delays may reflect time to open alternative gates to information that is already closely linked to specific locations in the overall structure of which the common material is a part (see General Discussion).

Assuming that the response latency increases are a result of some kind of preproduction planning, it is of interest to determine if such planning effects can

MEMORIZATION TIME

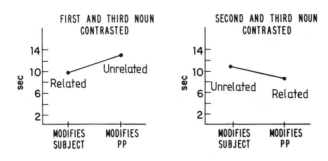

RESPONSE LATENCY

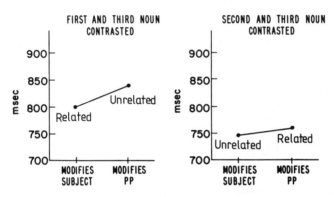

FIG. 31.2. Mean memorization time and response latency for Experiment 2 (Ehrlich & Cooper, submitted for publication).

be observed with more complex materials. Two experiments are reported here in which pairs of two-clause sentences are memorized.

An important question for research on speech production concerns whether sentence planning occurs on a clause-by-clause basis. Previous studies of speech errors (Garrett, 1975) indicate that planning of words later in a sentence can influence production of words earlier in a sentence, as when a speaker erroneously produces the phrase *salary and valley* when intending to produce *Valerie and Sally.* Such exchange errors rarely involve words that belong to separate clauses. The rarity of such cross-clause errors has prompted some psycholinguists to propose that the phonetic material of a sentence is programmed on a clause-by-clause basis (Garrett, 1975; Shattuck-Hufnagel, 1979). However, it is possible that speakers do preplan the words of a second clause at a lexical level under certain circumstances, such as when those words denote critical information differentiating two alternative sentences represented in memory. If, in our task, response latencies to begin producing two-clause sentences reflect the fact that contrasting words occur in the second clause, then evidence would be provided that decisions about lexical identity are made prior to the initiation of articulation. If, on the other hand, decisions concerning lexical content of a second clause are delayed until that clause is about to be produced, then contrasts in a second clause should not influence response latency.

EXPERIMENT 1: CONTRASTED PROPER NAMES

In this experiment, six base sentences were constructed that permitted four variations each. The base sentences were designed so that two contrasted words could either appear within the first clause or straddle the clause boundary of a two-clause sentence. In two other conditions, a single contrasted word appeared in the first clause, as shown for the following example.

TWO WORDS CONTRASTED

EARLY BOUNDARY

T   I like Chuck, and Mary and Sally respect him too.

B   I like Pete, and Katie and Sally respect him too.

LATE BOUNDARY

T   I like Chuck and Mary, and Sally respects them too.

B   I like Pete and Katie, and Sally respects them too.

ONE WORD CONTRASTED

EARLY BOUNDARY

T   I like Chuck, and Mary and Sally respect him too.

B   I like Pete, and Mary and Sally respect him too.

LATE BOUNDARY

T   I like Chuck and Mary, and Sally respects them too.

B   I like Pete and Mary, and Sally respects them too.

The subjects used in this experiment were 10 paid volunteers from the Harvard University Community. All subjects were native speakers of American English with no speech or hearing impairment.

At the beginning of the experimental session, an individual subject was seated facing a cathode-ray tube (CRT) and given instructions describing the procedure. In random order 24 practice trials and 24 experimental trials were presented to each subject.[1] In each trial, two sentences appeared on the screen, one above the

---

[1]The number of practice and test trials in these experiments was generally much smaller than in other reaction-time experiments. Typically, such experiments include a large number of practice

other, with a *T* printed on the left of the top phrase and a *B* printed to the left of the bottom phrase. The subjects were asked to memorize both sentences and to press a button as soon as they were sure they had memorized them. Upon the button press, the sentences disappeared from the screen and, following a 1-sec delay, an auditory precue beep was presented over headphones. This was followed 1 sec later by the appearance of a *T* or *B* on the screen. The speaker then produced whichever sentence was cued as quickly as possible into a microphone. The sequencing of stimulus presentations and the recording of memory and response times were controlled by a PDP-4 computer. The speakers were told to speak clearly and fluently, avoiding long pauses. High accuracy in producing the sentences was rewarded by cash bonuses. Although the subjects were instructed to avoid errors, it was stressed that they should not use any unusual mnemonic strategies for remembering the sentences but to remember them as if they were to be communicated to someone else. After the string was produced, the speaker pushed a button to begin the next trial. During the session, the experimenter monitored the speaker's output and recorded any speech errors. Aside from the initial instructions, no feedback about speech rate or onset time was given to the subjects. Speech rates appeared to be within a normal range.

Reaction time to initiate speech was measured by a voice key (Grason Stadler E7300-A1). Because each sentence began with the pronoun ''I,'' the onset of this vowel provided a consistent trigger for the voice key. The experimenter observed whether the voice key was appropriately triggered on each trial by observing whether the cue disappeared from the screen simultaneously with the onset of the subject's voice. A small number of trials were eliminated because the voice key was inappropriately triggered by the prespeech breath of the subject. The appropriateness of the onset delay setting and the gain setting for the voice key was examined visually using the *AUDITS* computer program (Huggins, 1969). With this program, it was possible to measure the time delay between the onset of the precue beep and the onset of the waveform of the subject's voice, displayed on a CRT.

For both memorization time and response latency, means were obtained across the six sentences and entered into a 2 (one versus two contrasts) × 2 (early versus late boundary) analysis of variance for repeated measures. Means, rather than individual responses, were analyzed in an attempt to constrain the variability of the data. Graphs of the memorization time and response latency results appear in Fig. 31.3. Memorization times longer than 40 sec and response latencies

---

trials in order to stabilize the subjects' response latencies, with large reductions in latency often accompanying the first 100 or so trials. We chose a relatively small number of practice and test trials in these experiments with sentences in order to render the task as natural as possible, still hoping to achieve some measure of response stability. The goals of stability of response and naturalness seem at odds in this experimental task, and our preference for naturalness is bought at the expense of large response variability, as indicated by the results, with large mean effects sometimes failing to reach statistical significance.

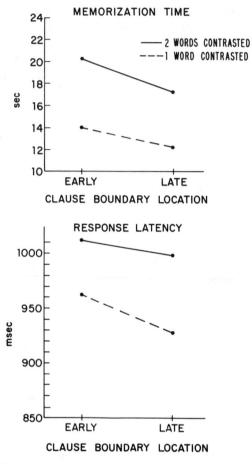

FIG. 31.3. Mean memorization time and response latency, Experiment 1.

longer than 1.5 sec (less than 4% of the responses) were eliminated from the data analysis because they were likely to reflect cases of disrupted processing.

The difference between one versus two contrasts was found to be significant for the memorization time variable, with sentences having two contrasts requiring about 5 sec longer to memorize, $F(1, 9) = 16.22$, $p < .005$. The result was the same both when the boundary occurred between the two contrasted words and when the boundary followed the two contrasts. The memorization times were longer when the boundary occurred early in the sentence, independent of the number of contrasts, $F(1, 9) = 6.04$, $p < .05$. The direction of effects for individual sentences was consistent with the overall pattern, with only one sentence showing longer memory time for one versus two contrasts, and only when the boundary occurred early in the sentence. The effect of location of boundary was consistent for all but 3 of the 12 cases.

The fact that the memorization times increased with the number of contrasts provides further evidence that subjects can create a complex memory representation that can encompass alternative words for particular locations without requiring duplicate representations of common material. The boundary location effect was not predicted and is difficult to interpret, except for the two-contrast case where the clause boundary might be seen as having a disruptive influence on the subjects' attempts to create a link between the words of each contrast pair.

Mean response latencies were also longer for two versus one contrasts, although the effect did not reach significance, $F(1, 9) = 2.41, p < .15$. The nature of the relationship between the two conditions for this variable is clouded by a great deal of response variability, a factor to be addressed in the General Discussion. The standard deviation averaged across the four conditions was 260 msec. The boundary variable produced a nonsignificant result, $F(1, 9) = .47$. In general, the mean effects for response latency are in direct conflict with the position that speakers delay decisions about words that are contrasted in a second clause.

EXPERIMENT 2: CONTRASTED PROFESSIONS

A second experiment was conducted to test the generality of the previous results for a situation in which the contrasted words were nouns denoting related professions rather than proper names. Professions permitted the generality of the previous results to be determined for sentences containing contrasted words that bear a natural semantic relationship to one another.

The experiment included 12 base sentences, very similar to those of the previous experiment but replacing proper names with related professional roles.

TWO WORDS CONTRASTED
EARLY BOUNDARY
T   I jog with the pitcher, and the umpire and Pete work out in the gym.
B   I jog with the mason, and the plumber and Pete work out in the gym.
LATE BOUNDARY
T   I jog with the pitcher and the umpire, and Pete works out in the gym.
B   I jog with the mason and the plumber, and Pete works out in the gym.
ONE WORD CONTRASTED
EARLY BOUNDARY
T   I jog with the pitcher, and the actor and Pete work out in the gym.
B   I jog with the mason, and the actor and Pete work out in the gym.
LATE BOUNDARY
T   I jog with the pitcher and the actor, and Pete works out in the gym.
B   I jog with the mason and the actor, and Pete works out in the gym.

For single-word contrasts, the second noncontrasted noun was unrelated to the contrasted nouns.

Ten speakers, none of whom participated in the previous experiment, were presented the task. In an attempt to restrict variability, subjects were told to memorize both sentences of a pair equally well.

The analysis of these data was identical to that of Experiment 1. The results are shown in Fig. 31.4, depicting the mean memorization and reaction times. As in the previous experiment, both memorization times and response latencies were substantially longer (5 sec and 69 msec, respectively) when the sentences contained two versus one contrasted words, and, in this study, the effects were statistically significant for both memorization times, $F(1, 9) = 15.89$, $p < .005$, and response latencies, $F(1, 9) = 6.54$, $p < .05$. The memory difference was

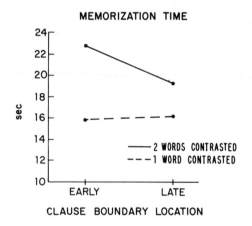

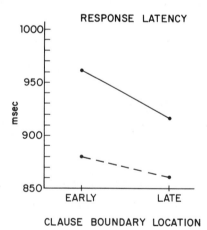

FIG. 31.4.   Mean memorization time and response latency, Experiment 2.

consistent across sentences, with 22 out of the 24 cases showing the same direction of effect. The response latency data showed more variability across sentences, with 15 of the 24 cases in the same direction. Thus, when the two contrasted words denote related professional roles, speakers apparently preplan both words prior to initiating speech. The standard deviation for response latency remained high, however, averaging 220 msec. Both memorization times and reaction times were longer when the two contrasted words straddled the clause boundary, although this effect was significant only for the memorization times, $F(1, 9) = 8.71$, $p < .05$, paralleling the previous experiment. Finally, a significant interaction was obtained for the memorization times (number of words contrasted $\times$ boundary location, $F(1, 9) = 9.15$, $p < .05$. This interaction is attributable to the fact that the difference between early versus late boundaries was confined to the case involving two-word contrasts. As in the case of Experiment 1, the clause boundary might have hindered memorization of the contrasted pairs here.

GENERAL DISCUSSION

The studies presented in this chapter represent a first attempt to use a response latency paradigm to examine the planning of sentences that are derived from a complex memory representation. The fact that memorization time was found to increase with the number of contrasted words suggests that subjects have an efficient means for representing similar sentences containing variable arguments, a means not requiring duplicate storage of material common to both sentences. The fact that response latencies also increased with the number of contrasted words in Experiment 2 strongly suggests that some decisions about word identity are made in the prearticulation interval and that such decisions are not delayed until a clause boundary has been reached during speech production. Such prearticulation decisions about the content of an utterance seem to be an important aspect of natural communication, not addressable by paradigms in which subjects memorize sentences out of context.

It is important to note that, although these results suggest that the contrasted words are processed in some way during the prearticulation interval, these results do not imply that all the material held in common between the phrase is likewise processed during this interval. It is possible that contrastive words alone are accessed but are not ordered with respect to common material at this early stage. Such prearticulation planning may tap the *functional* level of representation described by Garrett (1975). Drawing on data from speech errors, Garrett suggested that planning of functional relationships between words may operate independently from the planning of their serial order.

Given the potential utility of the choice reaction-time technique, it seems important to consider the extreme variability plaguing the response latency data.

A number of factors are likely to contribute to the variability. First, because the subject is presented with only two alternatives to memorize, there is a strong possibility that one of the possible alternatives is anticipated. (However, inspection of the data from both experiments reported here did not reveal a clearly bimodal distribution of responses.) When subjects anticipate the correct choice, then critical planning operations may occur before the interval that is being measured. One possible way to deal with this problem is to bias the experiment so that the "top" cue is much more likely to be presented to the subject. Under such conditions, subjects would be much less likely to anticipate the bottom response, and planning operations might be revealed more consistently for trials on which these bottom phrases are selected. Another factor possibly contributing to variability is that subjects might delay certain planning operations until mid-sentence (Cooper & Paccia-Cooper, 1980). Further research in which both response latency and mid-sentence pausing are studied may reveal that various conditions bias subjects to adopt either a preplanning or a mid-sentence planning strategy. A third possibility is that increased practice and a greater premium on fast responses may reduce the variability found in these studies, though it will be important to ensure that such practices do not encourage the use of unnatural strategies and processing operations.

The planning operations tapped by this procedure may be akin to operations observed in studies of pausing in spontaneous speech. Both Butterworth (1975, 1980) and Beattie (1977) have observed that speakers tend to produce speech in cycles such that a period of speech containing numerous long pauses is followed by a period containing only short pauses. It seems likely that decisions about content such as those made in the present experiments would be made during the planning phases described by these researchers. It is of particular interest that the "nonplanning" phases described by them often encompass more than one sentence. These data and our own results provide independent support for planning operations that cross clause boundaries.

Another important question involves the nature of the representation of the sentences in memory. Ehrlich and Cooper (submitted for publication) have suggested that two related messages might be represented by a linked structure encompassing both sets of alternative words. Upon receiving the cue, subjects might prime the appropriate nodes within the structure, and these primed nodes could act to guide production. Morton (1970) has suggested that the words of an utterance are loaded into a response buffer that might have capacity limitations. This response buffer might actually be created via the pattern of activation of the nodes within the linked memory buffer. Alternatively, a response buffer might simply contain the information of the sentence that is known in advance, with some kind of place holders for the contrasted words that would be stored independently. The set of contrasted words could actually be represented as primed items in the standard lexicon. Either of the descriptions given above is consistent with the introspection that there is a strong tendency to confuse the members of each pair when relational links are not available. If the sentences are stored in a linked structure, selection of the correct pairs of contrasted words would require an external link to be created between the members of a pair. If the contrasts are stored independently within the standard lexicon, search for those words might be slower if relational links between semantically related items are not available.

When longer sentences are to be spoken, the content of the response buffer (or the number of activated nodes) may be limited to the first part of a sentence. It was sometimes observed that subjects would forget the end of a sentence or produce the ending from a previous sentence after giving the correct contrasting pairs. This finding is consistent with the idea that subjects needed to reload the response buffer and that pointers to the new contents of the buffer were sometimes either lost or confused. Response latencies might also reflect the time to alter representations of sentences that have not yet been loaded into a limited capacity buffer if the cue designating the correct response is given far in advance of the time when the contrasted item is spoken. These and other possible variants in the structure of short-term memory representation and planning procedures are in need of further investigation.

ACKNOWLEDGMENTS

This work was supported by NIH Grant NS-15059. We thank Phil Barnard, David Green, and two anonymous reviewers for their comments on an earlier version of the manuscript. We also thank Scott Bradner and the Computer Based Laboratory at Harvard for facilities and programming and Trude Huber for help in running subjects and providing suggestions.

REFERENCES

Beattie, G. W. The dynamics of interruption and the filled pause. *British Journal of Clinical Psychology,* 1977, *16,* 283-284.

Butterworth, B. L. Hesitation and semantic planning in speech. *Journal of Psycholinguistic Research,* 1975, *4,* 75-87.

Butterworth, B. L. Evidence from pauses in speech. In B. Butterworth (Ed.), *Language production* (Vol. 1): *Speech and talk.* New York: Academic Press, 1980.

Cooper, W. E., & Paccia-Cooper, J. *Syntax and speech.* Cambridge, Mass.: Harvard University Press, 1980.

Drewnowski, A. Attributes and priorities in short-term recall: A new model of memory span. *Journal of Experimental Psychology: General,* 1980, *109,* 208-250.

Ehrlich, S. F., & Cooper, W. E. Memory determinants of response latency to produce speech. Manuscript submitted for publication.

Garrett, M. F. The analysis of sentence production. In G. Bower (Ed.), *Advances in learning theory and motivation* (Vol. 9). New York: Academic Press, 1975.

Huggins, A. W. F. A facility for studying perception of timing in natural speech. *Quarterly Progress Report of the MIT Research Laboratory of Electronics,* 1969, *95,* 81–83.

Johnson, N. F. On the relationship between sentence structure and the latency in generating the sentence. *Journal of Verbal Learning and Verbal Behavior,* 1966, *5,* 375–380.

Morton, J. A functional model for memory. In D. A. Norman (Ed.), *Models of human memory.* New York: Academic Press, 1970.

Shattuck-Hufnagel, S. Speech errors as evidence for a serial-ordering mechanism in sentence production. In W. E. Cooper & E. C. T. Walker (Eds.), *Sentence processing: Psycholinguistic studies presented to Merrill Garrett.* Hillsdale, N.J.: Lawrence Erlbaum Associates, 1979.

Sternberg, S. Memory-scanning: Mental processes revealed by reaction-time experiments. *American Scientist,* 1969, *57,* 421–457.

Sternberg, S., Monsell, S., Knoll, R. L., & Wright, C. E. The latency and duration of rapid movement sequences: Comparisons of speech and typewriting. In G. Stelmach (Ed.), *Information processing in motor control and learning.* New York: Academic Press, 1978.

Tannenbaum, P. H. & Williams, F. Generation of active and passive sentences as a function of subject or object focus. *Journal of Verbal Learning and Verbal Behavior,* 1968, *7,* 246–250.

IX STRESS AND AGING

32

Cognitive Psychology Needs Models for Changes in Performance with Old Age

Patrick Rabbitt
Department of Experimental Psychology
University of Oxford
Oxford, England

ABSTRACT

A very large literature describes applications of models and paradigms from human experimental psychology to the study of performance changes in old age. These experiments have yielded disappointing data. This is partly because gerontologists and clinicians trained in psychometric techniques rather than in experimental psychology have failed to recognize incompatibilities between these two research methodologies. More interestingly it is because models developed in cognitive psychology have failed to offer useful descriptions of change and of individual differences. Some drawbacks of current models are discussed and contrasted with the advantages of control system models that describe how people improve with practice, adjust to changes in task demands, and circumvent limitations to the efficiency of their perceptual discrimination and control of responses. Some recent experiments comparing efficiency of control in young and elderly people are briefly discussed.

INTRODUCTION

Since Galton (1885) published data collected in his anthropometric laboratory at the Wembley International Health Exhibition, there have been many studies of changes in performance in old age. The most comprehensive and insightful is Welford's (1958) account of the work of the Nuffield Unit for Research into Problems of Aging at Cambridge, U.K., between 1946 and 1956. Much of the work published over the last 50 years has been reviewed in two excellent hand-

555

books (Birren, 1959; Birren & Schaie, 1977), in collections of papers and in symposium proceedings (Hoffmeister & Muller, 1979; Talland, 1968; Tibbets & Donahue, 1962; Welford & Birren, 1965), in textbooks (Botwinick, 1967, 1973; Bromley, 1966), and in the *Annual Review of Psychology* (Baltes, Reese, & Lipsitt, 1980; Botwinick, 1970; Chown & Heron, 1966; Schaie & Gribbin, 1975).

It is painful to have to add that investigators trained in cognitive psychology will find this literature very salutary. One reason is that persistent methodological errors have flawed most age comparisons. Furthermore, studies of age changes have been confused by misapplications of models and techniques borrowed from psychometrics. But, most importantly, conceptual failures of human experimental gerontology reflect and reveal critical conceptual weaknesses in mainstream human experimental psychology. Models for human cognition and performance have been derived from experiments on small groups of young people highly selected for intelligence and fitness, where performance has typically been sampled at a single point, after little practice. Consequently our models describe static systems in some arbitrary "steady state" but do not explain differences between individuals nor change within an individual. They do not tell us why people perform more skillfully as they grow up, or as they are practiced, nor what makes them less skillful when they suffer from diseases like schizophrenia, or when they grow old.

In this chapter, rather than cataloging experiments that have already been comprehensively reviewed, we shall consider the methodological and conceptual difficulties that pervade research in aging. Because a list of these problems would otherwise be merely tetchy and unhelpful, we close with a brief account of recent experiments that attempt to provide bases for models for change—including models for changes accompanying old age.

SOME PERSISTENT METHODOLOGICAL ERRORS IN THE STUDY OF AGE DIFFERENCES

The Random Accumulation of Isolated Performance Differences

A survey of the gerontological literature immediately suggests that most studies are simply replications of briefly fashionable experimental paradigms on old and young subjects. The models from which these paradigms are derived are seldom discussed and, in any case, are usually not sufficiently developed to permit interpretation of the "age differences" that are invariably found. This "effect bagging" is a wasteful research strategy. It might only be justified on the assumption that we ought to be engaged in the compilation of an "Universal Engineering Handbook of Human Performance":—i.e., some vast accumulation of normative performance data for people of all ages and conditions on all possible experimental tasks, surely a sterile and time-wasting exercise of no theoretical value. No experimental paradigm can be said to be "theoretically neutral," and unless we relate our experimental comparisons to clearly specifiable models of performance and, in particular, of performance *change,* we deceive ourselves and waste our time.

Models and Experimental Paradigms in Cognitive Psychology Are frequently Misunderstood by those Investigating Individual Differences

Cognitive psychologists pay lip service to the need for investigating individual differences. In fact most investigations of individual differences have been initiated by clinicians and gerontologists untrained in human experimental psychology. Inevitably performance models and the paradigms derived from them have been misunderstood and misapplied. Trivial errors in the conduct and design of experiments or in the analyses of results are frequent. More interesting confusions arise when investigators develop explicit models based on clinical experience and then search the human performance literature for paradigms with which to test them. The most widely quoted paradigms are usually precisely those which require the most complex methodological and theoretical caveats in application. The history of misunderstandings of Broadbent's (1958) filter model for selective attention, leading to widespread misinterpretation of the results of dichotic listening tasks in schizophrenia, provides a connoisseur's example of this. Particularly intelligent and sophisticated misunderstandings of the performance literature by Broen and Storms (1964) and of signal detection theory by Broen and Nakamura (1972) also repay inspection.

Clinicians may be pardoned for believing that paradigms quoted in the human performance literature are "standardized." In fact, experiments are seldom replicated and each investigator seems obliged to demonstrate trivial creativity by making minor, unexplained emendations to conditions, by using yet another, arbitrary, level of practice or by cryptically adding yet another dependent variable. Faced with this muddle, clinicians either abandon laboratory investigations or falsely infer that paradigms in common use are so robust that no modification in their administration can affect results. Both these reactions hinder progress.

Radical Methodological Confusions Occur Because Aging Is Mistaken To Be a Single, Unitary Process that May Be Directly Equated with the Simple Passage of Time

Typical experiments made to examine individual differences compare target and control groups of 15 to 30 people. Helpful suggestions have been made on how the validity of such comparisons may be improved (Baltes, 1968; Baltes & Willis, 1979; Schaie, 1965, 1977). But a remaining, pervasive difficulty is that such comparisons assume that target populations such as those of "schizo-phrenics," "depressives," or "old people" are so homogeneous that samples of 15 to 30 individuals are representative. This is clearly not the case.

The neurobiology of aging is not well understood but we know that people may "age" at different rates and may exhibit a variety of different syndromes of aging associated with different pathologies. Performance measures support this picture of increased *diversity* in elderly populations. For example, the present author tested 1800 people on reaction time and memory tasks. Mean scores for cross-sectional decade samples declined by 20% from age 50 to age 80+. However intersubject variance increased by 160% over the same range.

Thus there may be several different *patterns* of aging, related to various neurophysiological changes or even associated with particular social and environmental factors. The importance of large, longitudinal studies has been underestimated. Only such studies can show whether age changes are continuous, as steadily falling averages for group decade samples may at first suggest, or whether changes are sudden and discrete, occurring at different ages for different individuals and merely becoming more *probable* as sample age increases. Only such studies can reveal whether we can identify different *patterns* of aging and whether different processes, with different aetiologies, affect performance in different ways.

THE UNFORTUNATE LEGACY OF PSYCHOMETRICS

Clinicians and gerontologists are usually more familiar with psychometric test batteries than they are with other measures of human performance. They have tended to use the human experimental literature as a source of paradigms that can be used as individual "tests" in "batteries" to obtain "performance profiles." These attempts run into several difficulties.

Paradigms in Human Experimental Psychology Are Extremely Specific

Paradigms developed in human experimental psychology are developed to test particular functional models of particular processes. No single paradigm provides a unique index of anything so global as "short-term memory efficiency," "information processing," or "response speed" because paradigms are designed precisely to decompose such global terms.

What is worse, human experimental psychologists have developed great cunning in testing their models, minimizing variance by selecting groups of subjects who show as little individual variation as possible, designing tests which are as insensitive as possible to any residual individual differences, and using arbitrary levels of practice at which intersubject variance is minimized. These achievements are incompatible with the requirements for well-constructed psychometric tests that should be sensitive to individual differences and should simultaneously measure as many components of an individual skill as possible.

Different Tests of Attention and Performance Yield Scores that Cannot Be Validly Compared

The comparison of two or more indices obtained from different tasks is hazardous because it requires a rationale for comparing relative decrements [e.g., X-msec change in choice reaction time (CRT) with $Y\%$ change in digit span]. The tests we use must be of equal sensitivity. Even if the ingenious normalization and standardization procedures suggested by Chapman and Chapman (1973a, 1973b) are adopted (and they never have been), one cannot be sure that any two tests will show equal sensitivity over their entire range. Two indices may be significantly correlated only because of independent, nonlinear relationships with a third. For example, CRT and digit span may positively correlate over part of a range because rehearsal rate may vary with CRT, and digit span is influenced by rehearsal rate. But such associations will disappear if unrehearsable material is presented or if rehearsal is inhibited by secondary tasks, by experimental instructions, or by a subject's choice of strategy.

Such mediated relationships between indices may also conceal hysteresis effects where one performance index P may change in step with another index Q, until a critical point at which any slight change in Q is accompanied by a sudden, catastrophic change in P. This is possible when both P and Q are affected by some third factor. For example, both complex tracking and choice reaction time may covary over a wide range of arousal. But at very high arousal levels performance at the more difficult task may show a sudden, sharp decline, while the simpler task remains unimpaired.

The problem is, unless we clearly understand functional relationships, we cannot use psychometric procedures to boot-strap ourselves into an understanding of individual differences in performance.

Psychometric Tests Do Not Necessarily Assume, nor Allow, Functional Models for Performance

Cognitive psychologists seldom replicate their paradigms on large, varied groups of subjects and almost never validate them against skilled performance in everyday life. They hope to frame abstract models for functional processes but ignore the fact that performance is never static, but continually changes and differs very widely between individuals. Psychometricians, on the other hand, are concerned to describe *change* and to define individual *differences*. This has forced them to be scrupulous about test validation and reliability. But they show curiously little interest or insight into the *reasons* for the correlations between the measures they use. It sometimes seems from the psychometric literature that if pitch of nose blowing had been shown to correlate highly with arithmetical ability an entire technology for design, validation, administration and interpretation of nose blowing tests would have burgeoned. Factor analyses would have been made to discover loadings of major nasal harmonics with components of arithmetical skill. There would be a flourishing "Journal of Rhinological Resonance," countless PhD theses would be under way, the corridors of Departments of Education would reverberate with trumpeting demonstrations, Albert Einstein's nasal acoustic spectrum would be familiar in elementary textbooks, and a subsection of the Piaget Institute would have been lavishly funded to investigate "sinus decalage." Moreover all such enterprises would prosper in the complete absence of any predictive causal explanation of the relationships on which they all depend.

Recently investigators have begun to try to relate psychometric theory and test performance to underlying functional processes.

Jensen (in press) claims negative correlations between IQ scores and mean correct RT. He seems to argue that RT is a sensitive measure of the efficiency of CNS units such as synapses and neurones, so that we might expect relationships between simple and complex performance measures. In the gerontological literature, Birren, Woods, and Williams (1979) have also argued that elderly people are relatively slower at difficult than at easy CRT tasks because neural transmission time may increase with age. Because people also perform worse on IQ tests as they grow older, this would also lead to a negative correlation between RT and IQ across large populations that might be taken to support Jensen's idea.

However, Jensen's (in press) experiments provoke severe methodological criticisms. Moreover, overall mean RT scores as used by Jensen (in press) and Birren et al. (1979) tell us little about individual differences. In these studies all subjects have had little practice or, when practiced, have shown surprisingly little change in performance. Rabbitt and Vyas (Rabbitt, 1980) showed not only that differences between young and old subjects may vanish with practice but also that interactions between age and task complexity predicted from simple neural lag hypotheses may also disappear.

Horn (in press) uses factor analyses of test batteries for "fluid" and "crystallized" intelligence to derive descriptive functional models of age changes, but attention and performance measures that he attempts to relate to standard intelligence tests seem arbitrary, and interpretation of indices derived from them is difficult. For example, a dichotic listening task is used to measure efficiency of "selective attention," though work by Caird (1966) and Inglis and Caird (1963) has shown that *selection* between concurrent strings of digits may not be impaired by age though *memory,* for unshadowed strings can fall off sharply. A visual search task developed by Rabbitt (1964) is included as a general test of "information-processing ability" though the elderly are known to improve with practice more than, and in different ways from, the young (Rabbitt, 1968a). We may ask whether global distinctions between "fluid" and "crystallized" skills are really useful when we try to capture the complex functional changes evident even in apparently trivially easy performance tasks.

Hunt (in press) has adopted a more molecular approach, analyzing particular subclasses of well-validated and reliable IQ test problems both in terms of abstract computer simulative procedures (Hunt, 1974; Hunt, Mavin, & Stone, 1973) and in terms of functional models developed in cognitive psychology (Hunt, in press; Shepherd & Metzler, 1971). In contrast to Horn's (in press) global approach, this seems a promising way to relate two very disparate fields of research.

Much attention has rightly been paid to the work of R. Sternberg (1977a, 1977b, in press), who pioneered the "componential analysis" of analogical reasoning tasks, syllogism solution, and other classes of problems used in IQ tests. R. Sternberg uses linear regression equations to obtain estimates of the relative proportions of total solution times consumed by each of a series of hypothetical, successive independent processes.

A general objection is that the work of Hunt (in press) and R. Sternberg (in press) is based on the convenient assumption that human information processing is carried on by linear, independent sequential processes (LISPS). It will be argued in the following that this assumption is questionable and has retarded progress in cognitive psychology.

FAILURES OF COGNITIVE PSYCHOLOGY TO DESCRIBE CHANGES IN HUMAN PERFORMANCE

Saccuzzo (1977) reviewed experiments in which paradigms drawn from cognitive psychology were used to test performance of normal young adults, elderly people, and schizophrenics. He points out that in all cases old people and schizophrenics show similar patterns of deficits. The present author came to the same conclusion after reviewing more than 300 such studies. It would surely be naive to conclude from this that aging and schizophrenia are functionally similar conditions. It rather seems that paradigms developed in human experimental psychology are poor measures of individual differences. Some reasons for this have already been discussed. The principal limitation seems to be that we have no models for change.

The CRT literature exemplifies this. Signal discriminability, variations in signal and response entropy, stimulus–response compatibility, and repetition and sequential effects may each account for up to 20% of the variance in tasks specially designed to study them. A vast literature has grown up around the effects of these variables and all our models are designed to discuss them. Yet in all experiments practice effects may reduce CRT by up to 60% and can account for 50% or more of the total variance in particular cases. More to the point, any of the variables that our models discuss may have its effects reduced or entirely abolished by practice (Duncan, 1976; Kristoffersen, 1977; Mowbray & Rhoades, 1959; Rabbitt, 1968c; Rabbitt, Cumming, & Vyas, 1979). Models by Crossman (1959) and recently by Newell and Rosenbloom (1980) describe the overall shape of practice functions in CRT experiments but do not specify particular functional alterations that may produce these changes. Careful experiments have been made to compare differences in CRTs between young and elderly people, but arbitrary levels of practice have been chosen and interactions of main effects with practice have not been examined. Yet the effects of age, and interactions of age with signal and response entropy, may be greatly reduced or entirely eliminated by only moderate practice (Rabbitt, 1980).

In my view our current models are restricted by a tacit assumption that discriminations between signals and consequent choices between responses always involve a linear sequence of independent successive processes (LISPS) (Rabbitt, 1979a, 1980, in press-a).

It is arguable that F. C. Donders (1868) put forward the first LISP model in psychology but that S. Sternberg (1969) was the first to state clearly the assumptions such models involve, to define the limited conditions under which they are plausible, and to test these assumptions elegantly in relation to his memory scanning paradigm. Rabbitt (1979a, pp. 124–129) has argued that failures to recognize these assumptions and limitations of applicability have weakened the conclusions that can be drawn from many empirical and theoretical studies (Baddeley, 1968; Broadbent, 1971; Rabbitt, Clancy, & Vyas, 1969; Woodhead, 1964; among others).

The main difficulty with LISP models is that they represent passive systems that respond to events as they occur rather than active systems that monitor and use feedback to control and optimize performance. We now know that even in very simple tasks, such as simple RT or easy serial CRT tasks, subjects exercise active control by monitoring feedback. As we shall see, once we postulate such active control, the operations of component subprocesses cannot be held to be independent from each other as LISP models demand.

In CRT tasks, subjects actively control their performance to tradeoff speed and accuracy, maximizing either as required (Pachella & Fisher, 1969; Pachella & Pew, 1968; Pew, 1969; Rabbitt & Vyas, 1970; Schouten & Bekker, 1967; Wickelgren, 1977). On a LISP model a person can only do this in two ways. He may regulate the total time spent on all successive transactions. In this case, independent component processes will compete for time and cannot be mutually independent since they jostle for a common resource. Alternatively a person may regulate overall speed and accuracy by controlling the speed and accuracy of each component process independently. To do this he must be able to assess the speed–error tradeoff for each process independently. He must not merely know when he makes errors in the cumulative execution of all processes but must know which particular process has failed because it has not had enough time allocated to it. We know that people can regulate their performance by detecting their errors and that they can detect perceptual errors as well as errors of response execution (Rabbitt, 1966a, 1966b; 1968b; Rabbitt, Cumming, & Vyas, 1978; Rabbitt & Vyas, 1970; in press-b). But there is yet no evidence that they know *why* each error occurs.

One could test this by running S. Sternberg's (1966, 1967, 1969) memory search paradigm to look at changes in overall mean RTs and changes in mean error RTs as functions of increasing target set size. Errors might occur in memory search or in other processes. Errors in memory search would probably affect the slope of error RT functions, while errors in other processes affected the intercepts of error RT functions. Those errors which fell on a function parallel to the correct RT function might be assumed not to be errors of memory search. Errors which fell on a function divergent from the correct RT function might be assumed to be memory search errors.

This would still be inadequate because it is likely that errors would be heterogeneous, some reflecting failures in one process, some in another, and some (no doubt) in both. It would then be necessary to test whether these classes of errors were equally detectable by the subject. This would involve a post hoc classification of errors into those that fell within confidence limits of an error function parallel to the correct RT function and those that fell within confidence limits of other functions divergent from the correct RT function. Differences in the probability of detection of these subclasses of errors might suggest answers to our question. Thus, in principle, decompositional analyses of errors are possible, though as is evident they would be very laborious and based on dubious methodological and logical assumptions.

But, even so, we would still have to ask whether subjects accept the same speed–error tradeoff risks and benefits for completion of each individual process or not. If they did not, this would indeed be a rigorous demonstration of independence of processes. But if they turned out to use the same cost and benefit analyses for all subprocesses, an assumption of complete independence of processes would again be hard to justify. No evidence to decide this question is yet available.

CONTROL SYSTEM MODELS ARE DESIGNED TO DESCRIBE CHANGE

In contrast to such a passive, LISP model, let us consider how people of various ages actually do control their speed and accuracy during CRT tasks.

Experiments and a Model for Changes in CRT with Practice and in Old Age

Rabbitt (1979a, 1980, in press-a) and Rabbitt and Vyas (1970) have pointed out that subjects in CRT tasks change their performance with practice to obey the extremely ambiguous experimental instruction "respond as fast and as accurately as you can.'' To do this they must first discover, and then observe, the RT ranges over which speed trades off against errors. Thus they must first respond fast enough to actually make errors and then delicately vary their response speed so as to precisely track an RT band just slower than the dangerous RT band at which errors are likely to occur. They must also know when they have made unnecessarily *slow* responses so that they can respond faster and reduce their overall mean RTs as instructed.

Thus overall mean RTs and percentages of errors are quite inadequate performance indices in CRT tasks. We need to know also the intercepts and slopes of speed–error tradeoff functions (SETOFs), the extent to which subjects risk errors by allowing their RT distributions to transgress their SETOFs, the accuracy with which they detect their errors, the extent to which they can reduce the positive skews of their RT distributions by avoiding unnecessarily slow responses and the precision with which they can vary RT from trial to trial so as to track optimal RT bands. Rabbitt (1979a) has discussed how the different patterns of errors and slow responses observed in serial RT tasks under stress by heat, alcohol, and loss of sleep (Broadbent, 1971; Wilkinson, 1959) make better sense when these indices are considered. Rabbitt (1979b) found that although old people have slower mean correct RTs than the young, mean error RTs do not slow with age, nor do numbers of errors always increase. The old show much greater positive skew to their RT distributions than the young. Their ability to detect errors is apparently unimpaired. Their computed SETOFs are only slightly slower. After other possibilities have been considered it seems that a main cause of age decrements in CRT is that the old cannot precisely track and adjust RTs to their SETOFs so as to optimize speed and accuracy. When they try to respond slightly faster they overshoot their SETOFs and make relatively fast errors. When they try to go a little slower they produce very long RTs, increase RT skew, and slow their mean RTs.

Note that this is a model for change. It describes how people improve with practice, why rates and patterns of improvement are different in old and young people, and what particular factors change with age. These advantages have come about because we have assumed that even in very simple tasks human beings do not behave as passive LISP systems but as active, self-regulating systems. Self-regulating systems must be able to set themselves goal states for a particular task, to monitor and adjust their performance to conform to these goal states, and to allow for drift in their own performance parameters. Unlike LISP systems that can only improve performance with practice by carrying out the same operations, in the same sequence, ever faster and more efficiently, self-regulating systems can learn new and better ways to do things and can accommodate to changes, for better or worse, in the efficiency of their own parameters.

Systems will fail to optimize when they can no longer accurately monitor, detect changes in, or adjust output to parameters set by task demands. This may happen when task demands become more severe or when the system's internal limitations change so that demands can no longer be met. In this case, failure may not represent a complete cessation of function but will rather be seen as divergence from optimality of function. In some cases systems may program around task demands, adjusting the nature of control so as to circumvent system limitations.

Such models allow us to ask how people improve their performance with practice or why they cease to be able to perform a task as well as they once did. We can further distinguish between changes in particular parameters of control (e.g., shifts of SETOF or accuracy of error detection) and changes in the overall control process (interpreting experimental instructions to set a goal state and managing use of feedback and adjustment of response speed in relation to that goal state). We can also consider the total range of strategies which a control system may actively test out before selecting the best. Finally we may discuss how the central control process acquires and stores information necessary to develop and select among such strategies.

These points may be clarified by concrete examples that illustrate how control of selective attention changes with age.

The Distinction between Acquiring, and Using, Probabilistic Information to Improve Control of Attention

Learning Where to Look.   Senders, Elkind, Grignetti, and Smallwood (1964), Senders (1977), and Moray (1976) show how young people can actively change their scanning of signal sources to approximate to theoretically optimal search strategies. Sanford and Maule (1971, 1973a, 1973b) have compared young and elderly people on simulated industrial process control tasks in which they have to interrogate up to three "locations" to detect "signals." Absolute and conditional probabilities of signals differ between locations and young people rapidly learn these differences and use them to develop optimal search strategies. Elderly people can also accurately *describe* variations in signal probability across locations but appear not to *use* this information to guide their interrogations.

Rabbitt (1979c) reports a visual search experiment in which targets occurred more often at some display locations than others. Young subjects learned this fact and made use of it to guide their visual scans of displays, detecting targets most rapidly at frequent locations. Elderly people learned and accurately *described* the three probable target locations in correct rank order but apparently could not use this information to guide search, because they found targets no faster at these locations than at others.

Guiding Search by Landmarks.   In an unfamiliar city center I may locate banks and post offices because experience has taught me that they will be near some structures and not others.

Rabbitt, Corcoran, and Vyas (1980) attempted to simulate such tacit knowledge of unfamiliar scenes by teaching subjects to scan displays in which clusters

Table 32.1

	Target among "Landmarks"	Target not among "Landmarks"
Young people	879 msec ($\sigma = 76$)	964 msec ($\sigma = 84$)
Elderly people	1078 msec ($\sigma = 114$)	1082 msec ($\sigma = 121$)

of particular background letters were likely to occur adjacent to target items. Targets thus were frequently, but not invariably, to be found among particular "neighbors." Young subjects used these constraints to locate targets more rapidly among probable than improbable "neighbors." Elderly subjects learned, and could list, probable "neighbors" but apparently could not use this information to guide their search (see Table 32.1).

Learning a Scanning Pattern. People learn to interrogate the visual world efficiently by making appropriate patterns of eye movements. Familiar objects or scenes are interrogated by characteristic, efficient, learned scanning patterns (Gippenreiter, 1978; Yarbus, 1968).

Rabbitt, Bishop, and Vyas (1980) examined how people learn efficient scanning patterns in visual search by training subjects to search for target letters among 20 to 30 letters that always appeared on the same spatial locations on a computer VDU. This familiar pattern of locations gave no clue as to whether or not a target was present or where the target might be. Subjects might simply use the familiar patterns to guide search.

Other displays had variable patterns in which display locations changed from trial to trial during a run. Familiar pattern displays occurred on 50% of trials during a run, interspersed in random order among variable pattern displays.

Young subjects found targets faster on familiar pattern displays, suggesting that they learned and used characteristic, efficient search patterns. This was confirmed by stability of rank order of target detection times across display locations. Elderly subjects found targets no faster on familiar pattern than on variable pattern displays (see Table 32.2) and their target detection times show

Table 32.2

	Times to Scan Familiar, Repeated Displays	Times to Scan Novel, Nonrecurrent Displays
Young people		
Target present	963 msec ($\sigma = 89$)	1063 msec ($\sigma = 91$)
Target absent	1143 msec ($\sigma = 94$)	1204 msec ($\sigma = 106$)
Elderly people		
Target present	1204 msec ($\sigma = 196$)	1219 msec ($\sigma = 201$)
Target absent	1421 msec ($\sigma = 207$)	1432 msec ($\sigma = 218$)

no consistent ordering across display locations. Elderly people recognize that some display patterns recur. They are even able to reproduce these display patterns quite accurately on squared paper; but again there is a gap between the *possession* of useful information and its *use* in the exercise of active control.

Basing Control on Immediately Past Events

We have seen how people can detect statistical regularities in a task and hold this information in long-term memory to guide their search. But in real life events change rapidly and, from moment to moment, decisions on what to do next must be based on what has just happened. In this case the information necessary for momentary control is a sample of the immediate past.

The Samples of the Immediate Past on which Momentary Expectancies Depend. Rabbitt and Vyas (in press-a) compared young and old people on a serial self-paced choice response task in which signals occurred with different probabilities. Young subjects recognized these differences and responded faster to the most frequent signals. Elderly subjects were not helped to the same extent. Rabbitt and Vyas analyzed their data to discover how long a series of previous signals and responses affected the RT on any current trial. Earlier studies by Remington (1969) and Kirby (1972) had shown that normal young adults are affected, on any one trial N, by the precise nature of the sequence of $N-3$ to $N-10$ responses that they had just made. Rabbitt and Vyas' young subjects showed sequential dependencies as far back as N-3, but their elderly subjects showed no sequential dependencies beyond N-1. This explains why elderly people were apparently less sensitive to the presence of sequential bias than the young. The precision with which differences in event probability can be detected varies directly with the square root of the sample of events on which a decision is based. Thus young people, acting on a larger event sample, could be more sensitive discriminators of absolute differences in signal probability than the old, who apparently based their judgments on shorter samples.

It is interesting that these assumptions lead to the counter-intuitive prediction that if a sudden, unheralded change in bias actually occurs young people may, at first, regard it as a random perturbation in event probability and take some time to decide that there has been a "real" shift. The elderly will treat brief, random local perturbations in signal probability as actual changes in bias but will also respond more rapidly when "real" changes in bias occur. Earlier results by Griew (1962) may now be taken to show that this is precisely what happens. Griew's young and elderly subjects were set to track abrupt changes in signal bias that occurred at random intervals during a serial CRT task. Elderly subjects, apparently, detected these changes more rapidly than the young.

Note that the young cannot be considered to be at a disadvantage because they *can* use longer samples of previous events to guide and update their monetary expectations. Because they *can* take longer samples they also can detect subtle changes in bias that the old cannot recognize. With appropriate incentives, or different experimental instructions, they may curtail their sample sizes if necessary. They would then mistakenly respond to local random perturbations but would also detect sudden real changes as rapidly as the elderly. Greater sample size simply means potential for greater *variability* of sample size, leaving the young with options that the old have lost.

Learning What To Look for Next.   Visual search in everyday life is usually part of a complex, running transaction with the environment in which a person who has found one thing must immediately begin to search for something else. In this case he may be thought to have a linear "program" of instructions in his long-term memory and to be able to access this program for conditional instructions of the type "find A, then look for B, find B, then look for C, etc." Rabbitt and Vyas (1980) have compared tasks in which subjects are either instructed to search simultaneously for any of the letters A, B, C, D, E, F, G, or H or to search first only for A and, having found it, for B and then for C, etc. Young people perform the second task more rapidly than the first, and, after practice, seldom make mistakes. Elderly people find the serial search task very difficult. They are relatively slow and continually make mistakes because they apparently forget what they are looking for (see Table 32.3). It becomes more difficult for both young and old people to follow such linear programs when the programs are complicated by the addition of repetitive items or of a complex "loop structure" (Rabbitt, in press-b, in press-c).

Such tasks illustrate one, very common, type of control process that people use to guide themselves through their everyday lives. They may develop, and have available in long-term memory, "programs" that can guide them through series of contingencies. But to use these programs correctly they must access them at a precise point when each contingency occurs. To do this they must retain, and constantly update, information about what they have just done in working memory (Baddeley & Hitch, 1974). Failures in control can occur because of loss of working memory capacity, failures of efficient indexing of the

Table 32.3
Twenty Young People (Aged 18 to 30 Years)
and Twenty Elderly People (Aged 70 to 76 Years) Matched for Verbal IQ Scores,
Searched Displays of Eight Letters to Locate Any One of Eight Targets
or Eight Different Targets in Turn

	Searching for Eight Targets at Once	*Searching in Turn for Each of Eight Targets*
Young: errors	1.4%	6.3%
Old: errors	1.6%	26.8%
Young: mean time per display	790 msec ($\sigma = 84$)	630 msec ($\sigma = 62$)
Old: mean time per display	972 msec ($\sigma = 138$)	896 msec ($\sigma = 152$)

long-term memory program by information in working memory, or loss of the long-term program.

Our experiments suggest that although old people may retain long-term memory programs they may not be able to *use* them to control their behavior because they often forget what they have just done or fail to index programs accurately.

Changes in the Locus of Control of Selective Attention with Age

Hamilton, Hockey, and Rejman (1977) have cogently argued that in any active self-optimizing system the locus of control of current operations may shift during the course of a task, so that at some periods the system is governed by decisions made at lower, peripheral levels and at others by decisions made at higher, more central levels where information from more than one source may be integrated. Norman and Bobrow (1975) make a similar point, noting that attentional processes may either be controlled by current sensory input (data-driven processes) or may be controlled by previously acquired information available in memory (memory-driven processes).

Rabbitt (1979c) reviewed contrasting tasks where selective attention is modulated from moment to moment by external events (data-driven control) and tasks where it is modulated by previously acquired information (memory-driven control). Young people can effectively cope with complex tasks by allowing their selective attention to be passively controlled by external events when this is useful and by breaking off to use active memory-driven control where necessary, rapidly shifting the locus of control of selective attention to meet task demands. It seems that as people grow old they can still benefit from appropriate data-driven control but become increasingly unable to exercise active memory-driven control. Thus they cannot respond as flexibly to task demands as the young, because they have fewer options of locus of control and they may be unable to rapidly switch between even their remaining options.

There is a broad parallel between this loss of flexibility of control over perceptual information processing and changes in flexibility of control of motor output with age. Bernstein (1967, pp. 92–93) points out that marked changes in gait appear in old age long before loss of muscle power or loss of joint flexibility make them inevitable. It seems that young adults exercise smooth *predictive* control of walking, adjusting their movements *before* feedback cues arrive. As people grow older, they increasingly lose the ability to exercise higher-level predictive control of locomotion and regress to lower level post hoc control based on corrective movements in response to feedback and on movements initiated and controlled by sequences of external cues. Thus, again, loss of higher-level active control reduces options of shifting locus of control to flexibly meet task demands. As age advances, we do not only lose precision of parameters of control—that is, precise evaluation of input and precise regulation of output—we also regress to less complex, less flexible, and less efficient control processes and impoverished choices of strategies.

CONCLUSIONS

Models in human experimental psychology have not been models for change. When these models, and the paradigms derived from them, have been applied to changes in performance in old age, they have yielded disappointing data. Models and techniques derived from psychometrics have also proved unhelpful.

We can now borrow models and techniques of data analysis from control systems theory—which is specifically designed to provide us with descriptions of systems adapting to external changes or to internal changes in their own capacities. These descriptions allow us to distinguish between changes in the efficiency of parameters of control and changes in the nature, source, and location of control processes within a system. Some preliminary applications of such descriptions to changes in performance with old age have yielded encouraging results.

REFERENCES

Baddeley, A. D. How does acoustic similarity influence short-term memory? *Quarterly Journal of Experimental Psychology,* 1968, *20,* 249-264.

Baddeley, A. D., & Hitch, G. Working memory. In G. H. Bower (Ed.), *The psychology of learning and motivation* (Vol. 18). New York: Academic Press, 1974.

Baltes, P. B. Longitudinal and cross-sectional sequences in the study of age and generation effects. *Human Development,* 1968, *11,* 145-171.

Baltes, P. B., Reese, H. W., & Lipsitt, L. Life-span developmental psychology. *Annual Review of Psychology,* 1980, *31,* 65-110.

Baltes, P. B., & Willis, S. The critical importance of appropriate methodology in the study of aging: The sample case of psychometric intelligence. In F. Hoffmeister & C. Muller (Eds.), *Brain function in old age.* Berlin: Springer-Verlag, 1979.

Bernstein, N. I. *The coordination and regulation of movements.* Oxford: Pergamon Press, 1967.

Birren, J. E. (Ed.). *Handbook of aging and the individual.* Chicago: University of Chicago Press, 1959.

Birren, J. E., & Schaie, W. (Eds.) *Handbook of the psychology of aging.* New York: Van Nostrand, Reinhold, 1977.

Birren, J. E., Woods, A. M., & Williams, M. V. Speed of behaviour as an indicator of age-changes and the integrity of the nervous system. In F. Hoffmeister & C. Muller (Eds.), *Brain function in old age.* Berlin: Springer-Verlag, 1979.

Botwinick, J. *Cognitive processes in maturity and old age.* New York: Springer, 1967.

Botwinick, J. Geropsychology. *Annual Review of Psychology,* 1970, *21,* 239-272.

Botwinick, J. *Aging and behavior.* New York: Springer Pub., 1973.

Broadbent, D. E. *Perception and communication.* Oxford: Pergamon Press, 1958.

Broadbent, D. E. *Decision and stress.* New York: Academic Press, 1971.

Broen, W. E., & Nakamura, C. Y. Reduced range of sensory sensitivity in chronic non-paranoid schizophrenics. *Journal of Abnormal Psychology,* 1972, *77,* 106-111.

Broen, W. E., & Storms, L. H. The differential effects of induced muscular tension (drive) on discriminations by schizophrenics and normals. *Journal of Abnormal and Social Psychology,* 1964, *68,* 349–353.

Bromley, D. E. *The psychology of human ageing.* Harmondsworth, England: Penguin Books, 1966.

Caird, W. K. Aging and short-term memory. *Journal of Gerontology,* 1966, *21,* 295–299.

Chapman, L. J., & Chapman, J. P. *Disordered thought in schizophrenia.* New York: Appleton-Century-Crofts, 1973. (a)

Chapman, L. J., & Chapman, J. P. Problems in the measurement of cognitive deficit. *Psychological Bulletin,* 1973, *79,* 380–385. (b)

Chown, S. M., & Heron, A. Psychological aspects of aging in man. *Annual Review of Psychology,* 1966, *17,* 417–450.

Crossman, E. R. F. W. A theory of acquisition of speed skill. *Ergonomics,* 1959, *2,* 153–166.

Donders, F. C. Die schnelligkeit psychischer processe. *Archiv der Anatomie und Physiologie,* 1868, 652–681.

Duncan, J. *Association and decision: S-R compatibility in choice reaction tasks.* Unpublished doctoral dissertation, University of Oxford, 1976.

Galton, F. On the Anthropometric Laboratory at the Late International Health Exhibition. *Journal of the Anthropological Institute,* 1885, *14,* 205–218.

Gippenreiter, I. B. *Dvizheniya chelovecheskovo glaza.* Moscow: Moscow University Press, 1978.

Griew, S. Learning of statistical structure: A preliminary study in relation to age. In C. Tibbets & W. Donahue (Eds.), *Social and psychological aspects of aging.* New York: Columbia University Press, 1962.

Hamilton, P., Hockey, E. R. J., & Rejman, M. The place of the concept of activation in human information theory: An integrative approach. In S. Dornic (Ed.), *Attention and performance VI.* Hillsdale, N.J.: Lawrence Erlbaum Associates, 1977.

Hoffmeister, F., & Muller, C. (Eds.). *Brain function in old age: Evaluation of changes and disorders: Bayer Symposium VII.* Berlin: Springer-Verlag, 1979.

Horn, J. In F. I. M. Craik & S. Trehub (Eds.), *Erindale symposium on ageing,* in press.

Hunt, E. Quote the Raven? Nevermore! In L. W. Gregg (Ed.), *Knowledge and cognition.* Hillsdale, N.J.: Lawrence Erlbaum Associates, 1974.

Hunt, E. In M. Friedman (Ed.), *York symposium on development of intelligence.* New York: Plenum Press, in press.

Hunt, E. B., Mavin, J., & Stone, P. J. *Experiments in induction.* New York: Academic Press, 1973.

Inglis, J., & Caird, W. K. Age differences in successive responses to simultaneous stimulation. *Canadian Journal of Psychology,* 1963, *17,* 98–105.

Jensen, J. In M. Friedman (Ed.), *York symposium on development of intelligence.* New York: Plenum Press, in press.

Kirby, N. H. Sequential effects in serial reaction time. *Journal of Experimental Psychology,* 1972, *96,* 32–36.

Kristofferson, M. The effects of practice with one positive set in a memory scanning task can be completely transferred to a new set. *Memory & Cognition,* 1977, *5,* 177–186.

Moray, N. The strategic control of information processing. In G. Underwood (Ed.), *Strategies of information processing.* London: Academic Press, 1976.

Mowbray, G. H., & Rhodes, M. V. On the reduction of choice reaction time with practice. *Quarterly Journal of Experimental Psychology,* 1959, *11,* 16–23.

Newell, A., & Rosenbloom, F. Mechanisms of skill acquisition and the law of practice. *Carnegie Mellon University, Department of Computer Science,* C.M.U.-CS-1980-145.

Norman, D. A., & Bobrow, D. G. On data limited and resource limited processes. *Cognitive Psychology,* 1975, *7,* 44–64.

Pachella, R. G., & Fisher, D. F. Effects of stimulus degradation and similarity on the trade-off between speed and accuracy in absolute judgements. *Journal of Experimental Psychology*, 1969, *76*, 19–24.

Pachella, R. G., & Pew, R.   Speed-accuracy trade-off in reaction times: Effects of discrete criterion times. *Journal of Experimental Psychology*, 1968, *76*, 19–24.

Pew, R.   The speed-accuracy operating characteristic. *Acta Psychologica*, 1969, *30*, 16–26.

Rabbitt, P. M. A.   Ignoring irrelevant information. *British Journal of Psychology*, 1964, *55*, 4–18.

Rabbitt, P. M. A.   Errors and error correction in choice response tasks. *Journal of Experimental Psychology*, 1966, *71*, 264–272. (a)

Rabbitt, P. M. A.   Error correction time without external error signals. *Nature*, 1966, *212*, 438. (b)

Rabbitt, P. M. A.   Age and the use of structure in transmitted information. In G. Talland (Ed.), *Human aging and behavior*. New York: Academic Press, 1968. (a)

Rabbitt, P. M. A.   Three kinds of error-signalling—responses in a serial choice task. *Quarterly Journal of Experimental Psychology*, 1968, *20*, 179–188. (b)

Rabbitt, P. M. A.   Repetition effects and signal classification strategies in serial, choice-response tasks. *Quarterly Journal of Experimental Psychology*, 1968, *20*, 232–240. (c)

Rabbitt, P. M. A.   Current paradigms and models in human information processing. In V. Hamilton & G. Warburton (Eds.), *Human stress and cognition*. London: Wiley, 1979. (a)

Rabbitt, P. M. A.   How old and young subjects monitor and control responses for accuracy and speed. *British Journal of Psychology*, 1979, *70*, 305–311. (b)

Rabbitt, P. M. A.   Some experiments and a model for changes in attentional selectivity with old age. In F. Hoffmeister & C. Muller (Eds.), *Brain function in old age*. Berlin: Springer-Verlag, 1979. (c)

Rabbitt, P. M. A.   A fresh look at changes in reaction times in old age. In D. Stein (Ed.), *The psychobiology of aging: Problems and perspectives*. N. Holland and New York: Elsevier, 1980.

Rabbitt, P. M. A.   Sequential reactions. In D. Holding (Ed.), *Advances in motor skills*. New York: Wiley, in press. (a)

Rabbitt, P. M. A.   In M. Friedman (Ed.), *York symposium on development of intelligence*. New York: Plenum Press, in press. (b)

Rabbitt, P. M. A.   How do old people know what to do next? In F. I. M. Craik & S. Trehub (Eds.), *Erindale symposium on ageing*. New York: Plenum Press, in press. (c)

Rabbitt, P. M. A., Bishop, D., & Vyas, S. M.   Age and patterns of search. Manuscript in preparation, 1980.

Rabbitt, P. M. A., Clancy, M., & Vyas, S. M.   Age, retrieval, storage, and recognition. *Proceedings of the International Congress of Gerontology*. Washington, D.C.: International Gerontological Society Monographs, 1969, No. 14.

Rabbitt, P. M. A., Corcoran, D. W., & Vyas, S. M.   Age and proximity cues to target detection in visual search. Manuscript in preparation, 1980.

Rabbitt, P. M. A., Cumming, G., & Vyas, S. M.   Some errors of perceptual analysis in visual search can be detected and corrected. *Quarterly Journal of Experimental Psychology*, 1978, *30*, 319–332.

Rabbitt, P. M. A., Cumming, G., & Vyas, S. M.   Improvement, learning and retention of skill at visual search. *Quarterly Journal of Experimental Psychology*, 1979, *31*, 441–459.

Rabbitt, P. M. A., & Vyas, S. M.   An elementary preliminary taxonomy of errors in choice reaction time tasks. *Acta Psychologica*, 1970, *33*, 56–76.

Rabbitt, P. M. A., & Vyas, S. M.   Looking for one damn thing after another. Manuscript in preparation, 1980.

Rabbitt, P. M. A., & Vyas, S. M.   Selective anticipation for events in old age. *Journal of Gerontology*, in press. (a)

Rabbitt, P. M. A., & Vyas, S. M.   Processing a display even after you make a response to it: How perceptual errors can be corrected. *Quarterly Journal of Experimental Psychology*, in press. (b)

Remington, R. J.   Analysis of sequential effects in choice reaction times. *Journal of Experimental Psychology*, 1969, *82*, 250–257.

Saccuzo, D. P. Bridges between schizophrenia and gerontology: Generalized or specific deficits? *Psychological Bulletin*, 1977, *84*, 595-600.

Sanford, A. J., & Maule, A. J. Age and the distribution of observing responses. *Psychonomic Science*, 1971, *23*, 419-420.

Sanford, A. J., & Maule, A. J. The allocation of attention in multisource monitoring behaviour: Adult age differences. *Perception*, 1973, *2*, 91-100. (a)

Sanford, A. J., & Maule, A. J. The concept of general experience: Age and strategies in guessing future events. *Journal of Gerontology*, 1973, *28*, 81-88. (b)

Schaie, K. W. A general model for the study of developmental problems. *Psychological Bulletin*, 1965, *64*, 92-107.

Schaie, K. W. Methodological problems in the design of gerontological experiments. In J. E. Birren & W. Schaie (Eds.), *Handbook of the psychology of aging*. New York: Van Nostrand, Reinhold, 1977.

Schaie, K. W., & Gribbin, K. Adult development and aging. *Annual Review of Psychology*, 1975, *27*, 65-96.

Schouten, J. F., & Bekker, J. A. M. Reaction time and accuracy. *Acta Psychologica*, 1967, *27*, 143-153.

Senders, J. W. Visual scanning behavior. In *Visual search*. Washington: National Academy of Sciences, 1977.

Senders, J., Elkind, J., Grignetti, M., & Smallwood, R. *An investigation of the visual sampling behavior of human observers*. NASA CR-434, 1964.

Shepard, R. N., & Metzler, J. Mental rotation of three-dimensional objects. *Science*, 1971, *171*, 701-703.

Sternberg, R. J. *Intelligence, information processing and analogical reasoning: The componential analysis of human abilities*. Hillsdale, N.J.: Lawrence Erlbaum Associates, 1977. (a)

Sternberg, R. J. Component processes in analogical reasoning. *Psychological Review*, 1977, *84*, 353-378. (b)

Sternberg, R. J. In M. Friedman (Ed.), *York symposium on development of intelligence*. New York: Plenum Press, in press.

Sternberg, S. High-speed scanning in human memory. *Science*, 1966, *153*, 652-654.

Sternberg, S. Memory scanning and recognition processes. In W. Wathen-Dunn (Ed.), *Models for the analysis of speech and visual form*. Cambridge, Mass.: MIT Press, 1967.

Sternberg, S. The discovery of processing stages: Extensions of Donders' method. *Acta Psychologica*, 1969, *30*, 276-315.

Talland, G. A. (Ed.). *Human aging and behavior*. New York: Academic Press, 1968.

Tibbets, C., & Donahue, W. (Eds.). *Social and psychological aspects of aging*. New York: Columbia University Press, 1962.

Welford, A. T., & Birren, J. E. *Behavior, aging and the nervous system*. Springfield, Ill.: Charles Thomas, 1965.

Wickelgren, W. Speed-accuracy tradeoff and information processing dynamics. *Acta Psychologica*, 1977, *41*, 67-85.

Wilkinson, R. T. Rest pauses in a task affected by lack of sleep. *Ergonomics*, 1959, *2*, 373-380.

Woodhead, M. M. The effects of bursts of noise on an arithmetic task. *American Journal of Psychology*, 1964, *77*, 627-633.

Yarbus, A. *Eye movements in vision*. New York: Plenum Press, 1968.

33

Effects of Two Counteracting Stresses on the Reaction Process

H. W. Frowein, D. Reitsma, and C. Aquarius
Institute of Perception TNO, Soesterberg, The Netherlands

ABSTRACT

The effects of an amphetamine and sleep deprivation were investigated in a visual two-choice RT task with reaction time (RT) and movement time (MT) as response measures. Independent task variables were time uncertainty and movement amplitude. The RT data showed that sleep deprivation lengthened RT and that this effect was nearly totally suppressed when amphetamine was administered. Also, the effects of both amphetamine and sleep deprivation were greater with high than with low time uncertainty. This was interpreted in terms of Sternberg's additive stage analysis. On the assumption that time uncertainty affects a motor adjustment stage preceding motor execution, it was inferred that this stage is affected by sleep deprivation as well as amphetamine. Furthermore, an analysis of morning versus afternoon sessions indicated that these effects were more prominent in the afternoon than in the morning. The movement data showed that both the speed and the accuracy of the movements was improved by amphetamine and impaired by sleep deprivation. However, there was no clear interaction between these two stresses and the possibility was suggested that they may affect different mechanisms during movement execution.

INTRODUCTION

This chapter describes an experiment about the effects on task performance of two counteracting stresses: sleep deprivation and amphetamine. Its aim is to relate these effects to some of the component processes involved in carrying out a

575

task, in this case a choice reaction task. We have tried to achieve this by investigating the relationship between the effects of these stresses and the effects of certain task variables.

The theoretical basis for this approach is provided by the additive factor analysis of stages in reaction time (Sternberg, 1969). In accordance with this approach, it may be assumed that reaction time reflects a series of independent processing stages, and it may be inferred that different task variables affect separate processing stages if their respective effects on RT are additive, whereas an interaction between different task variables would mean that they affect at least one common processing stage. Following Sternberg, a number of investigators have applied this method to arrive at a more complete picture of the reaction process. Comprehensive reviews of this research were presented by Sanders (1977, 1980b). For the present, the following findings are relevant to formulate a working model of the reaction process.

First, it has been consistently shown that visual stimulus degradation and S–R compatibility have additive effects on RT (Frowein & Sanders, 1978; Sanders, 1980a; Shwartz, Pomerantz, & Egeth, 1977; Sternberg, 1969). This indicates that they must affect different processing stages, which may be referred to as *stimulus encoding* and *response selection*.

Second, it has been shown that time uncertainty is additive with each of these two variables. Time uncertainty can be varied in different ways. If the reaction stimulus is preceded by a warning signal, time uncertainty can be increased by increasing the foreperiod between the warning signal and the reaction stimulus. If there is no warning signal, time uncertainty can be increased either by making the interstimulus interval longer or making it more irregular. In either of these cases, an increase in time uncertainty will bring about an increase in RT, and this effect appears to be additive with both visual stimulus degradation (Frowein & Sanders, 1978; Wertheim, 1980) and S–R compatibility (Frowein & Sanders, 1978; Posner, Klein, Summers, & Buggie, 1973; Sanders, 1977). This indicates that the stages involved in stimulus encoding and response selection are unaffected by time uncertainty and that time uncertainty must affect RT via some other stage in the reaction process. In this respect, Sanders (1977, 1980b) has postulated that time uncertainty affects a "motor adjustment" stage that would occur after response selection (i.e., if the subject knows when to expect the stimulus, he would be better prepared to respond, and the motor adjustment stage would proceed more quickly). This is also consistent with an experiment by Sanders (1980a), who instructed subjects to tense the muscles necessary to initiate the response. This instruction brought about a shortening of RT, and this effect was greater in the case of high time uncertainty. Furthermore, there is also some physiological evidence that time uncertainty affects the motor adjustment stage. Gaillard (1978) has shown that the amplitude of the so-called contingent negative variation (CNV) in the EEG, which is mainly found in the derivation from the motor cortex, varies as a function of time uncertainty but is unaffected by stimulus degradation.

A third relevant finding for our working model is that stimulus degradation, S–R compatibility, and time-uncertainty, which were found to have additive effects on RT, had no effect on the movement time (MT) when MT followed RT in a target-aiming response (Frowein & Sanders, 1978). This indicates that MT represents a separate process following on from stimulus encoding, response selection, and motor adjustment. However, this motor execution process should not be conceived of as necessarily consisting of only one stage. For short ballistic movements below 200 msec, motor execution may be conceived as consisting of one stage because there is not enough time for visual feedback to play a role, and it has been shown that other modes of feedback are not sufficient for adequate feedback control (Klapp, 1975). When movements become longer than 200 msec, it may be assumed that feedback starts playing a role that probably increases with the complexity of the movement. Thus, with the reservation that more mechanisms may be involved, we may represent motor execution as one process in our working model, pictured in Fig. 33.1.

This working model may serve as a framework to locate effects of stresses. If a stress and a task variable show an interaction in their respective effects on RT, it can be inferred that they affect a common processing stage; whereas additivity implies that they affect separate processing stages. Similarly, an effect of a stress on response execution can be inferred from its effect on MT.

In previous experiments in our laboratory we have investigated the separate effects of amphetamine and barbiturate in this manner. For the purposes of introducing the present experiment, it is useful to review some of the amphetamine findings. Here the following points are relevant:

1. There is no evidence that amphetamine affects the stimulus encoding stage; Frowein (in press) found that the effect of amphetamine on RT was unaffected by visual stimulus degradation. Also, Frowein and Sanders (1981) found no relationship between the effect of amphetamine and the effect of visual intensity.

2. The evidence regarding the effect of amphetamine on the response selection stage is more equivocal. Frowein (in press) found that there was a small but

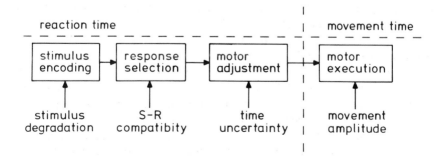

FIG. 33.1.   Model of the reaction process.

significant interaction of amphetamine with the effect of S–R compatibility on RT. It appeared in this case that amphetamine had an inhibitory effect on response selection: In the incompatible condition, amphetamine brought about longer RTs. However, a subsequent attempt to replicate this interaction proved unsuccessful (Frowein, 1979). In this experiment it was also found that the amphetamine effect on RT was additive with the effect of relative signal frequency. Because this variable has also been found to affect the response selection stage (Sanders, 1977), it appears that the weight of the evidence tilts toward concluding that amphetamine has no effect on the response selection stage.

3. Regarding the motor adjustment stage the evidence is more consistent. Trumbo and Gaillard (1975) found that the effect of amphetamine on RT increased with time uncertainty and this interaction has recently been replicated by Frowein (in preparation). Thus, assuming that time uncertainty affects motor preparation, there is consistent evidence of an amphetamine effect on that stage.

4. Finally, there is also consistent evidence that amphetamine affects motor execution. In two recent experiments (Frowein, 1979; Frowein, in press), with two different types of tasks and movement times ranging from about 120 msec to about 500 msec, it has been shown that amphetamine shortens the MT. Furthermore, in the second of these two studies, in which a task adapted from Fitts and Peterson (1964) was used with movement amplitude and target width as independent variables, the data showed that the amphetamine effect increased slightly as a function of movement amplitude but did not vary as a function of target width. Because the role of visual feedback was assumed to be greater with smaller targets, it was inferred that the amphetamine effect on MT could not be attributed to an amphetamine effect on visual feedback (i.e., encoding).

Thus, in summary, it appears that amphetamine selectively affects motor adjustment and motor execution. The present experiment investigates the effects on motor adjustment and motor execution of sleep deprivation as well as amphetamine. The task was again a two-choice task derived from Fitts and Peterson (1964) with reaction time and movement time as the main response measures. Time uncertainty and movement amplitude were the independent task variables.

Sleep deprivation was introduced as an extra stress because it has been shown in a variety of tasks that its effect on performance can be counteracted by amphetamine and that the size of the effect of amphetamine increases considerably in the presence of sleep deprivation (Weiss & Laties, 1962). Thus, if amphetamine and sleep deprivation have a similar relation in their effects on RT, it could be inferred that they affect at least one common processing mechanism. In terms of our working model this would mean either that these two stresses affect the motor adjustment stage or that they affect a common mechanism during motor execution or that both of these possibilities are true.

That it is not implausible to suggest that sleep deprivation affects both motor adjustment and motor execution was suggested by some prior evidence from the literature. First, it has been repeatedly shown that sleep deprivation affects RT (Glenville & Wilkinson, 1979; Lisper & Kjellberg, 1972). Second, the finding by Naitoh, Johnson, and Lubin (1973) that the CNV wave disappears as a function of sleep deprivation suggests that the latter has an effect on motor adjustment, because the aforementioned experiments by Gaillard (1978) indicate that the motor adjustment stage proceeds more slowly when the CNV is low or absent. Third, an effect of sleep deprivation on motor execution was suggested by an experiment by Buck (1975), who investigated the effect of sleep deprivation in a step-tracking task and found prominent effects on MT as well as RT.

In addition, the experiment also allowed an analysis of time-of-day effects. This variable was included in the analysis because the experimental tasks were carried out twice: first in the morning and subsequently in the afternoon.

METHOD

Subjects

The subjects were 32 healthy male students from the University of Utrecht. They were allotted to two groups of 16 subjects each: a sleep-deprived (S.D.) group and a control group. One week before participating in the experiment, all subjects received a medical examination and were informed about the nature of the drug treatment conditions and the experimental task. They were paid Hfl. 75.- for each day of experimentation and an additional Hfl. 75.- was paid for each night of sleep deprivation.

Drug Treatment

The drug conditions consisted of an amphetamine derivative (40 mg Phentermine HC1) and a placebo. The drug treatment was always administered by the subject himself by means of a suppository at either 9.00 or 9.25 A.M. The experimental sessions were started 1 hr after treatment and finished about 6 hr later. This ensures a relatively constant plasma concentration across experimental sessions (Vree, 1973). Allocation of the drug treatment was double-blind in the sense that neither the subjects nor the experimenter knew on which days the different treatments would be administered.

Sleep Deprivation

Sleep deprivation consisted of one night without sleep. Subjects in the sleep-deprived (S.D.) group were instructed neither to sleep nor to drink alcohol on days prior to sleep deprivation and to arrive at the laboratory at 11.00 P.M. During the night and during the rest periods of the following day, they were under constant supervision and kept busy playing various games (cards, Monopoly, etc.). Subjects in the control group were instructed not to use alcohol and to get a normal night's sleep on days prior to experimental days, and they were also kept busy with various games during the rest periods on experimental days.

Experimental Task and Apparatus

The experimental task was adapted from Fitts and Peterson (1964). The subject was seated at a sloping desk with (in his preferred hand) a lightweight stylus that rested on a slightly hollowed circular starting plate of 1-cm diameter. A red warning light (WL) of 1-cm diameter was mounted 5 cm above the starting plate. White reaction lights (RL) were mounted 2 cm to the right of the WL and 2 cm to the left of the WL. The subject's task was to fixate the WL and to hit the appropriate one of two metal target plates as quickly as possible when one of the two RLs came on. The target plates were positioned to the right and to the left of the starting plate and they were 0.7 cm wide and 10 cm long. Undershoot and overshoot plates of 3.5 cm wide and 10 cm long were positioned adjacent to each of the two target plates. The instructions specified that movements should be made without hesitation and that movements in the wrong direction should never be corrected during the movement. For each trial, the stimulus sequence was started with a 1000-msec WL that was followed by a 200-msec RL. The cycle duration (i.e., the onset–onset interval between consecutive RLs) was 7, 8, or 9 sec with a mean duration of 8 sec. The preprogrammed signal presentation and the registration of responses was performed by a PDP 11-03 computer with an internal clock. The reaction time (RT) was defined as the interval between the onset of the RL and the release from the starting plate, and the movement time (MT) was defined as the interval between the release of the starting plate and the touching of either one of the two target plates or one of the undershoot or overshoot plates that were mounted adjacent to the target plates. The task variables were movement amplitude and time uncertainty. Movement amplitude was either 10 cm or 30 cm as measured by the distance between the midpoint of the starting plate and the midline of the target plate. Time uncertainty also had two levels and was varied by means of varying the interval between the onsets of WL and RL. With low time uncertainty, the onset–onset interval between WL and RL was 1 sec, which was also the duration of WL. With high time uncertainty, the onset–onset interval was 4, 5, or 6 sec with a mean interval of 5 sec.

Design and Procedure

The independent variables were sleep deprivation (S.D. versus control), drug treatment (amphetamine versus placebo), time uncertainty (low versus high), movement amplitude (10 cm versus 30 cm) and time of the day (morning versus afternoon). Sleep deprivation was varied between two groups of 16 subjects, whereas the other independent variables were varied within subjects. For each group the program consisted of three separate days with 1 week in between days. The first day served as training day; the next 2 days served as experimental days. On nights preceding each of the experimental days, the S.D. group was sleep-deprived; for both the S.D. and the control group, drug treatment was varied between the two experimental days.

On each day, two pairs of subjects were run alternately in four morning sessions and four afternoon sessions of 20 min each. There was always a 60-min rest period between treatment administration and the beginning of the first session and a 30-min rest period between consecutive sessions. For half the subjects, treatment was administered at 9.00 and the sessions started at 10.00 and finished at 16.10; for the other half, treatment was administered at 9.25 and the sessions started at 10.25 and finished at 16.35. The rest period between the fourth morning session and the first afternoon session occurred from 12.50 to 13.20 for the first half of subjects and from 13.15 to 13.45 for the second half of subjects.

The task variables were varied between the morning sessions and again in the same order between the afternoon sessions. The order of presentation of the drug conditions and of the conditions of movement amplitude and time uncertainty were counterbalanced, with the sequence of high and low time uncertainty counterbalanced within each sequence of movement amplitudes and the sequence of movement amplitudes counterbalanced within each sequence of drug treatment conditions.

Thus for each subject the task conditions were the same for both the training and the two experimental days, with the exception that during the training sessions, subjects received feedback about their performance, that is, about the total times (RT + MT) and about the accuracy of their performance. They were also told that during the experimental days a bonus would be computed on the basis of their mean total time for correct responses but that no bonus would be paid for sessions with more than 10% errors (which included incorrect decisions, undershoots, and overshoots). During the experimental days no feedback was given.

The experimental task was always carried out in a sound-attenuating cubicle with dim ceiling illumination. Subjects could be observed by the experimenter via a TV monitor.

RESULTS

The dependent variables were mean RTs and MTs, and the percentages of incorrect decisions (left/right errors), missed responses, and movement errors (undershoot and overshoot). These measures were computed for each individual session and analyzed in separate analyses of variance.

Reaction Times

The effects of time uncertainty, time of the day, drug treatment, and sleep deprivation are shown in Fig. 33.2. There were significant main effects of time uncertainty, F (1, 28) = 90.33, p < .001, time of day, F (1, 28) = 59.31, p < .001, and drug treatment, F (1, 28) = 18.88, p < .01. The main effect of sleep deprivation was not significant, F (1, 28) = 1.54, N.S., but a planned comparison analysis with only the placebo condition included showed that sleep deprivation brought about a significant increase in RT when this effect was not counteracted by amphetamine, F (1, 28) = 14.86, p < .01. This was also supported by a significant interaction between the effects of sleep deprivation and amphetamine, F (1, 28) = 4.89, p < .05. Furthermore, the effect of sleep deprivation and the suppression of this effect by amphetamine were greater in the afternoon than in the morning. In the analysis of variance this was evident from significant interactions of sleep deprivation × time of day, F (1, 28) = 8.04, p < .01, and sleep deprivation × drug treatment × time of day, F (1, 28) = 5.20, p < .05.

Regarding the relationship of the effect of time uncertainty with the effects of drug treatment and sleep deprivation and time of day, there were significant interactions of time uncertainty × drug treatment, F (1, 28) = 9.96, p < .01, and time uncertainty × time of day, F (1, 28) = 6.58, p < .05. Although the analysis of variance did not show an interaction between time uncertainty and sleep deprivation, F (1, 28) < 1, N.S., a planned comparison analysis (with only the placebo condition included) indicated that the effect of sleep deprivation (when not suppressed by amphetamine) was greater with high time uncertainty, F (1, 28) = 7.72, p < .01. Furthermore, Fig. 33.2 also suggests that this interaction was greater in the morning than in the afternoon. In the analysis of variance this was indicated by a significant third-order interaction of sleep deprivation × drug treatment × time of day × time uncertainty, F (1, 28) = 6.19, p < .05.

The effect of movement amplitude on RT is not pictured in Fig. 33.2. In fact, the mean RTs preceding longer movements were about 11 msec longer than those preceding short movements. This small effect was significant, F (1, 28) = 11.14, p < .01, but showed no interaction with any of the other independent variables.

Movement Times

The effects of movement amplitude, drug treatment, sleep deprivation, and time of day are shown in Fig. 33.3. Movement amplitude had of course a highly significant main effect, F (1, 28) = 1364.83, p < .001, but none of the interactions involving movement amplitude were significant.

Similarly there were also significant main effects of drug treatment, F (1, 28) = 14.01, p < .01, and time of day, F (1, 28) = 5.65, p < .05, but none of the interactions involving either or both of these variables were significant.

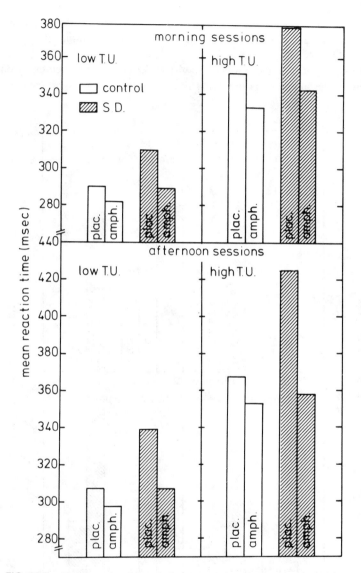

FIG. 33.2. Mean reaction time as a function of drug treatment, sleep deprivation, time uncertainty (T.U.), and time of day.

Sleep deprivation did not have a significant main effect on MT, F (1, 28) < 1, N.S., but a planned comparison analysis with only the placebo condition included was significant, F (1, 28) = 5.97, p < .05. Thus, if the effect of sleep deprivation was not counteracted by the effect of amphetamine, it appeared to lengthen MT.

Finally, as expected, there was no significant effect of time uncertainty on MT and none of the interactions involving time uncertainty was significant.

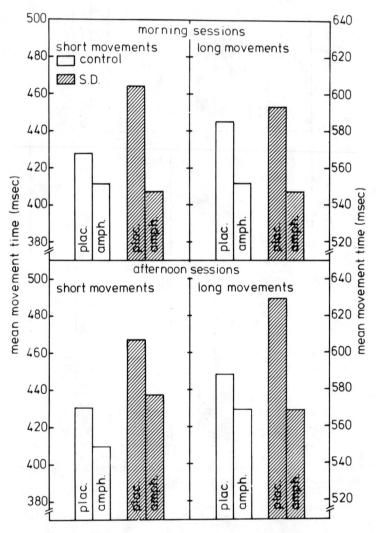

FIG. 33.3. Mean movement time as a function of drug treatment, sleep deprivation, and movement amplitude (short = 10 cm; long = 30 cm) and time of day.

Movement Errors

The percentages of movement errors (undershoots and overshoots) are pictured in
Fig. 33.4. The analysis of variance showed marginally significant effects of sleep
deprivation, F (1, 28) = 3.99, p < .10, and drug treatment, F (1, 28) = 3.29, p
< .10, but the interaction between these two variables did not approach signifi-
cance. Likewise there were no significant main effects or interactions involving
movement amplitude or time of day.

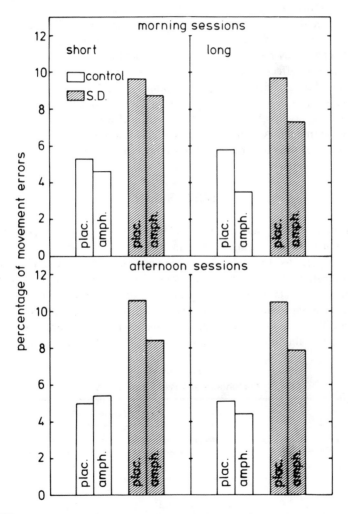

FIG. 33.4.   Percentage of movement errors as a function of drug treatment, sleep
deprivation, and movement amplitude (short = 10 cm; long = 30 cm) and time of
day.

Incorrect Decisions and Missed Responses

Incorrect decisions (left/right errors) and missed responses were computed separately. Incorrect decisions occurred very rarely (well below 1% for all conditions) and there was no evidence of an effect of any of the independent variables on these types of errors or of these variables affecting RT through changes in speed–accuracy tradeoff.

The percentages of missed responses are shown in Table 33.1. The analysis of variance showed significant main effects of sleep deprivation, $F (1, 28) = 6.30$, $p < .05$, and drug treatment, $F (1, 28) = 10.66$, $p < .01$, and there was also a significant interaction of sleep deprivation × drug treatment, $F (1, 28) = 16.62$, $p < .01$. As shown in the table, amphetamine reduced the percentage of errors in the S.D. conditions but not in the control condition. Time of day also had a significant main effect, $F (1, 28) = 6.25$, $p < .05$, and there was a significant interaction of time of day × sleep deprivation, $F (1, 28) = 5.97$, $p < .05$ (i.e., the effect of sleep deprivation was greater in the afternoon than in the morning). Other interactions involving time of day, sleep deprivation, or drug treatment were not significant. Also there were no significant main effects or interactions involving either time uncertainty or movement amplitude.

DISCUSSION

The RT data showed that the effect of sleep deprivation was greater in the afternoon than in the morning and that in both the morning and the afternoon this effect was nearly totally suppressed when amphetamine was administered. Furthermore, there were first-order interactions of the effect of time uncertainty with the respective effects of sleep deprivation and drug treatment and a third-order interaction among time uncertainty, sleep deprivation, time-of-day, and drug treatment. Thus, on the assumption that time uncertainty affects the motor adjustment stage, the most parsimonious conclusion is that sleep deprivation and

Table 33.1
Percentage of Missed Responses

S.D. condition:	Time of Day					
	Morning			Afternoon		
	S.D.	Control	Diff.	S.D.	Control	Diff.
Drug treatment						
Placebo	5.9	1.3	4.6	8.3	2.1	6.2
Amphetamine	2.5	2.3	0.2	5.9	1.8	4.1
Difference	3.4	−1.0		2.4	0.3	

amphetamine affect motor adjustment in opposite directions and that these effects are greater in the afternoon than in the morning.

However, it does not necessarily follow that motor adjustment is the only stage prior to motor execution that is affected by either amphetamine or sleep deprivation. With respect to amphetamine this conclusion is in fact not implausible because (as discussed in the Introduction) our previous research has shown little evidence of an amphetamine effect on either stimulus encoding or response selection. However, this is not true for sleep deprivation. A recent experiment by Sanders and Wijnen (in preparation) showed a strong interaction of sleep deprivation with visual pattern degradation and an additive relationship between sleep deprivation and S–R compatibility. Interpreting these data together with the present results, it appears that sleep deprivation affects the stimulus encoding stage as well as the motor adjustment stage but there is no effect of sleep deprivation on response selection. However an inconsistency of this interpretation with the present data is that amphetamine nearly totally suppressed the effect of sleep deprivation. If amphetamine counteracts the effect of sleep deprivation on motor adjustment but not on stimulus encoding, one would expect only a partial suppression. To account for this inconsistency it may be noted that the visual stimuli in the present experiment consisted of simple lights that would make little demand on the encoding stage. It would be expected that the suppression of the sleep deprivation effect by amphetamine would be less prominent if more complex stimulus patterns were used.

With regard to the effects of sleep deprivation and amphetamine on motor execution, the present data showed that sleep deprivation brought about longer MTs as well as more movement errors. Amphetamine, on the other hand, brought about shorter MTs and less movement errors. Thus, sleep deprivation and amphetamine had opposite effects on motor execution and this applied to the accuracy as well as the speed of movement. However, it is not clear whether these two stresses affect a common mechanism during motor execution. Although the figures suggest an interaction between sleep deprivation and amphetamine on MT as well as movement errors, this was not confirmed by the analyses of variance. A possible explanation of these results could go as follows. Because the movements in this experiment were always longer than 200 msec, it may be suggested that the first part is programmed before movement onset, whereas the second part is under feedback control. Thus, given this rather simple picture of motor execution, it may be postulated that sleep deprivation as well as amphetamine affect the first preprogrammed part and sleep deprivation alone affects the efficiency of visual feedback. The latter would be consistent with the experiments mentioned above that suggest that stimulus encoding is affected by sleep deprivation but not by amphetamine.

The effects of sleep deprivation and amphetamine on the missed responses appear to be of a different nature. It is clear that sleep deprivation increased the percentage of missed responses and that this effect was counteracted by the effect of amphetamine. However, it does not seem plausible to relate these effects to stages in the reaction process. For instance, the task variables in this experiment had no effect on the percentage of missed responses. Probably the simplest explanation is that the sleepy subjects started to catch little "micro-sleeps" (Dement, 1972). As it is well-known that amphetamine makes people less sleepy, it is not surprising that amphetamine would counteract this effect.

ACKNOWLEDGMENTS

This research was subsidized by the Netherlands Organization for Pure Research. I thank A. Krul for carrying out the statistical analysis and A. F. Sanders for his helpful and constructive comments on the manuscript.

REFERENCES

Buck, L. Sleep loss effects on movement time, *Ergonomics,* 1975, *18,* 415–425.

Dement, W. C. Sleep deprivation and the organization of the behavioral states. In C. D. Clemente, D. P. Purpura, & F. E. Mayer (Eds.), *Sleep and the maturing nervous system.* New York: Academic Press, 1972.

Fitts, P. M., & Peterson, J. R. Information capacity of discrete motor responses. *Journal of Experimental Psychology,* 1964, *67,* 103–112.

Frowein, H. W. Effects of amphetamine on response selection and response execution processes in choice reaction tasks. Institute for Perception TNO Report, Soesterberg, The Netherlands, 1979.

Frowein, H. W. Selective effects of barbiturate and amphetamine on information processing and response execution. *Acta Psychologica,* in press.

Frowein, H. W. Effects of stimulant and depressant drugs, time uncertainty and an auditory accessory on visual choice reaction time. Manuscript in preparation.

Frowein, H. W., & Sanders, A. F. Effects of stimulus degradation, S-R compatibility and foreperiod duration on choice reaction time and movement times. *The Bulletin of the Psychonomic Society,* 1978, *12,* 106–108.

Frowein, H. W., & Sanders, A. F. Effects of amphetamine and barbiturate on RT in a memory search task. Institute for Perception TNO Report, Soesterberg, The Netherlands, 1981.

Gaillard, A. W. K. *Slow brain potentials preceding task performance.* Amsterdam: Academische Pers, 1978.

Glenville, M., & Wilkinson, R. T. Portable devices for measuring performance in the field: The effects of sleep deprivation and night shift on the performance of computer operators. *Ergonomics,* 1979, *8,* 929–933.

Klapp, S. T. Feedback versus motor programming in the control of aimed movements. *Journal of Experimental Psychology: Human Perception and Performance,* 1975, *104,* 147–153.

Lisper, H. O., & Kjellberg, A. Effects of 24 hours sleep deprivation on the rate of decrement in a 10 min. auditory reaction time task. *Journal of Experimental Psychology,* 1972, *96,* 287–290.

Naitoh, P., Johnson, L. C., & Lubin, A. The effects of selective and total sleep loss on the CNV and its psychological and physiological correlates. *Electroencephalography and Clinical Neurophysiology,* 1973, *33,* 213–218.

Posner, M. I., Klein, R., Summers, J., & Buggie, S. On the selection of signals. *Memory & Cognition,* 1973, *1,* 2–12.

Sanders, A. F. Structural and functional aspects of the reaction process. In S. Dornic (Ed.), *Attention and performance VI.* New York: Academic Press, 1977.

Sanders, A. F. Some effects of instructed muscle tension on choice reaction time and movement time. In R. S. Nickerson (Ed.), *Attention and performance VIII*. Hillsdale, N.J.: Lawrence Erlbaum Associates, 1980. (a)

Sanders, A. F. Stage analysis of reaction processes. In G. E. Stelmach & J. Requin (Eds.), *Tutorials in motor behavior*. Amsterdam: North Holland Pub., 1980. (b)

Sanders, A. F., & Wijnen, J. The effects of sleep deprivation on signal degradation and S-R compatibility as choice reaction variables. Manuscript in preparation.

Shwartz, S. P., Pomerantz, J. R., & Egeth, H. E. State and process limitation in information processing: An additive factor analysis. *Journal of Experimental Psychology: Human Perception and Performance*, 1977, *3*, 402–410.

Sternberg, S. On the discovery of processing stages. In W. G. Koster (Ed.), *Attention and performance II*. *Acta Psychologica* 1969, *30*, 276–315.

Trumbo, D. A., & Gaillard, A. W. K. Drugs, time uncertainty, signal modality and reaction time. In P. M. A. Rabbitt & S. Dornic (Eds.), *Attention and performance V*. New York, Academic Press, 1975.

Vree, T. B. *Pharmacokinetics and metabolism of amphetamines*. Nijmegen: Brakkenstein, 1973.

Weiss, B., & Laties, V. G. Enhancement of human performance by caffeine and the amphetamines. *Pharmacological Reviews*, 1962, *14*, 1–36.

Wertheim, A. H. Information processing mechanisms involved in ocular pursuit. In G. E. Stelmach & J. Requin (Eds.), *Tutorials in motor behavior*. Amsterdam. North Holland Pub., 1980.

34 Task-Related Cardiovascular Stress

G. Mulder and L. J. M. Mulder
Institute of Experimental Psychology
University of Groningen
Groningen, The Netherlands

ABSTRACT

The experiments described in this contribution were inspired by the observation that the human cardiac rhythm becomes more regular as task difficulty increases. In contrast to previous studies, signal rate was kept constant but task difficulty was varied in three different ways. The amplitude of vasomotor oscillations (frequency between 0.06 and 0.14 Hz) in the cardiac interval signal served as the dependent variable. This component is relatively independent of respiratory rate and depth but is related to blood pressure control. It was concluded that the amplitude of the vasomotor oscillations is strongly reduced if a task continuously requires processing. This conclusion was substantiated with three experiments dealing, respectively, with sentence comprehension, visual and memory search, and maintenance rehearsal.

INTRODUCTION

Performance on mental tasks may be accompanied by phasic and tonic changes in cardiovascular responses. Phasic responses refer to short-term changes, those occurring within a few seconds; tonic responses refer to mean values over some longer interval (i.e., over minutes or hours). Both types of responses have been related to task difficulty. For example: A subject may be required to perform a paced-choice reaction-time task for 5 min. Over this period one can compute the mean interval between successive heartbeats (i.e., the mean cardiac interval) and the variability of these intervals. Normal variations in time between successive heartbeats are known as *sinusarrhythmia* and this phenomenon is believed to originate mainly from respiratory activity. Inspiration causes an increase in heart rate and expiration, a decrease. The more irregular respiratory activity, the more irregular heart rate will be and vice versa.

At the first conference on Attention and Performance, Kalsbeek and Sykes (1967) reported a reduction in sinusarrhythmia during continuous tasks. Their main task was a paced binary-choice reaction task, and task difficulty was changed by increasing the number of signals per minute. An increase in signal rate produced a decrease in heart-rate variability or sinusarrhythmia. The mean cardiac interval was not strongly affected. The authors proposed sinusarrhythmia as an index of mental effort. The main results of Kalsbeek and Sykes were replicated by other researchers (Blitz, Hoogstraten, & Mulder, 1970; Loos, 1968; Luczak, 1979; Mulder & Mulder-Hajonides van der Meulen, 1972, 1973). In all these reports, task difficulty was varied by changing signal rate. However, variations in signal rate in choice reaction-time tasks cause variations in response rate also. Thus task difficulty was confounded with muscular load. Subjects also tend to regularize their respiration in a manner synchronous with the imperative stimuli. The observed reduction is sinusarrhythmia may therefore in fact reflect a more regular respiratory pattern. If signal rate was kept constant and processing time varied (e.g., by changing the number of alternatives), sinusarrhythmia was either not affected or increased (Danev, Wartna, Bink, Ridder, & Luteyn, 1971; Mobbs, David, & Thomas, 1971; Mulder & Mulder-Hajonides van der Meulen, 1972).

In addition to these tonic measures, it is also possible to study momentary changes in heart rate (or other cardiovascular indices) between successive imperative signals in paced-choice reaction-time tasks. A very reproducible pattern of responses appears: for example, heart rate decelerates until the presentation of the stimulus, possibly reflecting preparatory processes, and accelerates in the interval between the presentation of the stimulus and response emittence (Mulder, in press). This pattern of heart-rate changes is sometimes called the evoked heart-rate response.

Spectral analysis of sinusarrhythmia reveals both types of responses. The cardiac intervals are subjected to Fourier analysis, and the resulting spectrum reveals several components. During rest, three major components may be observed: one at about 0.03 Hz, one around 0.10 Hz, and one corresponding to the mean respiratory frequency of the subject (usually between 0.25 and 0.40 Hz). During paced-choice reaction-time tasks, the frequency of respiration increases, and respiratory activity becomes more regular. Similarly, the respiration-related heart-rate component increases in frequency and diminishes in power. In addition, a new component appears in the spectra. The dominant frequency of this new component corresponds to the imposed signal frequency (Loos, 1968; Mulder, in press; Mulder & Mulder, 1980; Mulder & Mulder-Hajonides van der Meulen, 1973). This component originates from the evoked heart-rate response.

Fourier analysis of the respiratory signal reveals two components. One component reflects the mean respiratory frequency of the subject. This component shows a high coherence (0.85 on the average) with the corresponding heart-rate component. The other component corresponds to the imposed signal frequency. This component shows a moderate coherence (0.60 on the average) with the corresponding heart-rate component (Mulder, in press). Thus paced-choice reaction-time tasks strongly affect the pattern of respiration. Further, during performance on mental tasks, all spectral components may decrease in power, but spectral areas differ in amount of reduction. For example, in a recent experiment (Mulder, in press), we divided the cardiac interval spectrum of each subject into three areas: a band ranging from 0.02 to 0.20 Hz (according to Hyndman & Gregory, 1975, this band represents about 80% of the total spectral energy); a band ranging from 0.22 to 0.40 Hz, and finally a band ranging from 0.41 to 0.60 Hz. Two paced-choice reaction-time conditions, differing in task difficulty, were compared. In both conditions a signal was presented every 2 sec. In the band ranging from 0.42 to 0.60 Hz the decision-related spectral component appeared around 0.50 Hz. Mean RTs in the "easy" and "difficult" conditions were 606 msec and 830 msec, respectively. In the "difficult" condition (and when tasks were performed in the order difficult–easy) the total spectral power was significantly smaller than in the "easy" condition, but the p-values associated with the reduction in each of these areas were 0.01, 0.13, and 0.20, respectively. Thus only the power in the lowest-frequency band was significantly reduced. Similar observations have been made earlier (Hyndman & Gregory, 1975; Loos, 1968). The power in that area is believed to originate from nonrespiratory homeostatic processes involved in the regulation of body temperature and blood pressure (Hyndman, 1974; Hyndman, Kitney, & Sayers, 1971; Sayers, 1973, 1975). Hyndman et al. (1971) have argued that the spectral components at 0.03 and 0.10 Hz are a product of the homeostatic control system. The 0.10-Hz component constitutes most of the energy in the 0.02- to 0.20-Hz area. This component arises from oscillations in vasomotor tone. Its energy is spread between 0.06 and 0.14 Hz. In the rest of this contribution we shall call them *vasomotor oscillations*. The mean power density of this spectral component is not very sensitive to considerable changes in respiratory frequency (between 0.20 and 0.40 Hz) and depth (Mulder, in press) but its amplitude is related to the level of arterial pressure: A decrease in arterial pressure increases the dominant frequency and increases its power spectral density; an increase in arterial pressure decreases the dominant frequency and decreases its power density (Monos & Szücs, 1978). This spectral component may be entrained by external disturbances with a frequency near to its dominant frequency. For example, requiring a subject to make decisions at a very low frequency (e.g., one decision each 8 sec) may entrain the oscillations by producing an evoked heart-rate response with a period of about 8 sec (i.e., about 0.13 Hz). Selective entrainment may decrease the amplitude of the vasomotor oscillations.

The aim of our experiments was to investigate whether the amplitude of the vasomotor oscillations was affected by task difficulty. In two experiments (Experiments 1 and 2) we used signal rates that could also entrain the oscillations. In Experiment 3 the signal rate was beyond the area in which entrainment could occur. In Experiment 1 the subjects were required to carry out a sentence comprehension task; in Experiment 2 the subjects were required to search for memory items in a visual display. In both experiments the subjects had to decide each in 7.6 to 7.8 sec. In Experiment 3 the subjects were required to keep a running mental account of the status of either 1 or 3 counters. The status of each counter could need to be changed each 4 sec. In all experiments the power of five spectral points (points 0.06, 0.08, 0.10, 0.12, and 0.14), representing the amplitude of vasomotor oscillations in the cardiac interval signal, served as the dependent cardiovascular response. Reaction time and errors were the performance measures.

GENERAL METHODS

Subjects

All subjects who participated in the experiments were students of the University of Groningen. Their ages ranged between 18 and 30 years. They were paid for their cooperation.

Apparatus

The experiments were conducted in a soundproof cubicle. The timing of the stimuli, the exposure duration, and the measurement of RT and errors were under control of a PDP-8E computer. The electrocardiogram (ECG) was recorded from precordial leads, amplified, and filtered (time constant of the amplifier 0.10 sec, low pass filter at 35 Hz). The filtered signal was fed into a pulse-shaping device (Venables & Martin, 1967) that produced a pulse coincident with each R-wave in the ECG.

Procedure

There were always two levels of task difficulty called *easy* and *difficult*. Subjects were trained on both task levels until a satisfactory performance was obtained (see experiments). Both the easy and difficult tasks were preceded and followed by a very simple version of both tasks. These tasks were called "reference tasks." There were two orders of presentation of the main tasks: difficult–easy or easy–difficult. Thus the sequence of tasks was always as follows:

     Order 1   Rest—Ref 1—Easy—Ref 2—Difficult—Ref 3
     Order 2   Rest—Ref 1—Difficult—Ref 2—Easy—Ref 3

Order was a between-subject factor; task difficulty and Ref 1, 2, and 3 were within-subject factors. This design was used to separate two different effects:

1. A gradual increase over time both in mean cardiac interval and in amplitude of the vasomotor oscillations.

2. Task-induced changes in these parameters.

The first effect becomes visible during recording of the electrophysiological activity during the reference tasks. The second effect can be assessed by evaluating the task × order interaction (for details see Mulder, in press). All conditions lasted 5 min.

Because the reference tasks are the most simple versions of the main tasks, they can be compared to both the easy and difficult version. Comparisons were always made with the second reference task.

Data Analysis

The interval between successive heartbeats is measured in milliseconds. Because spectral analysis requires an equispaced signal, and the cardiac interval signal is typically nonequispaced, a Lagrange interpolation is carried out every 500 msec (for details, see Mulder, in press; Mulder & Mulder-Hajonides van der Meulen, 1973). The equidistant values are autocorrelated. The maximum lag K of the autocorrelation function is 10% of the total number of computed values (i.e., 500). The autocorrelation functions are Fourier-transformed and the obtained raw spectral densities are smoothed with a Hamming window. The highest frequency that can be observed with the used sample rate is 1 Hz. Spectral resolution is 0.02 Hz. From the smoothed spectra the power of five spectral points (points 0.06, 0.08, 0.10, 0.12, and 0.14 Hz) is derived. The power of these points is expressed in $sec^2 \times 10^{-6}$.

Analysis of variance is carried out on the mean correct RT and the natural logarithm of the power of five spectral points. The difference among the three successive reference tasks is evaluated by orthogonal polynomials (linear and quadratic trend). Only effects that reach at least the 0.05 level will be reported.

EXPERIMENT 1. SENTENCE COMPREHENSION

In a sentence comprehension task the subject is required to compare a statement about a situation, actually a stimulus configuration, with a picture. Carpenter and Just (1975) have presented a comprehensive model of the control operations in such a comparison. The model deals with the internal representation of both the sentence and the picture in working memory and with the processes that are applied to these representations. The model predicts that the total number of comparisons should increase linearly from true affirmatives (e.g., sentence: It's true that the dots are red; picture: red dots; K comparisons) to false affirmatives (e.g., sentence: It's true that the dots are red; picture: black dots; $K + 1$ comparisons) to false predicate negatives (e.g., sentence: It's true that the dots are not red; picture: red dots; $K + 2$ comparisons) to true predicate negatives (e.g., sentence: It's true that the dots are not red; picture: black dots; $K + 3$ comparisons) to false denials (e.g., sentence: It isn't true that the dots are red; picture: red dots; $K + 4$ comparisons) to true denials (e.g., sentence: It isn't true that the dots are red; picture: black dots; $K + 5$ comparisons). With the aid of this model two levels of task difficulty were created. In the easy task we used true and false affirmatives, requiring K and $K + 1$ comparisons, respectively. In the difficult task we used true negatives, false denials and true denials, requiring $K + 3$, $K + 4$, and $K + 5$ comparisons, respectively. According to data provided by Carpenter and Just (1975) we should expect processing time in the easy task to vary between 900 ($K + 1$) and 1100 ($K + 2$) msec; in the difficult task these values are 1300 ($K + 3$) and 1800 ($K + 5$) msec, respectively.

The reference task required only a physical match: The subject had to decide whether two successive visual stimuli were physically identical or not.

Method

The subject was seated at a distance of 2 m from a screen on which the stimuli were presented. A step-by-step film projector projected the items through a plane-parallel coated-glass window on the screen. Each item was projected for 3700 msec. The reference task contained an equal number of two different figures, a square and a circle, and the subject was required to match two successive stimuli. In 22 out of 46 pairs the successive stimuli did match and required the response *same;* in the other 24 cases, the stimuli did not match and required the response *different.* The subject was to press a key when he thought he found a match and to press a different key if he thought the stimulus did not match the sentence or the preceding stimulus.

In the easy version of the sentence comprehension task, sentences such as "It is true that the minus is above the plus" were used and these were followed by a configuration that either confirmed or contradicted the sentence. In 23 of the 47 pairs the successive stimuli matched and in the other 24 cases they did not. In the difficult version of the task, sentences were used such as: "It isn't true that the plus is above the minus," and these were then followed by a matching or nonmatching configuration. In 23 of the 47 pairs the successive stimuli matched and in the other 24 cases they did not. One day before the experiment the subjects were extensively trained on a paper-and-pencil version of the task in another experimental room. Training continued until the subject made no more than 10% errors.

A group of 20 subjects participated in the experiment. Ten subjects received the conditions in the order:

Rest—Ref 1—Easy—Ref 2—Difficult—Ref 3

The remaining 10 received the condition in the order:

Rest—Ref 1—Difficult—Ref 2—Easy—Ref 3

Results

Performance

The mean RT of correct responses in the easy and difficult condition of the sentence comprehension task were 1196 msec and 2095 msec, respectively. The mean difference in RT (899 msec) was highly significant, F (1, 18) = 160.26, p < 0.0001. The tasks also differed in the mean number of errors, 1.6 (3.6%) in the easy version and 6.4 (14%) in the difficult version. This difference was also significant, F (1, 18) = 31.04, p < 0.0001. The mean correct RT in the reference tasks did not differ significantly in either RT or errors. The results indicated that we were successful in designing three tasks differing greatly in processing demands.

Amplitude of Vasomotor Oscillations

In Fig. 34.1 the mean power densities, ranging from 0.06 to 0.14 Hz, are shown separately for the rest period, the easy (E), the difficult (D), and the mean of the three reference tasks. From this figure it is clear that entrainment has occurred: In all three conditions there is an increase in the spectral points, 0.12 and 0.14 Hz. Remember that the subject is required to decide each 7400 msec. However, the entrained frequencies 0.06, 0.08, and 0.10 are smaller in the most difficult version.

The total energy in the area ranging from 0.06 to 0.14 Hz decreases from 11.37 in the reference tasks to 11.07 in the easy sentence comprehension task to 10.85 in the difficult version of the sentence comprehension task.

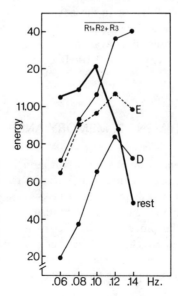

FIG. 34.1. Amplitude of vasomotor oscillations in the cardiac interval signal during four different conditions. $R_1 + R_2 + R_3$ refers to the mean value obtained during the three reference tasks: E refers to the easy sentence comprehension task; D refers to the difficult sentence comprehension task. Power is expressed in $^e\log \sec^2 \times 10^{-6}$.

The entrained frequencies 0.06 and 0.08 differentiated significantly (p = 0.017 and 0.0061, respectively) between easy and difficult conditions. If the difficult version of the sentence comprehension task is compared to the second reference task, corresponding to a difference of 1190 msec in mean RT, all spectral points (with the exception of 0.10 Hz) were significantly reduced [p ranged between 0.04 (point 0.06 Hz) to 0.003 (point 0.08 Hz)]. There was no significant task × order interaction.

Discussion

This experiment demonstrated that task difficulty affected the amplitude of the nonrespiratory component, ranging from 0.06 to 0.14 Hz, in the cardiac interval signal. The reader may wonder if other spectral areas were not also affected by the processing demands of the task. In a recent replication study, Van der Hoven, Smid, and Kerkdijk (1980) found the spectral components *beyond* the area ranging from 0.06 to 0.14 Hz not significantly attenuated. Only this latter area was significantly affected. The energy in the 0.06- to 0.14-Hz area was partly increased by selective entrainment. Requiring a subject to decide each 7400 msec (about eight decisions per minute) produced a new spectral component at 0.13 to 0.14 Hz. However, during very demanding tasks even this decision-related cardiac component is reduced in intensity. The processing demands of the present task were considerable. The picture verification time in the two conditions were 1196 msec and 2095 msec, respectively. Data from Hunt (1978) indicate that sentence comprehension takes about 2000 msec. This implies that the two conditions we used required, respectively, 55% (difficult) and 43% (easy) of the total time available (7400 msec). In the next experiment we required the subject to decide each 7600 msec. The processing time was, however, considerably smaller (about 10% of the total time available). The aim of the next experiment was to establish the sensitivity of the 0.10-Hz component to much smaller processing demands.

EXPERIMENT 2. MEMORY AND DISPLAY SEARCH

The time a subject is involved in short-term memory search may be another determinant of task difficulty. In this respect two types of tasks can be distinguished: memory and display search tasks. In a memory search task a single character called the *probe* is presented (usually visually) and the subject has to decide whether the probe is a member of a previously memorized set. Task difficulty is varied by changing the memory set size (Sternberg, 1969). In a visual search task, one single memory item is placed in short-term memory, and then the characters comprising the visual display (or frame) are presented simultaneously. The subject has to decide whether or not the memory set item is present in the visual frame. Task difficulty is varied by changing frame size (Atkinson, Holmgren, & Juola, 1969). In both types of tasks, reaction time increases about 40 msec for an increase of one item in either the memory set size (M) or the frame size (F). However, reaction time is less dependent on frame size if, for example, the subject has to search for a digit among letters or a letter among digits (Jonides & Gleitman, 1972). It is also possible to combine both tasks. Schneider and Shiffrin (1977) found that, during controlled memory and display search, reaction time was a function of the product of frame size (F) and memory size (M). The model that best fits their data assumes that during controlled memory and display search the subject first chooses a memory set item and then compares it each frame item in turn (in some order). Then the subject chooses another memory item and continues. A matching decision is made after each comparison. In our experiment we used two memory set size conditions of either 1 or 4 letters ($M = 1$, $M = 4$) and three frame size conditions ($F = 1$, $F = 2$, $F = 4$). The condition F_1M_1 was used as reference task; the easy condition was F_2M_4; the difficult condition was F_4M_4. In addition, we varied the nature of the distractors: In the same distractor condition the subjects searched for letters in a display containing 1, 2, or 4 letters; in the different distractor condition the subjects searched for letters in a display whose characters otherwise were numbers. We expected a considerable increase in search time in the F_4M_4 task in the same distractor condition but almost no effect of frame size in the different distractor condition. The amplitude of the vasomotor oscillations during these conditions should also be affected by these variations in task difficulty.

Method

Characters were presented on a cathode-ray oscilloscope at a distance of approximately 70 cm. The characters were arranged in a square around a central fixation dot. The characters presented could be digits, consonants, or random dot masks. If all characters were digits or consonants or a mixture, frame size was four. When frame size was less than four, all noncharacter positions were filled with random dot marks. The memory set ($M = 1$ or 4) was presented before a series of 42 trials. There was a probability of $p = 0.50$ that the frame contained a memory set item. The central fixation dot served as a warning signal (WS) and was presented 3800 msec before the frame (F). The frame time was 1000 msec. A new warning signal appeared 2800 msec after the moment the frame time expired. In the same distractor condition the subjects were required to search for consonants among consonants; in the different distractor condition the subjects had to search for consonants among digits. Subjects were randomly assigned to either the condition same or different. They were trained before the experiment on all three tasks (F_1M_1, F_2M_4, and F_4M_4) until they made no more than 5% errors.

A group of 24 subjects participated in the experiment. Twelve subjects received the tasks in the order:

$$\text{Rest}-F_1M_1-F_2M_4-F_1M_1-F_4M_4-F_1M_1$$

The remaining 12 received the tasks in the order:

$$\text{Rest}-F_1M_1-F_4M_4-F_1M_1-F_2M_4-F_1M_1$$

Within each order condition, 6 subjects were presented with the different and 6 subjects with the same distractor condition.

Results

Performance Measures

In Fig. 34.2 we have depicted the mean correct RT obtained in each of the three tasks (F_1M_1, F_2M_4, F_4M_4). In the same distractor condition, RT increased almost linearly from F_1M_1 to F_2M_4 to F_4M_4, with the slope of the negative responses being steeper than the slope of the positive responses. In the different distractor conditions, RT increased from F_1M_1 to F_2M_4, but there was only a very small increase from F_2M_4 to F_4M_4. Analysis of variance was applied to these latter tasks. There was a main effect of *distractors*, $F(1, 20) = 10.65$, $p = 0.039$. The mean correct RT in the different distractor conditions was 194 msec

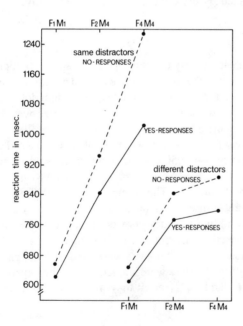

FIG. 34.2.   Reaction time as a function of distractor conditions and task load.

smaller than in the same distractor condition. There was a main effect of tasks, F (1, 20) = 32.89, $p < 0.0001$. The mean correct RT in the F_4M_4 task was 289 msec higher than in the F_2M_4 task. There was a main effect of response type, F (1, 20) = 36.26, $p < 0.001$. *No* responses were longer than *yes* responses.

There were three significant interactions: a task × distractor interaction, F (1, 20) = 18.82, $p = 0.0004$; a distractor × response type interaction, F (1, 20) = 5.05, $p = 0.0306$, and a task × response type interaction, F (1, 20) = 6.30, $p = 0.028$. In the different distractor condition the tasks (F_4M_4 and F_4M_4) differed by only 35 msec (this difference was not significant, $p = 0.3351$); in the same distractor conditions the tasks differed by 259 msec (this difference was highly significant, $p < 0.0001$). *No* answers were most sensitive to the differences in distractor conditions. Finally, the differences between the response latencies of *yes* and *no* responses were larger in the F_4M_4 than in the F_2M_4 task. The mean correct RT in the F_1M_1 was 633 msec. All tasks were carried out at a high level of accuracy. The mean percentage of errors in the F_1M_1 task was 3%. In the F_2M_4 task the percentages of errors were, respectively, 2% (different distractors) and 1% (same distractors). In the F_4M_4 task these values were 1% and 0.8%, respectively. There were no significant differences in RT or errors between the three successive reference tasks.

Amplitude of Vasomotor Oscillations

The three successive reference tasks (F_1M_1) did not differ significantly: Neither the linear nor the quadratic trends were sigificant. The pretraining in the same experimental situation was apparently long enough for the subjects to become to a certain extent habituated to the experimental environment. The total spectral energy decreased from 11.48 (F_2M_4, different distractors) to 11.43 (reference tasks) to 11.37 (F_4M_4, different distractors) to 11.00 (F_2M_4, same distractors) to 10.97 (F_4M_4, same distractors). In Fig. 34.3A, B, and C the main power of each of the five spectral points is depicted. Again selective entrainment occurred: In all conditions and tasks there was a large component at 0.12 to 0.14 Hz. In Fig. 34.3B and C the results are shown separately for the F_2M_4 and F_4M_4 tasks. There was a task × order interaction, F (5, 16) = 3.60, $p = 0.023$. In the order $F_4M_4 \rightarrow F_2M_4$ the tasks differed significantly from each other at 0.06 Hz ($p = 0.036$), at 0.08 ($p = 0.021$), and at 0.10 Hz ($p = 0.0023$). All points, with the exception of 0.14 Hz, were smaller in the F_4M_4 condition. On the other hand, in the order $F_2M_4 \rightarrow F_4M_4$, most spectral points were larger during the F_4M_4 task (significant only for 0.12 and 0.14 Hz). If tasks did not differ in their effects on the amplitude of the vasomotor oscillations, one should expect amplitude in the second task to be either the same as or larger than in the first (because of habituation). Thus the obtained interaction indicated that the F_4M_4 task had a small effect on the amplitude of the oscillations, but this effect was counteracted by habituation. In Fig. 34.3A we have depicted the mean power

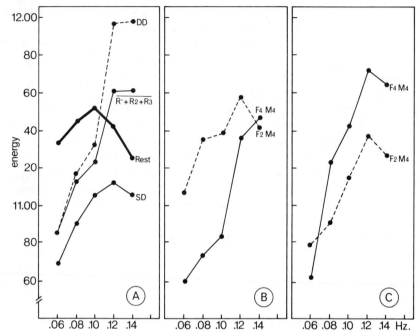

FIG. 34.3. Amplitude of vasomotor oscillations in the cardiac interval signal as a function of distractor conditions and task load. (A) The amplitude of the oscillations during different distractor conditions (*DD*), same distractor conditions (*SD*), and the three reference tasks ($R_1 + R_2 + R_3$). (B) The amplitude of the oscillations in the order $F_4M_4 \rightarrow F_2M_4$. (C) The amplitude of the oscillations in the order $F_2M_4 \rightarrow F_4M_4$. Power is expressed in $^{e}\log \sec^2 \times 10^{-6}$.

densities obtained during the two types of distractor conditions (averaged across F_2M_4 and F_4M_4). Though all spectral points were decreased during the same distractor conditions, only 0.12 Hz was significantly decreased, $F(1,20) = 5.05$, $p = 0.038$. The F_1M_1 task did not differ from any of the other tasks or conditions.

Discussion

The differences between the conditions in this experiment were smaller than in the preceding experiment. However, processing time required only a minor fraction of the total time available (from 10%, F_2M_4 DD to 11% F_4M_4 DD to 12% F_2M_4 SD to 15% F_4M_4 SD). In the preceding experiment these values were 43% (easy) and 55% (difficult), respectively. These results suggest that the load should be *continuous* before the vasomotor oscillations are reliably suppressed. The aim of Experiment 3 was to explore this suggestion further.

EXPERIMENT 3. MEMORY SEARCH AND REHEARSAL

The aim of the present experiment was to create two conditions, one condition (difficult) requiring the subject's full attention between the successive imperative signals. The task we used was designed after Massaro (1975) and is known as the QRST-task. In this task the subject is required to memorize a positive set, which then constitutes the memory load. In contrast to most experiments aimed to assess the effects of memory load on processing time, the subject is not required to indicate the presence or absence of a target (i.e., a member of the positive set) by pressing one of two buttons. In the present experiment the subject is told to set either 1 or 3 counters in memory, corresponding to the letters in the positive set. In contrast to Massaro's task, in our version not all letters in a series read off by the experimenter are members of the positive set. The probability that a letter is a member of the positive set is $p = 0.50$. If it is, the appropriate counter should be increased by 1. The updated values should be rehearsed in order to keep them in memory. Thus the subject is forced to keep a running mental account of the current status of each counter. The processing time required by memory search and comparison will depend on the number of counters in memory. At 40 msec per item the condition $M = 3$ will require 120 msec; $M = 1$, 80 msec less; the difference is too small to produce a reliable change in the amplitude of the vasomotor oscillations. The additional processes, updating and maintenance rehearsal, will mainly determine differences in task difficulty.

Method

A pilot experiment showed that the intersignal rate should be at least 4000 msec in order to enable the subject to perform the task without a substantial number of errors. Hence, the decision-related heart-rate response is outside the 0.06- to 0.14-Hz area.

The tasks and instructions were taped and presented to the subject by earphones. The subjects were trained on short versions of both tasks until the number of errors did not exceed the criterion of 1 error during a practice time of 1 min. In the condition $M = 3$, the probability of a target was, as in the $M = 1$ condition, 0.50, but the three targets differed in probability of occurrence. At the end of the task an auditory signal required the subject to report the status of each of the counters. A group of 20 subjects participated in the experiment. Rest periods substituted reference tasks. Ten subjects received the tasks in the order:

$$\text{Rest} — M = 1 — \text{Rest} — M = 3 — \text{Rest}$$

The remaining 10 received the tasks in the order:

$$\text{Rest} — M = 3 — \text{Rest} — M = 1 — \text{Rest}$$

Results

Performance

Both tasks were performed very accurately. During the $M = 1$ condition the mean percentage of errors was 1%, during the $M = 3$ condition, 4%.

Amplitude of Vasomotor Oscillations

The total energy in the area ranging from 0.06 to 0.14 Hz increases across the three rest periods from 13.06 to 13.34 to 13.41. The total energy is in the "easy" version 13.20 and 12.72 in the "difficult" version. The three successive rest periods differed significantly from each other in the lower spectral points (0.06 and 0.08). The power of these points increased gradually [linear trend is only significant for 0.06, $F(1, 19) = 11.94$, $p = 0.0027$, and 0.08, $F(1, 19) = 7.54$, $p = 0.013$)], and the dominant frequency shifted from 0.10 to 0.08 Hz. With the exception of 0.14 Hz all spectral points distinguished significantly (p ranging from 0.0133 to 0.0382) between the two memory set sizes. The intensity of the oscillations was reduced in the $M = 3$ task (see Fig. 34.4). There was no significant task $\times$ order interaction.

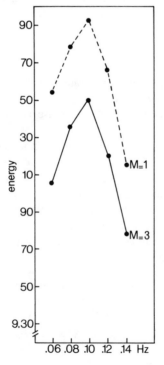

FIG. 34.4.   Amplitude of vasomotor oscillations in the cardiac interval signal during two versions of the QRST-task. $M = 1$ refers to a memory load of 1; $M = 3$ refers to a memory load of 3. Power is expressed in ^{e}log $sec^2 \times 10^{-6}$.

CONCLUDING REMARKS

The results of these three experiments suggest that the amplitude of the vasomotor oscillations between 0.06–0.14 Hz, a component in the cardiac interval signal that is relatively independent of changes in respiratory rate and depth, but related to blood pressure control, is reliably reduced if a task continuously requires processing. In general we concluded that this component is more suppressed the more a task requires controlled processing. With controlled processing we mean limited-capacity, serial, short-term memory operations (Schneider & Shiffrin, 1977). Elsewhere, (Mulder & Mulder, 1980) we have discussed mechanisms that can explain this attenuation. Also we have developed a technique to observe the oscillations from second to second during the performance of mental tasks. This technique can be used to observe the effects of momentary changes in task difficulty in the cardiac interval signal. First reports on the usefulness of this technique can be found in Mulder and Mulder (1980).

REFERENCES

Atkinson, R. C., Holmgren, J. E., & Juola, J. F. Processing time as influenced by the number of elements in a visual display. *Perception & Psychophysics*, 1969, *6*, 321–326.

Blitz, P. S., Hoogstraten, J., & Mulder, G. Mental load, heart rate and heart rate variability. *Psychologische Forschung*, 1970, *33*, 277–288.

Carpenter, P. A., & Just, M. A. Sentence comprehension: A psycholinguistic processing model of verification. *Psychological Review*, 1975, *82*, 45–73.

Danev, S. G., Wartna, G. F., Bink, B., Ridder, J. J., & Luteyn, I. Psychophysiological assessment of information load. *Nederlands Tijdschrift voor de Psychologie en haar Grensgebieden*, 1971, *26*, 23–29.

Van der Hoven, F., Smid, D., & Kerkdijk, G. J. *Fysiologische processen en informatieverwerking.* Een analyse van individuele verschillen bij de uitvoering van sentence-comprehension taken. Internal report. Groningen, Institute of Experimental Psychology, 1980.

Hunt, E. Mechanics of verbal ability. *Psychological Review*, 1978, *85*, 109–130.

Hyndman, B. W. The role of rhythms in homeostatis. *Kybernetic*, 1974, *15*, 227–236.

Hyndman, B. W., & Gregory, J. R. Spectral analysis of sinusarrhythmia during mental loading. *Ergonomics*, 1975, *18*, 255–270.

Hyndman, B. W., Kitney, R. I., & Sayers, B. McA. Spontaneous oscillations in physiological control systems. *Nature*, 1971, *233*, 339–341.

Jonides, J., & Gleitman, H. A. A conceptual category effect in visual search: O as letter or as digit. *Perception & Psychophysics*, 1972, *12*, 457–460.

Kalsbeek, J. W. H., & Sykes, R. N. Objective measurements of mental load. In A. F. Sanders (Ed.), *Attention and performance I.* Amsterdam: North-Holland Pub., 1967.

Loos, F. A. Onderzoek van de zintuigelijk-mentale belasting. Koninklijke Nederlandsche Hoogovens en Staalfabrieken N.V., IJmuiden, Holland, 1968.

Luczak, H. Fractioned heart rate variability. Part II: Experiments on superimposition of components of stress. *Ergonomics*, 1979, *22*, 1315–1323.

Massaro, D. W. *Experimental psychology and information processing.* Chicago: Rand McNally College Pub., 1975.

Mobbs, R. F., David, G. D., & Thomas, J. M. *An evaluation of the use of heart rate variability as a measure of mental workload in the steel industry.* BISRA, open report. London: The Corporate Laboratories of the British Steel Corporation, 1971.

Monos, F., & Szücs, B. Effects of changes in mean arterial pressure on the structure of short-term blood pressure waves. *Automedica*, 1978, *2*, 149–160.

Mulder, G. Sinus arrhythmia and mental workload. In N. Moray (Ed.), *Mental workload: Its theory and measurement*. New York: Plenum Press, 1979.

Mulder, G. *The heart of mental effort*. Thesis submitted to Groningen, 1980. To appear in G. Stelmach & P. Vroon (Eds.), *Advances in Psychology*. Amsterdam: Elsevier, in press.

Mulder, G., & Mulder, L. J. M. Coping with mental workload. In S. Levine & H. Ursin (Eds.), *Coping and health*. New York: Plenum Press, 1980.

Mulder, G., & Mulder-Hajonides van der Meulen, W. R. E. H. Heart rate variability in a binary choice reaction task: An evaluation of some scoring methods. *Acta Psychologica*, 1972, *36*, 239–251.

Mulder, G., & Mulder-Hajonides van der Meulen, W. R. E. H. Mental load and the measurement of heart rate variability. *Ergonomics*, 1973, *16*, 69–83.

Sayers, B. McA. Analysis of heart rate variability. *Ergonomics*, 1973, *16*, 17–32.

Sayers. B. McA. Physiological consequences of information load and overload. In P. H. Venables & M. J. Christie (Eds.), *Research in psychophysiology*. London: Wiley, 1975.

Schneider, W., & Shiffrin, R. M. Controlled and automatic information processing. I. Detection, search and attention. *Psychological Review*, 1977, *84*, 1–66.

Sternberg, S. The discovery of processing stages. In W. G. Koster (Ed.), *Attention and performance II*. Amsterdam: North-Holland Pub., 1969.

Venables, P. H., & Martin, I. *A manual of psychophysiological methods*. Amsterdam: North-Holland Pub., 1967.

35

State Changes and the Temporal Patterning of Component Resources

Robert Hockey and Allan MacLean
University of Durham, England

Peter Hamilton
University of Stirling, Scotland

ABSTRACT

A technique is illustrated for allowing direct analysis of the microstructure of components of a complex alphabet transformation task involving a variable memory load. Two experiments are reported using this technique to examine the detailed changes in the patterning of solutions when the state of the subject is altered by: (1) alcohol and (2) noise. Encoding (LTM access) and transformation phases are affected in opposing directions by the two stressors, but storage of transformed letters is seen to be more difficult under *both* these states compared to control performance. The data are discussed in relation to an evolving ''states'' view of mental functioning, in terms of patterning of mental resources, in contrast to a traditional arousal level interpretation.

Research on the effects of stress on performance has been heavily influenced by prevailing theories of the information processing system. Conversely, it has been very rare to find theories of the system being influenced by results of stress experiments, Broadbent's (1958, 1971) work providing a notable exception. In this chapter we argue for the adoption of a view of stressors that reflects the *differences* between their effects on both the biological substrate and on information processing resources. This contrasts with the current emphasis on the common changes associated with different stressors (Selye, 1956), normally expressed in terms of changes in the *level of arousal*. The arguments and methodology we have used represent an extension of those put forward in *Attention and Performance VI* by Hamilton, Hockey, and Rejman (1977).

607

STATE CHANGES AND PERFORMANCE PATTERNS

The view of stress that we have outlined in previous papers is based on the observation that changes in environmental conditions are associated with a complex pattern of observed effects on performance, rather than overall decrements or increments (Hamilton, Hockey, & Rejman, 1977; Hockey, 1979). Systematic analysis of performance across a number of task situations using a single manipulation of a stressor (in our case, loud noise) may indicate the presence of a constellation of performance changes of considerable complexity. Without restating this evidence here it is worth pointing out that we have observed changes comparable to those of noise (i.e., unique patterns of performance) in states produced by sleep deprivation, phase of the menstrual cycle and alcohol-induced hangover, although these data are by no means as extensive as those for noise.

What do we mean by "state" in this context? In one sense we are simply referring to the qualitative behavioral patterning associated with the internal and external environmental context of the person's activity. In this sense it is similar to the use of the concept to describe patterns of behavior in newborn infants (Prechtl, 1974; Wolff, 1966), as a constellation of vectors in a multidimensional behavioral space. As Prechtl argues, the attempt to use a single theoretical concept (arousal again) as an interpretation of these states is both logically invalid and singularly unsuccessful. The state is defined by the *pattern* of vectors associated with it, and not by the level of a single unidimensional process. Although we do not have space to develop the argument in this chapter we would also extend the concept of state to refer to: (1) the underlying pattern of physiological activity associated with the behavior profiles, and (2) the consequent balance of different processing resources comprising the *functional* state of the system.

With this broad viewpoint in mind, our aim is primarily to provide some rather direct and detailed evidence on the effect of state changes. Again we have focused largely on noise, but we also present some data collected from subjects in a state of alcoholic intoxication. There is no attempt to compare the two directly. Instead, we show how an analysis of the microstructure of performance enables the different detailed patterns of changes predicted by a state interpretation to be observed directly.

Our approach does not assume changes in system capacity in any state; rather a shift in the distribution of capacity across different resources. The alphabet transformation task that provides the empirical focus of this chapter, is designed to permit us to examine both the accessibility of each of its component resources (in terms of the time taken to complete each phase of the problem) and the effectiveness of the management of these resources as the task is made more demanding. It has been necessary to assume an essentially serial unfolding of components, since this is the only practical way we know of measuring these operations directly, though we have no particular commitment to a strictly serial model such as that of Sternberg (1969).

THE MICROSTRUCTURE OF PERFORMANCE

In our *Attention and Performance VI* paper (Hamilton, Hockey, & Rejman, 1977) we reported on the use of the alphabet transformation task in which we could independently manipulate the transformation size and memory load. Subjects were required to transform input letters by counting through the alphabet sequence an appropriate number of places (e.g., J + 4 = ?). The result of the transformation (N in this case) may be reported immediately (zero memory load) or held in memory until a number of letters have been similarly processed (JBRM + 4 = ????). In the latter case the subject must hold the results of the first three transforms in memory (memory load = 3) while he processes the last letter, then report the complete transformed sequence (NFVQ) as a single response.

In the pencil and paper versions of the task, two different effects of noise were apparent. Increases in the length of the required transform were dealt with more effectively under noise than quiet, but only when storage load was very low. Tasks involving a high storage load took longer to complete under the noise condition. These results were interpreted as representing the resultant effects of different changes in the system characteristics under noise, of which the two most relevant were increased rate of information transmission (throughput) and reduced holding capacity for currently activated inputs in memory. In the present paper we have attempted to measure the use of component resources *directly* by examining the temporal microstructure of self-paced problem-solving activity in this task.

Methodology and Analytic Techniques

The two task parameters we have manipulated are referred to as Memory Load (m) and Transform Size (t): m is defined as one less than the number of letters in the input, while t is the number of steps to be taken through the ordered alphabet squence. Figure 35.1 illustrates the sequence of operations that we have assumed in the solution of a problem of the type discussed above ($m = 3$, $t = 4$). Within this description there are a number of possible variations of strategy for the transfer of control between resources, depending on the degree of involvement of working memory, whether the response buffer may be accessed directly or only through the executive system, and so on. These possibilities are considered elsewhere (Hockey & MacLean, 1980), but do not materially affect the analysis of temporal patterns. We have referred to the last storage phase as one of retrieval since it is not apparent that the last transform has to be actively stored, like previous items. Instead it can be added to the previously stored sequence and produced as a response.

All experiments are run on-line, controlled by an IBM 1130 computer via a WDV interface, the stimuli being displayed on a Tektronix 603 monitor. Broadband noise is presented through Koss PRO-4A headphones by a Grason–Stadler

Button Presses	Screen	Principal Mental Operations	Code for Phases	Input Letter Cycle
	▢	(Signal that trial is available)		
BP_1	J	Encode - access LTM at ⓙ	E_1	I_1
	J	Transform ⓙ → "KLM<u>N</u>"	T_1	
	J	Store [<u>N</u>]	S_1	
BP_2	B	Encode - access LTM at ⓑ	E_2	I_2
	B	Transform ⓑ → "CDE<u>F</u>"	T_2	
	B	Retrieve store [N], update [N<u>F</u>], rehearse	S_2	
BP_3	R	Encode - access LTM at ⓡ	E_3	I_3
	R	Transform ⓡ → "STU<u>V</u>"	T_3	
	R	Retrieve store [NF], update [NF<u>V</u>], rehearse	S_3	
BP_4	M	Encode-access LTM at ⓜ	E_4	I_4
	M	Transform ⓜ → "NOP<u>Q</u>"	T_4	
	M	Retrieve store [NFV], update [NFV<u>Q</u>]	R	
BP_5		Prepare response [NFVQ]	P	
		Output response → "NFVQ"	O	
BP_6		(Signal to computer for end of trial)		

FIG. 35.1.   Summary of the task structure and hypothetical mental operations associated with each measurable phase. See text for explanation.

1702 audiometer. This is set at a level of 45 dBA for all conditions, except the noise condition in which the level was 95 dBA.

The subject sits in a soundproof cubicle wearing the headphones with a boom microphone attached, and holding a push button switch to control the presentation of the stimuli. Before each block of five trials a message appears on the screen reminding the subject of the condition about to be presented. A square subtending an angle of approximately 0.8 degrees appears before each trial to inform the subject that he may start the next trial. When the button is pressed the first letter appears on the screen (subtending an angle of approx. 1.5°). The subject then overtly transforms four letters forward in the alphabet, his speech being recorded on a computer-controlled TEAC A-3440 tape recorder, and passed on to the computer via a purpose built smoother-rectifier. When he is ready for the next letter in the sequence the subject presses the button again and the letter on the screen is replaced by a new one to be transformed. This cycle is repeated until he has seen and transformed all four letters. When he is ready to respond he presses the button once more to clear the screen and gives the response overtly. A final button press brings back the square and makes the next trial available. He may initiate this in his own time. The sequence of events is illustrated in Fig. 35.1. Timing of the occurrence of button presses and the beginning and end of the speech envelope enables us to time all three phases, either directly (T) or indirectly (E and S), by reference to these fixed points. The principal data for analysis are the sequences of durations of successive task phases for error-free trials.

After each trial the experimenter signals to the computer whether the response is correct or incorrect and notes any errors made. The experimental sessions are made up of blocks of a particular condition, each block consisting of five correct trials. All subjects are given considerable practice, so that they are familiar with the task structure and the various conditions they will meet (at least 1 hr, plus a second warm-up practice before the main sessions).

Summary of Normative Data

Several studies have been carried out under normal environmental conditions, primarily from the point of view of our interest in individual differences. Although these are not of direct relevance here it would be useful to illustrate the effects of the main task variables, m and t, where they have been manipulated in a parametric manner. A group of 9 well-practiced university students was tested on various versions of the task involving the independent manipulation of $m(0-3)$ and $t(1-5)$. Figure 35.2 summarizes the main effects of the two task variables, and those of Input position (Letter Cycle), on the time taken for each of the component processes. The data is presented here in the form of the mean of median times for each subject for the different components, over successive letter cycles of the task (I). For the purposes of the present paper the following observations are of particular relevance:

1. Encoding. Encoding times are increased as a function of the build up of items in store (I) and the number of items to be processed (m). There is also a lengthening of the E phase as t is increased from 1 to 3, but no further change as the transform phase is lengthened further.

2. Transformation. There is a linear relation between t and the time taken to carry out the transform phase. In addition, transform times are longer for larger values of m. The slope of average transformation time against t in fact shows a small but significant increase from 260 msec/item for $m = 1$ to values of 278 and 301 for $m = 2$ and $m = 3$.

3. Storage. Time for the storage phase increases considerably over successive letter cycles (though not for $t = 1$), and is longer for each cycle for larger values of m. Storage also takes longer when the transformation phase is extended by an increase in t from 3 to 5. The last (R) phase is short but also systematically affected by task parameters.

The effects referred to in this brief summary are all statistically significant,

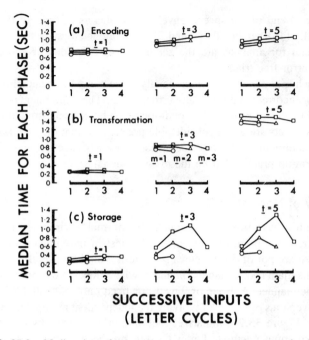

FIG. 35.2. Median times for separate components over the successive input cycles of the task. The two parameters are memory load, m (1, 2, or 3), and transform size, t (1, 3, or 5). For each panel $\bigcirc$ = $m(1)$, $\triangle$ = $m(2)$, and $\square$ = $m(3)$.

though we have not included the statistical data here. Clearly they demonstrate both separate effects of t and m on transformation and storage components respectively, and interactions between them, as well as effects of both on encoding latency. The increase in storage time as a function of I is what we would expect if this phase involved the updating and rehearsal of increasing amounts of material. The fact that subjects allow more time for this when the transform phase is lengthened suggests an adaptive strategy. Items are less likely to be forgotten during the increased time spent on other activities if they are rehearsed more thoroughly. A different effect of memory load is seen in the increased encoding latencies for conditions involving longer sequences of operations (increases in m). Time to begin transforming even the first letter seen is systematically affected by the number of letters anticipated. This may be interpreted as an example of ''planning'' or ''expected load.'' The effect is quite small (about 40–50 msec for each additional letter) but highly consistent, all 9 subjects showing such a pattern.

These observations are included here to provide a context of task phenomena in which to consider the effects of state changes. In the latter studies we have restricted ourselves to a much smaller range of task conditions. Although the temporal analyses summarized above clearly reflect the processing demands of the task as a whole it is important to note the existence of highly consistent differences in these patterns across subjects. These are considered elsewhere, along with more detailed analyses of these data (Hockey & MacLean, 1980).

EFFECTS OF STATE CHANGES

In addition to the baseline data discussed briefly in the last section we have so far studied the pattern of changes resulting from two stressors, a moderate dosage of ethyl alcohol (0.6 ml/kg body weight) and moderately loud (95 dBA) noise presented through headphones. Both studies employ the general methodology described above, except for details of design and procedure. In the next two sections we report the results of these two experiments. In the space available it has only been possible to highlight overall patterns of performance change, rather than consider formal detailed analyses of the data. We have thus presented standard errors, or standard errors of the difference (whichever is appropriate), as indices of the reliability of data points.

Effects of Alcohol

Background. This experiment was conducted primarily to test the sensitivity of the task to a quite substantial change of state, such as that produced by alcohol. We have not, hitherto, explored the alcohol state in any systematic way. It is well-established that speed is reduced, both in sensory processing and motor skill (Carpenter, 1961), though changes in the speed/accuracy function may sometimes result in an increase in errors (Wilkinson & Colquhoun, 1968). It seems fairly clear that memory is also affected quite severely. Birnbaum and Parker (1977) have shown, for example, that new material is more difficult to recall or learn in this state, though retrieval of items learned prior to induction of the state is unimpaired. In the absence of appropriate data on component effects of alcohol we designed the study to provide specific information about separate effects on transformation rate and memory span for letters, as well as performance in the combined task.

Design and Procedure. After a preliminary practice session involving 36 subjects, 10 pairs of subjects were selected by matching according to three criteria: (1) median solution times, (2) typical patterns of observed performance, and (3) sex. Others could not be easily matched, so were not used. All subjects were moderate social drinkers. In the main session subjects were given either 1.5 ml/kg bodyweight of commercial gin (40% alcohol by volume) mixed with fruit juice to drink over a 10 min period, or a "placebo" drink in which a small amount of gin (about 3 ml) was floated on the surface of the fruit juice and spread onto the rim of the glass. Subjects in each pair were randomly assigned to the two conditions. Testing (carried out between 40 and 70 min after beginning ingestion of the drink) involved the following versions of the task: (a) $m = 0$, $t = 1-5$; (b) $m = 1$, $t = 4$; $m = 3$, $t = 4$. In addition, following the letter transformation tasks subjects were given 15 trials of memory span. Sequences of 9 letters were presented on a VDU at a rate of 1/sec, and responses were written in prepared boxes according to a free position recall instruction.

Results and Discussion.   Figure 35.3 shows that alcohol increases transform time (with no memory load), $t(245) = 5.06$, $p < .001$. (This t-test is a pairwise comparison treating each trial for each subject as a separate data point, giving a maximum N of 250, reduced to 246 in this case because of missing data. A similar procedure is used for all subsequent comparisons.) It is clear that, as in all our data, rate of output of the alphabet sequence is approximately constant within each state but decreases from a rate of 330 msec/item under control conditions to 390 msec/item under alcohol. In addition, there is a small, but consistent, effect of alcohol on encoding time. This is reduced under alcohol by about 100 msec, $t(245) = 2.24$, $p < .05$.

Data from the memory span task are shown in Fig. 35.4, in the form of the proportion of errors at each serial position, analyzed as either item errors (intru-

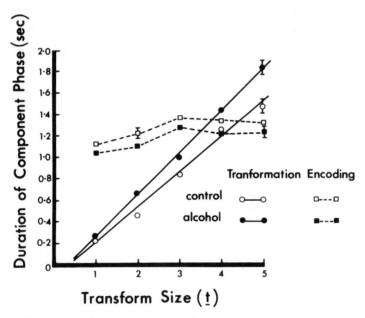

FIG. 35.3.   Transformation and Encoding times as a function of size of transform (t) for control and alcohol states, with linear functions fitted to the transformation data. Only the largest standard errors for each condition are shown.

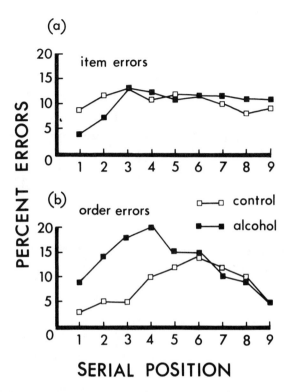

FIG. 35.4. Immediate recall as a function of serial position for control and alcohol conditions. The data are separated into errors of (a) failing to report an item presented in a particular position (item errors) or (b) reporting it in a different position (order errors). Both are expressed as a percentage of the number presented in each serial position, and scored with respect to the input rather than output.

sions or omissions) or order errors (transpositions), indicating that alcohol clearly impairs ordered recall of early items in the sequence, but does not affect item information.

The data thus show that the state produced by this dose of alcohol is unsuitable for *both* the transformation and ordered recall components involved in the complex transformation task, though encoding speed may be enhanced. Figure 35.5 expresses the sequential profiles of phase durations for the two memory load conditions ($m = 1$ and 3) as differences between the alcohol and control conditions (positive differences indicating a longer time being taken by the Alcohol group). The three points within each letter cycle refer to the separate phases of encoding, transformation and storage, as in Fig. 35.1. A somewhat surprising result is that there are no overall decrements (in total solution time, for example), though errors tend to be more common with alcohol. Differences appear, however, in the task profiles. In agreement with the data for the $m = 0$ condition

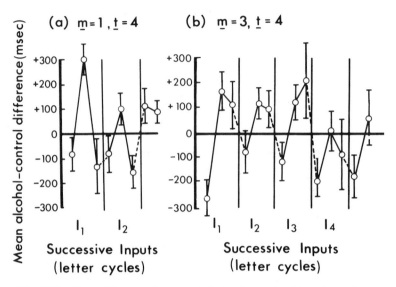

FIG. 35.5. Mean differences between alcohol and control subjects for each phase of (a) $m = 1$, $t = 4$ task (2 letter cycles), and (b) $m = 3$, $t = 4$ task (4 letter cycles), with estimates of standard errors of the differences for each phase.

(Figure 35.3), encoding is faster, $t(360) = 2.97$, $p < .01$ (pooling encoding times for the first letter cycle of $m = 1$ and the first 3 of $m = 3$), and transformation slower, $t(360) = 4.99$, $p < .001$, in both the more complex tasks. The increase in transform time varies somewhat, but is of the order of 100–200 msec, the same order of effect as in the $m = 0$ condition for the same degree of transformation ($t = 4$). The decrease in encoding time is also of the same magnitude across the different conditions. A difference emerges, however, in the effect of alcohol on storage. A small (though clearly nonsignificant) beneficial effect is present for the single storage phase of the two-letter ($m = 1$) task, but storage time is clearly prolonged for all three such phases in the longer four-letter ($m = 3$) version. Differences in both retrieval time and the report phases are inconsistent.

The patterns of temporal structuring of the various task components can be interpreted as generally reflecting underlying changes in the accessibility of these resources. The slower transformation rate and faster encoding /LTM access are preserved in the profile of the more demanding tasks. What then of the poorer memory span performance of the alcohol group, which is reflected in the effect on the storage component only in the $m = 3$ condition? It will be recalled from Fig. 35.4 that all of the impairment in memory span is confined to order errors on items seen quite early in the sequence. This may help to explain the observed difference between the two conditions. Only in the $m = 3$ condition are order errors likely to occur, since subjects must store three items in memory while carrying out the last transformation. In the $m = 1$ task only a single item must be held in store, so order preservation is not required. Further discussion is set aside until we have considered the noise study.

Effects of Noise

Background. The noise experiment reported here was designed to provide detailed information on the changes in resource accessibility suggested by our previous work (Hamilton, Hockey, & Rejman, 1977). In the paper-and-pencil version of the alphabet task we had found increasingly beneficial effects of noise as t was increased in the absence of memory load (i.e., a faster rate of processing single items) and detrimental effects with increases in m. It is not possible to tell from such data whether the facilitation for simple tasks is associated with an increase in the rate of the transformation process itself (as we have supposed), or with changes in the encoding or response processes involved in the task. Similarly, is the effect of memory load to impair all phases of processing in the noise state or only those associated with storage (or possibly memory access)?

Design and Procedure. Only 4 subjects were available for this experiment, each being tested in a total of 6 noise and 6 quiet periods, in an alternating manner. Testing was carried out in 4 1-hr sessions spread over the same day with 1-hr breaks between them (approximately 10-11, 12-13, 14-15, and 16-17 hours). Each session comprised an alternating sequence of 15-min periods of quiet-noise-quiet or noise-quiet-noise, with 5 min breaks between them. The order was kept the same for all subjects, beginning with quiet for sessions 1 and 3 and with noise on sessions 2 and 4. A background noise level of 45 dBA was used throughout, with the level increased to 95 dBA in the noise periods. Subjects were given 2 min to adjust to the noise before beginning each of these task periods. They were informed that they would be paid on an incentive scheme. Over and above the usual £1/hour they could earn up to an extra £2/hour by working quickly and accurately. This was based on the number of correct trials completed in the 15 min period with an additional small bonus for speed of transformation (in order to minimize the possibility of additional storage being carried out during this phase). Only the $m = 3$, $t = 4$ condition was used, in order to obtain highly stable strategies and reliable estimates of task profiles.

Results and Discussion. As was the case with alcohol, no consistent overall effects of noise were observed on either total solution times, which averaged 10.3 sec in quiet and 10.5 sec in noise, or error rates (19% and 20%). A different picture emerges, however, when we consider the changes that occur in the noise state in the temporal patterning of performance (Fig. 35.6). Here we can see clear and consistent increases in both encoding, $t(3074) = 5.06$, $p < .001$ (pooling first 3 letter cycles), and storage, $t(3074) = 2.52$, $p \simeq .01$, times with a complementary decrease in the time taken by the transformation phase, $t(3074) =$

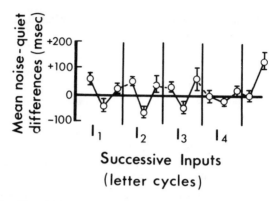

FIG. 35.6.   Mean differences between noise and quiet conditions ($m = 3, t = 4$), with estimates of standard error of the difference for each phase.

5.10, $p < .001$. Output tends to be slower as well. Note that, although this is consistent with the map of the noise state we have already sketched (Hamilton, Hockey, & Rejman, 1977; Hockey, 1979), the fine detail of this result could not be anticipated. An increase in the speed of simple transformations in a series of pencil-and-paper problems could, in principle, result from a facilitation of any of the component processes involved: encoding, transformation, or response production. The present data show that indeed the central transformation component is faster in this state.

Lack of space again prevents us from referring to differences between subjects. Although only 4 were tested, each one developed a unique and highly stable temporal pattern, but all showed a marked similarity to the cyclical effect of noise observed in Fig. 35.6 (see Hockey & MacLean, 1980).

GENERAL DISCUSSION

The data we have described can be interpreted at a number of levels. Taken at face value they at least confirm the view that changes in performance with stress are often rather subtle and depend on the intricate processing requirements of the task subjects are asked to carry out. On a more general level they raise some interesting issues for theories of mental functioning and the nature of stress.

State Changes and Performance Patterns

Considering the data as a whole, the main point we would wish to make is that a particular stressor affects performance by changing the balance of accessibility of underlying component processes. Alcohol and noise have a number of separate effects on performance, but those normally observed at the level of gross changes in a single performance criterion (such as overall indices of error rate or time) should more properly be regarded as the resultant effect of these separate changes. Noise can be seen to result in faster transformation but slower encoding and storage. Alcohol, on the other hand, slows down transformation rate and also impairs storage (where order preservation is important), but results in faster encoding. In neither case are there any clear effects on solution times or error rates. The data we have presented must be considered as exploratory rather than serving a more rigorous theory-testing function. Nevertheless, the consistency of the changes *within* successive letter cycles, particularly in the absence of changes in overall performance measures, is clearly encouraging. It reinforces our more broadly-based belief that effects of stressors on performance can only be properly understood in terms of their distinctive patterns of change across different mental processes.

Arousal and Stress: States versus Levels

We have stated that our view differs from the conventional interpretation of stress effects by emphasizing *differences* rather than similarities. In one sense this is a matter of degree rather than kind. We would, for example, agree that gross shifts in energetic aspects of mental functioning (from sleep to waking, or resulting from large doses of CNS stimulants) are likely to include a considerable change in the *level* of activity of the system.

We would argue, however, that such situations are rare in typical stress manipulations. Instead, stressors may be more typically regarded as changing the *functional state* of the system. While a shift in the overall level of activity may be a component of this under some circumstances, the primary feature of the change is a shift in the pattern of accessibility to different processing resources. Storage may be impaired under state *A* and under state *B*, rapid throughput impaired under *A* but facilitated under *B*, while both may be impaired in state *C*.

We feel that arousal theory, in its present form, is not adequately equipped to deal with these kind of data, though in the following we attempt to show how it might be applied to the results presented here. Alcohol, at least in the dosage administered, is usually considered to impair performance by reducing arousal level below the optimum for the task, while noise is assumed to increase arousal (Broadbent, 1971). The three results to be considered are: (1) Encoding speed is facilitated by alcohol and impaired by noise, (2) transformation is faster with noise and slower with alcohol, and (3) storage is impaired by both stressors. In order to account for these different effects it is necessary to assume: (1) that the optimum arousal level is highest for transformation and lowest for encoding, and (2) that the control state is roughly optimal for carrying out the storage phase, so that transformation is generally performed at a sub-optimal arousal level and encoding at a supra-optimal level. Given these, together with the usual assumptions about the inverted U function and optimal arousal, the pattern of results we have demonstrated can be accommodated within the arousal framework. Such an interpretation, or one like it, may of course be correct; the weakness of the theory is that it is equally capable of "explaining" almost any other pattern of observations. For arousal to remain useful in this context it must be required to provide independent evidence that the above assumptions hold. It is not clear how this could be achieved, though one possible test of the arousal level vs. state interpretation would make use of the methodology of stress combinations (Broadbent, 1971). If alcohol and noise merely alter the pattern of performance by changing arousal level in opposite directions, then a combination of the two might be expected to produce a level similar to that of the control conditions, thus removing all three effects. While we would not wish to assume that the state produced by such a combination was simply the sum of the two separate states, we would nevertheless expect the storage impairment, present in both, to remain or be increased under the combined conditions.[1]

The state approach, by contrast, makes no assumptions about optimality. We are concerned primarily at this stage in demonstrating detailed patterns of change in mental functioning. Stress, in this framework, refers to a departure from the "natural" pattern of mental activity that characterizes a particular individual. Any change in this state, whether brought about passively (by environmental factors such as noise or alcohol) or actively (by response to task demands), may be regarded as stress. For practical purposes, however, we would suggest that its use be confined to rather marked departures from this baseline state.

The multidimensional analysis of such effects may reveal important data about relationships between fundamental processing units and mechanisms involved in their management and control. Efficient use of such resources may, as we have demonstrated, become dissociated under stress. The relevant data for an approach such as that we have advocated are detailed patterns of such dissociation, rather than the direction and extent of changes in particular performance functions.

ACKNOWLEDGMENT

This research was supported by project grant no. HR 4987 from the Social Science Research Council of Great Britain awarded to the first author.

REFERENCES

Birnbaum, I. M., & Parker, E. S. Acute effects of alcohol on storage and retrieval. In I. M. Birnbaum & E. S. Parker (Eds.), *Alcohol and human memory*. Hillsdale, N.J.: Lawrence Erlbaum Associates, 1977.

---

[1]We are grateful to an anonymous reviewer for drawing our attention to this possibility.

Broadbent, D. E. *Perception and communication*. London: Pergamon Press, 1958.

Broadbent, D. E. *Decision and stress*. New York: Academic Press, 1971.

Carpenter, J. A. Effects of alcohol in some psychological processes: A critical review with special reference to automobile driving skill. *Quarterly Journal of Studies on Alcohol*, 1961, *23*, 274–314.

Hamilton, P., Hockey, G. R. J., & Rejman, M. The place of the concept of activation in human information processing theory: An integrative approach. In S. Dornic (Ed.), *Attention and performance VI*. Hillsdale, N.J.: Lawrence Erlbaum Associates, 1977.

Hockey, G. R. J. Stress and the cognitive components of skilled performance. In V. Hamilton & D. M. Warburton (Eds.), *Human stress and cognition: An information processing approach*. Chichester: Wiley, 1979.

Hockey, G. R. J., & MacLean A. *The sequential management of mental resources: An information processing approach to the analysis of individual differences in cognition*. Manuscript in preparation, 1980.

Prechtl, H. F. R. The behavioral states of the newborn infant (A review). *Brain Research*, 1974, *76*, 185–212.

Selye, H. *The stress of life*. New York: McGraw-Hill, 1956.

Sternberg, S. The discovery of processing stages: Extensions of Donders' method. *Acta Psychologica*, 1969, *30*, 276–315.

Wilkinson, R. T., & Colquhoun, W. P. Interaction of alcohol with incentive and sleep-deprivation. *Journal of Experimental Psychology*, 1968, *76*, 623–329.

Wolff, P. H. The causes, controls, and organization of behavior in the neonate. *Psychological Issues (Vol. 5, No. 1)*. Monograph 17. New York: International University Press, 1966.

Author Index

Italics denote pages with complete bibliographic information.

Subject Index